The Law of Contract
Fourth edition

Hugh Collins
Professor of English Law, London School of Economics and Political Science

LexisNexis™ UK

Members of the LexisNexis Group worldwide

United Kingdom	LexisNexis UK, a Division of Reed Elsevier (UK) Ltd, Halsbury House, 35 Chancery Lane, LONDON, WC2A 1EL, and 4 Hill Street, EDINBURGH EH2 3JZ
Argentina	LexisNexis Argentina, BUENOS AIRES
Australia	LexisNexis Butterworths, CHATSWOOD, New South Wales
Austria	LexisNexis Verlag ARD Orac GmbH & Co KG, VIENNA
Canada	LexisNexis Butterworths, MARKHAM, Ontario
Chile	LexisNexis Chile Ltda, SANTIAGO DE CHILE
Czech Republic	Nakladatelství Orac sro, PRAGUE
France	Editions du Juris-Classeur SA, PARIS
Germany	LexisNexis Deutschland GmbH, FRANKFURT, MUNSTER
Hong Kong	LexisNexis Butterworths, HONG KONG
Hungary	HVG-Orac, BUDAPEST
India	LexisNexis Butterworths, NEW DELHI
Ireland	Butterworths (Ireland) Ltd, DUBLIN
Italy	Giuffrè Editore, MILAN
Malaysia	Malayan Law Journal Sdn Bhd, KUALA LUMPUR
New Zealand	LexisNexis Butterworths, WELLINGTON
Poland	Wydawnictwo Prawnicze LexisNexis, WARSAW
Singapore	LexisNexis Butterworths, SINGAPORE
South Africa	LexisNexis Butterworths, DURBAN
Switzerland	Stämpfli Verlag AG, BERNE
USA	LexisNexis, DAYTON, Ohio

© Hugh Collins 2003

A CIP Catalogue record for this book is available from the British Library.

ISBN 0 406 94673 6

Typeset by Kerrypress Ltd, Luton

Printed and bound in Great Britain by Thomson Litho Ltd, East Kilbride, Scotland

Visit LexisNexis UK at www.lexisnexis.co.uk

LLLAM

The Law of Contract

Law in Context

Below is a listing of the more recent publications in the Law in Context Series

Editors: William Twining (University College, London) and
Christopher McCrudden (Lincoln College, Oxford)

Preface

Perhaps no other subject in the standard canon of legal education can claim such an august tradition, such rigour of analysis, and such sublime irrelevance, as the law of contract. The multitude of textbooks typically repeat an interpretation of the subject which has remained unaltered for a century or more in its categorization and organization of the legal materials. The latent values which inform these works include a priority attached to personal liberty, minimal regulation of market transactions, and a profound divide between private economic transactions and public control over the social order. This fidelity to nineteenth-century *laissez-faire* ideals, which is unmatched in other fields of legal studies, often remains concealed behind a presentation of the law which emphasizes the formal, technical, and historical qualities of legal reasoning.

The result of this fidelity to tradition is that students learn in their early years a misleading and almost entirely irrelevant set of rules. It is doubly misleading, for the values which support the law have altered, and the emphasis upon the formal qualities of legal reasoning tends to exclude any appreciation of how the law rests upon policy choices at all. The attempt to repeat the past guarantees the irrelevance of the subject, since it can only have rare practical applications, because most contractual relations will be governed by different rules from those stated in the books. My interpretation of the law of contract distances itself from these standard accounts of the subject in two ways.

The book defines the field of study by reference to the context of market transactions, rather than the traditional confines of the legal conceptual category of contracts. It delineates the subject as those rules which regulate trading practices and shape the permitted forms of market transactions. As well as compelling discussion of relevant parts of other aspects of private law, such as tort and unjust enrichment, this frame of reference also requires the introduction of statutory and regulatory materials. In particular, it requires an examination of how membership of the European Community and its single market is beginning to shape the rules which provide the basis for market transactions throughout Europe. By emphasizing the social context of market transactions, and identifying those rules and legal principles which have an important bearing on this context, the relevance of the subject to legal practice and social action becomes more assured. There remains a problem of generality, for most contracts are subject to particular regimes of law. But what a general introduction to the subject must achieve is an understanding of the criteria by which market transactions are differentiated from each other.

The second contrast with traditional accounts of the subject derives from the focus on these criteria of differentiation between contracts, which prompts a fundamental revision of the description of the values which underlie the modern law of contract. My interpretation of the legal materials emphasizes the way the law both establishes market transactions as an important site for citizens to acquire a sense of meaning for their lives, and controls the market for the sake of establishing and protecting public goods. I have referred to these goals compendiously as a conception of the 'social market'.

This fourth edition differs from the previous one principally in its inclusion of new statutory and case law material, together with European Community initiatives that increasingly set the regulatory framework for consumer contracts. Important new legislative material includes the Human Rights Act 1998, the Contracts (Rights of Third Parties) Act 1999, the Unfair Terms in Consumer Contracts Regulations 1999, the Consumer Protection (Distance Selling) Regulations 2000, the Electronic Communications Act 2000, the Sale and Supply of Goods to Consumers Regulations 2002 and the Enterprise Act 2002.

The primary focus of the book remains upon English law. But to understand the current regulation of market transactions in England, some aspects of European and international law have to be considered. I have also introduced frequent comparisons with jurisdictions from elsewhere in the common law world, either where these countries have addressed problems yet to be considered in England, or where their reasoning points to the future direction which English law is likely to take.

To avoid any misunderstanding of my purpose in writing this book, let me make a few concluding observations about its objectives. It is primarily a study of legal rules and doctrines, not an attempt to discover the way some aspect of society works through a study of the law. An examination of legal doctrine is interesting and important in its own right, for the law frequently supplies the location for conclusive settlement of debates about social justice, and so lawyer's interpretations of social phenomena and the values built into their analyses constitute a vital focus of study for anyone interested in how a society is constituted and how it may be reformed. This work offers an interpretation of the law which tries to make the best moral sense of these materials, to fit them into a coherent picture of the social policies which the law pursues in its regulation of market transactions. It is no part of my purpose to bring out contradictions and incoherence in the legal doctrine, though in formulating a sustained interpretation no doubt I brush over local difficulties of internal coherence in the law.

Lawyers trained in the traditional canon of contract law may find some of the concepts and categories of my interpretation unfamiliar, and they may be concerned that because the courts do not use exactly the same terminology, then my interpretation of the law must be misleading. But given that my interpretation suggests that the traditional account conceals more than it reveals about legal regulation of market transactions, some novelty in the terminology becomes essential. It serves the purpose of better expressing the principles which guide the legal reasoning.

A restatement of the law of contract has considerable potential importance, because students throughout the common law world learn from the subject many of their elementary legal skills. The way the subject is taught, described, and examined shapes most students' perception of how legal reasoning works, and what objectives the law normally tries to achieve. As long as students continue to receive the implicit message from traditional texts that legal reasoning comprises the formal application of rules gleaned from ancient precedents which embrace nineteenth-century *laissez-faire* values, their legal education commences on the wrong foot and never really recovers. Students should learn instead that contemporary moral and political values decisively shape each branch of the law, that legislation provides the key element in the legal regulation of social life, and that disputes about the law reveal conflicting interpretations of social values and how they should be realized.

Acknowledgements

One's debts in writing a work of this kind multiply over the years as it goes through successive editions, so one cannot hope to mention everyone who has assisted me by contributions and criticism. Special mention, however, should be made of Roberto Unger, who first inspired the project, and thanks go to Nick McBride and Colin Scott for their comments on the second edition, to Anna Edwards for her assistance on the third edition, and to Ed Brown for his help on this fourth edition.

Hugh Collins
March 2003
London School of Economics and Political Science

Contents

Page 310 collateral contract with diagram!

Table of statutes

Table of statutory instruments

Table of cases

PAGE

G

H

PAGE

I

J

T

PAGE

U

V

W

Decisions of the European Court of Justice

These decisions are also included in the preceding alphabetical list.

Table of EC legislation

Treaties and conventions

Directives

Chapter 1

Contract and market

A. Regulating markets
B. The classical law of contract
C. Towards a new conception
D. The market order
E. The constitution of the market

A. Regulating markets

The law of contract states the fundamental legal rules governing market transactions. In most societies markets serve as the principal mechanism for the production and distribution of wealth. This part of the law reveals some of the basic organising principles of their economic arrangements. It describes the elementary regulation of such key economic institutions as sale of goods, employment relations, arrangements for credit, and the provision of professional services. Individuals enter these market transactions for a variety of motives. The law of contract supports these practices by making transactions legally enforceable, but at the same time it places restraints on conduct, shapes the types of obligations which can be created, and limits the extent to which the parties may enforce their agreement by means of self-help or coercion from legal institutions.

A study of the legal regulation of the market system as a whole would require an examination of every branch of private law and other aspects of state regulation of the economy. Such an investigation would encompass the law of private ownership of property and the rules of tort law which require the observance of obligations to respect the economic and personal interests of others. Although no sharp distinction can be drawn, the law of contract focuses on the practices of entering transactions or exchanges, and of making binding commitments with respect to future economic behaviour. But this focus covers an enormous variety of market practices, ranging from consumer purchases in shops to international business transactions, or from the supply of a professional service to a major construction project.

These market practices may be examined from a variety of perspectives. An economic perspective analyses how transactions create wealth. A sociological perspective examines the patterns of behaviour of the parties to market transactions. A moral perspective might evaluate the conduct of the parties and the justice of the economic system. The legal perspective, like the others, serves to organise and rationalize our understanding of events. The objective of legal analysis differs, however, for its purpose lies ultimately in a determination of how these market practices should be governed by state regulation. The law of contract contains a set of legal concepts which are employed simultaneously to analyse the events of economic transactions and then to regulate the conduct of the parties.

Although the legal analysis of market transactions is distinct, it must be informed by the other perspectives. In order to achieve effective regulation, the law must take into account the likely response to its rules. It must also beware of regulation which damages the prospects of the market system for the production of wealth. For these reasons the legal analysis must be guided by sociological and economic perspectives. But this endeavour proves difficult, for each perspective tends to operate within its own closed system of analysis and evaluation. The concepts used in the legal analysis of contracts do not embrace economic or sociological ideas, so that the significance and effects of legal regulation cannot be immediately comprehended. The law of contract, therefore, constantly runs the risk of what Teubner calls 'the regulatory trilemma': either the legal rules may fail to have an impact on social practice, or they may subvert the desirable social practices by impractical demands, or the law may lose the coherence of its own analytical framework by seeking to incorporate sociological and economic perspectives in its reasoning.[1]

The legal analysis of market transactions may only represent a partial perspective, but it holds great interest because it displays the detailed ramifications of ideological debates within a society. Since the law can rely in the last resort upon a legitimate claim to the monopoly of violence in order to insist upon behaviour according to its vision, it becomes a principal site of disputes about the justice of the market order. The law's link to state power requires that its doctrines conform to shifts in the claims for legitimacy on which effective state power rests.

The legal analysis of market transactions holds particular interest, of course, for practising lawyers, who may be brought in to advise businesses on how best to organise their transactions. Lawyers devise contractual arrangements which give their clients the maximum legal advantage. This practice establishes a recursive process under which the courts and legislature observe how lawyers have reformulated contracts to escape legal restrictions on the pursuit of their clients' interests, and then seek to re-regulate contractual practices in order to restore the original policy decision. Lawyers also try to formulate standardised contracts that can be used over and over again. These standard form contracts preserve the

---

1 Teubner, 'After Legal Instrumentalism? Strategic Models of Post-Regulatory Law', in G Teubner (ed), *Dilemmas of Law in the Welfare State* (New York/Berlin, 1988) 299, at p 309.

wisdom of the firm of lawyers about the best way in which to handle recurrent problems of negotiation and performance. In the context of mass production of goods and services, this use of standard forms gives rise to the most significant new phenomenon in the practice of making contracts in the twentieth century: the application of mass contracts to consumer transactions. Lawyers devise a printed contract which businesses try to use in all their dealings with customers. With respect to consumers, businesses offer these standard form contracts on a take-it-or-leave-it basis, which has earned them the sobriquet of 'adhesion contracts'. One of the major challenges for legal regulation of markets during the twentieth century has been the requirement to restrict the advantages which businesses can obtain against consumers by deploying standard form contracts. This regulation has reached the stage where in simple retail sales there remains little or no scope for manipulating legal rights through the written contract, so in this context the standard form may gradually fall into disuse.[2]

The legal concept of contract law constantly evolves by expanding or contracting its scope, further differentiating its rules, and revising its basic principles. This evolution is prompted by changes in the social practices of the economy, the reception of new social policies and political ideals, and interactions with other fields of law. Despite this permanent evolutionary trajectory, we can discern in retrospect that during the nineteenth century lawyers in Europe and North America devised a new, radical system of contract law with which to interpret and regulate economic practices. This powerful vision persists in its influence today by providing the basic framework of the legal analysis of market transactions. Having considered the principal elements of this concept of contract law, however, I shall argue that it structures our thoughts about the market order in a way which once seemed so illuminating, but now seems to obscure, distort, and impede understanding and practical reasoning.

B. The classical law of contract

The new law of contract in the nineteenth century possessed two striking features. It was simultaneously sparse in content and imperialist in its ambitions of interpretation and regulation. These features have subsequently earned it the title of the 'classical law of contract'.

The simplicity and rigour of the doctrinal system of thought betrayed its dependence upon a relatively small set of fundamental principles. The nineteenth-century conception of contract law plundered highly selectively the antecedent intellectual traditions, thus abandoning their rich moral texture for a

2 Micklitz, 'Directive 93/13 in Action: A Report on A Research Project on Unfair Terms in Consumer Sales Contracts', in C Willett (ed), *Aspects of Fairness in Contract* (London, 1996) 77, at p 78

thin collection of organizing principles.[3] This impoverishment of the law permitted its restatement in a few terse rules.

A second distinctive characteristic of the nineteenth-century conception of contract law was the extent to which lawyers conceived so many different types of social relationships as falling within the conceptual framework of contracts. Together with the law of private property, the law of contract supplied most of the key principles through which lawyers sought to interpret and thence regulate every aspect of economic social relations. Obligations based upon status, trust and economic dependence were reinterpreted as contractual arrangements to be governed by the new organizing classification of contract law. The potential scope of this classification stretched from marriage to business, companies and employment, and from sales of private property to the provision of public services by governments. The new category of contract law threatened to subject nearly every kind of social and economic relation to its logic. The empire of the law of contract expanded in tandem with what Marx decried as the commodification of social life.[4]

We can discern both of these features of the law of contract developed in the nineteenth century in a case familiar to many law students: *Carlill v Carbolic Smoke Ball Co.*[5] The defendant manufacturer of these carbolic smoke balls placed an advertisement in a number of magazines which claimed that the product would cure all sorts of ailments including coughs, hay fever, loss of voice, asthma, influenza and many others. The defendant added that it would pay £100 in compensation to anyone who contracted influenza despite using the smoke ball according to the printed directions supplied with the ball, and, to demonstrate its sincerity, the defendant deposited £1,000 in a bank. Needless to say, the plaintiff caught influenza despite having purchased this quack remedy in a shop and having used it faithfully according to the directions. The Court of Appeal upheld the plaintiff's claim for £100, asserting that she had formed a contract with the manufacturer on the terms of the advertisement.

The amusing circumstances of the case should not obscure the surprising extent to which the court was prepared to conceive social relations in terms of contracts. The parties to the alleged contract had never met or communicated with each other directly. Nor had they exchanged goods, money or services between themselves. The law of contract is used by the court as an instrument for discouraging misleading and extravagant claims in advertising and for deterring the marketing of unproven, and perhaps dangerous, pharmaceuticals. The court protects the gullible and confused consumer by interpreting the events in the form of a contractual relationship giving rise to reciprocal obligations. In so doing

3   J Gordley, *The Philosophical Origins of Modern Contract Doctrine* (Oxford, 1991).
4   K Marx, *Capital* (London, 1867), Vol 1, ch 1.
5   [1893] 1 QB 256, CA; Simpson, 'Quackery and Contract Law: The Case of the Carbolic Smoke Ball' (1985) 14 *Journal of Legal Studies* 345.

it ignores alternative interpretations of these events, such as the idea that the misleading advertisement might constitute a civil wrong in itself, or that consumers who are ignorant of the properties of goods put on the market should be protected against any harmful consequences.

At the same time, the reasoning of the Court of Appeal in concluding that the plaintiff could succeed in her claim for £100 displays considerable analytical rigour based upon a terse set of rules. The court operates a checklist for determining whether an enforceable contract has been made. The judges run through a shopping-list of questions:

- Was there a promise?
- Was the promise serious and intended to be acted upon?
- Was the promise sufficiently definite and certain?
- Was the promise accepted by the plaintiff?
- Did the plaintiff perform some action in exchange for the promise?

If these questions, and others, are answerable in the affirmative, the court holds itself bound to find the existence of a legally enforceable contract. The legal reasoning thus takes the form of a brief and finite set of rules which must be applied to the facts of the case. The rules establish binary oppositions: either the test is satisfied, or it is not. No questions of degree, apportionment of blame, compromise of interests, or social policy imperatives will be considered.

Carlill v Carbolic Smoke Ball Co illustrates both the extensive province of the category of the nineteenth-century law of contract and its logical and formal reasoning process. The court employs its simple checklist of rules to interpret and regulate any kind of economic relationship. The generality and abstraction of the rules permit both the extensive utilization of this category of law and its application to the case, without any discussion of such matters as the moral claims of the parties, the nature of the market for pharmaceuticals and the problems generated by misleading advertising. The new textbooks on the law of contract in the nineteenth century both helped to create and to reinforce the construction of this category in the law.[6] The writers performed a crucial role in organizing the legal materials, individuating the rules and tests, and carving out this branch of the law from other categories such as the law of property rights, status, and civil wrongs. Most books on contract law have altered little since that time in their organization of the materials, their chapter headings, their identification of the rules and their conceptions of the scope of the subject. Although some significant challenges have been mounted against this classical system of thought,[7] the law of

---

6   Eg W Anson, *Principles of the Law of Contract* (Oxford, 1879); F Savigny, *System des heutigen Romischen Rechts* (Berlin, 1840–48).

7   Eg G Gilmore, *The Death of Contract* (Columbus, Ohio, 1974); Macneil, 'The Many Futures of Contract' (1974) 47 *Southern California Law Review* 691; Slawson, 'The New Meaning of Contract: The Transformation of Contracts Law by Standard Forms' (1984) 46 *University of Pittsburgh Law Review* 21; Feinman, 'Critical Approaches and Contract Law' (1983) *UCLA Law*

contract as it was constructed in the nineteenth century survives with an assurance – and even complacency – which renders it a daunting target for criticism.

The timing of the origins of this conception of the law of contract provides an important clue to its success. This category of the law supplied an essential tool for lawyers to understand the social and economic relations which were formed in the course of the explosion of a market economy. As markets became the dominant instrument for the production and allocation of wealth, the nineteenth-century conception of contract law created the tool by which these market relations could be understood and regulated. Such an understanding could perhaps have been achieved by a reworking of other categories of law concerning property and status. But the law of contract held a powerful attraction for lawyers. It offered both a framework for understanding the social relations thrown up by a market economy and a theory for the legitimate exercise of state power.

The latent social ideal of the nineteenth-century law of contract embodies a libertarian state, in which the law maximizes the liberty of individual citizens, encourages self-reliance and adopts an avowedly neutral stance with regard to permissible patterns of social life. The law of contract secures these goals perhaps more effectively than any other category of the law by facilitating the creation of legal obligations on any terms which individuals freely choose. We should recognize, therefore, that not only was the law of contract a convenient way of understanding the social relations of a market economy, but also it represented a particular theory of the legitimacy of state power, one which limited the exercise of such power in the name of respecting the liberty of citizens under the banner of freedom of contract.[8]

The fundamental analytical framework of the law of contract became one which focused upon the voluntary choices of individuals. The role of the law of contract was conceived principally as the facilitation of voluntary choices by giving them legal effect. To achieve this purpose, however, the law had to protect this social facility by identifying and declining to enforce those undertakings which were not truly voluntary. The textbooks described exhaustively what kinds of choices would be regarded as sufficiently voluntary to justify the imposition of legal obligations. The shopping-list of rules used by the court in *Carlill v Carbolic Smoke Ball Co* illustrates clearly how all the crucial questions were directed to ascertaining the choices of the parties concerned. The court ostensibly awarded a contractual remedy, not because the manufacturer of the smoke ball deserved to be made to pay up for its lies, but because it had voluntarily chosen to undertake that obligation. As a necessary corollary to this conception of the law of contract,

---

Review 829; P Atiyah, *Essays on Contract* (Oxford, 1988); T Wilhelmsson (ed), *Perspectives of Critical Contract Law* (Aldershot, 1993).

8 P Atiyah, *The Rise and Fall of Freedom of Contract* (Oxford, 1979).

the books excluded from consideration those instances where the law imposed obligations regardless of, or for reasons independent of, choice, such as those branches of law described today as tort and unjust enrichment (restitution), even though these sources of obligations have profound effects on the regulation of market transactions.

The unity and simple analytical framework of the law of contract, which was provided by the cardinal principle of respecting and enforcing voluntary choices, established a closed system of thought which necessarily excluded inconsistent rules and doctrines. There could be no place, for example, for a rule which insisted upon the fairness of the exchange between the parties, because that would contradict the fundamental assumption of this system of doctrinal thought that it was designed to facilitate and enforce the voluntary choices of individuals regardless of the wisdom or prudence of such choices. Nor could the traditional conception of contract law acknowledge the possibility of imposed contracts without the consent of the parties, for again that would contradict the basic tenets of the system. In some instances, of course, a court may have wanted to refuse to enforce a contract because of its shocking unfairness, or may have wanted to impose a contract regardless of consent for some instrumental purpose. In these cases, the integrity of the traditional doctrine prohibited any express recognition of such possibilities. The courts had to justify the results within the logic of the traditional doctrine. They had to argue in the case of unfairness that the choice was not truly a voluntary one; and in order to impose a contract, the court had to claim that the circumstances in fact revealed an agreement, as occurred in *Carlill v Carbolic Smoke Ball Co.*

This traditional conception of contract law persists in part because of the need to preserve the integrity and, hence, the legitimacy of this closed doctrinal system of thought.[9] Its doctrinal integrity helps to achieve legitimacy, because the law can be presented as objective and neutral, not a matter of politics or preference, but a settled body of rules and principles, legitimated by tradition and routine observance, and applied impartially and fairly to all citizens.

Even in modern accounts of the law of contract, therefore, one cannot ignore the traditional conception of contract law based upon the idea of facilitating voluntary choices. Its presence in the origins of the subject, the continuity of the tradition for more than a century, and its power as an analytical tool for understanding market relations and legitimating legal decisions, seem to render it almost immune from challenge. But challenge it we must. Whilst the legal presentations of the law of contract may have stalled, the market system and the content of legal regulation have altered dramatically. The classical concept of contract law now prevents us from understanding the significance of these developments by treating them as irrelevant or distorting their implications.

9   For this sense of integrity, see R Dworkin, *Law's Empire* (Cambridge, Mass, 1986).

C.   Towards a new conception

We have already glimpsed typical defects in the traditional conception of contract law in our discussion of *Carlill v Carbolic Smoke Ball Co*. Such an event, were it to occur today, would almost certainly be understood through the spectacles of the law in a radically different way. Legal regulation proscribes the marketing of dangerous or ineffective drugs through licensing systems and bans supported by criminal sanctions. These laws set limits to the range of products and services which can be offered in the market, and confine the number and type of persons who may engage in such transactions. More general criminal regulations prohibit unsafe products from being put on the market, and permit government agencies to intervene to prevent such products from being marketed.[10] A further array of criminal regulations control unfair marketing practices such as false and misleading advertising.[11] The relevant trade association insists upon certain standards of conduct from its members, and breach of these Codes of Practice might be given legal sanctions.[12] Furthermore, the events of *Carlill v Carbolic Smoke Ball Co* would have to be considered in the light of legislation and judicial decisions which have recognized increasingly that consumers need to be protected from their free choices, since these are so often based upon inadequate information and lack of expertise. Finally, we might observe that the economic relation between manufacturer and consumer has become the subject of mandatory laws which establish strict liability for defects resulting in personal injuries irrespective of the choice of the parties.[13] From this perspective, the relation between Mrs Carlill and the manufacturer might be regarded as one based not on voluntary choice but economic dependence, which in turn justifies the imposition upon the producer of compulsory duties of care with respect to the quality of the product and the information supplied about it. To interpret the events of the case as a voluntary choice to undertake an obligation was at the time regarded as stretching the category of contracts, but within the framework of today's laws and regulations it seems to provide a perverse understanding of the issues and problems to be addressed.

We need to construct a new conception of the law of contract.[14] It should provide a system of thought that illuminates present concerns of government, and that

10 General Product Safety Regulations 1994, SI 1994/2328; EC Directive 2001/95/EC on General Product Safety.

11 Control of Misleading Advertisements Regulations 1988, SI 1988/915; Trade Descriptions Act 1968.

12 Enterprise Act 2002, s 8.

13 Consumer Protection Act 1987, implementing EC Directive 85/374/EEC on Liability for Defective Products.

14 For other critical reformulations, see: Friedman and Macaulay, 'Contract Law and Contract Teaching: Past, Present and Future' (1967) *Wisconsin Law Rev* 805; Leff, 'Contract as Thing' (1970) 19 *American University Law Review* 131; Lewis, 'Criticisms of the Traditional Contract Course' (1982) 16 *Law Teacher* 111; Summers, 'Collective Agreements and the Law of Contracts' (1969) 78 *Yale Law Journal* 525; P Birks (ed), *Examining the Law Syllabus* (Oxford,

helps to analyse issues within an intellectual framework which has a place for all the relevant rules and doctrines. It should also provide a key for an interpretation of law's past, which simultaneously reconstructs the law and enables further transformations to take place.

The place to start no doubt, as did the Victorians before us, is with a desire to understand the market order. We still require legal systems of thought for interpreting, analysing, and guiding events and relations in the marketplace. The difference between our enterprise and theirs springs not from the site of the inquiry, but rather from the alteration in both the market order itself, and the nature of political and moral justifications for its legal regulation.

During the twentieth century, the state intervened to devise new principles to govern the operation and outcomes of the market. With respect to outcomes, the evidence is incontrovertible. Instead of permitting the distribution of wealth to be determined by voluntary choices to enter market transactions, the social security system which relieves poverty and all the other dimensions of the Welfare State, funded largely through progressive taxation, clearly affect the eventual outcomes of the distribution of wealth. What seems to be less generally perceived is that at the same time similar ideals of social justice have justified the channelling and regulation of market transactions. The purpose of these limits upon the exercise of voluntary choices lies in the realization of a compatible scheme of social justice.[15] The persistence of traditional descriptions of the law of contract no doubt contributes to this failure to perceive how the ground rules for the establishment of obligations in economic relations have been substantially altered in order that they may fit better with contemporary ideals of social justice.

How, therefore, should we conceive the law of contract today? It comprises those rules, standards, and doctrines which serve to channel, control, and regulate the social practices which we can loosely describe as market transactions. This branch of the law certainly facilitates the growth of the social practice of making economic transactions, especially those transactions where performance is not instantaneous; but it also sets limits to the exercise of voluntary choice. By emphasizing how modern ideals of social justice channel market transactions into approved patterns, this conception of contract removes the assumption that the law provides an open-ended facility for making binding commitments. Although some flexibility persists, especially with regard to the price, this freedom should be regarded as a privilege granted on stringent conditions, rather than a general licence to enter contractual obligations of one's choice.

1992); Frug, 'Re-reading Contracts: A Feminist Analysis of a Contracts Casebook' (1985) 34 *American University Law Review* 1065; D Campbell (ed), *The Relational Theory of Contract* (London, 2001); R Brownsword, *Contract Law: Themes for the Twenty-First Century* (London, 2000).

15 T Wilhelmsson, *Critical Studies in Private Law* (Dordrecht, 1992); R Brownsword, G Howells, T Wilhelmsson (eds), *Welfarism in Contract Law* (Aldershot, 1994).

As a consequence, the traditional contrast between imposed and voluntary obligations ceases to provide a crucial characteristic of the scope of the law of contract. Within the conception of the subject to be pursued here, we should define the field of inquiry by considering all those rules which serve to mould the form and content of market transactions, whether they be criminal offences, civil obligations of compensation imposed by the law, administrative regulations, or legislation which fixes the terms of obligations. It should be apparent that this conception of the subject incorporates many aspects of the law traditionally excluded from the classification of contract, because those topics cannot be derived from the concept of voluntary consent.

In one respect, however, this revised conception of contract law narrows the focus of study. Because the traditional conception offered to analyse so many types of relation within its logic, it lacked any determinate boundaries. Indeed, the subject became almost incoherent, because its expansive generality had to be constrained artificially by excluding such matters as marriage and property transactions in order to prevent it from occupying nearly all of private law. At the same time, the necessary generality of the traditional conception rendered it increasingly irrelevant to contractual disputes, where almost invariably some particular rules of law governed the transaction, such as the law governing sales, credit arrangements, and employment. In order to counter this incoherence and redundancy, the conception of contract law employed here focuses on the social context of market transactions, ie where people seek to acquire property or services by dealing with others. Whilst acknowledging that the law regulates these transactions by classifying them into particular types, this conception of contract law seeks to understand the general principles and social policies which inform and guide the legal classifications and regulation.

In the remaining sections of this chapter, we will examine the nature of the market transactions which the law seeks to regulate, the significance of market transactions in the social system, and the complex relation between the social system and legal regulation. In the following chapter, the values which inform the modern law of contract will be explored in greater detail by contrasting them with the traditional libertarian ideals briefly described above. We shall note how these changes have forced a modification in the form of the law and have drawn upon new sources of law.

D.   The market order

Every society creates an order of wealth and power. It establishes rules and institutions which direct the means for the creation and distribution of wealth and allocate power to certain individuals to control others. In modern western societies, market transactions play a central role in establishing the order of wealth and power. Consequently, the law of contract, which regulates these transactions, plays a leading role in determining the order of wealth and power.

Where considerable social division of labour exists in a market economy, wealth is normally created and distributed through the actions of selling, hiring and lending. These transactions tend to move commodities, services and capital towards those persons who value them most and who can exploit these factors of production efficiently. The bulk of most people's assets are purchased with income from contractual productive relations such as employment. Distributive relations reallocate this wealth through trade in commodities, securities and other forms of property. As well as the willingness to take risks with the resource of capital, superior information and expertise permit advantageous trading, resulting in a redistribution of wealth. Since the law of contract regulates both productive and distributive relations, it supplies a key ingredient in the determination of the distribution of wealth, although of course such laws as inheritance, taxation, social security payments and obligations of status (such as a parent's duty to care for a child) alter this pattern.

Not only does the market provide a principal mechanism for the distribution of wealth, it also establishes some of the significant relations of power in modern society.[16] Contracts provide the basis for the construction of many institutional arrangements which operate in the market. These institutions, be they firms, trade unions, or trade associations, can exert power over members of the organization, according to the licence of the contractual constitution. In addition, however, many market transactions that contribute to the system of production create power relations. Employees of a business usually accept the managers' contractual right to direct and control their efforts during working hours in return for the payment of wages. The firm enters into numerous agreements with suppliers of raw materials and components, often in the form of a requirements contract, which obliges the supplier to satisfy the needs of the firm, as determined by the firm, at a fixed price. Similarly, through franchise agreements with retailers and distributorships with wholesalers, a firm tries to secure reliable outlets for its product and the right to control price and exclude competition. Within this production network established by a variety of contractual relations, each party necessarily becomes heavily dependent upon the others for the proper performance of contracts: a distributor can be driven out of business by a refusal to supply the finished product, or a supplier or a group of employees can easily halt production unless alternative raw materials and employees are readily obtainable. Often these arrangements comprise symbiotic contracts,[17] where the economic interests of the parties are closely tied together so that wealth maximization depends upon intensive co-operation. The contractual rights and

---

16 I Macneil, *The New Social Contract* (New Haven, 1980), pp 32–35; H Collins, *Regulating Contracts* (Oxford, 1999), ch 10.

17 Schanze, 'Symbiotic Contracts: Exploring Long-Term Agency Structures between Contract and Corporation', in C Joerges (ed), *Franchising and the Law* (Baden-Baden, 1991).

duties both create and regulate the allocation and legitimate exercise of the powers required for efficient, co-ordinated production. Furthermore, even in a consumer's purchase of goods we can detect opportunities for the exercise of power, such as a retailer's refusal to repair defective goods or offer a replacement, which leaves a consumer in a weak position.

Standing back from these dimensions of power and wealth located in production and distribution relations, we can glimpse the main outlines of the market order. Every stable social system possesses an order of power and wealth but, unlike historically prior distributive schemes, the market order avoids the imposition of a detailed pattern. Instead of a structure of rank and privilege fixing entitlements to wealth and power, the distributive mechanism of the market allocates resources to those persons both able and willing to pay the highest price for them. Thus anyone with sufficient money may purchase a Rolls-Royce, or employ someone as a servant, or set himself or herself up in a country seat. The market order avows blindness to claims of privilege or force, so it recognizes no claims of an inherent right to govern or to possess superior wealth. Each transaction creates its own power relation and exerts an independent effect upon the distribution of wealth. In an employment relation, for instance, the level of wages and the employer's measure of control depend upon many factors, including the type of work, the effectiveness of union organization and the scarcity of labour. Each employment relation potentially differs from the next in its distribution of wealth and the range and oppressiveness of managerial control. Although certain patterns and regularities emerge in the course of the myriad of market transactions, their contingency upon the vector of market forces renders them always subject to renegotiation. The market order lets fly the centrifugal forces of radical individualism, permitting philosophers to celebrate the relative fluidity of its distributive outcome, and to legitimate it by appeals to the impervious mask of market forces. No other social order so successfully disguises the fact that it constitutes an order at all.[18]

In what sense should we regard the market as constituting an order of power and wealth? Under a regime of contract law which facilitates all types of voluntary transactions, it can be argued that individual choices determine distributive outcomes and the law does not impose any particular pattern of distribution of wealth and power. The justice of this distributive scheme can be defended either on the ground that each individual has chosen his or her lot, or on the ground that no justification is called for because the state does not seek to impose any pattern of distribution at all.[19] Both arguments resist the claim that the market constitutes an order of wealth and power in any strong sense. But these arguments are gravely flawed.

18 O Kahn-Freund 'Introduction', in K Renner, *The Institutions of Private Law and Their Social Functions* (London, 1949).
19 F von Hayek, *Law, Legislation and Liberty*, Vol 2 (London, 1976), pp 65–69; R Nozick, *Anarchy, State, and Utopia* (Oxford, 1974), p 159.

Even supposing that the law of contract might permit all voluntary transactions to take place, the effects of such a free market on the distribution of wealth and power are predictable. The decisions of the legislature and the courts to allow those predictable consequences to occur by abstaining from intervention in the market call for justification, just as much as attempts to control distributive outcomes.[20]

Moreover, the law of contract cannot avoid taking a stand on which distributive consequences should be permitted. In the legal rules which determine whether a voluntary transaction has taken place, as opposed to some coercive taking of property, the law necessarily takes a stand on the question of which bargaining chips may be used to a person's advantage in the marketplace. The law must determine what kinds of pressure may be used to secure better terms. It must determine the limits of fair dealing, so that certain types of lying and cheating cannot be used to gain advantage. Although all these rules may be described in the traditional understanding of the law of contract as rules designed to distinguish between voluntary and involuntary transactions, whatever rules may be chosen will inevitably have distributive consequences. They will determine the extent to which natural advantages, such as intelligence, strength and a facility for lying, and acquired advantages, such as ownership of resources and a monopoly position in the market, can be used to win further advantageous transactions and so redistribute wealth. Because the law cannot avoid taking a stand on these questions, the rules of contract law, even if conceived solely in terms of facilitating voluntary choices, have necessary and foreseeable distributive consequences.[21]

Of course the modern law of contract goes much further than simply distinguishing between voluntary and involuntary choices. It imposes compulsory terms on certain kinds of contractual relations, such as landlord and tenant, employment and consumer purchases. The law controls the remedies that the parties may enjoy to vindicate their contractual rights, which in turn determines the strength and effectiveness of those rights. Modern legislative interventions cannot conceal their distributive motives. All these rules shape the market order and produce foreseeable distributive outcomes.

The existence of all these rules alerts us, however, to the point that in one sense there is no such thing as the market order.[22] Market systems flourish under a

---

20 Collins, 'Distributive Justice Through Contracts' (1992) 45(2) *Current Legal Problems* 49; R Plant, *Modern Political Thought* (Oxford, 1991), pp 80–97.

21 Kronman, 'Contract Law and Distributive Justice' (1980) 89 *Yale Law J* 472; Alexander and Wang, 'Natural Advantages and Contractual Justice' (1984) 3 *Law and Philosophy* 281; Lucy, 'Contract as a Mechanism of Distributive Justice' (1989) 9 *Oxford Journal of Legal Studies* 132; Richardson, 'Contract Law and Distributive Justice Revisited' (1990) 10 *Legal Studies* 258; Ramsay, 'Consumer Credit Law, Distributive Justice and the Welfare State' (1995) 15 *Oxford Journal of Legal Studies* 177.

22 R Unger, *False Necessity* (Cambridge, 1987); P Hall and D Soskice (eds), *Varieties of Capitalism* (Oxford, 2001).

considerable variety of regulatory strategies. The degree and scope of regulation does not prevent the market from functioning as an efficient provider of goods and services, or at least as a system which proves more efficient than the alternative of state bureaucratic control. But each of these market systems shaped by different regulatory strategies imply different judgements about acceptable distributive outcomes. One legal system may, for example, fix a minimum wage for employees in order to alleviate poverty and provide an incentive for the efficient use of labour, whereas another system leaves wage levels alone but promotes the efficient use of labour by giving employees other rights to job security and profit-sharing. The market order does not have a single fixed content or a pure paradigm. Competition between markets to attract trade may compel a degree of convergence, and this movement may be strengthened by laws designed to remove obstructions to trade within free trade areas such as the European Community. But these legal measures do not rule out significant national divergences in the regulation of markets,[23] so that ultimately each legal system devises its own scheme for how the market should be permitted to operate.

An interpretation of the law of contract therefore becomes an interpretation of a particular distributive order contained in a legal system. A study of this branch of the law reveals the distributive principles which govern the allocation of rights and duties in the marketplace. The contests between different interpretations of the law of contract should therefore be understood as rival interpretations of the market order.

E.   The constitution of the market

What role does the law play in constituting the market order? What place does the law of contract have in influencing behaviour in the market on a day-to-day basis? Two polar opposite views often dominate reflection on these questions. On the one hand, it is argued that without the secure, calculable framework provided by the law of contract, a market order could not exist. This is the Hobbesian presupposition that the indispensable function of the law of contract is to provide the necessary insurance against breach of promise, for without a legal sanction, each party might seek to cheat and renege on the transaction.[24] On the other

---

23 EC law imposes a degree of harmonization under the EC Treaty, as interpreted in *Rewe-Zentral v Bundesmonopolverwaltung für Branntwein* (the *Cassis de Dijon* case) [1979] ECR 649, ECJ, but this does not prevent variations in trading conditions, as in the case concerning the opening of shops on Sundays: *Stoke-on-Trent City Council v B & Q plc* [1993] AC 900, [1993] 1 All ER 481, ECJ. See Weatherill, '1992 and Consumer Law: Can Free Trade be Reconciled with Effective Protection?' (1988) 6 *Trading Law* 175. Now the position is regulated by the Sunday Trading Act 1994; Maher, 'The New Sunday: Reregulating Sunday Trading' (1995) 58 *Modern Law Review* 72.

24 Thomas Hobbes, *Leviathan* (Oxford, 1955) (first published 1651), at pp 89–90 '... he that performeth first, has no assurance the other will perform after; because the bonds of words are

hand, it is observed that the vast majority of transactions are 'self-enforcing' in the sense that both parties will complete their side of the bargain out of self-interest.[25] People do not think about the legal aspects, but simply get on with their business. The truth lies somewhere between these extreme positions.

Markets can certainly flourish in the absence of a legal framework and effective sanctions. A withholding of performance or an insistence upon payment in advance normally suffices to discourage sharp practice. Indeed, studies of business contractors reveal that the most important implicit threat which they have at their disposal consists of a refusal to trade in the future with a particular person or business.[26] A person who examines fruit on a marketstall simply declines to purchase the goods if he or she suspects poor quality or excessive price. A carpenter will be discouraged from performing shoddy work by the threat of a deduction from the agreed payment. Whether or not any particular agreement is legally enforceable may not matter as much as the threat to withdraw from trading relations in the future and potential damage to business reputation from failure to perform as expected:

> Businessmen often prefer to rely on 'a man's word' in a brief letter, a handshake, or 'common honesty and decency' – even when the transaction involves exposure to serious risks.[27]

In practice, within some commercial contexts such as financial and commodity futures exchanges, the parties dispense with any reference to the legal system, but rely instead on trade associations to arbitrate disputes and discipline their members.[28] The diamond merchants of the Jewish community in New York City enter transactions of enormous value on the basis of a handshake, a practice sustained by the intense social ties of an immigrant community and supported by membership of a Bourse and a system of private arbitration which relies for its

too weak to bridle men's ambition, avarice, anger, and other Passions, without the fear of some coercive power; which in the condition of her Nature, where all men are equal, and judges of the justness of their own fears cannot possibly be supposed . . .'

25 Klein and Leffler, 'The Role of Market Forces in Assuring Contractual Performance' (1981) 89 *Journal of Political Economy* 615; Williamson, 'Calculativeness, Trust, and Economic Organization' (1993) 34 *Journal of Law & Economics* 453, at p 465; Telser, 'A Theory of Self-enforcing Agreements' (1980) 53 *Journal of Business* 27

26 Macaulay, 'Non-contractual Relations in Business: A Preliminary Study' (1963) 28 *American Sociological Rev* 55; Beale and Dugdale, 'Contracts Between Businessmen: Planning and the Use of Contractual Remedies' (1975) 2 *British Journal of Law and Society* 45, at p 48; Macaulay, 'Elegant Models, Empirical Pictures, and the Complexities of Contract', (1977) 11 *Law and Society* 507, at p 524; Weintraub, 'A Survey of Contract Practice and Policy' (1992) *Wisconsin Law Review* 1.

27 Macaulay, 'Non-contractual Relations in Business: A Preliminary Study' (1963) 28 *American Sociological Rev* 55, at p 58.

28 Simpson, 'The Origin of Futures Trading in the Liverpool Cotton Market', in P Cane and J Stapleton (eds), *Essays for Patrick Atiyah* (Oxford, 1991) 179; H Collins, *Regulating Contracts* (Oxford, 1999), ch 9.

effectiveness on the risk of harm to business reputation.[29] Even where the parties apparently rely upon elaborate written contracts, dealing may be much more informal in practice without reference to the legal documents. For the chartering of vessels through shipbrokers in London, for instance, the 'fix' is arranged by telephone, the ship sails and the 'paperwork' follows in the shape of a standard form charterparty, a practice sustained by the rules and standards established by membership of the Baltic Exchange. But do these observations entirely support the view that market transactions proceed independently of legal regulation, with the discipline of self-interest bringing the parties together and discouraging opportunism, leaving the law trailing along behind like the tail of a dog wagging in response to the stimuli of events?

If attention is turned to more complex transactions, such as the establishment of a partnership, a joint venture or a long-term supply contract, the role of the legal framework appears more central. In these transactions the parties are creating an institutional arrangement to govern their business dealings for the future. The law appears crucial in the process of constructing, refining and enforcing that institution, so that both parties can count upon it as the foundation for their business relation in the future. Similarly, in the construction of credit arrangements, the bank relies upon the documents that constitute the loan to define precisely its expectations and its potential remedies against a debtor. Despite the importance of contracts in shaping these kinds of relationships, we may still find that the real dynamic of co-operation and the incentives to comply with the contractual framework spring from visible commitments of the parties to the success of the transaction, such as specific investments, and the willingness to sacrifice immediate self-interest in favour of co-operation for the sake of maximizing joint gains and protecting business reputation in the long term.[30]

Empirical studies of contractual behaviour can perhaps best be understood as revealing that participants in markets orient their conduct to three competing frameworks of norms or standards of behaviour:[31]

(i)　　It is important to establish trust between the parties, which is the basis for the willingness to enter into a particular contract and to continue a long-term business relationship. For example, a supermarket needs to persuade customers that it sells good quality products at fair prices in order to induce them to select that shop and to return at frequent intervals.

(ii)　　It is important to ensure that the deal works for both parties in the sense that they will both feel better off as a result of successful performance. Unless

---

29　Bernstein, 'Opting Out of the Legal System: Extralegal Contractual Relations in the Diamond Industry' (1992) 21 *Journal of Legal Studies* 115.

30　Daintith, 'The Design and Performance of Long-term Contracts', in T Daintith and G Teubner (eds), *Contract and Organisation* (Berlin, 1986), p 164; Deakin, Lane, and Wilkinson, 'Contract Law, Trust Relations, and Incentives for Co-operation: A Comparative Study' in S Deakin and J Mitchie (eds), *Contracts, Co-operation, and Competition* (Oxford, 1997), p 105.

31　H Collins, *Regulating Contracts* (Oxford, 1999), ch 6.

the parties keep this framework in mind, the contract will lose its 'self-enforcing' quality, and one party will walk away.

(iii) The parties to the contract will look to any formal agreement as a source of rights and obligations between themselves.

The important point to note is that these three frameworks for guiding conduct will be present in every contractual relation. The extent to which one framework is emphasised over another will depend upon the type of transaction involved and what has occurred. For example, one party may be prepared to waive its legal rights under the contract in order to preserve the business relationship and to enable both parties to make a profit out of the deal, but if this behaviour fails to secure satisfactory performance, that party may begin to insist upon its strict legal rights under the contract. But when performance of the contract is proceeding satisfactorily, scant attention may be paid to strict legal entitlements, and indeed reference to the small print in a standard form contract may be regarded as sharp practice and a betrayal of trust. The move to insist upon a strict legal analysis of the relation or the dispute is likely to close down any further reference to norms of goodwill or co-operation between the parties, for it carries the implicit threat of a recourse to the power of the state to force observance of the contractual relations.[32]

What conclusion should we draw about the role of contract law from this analysis of the social practice of making contracts? Although contracts and markets can occur without a law of contract to support them, the law supplies a number of ingredients for a successful market order.[33] The law underpins the third framework, ie contractual rights and obligations, and the legal rules help to specify reasonable expectations under the contract. At the marketstall, the law specifies the expectation of the buyer that the goods should be of 'satisfactory quality',[34] and what the consumer should expect by way of remedy if the goods fail to meet that standard.[35] Although transactions at the marketstall could take place without law, it supplies a useful ingredient by giving an authoritative determination of the standards to be observed in case of dispute. The law also provides legal sanctions such as compensation for economic losses caused by a breach of contract. The availability of this remedy may supply some incentive for performance, but for the most part the other frameworks of maintaining the long-term relationship and making the deal work for all sides are likely to provide adequate incentives.[36] In any case, few parties have the time and resources to

---

32 Macaulay, 'Organic Transactions: Contract, Frank Lloyd Wright and the Johnson Building' (1996) *Wisconsin Law Review* 75, at p 114.

33 H Collins, *Regulating Contracts* (Oxford, 1999), ch 5.

34 Sale of Goods Act 1979, s 14(2).

35 Sale of Goods Act 1979, ss 48A–48D, as amended by the Sale and Supply of Goods to Consumers Regulations 2002, SI 2002/3045, reg 5.

36 Charney, 'Nonlegal Sanctions in Commercial Relationships' (1990) 104 *Harvard Law Review* 373.

litigate, and most lack an incentive in view of the potential for self-help by simple refusals to perform. What the law may achieve is to help the parties to make their commitments towards each other more credible despite the weakness of ordinary legal sanctions, and to strengthen the threat posed by opportunities for self-help.

The law provides techniques for taking 'hostages' against defective performance and then, in the event of breach of contract, the 'hostage' can be executed. The 'hostages' are called security: ie property rights such as a mortgage, a reservation of title clause or a deposit. These property rights can be asserted unilaterally, without the co-operation of the party in breach of contract, in order to punish or compensate for default.[37] The law also supports the use of alternative dispute resolution mechanisms, such as arbitration, which lower the cost of litigation, and therefore can increase the likelihood of a legal sanction for breach of contract. The most important alternative dispute resolution technique is simply one of discipline provided by the rules of the contract, such as dismissal for employees.

The law can also assist in constructing credible commitments. It produced the technique of guarantees provided by a wealthy third person, which more than doubles the chance of performance. International trade relied from the earliest times on transfers of money through negotiable bills of exchange, ie an offer of payment from a nominee trusted by the seller.[38] Attempts to enhance business reputation through misleading advertising or deceptive accounting can be policed and prohibited, so that the consumer can place greater confidence in information disseminated by businesses. Yet these devices and regulations amount to no more than marginal interventions in the market, for the law cannot confer a reputation for honesty and integrity on particular traders.

Although the law does not constitute the market order in the strong sense that transactions could not take place without it, it serves numerous roles in facilitating and strengthening the social practice of entering contracts. In so doing, the law articulates a detailed ideal of social justice in market relations by which people judge their behaviour and criticize others. An interpretation of these legal ground rules provides a representation of the scheme of distributive justice embedded in the market order. A fresh interpretation of those legal standards, the doctrinal expressions of fair trading and of justice in economic exchange, which alters our understanding of the market order and its implicit scheme of distributive justice, can claim in a sense to amount to a reconstitution of the market order itself. By altering our system of thought, thereby facilitating a new understanding of the economic sphere of social life, we can restate the legal doctrines, which in turn will serve to consolidate this new vision of the market order and its favoured distributive outcomes. This book will, I hope, make a

37 Llewellyn, 'What Price Contract? An Essay in Perspective' (1931) 40 *Yale Law Journal* 704, at p 724.
38 F Braudel, 'The Wheels of Commerce', *Civilization and Capitalism*, Vol ii, trans S Reynolds (London, 1982), p 142.

contribution to the development of a new interpretation of the law's standards of fair trading and justice in economic exchange, for the traditional interpretation born in the nineteenth century, with its root understanding of the law of contract as facilitating voluntary choices, seems to me to provide only a blinkered and distorted vision of the composition of those standards today.

Chapter 2

The transformation of the law of contract

A.   The transformation thesis

This chapter briefly describes the interpretation of the law of contract presented in this book. The claim advanced suggests that the modern law of contract differs from the classical tradition in its motivating ideals, in its methods of legal reasoning, and in its sources of law. When these differences are considered together, these developments amount to a transformation of the law of contract.

This discontinuity has been masked by the evolutionary pattern of legal developments. Change occurs through reinterpretation and differentiation rather than the invention of new principles of law:

- Reinterpretation of the law results from either redefinitions of basic legal concepts or the attribution of greater weight to principles which were occluded in the past. Traditional concepts such as consideration acquire new meanings rather than being abandoned or replaced. Alternatively, legal doctrines such as estoppel or undue influence acquire much greater force, so that they override traditional rules.
- Differentiation involves the exclusion of innovations from the canon of contract law, such as hiving off developments in consumer law or employment contracts. The transformation of the law of contract can only be perceived if the formal continuity of principle is examined in its practical applications and the process of differentiation is resisted.

The perception of transformation can be enhanced by reorganizing the elaboration of the legal principles by reference to concepts which emphasize the themes of the modern law. The chapters of this book, therefore, invoke untraditional concepts such as fairness and co-operation, which serve to highlight the thematic unity of the changes in the law.

The transformation thesis is controversial both as to its occurrence and as to its detail. Most texts on the law of contract persist in an attachment to the organizing categories of the classical law. Changes in legal principle are described as refinements or qualifications. Differentiation of legal rules becomes rife, so that the most common types of market transactions such as a sale of goods to consumer are attributed with marginal significance. This denial of change has received a boost from the methodology of economic analysis of law, which both supplies a new rationale for the traditional principles of law in terms of efficiency and provides plausible accounts of the justifications for the modern qualifications in terms of market failure. Even for those interpreters of the law who acknowledge the case for transformation, there is marked disagreement about the themes which underlie the evolution of the law. For some authors the alterations reflect merely a greater concern for the protection of consumers,[1] or a greater differentiation between commercial transactions and personal agreements;[2] whereas others detect a more fundamental reorientation of the values expressed by the law moving from an emphasis on rights and freedom to a concern for needs and economic dependence.[3] In arguing the case for a particular interpretation of the transformation thesis, therefore, this book encounters critics on all sides.

B.   The social market

A central element of the transformation thesis concerns the values which underlie the interpretation and application of the legal principles. A contrast can be drawn

1   J Adams and R Brownsword, *Understanding Contract Law* (London, 1987).
2   J Wightman, *Contract: A Critical Commentary* (London, 1996), ch 8.
3   T Wilhelmsson, *Critical Studies in Private Law* (Dordrecht, 1992).

between the importance attached to the slogan 'freedom of contract' in the nineteenth-century law and the search in modern law to regulate the market so that it offers worthwhile opportunities and satisfies needs. Whereas the former value system emphasized individual choice, the modern law conceives markets as a collective good which requires steering, channelling and supplementation. This contrast leads to different conceptions of contracts: the former regards contracts as a creation of individuals which is facilitated by the law; the latter regards contracts as structured obligations imposed by the law on people participating in markets.

In this section, we will first consider, in brief outline, the principal values underlying the nineteenth-century law of contract, then describe a modern restatement of those values drawn from economic analysis of law, before moving on to highlight the values which seem to lead to a transformation in modern contract law. The section concludes that a regulatory perspective helps us to appreciate the dynamics of the modern law.

1.   The justice of exchange

The governing ideal of the nineteenth-century law of contract is usually described as 'freedom of contract'.[4] This slogan was certainly a crucial political banner. It signified both a resistance to state interference in the economy and a desire to augment each individual's freedom of choice. It summarizes well some of the cardinal principles of the law: citizens enjoy a broad discretion to make contracts; the law routinely respects their choice of terms; and the voluntariness of their choices is protected against coercion and fraud. Yet respect for individual liberty comprises only one element in the ideals embedded in the Victorians' interpretation of the market order. In many respects, the ideal of individual liberty plays second fiddle to a deeper faith in the justice of an order of wealth and power established through exchange relations. This faith stems from the belief that the market order establishes both equality in place of social hierarchy and reciprocity instead of exploitation.

(a)   EQUALITY

Unlike social orders which distribute wealth and power by reference to such criteria as social status, political power, physical force, or moral worth, the market order claims to respect the ideal of equality. Each person enjoys the same opportunity to enter any kind of transaction, and through trade to improve his or her lot in life. This market order achieves a great social levelling, since the

---

4   P Atiyah, *The Rise and Fall of Freedom of Contract* (Oxford, 1979); L Friedman, *Contract Law in America* (Madison, 1965); M Horwitz, *The Transformation of American Law 1780–1860* (Cambridge, Mass, 1977), ch 6; D Miller, *Social Justice* (Oxford, 1976).

distribution of wealth and power depends upon success in trading under the regime of contract law, not upon social rank or military might. People transfer commodities according to voluntary agreements, not under imposed laws of political fealty. The market mechanism for the allocation of wealth and power is therefore fit for a democratic republic.

The ideal of equality which lies at the root of this conception of the market order is not, of course, one which insists upon an egalitarian distribution of wealth and power. It is not concerned with the ultimate distributive consequences of trade. It is concerned rather with formal equality and a narrow view of equality of opportunity. Formal equality requires that each person enjoys the same set of rights to enter contracts and to own property. The narrow view of equality of opportunity insists that each person in principle should be permitted to enter into any branch of trade and thereby to improve his or her position without limit. The law recognized some exceptions to formal equality with respect to children and the insane, and, more controversially, married women, but in general the rhetoric of the law admitted no distinctions of rank and privilege in determining contractual rights and duties.

Within this perspective there seems to be no serious concern that freedom of contract might be used, in combination with ownership of scarce resources and superior technical knowledge, to achieve relations of domination which subvert the equality of citizens. The belief seems to be that, provided that a person has freely consented to the terms of the contract, there is no danger that the contract establishes unjustifiable positions of power. Under this analysis, for example, an employer's right to give orders to his employees and demand obedience on pain of dismissal rests upon consent at the moment of hiring and is restricted to the scope of the duties envisaged in the contract. Such a limited, consensual obligation apparently runs little risk of establishing unjustifiable domination. Questions about the effects of inequality of bargaining power upon the terms of contracts, and thus upon the nature of social relations established by contracts, seem to be ignored or suppressed. It is as if positions of unjustifiable power over others simply cannot arise within the framework of freely chosen agreements.

(b) DISTRIBUTIVE JUSTICE

It is often overlooked that the nineteenth-century interpretation of the market order also proclaimed its fairness. The law insisted that only those transactions which involved an exchange could be enforceable. Both parties should give up something of value in return for something which was desired. This requirement of reciprocity, as defined by the doctrine of consideration (which will be examined in Chapter 4), established a distinction between, on the one hand, enforceable market transactions which had to be bargains or exchanges, and, on the other hand, instances of expropriation, domination, and exploitation. The nineteenth-century lawyers perceived a vital difference between an employment relation where wages are paid and one where no remuneration is given: the former constitutes a bargain struck between equals from which both parties expect to benefit, whereas the latter smacks of slavery and extortion. From this perspective, the presence of reciprocal rights and duties guarantees the fairness of productive and distributive relations.

This idea of fairness does not ensure an exact equivalence in the value of the performance supplied by each party to the contract. The courts did not believe that it was either possible or desirable to test the balance of the bargain. It was impossible because value depends upon a subjective appreciation by each individual, which differs from one person to the next, so the court could only assume that parties entering a contract had accepted at that time the fairness of the exchange. Any such interference would also be undesirable, for it would undermine the reliability of bargains which had been struck and pose a threat to freedom of contract. But above all, such intervention was unnecessary, because the presence of a freely chosen exchange ensured that the bargain was fair. No one enters a transaction voluntarily unless he or she expects to benefit from it, so that every voluntary bargain must be fair, because it should leave each party better off than before.

Some limited intervention was necessary, however, to ensure the preservation of competitive markets. It is readily apparent that someone holding a monopoly over a scarce and valuable item of commerce might use that bargaining position to impose contracts which were scarcely distinguishable from expropriation. Legislation against combinations and cartels, allied with the judges' development of the doctrine of restraint of trade, tried to preserve a competitive market. In addition, some legislation prevented owners of monopolies such as railways from charging unfair prices. But these were limited and necessary interventions in order to uphold the general ideal that contractual exchanges established fair economic relations and distributive outcomes.

Absent from this conception of fairness in the market order is the possibility that the distributive consequences of freely chosen agreements could be unjust in any but a few isolated instances of foolishness and carelessness. The idea that large groups of people entering transactions in competitive markets might all suffer a diminution of their resources from concluding bad bargains is simply dismissed as absurd. Tenants who pay high rents, borrowers who accept exorbitant rates of interest, workers who settle for wages below subsistence levels, all have only themselves to blame for errors of judgement. Nor does this concept of the market order recognize any need for a distribution of wealth which protects people against poverty and hardship. In particular, the classical law of contract believed that it should not concern itself with the ultimate distributive consequences of the market order.

(c)   FREEDOM OF CONTRACT

The slogan 'freedom of contract' both summarized vital elements of these ideals of equality and fairness, and then added to them an interpretation of the kind of freedom which the state should establish and protect. This idea of freedom insisted that individuals should be given the choice whether to enter contracts or not, which ruled out compulsory contracts and other legally imposed duties, and that individuals should also enjoy the freedom to choose the terms of their agreements. This idea of freedom contains a negative element, which rejects the interference of the state in the terms of market transactions, but also a positive element, for it sees in the general licence to enter binding contracts an enhancement of freedom, because this facility permits new forms of co-operative endeavours which last over a period of time.

The adherence to the negative aspect of liberty could not be absolute without endangering the justice of the market order. Parties entering into contracts had to be protected against threats of violence and fraudulent misrepresentations, but this intervention could be justified as being designed to protect freedom by ensuring the genuineness of the choice to enter the contract. It also seemed possible, although unlikely, that a person might freely choose to enter a contract which permanently circumscribed liberty, as in the example of a contract of slavery, and in such instances the courts insisted that such contracts would be unenforceable. The courts further declined to enforce certain transactions on the grounds that they exhibited gross immorality or criminal behaviour: liberty of contract could not be permitted to become a licence to misbehave. But the limited nature of these exceptions to the general ideal of freedom of contract reveals how strongly this ideal informed interpretations of the just market order in the nineteenth century.

Liberty, equality, and fairness in reciprocity: these ideals make up the conception of the just market order expressed by the law of contract as it was originally conceived in the nineteenth century. For convenience, this interpretation of the market order which informed the values embedded in the law will be called 'the justice of exchange'.

2.   *Efficiency and market failure*

In contemporary legal writing, a similar interpretation of the law of contract is presented using rather different concepts and values drawn from economics.[5] The central value is efficiency, or, more precisely, wealth maximization. The virtue of contracts is described as the opportunity presented by exchanges for

---

5   V Goldberg, *Readings in the Economics of Contract Law* (Cambridge/New York, 1989); A Kronman and R Posner, *The Economics of Contract Law* (Boston/Toronto, 1979); M Trebilcock, *The Limits of Freedom of Contract* (Cambridge, Mass, 1993).

both parties to enhance their wealth. If a transaction is freely chosen, the motivation for the exchange in obtaining something of greater value to the purchaser will ensure that both parties will be better off. For the purpose of maximizing the wealth of society, the law of contract should respect and enforce the choices of parties to enter exchanges. Although the modern rhetoric differs, it does support the traditional interpretation of the law of contract. Freedom of contract is essential in order to ensure that the transaction does maximize wealth, although freedom of contract is now regarded as an instrumental value rather than a value in itself.

It is recognized in economic theory, however, that in many circumstances this ideal cannot be realized in practice. Individuals and businesses simply do not have the time or the resources to acquire all the necessary information and to plan every aspect of their economic arrangements through detailed agreements. Within these constraints, which may generically be called 'transaction costs', we should expect that in many instances agreements will be left incomplete. Moreover, the impediment of transaction costs may lead to market failure in the sense that, by mistake, the parties may not enter into a wealth maximizing transaction. This result can occur, for example, where one party lacks vital information about market conditions or is unable to process the available information.

From this economic perspective, the law serves the useful regulatory function of overcoming the obstructions of transaction costs and preventing or reducing the occurrence of market failure. For incomplete contracts, the law can set 'default' rules to govern market relations to which the parties would have agreed themselves but for the impediment of transaction costs. To remedy market failure, the law can impose duties to disclose information or make it more accessible. In a consumer purchase of food, for instance, the law can establish such default rules about liability for lack of hygiene, and can improve access to information for the consumer by requiring clear labelling of contents on the packaging. Far from interfering with freedom of contract, these regulations can be presented in economic analysis as facilitating freedom of contract for the purpose of wealth maximization.

This economic interpretation of the law of contract can, at a pinch, provide a plausible account of modern developments in the law. Although at first sight rules which impose compulsory terms in contracts, such as the duty on a seller to supply goods of satisfactory quality to a consumer, appear to impede freedom of contract and restrain wealth maximization, such rules can be explained as a necessary response to transaction costs and market failure. The consumer lacks the expertise to judge the quality of a complex product and can only obtain the necessary information and expertise at considerable expense. This results in market failure in consumer purchases of such products, so that consumers acquire products which do not satisfy their preferences. The remedy lies in compulsory terms which restrict choice in order to protect consumers from their worst mistakes, and duties to disclose vital information to put consumers on their guard. These economic arguments always work as explanations of the interventionist character of modern law both because transaction costs are omnipresent and unquantifiable, and because market failures arising from shortage of information and expertise is endemic to most markets.

But they are weak explanations, because the economic arguments can also always support lesser regulation or no intervention at all. Market failures are always a matter of degree and transaction costs hard to quantify. Depending on assumptions about how gravely a competitive market is impeded by difficulties of acquiring or processing information, or how expensive it might be to create complete contracts that deal with every eventuality, it is possible to argue either in favour or against particular legal regulation. For example, is it justifiable to require banks, when making loans to consumers, always to state the rate of interest in a particular way known as the annual percentage rate (APR)? This intervention may address a market failure if consumers were unable, prior to the regulation, to make intelligent comparisons between rates of interest. Although this hypothesis seems plausible, the continuing wide variety of interest rates and the apparent willingness of consumers to borrow at extremely high rates of interest perhaps suggests that in fact the inability to make comparisons was not the problem but rather some other reason, such as urgent financial need, led consumers to enter into disadvantageous transactions. Economic analysis provides a useful tool for considering the need for restrictions on freedom of contract, but without evidence of the sources of market failure and the amount of transaction costs, it cannot provide a convincing account of modern regulatory interventions.

Most advocates of this economic interpretation of the law of contract do not in fact generally support restrictions on freedom of contract. On the contrary, they use economic analysis to identify certain interventions as undesirable and unjustifiable infringements of the market order, and propose deregulation instead. Price controls, for example, as occur sometimes in rented accommodation and on minimum wages, will normally be rejected on the ground that these do not respond to a market failure, but in fact create a market failure themselves. By artificially lowering the price of rented accommodation, the law will reduce the supply, thereby creating a problem of homelessness. Similarly, by artificially raising the price of wages, the law reduces employers' demand for labour, which in turn creates the market failure represented by unemployment. By analogy, the desirability and justice of many other types of interference in free contracts may be questioned, such as the imposition of compulsory terms in leases and contracts of employment, on the ground that they cause a market failure which in the long run leaves everyone worse off than before. In short, restrictions on freedom of contract, although occasionally justifiable under an economic analysis as a last resort to handle market failures, often create a market failure themselves, so should normally be avoided.

3.   The value of autonomy

Like the paradigm of the justice of exchange, the market failure approach shares a disregard for problems of power, distributive fairness, and the need to encourage co-operation in the realization of market opportunities. Its system of understanding the market order confines attention to the process of economic exchange and an assessment of how best to facilitate its efficient operation as a mechanism for the generation of wealth. This view represents a vital perspective on the market order, but this system of understanding seems to me to be impoverished in its appreciation of the issues raised by contractual disputes.

Consider, for example, the case of the unknown songwriter in *Schroeder Music Publishing Co Ltd v Macaulay*.[6] This young composer agreed to give all his songs to a publisher for a period of five years, renewable at the option of the publisher, in return for royalties on published work but no promise to publish the work. The House of Lords declared the agreement void under the doctrine of restraint of trade, arguing that the weak bargaining position of the composer had led to an unfair agreement under which the publisher undertook minimal obligations in return for total commitment by the composer. If one considers this decision from the perspective of market failure, it seems hard to justify. As Trebilcock points out,[7] there seems to have been a competitive market operating in this instance, with many music publishers competing for young talent. Nor can it be seriously suggested that the composer did not understand the terms of the agreement because they were too complex. In the absence of such grounds to suspect market failure, economic analysis suggests that the contract should be enforced, for any interference may disrupt the market opportunities for young composers in the future.

But these arguments, although sound in themselves, miss the real objections to this contract, which concern the dimensions of power, fairness, and co-operation, not the efficiency of the market. Because the composer's career was completely dependent upon the publisher's discretion for a period up to ten years, his degree of subordination to another represented an unjustifiable form of domination. The absence of an undertaking on the part of the publisher to publish any of his songs rendered the exchange too one-sided to be fair. In addition, because the composer could not terminate the agreement during its fixed period, he had no

6   [1974] 3 All ER 616, [1974] 1 WLR 1308, HL.
7   Trebilcock, 'An Economic Approach to Unconscionability' in B Reiter and J Swan (eds), *Studies in Contract Law* (Toronto, 1980), p 379.

effective sanction against the publisher to ensure that at least it made reasonable efforts to bring the venture to fruition by publishing and promoting his work.

These three themes – the concern about unjustifiable domination, the equivalence of the exchange, and the need to ensure co-operation – which seem to me to motivate the decision in *Schroeder Music Publishing Co Ltd v Macaulay*, form the core of the interpretation of law of contract presented in this book. The emphasis upon these values in the modern law signifies a new understanding and justification of the market order. The law's endorsement of those values does not represent the adoption of a socialist or communitarian political philosophy or a rejection of the market order. The constitution of the market by reference to these values, as well as the traditional concerns for liberty and competitive markets, merely represents a revised understanding of the market order and its justificatory principles, not a wholesale rejection of markets as the most efficient system for the satisfaction of wants.

The question of what political philosophy underpins this conception of the market order is more troublesome to answer. It cannot be the libertarian philosophies which underpin the justice of exchange paradigm, nor the wealth-maximization goal which seems to provide the main justification for the market failure interpretation. On the other hand, these values do not seem to be incompatible with certain liberal ideals, which it may be sensible to attribute to legislators and judges as the basis for their unarticulated political assumptions.

Perhaps the core principle in this interpretation of the market order consists in a revised notion of liberty or autonomy.[8] Whilst one should celebrate the liberating potential of a market order, because it offers considerable choices of occupation and consumption, we should recognise that not all choices seem so worthwhile and deserving of approbation. For instance, choices to harm the environment, to injure one's own body, to sell one's property at far less than its market value, and to enter into economic relations which give others discretionary power over major aspects of one's well-being, do not seem to be valuable choices which the law should respect and protect. If so, although the law should continue to support the facility of entering into binding commitments by voluntary choice, it should limit this facility to choices which are likely to prove worthwhile ways of pursuing one's life. The law can tolerate a considerable range of economic transactions and give the benefit of the doubt to activities which seem of little worth to most people, but the law sets limits to freedom of contract when the choices made do not appear worthwhile on any reckoning. In other words, the positive side of liberty, the ability to enter into binding commitments, is interpreted not as a general licence, but a power to be exercised for worthwhile purposes; and the negative aspect of

8   Perhaps closest to J Raz, *The Morality of Freedom* (Oxford, 1986). For similar views, see Brownsword, 'Liberalism and the Law of Contract' (1988) 36 *Archives for Philosophy of Law and Social Philosophy* 86; Smith, 'Future Freedom and Freedom of Contract' (1996) 59 *Modern Law Rev* 167.

liberty relaxes the constraints upon state intervention in the market to place limits on the types of contractual obligations which may be undertaken.[9]

Another way in which to make the same point is to interpret the modern law of contract as not regarding the market merely as a source of preference satisfaction, but as an opportunity to augment and contribute to the sense of 'meaning' of a person's life.[10] The purchase of a house, for example, although certainly sharing a dimension of preference satisfaction, will often mean so much more to an individual, for it offers security, a home and a base from which the rest of life may be organized. Similarly, the entry into a contract of employment will often mean more than simply the opportunity to earn cash for purchasing goods: it marks the entry into a career, the acquisition of status, and an opportunity to gain dignity and respect. To understand the realm of the market order merely in terms of preference satisfaction, as the sophisticated economic models tend to do, seriously misunderstands the significance of many market transactions.

When contracts have these qualities – of contributing in important ways to the sense of meaning in a person's life – the modern law of contract responds by securing that person's reasonable expectations. The concept of the social market appreciates how the market must be channelled and controlled to preserve its quality as an opportunity for individual aspiration. To perform this function so that the law can reflect in its standards the different satisfactions which may be derived from economic transactions, the unity of the law of contract must be sacrificed. Each type of transaction must be governed by its own distinctive standards, which seek to preserve and enhance the opportunities afforded by that type of transaction for the establishment of meaning.

(a) UNJUSTIFIABLE DOMINATION

One derivation from this more complex notion of liberty or autonomy concerns the power relations developed through contractual relations. Under the principles of the justice of exchange, with its idol of freedom of contract, the potentialities of ownership and knowledge can be realized into oppressive forms of domination to the extent that lawyers can devise complex organizational structures in the form of exchange relations. The main constraint upon the facility for domination lies in the limits of one's ability to persuade others to bind themselves by way of contract. But here the discipline of economic necessity operates to provide compelling inducements to contract. Since the principal source of wealth lies in the market in the form of wages and profits, few can afford to remain aloof. Consequently, the law of contract lies at the intersection of the market and state power, and it uses the coercion of the latter to reinforce the discipline of the former.

---

9   Sunstein, 'Disrupting Voluntary Transactions', in J Chapman and J Pennock (eds), *Markets and Justice* (New York, 1989), ch 10.
10 D Levine, *Needs, Rights and the Market* (Boulder, 1988).

One response to this risk of domination through contract is to limit freedom of contract to prevent persons from making such binding commitments. In some instances contractual rights will be superseded by a statutory framework of rights. For example, under English law an employee is granted a statutory right to challenge unfair dismissal from employment, which circumscribes the power of management to coerce the worker, and this right cannot normally be given up by contractual agreement. Although these rules still permit the individual to choose his occupation unfettered by law, they ensure that any choice will not be one which in effect establishes an unjustifiable level of subordination. In other instances mandatory terms shape the reciprocal obligations of the parties. Indeed, with little exaggeration, we can say that in most standard types of contracts made by ordinary persons, apart from the price, the parties have little choice over the terms of the agreement. The law adopts a number of model contracts, such as in purchases, loans, employment and leases, and describes a pattern for these economic relations which is imposed by a set of compulsory terms. For example, the seller of goods to a consumer must guarantee their satisfactory quality and fitness for their normal purpose, and any attempt to limit or qualify this guarantee in the terms of the contract will be void. Although businesses still enjoy a greater measure of freedom when contracting amongst themselves, even here the courts have powers to control unreasonable terms inserted in standard form contracts, and through interpretation of the terms of the contracts the courts may more subtly ensure conformity with unarticulated model agreements.

Another way in which to counter domination through contracts is to introduce a more substantive conception of equality. Although an ordinary consumer and a large business such as a retail chain store enjoy the formal equality to own property and enter bargains, it is clear that a business can often call upon much greater technical knowledge and legal expertise in order to secure favourable transactions. These disparities become particularly noticeable in complex transactions, as where the consumer requires a credit arrangement or a loan in order to complete the purchase, or when the item purchased involves complex technology as in the case of a car or electrical goods. But disparities appear in even a simple purchase of a can of beans at the supermarket, where the business is likely to have a much better understanding of the quality of the goods and the exact contents of the tin, which may include, besides the beans, various sauces, preservatives, colourings and so forth. The modern law recognizes these differentials in knowledge and expertise by introducing measures of consumer protection, and in so doing drops the presumption that citizens enter the market on equal terms. The credit arrangement must follow a prescribed explanatory form and cannot be extortionate; the seller of the car or electrical appliance must guarantee its quality, and the manufacturer will be liable for any injury caused to the purchaser; and the contents of the can of beans must be clearly labelled. The modern law replaces the commitment to formal equality by a recognition that each person enters the market from a different situation, and that to ignore those differences in knowledge, expertise, needs and command over resources is not to treat people equally but to treat unlike cases alike.

Behind these responses to unjustifiable domination lies a perception that the traditional separation between public and private spheres has become inadequate. Under the classical law, problems of power and domination were regarded as problems presented exclusively by the state. The role of public law was to combat state power by subjecting government bodies to controls over the exercise of discretionary power. Once it is recognised that similar problems of power arise in the context of contractual relations, especially those contracts which establish organizations such as firms, trade unions and trade associations, the case for extending controls over discretionary power to such private relations becomes pressing. We therefore discover the courts and the legislature inserting rules into such organizations which require them to follow fair procedures, to exercise discretion rationally and for lawful purposes, and to respect the rights of individuals. In other words, concepts and values formerly present exclusively in public law are applied to market relations where the contracts establish the potential for domination.[11]

(b) FAIRNESS OF THE EXCHANGE

A second derivation from this complex notion of liberty concerns the fairness of the price of exchanges. Although the modern law tolerates considerable disparity of prices, for this divergence reflects the different values which people choose to place on opportunities, it is sceptical about choices which amount to contracts setting a price significantly above or below comparable market prices or under which most of the reciprocal promises seem illusory. Such a choice does not amount to a worthwhile exploration of market opportunities, unless, of course, it signifies that an outright gift was intended. Statutes give the courts the power to revise or invalidate unfair transactions, either explicitly as in the case of extortionate credit bargains, or indirectly by monitoring whether the quality of the goods supplied lives up to the expected standard in the light of the price paid for them. The statutory power to invalidate unreasonable exemption clauses which limit or exclude liability for defective performance also contributes to equivalence in exchange, for it is no longer possible for one party to reduce drastically his or her obligations without a commensurate reduction in the price paid. Under the judge-made common law the courts deploy a battery of legal doctrines which tend to ensure an equivalence in exchange. When the circumstances surrounding the formation of contract signify the possibility of pressure or exploitation of a necessitous position or person's weak understanding

---

11 Beatson, 'Public Law Influences in Contract Law' in J Beatson and D Friedmann (eds), *Good Faith and Fault in Contract Law* (Oxford, 1995), p 263; Blades, 'Employment at Will vs Individual Freedom: On Limiting the Abusive Exercise of Employer Power' (1967) 67 *Columbia Law Review* 1404; Black, 'Constitutionalising Self-Regulation' (1996) 59 *Modern Law Review* 24.

of business, the court will rely upon the unfairness of the terms of the contract, judged by reference to other similar market transactions and the degree of disadvantage to the weaker party, in order to impugn the validity of the contract under the doctrines of duress and undue influence. These developments in the law of contract signify an abandonment of the presumption of fairness in exchanges.

(c) CO-OPERATION

A third derivation from this complex notion of liberty concerns the relation between the individual and others. The underlying image of the individual in the ideals of the justice of exchange was one who was antagonistic towards others and who entered transactions solely for the sake of his or her own interests. Indeed, from this perspective it is hard to find adequate justification for the enforcement of contracts against the will of the individual in the absence of clear economic harm to others. If, however, one regards the law of contract as offering an opportunity for entering into binding long-term commitments with others, an opportunity which augments the freedom of the individual, precise calculations of self-interest at every stage in the transaction should not be permitted to subvert the value of the institution of contracts. Instead, the law must impose certain duties of co-operation in the formation and performance of contracts, which reflect the need to secure reliable and worthwhile opportunities for market exchanges. These duties both expand and articulate the reciprocal duties implicit in a contractual relation.

Furthermore, this new interpretation of the relation between the individual and others introduces two kinds of limitations on the freedom to choose whether or not to enter a contract. In the first place, this freedom has been curtailed in order to ensure better equality of opportunity in the market. For this purpose, sex and race discrimination legislation deters refusals to enter contracts on the grounds of sex, marital status, race, nationality and other motives which display a lack of respect for the equality of others. In *Quinn v Williams Furniture Ltd*,[12] a married woman agreed to purchase a three-piece suite of furniture, paid a deposit, and then requested a loan arrangement for the balance of the price. The shop assistant said that the loan could not be made without her husband signing a collateral personal guarantee for the loan as well. The Court of Appeal decided that, since a similar guarantee from a spouse would not have been demanded by the shop in the case of a loan to a married man, this conduct constituted unlawful sex discrimination.

In the second place, the choice whether or not to undertake an obligation, although still a characteristic of contractual obligations, has in practice been significantly diminished by the expansion of alternative grounds for the

12 [1981] ICR 328, CA.

imposition of obligations. The law of tort, for instance, implies a duty of care between manufacturers and ultimate consumers regardless of their choice. This liability for negligence may extend to many kinds of relations of economic dependence, which, although not established by agreement between the parties, nevertheless are regarded as entailing an obligation to take care. For example, the decision in *White v Jones*[13] illustrates how a solicitor who negligently fails to draft a Will with the consequence that the testator's intentions are frustrated, will be held liable to the intended beneficiaries to the extent of their expected inheritance. Although the solicitor never entered a contract with these beneficiaries, he or she nevertheless owes them a similar duty to take care as that established in the contractual relation with the testator. The precise ambit of such tortious duties of care between parties who have not made agreements or bargains remains controversial, but the possibility of liability in tort in order to protect economic interests represents a major invasion of the freedom of individuals from obligations without their consent.

4. Conclusion – a regulatory perspective

The above discussion claims that the modern themes in the law of contract which I have identified as constituting a transformation in the market order may be derived from a sophisticated version of liberalism which relies upon a perfectionist conception of liberty or autonomy. It suggests that the modern law of contract should be understood by an examination of themes such as restrictions on the scope of contracts, mandatory terms, fairness, co-operation and imposed duties of care and responsibility. The details of this interpretation will be elaborated in the course of the book. But it is important to repeat that this transformation in values is masked at all times by the persistence of traditional legal categories and the differentiation of large fields of contractual practices, such as consumer purchases and employment, from mainstream discussions of the law of contract. Nor should I be understood as claiming that the modern values were completely unknown to the classical law of contract. No doubt courts in the nineteenth century occasionally found a way to permit a person to escape from an improvident bargain, to deter unco-operative or opportunistic behaviour that undermined the economic value of the transaction to the other party, or to give relief from an oppressive power relation established by contract. My point is rather that the modern values infuse the law at every point, encouraging the courts to evolve doctrines in new directions and providing the basis for a considerable body of regulatory intervention by legislatures.

This perspective on the law of contract can perhaps be given sharper focus by contrasting a traditional private law view with a modern regulatory perspective. Under the traditional private law view, which infused discussions of the classical

13 [1995] 2 AC 207, [1995] 1 All ER 691, HL.

law of contract, the law provided a facility for individuals to enter into voluntary binding commitments. The private ordering of individuals was respected and supported by legal enforcement of their agreements. In this modern perspective, however, the function of the law of contract is to regulate markets, market practices and the social practices of making contracts with a view to controlling the types of relationships established through contracts and their distributive consequences. This regulation of markets still pays considerable respect to private ordering, for the continuing strength of the law of contract is that it attaches great significance to the self-regulation of the parties established by their contractual agreement. Indeed, the law can contribute to the success of self-regulation by improving the operation of competitive markets and by steering contractual relations in ways that are likely to help to maximise the joint wealth of the parties. But this power of self-regulation is limited in most common transactions with a view to steering the outcomes of these transactions in ways that the values of the modern law wish to support.

C.   Contextual legal reasoning

The second element of the transformation of the law of contract concerns the method of legal reasoning. Of course the basic elements of legal reasoning have remained constant. The courts follow precedent, apply statutes and distinguish cases on their facts. Nevertheless, there has been a shift in the scope of reasoning and the complexity of the system of classification. The scope becomes broader as the courts acknowledge the relevance of a greater diversity of considerations. The system of classification becomes complex as different types of contractual relation receive differentiated treatment. In short, the formalism and unity of the classical law is replaced by contextual legal reasoning.

1.   Formalism and unity

We observed in Chapter 1 that in the nineteenth century the common law defined its conception of the law of contract in a simple set of rules. These rules comprised categories with logical relations between themselves. The application of these categories with their logical implications to the facts of a dispute determined the result. For example, for an enforceable contract the law required an agreement, comprised of an offer by one party and an acceptance by the other, so that the absence of either element prevented a binding agreement from arising. We examined this rule-governed and conceptual style of reasoning in the case of *Carlill v Carbolic Smoke Ball Co.*[14] Recall how in that case the court's reasoning towards the conclusion that the promise to pay £100 was enforceable proceeded

14 [1893] 1 QB 256, CA.

by listing the requirements of an enforceable contract, and by then ticking them off as each was satisfied on the facts. The formalism of the law of contract probably contributed to its certainty and predictability, which were desirable features for the law governing an expanding market economy.[15]

As a style of legal reasoning, legal formalism does not prevent the insertion of moral and political values into law. On the contrary, the technical rules are but clues to the submerged principles of the law, and it is these principles which express the governing ideologies of the legal control over the market order. Moreover, in the application of the rules to the particular facts of cases, the courts could manipulate the results for instrumental purposes. The *Carlill v Carbolic Smoke Ball Co* case itself illustrates this instrumentalism, for the court had to strain the requirements of offer and acceptance in order to conclude that, even in the absence of direct communication by the claimant with the manufacturer, they had in fact reached an agreement. Nevertheless, the underlying values and purposes of the rules and their manipulation for instrumental purposes was rarely acknowledged by the courts. They preferred to dispose of a case by reference to a narrow technical rule, without venturing into the field of basic principle or considering openly the consequences of the decision. This method conformed to a narrow conception of the political authority of judges under the Rule of Law, in which their job is, in principle, to enforce the law, not to create it. The judiciary seeks to appear neutral between conflicting interest groups and competing conceptions of the good life. This conception of the judicial role in developing the law of contract leads the courts to refer extensively to precedent, to present the law as a logical elaboration of ancient principles, and to frame the rules in terms avoiding reference to group interests.

During the development of this classical scheme of rules, the courts were not confronted with the whole range of possible contractual disputes. For the most part, these technical rules were designed to cope with disputes between persons who actually litigated, which generally meant businesses in the course of a series of commercial transactions rather than private individuals. The character of this site for the development of the classical rules had a number of consequences. The language of the technical rules reflects the world of commerce rather than consumer purchases. The categories of the law, such as offer and acceptance, presuppose a situation where the parties negotiate the details of their contract and reach a firm conclusion, rather than the more casual, everyday contracts, such as boarding a bus or purchasing a can of beans. As Lord Wilberforce has observed:

It is only the precise analysis of this complex of relations into the classical offer and acceptance, with identifiable consideration, that seems to present

15 M Weber, *Economy and Society* (G Roth and C Wittich (eds), Berkeley, 1968), Vol 2, ch 8, esp pp 687–688; Cotterrell, 'The Development of Capitalism and the Formalisation of Contract Law' in B Fryer et al (eds), *Law, State and Society* (London, 1981); H Collins, *Regulating Contracts* (Oxford, 1999), ch 8.

difficulty, but this same difficulty exists in many situations of daily life, eg sales at auction; supermarket purchases; boarding an omnibus; purchasing a train ticket; tenders for the supply of goods; offers of rewards; acceptance by post; warranties of authority by agents; manufacturers' guarantees; gratuitous bailments; bankers' commercial credits. These are all examples which show that English law, having committed itself to a rather technical and schematic doctrine of contract, in application takes a practical approach, often at the cost of forcing the facts to fit uneasily into the marked slots of offer, acceptance and consideration.[16]

More importantly, the common context of the decisions in business disputes permitted the insistence upon a unified law of contract. No matter what the substance of the transaction, nor the nature of the parties concerned, the general rules applied. The doctrine of consideration was the test of enforceability, for instance, regardless of whether the dispute concerned a transaction for the import of a valuable commodity, a loan from a bank, a claim of a reward offered in a newspaper, or an invitation to lunch. The law of contract was conceived as an abstract and general set of rules applicable to all transactions.

If we tie together these strands of the classical form of the law of contract, we find an unusual legal knot. The law comprises a unified set of formal rules which eschews any claims to a moral vision and which systematically suppresses as irrelevant questions about the distribution of wealth and power. The rules are technical, tied to precedent, and can be expanded by appeals to logic and rationality. Judges express the rules in the discourses of commerce and tend to describe all obligations in monetary values. This combination indubitably possesses a peculiar fascination for lawyers, particularly professors of law, for it presents a challenge for which raw intellect suffices. To write a classical treatise on contracts apparently involved no political or moral judgements; instead, the patient application of logic to the learning generated by reading precedents would reveal the majesty of the law of contract. The subject became the ideal instrument for acquainting students with the desired autonomous modes of legal reasoning and the sparring ground for the most talented lawyers of the age.

2. Differentiation and materialization

In contrast, legislatures have often provided the decisive innovations which constitute the modern law of contracts. Legislators can select openly between competing distributions of wealth and power. A legislature may treat types of contracts distinctly and is capable of discriminating between persons. It can identify consumers, employees, and tenants as categories of persons which deserve protection from the relations of domination established by freedom of

16 Lord Wilberforce, *New Zealand Shipping Co Ltd v A M Satterthwaite & Co Ltd (The Eurymedon)* [1975] AC 154, [1974] 1 All ER 1015, PC.

contract. This differentiation between types of contracts and the character of the parties to contracts is incompatible with the unity of classical contract law.[17] Many texts therefore limit their discussion of legislation to footnotes or tailpieces to chapters, and in the classroom the legislative interventions usually produce separate courses altogether on such matters as consumer law, landlord and tenant and employment law. But these methods of accommodating legislative innovations ignore their real impact on the general principles of the law of contract, for they demand a reconsideration of the fundamental assumptions of the classical model.

The novel legislative standards often delegate considerable discretion to the courts, because the laws often employ imprecise concepts such as reasonableness, fairness, good faith and unconscionability, the meaning of which must be elaborated in the ordinary run of cases.[18] Judges often find this task uncomfortable for it requires them to regulate market practices and to impose moral judgments on the behaviour of the parties. To avoid this difficulty, judges tend to appeal to normal practices in the market place to define standards of reasonableness and fairness. This weakens the impact of legislation, for it restricts the proscriptions of legislation to unconventional practices and perhaps indirectly legitimizes those standard practices which the legislation was designed to reform. In order to overcome this judicial inhibition, legislatures sometimes vest the task of interpretation of legislation in special courts such as rent tribunals, labour courts and trade commissions, although this technique enjoys only limited success in altering the behaviour of adjudicators.

To a limited extent, the courts have also participated in the elaboration of common law principles which fit better the modern values presaged by legislation. The contribution of the courts has been cautious, however, because they remain committed to the unity of the law of contract. They have resisted differentiation of the law according to context, so they have deprived themselves of a crucial tool in legal reasoning. For example, they could not distinguish between exclusion clauses in consumer contracts and in commercial contracts, so that they failed to create any protection for consumers against the deprivation of legal rights in the small print of standard form contracts. On the whole, lawyers prefer their legal doctrines to be stirred but not shaken.

17 J Wightman, *Contract: A Critical Commentary* (London, 1996), ch 8.
18 Some authors suggest that there is a connection between the values of the modern law and its form, particularly this dimension of materialisation: Kennedy, 'Form and Substance in Private Law Adjudication' (1976) 89 *Harvard Law Review* 1685; Adams and Brownsword, 'The Ideologies of Contract' (1987) 7 *Legal Studies* 205; Cockrell, 'Substance and Form in the South African Law of Contract' (1992) 109 *South African Law Journal* 40. Although there have been important concordances between changes in form and substance, these homologies seem to be contingent facts rather than logical relations: M Kelman, *A Guide to Critical Legal Studies* (Cambridge, Mass, 1987), ch 1. For example, our discussion of the case *Carlill v Carbolic Smoke Ball Co* in the previous chapter revealed that it was consumerist in orientation, but strictly formal, judge-made rules in its discourse.

Despite these important changes in the form of the law of contract, it is fair to say that they can easily be overlooked because the features of the bulk of litigated cases remain similar to those which provided the forge for the classical law. If a study of the law of contract is confined to the reported decisions of higher courts of appeal, the cases usually involve commercial organizations locked into disputes over large sums of money or large organisations such as banks seeking to collect their debts from individuals. To resolve these disputes the courts still rely heavily on the classical rules of the law of contract but, of course, this gives a misleading picture of the law of contract as a whole. Even in commercial litigation, we can discern significant adjustments to the style of legal reasoning employed by the courts. There is an unwillingness to apply the 'marked slots' of the classical categories without regard to the consequences of classification of the facts. Moreover, the relevant legislation often forces courts even in commercial disputes to have regard to looser terminology, such as standards of 'unconscionability' and 'reasonableness'.

Looking generally at the form of contract law we observe that, whereas the classical law assumes a style of autonomous legal reasoning, the modern law fails to draw a bright line between legal, political and moral argument. Legal discourse has shifted from a rhetoric of entitlements determined by the application of general rules to the facts of a case, to one of consequentialist reasoning and a balancing of moral values. This 'materialization' of the modern law of contract[19] both breaks down the generality of the rules by devising norms appropriate to specific classes such as consumer and employee, and it challenges the closed quality of formal legal reasoning by compelling courts and regulators to confront the social and economic consequences of their decisions in their interpretation of the law.[20] To grasp the transformation of legal thought and reasoning about contractual disputes which the modern law of contract engenders, we must abandon the old legal categories focused on entitlement and replace them with an articulation of the values and policies pursued by modern legal discourse. In order to capture the spirit of the modern law, instead of listing a set of rules which can be applied mechanically to resolve contractual problems, this book must present the dominant values which inform and direct legal reasoning.

D.   Globalization and sources of law

The third aspect of the transformation of the law of contract concerns the sources of law. The classical law was linked to the concept of 'nation state', each nation developing its own closed doctrinal system using distinctive concepts and rules.

---

19 R Unger, *Law in Modern Society* (New York, 1976), pp 192–216; G Teubner (ed), *Dilemmas of Law in the Welfare State* (New York/Berlin, 1988); J Habermas, *Between Facts and Norms* (Cambridge, 1996), ch 9.
20 H Collins, *Regulating Contracts* (Oxford, 1999), ch 3.

Now this insularity is breaking down under the pressure of globalization of markets and the evolution of international political structures to regulate these markets. Such developments expand the sources of the law of contract to encompass rules emanating from transnational legal orders. Furthermore, it accelerates the development of legal orders which are to a considerable degree autonomous from any nation state. Observe also the increasing emphasis placed on the international protection of human rights as the source of legitimacy in these international legal orders. This arena provides a new source of law for regulating contracts, one which may steer its values in new directions.

1. Sources of national law

The insularity of the classical law did not prevent each legal system from having a rich set of sources of law. The rules could be derived from the variety of jurisdictions within the national legal order, such as specialist commercial courts. In common law jurisdictions, such as the UK and the USA, the rivalry between common law courts and Chancery permitted the evolution of contrasting legal principles. When the jurisdictions were fused in the late-nineteenth century, the law of contract had to integrate into its doctrinal system both distinctive equitable doctrines such as undue influence, estoppel and relief from penalties, and also special equitable remedies such as specific performance and rescission. The process of integration continues to this day, and provides judges occasionally with the opportunity to seize upon the fertile principles of equity to justify some modern departure from classical common law precedents.

As well as separate courts, the classical law drew upon the intellectual resources provided by historical antecedents and comparative studies. The common law judges transplanted many doctrines, like the ideas of mistake, frustration and tests for the measurement of damages, from the scholarly tradition of natural law, whose own intellectual roots lay in Roman Law, but which culminated in the readily available Napoleonic Civil Code. These transplants overlapped with existing common law concepts, provoking some confusion and inconsistency.[21]

2. Transnational legal orders

With the advent of greater international trade, instantaneous electronic communications, multinational enterprises operating in global markets, and the creation of free trading blocks such as the single market of the European Community (EC), the source of legal regulation of markets now includes transnational legal orders as well as the regulation of nation states.

---

21 Simpson, 'Innovation in Nineteenth-Century Contract Law' (1975) 91 *Law Quarterly Review* 247; Nicholas, 'Rules and Terms – Civil Law and Common Law' (1974) 48 *Tulane Law Review* 946.

A typical example concerns the rules governing the legal system applicable to contracts. Under the general rules of private international law, the parties to a cross-border transaction can select which legal system should govern their contract. In the UK these conflict of laws rules applicable to contract are determined by the Contracts (Applicable Law) Act 1990. But this national statute merely incorporates the standards agreed in an international convention, the 1980 Rome Convention on the Law Applicable to Contractual Obligations. This convention is itself supplemented by EC rules which create exceptions for particular kinds of contracts.[22] The English courts have to produce interpretations of this law which conform to the interpretations placed upon it by other courts, including the European Court of Justice. Although English commercial law has been slow to adopt such international conventions through legislation,[23] in the long term the globalization of the economic system is likely to compel accession.

For English law, the most important development in transnational regulation of markets has been the creation of the single market of the EC. The scope of European regulation has expanded from the elimination of obvious barriers to trade between member states to include more subtle impediments such as the diversity in the laws of contracts. If this diversity inhibits trade within the single market, as it may, there is a case for devising a European uniform law of contract, or at least to seek approximation of the laws.[24] As a first step along such a road, a series of EC Directives has sought the harmonization of the legal rules governing consumer transactions in member states. The need for harmonization is arguably the greatest in consumer transactions and contracts of employment, for uniform transnational laws prevent regulatory competition between member states, which causes each state to minimize the legal obligations imposed on businesses in order to attract investment and trade.[25] For example, ordinary consumer purchases in the high street shops are now largely governed throughout the EC by uniform

22 EC Directive 92/49/EEC on Direct Insurance, Art 31, which imposes a mandatory duty of express notification of choice of law clauses in insurance contracts.

23 Steyn, 'A Kind of Esperanto?' in P Birks (ed), *The Frontiers of Liability* (Oxford, 1994), Vol 2, p 11, discussing the UN Convention on Contracts for the International Sale of Goods (the 'Vienna Convention') to which most of the EU, North America, and Australasia are already signatories.

24 Communication from the Commission to the Council and the European Parliament on European Contract Law, COM (2001) 398 final, OJ 2001 C 255/1; Resolution of the European Parliament on the approximation of the civil and commercial law of the Member States, COM (2001) 398 – C5-0471/2001; Communication from the Commission to the European Parliament and the Council, *A More Coherent European Contract Law: An Action Plan* (Brussels, 12.2.2003 COM (2003) 68 final; S Grundmann and J Stuyck (eds), *An Academic Green paper on European Contract Law* (The Hague, 2002); A Hartkamp *et al* (eds), *Towards a European Civil Code* (Nijmegen, 2nd edn, 1998); O Lando, 'Principles of European Contract Law' (1992) 56 *RabelsZ* 261.

25 T Bourgoigne and D Trubeck, *Consumer Law, Common Markets and Federalism in Europe and the United States* (Berlin/New York, 1987); Reich, 'Protection of Consumers' Economic Interests by the EC' (1992) 14 *Sydney Law Rev* 23; R Buxbaum, G Hertig, A Hirsh, K Hopt (eds), *European*

rules and principles. EC Directives have to be incorporated by each member state into national legislation, but the European source of the regulation will require the courts in each jurisdiction to ensure that their interpretations conform to the common pattern. For the future, therefore, European law will become a crucial determinant of the evolution of the law of contract in the UK. There is hardly a chapter in this book in which EC Directives do not steer some of the relevant legal regulation. What effect will this transnational regulation have on the common law of contract?

Will the values contained in EC Directives coincide with the ambitions of the social market described earlier in this chapter, or will the values differ? Since the driving force of the single market comprises the enhancement of competition by breaking down barriers to entry into markets, there is certainly a risk that laws which restrict choice in entering contracts and promote social goals will be regarded as obstructions to competition. For the time being, however, this danger has been avoided by framing EC Directives as minimum standards rather than compulsory levels of protection. There remains the deeper question whether the gradual replacement of national law by transnational regulation poses a challenge to the cultural identity of regions within the European single market and to their distinctive legal traditions.[26]

In some quarters there is strong support for the introduction of a European Code of Contract Law, perhaps based on model codes that draw upon all the different national legal systems.[27] Since the common law lacks a codified law of contract, its method of reasoning has never attained the same level of formalism as civil law systems. The formulation of rules derives from generalizations about previous decisions, so the description of the rule can always be reconsidered and qualified. The canon of rules is never fixed in the common law, for earlier lines of authority can be permitted to atrophy or can be resuscitated. The challenge posed by European regulation is that these pragmatic and inductive qualities of common law legal reasoning will be inhibited under the influence of the formal deductive style of reasoning characteristic of legal systems governed by codes.[28] From a less insular point of view, we must question whether a traditional code of private law is the most adequate regulatory technique for expressing the modern values and perspectives of the law of contract.[29]

Business Law: Legal and Economic Analysis on Integration and Harmonization (Berlin, 1991); Trachtman, 'International Regulatory Competition, Externalization, and Jurisdiction' (1993) 34 *Harvard International Law Journal* 47; Collins, 'Good Faith in European Contract Law' (1994) 14 *Oxford Journal of Legal Studies* 229; S Weatherill, *EC Consumer Law and Policy* (Harlow, 1997).

26 Collins, 'European Private Law and the Cultural Identity of States' (1995) 3 *European Review of Private Law* 353.

27 O Lando and H Beale (eds), *Principles of European Contract Law, Parts I and II* (The Hague, 2000).

28 Legrand, 'Against a European Civil Code' (1997) 60 *Modern Law Review* 44.

29 M Hesselink, *The New European Private Law* (The Hague, 2002).

3.   Commercial legal order

Beyond transnational legal regulation, international business transactions have always forged their own miniature legal orders. The first step in this development was the creation of commercial standard form contracts, which through their elaborate provisions created a novel set of legal relations suited to international trade. These contracts such as bills of exchange and bankers' commercial credits often fitted uneasily into the traditional doctrinal fabric of national contract law. They were designed to bind together numerous parties and to create a system of credit, and these objectives could not always be achieved consistently within the ordinary rules of contract law such as the doctrines of consideration and privity of contract. Recognizing the utility of these types of documents, however, English courts routinely gave effect to their intentions, either brushing aside doctrinal difficulties or inventing special categories of exceptions such as 'negotiable instruments' which could transfer contractual rights with the minimum of formality. But these commercial contracts remained tied to the national legal order insofar as they required state courts to supply effective sanctions.

The connection with national legal orders becomes more attenuated once the contracts allocate jurisdiction to arbitration tribunals. In effect the parties select their own judges, and define the mechanism by which the arbitrators may enforce sanctions. This development permits the arbitrators to draw upon sources of law which are not tied to a particular legal order. The parties to the contract may instruct the arbitrator to use the guidance of a code of rules specially devised for international business transactions. As international arbitration of commercial disputes becomes more common, the practice is developing its own standards which supplement any rules selected by the parties, but which are not based specifically on any one national legal system.[30] In this context, it is only the final sanction which must be backed by state power, but the remaining sources of law regulating the transaction derive from non-state, depoliticized institutions and customs. Where the effective sanction is exclusion from a private association such as a particular exchange or trading market, then even this tenuous connection with state law is sundered.

This form of private ordering is sometimes called a 'lex mercatoria'. Whether or not it should be regarded as a separate source of law governing international contracts remains a controversial issue. Since its standards remain ultimately dependent upon state sanctions for their enforcement, it can be discounted as merely an elaborate form of contract regulated ultimately by state law. On the

30 Teubner, 'Global Bukowina: Legal Pluralism in the World Society', in G Teubner (ed), *Global Law Without A State* (Aldershot, 1997), p 3; Mertens, 'Lex Mercatoria: A Self-applying System Beyond National Law?', in G Teubner (1997) *ibid*, p 31; B Cremades, 'The Impact of International Arbitration on the Development of Business law' (1983) 31 *American Journal of Comparative Law* 526; Y Dezalay and B Garth, *Dealing in Virtue: International Commercial Arbitration and the Construction of a Transnational Legal Order* (Chicago, 1996).

other hand, to the extent that the standards applicable to the contracts derive from other sources such as conventions, customs of business or rules of private associations, then it can be regarded as an independent source of legal regulation of contracts.

4. Human rights law

In the architecture of the emerging global legal order, the protection of human rights occupies the highest position. The protection of human rights provides the most powerful justification for judicial intervention. Many countries confer the power to protect human rights on judges through their constitutions, but they may also acknowledge the authority of transnational courts, such as the European Court of Human Rights that enforces the European Convention on Human Rights and Fundamental Freedoms against the signatory states. In the UK, the Human Rights Act 1998 confers on domestic courts the power to uphold the rights contained in the Convention against public authorities, and places a duty on the courts to interpret the law in ways that are consistent with Convention rights. This latter duty may occasionally influence the courts in the development of the common law of contract, for the Convention rights include in Article 11 the right to freedom of association, which might be interpreted to provide strong support for freedom of contract, and in Article 1 of the First Protocol to the Convention the right to peaceful enjoyment of possessions.

In the context of a discussion of the emergence of modern values in the law of contract, the danger presented by this emphasis on human rights is that legislation that pursues social purposes, even to the extent of overriding the rights of individuals, may be found by a court to be inconsistent with the Convention rights. In *Wilson v First County Trust Ltd (No 2)*,[31] for instance, the Court of Appeal made a declaration that the Consumer Credit Act 1974, s 127(3) was incompatible with the protection afforded by the Convention to the peaceful enjoyment of possessions. This statutory provision prevented the court from permitting a creditor to enforce a credit agreement against a consumer if the signed agreement failed to include certain prescribed terms. In this case, the creditor had made an error in the statement describing the amount of credit agreed between the parties. The purpose of making the agreement unenforceable by the creditor is, presumably, to compel creditors to ensure that documents are accurate, so that consumers can be fully informed about the risks and liabilities arising from a credit agreement. But the effect of the unenforceability of a credit agreement might be that the creditor would be unable to take possession of any promised security, in this case a car, and sell it in the event of the debtor's default. The Court of Appeal concluded that this interference with the proprietary interest of the creditor in the promised security by completely blocking any claim

---

31 [2001] EWCA Civ 633, [2002] QB 74, [2001] 3 All ER 229.

by the creditor amounted to a disproportionate interference with the creditor's right to a fair trial under Article 6 of the Convention. A proportionate interference would have permitted the court a discretion to do justice between the parties in view of the gravity of the error and the prejudice caused to the consumer (a power that is conferred with respect to other improperly executed agreements under the Consumer Credit Act 1974, s 127(1)). Although the error in this particular case was slight and had caused no prejudice to the consumer, the willingness of the court to declare the statutory sanction of unenforceability by the creditor as incompatible with the Convention rights should raise a concern about whether the courts might use their new powers under the Human Rights Act 1998 to interfere more widely with modern regulation in the name of protection of property rights and freedom of contract.

Chapter 3

Tests of enforceability

A. Purposes of tests of enforceability
B. Evidence and formalities
C. Illegality and public policy
D. Public and private undertakings
E. The contractualization of social life

A. Purposes of tests of enforceability

Should the law enforce all transactions? In a market economy, which depends for its success upon the prolific exchange of goods and services, we expect the law of contract to enforce nearly every undertaking. Although this proves correct in general, the law requires the transaction to comply with both formal and substantive tests of legal enforceability. In this chapter we consider the purposes served by these tests of enforceability, before turning in subsequent chapters to an examination of the details of these tests.

Tests of enforceability determine the scope of legally enforceable transactions. The tests play a role, therefore, in the legal constitution of markets. An agreement which does not satisfy the tests of enforceability might nevertheless be observed by the parties. They might conform to their agreement due to a sense of moral obligation, or from a fear of threats or a loss of reputation for fair dealing, or for some other kind of pragmatic reason. But failure to comply with the legal tests of enforceability removes the potential advantage of legal support for the transaction. Why does the law insist upon tests of enforceability which have the effect of excluding legal support for some voluntary undertakings?

Consider some illustrations which point to the need to confine the law of contract. In the first case a man agrees with his wife to wash up the dishes if she will go out and do the grocery shopping. On her return she discovers that her husband has failed to stir himself from in front of the television. Should she be able to sue her husband for breach of contract? In a second case, a politician agrees to cast his or her votes according to the instructions of a large multinational corporation in return for money to fund an expensive lifestyle.

Should the multinational be permitted to sue the politician when he or she disobeys instructions? In both of these instances the persons concerned reach an agreement, one which has been freely chosen, and from which they expect to benefit. Yet it seems unlikely that any legal system would regard these agreements as legally enforceable. In the first illustration, a court would simply decline to become involved in this matrimonial dispute, holding that the spouses did not intend to make a legally binding agreement.[1] In the second instance, not only would the agreement be unenforceable on the grounds of illegality and public policy,[2] but also it would probably trigger the application of criminal penalties for corruption.

These examples reveal some cases when it is appropriate for the courts to set limits to the possibility of contractual obligations. They also demonstrate that it would be improper for the courts to delegate entirely to the parties themselves the question of whether their agreement should be legally enforceable. These tests of enforceability must therefore contain mandatory rules. If we examine the reasons for having tests of legal enforceability, we can distinguish four purposes which they serve:

(i)   they prove the transaction;
(ii)   they deter criminal and immoral transactions;
(iii) they respect the privacy of social arrangements; and
(iv)   they control the scope of contractual self-regulation.

In the first instance, tests of enforceability address a practical problem. A court will sometimes be faced with a dispute about whether any undertaking, promise, or agreement has occurred at all. To resolve this dispute, the court requires evidence to prove the existence of the transaction. A test of enforceability indicates what kind of evidence suffices to prove the transaction. Such a test may indicate that the form of proof must be a written, signed document, or an oath sworn in front of witnesses or a public official such as a notary, or the registration of the contract in a public registry. If the law adopts any of these formal requirements, then failure to satisfy the relevant formality will prevent the transaction from being legally enforceable. Provided that the formalities required are well known and understood, this device immediately resolves most disputes about the existence of a contract.

Secondly, the law examines the content and purpose of agreements, for it will deny legal sanctions to transactions which it regards as improper on the ground that they involve activities which involve criminal or immoral conduct. This function requires an examination of the substantive content of the undertaking in order to determine whether or not it involves the kind of activity to which the law ought to lend its support. Easy cases where the law will deny a legal sanction

---

1   *Balfour v Balfour* [1919] 2 KB 571, CA; see Chapter 4.
2   *Amalagmated Society of Railway Servants v Osborne* [1910] AC 87, HL.

involve blatant criminal activity such as a contract for the murder of an individual. The harder cases present facts where the actions may be generally regarded as immoral, but against which there is no specific legal prohibition.

The third purpose of tests of enforceability is to set limits to the intervention of the state in the private activities of individuals. Here the object of the agreement may be unobjectionable, but nevertheless the law determines that the voluntary undertaking should not be supported by the sanctions offered by the state. Should the law, for instance, be prepared to enforce an agreement to meet a financial consultant, or to comment on a colleague's work? In an appropriate context, an agreement to attend a meeting or to give professional advice could be an acceptable scenario for regulation. But if the agreement consists in a casual, informal arrangement, an intervention by the state into the form of sanctions for breach of contract would be regarded as an excessive intrusion into the private lives of citizens. The agreement may be binding in morality or etiquette, but should not be the subject of state intervention. We might say in other words that these agreements are private rather than public matters. Disputes which arise from them should be settled by compromise or the deployment of informal social sanctions, rather than by coercion by the state in the form of awards of damages for breach of contract.

The final purpose of tests of enforceability is to govern the extent to which relationships may be reduced to a contractual form. In an agreement between a husband and wife over household jobs such as cleaning and shopping, the issue is whether contractual arrangements are appropriate to govern the obligations arising under the matrimonial relationship? To what extent should the law permit contractualization of social relations? The effect of permitting a contract to govern a relationship is that it tends to exclude any open-ended diffuse obligations arising from trust and friendship. The recognition of an enforceable contract suggests that the relationship can be created exclusively by express agreement and can be reduced to measurable obligations. Tests of enforceability police this boundary in order to exclude contractual obligations where these would subvert the values of the relationship.

Although these four purposes of the tests of enforceability are distinguishable, in a particular case before a court more than one of these issues might be raised. For example, if the agreement concerns an invitation to dinner at a friend's house, the legal enforcement of the transaction may be objectionable both on the ground that it would involve an undesirable contractualization of a relation of friendship and that it would lead to the imposition of a state sanction in an inappropriate private context.

Since the purposes of tests of enforceability are complex and overlapping, every legal system employs a number of legal doctrines to serve this function. These doctrines use both substantive and formal criteria. The substantive criteria examine the purpose of the agreement or the activities which it involves. These criteria include tests of whether the agreement involves illegality or acts contrary to public policy. The formal criteria examine the structure and form of the voluntary undertaking. With respect to the structure of the transaction, the test applies models of enforceable types of undertaking. In common law countries, the dominant structural model consists of the doctrine of consideration, which requires the transaction to consist of an exchange relationship under which each party undertakes an obligation requested by the other. The other type of formal requirement serves the evidentiary function of insisting upon a particular kind of documentary proof of the existence of the agreement.

B. Evidence and formalities

A tension plainly exists between the exigencies of a flourishing market economy and the need for clear proof of voluntary undertakings. The desire for proof of transactions points in favour of a requirement for formalities, such as an official record of a transaction, or at least a written document signed by both parties to the alleged contract. Yet such formal requirements might tend to stifle commercial transactions, where often agreements are concluded orally, perhaps on the telephone, with paperwork only being transmitted subsequently. Similarly, ordinary consumer transactions such as purchasing goods in a shop would be hampered if the law required an agreement in writing for the transaction to be legally efficacious. Of course, prudential considerations often cause parties to a major transaction to reduce their agreement to a written document. But this wise precaution, which avoids problems of proof with regard to the existence of the contract and reduces disputes about the terms of the agreement, need not become a legal requirement, without which the transaction would be treated as invalid.

This tension has been resolved in favour of the exigencies of a fluid market economy. As the market system has intensified, so the legal requirements of formalities have declined. At one time, by virtue of the Statute of Frauds (1677) and other legislation, most major transactions required at least evidence in writing, but this increasingly proved to be a trap for the unwary and an unnecessary impediment to transactions.[3] These evidentiary conditions have therefore been dismantled. Problems of proof of the existence of undertakings usually have to be resolved by examining all the evidence, including the actions and statements of the parties to the alleged contract. Two principal exceptions persist, one concerning transactions in land, and the other negotiable instruments, both of which must be in writing in order to be legally enforceable.

With respect to transactions involving land, the Law of Property (Miscellaneous Provisions) Act 1989, s 2(1) provides:

3 Law Revision Committee, Sixth Interim Report (Statute of Frauds and the Doctrine of Consideration), Cmd 5449 (1937).

> A contract for the sale or other disposition of an interest in land can only be made in writing and only by incorporating all the terms which the parties have expressly agreed in one document or, where contracts are exchanged, in each.

The scope of this provision is broad, because it includes not only sales of land, but also the creation or transfer of an interest in land, such as a lease or a charge.[4] In addition, the contract must be signed by or on behalf of each party.[5] The effect of a failure to comply with these requirements in an appropriate case will be a failure to conclude an enforceable contract on the intended terms. But these formal requirements do not apply to claims based upon proprietary estoppel,[6] so that informal promises concerning interests in land may still have some legal effects amounting in a few cases to the equivalent of enforcement of the contract.

With respect to negotiable instruments, the requirement of writing secures their purpose, which cannot be achieved by other means. One of the objectives of such documents as bills of exchange, promissory notes and bills of sale is to permit a simple transfer of credit rights from one person to another. Bills of exchange provide a credit arrangement, used especially in international trade, but an ordinary cheque drawn on a bank account is a simple commonplace example, where the credit may be transferred by indorsement of the document by a signature. This device only works, of course, if the bill is in writing and follows a specified form in identifying the creditors and debtors.[7] The observance of the particular form then prevents any doubts being raised about the validity, effectiveness, and meaning of the credit arrangement. Similar rules apply to bills of lading, which enable the transfer of ownership of goods by indorsement of a written document in a particular form. By virtue of the endorsement, the new owner enjoys all the rights and obligations of the previous owner, and the document serves as conclusive proof of transfer and shipment.[8]

Apart from these two exceptions, which require contracts to be in writing, the only other significant requirement of formalities to establish the existence of a contract concerns contracts of guarantee, which require evidence in writing and a signature.[9]

Modern consumer legislation also prescribes formal requirements for contracts, but the objective of the law is not so much to establish proof of the existence of the agreement, but to disclose to the consumer the nature of the transaction. In a consumer credit contract, for instance, a failure by the lender to comply with the

4   Law of Property (Miscellaneous Provisions) Act 1989, s 2(5) recognises some narrow exclusions to this requirement.
5   Law of Property (Miscellaneous Provisions) Act 1989, s 2(3).
6   See Chapter 5.
7   Bills of Exchange Act 1882.
8   Carriage of Goods by Sea Act 1992.
9   Statute of Frauds (1677), s 4.

formalities does not prevent the formation of a binding contract. Instead, the consumer may enforce the credit arrangement despite the absence of compliance with formal requirements, and the creditor may enforce the agreement if it can persuade a court that it would be unjust in the light of any prejudice and fault to refuse to enforce the contract in whole or in part.[10] The purpose of these formal requirements is not to determine the existence of the contract, but rather to provide information to the consumer concerning the terms of the transaction. These formalities are better considered in the context of duties of disclosure in Chapter 10. At this point we should note, however, that enabling legislation has been passed that permits this consumer protection legislation to be adjusted in order to permit contracts to be concluded by electronic means.[11]

C.   Illegality and public policy

The courts may exercise general powers to refuse legal enforcement to contracts which involve illegality or conduct which is contrary to public policy. Most instances of the exercise of statutory prohibition concern rules designed to secure fair trading conditions and to invalidate contracts which, in whole or in part, undermine competitive markets or create risks to personal safety and property. In addition to those rules, which will be considered in subsequent chapters, in some instances a statute may directly declare particular types of agreement to be void or unenforceable, as for example in the cases of gambling, the sale of parts of the body and flick-knives,[12] but more commonly a court has to infer the unenforceability of the contract from the purpose of the statute and general considerations of public policy. Thus an agreement to commit a criminal offence, which itself amounts to the crime of conspiracy, will be unenforceable on the ground of public policy regardless of whether or not any statute expressly so provides.

The precise effects of the illegality of a contract may vary. Sometimes the courts regard the contract as void, but more usually the contract is said to be unenforceable. Formerly, the courts were extremely reluctant to permit either party to enforce a contract tainted by illegality in order to deter such conduct.[13] In recent years, however, the courts have been moving rapidly towards a more subtle and flexible position, which examines whether enforcement of the contract would

---

10 Consumer Credit Act 1974, ss 65, 127.
11 Electronic Communications Act 2000, s 8(1); EC Directive 2000/31/EC on Electronic Commerce, Art 9: 'Member States shall ensure that their legal system allows contracts to be concluded by electronic means.'; EC Directive 1999/93/EC on a Community Framework for Electronic Signatures (implemented by the Electronic Communications Act 2000, s 7).
12 Gaming Act 1845, s 18; Human Organ Transplants Act 1989, s 1; Restriction of Offensive Weapons Act 1959, s 1.
13 Grodecki, 'In Pari Delicto Potior Est Conditio Defendentis' (1955) 71 *Law Quarterly Review* 254.

in fact undermine public policy, and whether enforcement or some restitutionary remedy would prevent injustice between the parties.[14] Although the House of Lords in *Tinsley v Milligan*[15] ruled out the exercise of a broad discretionary power to enforce contracts tainted by illegality if the court believes justice so requires, they recognised a broad power to permit restitution of proprietary rights provided that the entitlement could be established without reliance upon the plaintiff's own illegal conduct.

This move towards greater flexibility has been further encouraged by the ruling of the European Court of Justice in *Courage Ltd v Crehan*.[16] Under Article 81 of the EC Treaty, contracts which have as their object or effect the prevention, restriction or distortion of competition in the Common Market are automatically void. The case concerned a 'tied pub', where the contract provided that in return for the lease of a pub the tenant would purchase its beer exclusively from a large brewery. The brewery brought a claim for unpaid bills for deliveries of beer, but the tenant counter-claimed damages on the ground that as a tied pub the tenant had been charged higher prices than those charge to independent retail outlets. On the assumption that the tied pub arrangements violated Article 81 because the network of similar contracts had a cumulative effect which restricted competition,[17] the English Court of Appeal held that under English law the tenant, as a party to an illegal contract, could not maintain a claim for damages. But the European Court of Justice held that a decision which precludes either party to an unlawful contract from bringing a claim for damages was contrary to EC law. A party to such a void contract might obtain damages if, in view of its weaker bargaining position, it was not significantly responsible for the breach of competition law, and where an award of damages might improve enforcement of competition law. In the case of a tied pub, these conditions were likely to be satisfied, since the large brewery effectively determined the terms of the distribution system, and the risk to the brewery of facing claims from tenants for compensation for price discrimination would discourage these anti-competitive practices. Although this decision is limited to illegality arising from breach of EC competition law, it may encourage the English courts to examine more carefully their blanket refusal to award claims for damages for breach of contracts which are unenforceable for illegality in circumstances where an award of damages might help to deter the unlawful conduct. These conditions may only be rarely satisfied, because usually the weaker party will be adequately protected by the unenforceability of the contract and a claim for damages may be regarded by the court as a device to avoid what proved to be a bad bargain rather than an

14 *Saunders v Edwards* [1987] 2 All ER 651, [1987] 1 WLR 1116, CA; *Euro-Diam Ltd v Bathurst* [1990] 1 QB 1, [1988] 2 All ER 23, CA; *St John Shipping Corpn v Joseph Rank Ltd* [1957] 1 QB 267, [1956] 3 All ER 683, QBD; Law Commission, *Illegal Transactions: The Effect of Illegality on Contracts and Trusts*, Consultation Paper 154 (London, 1999).

15 [1994] 1 AC 340, [1993] 2 All ER 65, HL.

16 Case C-453/99 [2002] QB 507, [2001] All ER (EC) 886, ECJ.

17 Case C-234/89 *Delimitis v Henniger Brau* [1991] ECR I-935, ECJ.

instrument for strengthening the policy behind the law.[18] They may be satisfied, in a case of employment where the employer requires as a condition of employment that the employees should be paid in cash, without records and deduction of any taxes. Here, the possibility of the employee claiming unpaid wages and any statutory entitlements, thereby forcing the employer to disclose to the tax authorities the illegal employment, might serve to deter employers from engaging in this practice.

It is only possible here to illustrate some of the reasons for limiting the scope of markets on the ground of illegality. Some statutes control the entering into of contracts with family relations. It is no longer possible to enforce an engagement to marry.[19] Parental responsibility for children cannot be surrendered or transferred by contract, although it is possible for a parent to arrange for parental responsibility to be met by another person acting on his or her behalf.[20]

Another common purpose of statutory illegality is to protect the proper administration of the state and the machinery of justice. Contracts to pervert the course of justice will in general be illegal. For example, a contract under which a person agrees to hide information which may help to secure the conviction of a criminal offender of an arrestable offence amounts to the crime of compounding and will be an illegal contract.[21] Although clauses in contracts that require information to be kept confidential are in general enforceable, public policy may prevent the enforcement of agreements not to disclose information concerning breaches of regulatory offences.[22] Similarly, an agreement under which a person agrees to indemnify another against the consequences of criminal liability such as a fine will be illegal.[23] On the other hand, an agreement by a victim to accept compensation for loss or injury suffered in return for withdrawing information which may lead to a criminal conviction is probably not contrary to public policy.

Contracts involving corruption in governments will also be contrary to public policy. The sale of honours and offices will be illegal either under statute or at common law.[24] Bribery of officials will also violate public policy.[25]

Agreements under which one person agrees to fund another person's civil litigation in return for a share in the proceeds were regarded as unlawful champertous agreements. But this prohibition has been confined in recent years,

---

18 Monti, 'Anticompetitive Agreements: The Innocent Party's Right to Damages' (2002) *European Law Review* 282.
19 Law Reform (Miscellaneous Provisions) Act 1970.
20 Children Act 1989, s 2(9).
21 Criminal Law Act 1967, s 5(1).
22 *Initial Services Ltd v Putterill* [1968] 1 QB 396, [1967] 3 All ER 145, CA; Employment Rights Act 1996, s 43F, as amended by the Public Interest Disclosure Act 1998, s 1.
23 *Colburn v Patmore* (1834) 1Cr M & R 73.
24 Sale of Offices Acts 1551 and 1809; Honours (Prevention of Abuses) Act 1925.
25 *Lemenda Trading Co Ltd v African Middle East Petroleum Co* [1988] QB 448, [1988] 1 All ER 513, QBD.

so that it does not apply to 'no win, no fee' agreements.[26] A statutory reform in Britain permits some agreements with lawyers under which payment for litigation may be conditional upon a successful outcome and set at a percentage above the normal fees for such work.[27] In the USA, notoriously, agreements of this kind, and arrangements for lawyers to take a large percentage of any damages awarded, have long been permitted.

The courts have traditionally reserved to themselves a residual power to deny enforcement to a contract on the grounds that it involves immorality or contemplates actions contrary to the public interest. In the nineteenth century the moral scruples of judges led to the denial of enforcement to any agreement tainted with some type of immorality. In *Pearce v Brooks*,[28] the court declined to enforce a contract to hire out an ornate brougham to a prostitute, who planned to attract customers with it. Although extensive legislative control over contracts has considerably reduced the exercise of this residual moralistic power, it lies in wait as a resource for the courts to set the limits of the sphere of contracts.

A final strand of controls on the scope of markets worth noting concerns contracts which unduly restrict personal liberty. No doubt a contract which amounts to slavery will be contrary to public policy, but the limit on contracts extends to other severe restrictions on personal liberty. In *Horwood v Millar's Timber and Trading Co*,[29] a moneylender extracted an agreement from the borrower that he would not leave his job, borrow further money, dispose of his property or move house without the lender's consent. This agreement was illegal as it unduly restricted the borrower's freedom.

D. Public and private undertakings

For the sake of privacy the law should not enforce every voluntary undertaking, even where the substance concerns matters otherwise appropriate for market transactions. The law will not simply endorse some elementary principle, such as promises which ought to be kept or that people should act in good faith towards each other, for this would involve the intrusion of the state into private and intimate relationships. But how should this zone of private conduct, where voluntary undertakings do not give rise to legal obligations, be defined? What tests of enforceability does the law adopt to mark this boundary between public and private domains? Traditionally the common law has adopted formal and

26 *Thai Trading Co v Taylor* [1998] QB 781, [1998] 3 All ER 65, CA.
27 Courts and Legal Services Act 1990, s 58; Conditional Fee Agreements Order 1995, SI 1995/1674; Conditional Fee Agreements Regulations 1995, SI 1995/1675. Extended to arbitration proceedings in *Bevan Ashford v Geoff Yeandle (Contractors) Ltd* [1993] Ch 239, [1998] 3 All ER 238, Ch D.
28 (1866) LR 1 Exch 213.
29 [1917] 1 KB 305, CA.

structural tests of enforceability rather than directly confronting the issue of defining the zone of unenforceable voluntary undertakings.

The oldest test of enforceability comprises the satisfaction of the requirements of a deed. This is a formal test of enforceability which describes a ritual. A ritual may comprise oaths, the signing of particular types of documents or the presence of witnesses. All these elements are necessary, for example, to create a binding contract of marriage. A deed became the normal mechanism for entering enforceable contracts in a wide range of circumstances. Formerly a deed comprised a written document, signed by both parties, with a seal attached, and which was then delivered to the person who expected to acquire property under the contract. A valid deed no longer requires a seal under English law, but instead the document must be signed in the presence of a witness who attests the signature and the document must make it clear on its face that it is intended to be a deed.[30] The attraction of using a deed no doubt includes the prudential consideration of establishing proof of a particular transaction before a court. But here the important point to note is that whenever the formal test of the use of a deed is satisfied, a court will enforce the promises contained in the document, for the court assumes that the adoption of the formality provides a sufficient justification for the use of state sanctions.[31] The majority of jurisdictions in the USA have abolished this test of enforceability, perhaps because it is appreciated that the use of this formality should not be determinative of the province of the public sphere.[32]

The second test of enforceability which has become firmly established in common law countries is the doctrine of consideration. This doctrine, which will be considered in detail in Chapter 4, requires the parties to have agreed an exchange, such as the transfer of goods or the provision of services for money. An oral or informal agreement, therefore, can satisfy the doctrine of consideration. It excludes from enforcement, however, donative promises, which are promises to give or to do something without some bargained exchange in return. This doctrine therefore suggests that whenever the parties have agreed an exchange, rather than a donative promise, that the agreement is appropriate for legal sanctions. In practice this generalization has proved too sweeping, and the courts have supplemented the doctrine with an additional safeguard that in casual social contexts the courts will refuse to enforce bargains on the ground that the parties did not have an intention to enter legal relations.

A third test of enforceability is more controversial, for it has received only halting and partial recognition in English law. It leads to the enforcement of promises where the promise has induced detrimental reliance on the part of the promisee,

30 Law of Property (Miscellaneous Provisions) Act 1989, s 1.
31 Specific performance (an order of compulsory performance) may not be available if there is no consideration.
32 EA Farnsworth, *Contracts* (Boston, 1982), pp 83–85.

even though the promise was not contained in a deed and nor was it part of a bargain under which the promisee undertook an obligation in exchange. Often this test for the enforceability of promises is described as promissory estoppel or reliance-based liability. Doubts persist whether or not this is a test of the enforceability of contracts. It may be regarded as an alternative species of liability, arising in equity, with a distinctive set of rules and remedies. In Chapter 5, it will be argued that reliance-based liability is properly regarded as a species of contractual liability in some instances. Whatever the appropriate classification, the test of reliance justifies the application of state sanctions to a voluntary undertaking, and therefore draws another boundary between the public and private spheres.

The principal type of promise which these tests exclude from legal enforceability can be described as an informal donative promise. This is a gratuitous promise, not given in exchange for another, not contained in a deed, and not one which induces detrimental reliance. The exclusion of donative promises from the realm of legal enforceability makes sense, for normally such promises are given in informal social contexts. Promises to give another a lift to the station, or to give a particular book as a birthday present, are informal donative promises, and these promises characteristically fit into perceptions of the proper scope of the private sphere of promises where legal enforceability is inappropriate. In a business context one of the three tests of enforceability will almost invariably be satisfied.

The hard cases that test the boundaries of the public realm of enforceability fall typically into two kinds of situation. In the first, the promise occurs in a social context, but there are aspects of the promise, such as its degree of seriousness and expectations of reciprocal undertakings, which indicate that this promise should be classified in the public realm of enforceability. The second type of case occurs in a business context, but superficially it appears to be no more than an informal donative promise, an indulgence or an act of goodwill offered by one business to another. In these cases the courts are asked to recognize either the implicit exchange taking place or the reasonableness of the reliance upon the undertaking, and so enforce the promise. But it should be stressed that, despite the theoretical interest of these hard cases, in the vast majority of commercial transactions the tests of enforceability are routinely satisfied.

E.   The contractualization of social life

The final purpose of tests of enforceability concerns the extent to which contractual obligations should be permitted to regulate and define all types of social relations. The issue is whether contracts should be permitted to rewrite other types of obligations such as those arising from status, as in the relation between parent and child. The problem here is not whether the obligation is fit for state regulation; there will be legal obligations in place already. The question is rather whether a contractual obligation can be created which in some way supplants or modifies the existing legal obligations.

No specific legal doctrine addresses this aspect of the test of enforceability. Any attempt to govern a relationship through a contract can be defeated by the use of the doctrines which we have already mentioned, such as a finding of illegality or that the contract is contrary to public policy. More subtle approaches include a finding that the contract was not supported by consideration, or that the reliance was not reasonable.

However the legal analysis may be framed, the underlying issue is whether or not the practices and legal regulation of market transactions should be extended to govern a particular kind of social relationship. This poses the issue of whether certain aspects of social life should be excluded from legal regulation through delegation to consensual arrangements. We examine how the modern law answers this question in Chapter 6.

Chapter 4

Consideration and the exchange model

A. The concept of an exchange

Although historians can trace the doctrine of consideration back to early common law, in the nineteenth century the courts devised a rigorous formulation of it, which has since predominated. The fundamental concept is that each party must promise to give up, or actually give up, some right or liberty specified by the other as the price of the reciprocal undertaking:

> The general rule is that an executory agreement, by which the plaintiff agrees to do something on the terms that the defendant agrees to do something else, may be enforced if what the plaintiff has agreed to do is either for the benefit of the defendant or to the trouble or prejudice of the plaintiff. If it be either, the adequacy of the consideration is for the parties to consider at the time of making the agreement, not for the court when it is sought to be enforced.[1]

---

1 Blackburn J, *Bolton v Madden* (1873) LR 9 QB 55 at 56.

In a simple transaction, such as a sale of goods, the parties satisfy the doctrine of consideration by one party promising to deliver the selected goods in return for the requested price, and the other promising to pay the stated price in return for delivery of the specified goods. Notice that each promise must be supported by consideration: the promisor must receive in return for the promise a reciprocal promise to perform the act requested as the price of the promise.

This concept of an exchange serves as the general criterion distinguishing between public enforceable transactions and private unenforceable agreements. It identifies the donative promise, ie a bare promise to give something to another person in the future, as the type of promise which should be regarded as a private arrangement which can be broken with only moral sanctions brought to bear. To ensure the legal enforceability of donative promises, a particular type of formality should be adopted, such as a Will or a deed.

B. The concept of consideration

Due to its remarkable degree of abstraction, the doctrine of consideration does not tie legal enforceability to particular kinds of transactions or subject matter. In principle, it seems possible to satisfy the doctrine with any kinds of promises and acts, such as promises to keep quiet, to stop pestering someone, or to give some token which has negligible market value. The doctrine of consideration serves as a general test of legal enforceability because any human action or forbearance, from complex commercial deals to trivial consumer purchases, potentially satisfies the test. This degree of abstraction turns out to be the weakness of the doctrine, for it cannot cope with the subtleties of context which the distinction between the public and private spheres of conduct must examine.

1. Benefit and detriment

Although this formal structure of an exchange relation has constituted the predominant concept of consideration, it is possible to detect a slight variant or supplement in terms of benefit; and the concept of detriment has also played a role in legal reasoning. In the quotation above, Blackburn J says that the 'something' that the claimant has promised must either be for the 'benefit' of the defendant or to the 'trouble or prejudice' of the claimant. In normal exchange relations both parties expect to acquire a benefit at the price of a detriment, so the language of benefit and detriment provides a loose model of the exchange relation. Yet the introduction of the ideas of benefit and detriment entails two crucial differences for a purely abstract model of exchange.

First, the language of benefit and detriment may deflect emphasis from the significance of the request. In the abstract concept of an exchange, the detriment to the promisee must be that requested by the promisor as the price of receiving the benefit. The conferral of a benefit which has not been requested, or the suffering of a detriment which has not been requested as the price of a promise, cannot count as consideration. When the courts begin to emphasise the language of benefit and detriment, they often seek to minimize the requirement of request or consent. In *Carlill v Carbolic Smoke Ball Co*,[2] for instance, it was perhaps unclear what request the advertisement of the smoke ball contained, but the court found no difficulty in discovering consideration either in the trouble to the claimant of using the smoke ball or in the indirect benefit to the company in gaining an additional sale.

Secondly, the language of benefit and detriment suggests that the court will make a substantive evaluation of the promises to discover whether or not each party in fact suffered a detriment or received a benefit. Under the abstract exchange concept, however, the law assumes that if the act has been requested, it must confer some benefit. The formulation of the doctrine of consideration in terms of benefit and detriment tends to occur when the courts seek to deny legal force to an agreement where they perceive that despite the appearance of an exchange there is no real exchange of economic value. Most of the puzzling decisions involving a question of consideration represent instances where the courts are unwilling to pursue the logic of the abstract concept of exchange, and have slipped into the language of benefit and detriment in order to alter the result. Yet the formulation in terms of benefit and detriment cannot become the dominant conception for it necessarily implies that the test of enforceability contains a substantive conception of fairness. As we have seen, however, the ideal of the justice of exchange expressly denied that it was part of the role of the courts to judge the fairness of consensual bargains.

2.   Adequacy of consideration

In standard definitions of the doctrine of consideration, immediately after the language of benefit and detriment has been employed, the court insists that it will not assess the adequacy of consideration or the fairness of the exchange. The sole question is whether the action requested in return for the promise has either been promised or in fact performed. Although the doctrine of consideration requires an exchange of something, it leaves it to the parties to determine what they value and the price which they are prepared to pay for any item. It is accepted, for example, that the hire of a car in return for a 'peppercorn' rent, ie either a nominal sum or even literally a peppercorn, will provide consideration to support enforcement of the contract.[3]

---

2   [1893] 1 QB 256, CA.
3   But some statutes invalidate such transactions in order to protect creditors: eg Insolvency Act 1986, ss 238, 423.

It should follow from the abstract conception of exchange and the rule against judging the adequacy of consideration that a promise to perform an act which the promisor is already under a legal duty to perform should constitute consideration. For example, if one person succeeds in making two agreements with different people under which he promises to perform exactly the same task in return for payment, both agreements amount to an exchange relation, although clearly the second agreement involves no additional cost to the promisor. Both agreements should be enforceable under the doctrine of consideration, because it is up to the promisee to determine the value of the promise or act requested. Yet for a long time the courts were loath to accept the logic of the abstract concept of exchange in practice. They argued, using the supplementary concept of consideration in terms of benefit and detriment, that in the absence of any real detriment to the promisor, there was no consideration to support the second agreement. But this view, which was called the 'pre-existing duty rule', has gradually been discarded. Now a promise to perform an existing duty in return for payment, such as a mother's promise to the father of an illegitimate child to look after a child in return for payment,[4] or a promise to perform duties which the promisor is already bound to perform under a contract with a third party,[5] will amount to good consideration. Such agreements may, however, fail some other test of enforceability by violating public policy, as in the case of a promise not to hurt someone in exchange for money.

Where the courts find it most difficult to accept the abstract logic of the concept of exchange are in cases concerning modifications of existing contracts. One party may simply demand more money for performing the same service agreed under the original contract. Alternatively, one party may simply offer less in return for the agreed sum under the original contract. Under the subjective valuation of promises in the abstract concept of exchange, both of these types of modification should be supported by consideration if the change of terms is accepted. Yet the courts naturally baulked at the enforcement of such modifications, since they looked unfair and smacked of extortion. The courts demanded some 'fresh consideration', ie an additional detriment, no matter how trivial, in return for the promise to pay more or to accept a lesser payment. The continuing application of this requirement to modifications must now be doubted, as we will see when we examine the issue of modifications of contracts in Chapter 15. What seems clear is that if the promisor perceives a commercial advantage to be gained by offering to pay more for the same performance, that commercial advantage may be a sufficient benefit to justify enforcement of the modification.[6]

4 *Ward v Byham* [1956] 2 All ER 318, [1956] 1 WLR 496, CA.
5 *New Zealand Shipping Co Ltd v Satterthwaite & Co (The Eurymedon)* [1975] AC 154, [1974] 1 All ER 1015, PC; *Pao On v Lau Yiu Long* [1980] AC 614, [1979] 3 All ER 65, PC.
6 *Williams v Roffey Bros & Nicholls (Contractors) Ltd* [1991] 1 QB 1, [1990] 1 All ER 512, CA.

3.   Promises, actions and omissions

In an exchange relation both parties must promise to sacrifice, or actually relinquish, some dimension of their freedom or their rights. This broad concept of exchange permits the doctrine of consideration to be satisfied by a wide variety of types of promises, actions or omissions.

In the normal exchange, the promise contains an offer to give something or to perform a service; but it is also possible to promise to forbear to act, in which case freedom of action is sacrificed as the consideration for a reciprocal promise. One party may promise, for example, to refrain from using a right of way in return for payment, or relinquish any rights to sue for damage caused to his property by a contractor in return for a cheaper job, and in either case the promise constitutes good consideration for the other's promise. Settlements of legal claims are an important example of this kind of agreement to forbear from action.

As well as promises to perform or refrain from actions, another type of promise which satisfies the idea of sacrifice consists in a guarantee or warranty that certain facts are true or that certain claims will turn out to be true. This inclusion of warranties involves an extension of the idea of sacrifice of rights, for what is sacrificed is merely the freedom not to offer a warranty. Warranties normally comprise part of the consideration for a wider transaction, such as a sale of goods where the seller promises not only to supply the goods but also warrants their satisfactory quality. Occasionally, however, warranties comprise the main consideration for a transaction, as in the case of manufacturer's guarantees of products to consumers. For example, in *Shanklin Pier Ltd v Detel Products Ltd*,[7] the defendant assured the claimant that a certain paint manufactured by the defendant would have a life of at least seven years if it was applied to the claimant's pier. On the faith of this promise, the claimant instructed its contractors to purchase the paint and use it on the pier. When the paint lasted only three months, the claimant successfully claimed damages against the defendant on the ground of breach of warranty. The warranty constituted a promise in return for which the claimant acted by instructing the contractors to purchase the paint for use on the pier.

It has already been pointed out that exchanges may be constituted either by reciprocal promises or acts. The type of contract known as an unilateral contract consists of an exchange of a promise for an act.[8] The promisor offers to give up some right, if the promisee actually performs certain actions. For example, if I promise Pat that I will pay her £20 to tidy up my garden this afternoon, Pat may claim the money if she carries out the work even though she has made no formal promise to do so. The same analysis was applied to the facts in *Carlill v Carbolic Smoke Ball Co*, so that Mrs Carlill's regular use of the smoke ball rather than any

---

7   [1951] 2 KB 854, [1951] 2 All ER 471, KBD.
8   Pettit, 'Modern Unilateral Contracts' (1983) 63 *Boston University Law Review* 55.

promise to do so was the consideration for the promise to pay £100. In unilateral contracts, actual performance of the request by one party in exchange for a promise of payment by the other constitutes the consideration, and, until the promisee performs the requested task, it seems that the promise is not legally enforceable, since reciprocity of sacrifice occurs only once the promisee has performed the action.

4. Requests and conditional promises

Although unilateral contracts fit the concept of exchange, it will sometimes be difficult to distinguish them from conditional promises. In a conditional promise, there is a donative promise which is made contingent upon some event happening. In *Carlill v Carbolic Smoke Ball Co* there was both consideration, consisting of the requested action of using the smoke ball, and also a condition of the promise, namely on the event of Mrs Carlill catching influenza. If the court had construed the advertisement so that it merely declared a promise to pay a sum of money if anyone caught influenza whilst using the smoke ball, without in fact requesting use of the smoke ball, there would have been no exchange relation, but simply a conditional donative promise which would have been unenforceable. The difference between unilateral contracts and conditional donative promises turns simply on the issue whether the condition can be construed as amounting to a request to perform an action in return for the promise.

Although the conceptual distinction between unilateral contracts based on exchange and conditional donative promises is clear, many promises may prove hard to categorize. Behind this problem of categorization lies the court's attempt to grapple with the distinction between public and private spheres. In *Shadwell v Shadwell*,[9] an uncle wrote to his nephew in the following terms.

> I am glad to hear of your intended marriage with Ellen Nicholl; and, as I promised to assist you at starting, I am happy to tell you that I will pay to you £150 yearly during my life and until your annual income derived from your profession of a Chancery barrister shall amount to 600 guineas.

The uncle paid the money until his death, but the executors of his estate then declined to pay any further sums. This promise could only be regarded as an exchange if it could be construed as either requesting the nephew to marry or requesting the nephew to proceed with his profession as a barrister. In the absence of such implied requests, the promise had to be regarded as a conditional donative promise to pay an annuity until the nephew's income reached a certain level. A majority of the court upheld the nephew's claim, holding that the consideration for the promise of the annuity was the nephew's marriage. Byles J, dissenting, declined to find any request by the uncle for his nephew to marry or to practise at

9 (1860) 9 CBNS 159, 142 ER 62, Common Bench.

the Bar, so that the letter merely disclosed a conditional donative promise to pay an annuity until the nephew's income improved.

The case reveals how a degree of flexibility enters into the legal process of deciding which promises to enforce by virtue of the ability of the courts to interpret events as either including or omitting implied requests for reciprocal sacrifice. This flexibility is employed to fine-tune the public/private boundary. The majority of the court in *Shadwell v Shadwell* regarded the uncle's promise as falling into the public realm of enforceable contracts, so they invented the implied request in order to satisfy the doctrine of consideration in that case.

5.   Implied requests

What emerges most clearly from this examination of the doctrine of consideration is that it exhibits considerable flexibility as an instrument for policing the boundaries of enforceable contracts. The crucial device employed by the courts is to discover an implied request to perform an act whenever they wish to enforce a donative promise. They will almost invariably place such a construction on the circumstances of the case when it concerns business and commercial matters.

The courts will quickly infer the existence of such implied reciprocal promises in business contexts where, in the notorious absence of free lunches, it seems likely that the parties would have intended the benefits of the transaction to flow in both directions. For example, in the famous New York case, *Wood v Lucy, Lady Duff-Gordon*,[10] a designer of fashions agreed an exclusive agency arrangement with the plaintiff, such that the plaintiff had the right to market the designer defendant's creations (and styles which the defendant endorsed) for a year, in return for giving the defendant one-half of all profits. The defendant broke this agreement by endorsing styles without the plaintiff's knowledge and without sharing the profits. When the plaintiff sued the defendant for breach of the exclusive agency agreement, the defendant raised the defence that the agreement was unenforceable because the plaintiff had not promised to market the designs, but merely to share profits if he did. The majority of the court rejected the defence by inferring an exchange relationship under which by implication the defendant promised to use reasonable efforts to market her designs, for without such an implication the exclusive agency agreement made little commercial sense for either party. Here we see the court discerning an implicit exchange relation, which both makes sense of the commercial transaction and serves the purpose of bringing the agreement into the public realm of enforceable contracts.

To discover an implicit exchange in a commercial context, a court may also have to overcome the problem of vagueness of the reciprocal undertakings. Questions

10 222 NY 88, 118 NE 214 (1917).

may arise about the satisfaction of the doctrine of consideration in cases where the parties do not specify with precision the exact terms of their exchange. It may be argued in such cases that no real exchange was intended, so that no contract was formed. If one person asks another to deliver some goods, which he does, but no price was mentioned, it may appear that no exchange was envisaged. The courts are likely to infer in such situations, however, that an implied promise to pay for the goods was understood between the parties. There must have been an understanding that the requested action was to be remunerated. Under statute a court is empowered to fix a reasonable price as the consideration for sale or a reasonable charge for a service.[11]

But where the court regards the promises as falling outside the commercial sphere, we see a much greater reluctance to infer requests and to imply terms which specify the intended reciprocity of sacrifice. In *Combe v Combe*,[12] during divorce proceedings, a husband agreed to pay his wife an allowance of £100 per year. After several years the wife claimed arrears of payment, the husband never having paid the allowance. The Court of Appeal rejected the claim on the ground that the wife had given no consideration for the promise of an allowance. It would have been easy for the court to have implied a request from the husband that the wife should refrain from applying to the courts for maintenance. But the court declined to construct such an implied request, even though it would have been simple to do so in the context of a promise made during divorce proceedings. One reason for this reluctance may have been the court's sense that the husband's promise should be regarded as a private arrangement, which should not be legally enforceable. The court also observed that the wife's income exceeded that of her husband, so they hinted that in any case fairness considerations disinclined them to enforce the promise.

The construction of implied requests has also proved useful as a device for determining when benefits which have been conferred on another should be paid for. If a friend fixes my broken bicycle without discussing the matter with me first, despite the undoubted conferral of a benefit on me, the action will not create a contractual obligation to pay my friend because the service was not requested. The position might be different if the court could imply a request, as in the situation where I had asked my friend to mend my bicycle on previous occasions, so that a court might infer a kind of 'standing order' under which I requested my friend to fix the bicycle whenever it was broken. Another way of achieving the same outcome is to apply the law of restitution for the value of services conferred, where instead of demanding a request the court searches for 'free acceptance of the benefit'.

A similar technique is employed in cases often described under the heading of 'past consideration'. Here the court discovers an implied request to perform the

11 Sale of Goods Act 1979, s 8, Supply of Goods and Services Act 1982, s 15.
12 [1951] 2 KB 215, [1951] 1 All ER 767, CA.

work, and relies upon a later promise to pay a specific sum for the work in order to determine the content of the reciprocal obligation. On its face the subsequent promise looks like a donative promise, a promise to pay out of gratitude, but on closer inspection of the facts of the case the courts may reason that the subsequent promise merely renders concrete the reciprocal obligations envisaged in an exchange relation formed earlier. In *Re Casey's Patents*,[13] for instance, an employee provided his employer with several inventions. Later on, after the work was completed, the employer promised to give the employee a share in the intellectual property rights of the patents on the inventions. On the question whether this promise created any binding contract, the court decided that the promise was supported by consideration, for it concluded that both parties understood that the work would be paid for; so the later promise, although merely a donative promise in form, was in fact merely a way of giving greater precision to the earlier undertaking to enter an exchange relation.

Perhaps the most troubling instances of unrequested benefits concern those promises given out of gratitude for an important service such as a rescue. On occasion, American courts have proceeded so far as to undermine the doctrine of consideration by enforcing donative promises to pay for work rendered where the court senses a strong moral obligation to recompense the rescuer. For example, in *Webb v McGowin*,[14] the plaintiff was crippled for life in the course of saving the defendant from serious injury, and a month later the defendant promised to pay the plaintiff a fixed sum every two weeks for the rest of the plaintiff's life. The Court of Appeals of Alabama was prepared to enforce this contract on the ground that the doctrine of consideration was satisfied by the motive of gratitude, although clearly the defendant neither expressly requested to be saved nor was there a prior understanding that the act of heroism would be rewarded. No doubt the fact that a benefit had been conferred was crucial in leading to the conclusion that the promise should be enforced. The orthodox analysis which prevails in English law, however, insists that such promises to pay merely represent donative promises made in response to, but not in exchange for, the prior gift.

The conclusion which emerges from this examination of the doctrine of consideration is that, although the abstract concept of exchange contains an internal rigour and logic, in its application to particular circumstances the courts enjoy the discretion to construct events in ways which suit their sense of how the private/public boundary should be drawn. In commercial contexts, the doctrine of consideration will seldom present an insuperable burden to a claimant in order to establish a contractual claim. A court will rely upon its understanding of the implicit exchange, in order to construct the necessary implied request, and to fashion the detail of the reciprocal undertakings. We have also observed that, although the abstract concept of exchange should not be concerned with the

13 [1892] 1 Ch 104, CA.
14 168 So 196, 27 Ala App 82 (1935).

fairness of the reciprocal undertakings, the courts have often defied the logic of the concept, in order to avoid the enforcement of what they regard as unfair contracts. The use of the language of benefit and detriment is often a sign that the court is engaging in either a diminution of the element of request or a substantive evaluation of the fairness of the transaction.

C.   Intention to create legal relations

As a test of enforceability designed to delineate the boundary between the public and private spheres, however, the doctrine of consideration suffers from one major defect: it assumes that all exchange relations should fall within the public sphere of legal enforceability. Yet it is readily apparent that casual social arrangements can often take the form of an exchange and this creates the difficulty that the test of consideration suggests, disfunctionally, that such casual agreements should be enforceable. In *Bolton v Madden*[15] the claimant and defendant subscribed to a charity, the objects of which were elected by the subscribers by casting votes in proportion to their contributions. The two friends agreed that, if at one election the claimant would direct his votes to the defendant's favoured object, at the next election the defendant would reciprocate the favour. The claimant sued to enforce the agreement when the defendant failed to keep his side of the bargain. On the question of whether this agreement was enforceable, the court reached the inevitable conclusion that it fitted the exchange model of the doctrine of consideration. Nor could the court refuse to enforce the agreement on the ground of public policy, for it could see nothing improper in the arrangement. What the court lacked was a way of explaining that perhaps this agreement between friends should not be legally enforceable, because it was intended to be binding in honour only, and not subject to the public realm of enforceability.

To deal with this problem of private arrangements happening to satisfy the doctrine of consideration, the courts have developed a subsidiary rule under which they refuse to enforce private agreements on the ground of an absence of an intention to create legal relations. The doctrine of no intention to create legal relations will be employed to avoid the enforcement of casual social arrangements, promises made as jokes and informal domestic agreements. Pollock first suggested this test in English law when he wrote:

> If people make arrangements to go for a walk or to read a book together, there is no agreement in a legal sense. Why not? Because their intention is not directed to legal consequences, but merely to extra-legal ones; no rights or duties are to be created.[16]

15 (1873) LR 9 QB 55.
16 F Pollock, *Principles of Contract* (London, 1st edn, 1876), p 2.

After a period of gestation, courts accepted the rule that social arrangements are not binding because the parties do not intend to make a contract. The argument was raised, for instance, in *Carlill v Carbolic Smoke Ball Co*, where the company claimed that its advertisement was not intended to be taken literally. The court rejected the argument particularly because the advertisement had stressed the seriousness of the company by emphasising that money to pay any claims had been deposited in a bank.

Atkin LJ's famous remarks in *Balfour v Balfour*[17] illustrate this concern to limit the province of state intervention in family relations, which in this case involved a promise of financial support between an estranged husband and wife:

> It would be the worst possible example to hold that agreements such as this resulted in legal obligations which could be enforced in the courts ... Agreements such as these are outside the realm of contracts altogether. The common law does not regulate the form of agreements between spouses. Their promises are not sealed with seals and sealing wax. The consideration that really obtains for them is that natural love and affection which counts for so little in these cold courts. The terms may be repudiated, varied or renewed as performance proceeds or as disagreements develop, and the principles of the common law as to exoneration and discharge and accord and satisfaction are such as to find no place in the domestic code ... In respect of these promises each house is a domain into which the King's writ does not seek to run, and to which his officers do not seek to be admitted.

Similarly, in *Jones v Padavatton*,[18] a mother promised her daughter that if the latter would give up her well-paid job in the USA, the mother would give her £200 a month until she completed her studies for the English Bar. A majority of the English Court of Appeal declined to enforce the agreement, despite the presence of consideration, on the ground that the parties did not intend to create legal relations.

The requirement of an intention to create legal relations has been criticized, however, on a number of grounds.[19] One obvious objection points out that the references to intent are at best fictitious, since the parties probably did not consider the matter; and at worst, they are actually false, since in those cases which occur in the law reports at least one party has chosen to litigate, which suggests an original intention to make a legally binding contract. The rule also raises a more general question of principle, namely whether the realm of legal liability should depend exclusively upon the wishes of the parties. If, for example, an invitation to dinner contained an express clause stating that failure to attend once the invitation had been accepted would give rise to legal liability, should the

17 [1919] 2 KB 571, CA.
18 [1969] 2 All ER 616, [1969] 1 WLR 328, CA.
19 S Williston, *A Treatise on the Law of Contracts* (Mount Kisko, 3rd edn by Jaeger, 1967), section 21.

courts comply with the express intention of the parties and enforce the agreement? It seems unlikely that the courts would award damages for breach of this agreement, although the point has not been tested, for the reason that in the last resort the courts will insist upon the ultimate power to determine the scope of legally enforceable obligations.

Nevertheless, for the doctrine of consideration this resort to the intention of the parties neatly resolves the dilemma presented by some social arrangements. It preserves a realm of private conduct where legal obligations should not arise despite the presence of consideration.

D. Rationale of consideration

Although the doctrine of consideration, supplemented by the test of intention to create legal relations, marks the boundary between the public and private spheres of conduct, it remains a puzzle to know why the concept of exchange has been adopted as the test for determining this boundary.[20] The puzzle begins with the abstract nature of the test: why use this proxy rather than assess directly the context of the agreement in order to determine whether the agreement should be accorded legal sanctions? Given the use of an abstract test, however, the question becomes what policy is the law pursuing in determining that exchange relations almost invariably fall into the public sphere? The question can also be posed in the obverse way: why does the law regard donative promises almost invariably as falling into the private sphere?

It is clear that the doctrine of consideration does not comply with the idea that the state should enforce some elementary moral principle such as the principle that promises ought to be kept. Nor does the doctrine of consideration delegate to the parties the choice over whether or not the voluntary undertaking should be legally enforceable. Even when the doctrine is qualified by the test of intention to create legal relations, the courts are plainly not relying on the actual intentions of the parties but rather imposing some mandatory rules about the proper limits of the public sphere. The two most attractive explanations of the doctrine of consideration which we will consider, namely the harm principle and the goal of wealth maximization, both come close to an adequate justification for the doctrine, but neither fits the legal requirement precisely.

---

20 Cohen, 'The Basis of Contract' (1932) 46 *Harvard Law Review* 553; Patterson, 'An Apology for Consideration' (1958) 58 *Columbia Law Review* 929; Pound, 'Promise or Bargain?' (1959) 33 *Tulane Law Rev* 455; J Dawson, *Gifts and Promises* (New Haven, 1980); G Gilmore, *The Death of Contract* (Columbus, Ohio, 1974); P Atiyah, *Essays on Contract* (Oxford, 1988), ch 8; Eisenberg, 'The Principles of Consideration' (1982) 67 *Cornell Law Review* 646; Gordon, 'A Dialogue About the Doctrine of Consideration' (1990) 75 *Cornell Law Review* 987.

1. Harm principle

In JS Mill's interpretation of the idea of liberty, the proper role of the state should be confined to the prevention of harm being caused by one person to another.[21] In the context of economic transactions, this harm principle may be interpreted to mean that the law should impose a legal obligation where, as a result of misplaced reliance upon an undertaking, promise or agreement, some economic detriment has been suffered. In the absence of such detriment, under the harm principle, the law has no justification for intervention. Although the harm principle may have influenced the development of the doctrine of consideration, especially in connection with the language of benefit and detriment, it is hard to explain every aspect of the doctrine by this rationale.

The major problem is simply that not every type of detriment induced by a promise or voluntary undertaking counts as consideration. It is only when the detriment has been requested by the promisor that the test of consideration is satisfied. A donative promise may induce detrimental reliance, yet such a promise will not be enforceable under the test of consideration. We shall shortly see that perhaps the reliance model of enforceability fills this gap.

A second problem with this rationale is that consideration can be found even in the absence of any detriment. The outstanding instance is an executory contract, where agreement has been reached but neither party has commenced performance. If there has been any harm to the promisee in such a case, it must consist merely in disappointment of expectations, which may not be a sufficiently serious harm to justify the imposition of state sanctions for breach of contract.[22] Alternatively, if the disappointment of business expectations is regarded as a sufficient harm,[23] the question arises why this disappointment does not apply equally to donative promises in a commercial context (and why the courts do not award compensation for mere disappointment).

To deal with the problem of the enforceability of executory contracts, it may be argued that the harm caused by breach is the damage to the social practice of entering agreements for future market transactions.[24] This explanation of how the harm theory accounts for the enforcement of executory contracts involves a degree of circularity: the potential harm arises from a failure to enforce the agreement when enforcement is expected and relied upon. If these agreements were not enforced in general, then no such harm would arise. What this version of

---

21 JS Mill, *On Liberty and Considerations of Representative Government* (R McCullum (ed), London, 1946).
22 Fuller and Perdue, 'The Reliance Interest in Contract Damages', (1936) 46 *Yale Law Journal* 52, at p 373; Atiyah, 'Contracts, Promises and the Law of Obligations' (1978) 94 *Law Quarterly Review* 193.
23 G Treitel, *The Law of Contract* (London, 10th edn, 1999), p 66.
24 Raz, 'Promises in Morality and Law' (1982) 95 *Harvard Law Review* 916, at pp 933–938.

the harm principle really establishes is simply the proposition that once the law has adopted a test of enforceability it should stick to it firmly, for otherwise the market system may be damaged. Furthermore, the argument assumes that the social institution of making voluntary undertakings is coterminous with the legal tests of enforceability. Unless this is the case, we may find that the social institution is broader than that defined by the doctrine of consideration, so that harm to the social institution may occur through breaches of donative promises. If this is true, as seems likely because the moral principle of keeping promises extends beyond exchanges, the theory is incomplete, since it must explain why only some harms to the social institution of voluntary undertakings are redressed by the law.

It may be correct, however, that the presence of detriment or benefit will incline a court towards discovery of consideration. We have observed this tendency in the contrast between a requested exchange and a conditional gift, and in the discovery of an implied request when a benefit has been conferred. Similarly, in cases concerning modification of contracts, a promise to pay a greater sum of money for the same original performance may cease to appear like a donative promise, if the court perceives that the additional promise to perform actually secured some tangible benefit to the promisor. Atiyah uses this judicial practice of reference to actual detriment or benefit to try to link the doctrine of consideration closely to the harm principle,[25] but this step blurs the requirement of the doctrine of consideration that the detriment or benefit should be one which was requested by the promisor. Actions which involve detriment or which confer a benefit on the promisor cannot on their own give rise to contractual obligations under the doctrine of consideration. A person may foresee that as a result of a promise another may act to his or her detriment, but, unless those actions were requested by the promisor, the detriment cannot count as consideration to support the enforcement of the promise. It is to solve this problem that the reliance model of enforceability, to be considered in the next chapter, has been developed. For this reason, the liberal harm principle justification for the doctrine of consideration seems unsatisfactory, even though it may help to explain the considerations relevant to a court's interpretation of the facts of a case.

2. Wealth maximization

The economic analysis of law suggests that the boundary between the public and private spheres is drawn by the doctrine of consideration for the purpose of wealth maximization. The public sphere is coterminous with those agreements and voluntary undertakings which increase the total wealth of society. The doctrine of consideration serves this function well on the whole. It excludes from

25 P Atiyah, *Essays on Contract* (Oxford, 1986), chs 2 and 8.

enforcement donative promises, which are usually sterile transactions because they do not necessarily transfer property to another person who values it more highly.[26]

Unfortunately, the test of consideration cannot distinguish with sufficient precision between sterile and value-enhancing transactions. Sometimes donative promises may move property to persons who value it more highly, as in the case of a promise by a rich man to give an annual donation to a charity which desperately requires funds, for the charity places much greater value on the money than the rich man. Equally, sometimes exchanges will not satisfy the value-maximizing criterion, where, for instance, one party to the exchange has made a mistake in his original valuation of the property. It is possible, of course, to preserve the economic explanation of the doctrine of consideration in the face of these examples by acknowledging that the doctrine only provides a rough guide to value-maximizing transactions. Since the law must employ rules which are general in nature, these exceptions are bound to occur. Any difficulties which arise from use of the general rule can be dealt with by supplementary rules and exceptions. Even so, this chip in the economic explanation casts some doubt on its validity.

When we add to this the observation that the courts rarely acknowledge that the aim of the law is to promote value-maximizing behaviour, the economic explanation looks more doubtful. The underlying problem here is that the complex moral judgement which determines the proper limits of state action cannot be reduced to the single issue of wealth enhancement.

3. Conclusion

The doctrine of consideration thus presents a puzzle. None of the rationales which we might expect to justify a test of enforceability by describing the proper sphere of state intervention appears to fit exactly the established legal rules which comprise the doctrine. We might conclude from this discussion that the doctrine of consideration therefore should be abandoned as an historical anachronism without satisfactory justification. This is the view taken, for example, by Fried.[27] Alternatively, we might seek to redefine the doctrine of consideration so that it fits better one of the rationales for legal enforceability. Atiyah follows this course in some of his work by maintaining, according to the liberal rationale, that benefit and detriment should suffice for enforceability without the element of request.[28]

---

26 R Posner, *Economic Analysis of Law* (Boston, 4th edn, 1992), ch 4; Posner, 'Gratuitous Promises in Economics and Law' (1977) 6 *Journal of Legal Studies* 411; Eisenberg, 'Donative Promises' (1979) 47 *University of Chicago Law Review* 1; Farber, 'Contract Law and Modern Economic Theory' (1983) 78 *Northwestern University Law Review* 303.

27 C Fried, *Contract as Promise* (Cambridge, Mass, 1981), ch 4.

28 P Atiyah, *Essays on Contract* (Oxford, 1988), ch 8.

My own view is that the harm principle underlies the distinction between the public and private spheres, but the law does not take a simple material or economic view of harm. In devising a scheme for the legal protection of the interests of individuals, the law can construct the interests to be protected without being confined to instances of economic harm. This approach to the construction of protected interests fits into the perspective of the social market, for it appreciates that the motives for entering contracts cannot be confined to wealth enhancement. The motives can include the potential of the agreement to contribute to a particular way of life and to assist in the planning and achievement of personal goals.

Once the concept of a protected interest is expanded in this way, it becomes possible to justify a test of enforceability which sanctions executory contracts. Even though the breach of such agreements may not cause economic harm, it may disrupt plans and prevent the realisation of valued goals. If necessary, we can describe the loss in economic terms as an opportunity cost: by entering one agreement, which is broken, the opportunity to make another contract to achieve an objective may have been lost. It is better, however, to recognise that law is capable of constructing personal, non-material interests, which it then seeks to protect by the application of legal sanctions.

Chapter 5

Estoppel and the reliance model

A. Another test of enforceability?

Is there a second general structural test of enforceability in addition to the doctrine of consideration? The reliance model, as I shall call it in contrast to the exchange model represented by the doctrine of consideration, has received halting recognition in common law courts. It encounters resistance because it subverts the orthodox classical analysis that all contracts must be supported by consideration. Many texts, especially in the UK, relegate the reliance model to the role of either an equitable doctrine, outside the law of contracts, concerned with the informal allocation of property rights, or a minor supplement used to enforce an anomalous collection of donative promises. Moreover, uncertainty about the rationale and limits of this model leads to cautious and reluctant application, and a judicial preference to ground decisions on the basis of consideration wherever possible. Nevertheless, I will suggest that in practice courts use this second model as a subsidiary test of enforceability in the arena of market transactions for the same purpose of demarcating the division between the public and private spheres of conduct.

B.   The concept of reliance

The elements of the reliance model cannot be reduced to a brief set of rules. The modern style of legal reasoning prefers to establish the parameters of this test of enforceability by reference to broad standards which require contextual interpretation before application to particular cases. But these broad standards indicate that the English courts look for four main elements to establish an enforceable obligation, as follows:

(i)   The first element requires a deliberate encouragement of reliance by means of a promise or some other form of express or implied undertaking.

(ii)   The second element requires proof that the other party has in fact relied upon that undertaking by acting to his detriment.

(iii)   The third element is the perception that the detrimental reliance was reasonable in all the circumstances.

(iv)   The fourth element considers whether it would be unfair, or 'unconscionable', to permit someone to go back on his or her original promise or undertaking.

In practice, of course, these elements may prove hard to disentangle, for unreasonable detrimental reliance may not have been sufficiently encouraged under the first element, or alternatively it may not be unfair or unconscionable to go back on the promise in such circumstances.

A leading example of the application of this reliance model in English law is found in *Crabb v Arun District Council*.[1] The defendant council built a road along the boundary between its property and the plaintiff's land, and granted the plaintiff a point of access to the road. Later on the plaintiff decided to divide his land and sell one portion, but for this purpose he needed a second point of access to the road. During conversations with officers of the council, the plaintiff received the impression that he would be granted the second point of access. Subsequently, when the defendant council erected a fence along the road, it left two gates corresponding to the intended points of access. Although no legal grant of the right of way was ever completed, for that would have required the satisfaction of formalities and registration, the plaintiff proceeded to sell a portion of his land. The council then blocked the second gateway, leaving the plaintiff's land inaccessible, and asked the plaintiff for £3,000 for a right of access.

In seeking a remedy against the council, the plaintiff had to overcome the problem that he had not provided consideration for any alleged promise or undertaking to grant the right of way. During the conversations with the officers of the council, he had not promised to buy the right, so no exchange was contemplated. His detrimental reliance upon those conversations, albeit substantial because the sale of a portion of the land left the remainder inaccessible

1   [1976] Ch 179, [1975] 3 All ER 865, CA.

and useless, could not comprise consideration because, although it had been foreseen, it had not been requested by the council's officers. Nevertheless, the English Court of Appeal granted the plaintiff the right of way. Lord Denning MR expressed the principle which supported the plaintiff's claim in the following terms:

> Short of a binding contract, if he makes a promise that he will not insist on his strict legal rights – even though that promise may be unenforceable in point of law for want of consideration or want of writing – and if he makes the promise knowing or intending that the other will act on it, and he does act on it, then again a court of equity will not allow him to go back on that promise . . . Short of an actual promise, if he, by his words or conduct, so behaves as to lead another to believe that he will not insist on his strict legal rights – knowing or intending that the other will act on that belief – and he does so act, that again will raise an equity in favour of the other, and it is for a court of equity to say in what way the equity may be satisfied.

This statement of the reliance model of enforceability reveals many of the hesitations surrounding its adoption by the English courts. Lord Denning emphasizes how the principle serves as a qualification to the doctrine of consideration: the principle does not replace consideration as the major test of enforceability of contracts, but represents an equitable exception which supplements consideration in certain situations. Nor is Lord Denning willing to describe the council's obligation to give the right of way as a contractual obligation. He reserves that title to agreements supported by consideration. He draws instead upon equitable doctrines to establish by informal means certain kinds of proprietary rights. These have been conventionally called 'equitable estoppels', the central idea being that because of the defendant's misleading conduct, he or she is barred from insisting upon his strict legal rights. Nevertheless, Lord Denning is willing to enforce the council's undertaking in the same way as if it were a contractual undertaking, provided that the justice of the case requires that result. The decision thus supports in form the view of the classical law that binding contracts require consideration, but in substance acknowledges an exception to that view in appropriate cases.

Although few doubt the correctness of that decision, English lawyers demonstrate great caution in accepting that it represents more than a narrow exception to the doctrine of consideration, which might be classified as an equitable doctrine concerned with interests in land labelled as 'proprietary estoppel'. It is instructive to observe this cautious approach in a more commercial context. In *Baird Textile Holdings Ltd v Marks and Spencer plc*,[2] the claimant alleged that for 30 years it had been one of the principal suppliers to the defendant

2   [2001] EWCA Civ 274, [2002] 1 All ER (Comm) 737.

retailer. The parties worked within a 'supplier partnership' arrangement,[3] under which Marks & Spencer were closely involved each season in the design and manufacture of the garments to be supplied by the claimant, and the claimant organised its workforce and manufacturing capacity to respond swiftly to orders from the defendant. The claimant alleged that the defendant had terminated this relationship without notice, which was both contrary to representations made by the defendant that the relationship would be a long-term one, and contrary to an implied duty to deal in good faith and reasonably, which had resulted in losses to the claimant of about £50m. The question before the Court of Appeal was whether this claim revealed a cause of action. The court rejected the argument that any contract existed between the parties other than the particular orders for garments. The supplier partnership arrangement was not contractual, in part because the obligations were too vague, but mostly because the defendant had indicated clearly that it did not intend to enter into a long-term binding contractual relationship for the purchase of garments and its conduct was entirely consistent with that position. In the alternative, it was argued that the claimant could obtain compensation based upon the reliance model, because the claimant had acted to its detriment in reasonable reliance upon the encouragements of the defendant to expect a long-term relationship. The Court of Appeal rejected this application of the idea of estoppel, again partly because the obligation placed on the defendant seemed too uncertain, but mostly because the facts of the case fell outside the kinds of situations that had hitherto been considered suitable for the application of the idea of estoppel or the reliance model as the basis for a claim for compensation.

Such hesitation in the reception of the reliance model as a second test of enforceability is less marked in other common law jurisdictions. Many jurisdictions in the USA routinely apply a similar principle which is called 'promissory estoppel'.[4] Section 90 of the American Restatement (Second) of Contracts summarizes the principle applied by American courts thus:

> (1) A promise which the promisor should reasonably expect to induce action or forbearance on the part of the promisee or a third person and which does induce such action or forbearance is binding if injustice can be avoided only by enforcement of the promise. The remedy granted for breach may be limited as justice requires.

3   Collins, 'Quality Assurance in Subcontracting' in S Deakin and J Mitchie (eds), *Contracts, Co-operation, and Competition* (Oxford: 1997), p 285.
4   Boyer, 'Promissory Estoppel: Requirements and Limitations of the Doctrine', (1950) 98 *University of Pennsylvania Law Review* 459; Henderson, 'Promissory Estoppel and Traditional Contract Doctrine', (1969) 78 *Yale Law Journal* 343; Feinman, 'Promissory Estoppel and Judicial Method', (1984) 97 *Harvard Law Review* 678; G Gilmore, *The Death of Contract* (Columbus, Ohio, 1974); Knapp, 'Reliance in the Revised Restatement: The Proliferation of Promissory Estoppel', (1981) 81 *Columbia Law Review* 52.

In a typical application of this principle, in *Feinberg v Pfeiffer Co*[5] the plaintiff claimed that she was entitled to a pension from her former employers. Her claim was based upon a resolution of the board of directors of the company which specified that she would receive $200 per month when she chose to retire. She retired a year and a half later at 57 years of age, and received this pension for nearly seven years. Following a change in the control of the company, however, it now sought to extricate itself from the promise. The Missouri Court of Appeals could find no consideration for the promise because no action had been requested from the plaintiff in return for the promise. Nevertheless, the court enforced the promise on the ground of promissory estoppel. The court discovered ample detrimental reliance in the plaintiff's decision to retire and then neither to seek employment nor secure her financial position in other ways. The reasoning of the American court differs, however, from the English cases in numerous minor respects, which all flow from a greater disposition to accept promissory estoppel as a species of contractual liability equivalent to consideration.

In Australia as well, the courts have recently moved towards an acceptance of the reliance model of liability. In the leading case of *Waltons Stores (Interstate) Ltd v Maher*,[6] the company entered into negotiations for lease of property with its owner under which the owner was to demolish a building and construct a new one to the company's specifications. During these negotiations the owner made it clear to the company's solicitor that the agreement needed to be concluded promptly, so that building supplies could be ordered in time, and also that he would not want to demolish the existing building until it was clear that there were no problems with the lease. The company's solicitor drafted a lease incorporating some suggested amendments by the owner, saying that the company had notified him orally that they approved of the amendments, and that if there were any objections they would be raised the following day. No such objections were made. The owner then signed the lease and sent it to the company's solicitor by way of exchange. The owner then demolished the building. A week later the company began to regret the transaction, and, having been advised by its solicitor that it was not legally bound to proceed until signed contracts had been exchanged, it took no further action, except to tell its solicitor to 'go slow' on the negotiations, until a month later, after the new building was about 40% completed, when the company announced its intention not to proceed with the lease. The High Court of Australia accepted that no legally binding agreement had arisen because of the absence of the exchange of promises represented by the exchange of copies of the signed lease, but nevertheless held that the lease was binding on the ground of estoppel. Although differing slightly in their description of the relevant principle, the members of the court agreed that the company should be held to its implied promise to complete the contract because, knowing that the owner was exposing himself to detriment by acting on the basis of a false assumption, it was

---

5   (1959) 322 SW 2d 163.
6   (1988) 164 CLR 387, Aust HC.

unconscionable for the company to adopt a course of inaction which served to encourage him in incurring that detriment.

At the outset, I divided the elements of the reliance model into four elements. These should be considered in turn, whilst remembering the warning that the elements are bound to overlap. Moreover, these four elements may not apply with equal force to the different jurisdictions mentioned above. In particular, as the description of the American doctrine of promissory estoppel in s 90 revealed, the American courts tend to confine the reliance model to express promises and avoid references to such equitable terms as unconscionability. This results from the courts' greater confidence in regarding the reliance model as a species of contractual obligation. Whether this makes any substantive difference in the law is harder to judge, for of course promises may be implied from conduct and other statements, and the equitable considerations stressed by English and Australian courts may equally well surface in the American criterion of injustice. With these reservations in mind, we should now elaborate the four strands of the reliance model.

1. Encouragement

The first element examines the initial actions of the person who has allegedly entered into a voluntary undertaking. An express promise satisfies this element, but also actions short of a promise may suffice if they amount to the deliberate creation or encouragement of an expectation of future action. In *Crabb v Arun District Council*, this element was satisfied by the combination of the discussions with the council officers and the subsequent action of installing two gates in the fence. This requirement was satisfied in *Waltons Stores (Interstate) Ltd v Maher*, by the deliberate omission to inform the owner of the building of the change of heart in the knowledge that he was acting on the belief that the lease would be completed. The idea of encouragement which is central to these cases implies the requirement of actual knowledge or foresight of the reliance which the injured party will place upon the action.

This first element marks the crucial distinction between the exchange and the reliance models of enforceability. Although the difference between, on the one hand, encouraging someone to act in a particular way by promises and undertakings which create certain expectations and, on the other, requesting him or her to act in a particular way as the price of a reciprocal promise which engenders expectations, may not appear great, it marks the boundary between the two models of enforceability. The difference may be summarized crudely by saying that unrequested detriment may generate liability under the reliance model but not the exchange model. In *Crabb v Arun District Council*, for instance, because the council's officers had not requested the plaintiff to sell his land, this detriment could not count as consideration to support their alleged promise to grant the right of way.

Although this distinction is conceptually clear, it must be observed that the courts may often interpret a particular set of facts as falling under either model. The acts which amount to encouragement can be interpreted by a court as constituting an implied request that those acts should be performed. This style of interpretation of the facts may have been present in *Carlill v Carbolic Smoke Ball Co.*[7] The court construed the terms of the company's advertisement to amount to a request to use the smoke ball according to the instructions, but the action would have failed under the exchange model if the court had only found in the advertisements an encouragement to use the smoke ball. The absence of a developed reliance model as a test of enforceability in the classical law indubitably led to the practice of the courts becoming ever more ingenious in discovering implied requests to perform actions, in order to bring a deserving case within the exchange model of consideration. The decision in *Shadwell v Shadwell*[8] illustrates this practice. Although not all the facts of the case were beyond dispute, it was clear that the uncle, on hearing of his nephew's engagement to be married, had promised his nephew in a letter £150 per annum for a certain period to assist him. Unless this promise contained an implied request to go ahead with the marriage, however, it seemed that the nephew had not supplied any consideration to bring it within the exchange model. The majority of the court was prepared to impose this artificial construction on the promise in order to render it enforceable, but it is clear that what influenced the court was the sense that the nephew had acted to his detriment in undertaking the support of a wife owing to reliance on the promise. This strained process of discovering requests for detrimental reliance may become less frequent as the reliance model gains acceptance.

2.   Proof of detrimental reliance

The second element of the reliance model requires proof that the other party has in fact relied upon that undertaking by acting to his detriment. This strand in the reasoning can be subdivided into a causal test and a requirement of detriment. For causation to be established, it must be shown that the words and conduct of the other party were at least a substantial factor leading to the change of position, but the evidence of a promise followed by detrimental reliance creates a strong presumption of the causal connection.[9] The requirement of detriment is more controversial, since it is not always clear whether this constitutes a test of enforceability or merely the basis for the assessment of an appropriate remedy. Perhaps the best view is that detriment is necessary, provided that it is understood that the detriment can comprise not only out-of-pocket expenses and financial losses, but also the failure to safeguard a legal position caused by reliance upon the expectation generated by the promise, even though such reliance caused no

7   [1893] 1 QB 256, CA.
8   (1860) 9 CBNS 159.
9   *Greasley v Cooke* [1980] 3 All ER 710, [1980] 1 WLR 1306, CA.

financial loss in itself. In the latter instance, the absence of financial loss will defeat the claim eventually, either because it will not be unfair or unconscionable to go back on the promise, or because the remedy will be nil. In a case, for example, where a promise to give money induces the purchase of an extravagant item, the purchase itself may count as detrimental reliance in satisfaction of this element of the reliance model, but a remedy will not be forthcoming unless it was both unfair to revoke the promise and economic detriment can be shown resulting from reliance, as for example in the case of a forced resale of the item at a loss.

The Australian case, *Commonwealth of Australia v Verwayen*[10] illustrates this point. A former member of the Navy sued for personal injuries caused 20 years earlier during combat exercises. As a result of a stated policy decision, the Commonwealth did not initially plead the defence that the action was barred by lapse of time, but, after a change of policy two years later, it sought to amend its pleadings. The High Court, by a narrow majority, held that the Commonwealth could not dispute its liability to the plaintiff on this ground at this late stage. The main issue which divided the court was the remedy available to the plaintiff. Given that the lapse of time defence was bound to succeed if pleaded, unless the Commonwealth was held to its original decision not to plead the defence the plaintiff's only detriment comprised his legal costs over a period of two years. The minority members of the court accepted the majority's view that the reliance upon the Commonwealth's stated policy position for two years of litigation was sufficient to create an obligation under the doctrine of estoppel, but preferred to limit the remedy to the legal costs during this time. This case illustrates the point that a change of position, or a failure to safeguard a position, caused by a promise or encouraged by the other party, will suffice to amount to the relevant type of detrimental reliance, but that the remedy awarded will not necessarily coincide with the expectation, if the actual losses caused by the misplaced reliance can be compensated in some other way.

3.   Reliance was reasonable

The third element of the reliance model is the perception that the detrimental reliance was reasonable in all the circumstances. During negotiations for a commercial transaction, for example, the parties may incur substantial costs in preparing plans and providing estimates. Normally, businesses undertake the risk that these expenditures will be wasted if the negotiations break down, and the courts refer to this practice to raise a presumption that reliance in such situations is unreasonable. Yet this presumption can be rebutted, where one party encourages the other to incur unusual costs or change his position irretrievably, as

10 (1990) 170 CLR 394, Aust HC.

in *Waltons Stores (Interstate) Ltd v Maher*.[11] Disparities of business sophistication probably influence the standard of reasonableness, such as where one party takes advantage of the other's naivety in business matters by stringing him along. This element of advantage-taking undermines the defendant's claim that the negotiations had not yet reached the stage where it was reasonable for legal obligations to be imposed.[12] On the other hand, if the promisor makes it clear that the promisee will act at his own risk by indicating, for instance, that the agreement remains subject to a formal contract, such statements should prevent any reliance from being classed as reasonable.[13] This could have been a ground for rejecting the claim in *Baird Textile Holdings Ltd v Marks and Spencer plc*: at various times the defendants had expressly indicated their unwillingness to enter into legally enforceable obligations, and this warning would probably have rendered the reliance unreasonable.

What the courts will regard as reasonable reliance can, of course, only be indicated by reference to certain themes. The notion of reasonable reliance clearly functions to rule out the enforceability of undertakings which were not intended to be binding and could not reasonably be expected to be binding. Suppose that a person relies upon a published railway timetable to select a train which will take him to his destination in time to conclude a highly profitable business deal. The train runs late, the passenger misses the opportunity to clinch the deal, and the business is given to a competitor. It is reasonably foreseeable that passengers will place reliance upon timetables, but it is unlikely that a court would find the railway company liable to passengers for any loss arising from delays. The reason is surely that no one expects the publication of a train timetable to engender legal liability: it is a service offered to passengers without expectation of serious reliance. This interpretation of the requirement of reasonable reliance explains the result in the American case *Division of Labor Law Enforcement v Transpacific Transportation Co*.[14] For fifteen years an employer annually paid its employees a Christmas bonus, but a claim for a sixteenth bonus on the basis of an implied promise to pay derived from the settled practice was defeated. The court regarded the reliance as unreasonable, for employees were aware, or should have been aware, that the payment of future bonuses was conditional and uncertain, so any implied promise could not be reasonably relied upon.

In a similar way, the test of reasonable reliance functions like the test of 'no intention to create legal relations' to exclude legal liability in social and family contexts. English courts have also handled this aspect of the reliance model by focusing on the content of the promise itself. They insist that the promise should

11 (1988) 164 CLR 387, Aust HC.
12 *Crabb v Arun District Council* [1976] Ch 179, [1975] 3 All ER 865, CA; *Hoffman v Red Owl Stores Inc* 26 Wis 2d 683, 133 NW 2d 267 (1965).
13 *A-G of Hong Kong v Humphreys Estate (Queen's Gardens) Ltd* [1987] AC 114, [1987] 2 All ER 387, PC.
14 69 Cal App 3d 268, 137 Cal Rptr 855 (1977).

be directed towards a change of position which alters legal rights, such as a modification of an existing contract or an alteration in interests in property.

The test of reasonable reliance also serves to confine the range of liability to intended beneficiaries of the promise or undertaking. It would be unreasonable to rely upon a promise when it should have been clear that the promisor did not expect or intend a claimant who is not the promisee to be able to do so. This dimension of reasonableness parallels the requirement of privity of contract which rules out claims by persons who are not parties to the contract under the exchange model. But the test of reasonable reliance does not limit the range of responsibility to parties within an exchange relation. Under a complex division of labour in production or distribution, it will be possible to discover reasonable reliance upon promises outside the strict confines of actual or expected exchanges. This point can be illustrated by the American case, *Lusk-Harbison-Jones Inc v Universal Credit Co.*[15] A retailer of cars repossessed them after a purchaser had missed payments on the credit arrangement provided by a finance company (which in this case was a subsidiary of the manufacturer). The dealer omitted to insure the repossessed automobiles in reliance on a pamphlet distributed by the finance company, which said that the finance company would arrange insurance protection for the dealer's interest, and this would continue in force until the loan was liquidated. Unfortunately, after the cars were destroyed by fire, the dealer discovered that no insurance coverage had been arranged by the finance company. Notice that the relation between dealer and finance company was not based upon an exchange, even though they co-operated in securing sales, so there could be no contractual relation based upon consideration between them. Nevertheless, the Supreme Court of Mississippi held the finance company liable to the dealer to pay compensation for damage to the automobiles, because his failure to insure was caused by reasonable reliance upon the finance company. The case provides a commonplace illustration of how the division of labour in an advanced capitalist society cannot be grasped fully in terms of exchanges between autonomous traders, at least not without considerable artificiality and distortion of the exchange model. To fill this gap, the test of reasonable reliance permits the creation of binding obligations outside exchanges or contemplated exchanges.

4. Unconscionability

The fourth element of the reliance model considers whether it would be unfair, or unconscionable, to permit someone to go back on his or her original promise or undertaking. This requirement looks at the situation which has arisen as a result of the reliance, rather than at the acts and omissions which caused the reliance. The question to be addressed is whether the promisor's attempt to enforce his strict legal rights which defeat the expectation engendered by the promise or

---

15 164 Miss 693, 145 So 623 (1933).

undertaking should now be regarded as unjust. The normal source for this finding of unfairness or unconscionability will consist in the irretrievable economic harm which has resulted from misplaced reliance upon the undertaking, as in the case of the sterile land in *Crabb v Arun District Council*.

This element goes beyond an identification of actual financial loss suffered, however, for it can amount to a moral judgement about the behaviour of the promisor in all the circumstances. One illustration of this requirement concerns those cases where the absence of conformity to requirements of formalities in sales of interests in land presents an additional obstacle to the recognition of any binding obligation. The revocation of a promise or a course of conduct which encouraged the belief that the formalities would be satisfied will be regarded as unconscionable here if, to rely upon the requirement of formalities, would be to use the formal requirements as an instrument of unfairness to the injured party. The moral judgement will also extend to other dimensions of the conduct of the parties such as, in this case, the 'high-handedness' of Arun District Council. In *Pascoe v Turner*,[16] when a man deserted his mistress, he said, 'The house is yours and everything in it.' On the strength of this promise, the woman took no steps to secure her occupation of the property and spent £230 on improvements. In fact, he never arranged for a conveyance of the property and he eventually brought an action for possession. The English Court of Appeal held that the woman had a defence to the action for possession and, furthermore, ordered the man to execute a conveyance of the property. Here the 'ruthless' determination of the man to evict his former mistress from her home was added to the relatively meagre financial loss of the mistress to render the man's attempt to insist upon his strict legal rights unconscionable or unjust.

The presence of actual detrimental reliance on the promise is usually, but not invariably sufficient to persuade a court that it would be unconscionable for the promisor to go back on the promise. A common situation that arises in litigated cases concerns employers who encourage their employees to believe that at some point in the future, often on the death of the employer, the employee will receive a substantial benefit, such as a gift of the employer's business. Such a claim succeeded in *Gillett v Holt*,[17] where the employer, a farmer, had on many occasions assured an employee who had lived in the farmhouse and managed the farm for 25 years that the employee would succeed to the farming business including the farmhouse. The parties fell out, the farmer dismissed his manager and changed his Will. The Court of Appeal upheld a claim for the farmhouse, together with a sufficient sum to compensate the former manager for his exclusion from the rest of the farming business on the basis of what was described as proprietary estoppel. In this case, the farm manager demonstrated consider-able detriment, such as selling his own home, foregoing career opportunities,

16 [1979] 2 All ER 945, [1979] 1 WLR 431, CA.
17 [2001] Ch 210, [2000] 2 All ER 289, CA.

incurring substantial expenditure on the farmhouse and, an element which is common in these cases, accepting a low level of wages. This detriment persuaded the court that it was unconscionable for the farmer now to resile on his assurances. On the other hand, unless the assurances are strong and the detrimental reliance considerable, a court may conclude that the employer has not given up the normal right of a testator to alter a Will in the light of changing circumstances. Mere hints by an elderly person that something might be left in his or her Will would be insufficient to found an estoppel.

C.   The classification of the reliance model

In contrast to most jurisdictions in the USA, the English and, to a lesser extent, the Australian courts display a hesitation in regarding the enforcement of promises on the ground of reliance as equivalent to the enforcement of contractual obligations. This hesitation finds its sustenance in both good and bad reasons. It is worth considering these reasons further before examining the rationale for the reliance model of enforceability.

Let me commence my observations on whether the reliance model constitutes an example of contractual obligations by expressing my doubt, perhaps incongruously, of both the significance and interest of this question. For those who wish to organize the law of obligations into a tidy scheme of tight conceptual classifications, no doubt the issue becomes of paramount importance. But with the more contextual approach adopted here, where the interest lies in examining the grounds and scope of legal obligations arising in market transactions, the question of proper classification fades into insignificance. What seems far more important in this contextual approach is the fact that the reliance model does generate obligations to transfer property, to refrain from certain courses of action and to compensate others for their frustrated expectations during commercial dealings. It must be admitted that the issue does sometimes have some practical importance, where, for example, a statute insists upon certain formalities for the enforcement of contracts, and in order to avoid that requirement in the interests of justice courts have often found it convenient to deny that the reliance model counts as a contract. This instrumental reasoning, however, should not be permitted to elevate the question of classification into a matter of fundamental importance. The only significant aspect of this issue consists in the extent to which the courts are reluctant to classify these obligations based upon the reliance model as contractual, which leads to a deeper hesitation to acknowledge these obligations at all.

1.   Time-frame

The fundamental difference between contracts supported by consideration and those supported by reliance consists in the time-frame of the legal analysis.

Whereas in a bilateral contract, formed by an agreement, the contractual obligation comes into force immediately, in cases of reliance the obligation matures as a result of a series of actions referable to a relationship over a period of time. In the case of *Crabb v Arun District Council*, for instance, it is hard to say at what point the council's obligation to grant a right of way arose. The discussions with the council's officers would not suffice in themselves, for at that stage no reliance had occurred. The source of the obligation lay rather in the combination of measures by the council which encouraged the owner's belief that he would be granted a right of way, such as the erection of gates, the foreseen detrimental reliance evidenced by sale of part of the land leaving the remainder inaccessible, and the judgment that it would now be unjust for the council to insist upon its strict legal rights. Similarly, in *Waltons Stores (Interstate) Ltd v Maher*, the obligation did not arise at any fixed point of time but matured as a result of the combination of detrimental reliance, evidenced by the owner's demolition and construction work, and the company's awareness of these actions, together with its decision not to disabuse the owner of his mistake. At the end of the day the court regarded this as rendering the company's attempt to deny the lease as unconscionable.

The classical model of contract law tends to stress the way contractual obligations come into existence at a fixed point in time through the satisfaction of the rules of consideration and agreement. The reliance model runs against the grain of this perception of how contractual relations must be conceived, but this in itself does not appear to justify the exclusion of the reliance model from the realm of contracts. Indeed, the classical model was always forced to qualify this assumption in the case of unilateral contracts, for there the contract only becomes binding following completion of the requested act of consideration. For instance, in *Carlill v Carbolic Smoke Ball Co*, it was not until Mrs Carlill had used the smoke ball according to the instructions and had caught influenza that the company's contractual obligation to pay £100 arose. Once one accepts that contractual obligations may mature over a period of time in the manner of unilateral contracts, then there seems little reason to continue to insist that the reliance model should not be regarded as the basis of contractual obligations.

2.   Consistency with consideration

Another ground for hesitation at the inclusion of the reliance model in the fabric of contractual obligations concerns the worry that it tends to subvert the doctrine of consideration. It is true, of course, that acknowledgement of the reliance model prevents the apotheosis of consideration as the exclusive test of legal enforceability, but this does not necessarily mean that the rationale of consideration is thereby frustrated. In particular, we have noted that one clear effect of the doctrine of consideration is to prevent enforcement of donative promises. The reliance model apparently threatens to alter that result, and as a consequence challenges a central purpose of the doctrine of consideration. The reliance model only enforces a certain kind of donative promise, however: one that lacks consideration, but which has the other elements of encouragement of detrimental reliance, reasonable reliance and unconscionable conduct by the promisor. These additional elements create grounds for the imposition of legal obligations, which may not conflict with the rationale underlying the doctrine of consideration's rejection of donative promises, but merely supplement and refine that rationale.

3. Promises and statements

Is there a fundamental difference between the two models of enforceability, under which only the test of consideration permits the enforcement of promises of future action? Some of the origins of the reliance model lie in the doctrine of estoppel, and this doctrine was primarily designed to prevent persons from denying that a state of facts which they had asserted to be true was in fact true. These origins lead to the claim that the reliance model can only create obligations arising from statements of present fact, not create obligations with respect to the future. It is clear, however, that whatever the legal source of the reliance model, recent cases in the UK and elsewhere have overstepped this alleged boundary. The decision in *Crabb v Arun District Council* clearly concerned a promise or an expression of intention with respect to future action, namely the granting of a right of way, not a statement about the existing factual or legal situation. The High Court of Australia in *Waltons Stores (Interstate) Ltd v Maher* also did not disguise the point that it was enforcing an implied promise to complete the lease, not simply preventing the company from going back on any implied statement that it had already executed the lease.

It is perhaps possible to distinguish the cases which clearly enforce promises as to future conduct on the ground that they all concern dealings in interests in land. It is suggested that this species of estoppel, often called 'proprietary estoppel', does permit enforcement of promises for the future, but that, apart from dealings in land, such promises are unenforceable under the reliance model. This distinction seems highly improbable. No reason other than the certainty achieved by following scrupulously the limits of precedent decisions is given for treating the general grounds for enforceability of promises connected with interests in land any differently from those concerning goods and services. If applied systematically the proposed distinction might produce some strange anomalies. In *Pascoe v Turner*, for instance, it will be recalled that the man's promise to his mistress referred to both the house and its contents. It was not suggested in this case that the goods in the house did not belong to the woman as well, and, although this result may be explicable as a simple gift, it would surely have been an absurd result if, on the strength of the promise and the subsequent detrimental reliance, the woman had won the house but not its contents, because the latter do not comprise interests in land.

Unconvinced by the necessity for this limitation to proprietary interests, some English decisions trespass over this alleged boundary to the enforceability of promises under the reliance model. In *Re Basham (deceased)*,[18] the deceased had promised to give his stepdaughter his estate on his death, and this promise was enforced, despite the absence of a Will, even though the estate comprised both a house and a substantial sum of money in the bank. Similarly, in *Pacol Ltd v Trade Lines Ltd (The Henryk Sif)*,[19] following a breach of contract, the defendants encouraged the claimant to believe that the correct people to sue were themselves, whereas, in fact, due to complex commercial arrangements, they were not the party liable under the contract. By the time the claimant discovered the true position, the period of limitation for bringing legal actions against the correct party had expired. The court held the defendants responsible under the contract in view of their failure to disabuse the claimant of its reasonable misunderstanding and its subsequent detrimental reliance. Here the promise or undertaking which was enforced is unconnected with land, although the court also believed that the case could be decided the same way as a more traditional type of estoppel based upon a statement of fact.

The limitation of enforcement of promises to proprietary estoppel has never been part of the American doctrine. In recent years, the Australian courts have expressly dissented from the proposition. Casting aside most of the suggested limitations on the scope of the doctrine of estoppel, Mason CJ in *Commonwealth v Verwayen* summed up the principle in the following terms:

> The result is that it should be accepted that there is but one doctrine of estoppel, which provides that a court of common law or equity may do what is required, but no more, to prevent a person who has relied upon an assumption as to a present, past or future state of affairs (including a legal state of affairs), which assumption the party estopped has induced him to hold, from suffering detriment in reliance upon the assumption as a result of the denial of its correctness. A central element of that doctrine is that there must be a proportionality between the remedy and the detriment which is its purpose to avoid.[20]

It is surely only a matter of time before the English courts will also break down these artificial and unjustified limits on the application of the reliance model of enforceability.

4.   Remedies

One more substantial ground for hesitation at the introduction of the reliance model into the fabric of contract law concerns the type of remedies afforded by

18 [1987] 1 All ER 405, [1986] 1 WLR 1498, Ch.
19 [1982] 1 Lloyd's Rep 456, QB.
20 (1990) 170 CLR 394 at 413, Aust HC.

the courts. Whereas a contract supported by consideration will invariably, at the least, give a right to damages for breach of the agreement, the remedy for breach of undertakings under the reliance model appears to lie within a broad discretion of the court. As we saw in connection with *Crabb v Arun District Council*, English law insists that the remedy should be merely that which is necessary to satisfy equity in the case. Similarly, as in the statement of Mason CJ above, the Australian courts have stressed that the remedy should do what is required, but not more, to prevent a person who has relied upon a promise from suffering detriment, whilst at the same time precluding any injustice to third parties.[21] The American Restatement also stresses the need to enforce the promise only to the extent that is necessary to avoid injustice.

Nor have English courts so far been willing to award damages for breach of promises under the reliance model but have instead adopted equitable remedies, such as ordering the conveyance of the right of way in *Crabb v Arun District Council*. This approach reflects the origins of these types of estoppel in equity, but, given the fusion of common law and equity, together with the power of equity courts to award damages, any possible denial of damages seems to be a historical anachronism. Australian courts have ignored this limitation, as in *Waltons Stores (Interstate) Ltd v Maher*, where the court eventually ordered payment of damages in lieu of specific performance.

Now the force of this undoubted contrast between remedies for breach of contracts, supported by consideration, and those obligations, arising under the reliance model, depends upon how closely one links the concept of contractual obligations to a particular remedial scheme. A close linkage inevitably leads to the reasoning that if the remedies differ, then the type of obligation must differ also. It must follow on this view that the reliance model does not create contractual obligations, but some other species of equitable proprietary right. But this view seems riddled with inconsistencies. The logic of this position should also insist upon a sharp distinction between, on the one hand, contracts which can be specifically enforced (an equitable remedy entailing compulsory performance and sometimes the creation of equitable proprietary interests), and on the other, those where the sole remedy lies in damages at common law. Yet all these contracts, despite the difference in remedies available, are invariably classified as full contractual obligations. No reason is given for ignoring the differences created by the availability of equitable remedies in some cases, but then relying upon the practice of using equitable remedies in the reliance model in order to justify the exclusion of these cases from the realm of contractual obligations.

As well as the inconsistent treatment of the significance of equitable remedies, this focus on the remedies for breach of the obligations also produces some paradoxical conclusions. It is often asserted that the remedial difference reveals

---

21 Eg *Commonwealth of Australia v Verwayen* (1990) 170 CLR 394, Aust HC; *Giumelli v Giumelli* (1999) 196 CLR 105, Aust HC.

that, for contractual obligations supported by consideration, the courts will attempt to enforce the promise or undertaking, whereas for obligations under the reliance model the court will provide the minimum equitable protection necessary, which will be simply the measure of detrimental reliance or out-of-pocket expenses. In other words, contractual obligations protect expectations, but obligations under the reliance model merely compensate detrimental reliance. Yet it is readily apparent that in many instances of the reliance model the court concludes that the equitable remedy must comprise enforcement of the promise or expectation. In *Pascoe v Turner*, for instance, the deserted mistress received a conveyance of the house. Similarly, in *Crabb v Arun District Council*, the plaintiff received the expected right of way over the road. By contrast, for contracts supported by consideration, the injured party may not receive enforcement of the promise, but merely nominal damages if his losses cannot be proven.[22] This suggests that the remedial contrast between the exchange model and the reliance model does not rest upon a difference of principle, in the form that only under contracts supported by consideration should the injured party receive his or her expected performance. Although remedial differences do exist between the two models, there seems no good reason arising from this divergence to deny that both represent species of contractual obligation.

In so far as this question of the proper classification of the reliance model as a species of obligation deserves attention, therefore, the arguments against regarding it as representing a species of contractual obligation seem overstated and confused. Without denying the important differences of emphasis between the exchange and reliance models, particularly the contrast between time-frames, it seems a mistake to insist upon a conception of the market order constituted by the law of contract which excludes these reliance model obligations.

D.   Rationale of reliance model

The reliance model plainly draws a different line between the public and private spheres to that drawn by the doctrine of consideration. This difference signals that it has an alternative conception of the appropriate sphere of state action. But this difference springs, I suggest, not from a radical departure in values, but merely a refinement of the harm principle.

1.   Good faith

It seems wrong to attribute to the emergence of the reliance model a simple legal endorsement of moral standards such as the idea that promises ought to be kept.[23]

22 Eg *Lazenby Garages v Wright* [1976] 2 All ER 770, [1976] 1 WLR 459, CA.
23 C Fried, *Contract as Promise* (Cambridge, Mass, 1981).

Even if the reliance model is tied to express or implied promises, which seems doubtful from the cases on acts of encouragement, the model does not require that all promises should be enforced, or even that all serious promises should give rise to legal liability. Instead, only where the promise has induced reasonable reliance will the courts insist that the promise be kept. Nevertheless, the emphasis placed by the courts upon the fourth element of unfair or unconscionable results, as a condition for intervention, suggests that moral standards play an important role in determining liability and shaping the remedy. In this context, however, the term 'unconscionability' appears to contain two dimensions.

In the first place, it suggests a deliberate manipulation of another person's choices by provoking or not disabusing false impressions about future intentions. This is similar to fraud, but, instead of making statements of fact known to be false, the promisor in the reliance model encourages certain expectations with regard to his or her future conduct and these expectations are known by the promisor to be unfounded either at the outset or later on whilst the ensuing detrimental reliance is taking place. The moral ideal here seems to be a requirement of acting in good faith. But the law cannot be endorsing a moral requirement of conduct in good faith alone, for the reliance model insists upon the additional requirement of detrimental reliance.

The second dimension of the term unconscionability examines the exposed position of the person who has relied to his or her detriment on this false expectation. A denial that the expectation was justified becomes unconscionable if the promisee cannot revert to his or her former position without loss directly attributable to reliance upon the expectation. Stated in this manner, this second dimension of unconscionability is merely a restatement of the harm principle, making it clear that what is required is an irretrievable change of position which entails economic loss.

2. Wealth maximization

Can the reliance model of enforceability be explained as a technique for identifying value-enhancing transactions beyond the exchange model? Recall that the difficulty for the wealth maximization idea in connection with the doctrine of consideration was that some donative promises could increase wealth yet were excluded from the public sphere. Does the reliance model solve that problem by identifying those situations where a supplement is required in order to bring the tests of enforceability into line with the dictates of the principle of wealth maximization?

Many of the cases which employ the reliance model fit the pattern of grappling with complex economic associations between numerous parties which cannot be distilled into a series of discrete exchange transactions. This standard feature of the cases stands out in an American application of the reliance model in disputes between building contractors as illustrated by *Drennan v Star Paving Co.*[24] A general contractor, in preparing a tender for building work, solicited bids from specialist sub-contractors for portions of the work. The general contractor then computed all the costs of the work and submitted a bid for the whole job, which was accepted. One of the sub-contractors had made a mistake in the quotation for his specialized work and refused to carry it out. It was clear that the general contractor had not formally accepted the sub-contractor's bid, so the doctrine of consideration had not been satisfied, but all the parties were aware that the general contractor would rely upon the quotation in putting forward his tender. The California Supreme Court held that, despite the absence of reciprocal promises, the sub-contractor's bid was binding because it was reasonably foreseeable that it would be relied upon by the general contractor and had in fact been relied upon. These practices of the construction industry involve complex arrangements between numerous independent contractors, and, for this system of production to work effectively, sometimes parties must be protected in their reliance upon others at a point earlier than the establishment of formal exchange relations. To obtain the general efficiency advantages of a competitive tendering system for construction work, the general contractors must be able to rely upon the accuracy of bids by sub-contractors. To this extent, the reliance model may display a response to concerns for economic efficiency and value-enhancing market transactions.

The difficulty with this interpretation lies in the problem of accounting for its application in cases where the facts reveal no more than a donative promise followed by reasonable detrimental reliance. In cases such as *Pascoe v Turner*, for instance, the enforcement of the promise to convey the house looks like a sterile exchange, not deserving of support as a value-enhancing transaction. We noted above, however, that not all donative promises are sterile, for it is possible that the recipient of the intended gift will value the property more highly than the donor. This opens up the possibility that the presence of unrequested detrimental reliance reveals that in fact the donee values the property more highly than the promisor. On this view, the fact that the deserted mistress in *Pascoe v Turner* made improvements to the house evidenced the greater value which she placed upon the property. But even supposing that detrimental reliance does evidence the donee's greater valuation of the property, the argument must overcome the problem that the absence of detrimental reliance does not prove the contrary point that the donee places no greater value on the property. The presence or absence of detrimental reliance appears an inept test of the relative utilities of the property between the parties.[25]

24 51 Cal 2d 409, 333 P 2d 757 (1958).
25 Eisenberg, 'Donative Promises' (1979) 47 *University of Chicago Law Review* 1.

3. Harm principle

Fuller[26] first suggested that the reliance model could be justified within the framework of the harm principle.[27] The harm is described as misplaced reliance upon another causing detriment. Indeed, Fuller suggested that this description of the nature of the harm which the law regarded as a protected interest fitted the whole of the law of contract and much of the law of tort.

Where the reliance model differs from the exchange model of consideration is in the absence of a request to incur the detriment. This is significant, for it indicates a diminution of the requirement of consent to contractual obligations. But the difference does not affect the application of the harm principle, which focuses on the fact of detrimental reliance as the reason for intervention. The reliance model is utilized when it seems impossible on the facts of the case to imply a request to incur the detriment, yet nevertheless the detriment has been encouraged by the promisor. In this respect the reliance model represents the mirror image of cases where benefits have been conferred without a request. If the court is unable to imply a request, then it must resort to the law of restitution or unjust enrichment to justify the imposition of an obligation to compensate for a benefit conferred.

In drawing the scope of the public realm of enforceability, therefore, the reliance model imitates the doctrine of consideration in adopting an interpretation of the harm principle. But instead of employing the abstract notion of exchange to determine when interests have been harmed, the reliance model examines the whole course of conduct of the parties in order to determine the extent and causes of the detrimental reliance.

26 Fuller and Perdue, 'The Reliance Interest in Contract Damages' (1936) 46 *Yale Law Journal* 52, at p 373.
27 Collins, 'Contract Law and Legal Theory', in W Twining (ed), *Legal Theory and Common Law* (Oxford, 1986).

Chapter 6

The contractualization of social life

A. Contract as governance mechanism

This chapter examines the final purpose of tests of legal enforceability. This concerns the extent to which contractual obligations should be permitted to regulate and define all types of social relations. This issue does not raise the question of the proper limits of state regulation, but rather whether the form of regulation derived from the law of contract supplies the appropriate criterion for governance of the relation. In recent times, with the success of the market economy, it has become increasingly common to assume that contractual relations should enjoy priority over other obligations unless there is good reason to exclude them. Let us consider some of the reasons for the strength behind the belief in the virtue of freedom of contract, before considering in greater detail some of the justifications put forward for limiting markets and contracts.

B. The faith in markets

The contemporary resurgence of faith in markets springs from a number of sources. The success of markets in performing the task of efficient satisfaction of consumer wants is no doubt the major justification for the contractualization of social relations. This reason explains, for example, why public services have become increasingly approximated in their organization and financing to private contractual provision of services. Viewed in this light, any limit upon contracts and markets, such as a prohibition of the sale of parts of the body, or arrangements for prostitution, is likely to impede the efficient satisfaction of wants, and is therefore to be regarded as undesirable without strong justification. But there are deeper reasons for the strength of the faith in markets.

One attraction of markets is their seductive claim that they avoid any governmental choice with respect to the pattern of the distribution of wealth in society.[1] The stock of goods which a person possesses depends upon a myriad of market transactions rather than any conscious human agency which engineers a particular distributive pattern. The 'invisible hand' of market forces as a distributive mechanism has the apparent attraction that it requires no political justification for its outcomes. The government can absolve itself from responsibility, and simply claim that poverty and wealth are the result of market choices by individuals. Once again this thesis strongly supports an absence of limits to markets, for those limits will necessarily interfere with this neutral mechanism for the distribution of wealth.

Yet the deepest attraction of markets and contracts is, I believe, that they promise a solution to the problem of loss of confidence in the potential for institutionalized structures to give direction to people's lives. The preference for markets is symptomatic of a scepticism with respect to any claim to know best how social relations should be organized, what standards they should observe, and perhaps a fear that any institutionalized power of control over social relations will be abused and employed to destroy individuality. By permitting contractual relations to flourish, the state effectively delegates to individuals as many choices as possible as to the nature of the social relations into which they may enter. Instead of determining in advance the reciprocal obligations in cohabitation, for instance, the law leaves the parties to select their own property settlement and

1   F von Hayek, *Law, Legislation and Liberty* (London, 1976), Vol 2, pp 65–69; R Nozick, *Anarchy, State, and Utopia* (Oxford, 1974), p 159. See Chapter 13.

distribution of assets and responsibilities. This scepticism about the role of institutionalized direction of social standards thus gives considerable impetus to the extension of contractual relations.[2]

When these three forces are combined – the efficiency of markets, the avoidance of public responsibility for distributive patterns, and the escape from scepticism about imposed social standards – the question tends to become not what relations should be governed by contracts, but rather why should there be any limits to contracts and markets? Before considering potential answers to this question, let us consider the variety of legal techniques available for policing the scope of markets and contractual obligations.

C.   Legal techniques for controlling the scope of contracts

No particular legal doctrine serves as a general technique for confining the scope of contracts. The courts achieve this result by a combination of the legal doctrines which we have considered so far in previous chapters, especially the doctrines of illegality and public policy, consideration, and intention to create legal relations.

1.   Contracts in the family

Although the obligations between members of a family are determined in the first instance by obligations of status, such as the parental duty to support children, contracts have played an important supplementary role, especially in connection with the distribution of property entitlements. It was once common for the parties involved in a marriage and their parents to devise an elaborate settlement of the distribution of property by means of a legally enforceable contract. Parties to a marriage today normally leave the issue of the distribution of assets to be determined by statutory norms, either the provisions regarding spousal support in the event of separation or divorce, or the law of succession and inheritance with respect to death. Although the law often encourages the parties to agree a settlement in these cases, it will not tolerate agreements which violate the legislative standards of a fair distribution of assets.

One way the courts exclude contractual relations is to invoke a combination of the doctrine of consideration and the idea of intention to create legal relations. The court will argue that either there is no consideration to support the agreement, as in *Combe v Combe*,[3] or if there is consideration, there was no intention to create legal relations. The famous decision in *Balfour v Balfour*[4] illustrates a court using

---

2   Collins, 'The Sanctimony of Contract' in R Rawlings (ed), *Law, Society, and Economy*, (Oxford, 1997) 63, at p 75.
3   [1951] 2 KB 215, [1951] 1 All ER 767, CA.
4   [1919] 2 KB 571, CA.

both of these legal doctrines in order to establish a limit to the application of market justice to family relationships. Here the wife alleged that her husband, before leaving to resume his job abroad, promised her an allowance of £30 a month. Her action to recover the money under this agreement failed. One ground for the decision was the absence of consideration. The wife alleged that the consideration which she gave for her husband's promise was a reciprocal promise to refrain from enforcing her husband's legal obligation to maintain her. Warrington LJ denied that the wife had given any such promise, and nor could one be implied in the circumstances. Duke LJ agreed that there was no consideration, but on the ground that the wife's power to pledge her husband's credit was not a right but merely a permission granted by her husband, so that she was not giving up any right which it was in her power to dispose. In the same case, the court also relied upon the doctrine of intention to create legal relations. Warrington and Atkin LJJ agreed that there was no intention to enter a binding contractual arrangement. Atkin LJ insisted that even if consideration could be established, the court should not enforce this type of agreement:

> It is quite common, and it is the natural and inevitable result of the relationship of husband and wife, that the two spouses should make agreements between themselves, agreements such as are in dispute in this action, agreements for allowances by which the husband agrees that he will pay to his wife a certain sum of money per week or per month or per year to cover either her own expenses or the necessary expenses of the household and of the children, and in which the wife promises either expressly or impliedly to apply the allowance for the purpose for which it is given. To my mind those agreements, or many of them, do not result in contracts at all, and they do not result in contracts even though there may be what as between other parties would constitute consideration for the agreement ... Nevertheless they are not contracts, and they are not contracts because the parties did not intend that they should be attended by legal consequences.

The underlying objective of the court in keeping contractual relations out of this case was to ensure that the wife benefited from the open-ended statutory duty of maintenance based upon need rather than be confined to a fixed sum.

The same objection to contracts determining fixed sums of maintenance does not apply outside marriage, for there is no statutory duty to support a partner after separation. The courts have enforced express and implied contracts between cohabiting couples, which distribute property and arrange financial affairs. These contracts often replicate the financial arrangements, which would have applied, had the parties been married. In *Tanner v Tanner*,[5] a married man persuaded his mistress (who took his name) to move with their children from her rent-controlled tenancy to a house which he had bought as more suitable

5   [1975] 3 All ER 776, [1975] 1 WLR 1346, CA.

accommodation. Later the man married another woman and sought to evict his former mistress, so that he might live there himself with his new wife and family. At no time had the man and his partner made a formal agreement with regard to ownership of the house. Nevertheless, the Court of Appeal concluded that she had a contractual licence to live there until the children left school, and for breach of this contract the court awarded damages as well as setting aside the order for repossession. Although the court took considerable pains to fit the circumstances into the normal positive requirements for enforcement of contracts, such as agreement (by implication) and consideration (by giving up previous accommodation on request), the judgments, particularly that of Lord Denning MR, are also coloured by rhetoric which reflects a social context other than a market:

> The man had a moral duty to provide for the babies of whom he was the father. I would go further. He had a legal duty towards them. Not only towards the babies. But also towards their mother. She was looking after them and bringing them up. In order to fulfil his duty towards the babies, he was under a duty to provide for the mother, too.

The court ignores the previous objection to the enforcement of these contracts that they involve a dimension of immorality, namely the condonation of sexual relations outside marriage. This reflects, no doubt, a change in conventional moral standards under which cohabitation ceased to be an immoral arrangement akin to prostitution, and became instead a common basis for family life. Taking into account this alteration in moral standards, and in the absence of explicit legislative guidance on property distribution between cohabiting couples, the court permitted the enforcement of a contractual relation, which, in its effects on property entitlements, mirrored the standards applicable to marriage.

Even where explicit legislative guidance is available, the courts may sometimes use contractual techniques to permit family members to reach binding agreements which extend their legal commitments towards each other. Such agreements may seem on balance beneficial to the meanings established in the social sphere of the family, either because these agreements add to, rather than subtract from, the obligations of the family community, or because they permit the members of the family to mould the full dimensions of their commitment in perhaps an unconventional way, but which nevertheless provides valuable meaning to the participants. In *Ward v Byham*,[6] for instance, a father promised to pay £1 a week to the mother of his illegitimate child in return for her promise to keep the child well looked after and happy, and to allow the child to decide for herself whether she wished to live with her mother. Later the mother re-married and the father discontinued payments. Under the family law of the time, the mother but not the father was under an obligation to maintain the child. It was argued in defence to the mother's claim for arrears of payment that no consideration supported the father's promise, since the mother had only

6 [1956] 2 All ER 318, [1956] 1 WLR 496, CA.

promised to do what she was already bound to do. Brushing aside this technical problem of satisfying the doctrine of consideration, the Court of Appeal held that all the positive conditions necessary for the formation of a contract were satisfied, and no public policy was violated, so it awarded the mother the arrears of payment. A technical consideration could be discovered either in the mother's promises which went beyond the public duty of support, or alternatively, as Lord Denning MR insisted, simply in the benefit conferred on the father from the mother's promise to care for the child.

Behind the formal grounds for the decision in this case, we may conjecture that the court found the scheme of distributive justice envisaged by family law in these circumstances (ie the absence of a duty of maintenance imposed on the father of an illegitimate child) unattractive, and, perceiving that the father had acknowledged greater responsibilities of support and care for his child, the court did not hesitate to translate those duties into contractual obligations. The case illustrates the paradox that contracts may be used instrumentally to remedy perceived defects in the existing scheme of family entitlements, so that the family is treated like the market for the purpose of limited interventions which add to, rather than subtract from, the independent meanings to be constructed in the family sphere of social life. The court was prepared to enforce the contract, because the obligation which it imposed on the father fitted into a particular meaning for the social relationship which the court approved and sought to foster.

With respect to contracts in the family, therefore, we can see the boundaries of the scope of enforceable agreements being constantly subject to scrutiny and renegotiation. The limits to contracts spring from the concern to uphold public legislative standards of reciprocal obligations and fair distribution of assets, and from an unwillingness to condone contracts which contemplate breaches of conventional moral standards. But within this framework, the courts can permit enforceable contracts, provided that they do not upset the fair distributive scheme, and appear to give greater specificity to choices about how family obligations are to be constructed.

2. Contracts with the state

We have already noted that the operations of government have also typically been insulated from the market. An agreement by a public official to distribute a benefit, such as a construction contract, to a particular contractor who in return has given lavish entertainment will be regarded as improper invasion of market principles into the sphere of government, and such agreements will be unenforceable and the actions treated as the criminal offences designed to deter bribery and corruption. The role of the judicial branch of government is also insulated from market transactions, where either the agreement amounts to a conspiracy to pervert the course of justice, such as a bribe to commit perjury, or an attempt to oust the jurisdiction of the courts over the agreement altogether. This latter rule does not prevent the important practice of private arbitration of disputes, which is often chosen to reduce the costs of litigation, but the exclusion of the courts is subject to statutory safeguards.[7]

Aside from clear illustrations of contracts designed to corrupt the good administration of government, however, a more subtle difficulty arises with respect to contracts with the state. In pursuit of the common good, the state may enter into market relations in order to secure the efficient provision of services and supplies to the public. In recent years, the extent to which the operations of the state have been contracted out to private businesses has been enlarged, with, for example, franchises for the operation of prisons, refuse collection, and broadcasting. Yet, if for some reason these contracts turn out to be harmful to the common good, then should the contract be binding? It can be argued that the state should not make such binding commitments for fear that it may jeopardize its purpose. If so, the principles of the law of contract and the scope of markets should be narrowed to exclude these transactions.

The dilemma need not be so sharp. It is possible for the state to insist in its contracts upon a term which permits withdrawal at any time, or upon a condition precedent to obligations arising which protects the common good. Such terms, however, run the risk of losing the advantage of acquiring the service or supplies with the maximum efficiency to be obtained by using the market mechanism. A contractor with the state will naturally demand a higher price for services, if there is a risk that any investment will be lost by cancellation.

Consider, as an example of this problem, the nature of the legal relationship between civil servants and the Crown (for this purpose the legal identity of the state). The question is whether this relationship should be classified as a market transaction in the form of an ordinary contract of employment, or whether it should be conceived as an exercise of public power with special rules appropriate to the exercise of that power? The practical implications of these different interpretations of the legal position may be summarized by saying that if there is a contract of employment its terms would be enforceable, whereas, in the absence of a contract, the public law rules which ensure government according to the Rule of Law would provide the relevant regulatory framework regardless of the terms of employment. The difference might be revealed in the case of a soldier: should the legal rights and obligations of a soldier be fixed by whatever agreement is reached, or should the soldier's legal position be fixed by reference to the general discretionary power of the government to control its armed forces subject to basic constitutional rights? The latter view may appear to maximise the effectiveness of the army by leaving the government's powers over soldiers largely unfettered; but a contractual arrangement, by giving reliable promises, may serve to improve the quality and long-term retention of recruits, which in fact may improve the effectiveness of the army. The courts have gradually recognized that

7 Arbitration Act 1996; see Chapter 16.

the state may enter into binding market commitments for the efficient provision of public services without jeopardizing the public good. In each particular case, however, it is a matter for discussion whether the sphere of market justice should be permitted to govern the state's agreements.

3. Inalienable property

A final illustration of the exclusion of contract on the ground that contractual obligations are inappropriate for regulating the relation is that of inalienable property. Examples might include the sale of human organs, human sperm and ovaries, and endangered species of animals. The prohibition on such sales will be justified in law on the grounds of illegality or public policy.

D. Justifications for limits on contractual obligations

These three illustrations of limits to the extent of contractual obligations and market relations, discussed above, raise the question of the purpose of these legal controls. Can we discern a pattern which explains why the market is excluded from certain kinds of relations and subject matter in contracts? Although I personally believe that the best explanation requires a deeper understanding of the meaning of contractual relations, arguments have been put forward to explain these limits on the straightforward ground of efficiency and respect for individual liberty. We will consider those explanations before examining the deeper implications of the contractualization of social relations.

1. Externalities and market failure

In answer to the question of why such limits to markets should be imposed, it has been suggested that we should confine our attention to the potential defects of markets with respect to the efficient satisfaction of consumer preferences.[8] Any limits to the sphere of contracts and markets would have to be justified within this framework on the grounds that, for some reason, the market has failed or that the agreement was not freely chosen. It is certainly possible to justify many limits to the sphere of markets and contracts on these grounds. Moreover, we can detect that these considerations have played a role in guiding the courts and the legislature towards setting the limits to contracts and markets. The economic or market failure explanation of the limits of the sphere of market justice begins with a strong presumption in favour of freedom of contract. It identifies free markets

---

8 Calibresi and Melamed, 'Property Rules, Liability Rules, and Inalienability: One View of the Cathedral' (1972) 85 *Harvard Law Review* 1089; Epstein, 'Why Restrain Alienation?' (1985) 85 *Columbia Law Review* 970.

in all goods and services with liberty of the individual and the efficient satisfaction of human wants. Interferences with this freedom are undesirable as a general rule, because they normally create either shortages or black markets in order to evade prohibitions, which display undesirable properties of violence and fear to secure performance of undertakings. Yet the market mechanism has one systematic imperfection. It is likely to discount what are called 'externalities'.

These externalities comprise costs to the parties not involved in the transaction. Such potential costs might include environmental damage, death to an endangered species of animal, injury to health or quality of human life, disgust and offence. Two parties to an agreement may conclude a bargain which satisfies their own interests, but which incidentally imposes some of these externalities on others. These costs could only be taken into account if all affected parties were permitted to influence the terms of the transaction. But this is impracticable because of transaction costs. These are the costs of time and effort in bringing all these persons together to haggle over the deal. The solution in these instances of market failure will be for the law to impose limits upon the freedom of two parties to a contract, so that their transaction reflects the externalities involved. Limits to the scope of contracts and markets should be devised such that, where non-participants in a transaction would have been prepared to pay the parties enough to stop the transaction from taking place, then the law should prohibit this type of contract altogether. This legal rule ensures that the market serves the purpose of wealth maximization despite the obstruction presented by transaction costs.

This reasoning can explain most instances where the law forbids contracts for certain types of goods and services. For example, the law may forbid the sale of certain types of drugs on the ground that these contracts will eventually impose costs on the rest of the community in terms of health care. Similarly, the law may prohibit trade in child labour and bodily organs, prostitution and slavery on the ground that others find such transactions shocking and offensive. The assumption here is that other members of the community would have been prepared to pay the contracting parties sufficient sums not to trade in such items, so that it would no longer be wealth maximizing for the parties to enter such contracts. The legal prohibition, therefore, achieves the efficient result, the one which would have occurred but for the problem of transaction costs which prevent the incorporation of externalities into the calculation of wealth maximization.

Notice that this market failure approach finds nothing intrinsically wrong in the legal enforcement of any of these types of transaction. Legal prohibition is triggered by the market functioning inefficiently, so that where the market seems to produce efficient results, even taking into account externalities, then the prohibition will be unjustified. Provided that other members of the community would not be prepared to pay enough to put an end to the transactions in slavery, ivory from elephant tusks, political votes, child labour and so forth, then on this view the law should permit these transactions.

Like any argument based upon efficiency criteria, it is difficult to falsify its explanation of the limits of markets and contracts, since suitable configurations of externalities can warrant any or no legal limits to market transactions. What is striking about this explanation is the absence of moral criteria other than wealth maximization. Notice that under the market failure theory, the objection to the politician selling his or her votes to the highest bidder is not that the vote has been given on trust by the people to further the common good, but simply that not all persons were present at the auction, with the resulting risk of inefficiency that the electors as a whole would have been willing to pay more for the vote than the multinational corporation. Limits to markets and contracts are therefore set by reference to the presumed goal of markets in wealth maximization, without any concern to promote other kinds of social values.

It is the univocal nature of this theory of the limits of contracts which renders it unsatisfactory as an explanation of the law. Even if a concern for externalities sometimes motivates the courts in setting limits to contracts, it is clear that a wide range of other moral considerations and values lead to constraints being imposed as well. The court in *Balfour v Balfour* was concerned about externalities, for it was worried about the potential cost of widespread litigation over domestic disputes, but far more important was its concern that the distributive pattern settled by law for deserted spouses should not be subverted by contractual agreement. As a rationalization of the law setting limits to contracts and markets, the efficiency explanation may work; but, as an interpretation of the motives which lie behind the courts' judgments, it is plainly inadequate, because it fails to take into account the diversity of reasons for setting those limits.

2. Libertarian considerations

A libertarian explanation of the limits of markets shares the stance of doubting the intrinsic wrongfulness of transactions. It is prepared to allow the principles of market justice to operate wherever parties have genuinely chosen to make binding commitments, provided that the agreement does not interfere with the rights of others. This explanation relies upon the protection of individual rights as the key to setting the limits to markets. Enforceable contracts should not interfere with rights, including the right to choose whether or not to enter a binding contract.[9]

At first sight the libertarian explanation accounts satisfactorily for many of the limits to markets set by the legal doctrines of illegality. Most criminal laws can be

---

9 Kronman, 'Paternalism and the Law of Contracts' (1983) 92 *Yale Law Journal* 763, at pp 774–786.

interpreted as protecting the rights of citizens, such as the rights to private property, freedom, and personal security. Agreements which invade these rights, or contemplate an invasion, should not be enforceable, and will be rejected by the courts on the ground of illegality.

But this strand in the libertarian explanation encounters a problem of accounting for the ranking of individual rights. Since freedom of contract is a right itself, the libertarian theory must be able to explain when this right succumbs to the force of superior rights. Perhaps the resolution of this issue is simple in the case of a conspiracy to steal property, for we can say that the right to freedom of contract must always give way to the right to private property. In the case of agreements entailing slavery, however, the libertarian explanation must address the conundrum that a prohibition on such contracts both interferes with a basic right, namely freedom of contract, and simultaneously protects that right in the future and other aspects of liberty. Indeed, the whole legal institution of enforceable contracts presents a difficulty for libertarian accounts, for they inevitably both secure freedom but also constrain it once the bargain becomes enforceable.[10]

In addition, the libertarian explanation places great weight on the intention of the parties, so that the limits of contract are set by reference to the choice of the parties to enter a binding agreement. The crucial reasons for setting limits on the scope of contracts therefore comprise both the intention of the parties to enter a binding legal agreement, and the genuineness of the choice to consent to an agreement.

The libertarian explanation accounts for the presence of the doctrine of intention to create legal relations in the rhetoric of the courts. One of the reasons given in *Balfour v Balfour* for refusing to enforce the agreement was that the parties did not intend to enter a binding contract. In a few instances, the parties may have made it plain that they do not expect to be legally bound. It is a common practice in business, for instance, to issue 'letters of comfort' or 'letters of intent', which contain indications of likely future action and current business strategy, but these are not intended, without more, to create binding obligations, and the courts respect this choice not to enter the market sphere.[11] Similarly, it is normally stated expressly or implied by custom in the UK that the parties to a collective agreement between management and trade unions do not intend to create a legally enforceable agreement. Apart from these clear expressions of intent, however, the libertarian explanation seems to be fatally flawed.

In cases where the issue is litigated, it seems likely that one party intended a legal agreement and the other wanted the agreement to be merely morally binding. This contradiction removes any possibility of justifying the limits on contracts on

10 Collins, 'Contract and Legal Theory', in W Twining (ed), *Legal Theory and Common Law* (Oxford, 1986).
11 *Kleinwort Benson Ltd v Malaysia Mining Corpn* [1989] 1 All ER 785, [1989] 1 WLR 379, CA; *Rose and Frank Co v JR Crompton and Bros Ltd* [1925] AC 445, HL.

the basis of the joint intent of the parties. We are forced to the conclusion that the courts must rely upon hidden policy considerations when determining the intent of the parties. The libertarian focus upon the choice of the parties to make contracts in a family context runs the risk of ignoring the obligations imposed by law, which are designed to support the family as a way of life insulated from market considerations. Even if both husband and wife in *Balfour v Balfour* had seriously intended to make a binding contract, the agreement would surely not have been enforceable, because it was likely to subvert the distributive principles of family law, such as depriving the wife of her needs-based right to maintenance.[12] If so, this aspect of the libertarian explanation of how the courts set the limits to markets is plainly inadequate.

Another source of justifiable limits on the sphere of the market under the libertarian explanation springs from doubts about the genuineness of the choice to trade in a particular type of goods or service. It seems unlikely, for instance, that a person would really want to choose to be another's slave, whatever the inducement offered. Similarly, it might be argued that a wife would not wish to sell her right to maintenance by her husband, or that a politician would not wish to restrict his or her freedom of action by selling his or her votes in advance. We have reason to suspect in many of these cases that the contract has been secured by coercion or by some other form of unfair dealing.

But, of course, it is hard to discern as a practical matter whether or not such a genuine choice was made. As we shall see in the discussion of consent and coercion in Chapter 8, since every contract is entered into under certain constraints and motivated by needs, the dividing line between free choices and coerced invalid choices cannot be drawn sharply. Even in cases where elements of coercion are patent in the circumstances of the case, we should still need to draw the line between coercion sufficient to negative genuine consent and those ordinary pressures we must expect in life. Consider, for instance, the case of a poor man who sells a kidney in return for money to help his starving family. To doubt that this was a genuine choice requires one to believe that the man valued his kidney above the lives of his family, yet one could also argue that such a sale is plainly a desperate measure of last resort signifying the absence of any real choice.

This problem may be solved, admittedly with a degree of arbitrariness, by certain presumptions in the form of legal prohibitions against contracts which seem unlikely to be genuine choices. Recent statutes have certainly employed this technique of absolute prohibition. For instance, the Human Organs Transplants Act 1989 makes it a criminal offence for any person to make or receive payment for the supply of, or offer to supply, an organ removed or to be removed from any person, alive or dead. This rule against sale of bodily organs could be interpreted

12 *Hyman v Hyman* [1929] AC 601, HL; by statute the wife may now sue upon an express promise, but cannot undertake not to apply to a court for her right to maintenance as well: Matrimonial Causes Act 1973, s 34.

as an irrebuttable presumption against such choices being genuine, and in this way reconciled with the libertarian explanation of the limits of markets and contracts.

Such presumptions enshrined in rules, however, are normally an anathema to libertarians. They fear that such presumptions will disguise instances of paternalism, in which the state imposes on people particular views of how to lead their own lives on the ground that the state claims to know better what is in their own best interests. Such presumptions, therefore, can only establish suspect grounds for intervention from a libertarian perspective. To be consistent with the libertarian explanation, the law should always admit the possibility that a genuine choice has been made, in order to avoid the risk of unjustifiable paternalism, and this should leave the scope of the market unconfined. In this respect, the approach adopted in *Balfour v Balfour* of presuming the absence of an intention to create legal relations in agreements between spouses seems more consistent with libertarian principles: it permits exceptions to be found in cases, for instance, where the breakdown of matrimonial relations may indicate a genuine choice to enter a market transaction. One weakness of the libertarian explanation of the limits of the market order therefore comprises its inability to explain satisfactorily the presence of fixed limits to the scope of market transactions.

The underlying weakness of the libertarian explanation of the limits of markets and contracts is that it attempts to rely upon a few simple criteria for fixing the boundaries. Even though these criteria may account for some of the limits to markets, such as an express agreement to avoid legal enforceability, these criteria are inadequate to account for the reasons justifying the limits of markets in a wide range of different examples. To rely upon the choice of the parties in order to account for the prohibition against bribery of public officials seems to fly in the face of common understandings of the problem here, which is that the parties concerned may genuinely have wished to make the bargain, but that it should be deterred for the sake of the integrity of the political system. This final weakness of the libertarian explanation, which is shared with the market failure analysis, points to the need for a theory of the limits of markets and contracts which is sensitive to the wide range of considerations which lead courts to set boundaries.

E.   The purpose of markets

During my examination of the idea of the social market in Chapter 2, I suggested that markets and contracts should be regarded primarily as a facility for expanding valuable choices and as providing the necessary security for the pursuit of more detailed plans in life. This understanding of markets and contracts suggests that it is wrong to regard these institutions as simply mechanisms for satisfying preferences. The purpose of markets involves a selection between preferences, aiding those which contribute to the pursuit of valuable choices, but prohibiting or obstructing preferences which seem to involve an undesirable way of life.[13] Unlike the market failure and the libertarian explanations of the limits of the market, therefore, the idea of a social market does not commence with a basic disposition towards general freedom of contract, but instead regards freedom of contract as merely valuable within limits for the pursuit of worthwhile individual goals.

From this perspective, the limits upon contracts and markets, far from being potentially dangerous and undesirable infringements of liberty and efficiency, comprise some of the central features of the legal construction of markets as an institution through which individuals may pursue valuable choices in life. It is implicit that not every choice or agreement fits into a valuable way of life, so that these poor and worthless choices need to be identified and denied legal enforceability. An agreement involving slavery must be unenforceable because the choice to subjugate oneself to another cannot lead to a valuable life plan in which one develops personal capacities to the full.[14] Similarly, an agreement for prostitution should not be enforced because it cannot contribute to the development of worthwhile sexual relations. The important question, thus, becomes one of how should we ascertain those choices which the law should and should not support through the facility of binding contracts?

It is important to recognize fully what is at stake in this question. Contracts represent a delegation of power (or at least the acceptance of the rightful exercise of power) to individuals by which they can shape their lives. It is ultimately within the power of the state to expand or to narrow these delegated powers. In exercising this choice, the state must make a judgement about the relative advantages of granting individuals permission to shape their own lives, balanced against the alternative of determining or shaping those aspects of life through regulation either by the state or intermediate institutions. The state can, for instance, effect the education of children by removing market influences and replacing them with administrative regulations which ensure the supply of a necessary quantity and quality of education. Such a measure might be justified on such grounds as the need for an even provision of education across the population in order to ensure equality of opportunity, or a belief that professional teachers in fact understand better than parents what kind of education will equip children for life. Against this state control and exclusion of markets, it could be argued that it is best to leave to parents the choice of how to educate their children, for this will promote diversity in the culture, encourage efficiency through competition, and lead to greater preference satisfaction for the parents and possibly the children as well.

No simple answer will be available to such questions concerning the proper scope of markets. Not only will opinions vary over time with respect to the value of

13 Radin, 'Market-Inalienability' (1987) 100 *Harvard Law Review* 1849.
14 Smith, 'Future Freedom and Freedom of Contract' (1996) 59 *Modern Law Review* 167.

particular choices, but it is also a virtue of the market as an institution that it permits considerable experimentation in the kinds of life which people may choose to lead. It follows that the law of contract should recognize, as it does, the possibility of renegotiation of boundaries of enforceability, when it is the vehicle for interesting and potentially valuable new choices of the way to spend a life. It was in this spirit that the law of contract was allowed to govern the family relations in *Ward v Byam* and *Tanner v Tanner*.

There are two principal dangers which may be provoked by experimentation through contracts:

(i)   The law of contract analyses and evaluates social relations formed within its confines by reference to criteria which may lead to an undesirable distortion of the meaning of the social relation involved.

(ii)   The seductive attraction of avoidance of explicit distributive decisions by delegating outcomes to the market mechanism can pose a threat to important principles of distributive justice.

We will now examine these issues in detail.

1.   The meaning of contractualization

The significance of the contractualization[15] of social relations can be elucidated in four dimensions.

(a)   VALUATION OF CONDUCT

Contracts create a particular form of conduct valuation. They tend to measure conduct narrowly by reference solely to the terms recorded for the transaction. The terms purport to set the exclusive point of reference, which inevitably confines or truncates the perception of the obligations owed between the parties.[16] This perception then creates the possibility of a conflict between the agreed bargain and the reasonable expectations of the parties based upon informal understandings regarding co-operation, give-and-take and dealing in good faith. In some long-term business relations a strict insistence upon the terms of the contract will be regarded as a form of opportunism,[17] for this valuation of conduct contradicts the basis of the relation in good faith conduct which establishes a business reputation for fair dealing. Diffuse obligations of support, co-operation, reciprocity and sharing become harder to establish, with the effect

---

15 P Selznick, *Law, Society and Industrial Justice* (New York, 1969), pp 52–62; H Collins, *Regulating Contracts* (Oxford, 1999), ch 2.

16 P Goodrich, *Languages of Law* (London, 1990), p 154.

17 Beale and Dugdale, 'Contracts Between Businessmen: Planning and the Use of Contractual Remedies' (1975) 2 *British Journal of Law and Society* 45, at p 47.

that the dynamic and meaning of the social relation becomes altered. This was the fundamental reason which Atkin LJ gave for declining to enforce the agreement in *Balfour v Balfour*.[18] The problem becomes most striking in agency relations, such as employment, where the more that the employer seeks to control the employee's discretion about how to define and carry out tasks, the less the employer can call upon diffuse obligations of loyalty and professionalism to further the interests of the employer's business.

(b)   CURRENCY OF EXCHANGE

Contracts also establish social relations with a currency of exchange which is quantifiable and measurable. This permits the introduction of what Weber called 'formal rational economic behaviour' into any type of social relation contained in a contract.[19] The question asked about the relation is whether it increases the wealth of the parties or whether it satisfies their preferences. Other questions about the contribution of the relation to the meaning of the lives of the parties are rendered irrelevant because they cannot be incorporated into the measurement of success. In this vein, for instance, non-pecuniary losses such as vexation and disappointment caused by breach of contract cannot be the basis of a remedy in damages for they cannot be quantified.[20] Similarly, to view an invitation to dinner with a friend as a contract would suggest that the value of the invitation can be reduced to a monetary price, whereas the point of the invitation is to reinforce the ties of friendship which are not the product of formal rational economic behaviour. The insertion of contracts into such relations as friendship does not destroy those relations, but it does introduce a particular form of valuation of behaviour which may tend to exclude other types of measurement such as loyalty and trust.[21]

(c)   ATOMIZATION

A third feature of contractualization consists in the atomization of social relations, so that the effects of a transaction upon other people are regarded as irrelevant. For instance, if one employee of a business receives high pay, which compels the business to dismiss another for lack of funds, the connection between these two decisions is rendered opaque by separation of contractual relations. Similarly, the decision to permit employers to offer higher wages to workers who agree that their union should not represent them in collective bargaining, and keep constant the wages of those who insist upon being represented by the union, can be justified as an aspect of freedom of contract enjoyed by the employer and

18 [1919] 2 KB 571, CA.
19 M Weber, *Economy and Society*, eds G Roth and C Wittich (Berkeley, 2 Vols, 1978) 85, at p 669.
20 *Addis v Gramophone Co Ltd* [1909] AC 488, HL; see Chapter 17.
21 Duxbury, 'Do Markets Degrade?' (1996) 59 *Modern Law Review* 331.

the individual workers, but such a view overlooks the negative effects on union membership and the potential benefits of union solidarity for other employees.[22] Contracts as a form of social relation juxtapose themselves against ties of community or bonds of social solidarity.

(d)   DISCRETIONARY POWER

Finally, contractualization permits the formation of a particular type of power relation. Although the imagery of freedom of contract presents an egalitarian picture of two people negotiating the terms of their agreement, in practice most contracts constitute the opportunity for one party to create unilaterally a system of rules and governance.[23] The standard form consumer contract represents only the tip of an iceberg of these governance structures. Contracts can incorporate whole regulatory systems such as staff handbooks, works rules, railway byelaws and quality assurance procedures. These codes simulate the form of a contract, but they really represent the exercise of discretionary economic power by one party to the contract over the other, backed up by a system of economic sanctions specific to that relation, such as the discipline of the employee or the disqualification of a contractor. Markets create their own hierarchies through contracts.

(e)   CONCLUSION – CONFINING CONTRACTUAL RELATIONS

These four features of contractual relations as a form of social relation – the valuation in delimited terms, the measurement by a precise currency of exchange, the externalization of social effects and the unilateral rule-making power – reveal that the decision to delegate to individuals the power to construct their own social relations through the market mechanism is not such a neutral choice as it may appear at first. In the case of cohabitation agreements, for instance, we can welcome the empowerment to the parties concerned of being able to shape, through contracts, how their relation should be constructed. They may wish, for instance, to pool all their property, or alternatively to keep their financial affairs strictly apart with no assumption of maintenance obligations towards a partner. By permitting contracts to be made between the parties on such matters, the law facilitates this power of choice to construct social relations.[24] But it should be recognized that at the same time the contractualization of such social relations

22   *Associated Newspapers Ltd v Wilson; Associated British Ports v Palmer* [1995] 2 AC 454, [1995] ICR 406, HL.

23   Kessler, 'Contracts of Adhesion – Some Thoughts About Freedom of Contract' (1943) 43 *Columbia Law Review* 629.

24   Olsen, 'The Family and the Market: A Study of Ideology and Legal Reform' (1983) 96 *Harvard Law Review* 1497; Dalton, 'An Essay in the Deconstruction of Contract Doctrine' (1985) 94 *Yale Law Journal* 997, at p 1095.

will have the tendencies described above of emphasizing the values of preference satisfaction and a monetary currency of exchange between the parties. If we wish to insist that cohabitation arrangements should entail more open-ended commitments of sharing, reciprocity and loyalty, we may find that the intrusion of contracts subverts this goal.

At bottom, therefore, the proper scope of the market and contracts must turn on carefully balanced judgements about whether the valuable freedom for individuals to construct their own meaningful social relations should be restricted in particular instances, for the reason that, if the meanings are to be established through the market mechanism, it is unlikely in these instances that they constitute valuable and worthwhile choices in life. To prevent social relations with these undesirable properties from being constituted, it will be necessary to exclude markets and contracts. Just as the law must be wary about allowing the sphere of politics to intervene too meticulously in the market for fear of stifling the latter's properties as an efficient satisfier of human wants, so too the law must prevent the market from infringing upon other social spheres such as politics and the family to their detriment as sites and opportunities for meaning. This explanation of the limits of the market order, unlike the libertarian one, therefore justifies mandatory limits to the field of contracts.

Nevertheless, it remains a difficult question of degree and calculation of probable effects to determine whether the market should be excluded from a particular kind of social relation. We might reject, for instance, a market in babies, for fear that these transactions would lead to a perception of babies as products to be evaluated in monetary terms by their characteristics, rather than as independent persons to whom the parents owe duties of care and nourishment. The case where a couple tried to exchange their baby for a used car raises the spectre that all children might become valued, and value themselves, according to their exchange value in the market, which might depend on colour, size and likely inherited genetic traits, rather than being valued for themselves and their many qualities.[25]

But the same fears might not extend to a surrogacy transaction by which a woman, in return for payment, agrees to bear and hand over a child to a childless couple. Although in form this resembles the sale of a baby, it does not so much signify an economic valuation of the child but a valuation of the service of gestation in the womb. Again we may fear the commercialization of this dimension of motherhood, but against this we must recognize that the transaction is intended not to thwart the values of the social sphere of the family but to extend the

25 *Toronto Star*, 5 September 1980; E Landes and R Posner, 'The Economics of the Baby Shortage' (1978) 7 *Journal of Legal Studies* 323.

opportunity to establish meaning in that sphere for a childless couple.[26] We may also be concerned that financial inducements may lead poor women to become surrogate mothers to earn a living, which some may not regard as a worthwhile way of spending one's life, although others may take a different view of the gift of childbearing. Under the Surrogacy Arrangements Act 1985 the practice of surrogacy is not prohibited, but it is a criminal offence to initiate or take part in any negotiations, or to offer or agree to do so, with a view to making a surrogacy arrangement on a commercial basis. This measure prevents businesses from establishing a market for surrogacy, but permits voluntary organisations to put childless couples in touch with potential surrogate mothers. The Human Fertilisation and Embryology Act 1990, s 30 forbids a court to grant a parental order to the biological parents if it finds that the biological parents had paid or agreed to pay for the surrogacy, except in so far as the payment represents expenses reasonably incurred. The law, therefore, tries to draw a distinction between the sale of a baby and a commercial surrogacy arrangement, which is ineffective, and a charge for the expense of having a baby, which might include loss of income by the surrogate mother. This proves to be a delicate distinction in practice, as in *Re C Application by Mr and Mrs X*,[27] where the court permitted a parental order to be made in favour of the biological parents, even though they had agreed to pay the surrogate mother £12,000 for expenses in circumstances where the surrogate mother had been claiming income support payments at all times, thus incurring little actual financial loss. We may be witnessing in such decisions a gradual revision of the boundaries of contractualization in favour of permitting contractual surrogacy arrangements.

This explanation of the limits of the market order in terms of balancing the arguments for and against the contractualization of aspects of social life cannot produce bright lines to define the limits of social spheres, for the boundaries depend in the final analysis upon uncertain predictions about the deleterious effects of the extension of contractualization to particular kinds of social relations.[28]

2. Distributive justice

A second major consideration which determines the scope of markets and contracts returns to the problem of social justice. We noted above the seductive

---

26 Hollinger, 'From Coitus to Commerce: Legal and Social Consequences of Noncoital Reproduction' (1985) 18 *University of Michigan Journal of Law Reform* 865; Note, 'Rumplestiltskin Revisited: The Inalienable Rights of Surrogate Mothers' (1986) 99 *Harvard Law Review* 1936; E Jackson, *Regulating Reproduction* (Oxford, 2000).

27 [2002] EWHC 157 (Fam), [2002] 1 FLR 909.

28 Radin, 'Market-Inalienability' (1987) 100 *Harvard Law Review* 1849; Mack, 'Dominos and the Fear of Commodification', in J Chapman and JR Pennock (eds), *Markets and Justice* (New York, 1989).

attraction of the market mechanism as a distributive solution which avoids direct state intervention and responsibility for the distribution of wealth. Nevertheless, it has to be recognized that the market mechanism has foreseeable distributive effects. Those with strong bargaining power derived from wealth, special talents and other resources, can usually employ the market mechanism to their relative advantage. Although perhaps not objectionable in general, in particular instances the use of bargaining power to achieve superior distributive outcomes may conflict with important distributive principles which we wish to protect from market manipulation.

By permitting markets to enter particular kinds of social relations, what becomes possible is the use of resources which are valuable in the commercial and economic spheres of social life in order to gain distributional advantages in other spheres of life. If, for example, a rich man is permitted to buy votes, then he is able to convert his wealth into political power by use of the market mechanism. Walzer in his book, *Spheres of Justice*,[29] argues cogently that the limits to markets and contracts should be set in order to protect the integrity of the distributional principles appropriate to different spheres of social life. Hence the rich man may use his wealth to acquire expensive goods, but should not be permitted to buy votes, because this practice interferes with the egalitarian principle for the distribution of political power envisaged in a democracy. To achieve this separation and integrity of different spheres of distributive justice, limits to contracts and markets must be established.

Once again, of course, the extent to which the market mechanism should be permitted to influence distributive outcomes will be controversial and constantly subject to revision. Indeed, this debate often lies at the heart of contemporary political disputes. Should access to health care for the sick, or education for children, or fertility treatment, or law school be dependent upon ability to pay, or should some non-market distributive principle such as need or equality of opportunity be adopted to govern access to these scarce resources?

The presence of these distributive considerations is evident in some of the earlier examples. One of the reasons for the court's reluctance to enforce the agreement in *Balfour v Balfour* was the concern that the market might be employed to undermine the distributive scheme for families arranged through the law of maintenance. Similarly, the rejection of bribery and political influence obtained through contracts reflects a desire to keep the sphere of politics relatively immune from the distributive pattern established by markets. These distributive considerations, and in particular the desire to prevent the conversion of market power into other forms of favourable distributive outcomes in different social spheres, thus accounts for many of the significant limits on markets and contracts.

29 (Oxford, 1983).

Chapter 7

Ascription of contractual responsibility

A. Voluntary responsibility

How does a person become bound to a contractual obligation? This is the question of the attribution or ascription of contractual responsibility. The traditional principle insists that a person's consent or agreement is an essential prerequisite to the ascription of contractual responsibility. This requirement of consent derives from the idea that a contractual obligation constitutes a voluntary assumption of an obligation, which is additional to the general obligations imposed by the law upon everyone.

The foundation of contractual responsibility in consent also serves to provide a rough distinction between contractual obligations and those deriving from other branches of private law such as tort, restitution and property. Although issues concerning consent may be relevant to those other sources of obligations, the law of contract is distinctive in the way in which it seeks to attribute the source of the obligation to the consent of the parties. In the law of tort, for instance, a duty to exercise reasonable care will be imposed by virtue of the relationship between the parties, and the role of consent may be confined to limiting the scope of that obligation. In the law of contract, however, the existence of a similar duty of care will be founded on the agreement of the parties to the creation of such an obligation. This contrast can never be drawn sharply, however, for, as we shall see, it is possible to infer consent from the nature of a relationship or a course of dealing, and equally other sources of obligation employ concepts which are closely analogous to consent, such as the idea of 'free acceptance' in restitution, or the idea of 'voluntary assumption of responsibility' in tort.

B.   The idea of consent

The idea of consent is central to the attribution of contractual responsibility. Indeed, many of the complexities in the classical law of contract derived from the attempt to deal with a variety of issues by reference solely to the idea of consent. As a result, the law's concept of consent became muddled and at times contradictory.

The breathtaking range of issues which the classical law attempted to resolve by reference to the idea of consent included the following:

- How does a person become bound to a contractual obligation? By consent to an agreement.
- When does a person become bound by a contractual obligation? Liability begins at the moment when both parties have consented to an agreement.
- What is the content of the contractual obligation? The terms of the contract to which consent has been given.
- Who is bound by the contractual obligation? Only the persons who have consented to the agreement can obtain rights or incur obligations under the contract.
- When will the use of threats or lies by one party towards the other prevent a contractual obligation from arising? When those threats or lies invalidate the apparent consent given to the contract.
- When will mental incapacity or immaturity prevent a person from entering a contractual obligation? When that incapacity prevents consent from being given to the contract.

This emphasis upon the idea of consent contributed to the elegance and simplicity of the classical law of contract, but a brief reflection on the variety of issues handled by the idea reveals that they present rather different problems for the law to handle. For example, even though entry into a contractual obligation may require consent, there may be good reason to answer the question about the content of the obligation by reference to criteria other than by the consent of the parties, so that the content of the obligation may be either supplemented or confined by reference to considerations of fairness, efficiency or social policy. Similarly, there may be good reasons of fairness or efficiency to extend the range of liability beyond the parties to the contract where third persons were intended to benefit from performance of the contract.

Indeed, as we consider these different issues, we will discover that despite the lip-service paid to the idea of consent, the law handles them effectively by other rules and standards. The absence or presence of consent tends to be the conclusion of a process of reasoning, in which the idea of consent has played no role at all. In the case of fraud, for instance, the law examines the kind of statement which was made, whether or not it was false and whether it induced entry into the contract, and if these tests are satisfied, the contract will be avoided because fraud has vitiated consent. In this reasoning process, the lack of consent to the contract represents the conclusion of the argument, but serves no function in determining whether or not a valid contract has been created.

Similarly, the classical law analysed the incapacity of children and artificial bodies such as corporations and public authorities to enter contracts as a result of a lack of ability to give consent. But the modern rules do not conform to the logic of consent at all. With respect to children, ie minors under the age of 18, the general rule is that the contract is not binding on the child, but the rule is severely qualified by exceptions designed to protect the trader who deals with a child in good faith and fairly, and where an incapacity would prevent the minor from making contracts which are necessary for his or her own welfare. In practice this has the effect that everyday contracts with children which are fair are binding.[1] For corporations, the traditional position denied the power to consent to contracts outside the capacity conferred by the constitutional documents which established the artificial entity.[2] This link between capacity and the ascription of contractual responsibility proved a trap for the unwary in dealings with corporations, so now they are presumed to have contractual capacity.[3] Limits on the capacity to contract may, however, still apply to government agencies and other statutory corporations under the doctrine of 'ultra vires'. The courts appear to assume that if a contract was outside the powers of a public authority to give consent, it should be regarded as void for the sake of the public interest. Yet the public interest could be protected better by permitting those who have entered into contracts with public authorities in good faith to enforce their contracts, for

1   Sale of Goods Act 1979, s 3; Minors' Contracts Act 1987.
2   *Rolled Steel Products (Holdings) Ltd v British Steel Corpn* [1986] Ch 246, [1985] 3 All ER 52, CA.
3   Companies Act 1985, ss 35, 35A, as amended by the Companies Act 1989, and EC Directive 68/151/EEC on the Protection of Interests of Members.

this would avoid the deterrent to making contracts with public authorities which the doctrine of ultra vires creates, whilst at the same time devising appropriate sanctions for those public officials who act beyond the scope of their powers. The idea of consent gives a spurious unity and coherence to the legal doctrines concerning capacity, but on closer examination it rarely performs any significant part in determining the validity of contracts. It might be better to abolish the doctrine of capacity altogether and replace it with appropriate rules governing the circumstances when contracts should be unenforceable against certain types of parties.

The emphasis upon the idea of consent is not only misleading but also confusing. As the law addresses the different issues, the concept of consent twists and turns in its meanings. The unity of the classical law therefore turns out to be a mirage, for the meaning of the requirement of consent alters according to the context of the problem and the relevant policy issues which the court must consider. As an example, consider two cases concerning the purchase of a vehicle. In the first, the dealer lies about the qualities of the car, and the contract can be invalidated because the fraud negatives consent. Here the idea of consent suggests that the purchaser did not give consent to the contract because he did not know the full facts of the matter. In the second case, the car has a latent defect which is a breach of warranty by the dealer. If we applied the idea of consent in which the purchaser must have full knowledge of the facts of the case to this problem, we would conclude that no contract had been formed at all, since the purchaser would not have bought the car with a latent defect. The law will certainly conclude, however, that a contract was made in the second case despite the mistake, although the purchaser will be entitled to reject the car and receive back his money. The idea of consent therefore shifts radically according to the problem to be addressed.

In this chapter, the issue to be considered is how a person becomes bound by a contractual obligation. The simple answer is by consent to an agreement, but a more perceptive answer will include an examination of the idea of consent employed in this context and an investigation of the extent to which the idea of consent plays any real function in the determination of contractual responsibility. Since the idea of consent is regarded as the hallmark of contractual obligations, we will also take the opportunity to consider how far this idea of consent serves to distinguish contractual obligations from other sources of obligations in tort, restitution and property law.

C.   Objective test of consent

It must be rare for parties entering a contract to make a declaration in the form 'I consent to this contract'. The shopper in a store simply presents the goods selected and a method of payment, and the sales assistant registers the sale on the till. When a person travels by public transport, she simply purchases a ticket. In complex commercial transactions with reams of written documents, all that happens is a signature on a document and perhaps a handshake. In the normal case, therefore, the law must infer consent to a contract from the words and conduct of the parties.

A signature on a document, for example, will normally be regarded as an expression of consent to the contract.[4] But we should be aware that even in this case of clear evidence of consent, we must go through a process of inferring consent from conduct. The signature on a document is regarded as a sign that consent has been given to the undertaking of the contractual responsibility contained in the document. The meaning of a signature has been established by convention, a common practice which the law recognizes as effective to attribute contractual responsibility to the signatory. Outside such clear conventions, however, the law must examine the conduct of the parties to discover whether consent to a transaction may be inferred. The problem confronting the law is to decide which forms of words and conduct should be regarded as signifying consent to a contract.

Since the law infers consent from conduct, the approach is often described as an objective test. The law examines the evidence which is verifiable by observation rather than speculating upon the actual state of mind of the parties. The law must therefore cope with the problem presented by a person whose conduct indicates consent to a contract, yet who asserts that he had no intention to enter any contract. The objective test denies any strength to such secret reservations. Blackburn J summarized both aspects of this objective test in a celebrated statement of principle in *Smith v Hughes*:[5]

> If, whatever a man's real intention may be, he so conducts himself that a reasonable man would believe that he was assenting to the terms proposed by the other party, and that other party upon that belief enters into the contract with him, the man thus conducting himself would be equally bound as if he had intended to agree to the other party's terms.

It follows from the objective test of consent that apparent consent to an agreement suffices to establish contractual responsibility, and that actual consent in the sense of an intention to enter a contract is not strictly necessary. It is no good, for instance, to fill up a car with petrol at a self-service petrol station, and subsequently claim that no contract for the sale of the petrol was made because you did not intend to make the contract. A court will infer from the conduct of filling up the car with petrol that consent was given to a contract for the sale of petrol. Equally the court will infer from the conduct of the garage proprietor of permitting the tank to be filled that the proprietor consents to the sale of the petrol.

4   *L'Estrange v F Graucob Ltd* [1934] 2 KB 394, DC.
5   (1871) LR 6 QB 597.

By permitting inferences of consent to be drawn from conduct, the law certainly facilitates transactions by avoiding unnecessary obstacles such as a requirement for contracts to be in writing or constituted by express statements. Inevitably, however, the courts will encounter situations where the conduct is ambiguous and could be regarded either as consent to a contract or a rejection of a contract. The test propounded by Blackburn J to cover these cases, that the court should examine the facts from the point of view of the other party to see whether it was reasonable for that other party to infer consent, provides useful but incomplete guidance.

1. Standard form contracts

The most important practical effect of the objective test of consent concerns the validity of standard form contracts. In many consumer and business transactions, the contract will be concluded on the basis of a printed document which purports to contain all the terms of the contract. In some cases the printed document will be signed by both parties, but often it is merely handed over or posted at the time of the formation of the contract. Some doubt has been expressed about the validity of such standard forms to count as contracts.[6] The process often resembles an imposition of will rather than mutual consent to an agreement, so these transactions have been described as 'contracts of adhesion'.

The use of standard forms responds to two economic pressures. They reduce the transaction costs of contracting by making available at no extra cost a suitable set of terms. In addition, the printed form permits senior management of a firm to control the contractual arrangements made by subordinate sales staff.[7] For these reasons, it makes sense to permit the use of standard forms, but to control the content of the terms of the contracts. The objective test of consent ensures that normally standard forms count as a contractual agreement between the parties.

2. Inaction and silence

The objective test helps to resolve cases where consent has been inferred from inaction or silence. If an offer is sent by post but the offeror receives no reply, it is not reasonable to infer from that silence that consent has been given, for the silence might equally or even more probably signify a rejection of the offer.

---

6 Kessler, 'Contracts of Adhesion – Some Thoughts About Freedom of Contract' (1943) 43 *Columbia Law Review* 629; Slawson, 'Standard Form Contracts and Democratic Control of Lawmaking Power' (1971) 84 *Harvard Law Review* 529; Slawson, 'The New Meaning of Contract: The Transformation of Contracts Law by Standard Forms' (1984) 46 *University of Pittsburgh Law Review* 21; Johnson, 'Autonomy and Contractual Liability' (1983) 2 *Law and Philosophy* 271.
7 Rakoff, 'Contracts of Adhesion: An Essay in Reconstruction' (1983) 96 *Harvard Law Review* 1174; Macneil, 'Bureaucracy and Contracts of Adhesion' (1984) 22 *Osgoode Hall Law Journal* 5.

Evidence to the effect that the recipient of the letter did intend to agree to the proposed contract is irrelevant under this objective test, for unless this evidence had come to the attention of the offeror he could not reasonably infer consent from silence. Hence in *Felthouse v Bindley*,[8] following muddled and inconclusive negotiations for the sale of a horse, the claimant wrote to his nephew offering to buy the horse at a fixed price, adding, 'If I hear no more about him, I consider the horse is mine at £30 15s.' His nephew did not reply to this letter, but a few weeks later he informed an auctioneer of his stock that the horse had been sold. Unfortunately the horse was inadvertently sold by the auctioneer to another person, and the claimant pursued damages against the auctioneer for the loss of his property. The claim failed on the ground that no valid contract of sale for the horse to the uncle had been concluded, for the nephew's consent could not be inferred from his silence to the claimant, even though it was apparent that the nephew had intended to agree to the contract. Under the objective test, this case can be interpreted as confirming the point that the claimant could not reasonably infer consent from silence, although it leaves open the possibility that if the claimant had heard of the nephew's intentions in some other way, consent might have been reasonably inferred.

The problem of determining consent from inaction becomes particularly acute when the alleged consent is to a contract which modifies an existing legal relation. In this context we can expect informal dealings between the parties, so that it may become reasonable to infer consent from inaction. For example, if a buyer does not receive the promised goods on time, but raises no objection when they are delivered late, it might be inferred from this conduct that the buyer has agreed to a modification of the contract. In this context of inaction during an existing contractual relation, where it was argued that the inaction signified consent to terminate or abandon arbitration proceedings for breach of contract, Lord Brandon suggested that the test of consent should be that:

> the conduct of B, as evinced towards A, has been such as to lead A reasonably to believe that B has abandoned the contract, even though it has not in fact been B's intention to do so, and that A has significantly altered his position in reliance on that belief.[9]

3. Inertia selling

The objective test may provide the opportunity for an unscrupulous trader to send unsolicited goods to a consumer or another business, together with an invoice, in the hope that the consumer or business either may pay for them or at least use the goods in such a way as for it to be possible to infer consent. To

8   (1862) 11 CBNS 869, 142 ER 1037.
9   *Paal Wilson & Co A/S v Partenreederei Hannah Blumenthal (The Hannah Blumenthal)* [1983] 1 AC 854, [1983] 1 All ER 34, HL.

prevent enforceable contracts from arising from such inertia selling, the Consumer Protection (Distance Selling) Regulations 2000, reg 24[10] permits the consumer to use, deal with or dispose of the goods as if they were unconditional gifts. For businesses that receive unsolicited goods, this protection is provided only if the recipient had no reasonable cause to believe that the goods were sent with a view to their being acquired by the business. In both cases, however, demands by the seller for payment knowing that the goods were unsolicited and payment has not been agreed constitute a criminal offence.

4. Express reservations

It follows from the objective test that express reservations indicating an unwillingness to enter a contract will normally prevent an inference of consent. The presence of the express reservation renders it unreasonable to suppose that consent to the contract has been given. Thus a statement that any agreement should be regarded as provisional and will be 'subject to contract' negatives consent,[11] for this disclaimer makes the unwillingness to make a contract clear.

Less explicit statements will also suffice to negative the intention to enter a contract. In *Gibson v Manchester City Council*,[12] the council sent to its tenants details of a scheme under which they might purchase their homes. The appellant filled in a form indicating interest in this opportunity. The city treasurer then sent him a letter which stated that 'the corporation may be prepared to sell the house to you at the purchase price of . . . £2,180' and finished by saying, 'If you would like to make a formal application to buy your council house, please complete the enclosed application form and return it . . . ' The appellant returned the completed application form (after some further communications) and claimed that a contract for the sale of the house had been concluded. But the House of Lords decided that the letter from the city treasurer did not indicate a willingness to consent to a contract. Their interpretation of the letter was to the effect that it expressly negatived an intention to enter a contract.

5. Implied reservations

A court may be asked to draw a similar inference about a reservation to enter into a contract from the context and the statements made by the parties. This inference will customarily be drawn, for instance, when construction work is put out for tender. Here the normal course of events consists of work being advertised as being up for tender, the competing bids for the work are received from

10 SI 2000/2334; implementing EC Directive 97/7/EC on Distance Selling.
11 *A-G of Hong Kong v Humphreys Estate (Queen's Gardens) Ltd* [1987] AC 114, [1987] 2 All ER 387, PC.
12 [1979] 1 All ER 972, [1979] 1 WLR 294, HL.

different construction companies, and then finally one of these bids is accepted. In these cases a court will normally decide that no contractual responsibility arises until one of the bids has been accepted, for this bidding process is designed to facilitate a competitive market, and so no inference of consent to any particular contract should be drawn until a bid is accepted.[13]

Advertisements in newspapers and magazines often present a similar kind of problem. If a person responds to the advertisement in the terms specified, such as placing an order, or, as in *Carlill v Carbolic Smoke Ball Co*,[14] using the smoke ball, should this conduct suffice to create contractual responsibility? On the one hand, it may be argued that the advertisement has all the appearance of consent to a contract on the terms specified but, on the other hand, it may be argued that it is merely intended as a publicity exercise and that any contracts should be formed by express dealings between the parties. In accordance with the principle of the objective test propounded by Blackburn J, the answer must depend in each particular case on whether a reasonable person would infer from the terms of the advertisement that it evidenced consent to a contract on satisfaction of any conditions. For example, a typical small advertisement in a newspaper may read, 'Flat for rent, Camberwell, £100 pw tel: 123'; it would not be reasonable to construe this as consent to a contract with the first person who telephoned. It should be expected that the landlord might wish to interview the potential tenants or at least establish their suitability before agreeing to the contract. On the other hand, an advertisement which is sufficiently explicit and without reservation, as in *Carlill v Carbolic Smoke Ball Co*, may well be regarded as an expression of consent to a contract.

When examining these examples of inferences of consent and implied reservations or conditions, it is important to be alert to the possibility that several contracts may be contemplated between the parties. In the case of tendering, for example, although the tenderer may expressly or by implication reserve the right to decide whether or not to enter into any contract at all with any bidder, the tenderer may at the same time indicate consent to other contractual obligations, such as an obligation to award the job to the lowest bidder if the job is awarded to any bid at all,[15] or an obligation to consider all bids which have been submitted in proper form at the appointed time and place.[16] These subsidiary or collateral contracts can be formed by consent tested objectively, even though the main contract which is contemplated for the building works is never formed between the parties.

13 *Spencer v Harding* (1870) LR 5 CP 561.
14 [1893] 1 QB 256, CA.
15 *Harvela Investments Ltd v Royal Trust Co of Canada Ltd* [1986] AC 207, [1985] 2 All ER 966, HL.
16 *Blackpool and Fylde Aeroclub Ltd v Blackpool Borough Council* [1990] 3 All ER 25, [1990] 1 WLR 1195, CA.

6.   Consent or reliance?

From this discussion of the objective test of consent, it is plain that a very thin theory of consent is applied by the law. Although in most instances no doubt the entry into a contract coincides with an intention to make a contract, such an intention is not required. Nor does the objective test of consent require complete knowledge or understanding of the terms of the proposed contract. The signature on a document or the receipt of the standard form contract counts as conduct which evidences consent to the contract. The question arises whether the objective test of consent is really a test of consent at all?

We could say that in reality consent is irrelevant: what matters is whether it was *reasonable* for the other party to rely upon the existence of contractual responsibility in view of the observed conduct. This hypothesis translates the test for ascription of responsibility from one concerning consent by one party to another test of reasonable reliance by the other.

This reinterpretation of the cases raises a question of principle, for the reference to reasonable reliance reduces the respect paid by the law to freedom of contract and the choice whether or not to enter a contract. It also suggests that consent should not be regarded as the distinguishing quality of the source of contractual obligations. Instead, the origin of contractual responsibility appears to lie in a special type of reliance on another's conduct where that conduct indicates that the party has voluntarily undertaken a special obligation.

This view is strengthened by a comparison with the reliance model of the test of enforceability. It will be recalled that to satisfy the reliance model, one party must encourage the other to believe that rights have been granted or will be granted, and the other party must act to his detriment on the faith of that encouragement. This requirement is similar to the ordinary contractual idea of reliance on the other's conduct which indicates the voluntary undertaking of an obligation. In both cases attention shifts from the state of mind of the promisor, which is the emphasis in the traditional idea of consent, to the reasonableness of the reliance of the promisee in the light of the promisor's conduct. This parallel in the determination of the ascription of responsibility between the two structural models of enforceability adds weight to the view that the origin of contractual responsibility lies in special instances of reliance rather than consent.

D.   Common mistake

Can consent to a contract be negatived by a fundamental mistake about the circumstances surrounding the transaction?[17] If I agree to purchase a car but,

---

17 Slade, 'The Myth of Mistake in the English Law of Contract' (1954) 70 *Law Quarterly Review* 385.

shortly before the agreement and unknown to both parties, the car was completely destroyed in an accident, is the agreement invalid? If the agreement is invalid, is this due to the absence of consent to the contract? The objective test of consent should rule out this latter possibility, for the evidence supports consent to a contract. The nature of my relief from the contract should depend upon the allocation of risk in the contract with regard to the destruction of the car. Nevertheless, there have been occasional suggestions that the contract is invalid owing to the absence of consent.

The logic behind this argument depends upon the forging of a link between the ideas of consent and intent. In the ordinary usage of the word 'intent', we usually recognize that a mistake about the facts will negative intent. If I take a raincoat from a hook, believing it to be my own, whereas in fact it is a similar one belonging to someone else, we would not say that I intended to take the other person's raincoat. The mistake about the ownership of the raincoat negatives my intent to take another's property. Similarly, it may be argued that a mistake about the circumstances surrounding a transaction may negative consent to the agreement, if the consent would have been withheld had the true state of affairs been known. Thus it might be argued that my mistake about the state of the car negatives my intention to make the contract, and therefore invalidates my consent. This argument overlooks the point that the objective test of consent sunders the connection between consent and intent in the context of the ascription of contractual responsibility. The actual intent of the parties is not crucial for the ascription of contractual responsibility. What matters is the appearance of consent to a contract, which may be inferred from words and conduct, regardless of the intentions of the parties.

Nevertheless, in a perplexing judgment in *Bell v Lever Bros*,[18] Lord Atkin claimed that there existed a narrow doctrine of mistake with regard to the subject matter of a contract:

> In such a case a mistake will not affect assent unless it is the mistake of both parties and is to the existence of some quality which makes the thing without the quality essentially different from the thing as it was believed to be.

Having stated this principle, however, Lord Atkin was unable to find either much authority from cases to support it, or examples to illustrate it. He was able to point to the Sale of Goods Act 1893 (now 1979), which declares in s 6 that a sale is void if the seller was ignorant of the fact that the goods had already been destroyed. This statutory provision was itself based upon a misreading of earlier cases, such as *Couturier v Hastie*,[19] which had not declared the contract void for mistake, but had simply denied the seller any remedy on the ground that the seller had failed to

18 [1932] AC 161, HL.
19 (1856) 5 HL Cas 673.

perform his side of the bargain because no goods had been delivered. There is also authority which suggests that a sale to a buyer who already owns the property will be voidable,[20] but as Lord Atkin himself observed, normally a seller will be understood to warrant that he owns the goods or property, so the sale can be terminated for breach of this warranty, which suggests that a binding, not a void, contract has been formed.

It is also possible to view these authorities as merely deciding that where a contract contains an express or implied term that it will only be enforceable if a particular circumstance or state of affairs exists, the failure of this condition precedent will prevent a binding contract arising. Strictly speaking, however, on this analysis a contract has been entered into, but one of its terms, which is enforceable, declares that certain events shall render the contract unenforceable and without any legal effect. There is ascription of contractual responsibility to a conditional contract, and, on failure of the condition, the contract provides that it should have no legal effect. This analysis has the potential to explain all the English cases which seem to give credence to the doctrine of mistake. For example, in *Griffith v Brymer*,[21] the claimant agreed to hire a room to view a Coronation procession an hour after it was decided to operate on the King and therefore cancel the procession. The claimant recovered the rent he had paid. Although the decision can be interpreted as an application of Lord Atkin's principle of common mistake, Lord Atkin himself seems to have regarded the Coronation cases as an example of an implied condition about a state of facts, so that on failure of the condition the contract had no legal effect. This analysis also fits coherently into the general principles governing ascription of responsibility, for it holds the parties bound to a contract by virtue of their apparent consent, but then out of respect for their autonomy permits the parties to determine the effects of their transaction in the event of mistakes being discovered.

The remaining illustrations of the doctrine of mistake offered by Lord Atkin all display the perverse characteristic that they invariably indicate that the doctrine has no application. For example:

> A buys a picture from B: both A and B believe it to be the work of an old master, and a high price is paid. It turns out to be a modern copy. A has no remedy in the absence of misrepresentation or warranty.

Nevertheless, Lord Atkin's statement of principle stands, has often been judicially approved, and may occasionally find some application.

A revealing application of the doctrine occurred in *Associated Japanese Bank (International) Ltd v Crédit du Nord SA*.[22] An engineering company arranged with the claimant bank a sale and leaseback transaction with respect to four precision

---

20 *Cooper v Phibbs* (1867) LR 2 HL 149, HL.
21 (1903) 19 TLR 434.
22 [1988] 3 All ER 902, [1989] 1 WLR 255, QB.

machines. The defendant bank gave a guarantee to the claimant for the repayments by the engineering company under the leaseback. It turned out that the engineering company had perpetrated a fraud, for it never owned any such machines. The claimant tried to enforce the guarantee given by the defendant when the engineering company failed to keep up its repayments. The defendant, however, succeeded in arguing that the guarantee was subject to a condition precedent that the machines existed, so that it was unenforceable on failure of the condition. As an alternative ground for the decision, the court was also prepared to apply the doctrine of common mistake formulated by Lord Atkin. Steyn J held that the mistake about the existence of the machines rendered the nature of the guarantee essentially different. He added, however, that the defendant would not have been able to rely upon the mistake if it had had no reasonable grounds for belief in the existence of the goods. This decision supports the earlier point that all cases on common mistake can be explained by means of construction of implied conditions precedent. But it also gives credence to the existence of a doctrine of common mistake.

The doctrine of common mistake is not only inconsistent with the objective test of consent and based upon little authority, but also the problems in such cases are better handled through construction of the express and implied terms of the contract. This latter approach is superior because it addresses more directly the question whether the parties have allocated the risk of mistakes in a particular way. The danger posed by the doctrine of common mistake is that it will upset a fair allocation of the risks made by the contracting parties. The doctrine was rejected for this reason in *McRae v Commonwealth Disposals Commission*.[23] The Commission sold the wreck of an oil tanker to the defendant for salvage, but after a fruitless search by the defendant, it emerged that no such wreck existed. The Commission tried unsuccessfully to defend an action for breach of contract on the ground that both parties were mistaken about the existence of the wreck. The High Court of Australia rejected the defence, arguing either that mistake could not be relied upon because it was entirely due to the Commission's negligence, or that the doctrine of mistake was excluded by the express warranty of the existence of the wreck made by the Commission.

It is clear from these authorities that the doctrine of common mistake that prevents a contract from arising between the parties despite their ostensible agreement is most unlikely to occur. The courts examine first the terms of the contract to ascertain whether the risk of the mistake had been allocated between them. If the terms allocate the risk, the courts will not use the doctrine of mistake to upset the agreement. If the contract cannot be construed as having allocated the risk, and if the mistake was shared by both parties and was not attributable to fault of either party, and if the effect of the mistake is to render it impossible to perform the contract or the essential obligations under the contract, a court may

23 (1950) 84 CLR 377, Aust HC.

declare the contract void.[24] But in practice these conditions are unlikely to be satisfied, and the nature of the conditions reveals that this doctrine has little to do with consent.

E.   Consent by remote parties

The problems of the ascription of contractual responsibility which we have considered so far involve two persons entering negotiations and contracts. In practice, however, it is extremely common for difficult issues of ascription of contractual responsibility to arise when three or more persons are involved. In a typical instance, a householder employs a builder to effect repairs, and the builder enters a sub-contract with a specialist electrician to carry out part of the required works. Although there are plainly two contracts in this case, one between householder and builder, and another between builder and electrician, is there a third between householder and electrician? This issue might become important if the electrician is injured, or if the electrician is careless and burns down the house.

The application of the objective test of agreement to such cases normally results in the conclusion that no direct contract between householder and electrician has been formed. The evidence is likely to demonstrate that there was no direct contact between householder and electrician, or if they had conversations, they were not about the terms of a contract. There is nothing from which an inference of consent to a contract could be drawn.

Looking at this scenario in another way, however, does suggest the possibility of a contractual relation. It might be argued that a direct contract between householder and electrician was formed via the builder as an intermediary. This argument will be successful if it can be established that the builder acted as the householder's agent for the purpose of making the sub-contract for electrical work. We consider the topic of agency below, but the technique of agency does not necessarily exhaust the possibilities of discovering a direct contract between householder and electrician. Can an implied direct contract be inferred from evidence such as the fact that the householder knew and consented to the proposal that the builder should use a sub-contractor for the electrical work, and from the fact that the electrician knew that the ultimate employer for whom the work was being performed was the householder?

By way of a preliminary remark to these topics, however, it is important to observe that as a general principle contractual responsibility will not attach to remote parties. At bottom, this principle concerns a respect for the liberty of the

---

24 *Great Peace Shipping Ltd v Tsavliris Salvage (International) Ltd* [2002] EWCA Civ 1407, [2003] QB 679, [2002] 4 All ER 689.

individual. A person should not have additional onerous obligations imposed without consent. It would be a gross infringement of liberty if two persons were able by agreement to impose substantial contractual obligations upon another. That would permit, for instance, two persons to agree that another should perform an arduous task, and that third person then to be in breach of a contractual obligation for failure to do so. In our earlier example, it might suggest that the agreement between householder and builder imposed the obligation on the sub-contractor to perform the work, or that the agreement between builder and electrician imposed an obligation on the householder to pay the agreed price to the electrician. Such conclusions will normally be rejected in principle as amounting to the imposition of a contract without consent. This general principle is often described as an aspect of the doctrine of privity of contract, which will be considered in Chapter 14, but in fact it flows directly from the requirement of consent to contracts. The principle only applies to contractual obligations, of course, so it does not rule out the possibility of tortious or proprietary obligations between remote parties, for these obligations can arise without consent.

1. Agency

The major exception to this principle is the doctrine of agency. Here the third party authorizes one of the parties to the negotiations to make the contract on his or her behalf. In our example, the householder would ask the builder to enter into a contract on behalf of the householder with the electrician. The third party is described as 'the principal' and the authorized negotiator 'an agent'. Because the agent is not making the contract for himself but for the principal, the legal analysis insists that the principal but not the agent is the party to the contract, and that consent by the principal to the contract is achieved through the authorized agent as an intermediary. As a result, it is the principal but not the agent who incurs contractual responsibility.

It is extremely common for contracts to bind third parties as principals by virtue of agency relations. Every time a contract is made with a company the doctrine of agency applies. The company, as an artificial legal entity, must act through human agents, usually either directors or employees. The contracts made by these agents bind the company as a principal to the contract. Within companies, a wide doctrine of agency normally applies, so that directors and employees will be regarded as enjoying the authority to make those contracts, which by virtue of their positions in the company they possess ostensibly or apparently the authority to enter. To take a simple example, a shop assistant has the ostensible authority to bind the shop to sales of its wares by virtue of his or her position, so such a sale will bind the shop as a principal. But if the transaction concerns the sale of the premises of the shop, the assistant will lack ostensible authority: such a major transaction will normally require the authorization of the board of directors of the company, which can be presumed to have authority to bind the company on any matter.[25]

Although an agent entering a contract on behalf of a principal will not incur personal contractual liability, it is possible that a complex transaction will involve several contracts under which a person acts both as agent and as principal. For example, a person may sign the main contract merely as an agent for another, but at the same time undertake a personal obligation under a collateral contract such as a contract of guarantee.[26] Thus, a carrier of goods on a ship may both enter a contract with the owner of the goods as a principal to carry the goods, but at the same time act as an agent to make contracts on behalf of other persons, such as the ship's crew and the stevedores who will load and unload the goods onto and from the ship.[27]

Although the details of the law of agency will not be examined here, one important limitation upon the ostensible authority of agents should be considered. The question arises whether the principal may limit the ostensible authority of an agent, such as the employee of a company. It is insufficient for the principal to prohibit the agent from making certain types of contract, for that will not diminish the agent's apparent authority.[28] But if the principal notifies the other contracting party in advance that the agent's ostensible authority is limited in certain respects, that notification can suffice to prevent ascription of contractual responsibility to the principal.[29] It is common, for instance, for employers to rely upon notices or terms of printed contracts which contain a statement to the effect that their employees do not have any authority to vary or add to the terms and conditions. In theory, such a statement should suffice to negative the ostensible authority of the agent. In consumer standard form contracts, however, such disclaimers of ostensible authority may be regarded as unfair terms, not binding on the consumer under the Unfair Terms in Consumer Contracts Regulations 1999.[30] The consumer is therefore entitled to rely on promises given within the ostensible authority of employees of a company.

Hence, the application of the notion of ostensible agency creates the possibility of contractual responsibility without express consent. Although in cases of actual authority, we may say that in effect the principal has consented to the contract by giving the agent the authority to make the contract on his behalf, it is quite

---

25 Companies Act 1985, s 35A, as amended by the Companies Act 1989.
26 *Elpis Maritime Co Ltd v Marti Chartering Co Inc (The Maria D)* [1991] 2 Lloyd's Rep 311, HL.
27 *New Zealand Shipping Co Ltd v Satterthwaite & Co Ltd (The Eurymedon)* [1975] AC 154, [1974] 1 All ER 1015, PC
28 *Watteau v Fenwick* [1893] 1 QB 346.
29 *Overbrooke Estates Ltd v Glencombe Properties Ltd* [1974] 3 All ER 511, [1974] 1 WLR 1335, Ch.
30 SI 1999/2083, Sch 2, para 1(n). Decisions by the courts at common law had foreshadowed this regulation: *Mendelssohn v Normand Ltd* [1970] 1 QB 177, [1969] 2 All ER 1215, CA.

possible in cases of ostensible authority that the principal did not wish to make the contract, or had indeed forbidden the making of the contract, yet will nevertheless be bound by it.

2.   Implied consent

Aside from agency, the principle that contractual obligations cannot be incurred without consent normally prevents the ascription of contractual responsibility to remote parties. It may be possible, however, to imply consent to a contract in the circumstances of the case by reference to the conduct and knowledge of the remote party. An implication of consent may be drawn where the remote party is aware of the contract and has encouraged its making because it serves the remote party's interests. This implication may be drawn, for instance, in a context where an employer encourages the main contractor to enter into a sub-contract in order to complete a particular job for the employer. In *Charnock v Liverpool Corpn*,[31] the claimant took his car to a garage for repairs which were to be paid for by his insurers. Although the main contract for repairs was between the insurance company and the garage, the Court of Appeal found an implied contract between the claimant and the garage under which the garage undertook to carry out the repairs in a reasonable time. The garage had consented to this contract by implication when it received the car delivered by the claimant.

This reasoning has been applied to cases involving work by a sub-contractor in relation to the employer's goods. In *Morris v CW Martin & Sons Ltd*,[32] the claimant instructed a furrier to clean her mink stole, but the furrier explained that he did not clean furs, so instead he undertook to send it to be cleaned by the specialist defendant cleaners, and the claimant agreed to this arrangement. One of the defendant's employees stole the fur, and the claimant sued the defendant for damages. As a defence to this claim, the defendant relied upon the terms of its contract with the furrier. These terms included a provision that the defendant should 'not be responsible for loss or damage however caused' to 'goods belonging to customers'. One question was whether the claimant could be bound by the terms of the sub-contract, even though she had never agreed to those terms or been a party to the agreement. There would be no difficulty, of course, if the furrier had acted as the claimant's agent, but it was clear in fact that two separate contracts had been made. Lord Denning MR held the claimant bound by the terms of the sub-contract, because she had impliedly consented to the furrier making a contract for cleaning on the terms usually current in the trade. Nevertheless, the claimant's suit for damages succeeded, because on a strict interpretation of the exclusion clause it only disclaimed liability for goods belonging to customers of the defendant, and the claimant was not the customer,

31 [1968] 3 All ER 473, [1968] 1 WLR 1498, CA.
32 [1966] 1 QB 716, [1965] 2 All ER 725, CA.

but merely a customer of a customer, the furrier. The same argument has been applied to a contract for the international carriage of goods, where the carrier sub-contracted the work of transporting the goods to a shipowner, whose ship then sank causing the destruction of the goods. The owner of the goods was held to have consented by implication to the terms of the sub-contract between carrier and shipowner, for in the contract between owner and carrier the owner had consented to permit the carrier to sub-contract the work of handling, storage and carriage 'on any terms'.[33]

An interesting question is whether or not such reasoning could be extended to the context of construction, where the owner of the building consents to sub-contracts for specialist work. In principle, this argument should work provided that there is sufficient evidence either from conduct or in the main contract that the owner of the building has authorized the sub-contract and acquiesced to its terms.

The dilemma confronting the law is this: although it is contrary to principle to ascribe contractual responsibility without consent, an implied contract may appear to conform to the intentions of the parties and represent a fair allocation of the risk. In *Morris v CW Martin & Sons Ltd*, for instance, the sub-contractor only agreed to perform the work of cleaning the fur on its standard terms. The price for the work no doubt reflected the content of these terms. Although these terms bound the cleaner as the other party to the contract, these terms could not affect the employer – ie the owner of the mink stole – without stretching the normal principles for ascription of responsibility. Yet this result seems only fair because either all the parties would be forced into the costly procedure of making direct contracts with each other, or other sources of obligations, particularly the law of tort, would in effect circumvent and undermine carefully constructed contractual arrangements. In this instance, a claim in tort might permit the owner of the fur to claim compensation from the sub-contractor directly, thereby avoiding altogether the restriction on liability for which the sub-contractor had bargained.

3. Equitable proprietary interests

Remote parties may be bound by contracts when they receive property in the knowledge that under a contract another person has acquired rights over that property. A typical example arises where a tenant assigns a lease to another, and the new tenant or assignee is then bound by any rights of the landlord over the property created by the original lease of which he receives notice. In a loose way of speaking, the new tenant must respect the contractual rights of the landlord merely by virtue of his knowledge of those rights. In formal legal analysis, however, the argument is rather that the new tenant must respect the property

33 *KH Enterprise v Pioneer Container (The Pioneer Container)* [1994] 2 AC 324, [1994] 2 All ER 250, PC.

rights of the landlord, which avoids a direct clash with the normal principles governing the ascription of contractual responsibility. This reasoning is not confined to interests in land.

A contract may establish a proprietary right in any kind of personal property, and, provided that this contract is specifically enforceable, any subsequent purchaser of the property who has notice of the proprietary interest in it will be bound to respect that interest.[34] This principle was applied, for instance, to a ship in *Lord Strathcona Steamship Co Ltd v Dominion Coal Co Ltd*.[35] The purchaser of the ship bought it with knowledge that it had been chartered out already by the previous owner. The charterer was able to defend his contractual rights against the new owner, even though the new owner had not agreed to the contract. The case may not be a correct application of the principle, however, for it is unclear whether the charter contract intended to confer a proprietary interest in the ship on the charterer, and it is unlikely that the contract was specifically enforceable.

Manufacturers have attempted to take advantage of similar legal reasoning in the absence of vertical integration of their distributive system, in order to prevent retailers at the end of a chain of supply from selling their products at substandard quality or beneath recommended prices. By attaching obligations to the product in contracts with wholesalers or distributors, which purport to bind anyone who deals with it after notice of those conditions, the manufacturer seeks to protect its trading reputation and keep up the market price of its product. Although unable to draw a principled distinction between cases concerning obligations attached to goods from those of covenants attached to land, with few exceptions the courts rebuff manufacturers' attempts to gain the advantages of vertical integration without the financial risks entailed in ownership of retail outlets. Moreover, statutes outlaw attempts to establish minimum resale prices of goods in order to protect consumers.

F.   The boundaries of contract

The requirement of consent, as defined by the objective test, marks the traditional boundary of contractual responsibility. This boundary is by no means sharply defined, for the objective test permits inferences of consent to be drawn in circumstances where at least one party had no intention of consenting to a contract. In such borderline cases, where consent has to be construed from slim evidence, the court may prefer to recognize the existence of another species of obligation drawn from unjust enrichment (restitution), equity or tort. This

---

34   *Swiss Bank Corpn v Lloyds Bank Ltd* [1979] Ch 548, [1979] 2 All ER 853, Ch; revsd on other grounds [1982] AC 584, [1980] 2 All ER 419, HL; Chafee, 'Equitable Servitudes on Chattels' (1928) 41 *Harvard Law Review* 945; Gardner, 'The Proprietary Effect of Contractual Obligations under *Tulk v Moxhay* and *De Mattos v Gibson*' (1982) 98 *Law Quarterly Review* 389.

35   [1926] AC 108, PC.

approach has the advantage of doing less violence to the integrity of contract doctrine and its attachment to the idea of consent, and, at the same time, much the same result may be achieved. We should briefly illustrate these possibilities here and reflect upon their implications for the modern law's conception of contractual responsibility.

1. Unjust enrichment

In the absence of conduct from which consent to a transaction may be inferred, it may be possible to impose liability on the basis of unjust enrichment. For example, if, without my consent or request, a person performs a service which necessarily enriches me, such as mending my broken bicycle, a court may impose liability to compensate the mender for the value of the service on the ground of unjust enrichment. There is a hazy borderline here between cases where a court is prepared to infer consent, and thus contractual responsibility, from conduct such as standing by watching the mechanic perform his work, and other cases where consent is not inferred so the cause of action is classified as unjust enrichment. Many restitutionary claims for unjust enrichment rest upon facts similar to unilateral contracts, except that no fixed remuneration for the service has been promised: the court simply adds a term providing for payment of a reasonable price. Hence a request to perform a task without any further terms being settled suffices to ascribe responsibility in restitutionary claims such as 'quantum meruit', so that it matters little whether or not contractual responsibility can be based upon inferred consent.

2. Reliance model

Similarly, under the reliance model of liability discussed in Chapter 5, if these obligations are not considered to be part of contract law, their importance should nevertheless be recognized as an important qualification to the test for ascription of contractual responsibility. Under the reliance model of liability, a claim may be founded on conduct from which consent may not be inferred, yet upon which it was reasonable to rely. In *Crabb v Arun District Council*,[36] the English Court of Appeal granted the claimant a right of access to his property from the council's adjacent road in the absence of an inference of agreement, because his land had become inaccessible as a result of a sale of part of it induced by reliance upon the statements of intent and conduct of the council's officers, especially the fact that they had left a suitable gap in the road's fence in anticipation of the proposed right of access. Similarly, in the American case of *Hoffman v Red Owl Stores Inc*,[37] the parties never reached an agreement for a franchise, but, since the defendants had

36 [1976] Ch 179, [1975] 3 All ER 865, CA.
37 26 Wis 2d 683, 133 NW 2d 267 (1965).

encouraged the claimant to incur expenses in the expectation that he would be granted a franchise, they were bound to compensate him for that wasted expenditure.

The conduct which engenders this kind of reliance-based liability will normally consist of words and positive acts, but it is possible for responsibility to arise from omissions to act where there is knowledge of the misplaced reliance upon the omission. When a landowner watches another build a house on his land, knowing that the builder labours under a mistake as to the ownership of the property or his permission to build there, the landowner cannot evict the builder without at least compensating him for his wasted expenditure.[38] An adequate warning from the landowner will negative this potential source of liability.[39]

3. Duty of care in tort

Finally, we should note the striking possibilities offered by the introduction into this field of the law of negligence in tort. Consider the case discovered by Atiyah: *Crossan v Ward Bracewell*.[40] Here the claimant, who had been charged with the criminal offence of reckless driving after having caused a serious road traffic accident, visited the defendant solicitor, who told him that he could either plead guilty, in which case he would not need a solicitor, or he could plead not guilty, but then the defendant would only provide the necessary legal advice on payment of £50 in advance against the defendant's costs. The claimant decided to plead guilty and to dispense with a lawyer's services. The claimant was subsequently sued for compensation for the damage which he had caused in the road accident, and under a term of the claimant's insurance policy the insurers disclaimed liability, because they had not been duly notified of the criminal charge of reckless driving. The claimant then sued the defendant solicitor for his failure to alert him to this risk of forfeiting his insurance cover against claims for civil liability. The court held the defendant liable in tort for failing to take reasonable care in advising the claimant. This liability was established despite the clear finding that no contractual responsibility had been created, because the defendant made it abundantly clear that he was not prepared to act without the prepayment. Yet the tortious duty of care was exactly the same duty as that which would have been owed if a contract had been concluded. Decisions such as this clearly eviscerate the principle of freedom of contract, for they indicate that, even in the absence of consent, liability in tort equivalent to contractual responsibility may arise from conduct.

38 *Ramsden v Dyson* (1866) LR 1 HL 129, HL; *Willmott v Barber* (1880) 15 Ch D 96, Ch.
39 *A-G of Hong Kong v Humphreys Estate (Queen's Gardens) Ltd* [1987] AC 114, [1987] 2 All ER 387, PC
40 [1986] NLJ Rep 849, discussed in P Atiyah, *Essays on Contract* (Oxford, 1990), p 381.

G.   Autonomy and responsibility

This brief survey of alternative sources of responsibility draws out some vital points. Although the courts preserve the boundary of contractual responsibility by reference to the idea of consent, it has become clear that the objective process of inferring consent from conduct introduces considerable flexibility in that boundary, especially in cases of collateral contracts. The analysis also reveals that alternative sources of obligation may impose exactly the same or equivalent responsibilities to those founded in contract. It will often matter little, therefore, whether a court chooses to combat deceptive practices by manipulating the objective test of consent or by recognizing some alternative source of legal obligation.

Given the diversity and power of these alternative sources of liability, the boundary of the ascription of contractual responsibility on the basis of consent may have been shorn of any practical implications. The question of what theory lies behind the limitation of contractual responsibility therefore loses much of its interest. What we can usefully say is that, although one of the best justifications for compromising personal autonomy by imposing legal obligations remains an act of consent to an agreement, since that act of consent to an agreement is in itself an exercise of the freedom granted out of respect for personal autonomy, in the modern law personal autonomy can also be compromised by other types of conduct which can be regarded as a deceptive practice. The modern law expands the horizon of these deceptive practices, so that they go beyond secret reservations of unwillingness to contract. They include many forms of conduct which induce reasonable reliance, without there being any intention to deceive. To this extent we should interpret the modern law as reducing the importance of the value of freedom to choose to enter a contract, by qualifying this value with a demand to respect the interests of others in many circumstances and to refrain from conduct that misleads another into believing that some undertaking has been made.[41]

---

41 Collins, 'The Transformation Thesis and the Ascription of Contractual Responsibility', in T Wilhelmsson (ed), *Perspectives of Critical Contract Law* (Aldershot, 1993), p 293.

Chapter 8

Coercion and competitive markets

A. Involuntary consent
B. Duress
C. Undue influence
   1. Where the dominant party is deemed to have gained an ascendant position
     (a) Choice is entrusted to another
     (b) Pressure to compel choice
     (c) Taking advantage of business ignorance
     (d) Taking advantage of effective monopoly
   2. Rebutting the charge – independent advice
   3. Role of third parties and constructive notice
D. Affirmation and bars to rescission
E. Protection of competitive markets
   1. Unlawful invasion of rights
   2. Anti-competitive practices

A. Involuntary consent

Coercion may negative consent to a contract. If someone holds a gun to my head and says that unless I sign a contract then he will shoot, clearly my freedom to choose whether or not to enter the contract is gravely impaired. In a more commonplace example, a vendor of double-glazing arranges a visit on the telephone, and once in the house it seems impossible to get rid of him unless you sign some lengthy printed document, which turns out to amount to an expensive contractual commitment. In both examples the contract is likely to be regarded as invalid or voidable. To protect the institution of contracts as an exercise of autonomy, the law must distinguish between consensual transactions and coercive taking: it must do so both by prohibiting acts of coercive taking, by means of criminal laws against theft and blackmail, but also by invalidating any apparent contracts produced by coercion. Without such a distinction, there would be no safeguard to ensure that market transactions are wealth enhancing in the long run. Moreover, unless coercion is prevented, the law of contract would cease to be a legal institution for augmenting individual autonomy: it would be a cloak for oppression. The central difficulty confronting the law is where to draw the line between consensual transactions and coerced taking.

To some degree, every contract is the product of constrained choice. There are three types of constraints upon the freedom to choose whether or not to enter a contract. One constraint derives from each person's shortage of resources when entering the market. Without unlimited finance to acquire information and advice, together with time to search and consider all market opportunities, each person must necessarily make contractual agreements in the absence of unrestricted freedom to choose between all the various possibilities. A worker seeking a job could in theory look for the best offer throughout the European Community, but in practice the costs of searching limit the choice to a locality or region. A second source of constraint derives from limits on choice in the market itself. Although few pure monopolies can persist in a market economy without government support, bargaining positions that benefit from what is in practice an effective monopoly may be common. The single shop in an isolated village can charge high prices, if it is expensive and time-consuming to travel to town to purchase goods elsewhere. A third source of constraint occurs when one person feels compelled to subordinate his wishes to another's. A parent may feel obliged to put the interests of the children first, or a member of a religious community may be held under oath to place the interests of the group above his own. No one can act entirely freely from all such constraints.

To accept that all these types of constraints on choice will always negative consent to contracts, however, would be to question the legitimacy of the market order itself. The law cannot accept, for instance, that poverty constrains choice sufficiently to justify invalidating contracts, for this stance would challenge the enforceability of many common instances of contracting, such as employment, tenancies, and purchases of food. The law must exclude from its evaluation of whether or not consent was coerced most of the factors which in practice constrain choice. Support for a market order requires the law to regard the contracting parties for the most part as disembodied, unsituated persons, the abstract 'A's and 'B's of contract textbooks, and ignore the effective constraints upon action experienced in everyday life.

Yet the law must draw a line at some point to protect the institutions of the market against coercive taking. Is it possible, however, to develop a sharp conceptual distinction between those types of coercion which should negative consent to a contract and those which do not? Can we distinguish clearly those constraints upon freedom which are acceptable, in the sense of being necessary to tolerate for the sake of enjoying the fruits of the market order, from those constraints which negative the ascription of contractual responsibility?

The common law, following the civil law tradition, sought to answer these questions by drawing distinction between voluntary and involuntary consent to a contract. If consent was involuntary, contractual responsibility could not arise. English law developed two doctrines to identify instances of involuntary consent. The common law invalidated contracts under the doctrine of duress. This doctrine was supplemented by the equitable doctrine of undue influence, which extended the definition of involuntary consent. These doctrines are conventionally presented as the rules that identify involuntary actions in connection with contract. If duress or undue influence was present at the formation of the contract, consent was deemed to be involuntary, so the victim could ask a court to rescind the contract.

Yet this explanation of these private law doctrines in terms of a distinction between voluntary and involuntary consent was never convincing. In ordinary language, an involuntary action is one that has not been chosen, but the absence of choice is not the problem in cases of coercion to enter contracts. A signature on a contract at gunpoint is certainly an action that was chosen: indeed, at the time of signing the document, there was nothing the signatory would rather have done. The problem of coercion seems to be rather that options are severely constrained, so that no other course of action except death or some other unpleasant consequence is available to the signatory. The law needs to identify cases of constrained choice, where the degree and source of constraint justifies the unusual step of invalidating apparent consent to a contract. The law must be interested not in the state of mind of the victim who alleges that his or her consent was not voluntary, but in the external conditions and the conduct of the other party for the purpose of identifying situations which should be regarded as negativing consent to a contract.

It is not easy to explain under a simple principle those circumstances where, either as a result of market conditions or the conduct of the dominant party, or a combination of both, consent to a contract will be regarded as invalid. The underlying idea, I suggest, is that binding contracts should only be concluded in circumstances of fair competition. Pointing a gun to someone's head unless she signs a contract creates a situation of unfair competition, by means of constructing an overwhelming bargaining position: the victim has little choice but to consent. Similarly, the doorstep seller of encyclopaedias, who refuses to leave your home until you have purchased the set, also constructs a non-competitive market, since there is little chance for the customer to ascertain whether or not the price reflects the market rate and, moreover, the pressurizing sales technique prevents the customer from remembering that she would rather spend her money on something else. But the general standard of unfair competition cannot provide detailed guidance on the lawfulness the huge variety of ways in which traders try to construct a position of dominating bargaining power or to take advantage of another's weakness.

Our examination of the law will try to identify the more detailed rules governing the lawfulness of bargaining tactics and abuses of a dominant position with a view to articulating the standard for fair competition. As well as the judge-made doctrines of duress and undue influence, we need also to complete the picture by including numerous instances of regulation of particular market sectors, and also by situating this discussion within the broader principles of competition law that seek to address structural problems, such as monopolies which undermine the competitiveness of markets.

B. Duress

The common law doctrine of duress requires an illegitimate act performed by one party that causes the other to consent to the contract. This test for rescinding contracts on the ground that consent was negatived by coercion focuses on two criteria:

(i)   the requirement of causation; and
(ii)   the illegitimate act.

In order to satisfy the requirement of causation, the illegitimate act must be at least one reason why the contract was concluded, although other considerations may have played a part in the decision to give consent.[1] Duress is ineffective as a ground for invalidity if another reasonable course of action – other than making the contract – was available. But the courts understand that commercial considerations such as business reputation and compliance with other contracts will often make it inadvisable for one party to decline to make a contract and seek other means of protection against the threatened unlawful act. This causation requirement is therefore trying to ascertain whether, as a result of the illegitimate conduct of the dominant party, the choices of the weaker party were effectively curtailed, leaving only the option of consenting to the contract as the rational one to make.

In its earliest formulations, the requirement of an illegitimate act was confined to threats of unlawful violence against the person. After a period of doubt, it has become clear that threats of damage to property or of unlawful seizure of it will also negative consent. Although examples in cases are sparse, it seems likely that any unlawful tortious act can satisfy the requirement of an illegitimate act.[2] For example, the doorstep salesman who refuses to leave is likely to be committing the tort of trespass, which should suffice to amount to an illegitimate act that permits the purchaser of the encyclopaedia to avoid the transaction (provided the causation requirement is also met).

1   *Barton v Armstrong* [1976] AC 104, [1975] 2 All ER 465, PC.
2   Beatson, 'Duress as a Vitiating Factor in Contract' (1974) *Cambridge Law Journal* 97.

What seems less certain is whether the common law of duress requires the illegitimate act to be unlawful, or whether some conduct may be regarded as illegitimate even though strictly speaking not amounting to a tort or some other breach of statutory obligation. In *Universe Tankships Inc of Monrovia v International Transport Workers' Federation (The Universe Sentinel)*[3] a trade union organized industrial action, so that a ship became immobilized. The plaintiff secured the release of the ship by reaching a collective agreement with the union. A term of the collective agreement provided that the plaintiff should pay a sum of money into the union's welfare fund. Having paid, the plaintiff later sought recovery of this money. The trial court determined that the collective agreement was reached under severe economic compulsion, because of the potentially disastrous effects of the industrial action upon the plaintiff's business. But the crucial question was whether the union had committed an illegitimate act in order to induce the payment. Although the union's action constituted under the ordinary law of tort an unlawful interference with business, statute law protects a worker's right to strike by granting immunity from an action in tort under certain conditions. The House of Lords decided that the money was recoverable, but only because the statutory conditions had not been satisfied. If the industrial action had been lawful, so that the strike action that constituted the coercion was not actionable in tort, the plaintiff could not have relied upon duress to negative consent. This decision suggests that the illegitimate act must also be unlawful. It is true that Lord Scarman in that case suggested that the nature of the demand itself, rather than the pressure exerted, may render the act illegitimate. He had in mind the example of blackmail, where the threat may be to perform a lawful act such as to inform the police of criminal conduct unless money is paid. But it is far from clear that such instances of extortion will not themselves amount to unlawful conduct, either the crime of blackmail or the tort of intimidation.

It is clear, however, that the unlawful act need not amount to a tort. Where one party threatens to breach an existing contract unless he is given some further advantage, then, although this threat does not amount to a tort, it satisfies the requirement of an illegitimate act. The threat to breach an existing contract between the parties is known as a type of 'economic duress'. Provided that the causation requirement is also satisfied, the victim of economic duress may rescind any modification to the agreement and insist upon performance of the contract according to the original terms of the contract. For the purpose of the law of duress, not only the unlawful act of breach of contract, but also the threat to do so, amounts to an illegitimate act. But as we shall see in Chapter 15, the application of the law of duress in the context of modifications of contracts requires special consideration of the need to promote co-operation between the parties during performance of a contract. Not every request to vary the terms of an existing contract will be regarded as illegitimate conduct.

3   [1983] 1 AC 366, [1982] 2 All ER 67, HL.

The hardest question about the scope of the law of duress remains whether the requirement of an illegitimate act includes conduct which is not unlawful in itself.[4] Consider an example where a walker in the hills becomes lost, the night closes in, and the weather turns sour. The walker stumbles across a remote track and flags down a four-wheel drive vehicle. The driver offers to take the walker to the nearest inn, in return for a payment of £100. The walker agrees to the fee reluctantly, but, on discovering that the inn was in fact only a few hundred metres away, subsequently refuses to pay. If the law of duress requires a unlawful act, this agreement must escape its province, for the driver of the car in offering a lift in return for payment has not committed any legal wrong. The implicit threat not to make a contract to carry the passenger cannot comprise an unlawful act, for such a step would negate the general freedom to choose whether or not to enter contracts which protects competitive markets. Yet this conclusion seems tough: the driver took advantage of his position to rip off the helpless hiker. Should such a contract really be binding?

To put the question more abstractly, does the law of duress extend to cases where one party to a contract has exploited an effective monopoly position, originating from the necessity of the other combined with the absence of other opportunities to satisfy the need, in order to obtain a highly advantageous transaction? Some authorities suggest that duress may extend to such instances. In *The Port Caledonia and The Anna*,[5] a captain of a ship, which was about to hit another boat, agreed to the demand of a master of a tugboat for a charge of £1,000 to tow the ship out of danger. The court permitted the captain of the ship to resist the claim for £1,000 on the ground that he was forced under compulsion to agree to an extortionate bargain, although he was required to pay a reasonable fee of £200. Here it was the costs of inaction, compounded by the state of necessity and the effective monopoly position of the master of the tug-boat, which vitiated the captain's consent. Perhaps a more typical example these days of exploitation of a monopoly position is that found in the American case of *SS & O Corpn v Township of Bernards Sewerage Authority*.[6] Here, the Supreme Court of New Jersey invalidated an agreement between a real estate developer and a municipal authority for payment of excessive charges for connecting new houses to the sewerage system, exacted by threats of refusal to supply the service. Duress in the form of a threat to refuse to enter a contract imposed by persons clothed with official authority exacerbates the exploitation of a monopoly position in such cases.

Although these decisions lend support to the idea that duress can be satisfied without a tortious act, there is reason to doubt whether they are examples of the removal of the requirement of an unlawful act entirely. In the instances of public authorities demanding exorbitant payments, there is usually a violation of law, for the regulations that establish their powers, foreseeing the risk of exploitation of

4   Dawson, 'Economic Duress – An Essay in Perspective' (1947) 45 *Michigan Law Review* 253.
5   [1903] P 184.
6   62 NJ 369, 301 A 2d 738 (1973).

the monopoly powers, place limits on the authority's discretion. In *SS & O Corpn v Township of Bernards Sewerage Authority*, the law provided that all houses should be connected to the sewerage system without discrimination, so it was unlawful under the terms of this power to demand higher rates of payment from one construction company than another. Statutory limits on public monopoly powers often forbid any supplementary demands for money,[7] require non-discrimination between citizens, or require that a reasonable rate be charged for the service.[8] These cases support the view that a tortious act is not required for duress, but at the same time they indicate that some other kind of illegal action is necessary to establish duress in the formation of contracts. This requirement of at least a breach of regulation explains why the exploitation of a public monopoly position did not constitute duress in the Australian case of *Smith v William Charlick Ltd*.[9] The plaintiff was informed by the Wheat Harvest Board that unless he paid a premium on the wheat he had already bought from them, no further supplies of wheat would be forthcoming, which would have put the plaintiff out of business. The plaintiff failed in his claim for recovery of premium payments, the main ground for the decision being that the Wheat Harvest Board had not acted unlawfully but had been within its powers. These decisions therefore support the requirement of an unlawful act, although it need not be a tortious one.

On the other hand, the cases concerning salvage agreements, such as *The Port Caledonia and The Anna*, cannot be so explained as requiring an unlawful act. The master of the tugboat does not commit a legal wrong by threatening not to make a contract. Usually lawyers suggest a different interpretation of these cases, which takes them outside the doctrine of duress altogether. In the case of salvage, the specialist admiralty courts developed doctrines governing salvage agreements that ensured that rescuers always received a fair rate of remuneration for their services. Thus a contract could be set aside for being agreed at a price which was either too high or too low. In establishing a fair rate of remuneration, the court would take into account such factors as the danger to the cargo, the risk to the salvors and the amount of work involved, together with the general consideration that the rate must be set at a level sufficiently high to provide a reasonable incentive for persons to enter the salvage business.[10] The salvage cases can be explained not as representing an extension of the law of duress but as the application of a special regulatory regime created by the courts of admiralty. This regime can be seen as analogous to the implied obligation placed on common carriers, such as railways and other public transport services, to accept and convey all goods delivered to them according to their line of business on being paid a reasonable remuneration for their services. The emphasis in these doctrines upon

7   *Steele v Williams* (1853) 8 Exch 625.
8   *Parker v Great Western Rly Co* (1844) 7 Man & G 253; *Great Western Rly Co v Sutton* (1869) LR 4 HL 226, HL.
9   (1924) 34 CLR 38, Aust HC.
10   *The Henry* (1851) 15 Jur 183.

a fair market price for services rendered suggests that the real ground for the salvage decisions was not so much the exploitation of an effective monopoly position, but rather the unfairness of the terms concluded. In which case, these decisions would be better considered in connection with standards of fairness in general, and they could be regarded as irrelevant to the question of whether the law of duress always requires an unlawful act.

Although the legal authorities may be so limited, thereby placing the example of the walker paying a high price for a lift outside the scope of the law of duress, this conclusion seems unsatisfactory. The presence or absence of some technical illegality can often be the product of the accidents of legislation. If the regulators foresee the problems posed by monopolies, they may enact appropriate qualifications on the powers to make contracts, but it is apparent from cases such as *Smith v William Charlick Ltd* that the controls may prove less than complete. Similarly, although the law may have developed adequate controls over prices with respect to common situations such as salvage and common carriers, this established regulation should not mean that the law is unable to intervene in the unusual instance of exploitation of an effective monopoly position falling outside these established categories. It therefore remains possible that duress may in some instances be constituted by lawful acts, especially if the court detects what it regards as conduct in bad faith.[11] Fortunately, the extension of the common law doctrine of duress to such cases is usually an unnecessary issue for the courts to consider, for it is clear that in equity, under the doctrine of undue influence, there is no requirement of an illegitimate act, so that contracts may be rescinded in response to more subtle coercive techniques.

C. Undue influence

Courts exercising an equitable jurisdiction have developed an elaborate, although often elusive, conception of the types of coercion which may negative ascription of contractual responsibility. Although the term 'undue influence' is the one most frequently employed to describe this jurisdiction, the courts also use a variety of terminology including 'equitable' or 'constructive' fraud, 'unconscientious dealing', and sometimes, especially in the USA 'unconscionability'.[12] Viewed as a whole, the equitable jurisdiction encompasses many subtle forms of domination and pressure, which the common law of duress, confined by the requirement of illegitimate acts, excludes from relief. Equity recognizes that choice can be

11 *CTN Cash and Carry Ltd v Gallaher Ltd* [1994] 4 All ER 714, CA.
12 Under the unconscionability provision of the American Uniform Commercial Code, s 2-302, courts decline to enforce contracts where the terms are grossly unfair in circumstances where the purchaser was illiterate or naive in business matters (*Frostifresh Corpn v Reynoso* 54 Misc 2d 119, 281 NYS 2d 264 (1967)), or on the broadest statement of the test of unconscionability, where there is 'an absence of meaningful choice' (*Williams v Walker-Thomas Furniture Co* 350 F 2d 445, 449 (DC Circ 1965)).

impaired from all three types of constraint identified at the beginning of this chapter – shortage of resources, effective monopolies and personal subordination. The doctrine of undue influence identifies aberrant instances where the behaviour of the stronger party removes the case from the normal market conditions.

To establish a claim that a contract should be rescinded for undue influence, the weaker party has to establish two elements. First the weaker party has to demonstrate that the dominant party had gained an ascendant position. This position may have been obtained by subtle coercive techniques or by encouraging the weaker party to place trust in the dominant party. A complete list of such aberrant situations of ascendancy could never be drawn up, for new methods of persuasion and domination may always be discovered. Nevertheless, four broad types of situation where relief has been given have been identified, as follows:

(i)   where the subordinate party entrusts the choice whether or not to enter the contract to another party;

(ii)   where the dominant party exerts pressure on the weaker party, short of duress;

(iii)   where the dominant party takes advantage of the weaker party's business ignorance; and

(iv)   where there is an effective monopoly.

These situations are discussed in greater detail below.

Having established the claim that the stronger party had gained an ascendancy over the weaker, the equitable doctrine requires, as a second element for proving the claim for rescission, evidence that the stronger party in fact took advantage of its position. This evidence might be found, for instance, in showing that the weaker party was induced to enter a contract which he would not otherwise have chosen in the ordinary course of events, or that the transaction itself was on such unfavourable terms that it seems probable that it was extracted by the use of undue influence. The terms of the contract may evidence a harsh bargain, such as property being sold at far less than its market value, or the charging of an exorbitant interest rate on a loan which far exceeds comparable market rates.

However, proof of unfair terms or the fact that the transaction was to the manifest disadvantage of the weaker party is not a necessary requirement.[13] Proof that undue influence was exercised may be discovered in the fact that the transaction was not one which an ordinary businessperson would regard as prudent. In *Lloyds Bank Ltd v Bundy*,[14] a farmer mortgaged his home to a bank in return for a loan by the bank to his son's business. Having established the potential for undue influence, the farmer argued successfully that this influence had been exercised, not because the interest rate on the loan was unfair in any way, but because the

13 *CIBC Mortgages plc v Pitt* [1994] 1 AC 200, [1993] 4 All ER 433, HL.
14 [1975] QB 326, [1974] 3 All ER 757, CA.

mortgage had been agreed in circumstances where, to the knowledge of the bank, the prospects for his son's business were so poor that the risk amounted to an unsound commercial prospect, which no businessperson would have recommended.

In order to provide compelling evidence that the stronger party has taken advantage of its position, the disadvantage must be sufficiently great that, 'it would have been obvious as such to any independent and reasonable persons who considered the transaction at the time with knowledge of all the relevant facts'.[15] Evidence of the unfairness or the imprudence of the transaction, although not essential, creates a presumption or a strong case to persuade the court that the stronger party has taken unfair advantage of its position. Nevertheless, it always remains possible for the stronger party to try to demonstrate in some way that in fact no advantage was taken or no undue influence exercised. However, 'the greater the disadvantage to the vulnerable person, the more cogent must be the explanation before the presumption will be regarded as rebutted.'[16]

1. Where the dominant party is deemed to have gained an ascendant position

(a) CHOICE IS ENTRUSTED TO ANOTHER

The most common instance of undue influence concerns those forms of constraint over freedom of contract which arise from personal authority and subordination. Undue influence arises 'where influence is acquired and abused, where confidence is reposed and betrayed'.[17] The court requires proof that one party acquired a dominating influence over the other, such that in effect choices whether or not to enter into contracts were entrusted by the subordinate party to the other.

This requirement of a dominating influence over choice to enter contracts can be established in many ways. In some cases a person may become a trusted commercial adviser, so that the subordinate party effectively permits himself to be guided in business transactions by the adviser. In many common instances of this type of dominating influence, equity subjects the adviser to fiduciary duties and presumes that the first requirement is satisfied. This will be true in such relationships as solicitor and client, guardian and ward, and religious adviser and disciple.

But the dominating influence may arise in special circumstances in many other commercial relationships. Although in general a bank manager will not have acquired such a dominating influence over a client, it is possible for such a

---

15 *Bank of Credit and Commerce International SA v Aboody* [1990] 1 QB 923, [1992] 4 All ER 955, CA.
16 Lord Nicholls, *Royal Bank of Scotland plc v Etridge (No 2)* [2001] UKHL 44 at [24], [2002] 2 AC 773, [2001] 4 All ER 449.
17 *Smith v Kay* (1859) 7 HL Cas 750 at 779.

relationship to develop. In *Lloyds Bank Ltd v Bundy*, the reason why the farmer was able to establish a relation of undue influence was that this elderly man had relied upon the manager of the bank to advise him on business matters over a number of years. The farmer wanted, for reasons of family loyalty, to assist his son's ailing business, but the manager explained that the bank would only make a further loan to the son's business if the farmer secured it by a charge over his home. When agreeing to this loan, the farmer was relying on the bank manager for advice, and although the manager was aware of this, and also was aware that the son's business position was grave, the manager did not suggest that the farmer should obtain independent advice. On these special facts, the necessary elements of a dominating influence were established. The manager was aware that the farmer was relying upon him to make the decision whether or not to mortgage his home. Of course, such a relation of trust and confidence rarely applies to the relations between banks and their customers. Bank managers may advise their customers, but their relationship usually remains one of arm's length dealing, and the customer ultimately makes up his or her own mind whether to enter into any proposed transaction. In order to trigger the doctrine of undue influence, courts of equity look for an instance when the decision to enter the contract has effectively been entrusted to the other party with a dominating influence.

Such cases where choice has been entrusted to the other party are most likely to arise in non-commercial relations within the family. A wife may permit her husband to make all the household financial decisions, and sign any contracts that he presents to her. Even adult children may routinely obey their parents and follow their parent's instructions on how to dispose of their property.

(b)   PRESSURE TO COMPEL CHOICE

Short of a tortious act of intimidation which would satisfy the common law of duress, equity may recognize that pressure was exercised to such an extent as to deprive the weaker party of any real freedom of choice whether or not to consent to a contract. Ordinary commercial pressures will not suffice: the court requires aberrant conduct which it can describe as wrongful, unfair or unconscionable. This requirement might be satisfied in a case where a man bullies and cajoles his wife so persistently that she gives in to his instructions and permits him to manage her affairs. In *Williams v Bayley*,[18] a father agreed to pay his son's debts to a bank (by way of executing a mortgage) when the bank showed him documents which clearly exposed his son to a criminal charge of forgery. Here the father naturally subordinated his interests to those of his son, and consequently he enjoyed little control over the decision whether or not to meet the bank's demands, so the court rescinded the contract. This type of undue influence has been used only rarely, because the pressure employed normally falls within the scope of the law of duress since it is likely to involve an unlawful act.

18 (1866) LR 1 HL 200, HL.

(c) TAKING ADVANTAGE OF BUSINESS IGNORANCE

In the early days of the equitable jurisdiction, the courts frequently came across instances of transactions with naive, often illiterate, people who had been persuaded to part with property at greatly less than its market value. To give relief in these circumstances, the courts either inferred fraud, or stated that there had been unconscientious dealing with either a poor and ignorant person or a youthful and inexperienced one. This emphasis upon the type of shortage of resources stemming from ignorance of business matters could obviously apply to a large section of the population in modern society as well. But such an expansion would threaten the validity of many common market transactions.

The necessary limits on this type of equitable jurisdiction, however, remain obscure. In *Cresswell v Potter*,[19] a woman obtained rescission of a contract with her husband, under which she agreed to give him her interest in the matrimonial home in return for his promise to repay all outstanding debts on the property. But these debts were small in comparison to the value of her share in the house, so her advantage from the transaction was illusory. The court based its grant of rescission on the ground that the wife counted as a poor and ignorant person because she had only a modest income and was ignorant of property transactions, and that the sale had proceeded without independent advice at considerable undervalue. The difficulty presented by this ground for the decision is that these conditions might apply to a wide range of transactions, but it seems likely that whenever a contract involves the sale of property at considerable undervalue these conditions may be met. The decision in *Cresswell v Potter* appears to dispense with any need to prove unconscientious dealing by the other party, such that he has deliberately taken advantage of the other's ignorance of business matters.

Although the decision in *Cresswell v Potter* certainly reflects ancient authorities, in other cases this decision and the authorities on which it was based have been reinterpreted to fit into the general framework of the law of undue influence by requiring evidence of a conscious abuse of an ascendant position. In a similar situation in *Barclays Bank plc v O'Brien*,[20] where a husband had lied to his wife about the financial risks of a transaction, it was suggested that undue influence could be found in the way that the husband had taken advantage of his wife's lack of adequate understanding of financial affairs, ie the nature and consequences of a proposed transaction, in order to persuade her to enter into an imprudent undertaking. A similar interpretation might apply to cases where a person takes advantage of his elderly parents' ignorance of business matters to induce them to enter into an improvident bargain.[21] A requirement of unconscientious dealing

19 [1978] 1 WLR 255n, Ch.
20 [1994] 1 AC 180, [1993] 4 All ER 417, HL.
21 *Avon Finance Co Ltd v Bridger* [1985] 2 All ER 281, CA.

was stressed in *Hart v O'Connor*,[22] where an unfair transaction with a person of unsound mind was not rescinded on the ground that this lack of capacity was unknown to the other party to the transaction, so that he could not be said to have taken advantage of it.

These decisions suggest that it is insufficient for the purposes of the law of undue influence merely to point to the inability of a person to understand the nature of the transaction and its unfairness. What seems to be required as well is evidence of an intention by the stronger party to take advantage of the other's weakness. Proof of this intention may be found in all the circumstances of the transaction, and it seems likely that it will be sufficient to demonstrate that the stronger person should have been alerted to the inability of the weaker party to handle his or her own affairs during the course of the discussions leading up to the contract.[23] The manifestly disadvantageous nature of the transaction, of course, helps to prove that those conditions were present.[24]

(d)   TAKING ADVANTAGE OF EFFECTIVE MONOPOLY

In the context of the law of duress, we noted that the common law does not give relief from contracts formed under conditions of effective monopoly, except where there is illegitimate conduct or the parties are purporting to modify an existing contract. But the equitable jurisdiction has strayed beyond these limits. It recognizes that some contracts should be set aside where there has been an unconscientious use of bargaining power arising out the necessitous circumstances of the weaker party. These grounds for equitable relief arose in *Aylesford v Morris*.[25] A young nobleman, in need of cash to pay his debts, obtained a loan from a moneylender at 60% interest on the security of his future inheritance. The young man had to conceal the transaction from his father, so was unwilling to seek independent advice or pursue other possible opportunities to borrow money. There was an effective monopoly in such circumstances, and the moneylender had clearly taken advantage of the situation. The court rescinded the transaction on the ground that there was a kind of equitable fraud both against the young man and his father, although it ordered repayment of the debts with 5% interest. Whilst this case should be read in the context of the courts seeking to protect the fortunes of the aristocratic and governing families of the country against moneylenders, it can also be regarded as an instance where the equitable jurisdiction extends to give relief where advantage has been taken of an effective monopoly. It might apply in a modern context where a large multinational corporation can effectively insist upon extremely advantageous terms against a

22 [1985] AC 1000, [1985] 2 All ER 880, PC.

23 *Barclays Bank plc v O'Brien* [1994] 1 AC 180, [1993] 4 All ER 417, HL.

24 *Boustany v Pigott* (1993) 69 P & CR 298, PC; *Ayres v Hazelgrove* (9 February 1984, unreported), Ch, discussed in P Birks, *Restitution – The Future* (Sydney, 1992), p 50.

25 (1873) 8 Ch App 484.

small business because, under the prevailing business context, the small business has no choice but to enter the contract with the multinational.[26]

Some legislation pursues this dimension of the equitable jurisdiction by identifying particular problem instances of taking advantage of effective monopolies. For example, most jurisdictions regulate door-to-door sales or contracts negotiated away from business premises such as a person's home,[27] because of the widespread evidence of the high pressure sales techniques employed which prevent the consumer from making price comparisons. The legislation grants a consumer a 'cooling-off' period during which time the contract can be cancelled.

An interesting question is whether this dimension of the equitable jurisdiction might have a role to play in cases such as the lost walker who accepts a lift at a high price, for a court of equity might regard the conduct of the driver as an unconscionable taking advantage of the necessity of the walker, and so rescind the contract.

2. Rebutting the charge – independent advice

In all these four types of undue influence, it is always possible for the party in the ascendant position to try to rebut the charge that advantage was taken of the weaker party. In some instances it might be argued that when examined in all the circumstances the contract was to the benefit of the weaker party and was not the product of the abuse of a dominating position. A more reliable defence is to show that the weaker party received independent advice. If an independent lawyer or business advisor had recommended that the weaker party should enter the contract, this evidence tends to rebut the argument that the dominant party has subtly coerced the weaker party into making the contract. If, for example, the farmer in *Lloyd's Bank plc v Bundy* had obtained independent advice from an accountant with access to the financial records of his son's business, the bank could not be said to have taken advantage of its dominating position. The court must be persuaded that, despite the dominating position and the apparently disadvantageous contract, the choice to enter it was influenced not by the dominant party, but influenced only by the independent advisor. If the independent advisor is demonstrated to have been incompetent, the remedy must lie in damages against the advisor, not in rescission of the contract for undue influence.

---

26 *Lobb (Alec) (Garages) Ltd v Total Oil GB Ltd* [1985] 1 All ER 303, [1985] 1 WLR 173, CA; the argument was rejected on the facts in this case.
27 EC Directive 85/577/EEC on Contracts Negotiated Away from Business Premises; Consumer Protection (Cancellation of Contracts Concluded away from Business Premises) Regulations 1987, SI 1987/2117; Consumer Credit Act 1974, ss 67–68; *Faccini Dori v Recreb Srl* (Case C-91/92) [1995] All ER (EC) 1, ECJ.

It is unclear whether it might be sufficient to rebut the inference of undue influence if the stronger party demonstrates that it warned the weaker party to obtain independent advice. Is a warning sufficient, or must the stronger party, having become aware of its dominant position, refrain from entering a contract until it is reasonably satisfied that independent advice has in fact been given? In some instances of undue influence, the giving of a warning and the opportunity for a period of reflection may be sufficient to persuade the court that the transaction was concluded free from the taint of undue influence. In general, however, confirmation that independent advice was received by the weaker party will be required in order to rebut the inference from the circumstances that undue influence was probably exercised.

3. Role of third parties and constructive notice

The effects of undue influence are not confined to the stronger and weaker parties to the contract. In many cases the stronger party has exercised the influence in order to obtain credit from a bank secured on the weaker party's property. In these circumstances the bank will be unable to enforce the security against the weaker party either if the bank had authorised the stronger party to act as its agent,[28] or if it had actual or constructive notice of the undue influence.

The idea of 'constructive notice' evolved in a series of cases where, in each case, the husband persuaded the wife to give her property interest in the matrimonial home as security for a bank loan to provide capital for the husband's business. On the failure of the husband's business, the bank would try to realise its security by selling the house. Wives tried to resist the action for possession by arguing that the husbands had exercised undue influence in order to obtain the wife's consent to stand surety for the loan by charging her property. Banks resisted this defence on the ground that, as the husband had not acted their agent and as they were unaware of the husband's conduct that amounted to undue influence or misrepresentation, they were not participants in any wrongdoing and should therefore be able to enforce the charge. In *Barclay's Bank plc v O'Brien*, the House of Lords decided that a bank would be unable to enforce the security if it had constructive notice of the husband's exercise of undue influence or misrepresentation. Constructive notice arises when the bank ought to have realised from the nature of the relationship between the parties and the unfavourable content of the transaction for the weaker party that there was a risk of undue influence.

The innovation of the doctrine of constructive notice was designed to reconcile two powerful interests. On the one hand, the courts recognised that in general secured loan transactions must be enforceable by banks if they have obtained signed consent to the contractual documents. Through these loans, banks provide capital to small businesses. Without security such as a charge over

28 *Coldunell v Gallon* [1986] QB 1184, [1986] 1 All ER 429, CA.

physical assets, banks would be unwilling to make such loans or charge higher rates of businesses. For many small businesses, the only security that may be available is the family home owned jointly by husband and wife. Since small businesses represented about 95% of all businesses in Britain, and account for nearly one-third of employment, the courts were unwilling to place obstacles in the way of these businesses in obtaining the necessary capital. On the other hand, the courts recognised that in some cases the husband had exercised undue influence over his wife or had misrepresented the risks of the loan agreement, and they tried to provide some protection for wives against these wrongs. The limited protection afforded by the doctrine of constructive notice reduces, but does not eliminate, the risks that wives will lose their property as a result of their husbands' wrongdoing.

Under the doctrine of constructive notice, a bank is put on notice that there is a risk that a signature has been obtained by undue influence or misrepresentation if:

(i)   the transaction is on its face not to the financial advantage of the person providing the security (the 'surety', in these instances the wife); and

(ii)   by the nature of the relationship between the recipient of the loan and the surety.

A transaction is not on its face to the financial advantage of the surety if the loan of money is made not to the surety but another legal entity such as the husband's business. Even if the wife owns some shares in the husband's business or is a director of the company, this condition is likely to be satisfied because in practice it is often the case that the husband has effective control over the management of the company. In contrast, see *CIBC Mortgages plc v Pitt*[29] where the bank was told falsely by the husband that the loan was for the purpose of purchasing a holiday home to be owned jointly by husband and wife: here, the condition that the transaction should be on its face not to the advantage of the wife was not satisfied.

For the second requirement, the nature of the relationship must be one where there is risk of undue influence. In non-commercial relationships, such as those between husband and wife, cohabiting couples or parent and child, this risk is always present. The risk may arise wherever emotional ties may induce the weaker party to trust the other. This risk may also be found in other domestic arrangements, as in the case of a secretary-companion taking advantage of her elderly employer.[30] Other relationships that may involve a degree of subordination, such as that between employer and employee,[31] should also place the bank on notice that the relationship may create the opportunity for the exercise of undue influence.

If those two conditions are satisfied, the bank must take reasonable steps to ensure that consent to the contract was properly obtained. In *Barclay's Bank plc v O'Brien*,

29 [1994] 1 AC 200, [1993] 4 All ER 433, HL.
30 *In Re Craig, dec'd* [1971] Ch 95, [1970] 2 All ER 390.
31 *Credit Lyonnais Bank Nederland NV v Burch* [1997] 1 All ER 144, CA.

the House of Lords suggested that these reasonable steps should normally include direct contact with the weaker party for the purpose of informing the weaker party of the exact nature of the transaction, the extent of liability which it entails, the risk of liability and to advise the weaker party to take independent advice. The banks, however, bitterly contested this requirement as placing too onerous a burden on them. In a case involving eight consolidated appeals, *Royal Bank of Scotland plc v Etridge (No 2)*,[32] the House of Lords accepted that the general practice of the banks was sufficient. The banks avoided a private meeting with the wife or surety, because they were concerned that subsequently the surety might allege misrepresentation or negligence in the quality of advice given. Instead the banks wrote to the wife or surety warning them to obtain independent advice from a solicitor, and insisting on written confirmation that such advice had been obtained. The House of Lords accepted that this practice amounted to reasonable steps by the bank to reduce the risk of undue influence, provided that the bank disclosed to the solicitor or independent advisor all the information relevant to the transaction, and that the solicitor gave written confirmation to the bank that he or she had brought home to the surety the risks involved in the transaction.

The effect of this decision is to reduce the burden on the banks, but at the same time it shifts the risk onto the solicitor or independent advisor. But the duty on the solicitor is not to ensure that no undue influence has been exercised: the duty is limited to providing the surety with an explanation of the nature and effects of the transaction. If during this explanation the solicitor becomes aware that the surety is in fact being compelled to consent to the transaction by undue influence, the solicitor must decline to confirm to the bank that the surety is acting with independent advice.

D.   Affirmation and bars to rescission

Through the doctrines of duress and undue influence, the law recognizes that coercion may vitiate consent to a contract. But the effect of these doctrines is not to prevent a contract from arising; rather they lead to a conclusion that the contract may be avoided by the weaker party, usually by an action for rescission of the contract.

The main reason for this rule lies in the point that the coercion may dissipate after the contract has been formed and, once the coercion has been removed, the weaker party may nevertheless indicate a willingness to be bound by the contract. In these circumstances, a court may declare that the contract has been affirmed, so that the right to avoid it has been lost. In *North Ocean Shipping Co v Hyundai*

---

32 [2001] UKHL 44, [2002] 2 AC 773, [2001] 4 All ER 449.

Construction Co (The Atlantic Baron),[33] a contract for the supply of a ship had been modified to increase the price at the insistence of the supplier, who threatened not to deliver without the increase. The court decided that this pressure amounted to economic duress, but nevertheless declined to void the contract on the ground that the buyer had subsequently affirmed the contract. The buyer had taken no steps to avoid the contract for seven months after delivery of the ship, and nor had it entered any protest at the time of making the final payments. The court judged the question of affirmation by the objective test of consent, finding that the buyer's conduct indicated to a reasonable man that it consented to the amended contract price.

Pragmatic considerations will also influence a court to resist an application for avoidance of a contract. If a substantial period of time elapses between the formation of the contract and the suit to avoid the contract, to upset the contract may have adverse effects on third parties and pose considerable problems in unravelling the transaction. For these reasons, actions to avoid a contract on the ground of coercion may be barred by reason of lapse of time, the impossibility of putting the parties back into the position which they held prior to the formation of the contract, and the necessity of protecting the interests of innocent third parties. The weaker party must seek relief within a reasonable time after the removal of the coercion.[34] Restitution must be possible to ensure that the parties are placed in more or less the same financial position as they enjoyed prior to the formation of the contract, but for this purpose it is acceptable to require payments of money to be made in order to compensate for property which cannot be returned and valuable services which have been rendered.[35] Third parties who have not knowingly taken advantage of the coercion will be protected by the court declining to avoid the contract if this would adversely affect them.

E.   Protection of competitive markets

This analysis of the law of duress and undue influence reveals that various types of constraint on freedom to choose to enter a contract suffice to negative consent and to prevent the ascription of contractual responsibility. The law must draw a line between the ordinary pressures and disadvantages experienced by people entering market transactions from aberrant cases when no transaction should be enforceable. Without this line, the commonplace inequalities of bargaining power between parties entering into contracts would suffice to invalidate contracts, which in turn would destroy the utility of the law of contract in providing a foundation for a market economy. The question to be addressed in

33 [1979] QB 705, [1978] 3 All ER 1170, QB.
34 *Allcard v Skinner* (1887) 36 Ch D 145, CA.
35 *O'Sullivan v Management Agency and Music Ltd* [1985] QB 428, [1985] 3 All ER 351, CA.

concluding this chapter is whether or not the legal doctrines of duress and undue influence reveal a coherent basis for drawing this line.[36]

As we observed at the outset, it is unsatisfactory to claim that the line has been drawn on the basis of the concept of voluntary consent alone. The doctrines of duress and undue influence clearly introduce more specific criteria by which to distinguish those cases where consent is vitiated by coercion. The doctrine of duress insists upon an illegitimate act, and the equitable jurisdiction confines relief to recognizable patterns of aberrant situations where the weaker party has been exploited. Although the courts insist that the reason for granting rescission of the contract is that consent has been negatived, proof of unwillingness to enter the contract does not suffice. The weaker party has to point to acts that constitute duress or undue influence by the stronger party for rescission to be granted. On what basis is it possible to justify these particular criteria for intervention?

1. Unlawful invasion of rights

It is tempting to try to synthesize the legal doctrines by suggesting that in their different ways both duress and undue influence require an illegitimate act on the part of the stronger party, which induced consent to the contract. The underlying idea is that the law posits a realm of private autonomy, guarded by the normal rights of citizens under the common law. Within this realm of protected private autonomy, all actions are presumed to be voluntary. Interference with the rights that protect private autonomy involves unlawful behaviour. Hence, proof of unlawful interference with private autonomy provides the dividing line between situations where consent is negatived and cases where the pressures to contract are those that everyone is expected to withstand.[37]

The reasoning here is analytically suspect. In the terminology of Hohfeld,[38] from the interference with a claim-right of the weaker party, it is assumed that the different privilege or liberty-right to enter contracts of one's choice has been removed as well. The false logic of this argument can be illustrated in the instance of a settlement of a valid claim. In a case where one party is guilty of committing a nuisance such as pollution against a neighbour's property, a settlement between the parties, which provides compensation to the injured party, will be binding despite the fact that rights were invaded. It is clear that an invasion of the rights of the weaker party does not necessarily involve a deprivation of the freedom to choose whether or not to enter a contract. It is for this reason that the causation

36 Kronman, Contract Law and Distributive Justice' (1980) 89 *Yale Law Journal* 472; Hale, 'Bargaining, Duress and Economic Liberty' (1943) 43 *Columbia Law Review* 603.
37 Epstein, 'Unconscionability: A Critical Reappraisal' (1975) 18 *Journal of Law and Economics* 293; Eisenberg, 'The Bargain Principle and its Limits' (1982) 95 *Harvard Law Review* 741; C Fried, *Contract as Promise* (Cambridge Mass, 1981), ch 7.
38 W Hohfeld, *Fundamental Legal Conceptions as Applied in Judicial Reasoning* (ed W Cook, 1923).

element in duress requires that the illegitimate act presents the weaker party with no reasonable choice but to make the contract. Illegality on its own cannot suffice to justify the rescission of contracts.

A more obvious weakness in this justification for controlling intervention by reference to the touchstone of illegality is its difficulty in accounting for the breadth of the equitable jurisdiction. The grounds for invalidating contracts under the doctrine of undue influence extend beyond ordinary examples of tortious or criminal conduct and, although a loose analogy may be drawn with fraud in many of these instances, the normal tests for fraud will not necessarily be satisfied. At best, therefore, this explanation in terms of the interference with the rights of the weaker party will only account for the common law doctrine of duress, and we require another justification for the equitable jurisdiction.

2. Anti-competitive practices

A more promising justification for the scope of the doctrines of duress and undue influence links this branch of the law of contract to a more general legal policy of the protection of competitive markets. On this interpretation, it is recognized that many different kinds of constraints serve to limit the freedom to choose whether or not to enter contracts. But these constraints only become impermissible if they prevent the operation of a normal competitive market. The law has to address both structural flaws in market sectors and particular instances of behaviour which frustrate the operation of normal competitive markets. The law addresses structural flaws through the law of competition, so that measures are taken to ensure that in relation to any one product sector no one producer can obtain a near-monopoly position. But the law must also address particular types of behaviour which subvert the operation of a competitive market. The law of duress and undue influence serve to identify those types of behaviour, drawing a boundary for unacceptable anti-competitive practices.

Under Article 78 of the EC Treaty, which is one of the foundations of competition law, an abuse of a dominant market position occurs when a business practice has the effect of reducing or eliminating competition in a particular market. One example is price discrimination by a supplier between different distributors. If the supplier favours one distributor over others by offering lower prices or rebates, this price discrimination has the effect of reducing competition between distributors and is forbidden.[39] Similarly, a refusal to supply an existing customer, thereby making it difficult or impossible for the customer to trade in that market, will be unfair competition.[40] A glaring example will be the refusal by a

---

39 *Hoffman–La Roche v EC Commission*, Case 85/76 [1979] ECR 461, [1979] 3 CMLR 211, ECJ.
40 *Instituto Chemioterapico Italiano SpA and Commercial Solvents v EC Commission*, Case 6/73 [1974] 1 CMLR 309, ECJ.

manufacturer to supply spare parts to a particular distributor or retailer.[41] Notice that, in these instances, a competitive market for the benefit of consumers may not be thwarted. EC law objects to practices which prevent particular businesses from entering markets on equal terms.

The private law of duress and undue influence appears to share a similar purpose. Its objective is to protect businesses and individuals in their freedom to trade. When economic resources are deployed to prevent equal competition, then this anti-competitive practice will be prohibited. Competition law provides an active remedy which permits prevention of such practices. The private law of duress and undue influence serves to invalidate contracts which have been entered into under such conditions of unfair competition.

The strength of this interpretation of the law lies in its ability to account for the design and complexities of the legal doctrines. Firstly, it explains why the law focuses on the behaviour of the stronger party rather than the state of mind of the weaker. This emphasis can be explained as revealing the fundamental concern to protect the integrity of a competitive market against anti-competitive trading practices. The scope of the intervention by private law is determined by a consideration of what types of behaviour are likely to create situations of unfair competition. Secondly, this interpretation explains why the equitable jurisdiction of undue influence extends beyond illegitimate acts. Unacceptable anti-competitive behaviour will include unlawful acts such as torts, but it can extend to more subtle forms of pressure. Thirdly, this interpretation explains why the equitable jurisdiction places such emphasis on the evidence of a manifest disadvantage. The equitable jurisdiction poses the hypothetical question of whether this contract could reasonably have been agreed under competitive conditions. If it could have been concluded on the same terms under competitive conditions, despite the existence of pressures or abuse of confidence the contract does not evidence any advantage having been taken of the anti-competitive behaviour, so it should be permitted to stand as valid.

What this interpretation of the law cannot provide is any sharp line that identifies prohibited types of anti-competitive behaviour. As in the equitable jurisdiction, the law must examine all the facts of the case to determine whether the behaviour effectively secured the result that advantage was taken of an uncompetitive market. It is plainly not sufficient, however, that the parties enjoyed different degrees of bargaining power in the sense of better resources or an advantageous trading position due to possession of some scarce commodity. What is crucial is rather that the superior bargaining position was used to establish the situation of an uncompetitive market, and then that situation was exploited in order to impose a disadvantageous transaction on the other weaker party.

41 *Hugin Kassaregister AB v EC Commission*, Case 22/78 [1979] ECR 1869, [1979] 3 CMLR 345, ECJ.

An interpretation of the doctrines of duress and undue influence in terms of the preservation of competitive markets marks a break from explanations that try to remain faithful to the ideas of the classical law of contract.[42] Instead of attempting to account for the legal doctrines as an elaboration of the idea of the voluntary consent, the doctrines are perceived as serving the function of protecting competitive markets.

---

42 Compare: Birks and Chin, 'On the Nature of Undue Influence', in J Beatson and D Friedmann (eds), *Good Faith and Fault in Contract Law* (Oxford, 1995), ch 3; Bigwood, 'Undue Influence: "Impaired Consent" or "Wicked Exploitation"?' (1996) 16 *Oxford Journal of Legal Studies* 503.

Chapter 9

The moment of responsibility

A. Consenting to contracts

At what point does contractual responsibility arise? The answer given by the classical law is that both parties must consent to the contract. In simple cases, this rule presents no problem. If two persons each sign a contract in the presence of each other, the contract is formed at the moment of the second signature. When the consent must be inferred from conduct with less precise meaning than a signature on a document, however, the exact moment at which contractual responsibility arises may prove more difficult to determine.

Imagine that a person is waiting for a bus at a bus stop. The bus lumbers into view, and the intending passenger waves it down. The doors open, the passenger steps inside, pays the fare, and takes a seat in the interior. At what moment in time was the contract of carriage completed? Payment of the fare clearly evidences consent to the contract, but it is arguable that boarding the bus, and even waving it down, also constitute acts of consent to the contract. Does it matter when the contract is formed? In most cases it does not, but it is not hard to invent problems where the precise timing of the formation of a contract makes a difference. Suppose, for example, that the bus driver failed to stop to pick up the passenger: if the contract was formed by waving the bus down, the driver would have broken the contract of carriage. In another case, suppose that the passenger's shopping is damaged on boarding the bus, perhaps because the door suddenly shuts and squashes a bag of fruit, the question of a possible claim for damages would be governed by the contract of carriage if the contract had been formed, or by the ordinary law of negligence in tort if it had not.

To decide when consent has been given by both parties to a contract, the authors of traditional contract textbooks devised an intricate set of rules employing the concepts of offer and acceptance to fix the moment of responsibility. These rules typify the formalist qualities of classical law: they are detailed, technical and mysterious, yet claim logical derivation from the idea of agreement. Judges quickly appreciated the rigour of this analytical framework, and in the nineteenth century they adopted most of the terminology from the textbooks. They would approach the question of when the contract of carriage had been formed in the above example by asking whether the bus company had made an offer, and if so, when the offer had been accepted by the passenger. In some instances this formulation of the issue can be helpful, as in the case where one person offers to sell his car and the other says 'I accept your offer'. But in the example of the bus passenger, the words 'offer and acceptance' are not employed, so clearly a court must attach these concepts to the facts by reference to further criteria. Even if the words of 'offer and acceptance' are used, they will not inevitably prove determinative, if the court's analysis of the moment of contractual responsibility differs. The fact that the use of the words offer and acceptance is not determinative indicates that the courts use further criteria by which to ascertain the moment of the formation of the contract.

In this chapter we commence by examining the details of the rules of offer and acceptance as they have been developed by the courts and the treatise writers. These rules usually purport to constitute no more than an elaboration of the principle that both parties should consent to an agreement in order to create a contract. Yet the rules of offer and acceptance are not always easy to reconcile with the simple principle of consent, which suggests that these rules are designed to serve other purposes as well.

Furthermore, we will quickly notice that even the formal rules of offer and acceptance are sometimes subverted and ignored. This deviation suggests that, despite the conventional lip-service paid to the rules of offer and acceptance, a court will often determine the moment of contractual responsibility by reference to the practical implications of its decision. In other words, in the example of the bus passenger, the court will determine the moment of contractual responsibility by reference to the effects of its decision on the rights and liabilities of the parties. If the court wishes to discourage bus drivers from passing bus stops with passengers waiting, it can hold that the contract is formed by the passenger waving down the bus. If the court wishes to permit the bus company to be able to rely on its standard form contract which excludes or limits liability for damage to personal possessions, it can hold that the contract was formed when the passenger stepped onto the bus, and not later when he paid his fare. If, on the contrary, the court seeks to avoid the application of the bus company's standard terms of carriage, it can hold that the contract was formed on payment of the fare. In *Wilkie v London Passenger Transport Board*,[1] Lord Greene MR suggested that the contract was concluded when the passenger was fully inside the bus and in a position to pay his fare, which had the effect (at that time) of entitling the bus company to avoid liability for personal injuries. This chapter concentrates upon an exploration of the instrumental purposes which influence the courts' determinations of the moment of formation of contracts.

The chapter concludes with a brief discussion of the sources of legal liability which may arise prior to the formation of a contract. In the case of the bus passenger, for instance, the general duty of care owed under the law of tort can be relied upon as a basis for recovery of damage to goods before the contract has been formed. These sources of pre-contractual responsibility will be considered in greater depth in Chapter 10.

It must be observed at the outset of this discussion, however, that the emphasis upon this issue of the moment of responsibility gives a misleading impression of its importance. In practice, informal understandings are likely to be observed even though the rules of offer and acceptance have not been satisfied. This conformity to implicit understandings is likely to occur for fear of damage to business reputation or loss of future contracts.[2] The withdrawal of an offer in circumstances where it has not yet been accepted although it has been acted upon in some respects may be regarded as bad faith conduct which will be sanctioned by a refusal to deal with that party in the future.[3] These non-legal sanctions will therefore establish a sense of obligation some time prior to the formation of the contract according to the strict legal analysis. Where this gap emerges between the application of the formal legal rules and the informal understanding, then we are likely to discern an attempt by the courts to bridge that gap by employing ideas of pre-contractual responsibility. Whether or not the courts should try to

1   [1947] 1 All ER 258, CA.
2   Lewis, 'Contracts Between Businessmen: Reform of the Law of Firm Offers' (1982) 9 *British Journal of Law and Society* 153.
3   Schultz, 'The Firm Offer Puzzle: A Study of Business Practice in the Construction Industry' (1952) 19 *University Chicago Law Review* 237.

bridge that gap appears to be an issue which divides the classical law with its respect for autonomy and the modern law's commitment to the value of co-operation.[4]

B.   Offer and acceptance

The classical law determines when the parties reach an agreement by imagining that they enact a short scene in which one makes an offer which the other accepts. The parts may be either spoken or mimed, for the offer and acceptance can be written, spoken, or even inferred from conduct. The law requires no special incantations, so the parties may improvise the manner of expression. The opening requires a clear offer, an expression that indicates a willingness to be bound to a particular proposal for a contract. In a commercial context, the offer will almost certainly be preceded by a prologue in which there are invitations to negotiate the contract, or, as lawyers say, an 'invitation to treat'. Once the negotiations have been concluded, an offer is made. The climax of the drama unfolds when one person pronounces his acceptance, for at that moment, precisely, contractual responsibility makes its entrance and seizes both players. Classical theory writes this script as the logical denouement of the principle that an agreement, as the basis of responsibility, is the product of an exercise of will by two parties. When an exercise of will signifies acceptance of the terms of the offer, there is a 'meeting of the minds' or an agreement.

We have already considered the question of what amounts to an act of consent to a contract. Under the objective test of agreement, the words or conduct must be reasonably understood by the other party to signify assent to the contract. The question to be considered here is when do those manifestations of consent coalesce into a binding agreement? The answer lies according to classical analysis when an acceptance is given to an offer.

1.   The test of acceptance – key rules

Three key rules determine which significations of consent succeed in forming a contract. These rules define three qualities of an act of will, which are essential if it is to count as an acceptance.

(a)   CORRESPONDENCE

An acceptance must correspond exactly to the terms of the offer. Accordingly, a purported acceptance containing terms which differ from the original offer fails to create contractual responsibility.

---

4   Charney, 'Nonlegal Sanctions in Commercial Relationships' (1990) 104 *Harvard Law Review* 373, at p 449.

At most, the purported acceptance constitutes another offer, a counter-offer, to make a contract on different terms. A counter-offer also has the effect of terminating the original offer, so that it can no longer be accepted.[5] In *Gibson v Manchester City Council*,[6] it will be recalled that the city treasurer wrote to the claimant stating that the City may be prepared to sell his rented council house to the claimant for £2,180. The House of Lords decided that the treasurer's letter did not even constitute an offer of sale because of its guarded terms. In the Court of Appeal, the majority had decided that a binding contract had been formed because the parties were agreed on all material terms. In a dissenting judgment, Geoffrey Lane LJ held that no contract had been formed because the claimant, instead of accepting the treasurer's offer immediately, had in fact written a counter-offer of a lower price to take into account repairs needed to the house, which was rejected by the treasurer. It was only later that the claimant had purported to accept the treasurer's original offer, by which time the claimant's counter-offer had annulled it, so there was no subsisting offer from the treasurer for the claimant to accept.

This rule, stated bluntly, has the implication that under English law even a minor suggested alteration in the terms for the contract turns what purports to be an acceptance into a counter-offer, thereby preventing a contract from arising.[7] If, for example, the modification concerns not the price of goods, but merely an alteration by the buyer of the place where they are to be delivered, a strict application of the rule would lead to the conclusion that no contract is formed unless the counter-offer is itself accepted. But this technicality might not be observed if the modification appears minor, unobjectionable, and immaterial to the seller of the goods. Some judges would certainly hold there to be a contract despite the absence of a formal acceptance of the counter-offer, provided that the modification was not so material that it would affect the price.[8] Alternatively, the seller's action of sending the goods to the buyer's chosen location could be treated as an act of consent to the modified terms to be inferred from conduct.[9]

(b) NEXUS

An acceptance must be in response to an offer. Unless the offeree knows that an offer has been made, and attempts to accept it, no agreement takes place. For example, if a person supplies information to the police leading to the apprehension of a person for whom a reward has been offered, the reward may

5 *Hyde v Wrench* (1840) 3 Beav 334, 49 ER 132, Rolls Court.
6 [1978] 2 All ER 583, [1978] 1 WLR 520, CA; revsd [1979] 1 All ER 972, [1979] 1 WLR 294, HL.
7 Compare: Uniform Laws on International Sales Act 1967, Sch 2, para 7.
8 For example Lord Denning MR in *Butler Machine Tool Co Ltd v Ex-Cell-O Corpn (England) Ltd* [1979] 1 All ER 965, [1979] 1 WLR 401, CA.
9 *Brogden v Metropolitan Rly Co* (1877) 2 App Cas 666, HL.

only be claimed by the informant if he is aware of the offer of the reward. Similarly, the balance of legal authority holds that two offers, identical in their terms, made at the same time or which cross in the post, will not create a contract, because neither offer counts as an informed acceptance of the other.[10] The justification for this rule commonly given is that, without an acceptance of a known offer, neither party can be sure whether the other regards himself as being bound.

(c) COMMUNICATION

An acceptance must be communicated to the offeror. Thus a mere intention to agree to an offer does not create responsibility: the offeror must be informed of the acceptance of his offer. This rule must be interpreted with two important qualifications in mind. First, because the courts will infer consent from conduct, an acceptance can be constituted by conduct which comes to the attention of the offeror, such as part performance of the contract.[11] Secondly, the offeror has the power to specify in the offer the manner in which acceptance must be made. This right gives the offeror both the power to insist upon strict observance of an elaborate procedure, such as the requirement that any acceptance must be received by a particular method of transmission at a particular time and place,[12] but also the power to weaken the requirement of communication of acceptance to vanishing point. These qualifications were combined in *Carlill v Carbolic Smoke Ball Co*.[13] Under the terms of the offer in the newspaper, acceptance was constituted by the purchase and use of the smokeball according to the manufacturer's instructions. Compliance with this condition therefore counted as acceptance, for the performance evidenced consent, and the requirement of communication had been waived by the terms of the offer.

2. Justification of the rules

Whilst these three rules defining the concept of an acceptance purport to be derived from the principle that agreement generates responsibility, when we examine them closely, the connection between the rules and this justification appears weak. Although the first rule requiring correspondence does make sense as a requirement dictated by the need for agreement, since it ensures that the parties are intending to contract on the same terms, the second and third rules,

10 *Tinn v Hoffman* (1873) 29 LT 271, Ct of Exch Ch.
11 *Brogden v Metropolitan Rly Co* (1877) 2 App Cas 666, HL; *Robophone Facilities Ltd v Blank* [1966] 3 All ER 128, [1966] 1 WLR 1428, CA.
12 *Holwell Securities Ltd v Hughes* [1974] 1 All ER 161, [1974] 1 WLR 155, CA; *Manchester Diocesan Council for Education v Commercial and General Investments Ltd* [1969] 3 All ER 1593, [1970] 1 WLR 241, Ch.
13 [1893] 1 QB 256, CA.

concerning nexus and communication, make it abundantly clear that an agreement is not created by a shared intention, or a meeting of minds. The rules require not simply agreement in fact, and not only conduct evidencing consent, but also conduct which both evidences that the consent was induced by the offer of the other party and which has been drawn to the other party's attention.

What is the purpose of these additional rules, if it is not to ensure that the parties have reached agreement? The underlying purpose of the rules governing acceptance is to determine the moment at which both parties can rely upon the existence of a binding contract between them. On the basis of this reliance, either may then incur expenditure in preparing for, or actually performing, the agreement. They may also forgo other opportunities to make contracts, believing that they are now bound by the contract. Goods may be withdrawn from sale, or a person may desist in seeking employment for his or her services. The rules governing acceptance of contracts determine at which point it is reasonable to act in these various ways in reliance upon the binding contract. They also transfer the risk of that reliance to the other party, so that if that other party breaks the contract, he or she will incur liability for any wasted expenditure or forgone opportunities. On this analysis of the test of acceptance, therefore, the fundamental issue is not whether or not there is agreement between the parties, but whether or not the negotiations and conduct have reached such a point that both parties can reasonably suppose that the other is committed to the contract so that it can be relied upon.

This analysis explains why proof of agreement, in fact, is not crucial to the decision whether or not the moment of contractual responsibility has been reached. The courts can decline to find a contract in circumstances which indicate a shared intention to carry out a transaction without any observable action of acceptance. This is true in the instance of cross-offers. It is also true in the case where the offeree first makes a counter-offer, and then purports to accept the original offer: the parties may be in agreement, but, in the light of the history of the negotiations, the courts regard this as an unsafe basis on which to claim that reliance upon a binding contract was reasonable. Similarly, in *Felthouse v Bindley*,[14] the claimant wrote to his nephew offering to buy his horse for £30 15s, saying, 'If I hear no more about him, I consider the horse mine at that price.' The nephew failed to reply to this letter, although he instructed an auctioneer to withdraw the horse from a forthcoming sale of his stock. The Court of Common Pleas found that no contract had been formed, insisting that direct and unequivocal evidence of acceptance is essential for contractual liability. Although the facts of the case revealed that the parties were in fact in agreement, the court could not accept that it was reasonable for the uncle to assume so without a further communication from the nephew.

14 (1862) 11 CBNS 869.

The differing decisions of the courts in *Gibson v Manchester City Council* illustrate this function of the rules of offer and acceptance most clearly. Lord Denning MR in the Court of Appeal was probably correct to say that the parties were agreed on all the material terms of the proposed sale of the council house. But he was mistaken to infer from this agreement that the moment of contractual responsibility had been reached. He slipped into the error of thinking that the test of the moment of contractual responsibility is when the parties have reached agreement, yet the test imposes additional hurdles such as communication of the acceptance, because its function is to determine at what point it is reasonable for both parties to rely upon the existence of a binding legal commitment. Mr Gibson had jumped the gun in believing that he had a binding legal commitment from the council, for it had not formally accepted his offer, even though it no doubt intended to do so. What the technical rules governing acceptance seek to achieve is to determine the moment of time at which it is reasonable to act in reliance upon the existence of a binding legal contract, not merely to ascertain whether in fact the parties were in agreement.

Exponents of the classical theory of contract were aware that the rules governing acceptance created a problem for their analysis of contract rules based upon agreement. The rules governing acceptance occasionally produced the result that, despite the parties being in agreement in fact, there was no contract. They attempted to explain this disparity by reference to the problem of proving intent or will. The need to communicate acceptance was regarded as a necessary element in the proof of consent, 'for the devil himself knows not the thought of man'.[15] As well as being theologically suspect, this response is unconvincing, for the rules about nexus and communication can prevent the formation of a contract, even though the evidence based upon proven observable facts points unambiguously towards the conclusion that the parties were in agreement. This was the position in *Felthouse v Bindley*, where the nephew had withdrawn the horse from auction and told the auctioneer that it had been sold, leaving little doubt that he believed himself to be bound by a contract with his uncle. This disparity between the tests of acceptance and the foundational principle of agreement in classical law therefore leads writers such as Anson to doubt decisions like *Felthouse v Bindley*, insisting that 'there seems to be no convincing reason why a contract should not come into existence', given that intention could be proven.[16]

The function of the rules governing acceptance is therefore not to serve as an evidentiary device. This function is already performed by the rules governing consent and the inference of consent from conduct. The rules of acceptance mark the point at which reliance can be placed upon the existence of a binding contract

---

15 Brian CJ, *Anon* (1477), YB Pasch 17 Edw IV, f 1, pl 2.; this dictum was frequently repeated in formation of contract cases in the nineteenth century: eg *Brogden v Metropolitan Rly Co* (1877) 2 App Cas 666, per Lord Blackburn.

16 This verdict has been preserved by the editors: J Beatson, *Anson's Law of Contract* (Oxford, 28th edn, 2002), p 48.

between the parties. The requirement of nexus follows logically from that purpose, because it cannot be reasonable to rely upon the existence of a contract between the parties if one is unaware of the other's offer. The general requirement of communication of acceptance makes sense as marking the point in time when both parties are likely to be aware that the other is now reasonably relying upon the existence of a contract between them. It is also clear, however, that the offeror may dispense with the requirement of communication of acceptance, if he or she is content to assume the risk of liability under the contract without notification of acceptance, as in the case of *Carlill v Carbolic Smoke Ball Co*. One can consistently claim, therefore, that the source of contractual responsibility lies in an exercise of will or an agreement, and at the same time maintain that the moment of responsibility is deferred until both parties know of the agreement. The classical lawyers, however, resisted this separation of the issues of ascription of responsibility and the moment of responsibility, and consequently failed to mount an adequate defence against the criticism that the rules defining the concept of acceptance do not conform to the principle that basis of responsibility lies in agreement or consent.

3. Avoidance of the rules

The problem which these well-established rules governing acceptance present to the courts is that, from time to time, they support the view that the moment of responsibility has been reached even though, under the normal tests of acceptance, some element is missing. To justify the conclusion that a contract was formed, the courts have two choices. Either they may subvert the three rules of acceptance, and maintain that a contract was formed despite the failure to comply with one or more of the rules: to achieve this result, they must adopt a surprising view of the facts of the case, in order to bring them into conformity with the rules. Alternatively, the courts may alter the category of the legal analysis, choosing to impose a different form of liability in order to compensate the misplaced reliance.

(a) TWISTING THE FACTS

Under the first method of judicial avoidance, the court pays lip-service to the rules of acceptance, but it is hard to see how the facts of the case can satisfy those rules. This has often been the problem, for instance, in cases known as the 'battle of forms', where the court must strive to fit the facts under the correspondence rule. Businesspersons prefer to make contracts on their own standard terms of business for the sake of simplicity and efficiency. Between two such persons, even after a number of exchanges of offers, quotations, tenders, invoices, orders and so forth, it is possible that they will have failed to achieve a coincidence of offer and acceptance because of the incompatibility of their respective standard terms. Nevertheless, the courts strive to impose contractual responsibility once performance has commenced, since it seems reasonable at that point to transfer the risk of reliance upon the contract; but this result compels the court to ignore the first rule of correspondence.

Such a flaunting of the rule happened in *Butler Machine Tool Co v Ex-Cell-O Corpn (England) Ltd*.[17] The claimant offered to manufacture and deliver a machine tool for £75,535 on two conditions, which were that orders were accepted only on the terms set out in the quotation and, secondly, that a price variation clause should apply whereby the defendant would be charged at the prices ruling at the date of delivery. The defendant then placed an order including its own terms and conditions which contained no price variation clause. The order had a tear-off acknowledgment for signature, which accepted the order on the terms it contained. The seller signed and returned the acknowledgment with a covering letter stating that delivery was to be in accordance with the terms of the original quotation. On delivery of the machine tool, the seller invoked the price variation clause and charged an extra £2,892. The English Court of Appeal denied the seller's claim for the extra sum, holding that the return of the signed acknowledgment form on the buyer's terms which excluded any price variation constituted the binding contract. Yet this conclusion is evidently artificial,[18] for the covering letter made it plain that the price variation clause contained in the original quotation was intended to remain part of the agreement. In truth, the parties never reached an agreement which satisfied the requirement of correspondence, for each purported acceptance really constituted a counter-offer. The court adeptly excluded a part of the written evidence in order to bring the facts under the established rules of acceptance. This achieved the result of confirming that a contract had been formed, a conclusion which the court no doubt believed was warranted because of the extent of the reliance upon the contract by both parties.

The courts similarly manipulate facts to fit the rule concerning the nexus of agreement, and perhaps even ignore it. For example, many cases involving a claim for a reward succeed, even though the claimant cannot establish that he intended to accept the offer because he was unaware of it.[19] Sometimes courts will interpret the events in such a way that the informant is presumed to have heard of the reward moments before supplying the information. Another technique involves interpreting the terms of the offer to apply whether or not the informant was motivated by knowledge of the reward. Many judges simply ignore the nexus rule completely, encouraged perhaps by the belief that an informant, who acted in an exemplary fashion and without mercenary motives, should be able to recover the

---

17 [1979] 1 All ER 965, [1979] 1 WLR 401, CA.
18 P Atiyah, *An Introduction to the Law of Contract* (Oxford, 5th edn, 1995), p 67.
19 Eg *Gibbons v Proctor* (1891) 64 LT 594; Hudson, 'Gibbons v Proctor Revisited' (1968) 84 *Law Quarterly Review* 503.

reward as payment for his services even though he was ignorant of the offer. Of course, these decisions infuriate and torment the classical theorists. Listen to the outraged Anson:

> One who does an act for which a reward has been offered, in ignorance of the offer, cannot say either that there was a *consensus* of wills between him and the offeror, or that his conduct was affected by the promise offered. On no view of contract could he set up a right of action.[20]

Anson dismisses cases to the contrary as uncertain on their facts, or simply wrong. Other writers list a number of special cases or exceptions which do not fit the general rule. As the list of exceptions to the requirement of nexus lengthens, or the dogmatic assertions of judicial error multiply, one is entitled to doubt whether the courts really accept the importance of the nexus rule as a determinant of the formation of contractual responsibility.

Of the three rules, the last one concerning the requirement of communication of the acceptance retains perhaps the shakiest hold on judicial practice. The courts can infer that the acceptance has been communicated from any conduct which is referable to a concluded contract and comes to the notice of the offeror. In *Brogden v Metropolitan Rly Co*,[21] after negotiations between the parties, the railway company sent a requirements contract to the coal merchant. The latter signed the agreement after making some alterations and returned it. The company's agent then put the document in a drawer. Both parties subsequently acted upon the agreement by ordering and supplying coal. The coal merchant's alterations of the document turned it into a counter-offer, and so at first sight the company had never communicated its acceptance by simply putting it into a drawer. Nevertheless, the House of Lords held that a contract had been concluded by virtue of the subsequent orders for, and delivery of, coal. In effect the courts are prepared to look at later events and the conduct of the parties in order to determine whether a contract was formed, sliding over the logical difficulty that subsequent conduct cannot prove that the original acceptance was ever communicated.

A celebrated source of difficulty with the requirement of communication of acceptance involves contracts concluded by post. Acceptance of a contract by post is permissible unless the offeror specifies a contrary method or it is not reasonable in the circumstances. It will not be reasonable usually if the offer is made by a method of instantaneous communication, such as telephone, fax or electronic mail, in which case a court will normally regard it as only reasonable to reply by using a similar instantaneous medium. An acceptance by one of these instantaneous methods of communication will therefore only conclude the

20 W Anson, *Principles of the Law of Contract* (Oxford, 10th edn, 1903), p 23; (Oxford, 28th edn, J Beatson, 2002), pp 48–49.
21 (1877) 2 App Cas 666, HL.

contract when it is received by the offeror.[22] Assuming, however, a postal acceptance is reasonable, at what point in time is the contract concluded? Under the third rule requiring communication of acceptance, one would expect the English rule to be that the letter has to be received by the offeror. Since the early part of the nineteenth century, however, the courts have followed the anomalous rule that the acceptance is complete when it is posted.[23] The justification for this anomaly was said to be that the Post Office acted as the agent for the offeror, so in effect the posting of the letter of acceptance simultaneously constituted receipt by the authorized agent of the offeror.[24] This fits the facts into the rule requiring communication of acceptance, but at the price of considerable distortion, for if the Post Office acts as an agent for sending and receiving communications at all, which seems improbable because it does not otherwise act like an employee of the parties, it is surely the agent of the offeree who pays for the service rather than the offeror.

The central difficulty in these cases of postal acceptance is to identify a moment at which it is reasonable for both parties to be able to rely upon a concluded contract. In favour of selecting the moment at the time of posting the letter, it can be said that from that time onward the offeree cannot alter his mind and will reasonably suppose that the letter will reach its destination and so conclude the contract.[25] Against this view it can be argued that until the offeror receives the letter, he cannot act in reliance upon the conclusion of the contract; moreover, if the letter goes astray or is misdirected, the offeror may only learn of the conclusion of the contract when he has irretrievably harmed his own position.[26] In favouring the former solution, the courts appear to have decided that an offeror who is prepared to accept the risk of a postal acceptance without protecting himself in the terms of the offer, should also take the risk of misdirection or loss of letters, which is a harsh conclusion given that the failure to communicate the acceptance may prove to be the offeree's fault. The lesson has, however, been learned by offerors, who normally specify a requirement of communication of the acceptance in the terms of an offer, which prevents the postal rule from operating.[27]

The question has been raised, but not yet answered by the courts, of when contracts are made during transactions on the Internet. In particular, does the anomalous postal rule apply as a default provision to e-mails?[28] Some of these purchases are formed by e-mail, which operates like a letter, since the medium is

22 *Entores Ltd v Miles Far East Corpn* [1955] 2 QB 327, [1955] 2 All ER 493, CA.
23 *Adams v Lindsell* (1818) 1 B & Ald 681.
24 Eg Thesiger LJ, *Household Fire Insurance Co v Grant* (1879) 4 Ex D 216, CA.
25 *Brogden v Metropolitan Rly Co* (1877) 2 App Cas 666, HL, per Lord Blackburn.
26 See Bramwell LJ in *Household Fire Insurance Co v Grant* (1879) 4 Ex D 216, CA.
27 Eg *Holwell Securities Ltd v Hughes* [1974] 1 All ER 161, [1974] 1 WLR 155, CA.
28 Murray, 'Entering Into Contracts Electronically: The Real W.W.W.', in L Edwards and C Waelde, *Law & The Internet: A Framework for Electronic Commerce* (Oxford, 2000), p 17.

not instantaneous, although usually very quick, and also e-mails sometimes go astray. But a more common method today of transacting on the Internet is on-line instantaneous completion of a form followed by pressing or clicking on the 'Submit' button. In practice, traders who use the Internet usually try to safeguard their position by stating that the contract is only concluded when they acknowledge the customer's order (thereby rendering the order an offer, and the acknowledgement an acceptance). The EC Directive on Electronic Commerce, however, requires that a business should acknowledge receipt of a consumer's order by electronic means and that the consumer only receives this acknowledgement when the consumer can access it.[29] This provision does not expressly state a rule for determining the moment of contractual responsibility, although perhaps it implies that no binding contract is concluded until the consumer can access the acknowledgement of the receipt. In the UK, however, the implementing regulations merely give consumers the right to cancel the contract for breaches of the regulations and prevent businesses from enforcing contracts in the event of significant breaches of the rules.[30] This cancellation right implies that the contract has been formed even without the acknowledgement of the trader, thereby suggesting that the consumer's action of clicking on the 'Submit' button or sending an e-mail completes the formation of the contract by acceptance.

(b)   NEW CATEGORIES OF LIABILITY

The drama of offer and acceptance, as it is recounted in the classical texts, takes as its paradigm a series of oral negotiations leading to an express agreement between the parties. As the facts of cases move beyond this paradigm, as in the case of postal communications, or promises which induce reliance, the courts are forced to make the choice between twisting the facts to fit them into the rules, or to recognize new categories of liability for which the formal rules of offer and acceptance do not apply.

The most important example of this latter technique concerns unilateral contracts. Living in a hybrid world between the exchange model and the reliance model of contractual enforceability, these contracts are valid despite the absence of conduct which satisfies the rules of acceptance. Although it is possible to say in *Carlill v Carbolic Smoke Ball Co* that the company waived its right to have acceptance of its offer communicated to it, this is an artificial way of reconciling unilateral contracts with the rules of acceptance. It is better to recognize that the courts can use the category of unilateral contract when they believe that the moment of contractual responsibility has been reached even though there was no communication of acceptance. This device is frequently employed in commercial contexts to overcome the problem that in networks of contracts between several

29 EC Directive 2000/31/EC on Electronic Commerce, Art 11.
30 Electronic Commerce Regulations 2002, SI 2002/2013, reg 15.

parties there may not be any direct communication between the parties in dispute, or indeed any precise knowledge of the terms of any offer, with the effect under the rules of acceptance of preventing the conclusion of any contract. But a unilateral contract between parties who have never communicated may be discovered from an offer which is acted upon.[31] This device was used, for example, in *New Zealand Shipping Co Ltd v Satterthwaite & Co Ltd (The Eurymedon)*,[32] so that a contract was formed between the owner of goods and the stevedores who unloaded them, even though they had never communicated with each other, but in fact made separate contracts with the carrier of the goods.

As well as unilateral contracts, the courts can also utilise upon the reliance model of contractual liability, by holding the parties estopped from denying contractual responsibility. This technique can overcome the problem of the absence of a communication of an acceptance when one party is induced to act to his detriment by the acts of the other, even though those acts cannot be characterized as a communication of the acceptance. This was the technique employed by the High Court of Australia in *Waltons Stores (Interstate) Ltd v Maher*,[33] in order to overcome the problem that no formal acceptance of the contract had ever been sent, and no acceptance could be inferred from conduct in the circumstances. Nevertheless, there were acts and omissions which led the other party to believe that he could reasonably rely upon the contract being concluded.

C. Instrumentalism

Even where the traditional rules of offer and acceptance are applied, it is apparent from our earlier examples – such as that of the bus passenger – that the facts do not conveniently label themselves as 'offers' and 'acceptances'. On the contrary, a hidden element of discretion permits the courts to label the facts with the terminology of offer and acceptance, whenever they believe it is fair and reasonable to impose contractual liability.

Consider, for example, the purchase of goods in a self-service store. At what point is an agreement completed by an acceptance? Does the customer accept the offer when he or she places the goods in the wire basket? Or does acceptance take place when the customers present the goods to the assistant at the cash register? Alternatively, we can even argue that the assistant accepts the offer to buy by ringing up the prices of the goods on the cash register. Or is that merely an offer, accepted by the customer by the presentation of the right amount of money? Since each interpretation is plausible, a court must make a discretionary choice between them, concealing the real grounds for the decision by the formalist

31 *Clarke v Earl of Dunraven* [1897] AC 59, HL.
32 [1975] AC 154, [1974] 1 All ER 1015, PC.
33 (1988) 164 CLR 387, Aust HC.

reasoning of offer and acceptance. In this brief section we cannot hope to identify all the relevant considerations which a court takes into account. Instead we will illustrate the surprising variety of such considerations in order to reveal the complexity of the issues.

The variety of potentially relevant considerations emerges with a brief review of conflicting decisions from different jurisdictions concerning the moment of formation of a contract of sale in a self-service store. Sometimes the courts desire to make the moment of responsibility as late as possible, in order to avoid making the customer liable to pay for the goods before he or she has had a chance to inspect them and compare the price between different brands. Courts encourage this consumer circumspection by holding that the customer forms the contract by presenting the goods at the cash register.[34] In contrast, in other cases courts insist that the parties enter a contract when the customer places the goods in the wire basket, if for instance this result strengthens the legal position of a customer injured by a bottle exploding as it is placed in the basket.[35] The relative advantage to a customer of being allowed a contractual claim against the shopkeeper for personal injuries depends upon the state of the law of tort governing the liability of owners of premises towards those injured upon them, so courts in different jurisdictions react in the light of the background law applicable to personal injuries.

Another reason for deferring the moment of acceptance emerges in cases involving charges of shoplifting. If the customer completes the contract when he or she removes goods from the shelf, the shoplifter could defend himself or herself against a charge of theft by arguing that he or she had purchased the goods before taking them from the store. Of course, the shoplifter would in these circumstances be liable to pay the price of the goods, and might also be guilty of another criminal offence involving fraud. But the shoplifter would avoid liability for theft if the contract is formed by taking the goods from the shelf, for logically one cannot steal goods which belong to oneself as a result of a contractual purchase. For this reason, the court is likely to defer the moment of formation of the contract until the goods have been paid for.

These conflicting considerations which influence the determination of the moment of contractual responsibility in a simple case of supermarket purchases explain why courts reach such different results. They also illustrate how difficult it is to anticipate all the relevant considerations. Further complications are introduced in the leading English case, which illustrates how special statutory provisions give added legal significance to a particular result. In *Pharmaceutical Society of Great Britain v Boots Cash Chemists*,[36] the self-service store was required to demonstrate that it satisfied a statutory requirement that all sales of certain

34 *Lasky v Economy Grocery Stores* 65 NE 2d 305 (Supreme Court of Mass, 1946).
35 *Sancho-Lopez v Fedor Food Corpn* 211 NYS 2d 953 (1961) (City Court, New York).
36 [1953] 1QB 401, [1953] 1 All ER 482, CA.

non-prescription drugs should be made under the supervision of a registered pharmacist. The store argued that it complied with the statute by posting a pharmacist in the vicinity of the cash register, as opposed to stationing one near all the display shelves. The Court of Appeal facilitated the development of self-service pharmacies, and incidentally reduced the need for registered pharmacists whose professional body had commenced the action, by concluding that customers made contracts of sale at the cash register and therefore the store complied with the law. The reason given by the court for its decision was simply one of permitting customers to inspect the goods and change their minds in the shop. But one wonders also how impressed the court was by the desire of the pharmacists to retain their restrictive practices, although this consideration was not explicitly acknowledged.

Whilst this discussion of the self-service store demonstrates how difficult it is to list in advance all the policy considerations which influence the determination of the moment of contractual responsibility, we can identify some of the factors which frequently weigh heavily in the exercise of judicial discretion. Lord Wilberforce has acknowledged the balancing process at the heart of this determination of the moment of contractual responsibility when he remarked that:

> No universal rule can cover all such cases: they must be resolved by reference to the intentions of the parties, by sound business practice and in some cases by a judgment where the risks should lie.[37]

The following list comprises the most popular considerations acknowledged by courts in commercial contexts.

1.   Room for manoeuvre

Courts recognize that negotiations may be carried out over a considerable period of time without any binding commitment being assumed by either party. These exploratory discussions perform a valuable service, for the parties become better informed about the details of the transaction, and they resolve possible ambiguities. They also use this period of time to consider alternatives, and to check up on the reliability of the other party. In a typical building contract, for example, the investor seeks tenders from a number of contractors, and only when all the bids have been considered will one particular contractor be selected. The investor will obviously be attracted to the least expensive bid, but on closer scrutiny may decide to select another more conscientious and skilled contractor. The courts examine these cases with a disposition towards granting both parties room for manoeuvre, although naturally this licence must not be abused by the

---

37 *Brinkibon Ltd v Stahag Stahl GmbH* [1983] 2 AC 34, [1982] 1 All ER 293, HL.

kind of sharp practice where one party leads another on by letting the other believe that a binding commitment has been, or shortly will be, made.

The courts employ a variety of conceptual tools to effectuate this policy. At the simplest level, the court reaches a conclusion on the basis of whether or not an acceptance was made, although this determination will depend upon the court's judgment of whether the offeror was genuinely seeking room for manoeuvre. Sometimes the courts adopt a more elaborate conceptual structure. In the example of a building contract described above, courts normally characterize the investor's request for tenders as 'an invitation to treat' rather than an offer, and regard the tenders placed by building contractors as offers, leaving the selection of a contractor as the acceptance which forms the contract. A similar analysis works for the purchase of goods in a self-service store, where the courts preserve the customer's freedom for manoeuvre by characterizing the display of goods on the shelves not as an offer but as an invitation to treat. A third technique for delaying the moment of responsibility denies legal enforcement to uncertain agreements. A vague agreement can be valid provided that a court can infer that the parties intended to supplement their informal understanding according to the normal terms of the trade. But where the parties deliberately leave open terms for future negotiation, thereby exhibiting a desire to preserve their freedom for manoeuvre, a court will decline to enforce this uncompleted agreement on the ground of uncertainty.[38]

2. Discouragement of opportunism

The courts prevent manipulation of the time at which the parties reach an acceptance in order to stop one party from exploiting alterations in market price to his or her advantage. In the simplest example, a seller may discover after making an offer to sell at a fixed price that the market price for the goods has risen. The policy of the courts is to disallow revocation of the offer where the purchaser has already taken steps to indicate completion of the bargain, in order to prevent the seller from gaining an advantage. Courts carry out this policy through the terminology of offer and acceptance, although at the cost of a further distortion of the underlying principles of responsibility.

The courts place obstacles in the way of revocation of offers, so that they may conclude that the acceptance was completed prior to the revocation of the offer. In particular, the courts adopt the rule that the offeror must communicate any revocation of an offer to the offeree. In *Byrne & Co v Leon van Tienhoven & Co*[39] the defendant posted a letter from Cardiff to New York offering to sell 1,000 boxes of tinplates at a fixed price. Before the letter reached New York, the defendant posted a revocation of the offer, explaining that there had been, 'a regular panic in

38 *Courtney & Fairbairn Ltd v Tolaini Bros (Hotels) Ltd* [1975] 1 All ER 716, [1975] 1 WLR 297, CA.
39 (1880) 5 CPD 344.

the tinplate market during the last few days, which has caused prices to run up about twenty-five per cent'. The claimant in New York accepted the offer by post when it arrived, and only later received the revocation of the offer. Lindley J held that the revocation of the offer was inoperative until it was communicated to the claimant, so the claimant had successfully accepted the offer according to the postal acceptance rule described above. This result prevented the offeror from waiting to see which way the market moved, in order to choose whether or not to go forward with the transaction.

The rule that a revocation of an offer must be communicated cannot be squared with the theory that contracts are created by agreement, for clearly the offeror no longer intends to make the agreement once he tries to withdraw his offer. In his judgment, Lindley J acknowledges this problem, but argues that under the principles of the common law, 'a state of mind not notified cannot be regarded in dealings between man and man'. Of course, he promptly ignores this justification by applying the rule that the letter of acceptance completes the transaction when it is posted, not when it arrives in the hands of the offeror. Given this inconsistency, it is better to admit that the policy behind the rule that revocations of offers have to be communicated is one which discourages offerors from taking advantage of market fluctuations retrospectively.

3. Partial performance

The courts hesitate to conclude that no contract was ever formed when one party has partially performed his side of the bargain. This policy is even more insistent when performance has been completed. We have already noticed one example of this policy being applied in the 'battle of forms' cases. The same policy applies to partial performance of unilateral contracts. In the classic statement of the problem, the offeror promises to pay a sum of money if another walks from London to York. Can the offeror revoke his offer once the walker has set out on his journey? According to the logic of the rules of offer and acceptance, performance of the contract constitutes acceptance by the offeree, but, until the walker completes performance, he has not accepted the offer, and so no contractual responsibility arises. This result causes injustice where the walker has travelled a substantial proportion of the journey. The courts therefore strive to find a means to invalidate the revocation of the offer. One way to achieve this result involves the finding of a collateral contract, under which the offeror promises to keep the offer open until the journey has been completed or abandoned.[40] Another analysis suggests that the walker accepts the offer prior to setting out on his journey, thereby transforming a unilateral contract into a bilateral one. Sometimes courts simply insist that the offer cannot be revoked

40 *Errington v Errington and Woods* [1952] 1 KB 290, [1952] 1 All ER 149, CA.

once the offeree has embarked upon performance,[41] which has the merit of being straightforward, although once again it creates an exception to the idea that contractual responsibility is based upon consent. Whichever method the courts adopt, however, the policy remains the same: to provide the protection of contractual rights to a party who partially performs an anticipated contract.

4. Protection of ancillary reliance

Ancillary reliance involves acts of expenditure incurred in anticipation of the formation of a contract, or as a result of a mistaken belief in the existence of a contract, where this expenditure does not count as partial performance of the anticipated contract. Where such detrimental reliance has taken place, the courts may lean towards the discovery of contractual responsibility. In *Gibson v Manchester City Council*[42] Lord Denning relied upon the ancillary reliance of the purchaser of the council house, who had effected repairs and improvements to the property, in order to justify his conclusion that a contract had been formed. The difficulty of this reasoning is that the court cannot easily infer acceptance of an offer from the conduct, since it does not comprise partial performance. For this reason, the protection of ancillary reliance will often have to be achieved by means of some different category of contractual liability, such as estoppel under the reliance model.

In the leading American authority, *Drennan v Star Paving Co*,[43] a general contractor, in preparing a tender for building work, relied to his detriment upon a mistaken bid from a specialist sub-contractor for a portion of the work. The California Supreme Court held that, despite the absence of agreement, the sub-contractor's bid was binding, because it was reasonably foreseeable that it would be relied upon by the general contractor. Once this principle is admitted into the law, it provides a means for effecting the policy of protecting ancillary reliance without any distortion of the traditional rules of offer and acceptance. Whilst the American courts have followed this course, English courts have preferred to manipulate and distort the classical rules in order to achieve the same result.

By listing these policy considerations which influence the courts in determining the moment of contractual responsibility, we have inevitably touched upon only a small proportion of the relevant considerations. Our aim, however, has not been to supply a complete list, but rather to indicate some of the most common policy factors. We have also noticed that these policies often conflict and that the courts must balance the rival considerations in each case. The important point to grasp is

41 *Daulia Ltd v Four Millbank Nominees Ltd* [1978] Ch 231, [1978] 2 All ER 557, CA.
42 [1978] 2 All ER 583, [1978] 1 WLR 520, CA.
43 51 Cal 2d 409, 333 P 2d 757 (1958).

that the application of the rules of offer and acceptance involves a seldom acknowledged discretionary judgment in which the competing policies are weighed.

D. Pre-contractual responsibility

In many of the cases which we have considered in this chapter, the doctrinal analysis assumes that either contractual responsibility has arisen, or that the parties have no legal rights against each other at all. In the classical law, prior to the moment of acceptance, the parties owe no voluntarily undertaken duties towards each other. Yet in these situations an equitable solution might be to refuse to create contractual responsibility, but nevertheless provide a measure of compensation in deserving cases for misplaced reliance. This solution might have been appropriate in *Gibson v Manchester City Council*.[44] The claimant could have been compensated for the costs of his repairs to the property without being granted a contractual right to purchase his house. This result would respect the normal freedom of manoeuvre during negotiations, but at the same time satisfy the policy of protecting ancillary reliance. In short, all relevant policies would be satisfied by the adoption of pre-contractual liability, whereas the normal pattern of the common law tends to insist upon the triumph of one policy over the other.

A similar attractive solution presents itself for the problem of the revocation of offers during the course of performance of unilateral contracts. In the case of a man who has walked half-way to York on the strength of an offer to pay him £100 when he reaches the city, pre-contractual responsibility would require the offeror to compensate the walker for his time and trouble until the revocation of the offer, without requiring full payment of £100. Here the policy of compensating partial performance could be satisfied, without undermining the normal freedom to revoke offers entirely.

On the whole, however, the courts have ignored this attractive compromise. The main reason for their reluctance to accept a form of pre-contractual responsibility stems from the sense that such a step would subvert the basic value of freedom to contract which colours the whole theory of individual responsibility. By permitting liabilities to arise before agreement has been reached, the courts sense a danger that this would amount to the imposition of responsibility without consent. This fear is misplaced, for in effect the courts already subvert the value of liberty by determining the moment of responsibility by reference to such considerations as ancillary reliance and partial performance. Even so, the modern law has yet to achieve a coherent doctrinal basis through which the compromise of pre-contractual responsibility could be effectuated.

44 [1979] 1 All ER 972, [1979] 1 WLR 294, HL.

One possible legal category which could be nurtured towards establishing a legal basis for unilateral responsibility prior to the formation of a contract is liability for negligence in tort. Courts could impose a duty of care upon the parties during the course of negotiations. Whenever it could be demonstrated that, through the fault of one party, the other was induced to act to his detriment, a duty to compensate wasted expenditure might arise. As we shall see in Chapter 10, the courts have been edging towards this position. Another possible source for pre-contractual responsibility lies in the development of the reliance model and the doctrine of estoppel. Here, instead of the fact of detrimental reliance grounding full contractual rights as it did in *Drennan v Star Paving Co*, the estoppel technique would merely permit recovery for wasted expenditure. This method was used in the American case *Hoffman v Red Owl Stores Inc*,[45] where the plaintiff wasted large sums of money in anticipation of a franchise agreement which never materialized. His remedy was an award of damages commensurate with his wasted expenditure, not the award of the franchise agreement. No English case precisely replicates this use of estoppel to compensate pre-contractual reliance, but *Crabb v Arun District Council*[46] verges on this result, even though the claimant there was awarded the right of access which he thought he had been promised. In the circumstances, the only sensible way in which the claimant could be compensated for his inaccessible land was the award of a right of access, and the court indicated that they thought that the claimant's loss during the period of inaccessibility was roughly equivalent to the commercial value of the right of access.

Normally, however, common law courts impose pre-contractual responsibility through the law of restitution or unjust enrichment. Where one party confers a benefit upon the other in anticipation of a binding contract, he may recover the value of his work if the contract never materializes. For example, if it emerges after a battle of forms that the parties never reached an agreement prior to performance, each may recover from the other in an action for quantum meruit the value of any property transferred or services performed.[47]

As we shall discover in the next chapter, these cases of tort, estoppel and restitution provide an embryonic form of pre-contractual responsibility for the common law to develop. It certainly makes sense to recognize this compromise source of liability, as many other legal systems do, for it permits a more satisfactory reconciliation of the relevant policies already entertained by the courts.

45 26 Wis 2d 683, 133 NW 2d 267 (1965).
46 [1976] Ch 179, [1975] 3 All ER 865, CA.
47 *British Steel Corpn v Cleveland Bridge and Engineering Co Ltd* [1984] 1 All ER 504, QB.

Chapter 10

The duty to negotiate with care

A.   A general principle?
B.   Misleading statements
        1.   Reasonable reliance
                (a)   Statements of law and contractual terms
                (b)   Statements of future intentions
                (c)   Statements of opinion
        2.   The standard of care
                (a)   Burden of proof
                (b)   Reasonable care
        3.   Remedies
                (a)   Rescission
                (b)   Damages
                (c)   Regulatory offences
                (d)   Administrative injunction
C.   Failure to disclose information
        1.   Disclosure of terms
        2.   Disclosure of facts
                (a)   Misrepresentation
                (b)   Implied terms
                (c)   Regulatory offences
                (d)   Mistaken identity
D.   Abuse of position of trust
        1.   Contracts uberrimae fidei
        2.   Fiduciary relations and relations of trust
E.   Misuse of confidential information
F.   Misleading implied promises
        1.   Collateral contracts
        2.   The reliance model
        3.   Damages
G.   Rationale for the duty to negotiate with care

A.   A general principle?

Prior to the formation of a contract, particularly in a commercial context, lengthy negotiations may take place. During these negotiations, the parties may give explicit or implicit undertakings, and may incur considerable expenditure in anticipation of the concluded contract. As we saw in the previous chapter, the law fixes the moment of contractual responsibility at the time when it is reasonable for the parties to rely upon the existence of a binding contract between them as a result of having reached agreement and having communicated their acknowledgment of the obligation. But prior to that moment, during the negotiations, the law also imposes obligations, which are the topic of this chapter.

The common law has exhibited a persistent reluctance to impose pre-contractual obligations. The main reason for this reluctance is a concern to protect the parties' freedom to choose whether or not to enter a contract. If obligations were to arise as soon as negotiations commence, then parties would discover that they had undertaken obligations unexpectedly and without due deliberation. Moreover, as we discovered in Chapter 9, the law recognizes the need to protect the parties' room for manoeuvre. It permits, for instance, revocation of an offer at any time until the offeree has communicated an acceptance. Exploratory discussions serve many useful purposes, such as permitting individuals to discover all the market opportunities before making any commitment, which will assist the competitiveness of the market. For these reasons, pre-contractual obligations require a justification which has sufficient weight to overcome objections based on the protection of freedom of contract and the efficient operation of the market.

Such justifications can be established, however, in many instances. Where one party lies to another during the negotiations, or carefully conceals some vital information, then this misconduct can be regarded as forfeiting the protection of freedom to contract and as frustrating the operation of market competition. Similarly, where one party deliberately induces another to incur expenditure or to disclose confidential information, without any intention of making a contract, then again we can regard this conduct as an abuse of the freedom to negotiate without incurring obligations. Many other examples will be considered in this chapter where these and analogous reasons justify the imposition of pre-contractual obligations.

Do all these instances of pre-contractual obligations rest upon general principles, or do they represent minor, pragmatic exceptions to the general policy of declining to recognize pre-contractual liabilities? In some legal systems, the codes of contract law declare the existence of a general duty to bargain in good faith.[1] It can be argued that English law, and even more strongly US law, respects

---

1   Eg Italian Civil Code, Art 1337; Israeli Contracts (General Part) Law 1973, s 12(a).

the same principle once all the different strands of pre-contractual obligations are gathered together.[2] But this argument encounters two difficulties.

In the first place, the courts have been reluctant to acknowledge any such general principle, proceeding rather by reference to narrower doctrines such as misrepresentation, undue influence, collateral contracts and equitable estoppel. The results may be similar to other legal systems with an acknowledged principle of good faith in bargaining, but English lawyers have never systematized their particular doctrines under this principle.[3]

The second difficulty for English law concerns the idea of good faith itself. The meaning of the idea is obscure. It tends to function, as Summers suggests,[4] as a negative concept in practice, so that various sorts of conduct are labelled as negotiation in bad faith, without any clarity about the positive duty which is envisaged by the concept. But worse than obscurity, the idea of good faith implies a content to the duty which is far too narrow. In its ordinary legal usage, the standard of good faith requires honesty or conduct which does not deliberately deceive or harm another. It does not include negligent or careless behaviour which has the same effect. But many of the pre-contractual obligations arising under English law, such as the duty not to misrepresent facts, require more than honesty. They require carefulness in giving information, so that reasonable care must be taken to ensure its accuracy. For this reason, the terminology of good faith proves unsatisfactory as an indication of the reach of pre-contractual obligations.

This chapter argues that the sources of pre-contractual obligations can be usefully conceived as deriving from a general principle. The principle serves to bring coherence to a diverse collection of legal doctrines and to bring their weaknesses and anomalies to light. But the principle concerned is better described as a duty to negotiate with care, not one to bargain in good faith. What English law requires of parties is carefulness towards each other during the period of negotiation. The modern law rejects the strong protection for freedom of contract afforded by the absence of pre-contractual obligations, and instead recognizes that some obligations of respect for the interests of others should be

2   Kessler and Fine, 'Culpa in Contrahendo, Bargaining in Good Faith, and Freedom of Contract: A Comparative Study' (1964) 77 *Harvard Law Review* 401; Finn, 'Equity and Contract', in P Finn (ed), *Essays on Contract* (Sydney, 1987), p 104, at p 105; Reiter, 'Good Faith in Contract', (1983) 17 *Valparaiso University Law Review* 705.

3   Bingham LJ in *Interfoto Picture Library Ltd v Stiletto Visual Programmes Ltd* [1989] QB 433, [1988] 1 All ER 348, CA; Bridge, 'Does Anglo-Canadian Contract Law Need a Doctrine of Good faith?' (1984) 9 *Canadian Business Law Journal* 385; Farnsworth, 'Precontractual Liability and Preliminary Agreements: Fair Dealing and Failed Negotiations' (1987) 87 *Columbia Law Review* 217.

4   Summers, 'Good Faith in General Contract Law and the Sales Provision of the Uniform Commercial Code' (1968) 54 *Virginia Law Review* 195

owed during negotiations. There are two principal justifications for the common law to adopt this limited duty of respect for the interests of others during negotiations.

In part these rules serve to protect the operation of a competitive market. False or misleading claims about products and the terms of contracts obstruct competitive markets, for they make it difficult to acquire accurate information about the merits of different opportunities. Moreover, such behaviour will place other traders at a competitive disadvantage unless they also employ deceptive practices, which would escalate the harm to the competitive market.

In addition, the duty of care during negotiations recognises that even in the absence of a concluded contractual relation, the parties may enter a relation of dependence during negotiations where the actions of one party may foreseeably cause economic harm to another unless care is taken. Promises, statements, and conduct may induce the dependent party to act to his detriment, and where this action was one of reasonable reliance upon the promises, statements or other conduct, then the law is likely to impose a duty to compensate for the losses incurred. This duty of care during negotiations fits into the broader scheme of the law of tort where obligations are owed to prevent harm to the interests of others, but it receives a specialized articulation in the context of negotiations towards a contract.

To complement these general justifications for a duty of care during negotiations, the modern law has sought to promote the social market by means of specialized legislative interventions. One important theme of this legislation has been the development of duties imposed upon businesses during negotiations with consumers which aim to educate consumers about the nature of the transaction and the qualities of the products and services on offer. With the sale of a car, for instance, the manufacturer or retailer can be required to supply certain kinds of information about fuel consumption per mile in a standard form. This information enables the consumer to become knowledgeable about a particular product, and thereby make a more rational choice about whether its acquisition fits harmoniously into his or her chosen plan of life.

This chapter considers the diverse doctrinal and legislative sources of this duty to negotiate with care before returning in the conclusion to an examination of the question whether they are united by this general principle. It organizes the materials under brief factual descriptions of the types of conduct which constitute a breach of the duty to negotiate with care.

B.   Misleading statements

The law imposes a duty of care on parties to negotiations for a contract when they make statements to each other. The duty requires that statements of fact are made with reasonable care in the light of the specialized knowledge and expertise of the representor. This duty is broken by making a statement which is false or misleading because insufficient care was taken. The breach of duty can be sanctioned both by an award of damages to compensate for losses arising from misplaced reliance upon the statement, and by rescission of any contract which is induced by reliance upon the representation. In addition, many such misleading statements constitute criminal offences if made by a person in the course of a trade or business to a consumer.

This duty of care in making statements during negotiations qualifies to a considerable extent the freedom of parties to avoid obligations until the moment of formation of contract. Given that in practice most negotiations will involve the making of various representations about the quality and variety of products and services on offer, the duty will normally be triggered and circumscribe the parties' freedom to avoid obligations during the bargaining process. This duty provides a strong example of the more general principle of a duty to negotiate with care. But the duty of care in making statements is confined by numerous technical requirements, which betray the diverse sources of the duty in common law, equity and statute.

1. Reasonable reliance

The obligation to take care in making statements is confined to statements on which it is reasonable to place reliance. In developing the common law and interpreting statutes, the courts have attempted to define the types of statements on which it will not be reasonable to rely, excluding for instance statements of law, expressions of opinion and statements about future conduct. But these classifications can be misleading, unless one bears in mind the point of the classification, which is to limit the obligation to take care to statements on which it is reasonable to rely. The statutes governing criminal offences offer more specific lists of the kinds of statements made by traders on which it is reasonable for consumers to rely, but this leads to extensive, detailed and confusing regulation, which itself creates problems for compliance by traders.[5]

These attempts to reduce to the form of rules the situations and contexts when it will be reasonable to rely upon pre-contractual statements look doomed to failure for two reasons. In the first place, the reasonableness of reliance must depend upon numerous features of the particular case, such as the relative expertise and knowledge of the parties, and the context in which a statement is made. For example, a statement about the legal effect of a document such as a Will might be reasonably relied upon if made by a qualified lawyer to a client, but not if made by someone without legal expertise, and nor perhaps if made by a lawyer in informal

---

5   I Ramsay, *Consumer Protection* (London, 1989), p 257. See also the Property Misdescriptions Act 1991; Property Misdescriptions (Specified Matters) Order 1992, SI 1992/2834.

circumstances such as a casual conversation on a train. The common law attempts to distinguish these different cases by saying that some are statements of fact, whilst others statements of law and opinion on which no reliance can be placed. But, since the statement remains identical in every case, it is clear that these distinctions merely represent conclusions of law about whether or not reliance was reasonable in the circumstances rather than an analysis of the words employed.

We should also be aware that the issue of whether it was reasonable to rely upon a statement is not simply a question of fact. It involves a normative judgement about which kinds of statements negotiating parties ought to be able to rely upon. For example, every consumer is familiar with misleading statements about the price of goods. Blaring notices proclaim that the goods are on special offer, their prices have been slashed, or there is extra value and a great bargain, and so on. It is doubtful whether most consumers place much trust in such claims, and they will try to make their own price comparisons. Nevertheless, there is good reason for traders to be held to such claims if any substance can be given to them at all. The proliferation of such claims obstructs a competitive market, making it increasingly difficult to make accurate price comparisons, and there is always a risk that an unsophisticated consumer will be genuinely misled and waste his money. For these reasons the Consumer Protection Act 1987, s 20 renders the giving of misleading price indications a criminal offence. We may not regard it as sensible to place much faith in such misleading price claims, but nevertheless the law deems it to be reasonable to rely upon such statements, in order to regulate the market towards competitive practices and to protect even instances of unreasonable reliance by consumers. This regulation reveals that the question of whether or not reliance was reasonable not only depends upon all the circumstances of the case, but also requires a normative judgement about which statements should become reliable for the sake of improving market competition and protection of the weak from the unscrupulous. In the light of these general observations about the test of reasonable reliance, we should look more closely at the formal rules which the courts employ to draw these subtle distinctions.

(a) STATEMENTS OF LAW AND CONTRACTUAL TERMS

It is probably not reasonable to rely upon someone's opinion of the law in general, since it is advisable to seek one's own advice about legal rights and responsibilities. For this reason the common law holds that statements of law as opposed to statements of fact may not be relied upon. But there will be many special cases where reliance can be placed reasonably upon express and implied statements of law. For instance, a misleading statement about the law by a lawyer to a client as a result of carelessness will count as a statement on which it is reasonable to rely.

During negotiations for a contract one party may make misleading statements about the content and meaning of the terms of the contract. The precise interpretation of a contract is ultimately a question of law, so it might be supposed that such statements could not be relied upon. In addition, it may not be reasonable to rely upon such statements in general, for each party should read the terms of the contract for himself or herself.

Nevertheless, there will be many circumstances in which statements about the effects of a legal document can be relied upon. For instance, a statement about the legal effects of a document from a person who should understand those effects will be treated as a representation on which reliance can be placed. What is crucial is the difference in relative expertise between the parties. The person giving the statement may be relied upon because that person has greater legal expertise or business experience. In *Cornish v Midland Bank plc*,[6] a bank clerk gave advice to a customer about the effects of a mortgage upon her home to which her husband wanted her to agree. The advice was misleading in that it omitted to explain the full effects of the document. The customer obtained damages for losses resulting from this negligent advice. Similarly, a statement about the legal effects of a contract can be relied upon where the representation is made by a party seeking to invoke a standard form contract. In *Curtis v Chemical Cleaning and Dyeing Co*[7] the claimant took her wedding dress to the defendant's shop to be cleaned. She was required to sign a contract, which, she was told by an assistant, disclaimed liability for certain specified risks to the beads and sequins which adorned the dress. In fact, the contract contained a clause which exempted the defendant from liability for any damage to the dress, howsoever arising. The claimant subsequently sued for damage to her dress comprising a stain of uncertain origin. The English Court of Appeal held that the defendant could not rely upon the full width of the exclusion clause on account of the misrepresentation by its employee of the meaning and content of the terms.

One of the most common kinds of misleading statement about the terms of the contract concerns the price of goods or services. These have been singled out for detailed regulation by the Consumer Protection Act 1987.[8] Section 20 makes it a criminal offence if a person in the course of a business of his gives by any means to a consumer a misleading indication of the price of goods, services, accommodation or facilities. The statute adopts a broad interpretation of such misleading statements by not requiring the statement to be false, but rather for a court to ask whether consumers might reasonably be misled by the indication of price. The offence is committed, for instance, when a shop fails to honour an advertisement which claims that it will 'beat any TV Hi-fi and Video price by £20 on the spot'.[9]

6   [1985] 3 All ER 513, CA.
7   [1951] 1 KB 805, [1951] 1 All ER 631, CA.
8   See also the Consumer Protection (Code of Practice for Traders on Price Indications) Approval Order 1988, SI 1988/2078.
9   *R v Warwickshire County Council, ex p Johnson* [1993] AC 583, *sub nom Warwickshire County Council v Johnson* [1993] 1 All ER 299, HL.

(b)   STATEMENTS OF FUTURE INTENTIONS

It is also, in general, unreasonable to rely upon promises about future conduct. Such promises should be part of a binding contract before they can be relied upon. But that leaves open the question whether such promises themselves may constitute an independent or collateral contract or establish facts sufficient to ground an equitable estoppel. We will examine these possibilities below when we consider misleading implied promises.

Yet statements about future intentions can involve simultaneously implied statements of fact. The expression of intention may indicate that the representor has taken reasonable care to ascertain certain facts which are material to the negotiations. If the representee has reasonably relied upon these implied statements of fact, then an action for misrepresentation may succeed. In *Box v Midland Bank plc*[10] a businessman sought an overdraft facility in order to finance an export contract which would save the business. During discussions of the proposal, the bank manager advised the claimant businessman that, although he would require approval from head office for the loan, the process would be a mere formality. But the head office scrutinized the transaction and rejected it. As a result the claimant's business collapsed and he sought a remedy for misrepresentation against the bank. The court accepted that the bank manager had failed to take reasonable care in indicating that the loan would be forthcoming, for he ought to have realized that under the bank's rules there was never the slightest possibility of the overdraft facility being made available. Since the claimant would have sought a loan elsewhere if the bank manager had provided a careful prediction of the outcome, the bank was held liable for £5,000 to cover the claimant's additional costs of borrowing to finance the export sale at a late stage, although not for the whole cost of the collapse of the business. In this instance liability for misrepresentation comes close to holding the bank liable for its informal promise to make the overdraft facility available during negotiations, but the measure of damages makes it clear that the true basis of liability consists in the opportunity costs incurred as a result of misplaced reliance upon a statement.

(c)   STATEMENTS OF OPINION

It will also be unreasonable to rely upon vague statements of opinion and inflated sales talk. Hence if I persuade someone to buy my car by claiming that it is the fastest red Peugeot 104 on the road, the purchaser can rely upon my statements of fact about the colour, make and model of the car, but he or she should treat my claim about its speed with more circumspection, since a court would probably regard it as 'mere puff', like an advertising slogan which claims that a detergent will make clothes 'whiter than white', and therefore not a statement upon which

10 [1979] 2 Lloyd's Rep 391, QB.

reliance may be placed. But it is wrong to suppose that every statement of opinion will be excluded, or that every apparent statement of fact can be reasonably relied upon.

Some statements of opinion imply that the representor knows facts on which his opinion is based, and a failure to take reasonable care in ascertaining these facts which renders the opinion false will constitute a breach of the duty of care. When, in *Smith v Land and House Property Corpn*,[11] the landlord who was selling property declared that it was 'let to a most desirable tenant', knowing in fact that the tenant was in serious arrears with the rent, the court treated this as a statement of fact, because the landlord could know better than the purchaser the qualities of the tenant, and it was therefore reasonable for the purchaser to rely upon this vague statement. Moreover some statements of opinion will be given by experts who hold themselves out as being in a position to make reliable statements, and again these opinions will be treated as giving rise to the duty of care. This analysis will be applied, for example, to medical opinions. It was also applied in *Esso Petroleum Co Ltd v Mardon*,[12] where the defendant took on the tenancy of a petrol station on the basis of an opinion of an expert representative of the oil company as to the probable turnover of the station. The court rejected the oil company's defence that the forecast was merely an expression of opinion. It was a statement which could be relied upon because it was made by a person with special knowledge and skill, and, although in form it was an opinion, the statement implied that it was founded upon facts known to the representor. Lord Denning MR summarized the principle:

> If a man, who has or professes to have special knowledge or skill, makes a representation by virtue thereof to another – be it advice, information or opinion – with the intention of inducing him to enter into a contract with him, he is under a duty to use reasonable care to see that the representation is correct, and that the advice, information or opinion is reliable.

It follows, of course, that some apparent statements of fact cannot be relied upon, if they do not draw upon special expertise or knowledge. For example, in *Bisset v Wilkinson*,[13] the seller asserted that a piece of farm land was sufficiently fertile to support 2,000 sheep. The court decided that this was a statement of opinion which could not be reasonably relied upon, for the parties were both farmers who could make their own judgements about the fertility of the land.

These decisions reveal that the question of whether or not a statement which looks like an opinion rather than a statement of fact can be reasonably relied upon involves a complex determination of several factors. One important factor will be the relative expertise or knowledge of the parties, so that it will be more

11 (1884) 28 Ch D 7, CA.
12 [1976] QB 801, [1976] 2 All ER 5, CA.
13 [1927] AC 177, PC.

reasonable to rely on statements when the representor enjoys superior knowledge or expertise. The circumstances in which the representation is made will also colour the court's judgment, so that casual remarks or statements made on social occasions should not be relied upon, although the same statements made in a professional or commercial context could amount to a breach of the duty.

When devising the Trade Descriptions Act 1968, Parliament attempted to produce more specific regulations which would determine which statements involved a breach of duty and, therefore, a criminal offence. The Act is limited by s 1 to statements made by a person in the course of a trade or business. Section 2 lists the kinds of statements about products which are covered by the Act, including such matters as its quantity, composition, fitness for purpose, strength, performance and the history of the product. Statements are caught by the Act even though they are not false, but merely misleading, that is to say, likely to be taken as an indication of some quality referred to in the list of kinds of statements covered by the Act. This provision permits the courts to punish broad statements which imply particular qualities for the goods. In *Robertson v Dicicco*[14] the defendant advertised a used car claiming that it was a 'beautiful car'. The court found that although the external appearance of the car was indeed attractive, the statement that the car was beautiful also implied that the car was fit for its normal purpose. In fact the car suffered from serious corrosion and was thoroughly unroadworthy. This is an example of a statement which, although literally true, could be understood to imply further statements of fact which were false.

In formulating the Trade Descriptions Act 1968, Parliament sought to provide consumer protection against an extremely broad range of misleading statements. The legislation seems to take as its model an unsophisticated and credulous consumer, who is likely to be misled by sales talk. The common law, however, developed a narrower picture of the circumstances in which reasonable reliance might take place, so that a statement that a car was 'beautiful' would almost certainly be treated as 'mere puff' and therefore not a statement which could found a breach of duty. It is unfortunate that this divergence of statutory and common law standards may have developed. It is to be hoped that courts will view the 'mere puff' defence circumspectly in the context of consumer transactions in future.

Unfortunately, what may have happened occasionally is exactly the reverse. Steeped in the common law tradition of evaluating reasonable reliance, the courts may have ignored the point that the statutes aimed at consumer protection intended to include within their ambit even some instances of foolish reliance, in order to further the policies of consumer protection and enhance the competitive market. In *Cadbury Ltd v Halliday* [15] consumers could find in retail shops two types of bars of chocolate. One sort of bar bore a 'flash' sign on its wrapper stating that

14 [1972] RTR 431, DC.
15 [1975] 2 All ER 226, [1975] 1 WLR 649, DC.

the bar was 'extra value'. Close inspection revealed, however, that the other sort of bar on sale in fact contained more chocolate and was cheaper. The company was prosecuted for a misleading price claim, but successfully appealed against conviction on the ground that the phrase 'extra value' conveyed no identifiable factual meaning. The court regarded the phrase as a matter of opinion, a mere puff, on which no reliance could reasonably be placed.

It may be true, of course, that prudent consumers place no reliance upon such statements, but to confine the legislation in this way defeats its objective. The statute seeks to eliminate such confusing statements from the market, in order to foster genuine competition and at the same time to protect even the gullible consumer. The phrase 'extra value' could easily be attributed a more definite meaning, such as more chocolate for the same price, and in this sense it would have been misleading. By sticking to the common law standard of reasonable reliance, and not realizing that consumer protection measures will often take a broader view of which statements may reasonably be relied upon, the court managed to defeat the purpose of the legislation in this case.

2. The standard of care

A negligence standard applies to those who make pre-contractual statements. It requires reasonable care to be taken to ensure the accuracy of the statement and facts on which it is based. This standard may be contrasted with fraud and strict liability. In the case of fraud the statement is made either knowing that it is false or being aware that it is likely to be false. Of course, fraudulent statements will also involve a breach of the duty to negotiate with care. But the duty does not set the standard of strict liability under which a false or misleading statement is a breach of duty even though it was made honestly and despite the use of reasonable care.

In defining the standard of care, however, the courts and the legislature have some latitude in raising or lowering the requirements experienced in practice by manipulating two factors. The first factor concerns the burden of proof of negligence. Since it will often be difficult to ascertain the facts on which it may be possible to assert that a statement was made carelessly, if the burden of proof is reversed, this will give the party who has relied upon a false or misleading statement an immense practical advantage in establishing a breach of the duty. The second concerns the standards by which reasonable behaviour is set. These could range from the highest and most careful standards of any trader to the lowest practices.

(a) BURDEN OF PROOF

The common law traditionally requires a person alleging negligence to prove that lack of reasonable care was taken. But for most practical purposes this burden has been reversed in the context of statements made during negotiations. To obtain rescission of the contract at common law, a party to the contract merely has to show that it was reasonable to rely upon the statement and that it was false, without the further need to prove negligence. To obtain damages for losses resulting from misplaced reliance upon the statement, the Misrepresentation Act 1967, s 2(1) requires the representor to prove that he had reasonable ground to believe and did believe up to the time when the contract was made that the facts represented were true. This provision reverses the normal burden of proof once the statement has been shown to be false and one which was reasonably relied upon.

The statutory offences offer a different framework, which in effect also reverses the burden of proof. Although the Trade Descriptions Act 1968 and the Consumer Protection Act 1987 impose strict liability upon traders for making false and misleading statements (except in the anomalous case of statements about services),[16] traders have open to them a number of special statutory defences, including the general one of 'due diligence'. This defence permits the evasion of liability, if the trader can show that he or she took all reasonable precautions and exercised all due diligence to avoid the commission of the offence by himself or herself or any person under his or her control.[17]

(b)   REASONABLE CARE

The question of what amounts to reasonable care, adequate precautions, or due diligence leaves the court considerable scope for adjusting the standard of the duty to negotiate with care. As in the ordinary law of negligence in tort, the courts are likely to rely upon standard trading and professional practices as a guide to what should be regarded as reasonable care. For example, in *Cornish v Midland Bank plc*, on the question whether the bank clerk had taken reasonable care in describing the terms of the mortgage accurately, the court used the bank's own internal instructions to employees as a useful guide to standard banking practice. Similarly, the standard of care for doctors and surgeons will be set by the normal practices of the profession. But there is a danger in merely endorsing established trade practices, if these fall below what a court regards as reasonable.

The standard of care required will also be affected by the particular skill and knowledge of the representor. If the representor is in a special position to know the true facts or to ascertain them, then the care required will normally involve taking advantage of this special position. In *Howard Marine and Dredging Co Ltd v*

---

16 Trade Descriptions Act 1968, s 14; for criticism, see Director General of Fair Trading, *Review of the Trade Descriptions Act 1968* (London, 1976), pp 18–20.

17 Trade Descriptions Act 1968, s 24; Consumer Protection Act 1987, s 39; Property Misdescriptions Act 1991, s 2.

A Ogden & Sons (Excavations) Ltd,[18] during negotiations for the hire of some barges, the owner's agent stated their freight capacity on the strength of an inaccurate entry in the Lloyd's Register of ships, and omitted to check the owner's records of capacity. The agent was held liable for a negligent misrepresentation because he was in a position to check the accuracy of the registers, whereas other persons could have made the same statement without negligence, for normally the Lloyd's Register is a reliable guide. Similarly, special expertise in judging the accuracy of information is likely to heighten the precautions required. In the sale of used cars for example, statements about their qualities such as age made by a dealer will have to be made with considerable care, whereas an ordinary consumer selling a car with no special knowledge of the facts should be able to rely upon the appearance and records of the car.[19]

The most troublesome issue in determining the standard of care required concerns the liability of employers for negligent employees. The false statement may be made by an employee or an agent, even though the employer has taken care to instruct employees not to make such statements. Should the employer be held responsible for such inaccuracies? When the claimant's action concerns civil law remedies of rescission of the contract or damages, the employee making the false statement will normally be regarded as an agent acting within the scope of his authority, so the employer will be vicariously responsible for the agent's statements. When the case involves a criminal prosecution, however, the legislature and the courts have proved reluctant to hold the employer strictly liable for the acts of employees.

Under the Trade Descriptions Act 1968, s 24, the employer may establish a defence that the statement was made by an employee even though the employer had exercised all due diligence to prevent the employee from making the false statement. The employer can escape conviction, therefore, if it can impress the court with the elaborate details of its staff manuals and procedures for ensuring that consumers are given accurate information, even though, of course, the procedures failed in this particular case.[20] A similar position prevails with respect to misleading prices under the Consumer Protection Act 1987. Here criminal liability is confined to employers,[21] but the employer can avoid liability for a misleading price statement made by an employee by claiming that the employer took all reasonable steps and exercised all due diligence to avoid committing the

---

18 [1978] QB 574, [1978] 2 All ER 1134, CA.
19 Compare: *Dick Bentley Productions Ltd v Harold Smith (Motors) Ltd* [1965] 2 All ER 65, [1965] 1 WLR 623, CA, with *Oscar Chess Ltd v Williams* [1957] 1 All ER 325, [1957] 1 WLR 370, CA.
20 *Tesco Supermarkets Ltd v Nattrass* [1972] AC 153, [1971] 2 All ER 127, HL; T Ison, *Credit Marketing and Consumer Protection* (London, 1979) p 375; I Ramsay, *Consumer Protection* (London, 1989), p 249.
21 *R v Warwickshire County Council, ex p Johnson* [1993] AC 583, sub nom *Warwickshire County Council v Johnson* [1993] 1 All ER 299, HL.

offence.[22] No criminal offence will be committed if the employee makes an unauthorized misleading price statement which the employer had taken reasonable steps to prevent.

This reluctance to convict employers of criminal offences reveals how strongly the law remains attached to a requirement of blameworthiness in the criminal law. But this attachment may serve in this context to frustrate the operation of the legislation, for if the employer can succeed in this defence too easily, little incentive remains to check upon employees to the benefit of consumers. It could be argued that any false statement by an employee represents a failure by the employing organization to establish procedures ensuring due diligence by employees, so that employers should normally be held vicariously liable under criminal regulatory offences, as under civil law.[23]

3.   Remedies

(a)   RESCISSION

The remedy of rescission for a false or misleading statement aims to avoid the contract and to put the parties back into the position which they held prior to the formation of the contract. The remedy is available to the representee if the misrepresentation was a material inducement to enter into the contract, subject to a number of equitable bars. Until the contract has been rescinded, it is merely voidable, not void, so that it may transfer property rights. The contract may be rescinded either by a court declaration or by giving notice to the representor.[24]

The right to rescind a contract will be barred in four main circumstances. These rules apply generally whenever a contract is voidable:

(i)   Where the representee cannot make restitution of what he has received under the contract, he may be prevented from rescinding the contract. But precise restitution is not necessary. Rescission will be available provided that the subject matter transferred under the voidable contract can be substantially restored, and that due allowance in the form of compensation can be paid for any deterioration and any profits obtained by dealing with the property.

(ii)   Third party interests will be protected by preventing rescission if property transferred under the contract has already been sold to an innocent third party.

---

22 Consumer Protection Act 1987, s 39.

23 Cartwright, 'Defendants in Consumer Protection Statutes: A Search for Consistency' (1996) 59 *Modern Law Review* 225.

24 In the case of fraud where the representor has deliberately disappeared, it may be possible to rescind the contract by giving notice to the police and other affected parties: *Car and Universal Finance Co Ltd v Caldwell* [1965] 1 QB 525, [1964] 1 All ER 290, CA; criticized by Law Reform Committee 12th Report (1966) Cmnd 2958 para 16.

(iii)   The right to rescind the contract can be lost by affirming it after the truth has been discovered.

(iv)   The right to rescind will be lost by the lapse of time,[25] except perhaps in the case of fraud where lapse of time after discovery of the truth will merely amount to evidence of affirmation.

Under the Misrepresentation Act 1967, s 2(2), a court also has a discretion to refuse rescission and award damages instead. This broad equitable discretion is likely to be exercised if the misrepresentation is not fraudulent, is relatively minor, and the losses likely to be caused to the representor by rescission far exceed the losses to the representee if the contract is upheld. The measure of damages will be the cost of curing the defect or the diminution of the value of the property.[26]

(b)   DAMAGES

The slow and grudging acknowledgement by the courts of a pre-contractual duty to be careful in making statements led to an extraordinarily complex body of law governing the award of damages. Even today, after statutory reform, many doubts remain about the principles on which damages will be awarded for breach of the duty.

Most claims for damages for misrepresentation will today be brought under the Misrepresentation Act 1967, s 2(1). This statutory remedy has several advantages. It provides a clear basis for recovery, unlike the confusing common law position. Claimants can take advantage of the reversal of the burden of proof in establishing negligence. Finally, recent cases indicate that the statute provides the most advantageous measure of compensation.

But the statutory claim for damages has not eliminated the common law, which still persists and may sometimes be employed. In particular, the statutory claim for damages only applies if the parties have entered a contract which subsequently causes loss, whereas the common law claims do not depend upon entry into a contract. At common law damages are available for fraudulent misrepresentation, but this claim requires proof of the defendant's knowledge of the falsity of the statement which will often not be practicable.[27] The law of tort also provides a remedy of damages for negligent misrepresentation, although the limitations and conceptual complexity of this claim render it less attractive than the statutory action.[28] Prior to the statute, the most common basis for a claim for damages

---

25 *Leaf v International Galleries* [1950] 2 KB 86, [1950] 1 All ER 693, CA.
26 *William Sindall plc v Cambridgeshire County Council* [1994] 3 All ER 932, [1994] 1 WLR 1016, CA.
27 *Derry v Peek* (1889) 14 App Cas 337, HL.
28 *Hedley Byrne & Co Ltd v Heller & Partners Ltd* [1964] AC 465, [1963] 2 All ER 575, HL; *Caparo Industries plc v Dickman* [1990] 2 AC 605, [1990] 1 All ER 568, HL.

consisted of an allegation of the existence of a collateral contract. Under this implied contract, the statement became a warranty and the consideration given for it was entry into the main contract.[29] Both the common law claim for negligent misrepresentation and the claim for a collateral warranty succeeded, for instance, in *Esso Petroleum Co Ltd v Mardon*.

The courts insist that the measure of damages in tort and under the Misrepresentation Act 1967 should not be the same as for breach of contract. In particular, the claimant should not receive damages to compensate for the loss of profits which the claimant expected from entry into the contract. The courts have insisted that a tort measure of damages is more appropriate for misrepresentation, either for claims at common law,[30] or under the Misrepresentation Act 1967, s 2(1).[31] But that conclusion leaves open the question of how the tort measure should be calculated.

The claimant's losses in the situation of a pre-contractual misrepresentation that induces the formation of a contract can be described in three ways:

(i)   The loss can be conceived as the original entry into the disadvantageous contract, so that the claimant should be put back into the position he held prior to the formation of that contract. In the case of a purchase of a hotel on the strength of a false statement about its occupancy rate, for instance, the purchaser would receive back any money paid for the hotel, a purely restitutionary remedy.

(ii)   The loss can be described as the difference in the claimant's situation between the statement being true and false. Here the damages would amount to the difference between the actual value of the hotel at the time of purchase and its value if the statement had been true.

(iii)   The loss could be conceived as the difference between the claimant's situation in entering this contract and his likely situation if he had entered another similar contract, which might have been made but for the fraudulent misrepresentation. In the case of a purchase of a hotel, the losses would then include the profits which would have been made by the exploitation of an alternative hotel which had the qualities described in the misrepresentation, a measure of damages which includes opportunity costs. This third measure of damages could greatly exceed the others, for it encompasses the profits which would have been made under an alternative contract. It differs only slightly from the measure of damages for breach of contract, which would include in principle the profits which would have been made if the representation about the hotel had been true.

29 *Evans & Son (Portsmouth) Ltd v Andrea Merzario Ltd* [1976] 2 All ER 930, [1976] 1 WLR 1078, CA.
30 *Esso Petroleum Co Ltd v Mardon* [1976] QB 801, [1976] 2 All ER 5, CA.
31 *Royscott Trust Ltd v Rogerson* [1991] 2 QB 297, [1991] 3 All ER 294, CA.

There is support in the decided cases for each of these approaches to the quantification of damages for misrepresentation, usually depending on what has been claimed and can be proven. Most cases apply the second measure, ie the difference in value of the goods or property between their actual market value at the time of the misrepresentation and their value if the representation had been true. For example, in *South Australia Asset Management Corpn v York Montague Ltd*,[32] a careless over-valuation of a large commercial property induced lenders to advance money to borrowers for the acquisition of the property. When the property market collapsed and the borrowers were unable to repay the loan, it emerged that the property given as security for the loan was worth much less than the sum advanced. The lenders claimed their losses from the valuers. The House of Lords permitted the second measure of recovery, namely the difference between the valuation figure and the actual market value at that time, which amounted to about £10m. But the claim for the difference between the valuation figure and the actual value at the time when the lenders sought to realise the asset, which amounted to £12.5m was rejected on the ground that the subsequent fall in the value of the property was not attributable to the valuer's breach of duty.

Yet it is also clear that the third measure of damages is a possibility in some instances. In *Esso Petroleum Co Ltd v Mardon*, for instance, the tenant of the garage which had a lower turnover than predicted by the landlord oil company received as his measure of damages, not only his capital loss from investment in the business and his operating losses, but also the return that he would have made from investment and work in another comparable business. Similarly, in *East v Maurer*,[33] in a claim for fraud at common law, the third measure of damages was awarded. Here the claimants had purchased the business of a hairdresser for £20,000, on the faith of a fraudulent representation by the hairdresser that he would not continue a competing business in the town. The business was a failure as a result of the continuing competition, leading to trading losses, and eventually a sale of the business which realised only £5,000. As well as awarding compensation for the difference in value of the business between the purchase price and its true market value, and for the trading losses, the court awarded a further £10,000 for the loss representing the profits which would have been made if an alternative hairdressing business had been purchased in another town. Of course, this loss of profits is likely to be much the same as the expected profits from the business which was in fact purchased, so there is little difference, if any, between this measure of recovery and an ordinary action for breach of contract.

Section 2(1) does not give any clear indication of the measure of damages to be awarded. But the section does suggest that the measure should be the same as the common law of fraud, since it states that the liability for damages for misrepresentation should arise as if the statement had been made fraudulently.

32 [1997] AC 191, [1996] 3 All ER 365, HL.
33 [1991] 2 All ER 733, [1991] 1 WLR 461, CA.

This 'fiction of fraud' has been taken to mean that the measure of damages under the statute should be the tortious measure,[34] not a contractual measure, and the cases on fraud invariably apply the third, most generous, quantification of damages.

A second difficulty in determining the measure of damages is whether the ordinary limits on the types of loss recoverable in cases of breach of contract should apply to actions for misrepresentation. In particular, damages are not normally awarded in actions for breach of contract to cover disappointment and distress, but only for actual financial losses incurred by extracting oneself from a bad bargain. But this limitation has not been observed in claims for losses resulting from fraud. In *East v Maurer*, for instance, the court awarded £1,000 as general damages for disappointment and inconvenience.

The third difficulty in calculating damages arises from the question of whether the rules should differ between fraudulent and negligent misrepresentations. In particular, some losses resulting from a misrepresentation may seem so remote and unforeseeable that compensation for those losses should only be awarded, if at all, in cases of deliberate fraud. Although the common law adopts this division,[35] the statutory claim for damages for negligent misrepresentation under the Misrepresentation Act 1967, s 2(1) appears on its wording to insist upon identical treatment for cases of fraud and negligence, and it has been so interpreted by the courts.[36]

The strange result of these decisions concerning the quantification of damages is that a person may gain a higher measure of damages for a claim for negligent misrepresentation during pre-contractual negotiations than could be obtained for a simple claim for breach of contract. Under the third version of the tort measure, which includes opportunity costs, in a competitive market this measure should always approximate to the profits which were expected under the contract which was undertaken. In addition, the claimant in an action for negligent misrepresentation under s 2(1) can also avoid the rules barring recovery in an action for breach of contract for claims concerning disappointment and inconvenience and for remote and unforeseeable losses. This strange conclusion results from the courts' adhesion to a sharp conceptual distinction between the measure of damages in contract and tort, and then its relentless application of the tort measure to pre-contractual representations. This conceptualism ignores the context of these claims, which is essentially one concerned with pre-contractual arrangements. What the law requires is the recognition of a distinct species of liability, which is neither precisely contract nor tort, but which addresses directly the proper measure of the sanction for breach of a duty to negotiate with care.

34 *Royscott Trust Ltd v Rogerson* [1991] 2 QB 297, [1991] 3 All ER 294, CA.
35 *Doyle v Olby (Ironmongers) Ltd* [1969] 2 QB 158, [1969] 2 All ER 119, CA.
36 *Royscott Trust Ltd v Rogerson* [1991] 2 QB 297, [1991] 3 All ER 294, CA.

(c) REGULATORY OFFENCES

We have noted how the duty of care in making statements during pre-contractual negotiations has been buttressed by criminal sanctions in many consumer contexts. The justification for this regulation, in addition to the sanctions of private law in rescission and damages, lies in the general problem of enforcement of private rights in small consumer transactions. The costs of obtaining a remedy such as damages for a misrepresentation with respect to a consumer purchase may well far exceed the likely measure of recovery and the value of the item purchased. The expense and trouble of litigation, combined with the likely unsatisfactory outcome, will deter most consumers from asserting their legal rights beyond a letter of complaint. The result will be that few traders will be deterred from making misleading claims about products and prices and, in turn, this will harm consumers and obstruct a competitive market. A number of possible solutions to this problems can be imposed.

Private law rights could be enhanced and made more effective. For this purpose the measure of compensation could be augmented and access to justice improved by provision for inexpensive means for enforcing rights.

Alternatively, and this is the route chosen in most jurisdictions, a criminal sanction is introduced as a deterrent. The criminal sanction has the advantage that the costs of policing the market are borne by state agencies and that the sanction, because it exceeds mere compensation, should eliminate the deceptive trade practices. But the effectiveness of such measures depends ultimately upon consumers passing along complaints to the public authority, and then the authority acting vigorously upon them through enforcement mechanisms. Studies of these procedures often reveal a marked lack of effective monitoring and enforcement of standards. The criminal penalties also can prove meagre and therefore lack any real deterrent force. A criminal sanction can be combined with a power vested in the courts to award damages to individuals adversely affected by a misleading trade practice, as in Australia.[37]

(d) ADMINISTRATIVE INJUNCTION

The Control of Misleading Advertisements Regulations 1988[38] established a novel procedure for English law under which complaints about misleading business advertising should be made to a public official, the Director General of Fair Trading. Unless the complaint can be settled by informal means, such as

---

37 Australian Trade Practices Act 1974, s 82. This law also differs from the English regulation by including a general regulation against misleading practices which is described as 'conduct that is unconscionable within the meaning of the unwritten law': s 51AA. Harland, 'The Statutory Prohibition of Misleading and Deceptive Conduct in Australia and its Impact on the Law of Contract' (1995) 111 *Law Quarterly Review* 100.

38 SI 1988/915, implementing EC Directive 84/450 EEC on Misleading Advertising.

control by self-regulatory bodies, the Director may apply to a court for an injunction against any person concerned in the publication of the misleading advertisement. If the court agrees that the advertisement is misleading,[39] and likely to cause economic detriment to consumers, it issues an injunction against publication. This injunction procedure avoids the use of criminal penalties and emphasizes prospective prevention of misleading advertisements. The employment of the Director as a substitute litigator for the ordinary consumer overcomes many of the weaknesses of control of deceptive practices through private law. The same procedure has now been adopted by the European Community for all its consumer protection Directives.[40] In addition, the power to bring a claim for an injunction has been extended to other regulators and the Consumers' Association.[41] This injunction procedure, known colloquially as 'stop now orders', is rather cumbersome with its requirement of the need to make attempts to negotiate a change in practice with the trader before seeking an injunction in court. Nevertheless, the mere threat of possible proceedings may give the Director General and other regulators sufficient bargaining power to negotiate the withdrawal of most instances of plainly misleading advertisements.

C.   Failure to disclose information

To what extent are the parties to negotiations for a contract required to disclose information in their possession? The law's answer to this question draws a sharp distinction between two sorts of information. On the one hand, the law displays a reluctance to require disclosure of information about the circumstances surrounding the transaction, but on the other hand it provides considerable incentives to disclose information about the terms of the proposed transaction. This distinction can be justified by the need to protect and enhance a competitive market.

The efficiency of markets will be enhanced if the law provides incentives for the discovery of commercially valuable information. This information tends to ensure that goods will move to those who value them most. For example, if one trader discovers that a commodity is in short supply in one region so that prices have gone up, then with the benefit of this information the trader can purchase the commodity and resell it in the place of short supply. The inducement of profits ensures that the market operates competitively and efficiently, so that goods are quickly moved to those who value them the most. This process would be obstructed, however, if the trader were required to disclose his or her knowledge of market shortage on the initial purchase. Following such disclosure, the information would become public knowledge, permitting others to exploit it.

---

39 *Director General of Fair Trading v Tobyward Ltd* [1989] 2 All ER 266, [1989] 1 WLR 517, Ch.
40 EC Directive 98/27/EC on Injunctions for the Protection of Consumers' Interests.
41 Enterprise Act 2002, s 213.

The trader would be prevented from taking advantage of the information, which would in turn discourage him or her from obtaining the information in the first place. Without giving the trader an incentive to acquire the information by promising the trader the commercial benefits of that information, it seems likely that much less information will be produced, leading to inefficiency in the operation of the market. For this reason, it seems inadvisable to require disclosure of commercially valuable information during negotiations for a contract.

The same policy considerations, however, argue for disclosure of the content of the terms of the contract. In an ideal competitive market parties should become fully aware of the proposed terms of the transaction, so that they can compare the relative advantages of different market opportunities. This comparison will enable them to conclude the most efficient contract available on the market. Although these conditions will be satisfied in specially negotiated contracts, in the majority of contracts concluded on standard forms businesspersons and consumers will have neither the time nor the expertise to evaluate the full meaning of all the terms of the contract. To enhance the competitiveness of the market, therefore, the law can require a party relying upon a standard form contract to ensure that the principal terms and any unusual terms are brought to the other party's notice.

This distinction explains the general pattern of the law on disclosure which displays a much greater readiness to require disclosure of the terms of a contract than other kinds of commercially valuable information. But these simple economic models cannot capture the complexity of the issues at stake. The economic model of the operation of commodity markets described above provides an inadequate picture of how markets operate in general. In many instances one person enters into a transaction with another relying upon the other's expertise and superior information. For example, a consumer contracts with a stockbroker for the purchase of some shares relying upon the stockbroker to exercise normal professional skills. If the stockbroker knows or ought to know of information which is about to send the value of the shares plummeting, the consumer may assert that the failure to disclose this information amounted to a breach of a duty of care owed to him. To deny that such a duty was owed would place the stockbroker in the contradictory position of simultaneously asserting that, on the one hand, it is advisable to make the contract with him or her because of his or her special skill and knowledge, and on the other, denying that the skill and knowledge need be exercised for the benefit of the consumer. What this example shows is that, whilst the law may turn its face against a general duty of disclosure of information, it may discover many situations where, by virtue of the relation of dependence between the negotiating parties, at least some measure of disclosure should be required. The difficulty confronting the law is to identify those situations which justify a departure from the general rule against disclosure.

The concept of a relation of dependence is useful in describing the general pattern of the law governing disclosure of information of facts other than the terms of the contract. The paradigm instance consists of the negotiating relation between a person who regularly conducts the kind of business involved in the transaction and a person who lacks equivalent experience, skill and knowledge. This relation of dependence will trigger legal duties of disclosure where reasonable reliance has been placed on the exercise of this experience, skill and knowledge to the extent of disclosure of information. The crucial normative judgement of when it is reasonable to expect disclosure of information must depend, in the absence of explicit legislative guidance, on a careful investigation of the facts of each case.

1.   Disclosure of terms

The general pattern of the law requires disclosure of the terms of the contract, and failure to do so will render the contract unenforceable either as a whole or in part. The source of this principle lies in the common law, but it is supplemented by numerous statutory requirements aimed at informing consumers of the terms of standard form transactions. With the development of a single European market, these rules are increasingly being harmonized throughout the EC.

The common law's requirement of disclosure derives from a number of particular principles:

(i)   For a standard form to be treated as the terms of the contract, it must be communicated before the contract has been concluded.[42]

(ii)   The objective principle for determining the content of the terms of the contract has the effect that confusing or obscure terms should be interpreted by reference to the reasonable promisee's understanding of the terms. Failure to disclose the terms clearly may therefore result in the proposed terms being enforced with a meaning contrary to the profferor's intention or even in the conclusion that no binding contract was reached at all.[43]

(iii)   A failure to disclose the full import of the terms of a contract can be treated as a misrepresentation where statements about the content of the terms are made which omit some material element of the proposed contract. This liability for an omission was one of the grounds for the liability of the bank in *Cornish v Midland Bank plc*.[44]

(iv)   As Dillon LJ stated in *Interfoto Picture Library Ltd v Stiletto Visual Programmes Ltd*:[45]

---

42 *Thornton v Shoe Lane Parking Ltd* [1971] 2 QB 163, [1971] 1 All ER 686, CA; *Hollier v Rambler Motors (AMC) Ltd* [1972] 2 QB 71, [1972] 1 All ER 399, CA; *Olley v Marlborough Court Ltd* [1949] 1 KB 532, [1949] 1 All ER 127, CA.

43 *Scriven Bros v Hindley & Co* [1913] 3 KB 564, QB. See Chapter 11.

44 [1985] 3 All ER 513, CA.

45 [1989] QB 433, [1988] 1 All ER 348, CA.

If one condition in a set of printed conditions is particularly onerous or unusual, the party seeking to enforce it must show that the particular condition was fairly brought to the attention of the other party.

In that case, under a standard form contract for the hire of some old photographs, there was a provision which imposed heavy charges for late return of the photographs after the period of hire had expired. The Court of Appeal declined to uphold a claim for these heavy charges on the ground that this term in the contract had not been drawn to the attention of the hirer.

The sum of all these rules is to require the parties to disclose the terms of a proposed contract in good time for their consideration, clearly, fully, and drawing the other party's attention to any unusual and onerous clauses.

These common law principles are supplemented by legislation with respect to most consumer transactions which imposes more particular duties and incentives for disclosure of information about the terms of a transaction. The objectives of these rules are twofold:

(i)   to promote a competitive market by making comparisons between contractual terms simple; and
(ii)   to reduce the risk that consumers will enter contracts which are inadvisable in their particular circumstances, such as taking out loans which they cannot afford to pay back.

These objectives can be served by a huge variety of measures including the requirement of terms which are written down, easily legible, in plain English, with a copy handed to each party to the transaction; the adoption of the same form of words for the terms in every contract of a particular type such as consumer credit transactions; certain terms being highlighted by being printed in a different colour or placed in a conspicuous position; and 'cooling-off' periods during which a consumer has a right to cancel the contract, which permit examination of the terms and comparisons to be made. For example, the Price Marking Order 1991[46] requires retailers to display or mark the selling price of goods in a way which is unambiguous, easily identifiable, and clearly legible.

A general principle governing disclosure of terms in consumer contracts derives from the Unfair Terms in Consumer Contracts Regulations 1999, which in reg 7 proposes:

(1)   A seller or supplier shall ensure that any written term of a contract is expressed in plain, intelligible language.

---

46 SI 1991/1382, implementing EC Directives 88/314/EEC and 88/315/EEC on Consumer Protection in the Indication of Prices.

(2) If there is doubt about the meaning of a written term, the interpretation most favourable to the consumer shall prevail . . . [47]

Although the Regulations do not spell out the consequences of breach of this provision, it seems that not only does para (2) provide a rule of interpretation, often called the 'contra proferentem' rule, but also para (1) suggests that a written term which fails to pass the test of being expressed in plain, intelligible language is likely to be regarded as an unfair term and therefore unenforceable. This risk of invalidity creates a strong incentive for traders to rewrite their standard form contracts in a 'user-friendly' style, which in turn should serve the purpose of disclosure of information about the terms of the contract.

In English law the most elaborate provisions of this kind apply to consumers' financial transactions, such as credit arrangements for the purchase of goods or a home. Under the EC Directive on Consumer Credit,[48] member states must enact legislation to ensure in consumer credit arrangements that they are in writing, that the consumer receives a copy of the agreement, and that the agreement clearly states the annual percentage rate of interest and other essential terms of the contract. The Consumer Credit Act 1974, ss 60–65, enacts these requirements,[49] so that a creditor's failure to comply with these formalities makes the agreement unenforceable against the debtor except by court order.[50] Under these regulations, for instance, the lender is required to describe the cost of borrowing according to a uniform measure, the annual percentage rate (APR). The objective of this requirement to disclose credit terms in a particular way is to enable the consumer to compare the cost of credit, which in turn should promote a competitive market.[51] It also reflects a view that the APR is the most rational way to compare the cost of credit,[52] even though consumers are likely to measure instead the actual cost of weekly or monthly repayments. The intensity of the controls in this financial sector presumably reflects the sense that the terms of these transactions are likely to be complex and involve concepts with which the ordinary consumer is unfamiliar. In addition, the consequences of breach of these contracts may cause considerable hardship, such as loss of possession of a home, so it is useful to warn the consumer of these risks clearly in advance.

47 SI 1999/2083, implementing EC Directive 93/13/EEC on Unfair Terms in Consumer Contracts, Art 5.
48 EC Directive 87/102/EEC.
49 Further detailed requirements are contained in Consumer Credit (Agreements) Regulations 1983, SI 1983/1553.
50 Consumer Credit Act 1974, s 127.
51 Report of the Committee on Consumer Credit (Crowther Committee), Cmnd 4596 (1971), para 3.8.3.
52 Whitford, 'The Functions of Disclosure Regulation in Consumer Transactions' (1973) *Wisconsin Law Review* 400, at pp 423–425.

As well as consumer transactions, legislation regulates the disclosure of terms in other standard types of contract. Under EC law, for instance, an employer must provide employees with a written statement of the terms of the contract.[53]

The effectiveness of the legislative provisions for the protection of consumers has been questioned. Even with all this information about the terms of the contract, it must be doubted whether most consumers take the trouble to read the contract, or fully comprehend its implications if they do.[54] Nevertheless, provided that a substantial group of relatively sophisticated consumers take advantage of the ability to scrutinize the information and make comparisons, this is likely to improve the competitiveness of the market overall.[55] The provision of information cannot of course prevent some consumers from entering extremely disadvantageous transactions, but the remedy for this must lie elsewhere in the control over the content of the terms and challenges on the ground of unfairness.

Against these advantages of disclosure requirements about the terms of standard form contracts to the consumer, however, must be set the costs of compliance to businesses and the expense of enforcement mechanisms. In the main, the disclosure requirements can be satisfied by standard form contracts and printed publicity material at little extra cost, but when regulation goes beyond such easily satisfied requirements, then it seems likely to become unworkable. For example, the regulation of the advertising of credit under the Consumer Credit Act 1974, ss 43–47 seems to deter anything but rudimentary statements, for the costs of full compliance with the regulation would push up advertising costs and lead almost inevitably to unintended breaches of the complex regulations.[56]

2.   Disclosure of facts

In what circumstances does the law require disclosure of facts other than the terms of the contract?[57] As we have noted, arguments based upon the enhancement of competitive markets favour a general rule against a duty to disclose facts. But these arguments cannot prevail in every case, because markets are permeated with situations where one party relies upon the other to exercise care and skill. Where such a relation of dependence exists it may be appropriate to impose a duty of disclosure as part of the broad duty to negotiate with care. We

---

53 Employment Rights Act 1996, s 1; EC Directive 91/533/EEC on Employers' Obligations; Clark and Hall, 'The Cinderella Directive? Employee Rights to Information about Conditions Applicable to their Contract or Employment Relationship' (1992) 21 *Industrial Law Journal* 106.

54 I Ramsay, *Consumer Protection* (London, 1989), pp 330–331, discussing the report of National Consumer Council, *Consumers and Credit* (London, 1980).

55 Schwartz and Wilde, 'Intervening in Markets on the Basis of Imperfect Information: A Legal and Economic Analysis' (1979) 129 *University Pennsylvania Law Review* 630.

56 I Ramsay, *Consumer Protection* (London, 1989), pp 333–334.

57 Nicholas, 'The Precontractual Obligation to Disclose Information' in D Harris and D Tallon (eds), *Contract Law Today* (Oxford, 1989), p 166.

examine in this section the situations where such a duty to disclose information will arise. The principal legal techniques for creating such duties of disclosure comprise development of the law of misrepresentation and reliance upon the implication of terms into contracts. These are supplemented in some instances by regulatory offences.

(a)   MISREPRESENTATION

In many cases of relations of dependence, the party with superior knowledge or expertise will give advice to the weaker party. We have noted that if this advice is false or misleading, then liability for misrepresentation will protect the weaker party. One significant way in which advice may be misleading is that it omits to mention certain material facts. These omissions to disclose information will be treated as a misrepresentation, and the normal rules governing misleading statements will be applied. The test is whether in the circumstances of the case, including any statements made, the fact not disclosed is such that it is impliedly represented not to exist.[58] In *Nottingham Patent Brick and Tile Co v Butler*,[59] during negotiations for the sale of land, the vendor's solicitor stated in response to a question that he was not aware of any restrictive covenants inhibiting the use of the land. The solicitor failed to acknowledge, however, that he had not studied the relevant deeds, so although his statement was true it was misleading by virtue of this omission.

The reasonable expectation of disclosure in a relation of dependence will also arise when a statement is made which, although true at the time it is made, subsequently becomes false prior to the formation of the contract. Having established the relation of dependence through reliance upon the statement, it becomes reasonable to expect disclosure of information which reveals the statement no longer to be true. During negotiations for the sale of a medical practice in *With v O'Flanagan*,[60] the vendor affirmed the current value of the practice, but prior to conclusion of the sale it dropped substantially in value due to the illness of the vendor. The failure to disclose this change in circumstances was treated as a misrepresentation entitling the purchaser to rescind the contract.

The full extent of this potential liability in misrepresentation for omissions was revealed in our earlier discussion of *Crossan v Ward Bracewell*.[61] It will be recalled that the claimant visited a solicitor to obtain advice, but after preliminary negotiations decided not to employ the solicitor because of the cost and doubts about the necessity for legal advice. Because the solicitor failed to alert the claimant to risks of loss from civil liability, the solicitor was held liable in

58 *Lee v Jones* (1864) 17 CBNS 482, 144 ER 194.
59 (1886) 16 QBD 778, CA.
60 [1936] Ch 575, CA.
61 [1986] NLJ Rep 849.

negligence despite the absence of a concluded contract. The duty of care arose despite the absence of any contract for services, because the advice was given in a relation of dependence.

The same reasoning can apply to cases of misrepresentation by conduct. Covering up and deliberately concealing faults and information can amount to a misrepresentation, if the effect is to imply a false representation. If, for example, the seller of a used car carefully conceals important defects then, unless he or she discloses the true state of the car, he or she will be treated as having made a representation that the car conforms to its appearance. The difficult question here is to determine what implied representations should be inferred from conduct. Should it be inferred, for example, from the fact that a trader offers a used car for sale that he or she impliedly represents that he or she has taken reasonable care to ensure that the car is safe and free from major defects? The decided cases indicate that perhaps the representation that the trader has taken reasonable care to check that the car is safe is one which can be implied from this conduct, but that the representation that checks have been made to ensure no major defects is too broad.[62] The latter kind of information can lead only to economic loss, and here the argument for enhancing the competitive market by allowing traders to profit from information acquired from the development and exercise of expertise points strongly against imposing a duty of disclosure.

In cases where a duty of disclosure has been established through the law of misrepresentation, the question may arise whether some limited form of disclosure has satisfied the duty. In particular, the person under the duty of disclosure may have made some general declaration purporting to deny that any implied representations have been made and warning the other party to seek independent advice. The courts have permitted such general statements to negative the breach of the duty to disclose information.[63] Such general clauses would now, however, be treated as exclusion clauses subject to a requirement of reasonableness under the Misrepresentation Act 1967, s 3.

(b)   IMPLIED TERMS

The most important regulation of disclosure of information under the common law derives from the use of implied terms in contracts. In construing a contract a court may imply a term on the ground that it is reasonably necessary to give efficacy to the transaction. This term may constitute a warranty about, for example, the quality of goods and services, or that reasonable care has been taken in the preparation of advice or manufacture of goods. To avoid this potential liability a trader must either seek to exclude such implied terms from the contract

---

62 *Bodger v Nicholls* (1873) 28 LT 441; *Ward v Hobbs* (1878) 4 App Cas 13, HL; *Hurley v Dyke* [1979] RTR 265, HL.

63 *Ward v Hobbs* (1878) 4 App Cas 13, HL; *Hurley v Dyke* [1979] RTR 265, HL.

by express terms, or alternatively supply information during the negotiations which alerts the other party to the true state of affairs. These implied terms therefore provide an incentive to supply information, with the potential sanction that if information is not given then liability for damages for breach of contract may arise.

In contracts for the sale of goods, for example, the Sale of Goods Act 1979, s 14 implies terms to the effect that a seller acting in the course of business warrants that the goods are of satisfactory quality and are reasonably fit for their normal purpose. These provisions give several incentives for disclosure of information. The seller can avoid liability if any defects are specifically drawn to the buyer's attention before the contract is made, or if the buyer examines the goods and the defects ought to have been apparent. The buyer has an incentive to disclose any particular purpose for which the goods are being bought, for then the seller will be held to imply a warranty of fitness for that purpose, except where the circumstances show that the buyer does not rely, or it is unreasonable for him to rely, on the skill or judgement of the seller, ie where there is no relation of dependence. In sales to consumers, these implied terms cannot be excluded by virtue of the Unfair Contract Terms Act 1977, s 6. In other contracts, such exclusions will be subject to a test of reasonableness.

The strength of this incentive to disclose information in order to avoid liability for breach of an implied term of the contract depends upon the extent to which implied terms will be imported into contracts, a topic to be considered in Chapter 11. In sales of land and houses, for instance, there is no established implied warranty akin to the standard of satisfactory quality.[64] Thus, the housing market operates with this incentive to disclose defects in the property.

The extent of the incentive to disclose information under implied terms will depend also on the exact meaning of the implied term. Under the sale of goods provisions, for example, goods can be of satisfactory quality even if defective, provided that the seller through any description and the price charged indicates that the goods may be substandard. Similarly, the goods may be of satisfactory quality even though they do not conform to the buyer's expectations, provided that they are fit for the normal purpose for which such goods are intended. In a contract for the supply of professional services, the implied term that reasonable care has been taken to establish the facts on which advice has been given may also fall short of the purchaser's expectation, if the standard of reasonable care which is set by professional customary practice does not require detailed investigations.

(c)   REGULATORY OFFENCES

To make a crime out of a failure to disclose certain information during negotiations leading to a contract encounters the reluctance in the general

---

64 In sales of a new house a builder is liable for latent defects: Defective Premises Act 1972.

criminal law to make omissions a criminal offence. It is not a crime under English law, for instance, to fail to rescue a drowning swimmer, even though a rescue could have been easily effected with no risk. But the dividing line between omissions and acts is hard to draw in the context of misleading statements, for, as we have seen, the failure to give some information whilst giving the remainder can readily give a misleading impression. Thus the regulatory offences which condemn misleading statements can often encompass liability for omissions.

Under the Financial Services and Markets Act 2000, s 397, for instance, a person who makes a statement, promise or forecast which he knows or realizes is likely to be misleading, false or deceptive, or dishonestly conceals any material facts, for the purpose of inducing another to enter into an investment, commits an offence. To avoid the commission of this offence an investment broker would have to ensure that any statement about the investment prospects fully disclosed all material facts to a potential investor, or at least could not reasonably give any false impression.

A similar potential liability for omissions will arise in the context of other consumer protection legislation which we have already considered due to the extensive meaning given to the idea of misleading statements. Because the state-ment need not be in fact false under the Trade Descriptions Act 1968, s 3 and the Consumer Protection Act 1987, s 21, but merely give a misleading impression, statements which are economical with the truth, which in other words make certain claims but fail to make clear that certain implications which might be drawn from those claims by an unwary consumer should not be drawn, will be caught by the legislation. For this reason, in *Robertson v Dicicco*,[65] the statement that the second-hand car was a 'beautiful car', although perhaps literally true since the car had an attractive external appearance, amounted to a misleading statement, for it implied falsely that the car functioned satisfactorily as well.

A more explicit requirement to disclose information arises in connection with unsafe products. A producer of a product sold to consumers is required to provide consumers with the relevant information to enable them to assess the risks inherent in a product throughout the normal or reasonably foreseeable period of its use, where such risks are not immediately obvious without adequate warnings, and to advise them on appropriate precautions.[66] Clear labelling and warnings on products is likely to be the most effective way of complying with this duty of disclosure.

(d) MISTAKEN IDENTITY

A particular problem for consumers is the difficulty of knowing precisely with whom they are dealing. The problem becomes acute when transactions are

---

65 (1972) 70 LGR 589, DC.
66 General Product Safety Regulations 1994, SI 1994/2328, reg 8; A Ogus, *Regulation: Legal Form and Economic Theory* (Oxford, 1994), ch 7.

conducted at a distance by post, as in the mail order business, or by telephone, by e-mail or on interactive television. Regulations require businesses that approach consumers in these ways to ensure that they supply to the consumer prior to the formation of the contract information about the supplier's identity, and if the contract requires payment in advance, the supplier's address.[67] Failure by businesses to do so entitles the consumer to cancel the contract within a 'cooling-off' period.[68] In the case of advertisements, it will often be difficult for consumers to ascertain whether or not they are dealing with a business, with all the protection and risks which that creates, or merely another private individual. To put consumers on their guard, advertisements by businesses must reveal their true identity,[69] although this law appears to be widely flouted.

Other than these limited regulatory interventions, however, the law provides little protection against mistakes as to the identity of the other transacting party. Apart from a deliberate misrepresentation, which will permit rescission of the contract,[70] the consumer must be careful to make diligent enquiries as to the attributes such as credit-worthiness of the person with whom he or she is dealing. There is old authority in *Cundy v Lindsay*,[71] which supports the proposition that a contract will be void for the lack of agreement if a person purports to accept an offer sent by post which was made not to him but to a different person. If the contract is void, the victim can recover goods and money passed under the apparent contract, even if the rogue has already transferred them to an innocent third party. The courts have been reluctant to extend this authority, however, since they wish to protect the innocent third party and often take the view that the victim should have been more cautious.[72] The courts usually infer that a person intends to deal with the person who is physically present, even if the rogue has lied about his name or other attributes. The victim may rescind the contract for misrepresentation, but once the rogue has disposed of the property to an innocent third party, the sole remedy will be against the rogue, who no doubt has long since disappeared. Nevertheless, the old doctrine that the contract may be void for lack of agreement was applied, perhaps unsatisfactorily, by the Court of Appeal (Sedley LJ dissenting) in *Shogun Finance Ltd v Hudson*.[73] Having obtained another person's driving licence, a rogue persuaded a car dealer to sell him a car on hire purchase through the claimant finance company. The following day the defendant purchased the car in good faith from the rogue. The Court of Appeal upheld the finance company's claim to the car on the ground that the signature on the hire-purchase agreement was forged, so that no contract was made between the finance company and the rogue. The car dealer had acted merely as an intermediary, not an agent for the finance company,

67 Consumer Protection (Distance Selling) Regulations 2000, SI 2000/2334, reg 7.
68 Consumer Protection (Distance Selling) Regulations 2000, SI 2000/2334, regs 10–12.
69 Business Advertisements (Disclosure) Order 1977, SI 1977/1918.
70 *Car and Universal Finance Co Ltd v Caldwell* [1965] 1 QB 525, [1964] 1 All ER 290, CA.
71 (1878) 3 App Cas 459, HL
72 *Lewis v Averay* [1972] 1 QB 198, [1971] 3 All ER 907, CA.
73 [2001] EWCA Civ 1000, [2002] QB 834, [2002] 4 All ER 572.

so the contract was made at a distance by fax, not between parties who were physically present. The problem caused by this decision is that innocent purchasers may find they have lost all their money, and there is little they can do to protect themselves, whereas the finance company could take more precautions in checking on the identity of their customers.

D.   Abuse of position of trust

Numerous positive duties to act in good faith and with care during negotiations for a contract arise from special relationships of trust between the parties. Here the relationship of the parties is distinguished at the outset from the normal market of strangers bargaining at arm's length. Instead, the law identifies a relation of confidence and trust which requires a duty to provide full disclosure of information, to give careful advice and to avoid any conflicts of interest. The exact boundaries of these relations of confidence and trust have been established in part by the classification of certain types of legal relation, and in part by the examination of particular cases. The classification by reference to types of legal relation takes two forms.

1.   Contracts uberrimae fidei

One source of classification depends upon the nature of the contract which is being negotiated. Some contracts have been identified as always requiring good faith during negotiations, and these are known as contracts 'uberrimae fidei'. The most important example is a contract of insurance, where the assured has to reveal any facts which he knows, or ought to know, which a reasonable and prudent insurer might regard as material to the estimation of the risk.[74] A failure to disclose such information will entitle the insurer to avoid the contract and refuse to pay any claims under it.

The justification for this special classification of contracts of insurance is that only the insured is in a position to know the facts on which the risk must be estimated. Although this is true, this justification is perhaps inadequate to support the duty of disclosure, for of course it is open to the insurer to ask questions about the risk, and any inaccuracy and omission in the insured's reply could be treated as a misrepresentation. Moreover, the duty placed upon the insured seems excessive, since it assumes that the insured should recognize any features of his or her situation which might affect the insurer's estimate of risk, even though only the insurer possesses this specialized information. For example, a person convicted of robbery ten years before taking out fire insurance for a house was held in *Woolcott*

---

74 *Lambert v Co-operative Insurance Society* [1975] 2 Lloyd's Rep 485, CA; *Pan Atlantic Insurance Co Ltd v Pine Top Insurance Co Ltd* [1995] 1 AC 501, [1994] 3 All ER 581, HL.

v Sun Alliance and London Insurance Ltd[75] to have failed to have disclosed this pertinent fact so that his fire insurance was invalidated. Here it can be objected that since the insurance company (through its agent, a building society) did not ask any questions bearing on the insured's moral character or criminal convictions, and since it is not immediately obvious why a conviction for robbery could affect the risk of a house catching fire, the burden of disclosure imposed upon the insured is excessive and unpredictable in its effects.

In response to this criticism, the Association of British Insurance has issued a statement of good practice suggesting that insurers should give clear indication of those matters which the insurers regard as material to the risk, and should not repudiate liability to indemnify an insured on the ground of non-disclosure of a material fact which the insured could not reasonably be expected to have disclosed. This statement of practice, although not altering the strict law, represents a fairer rule for consumers, which might have prevented the avoidance of the fire insurance in *Woolcott v Sun Alliance and London Insurance Ltd.*

The duty to disclose information applies to both parties to a contract uberrimae fidei. The duty of the insurer extends at least to the disclosure of all facts known to the insurer which are material either to the nature of the risk sought to be covered or the recoverability of a claim under the policy which a prudent person seeking insurance would take into account in deciding whether or not to place the risk for which cover is sought.[76]

2. Fiduciary relations and relations of trust

The second source of classification comprises the identification of fiduciary relations. It is well established that many commercial relations impose a fiduciary relation between the parties, as in the case of principal and agent, partners in a business, and directors of companies. In any contract between these parties, the fiduciary duties require the highest standards of good faith in dealing, which certainly includes full disclosure of any information. Failure to disclose information will result in the contract being voidable, and may also impose a duty on the party in breach of the fiduciary relation to account for any profits made as a result of the failure to disclose.[77]

As well as these established instances of fiduciary relations, the equitable jurisdiction to avoid contracts on the ground of undue influence can be employed to identify special circumstances which trigger a duty to disclose information. We saw in *Lloyds Bank Ltd v Bundy*,[78] for instance, how a bank assumed a relation of

---

75 [1978] 1 All ER 1253, [1978] 1 WLR 493, QB.
76 *Banque Keyser Ullmann SA v Skandia (UK) Insurance Co Ltd* [1990] 1 QB 665, sub nom *Banque Financière de la Cité SA v Westgate Insurance Co Ltd* [1989] 2 All ER 952, CA.
77 *Boardman v Phipps* [1967] 2 AC 46, [1966] 3 All ER 721, HL.
78 [1975] QB 326, [1974] 3 All ER 757, CA.

trust and confidence as a result of dealings for many years with a farmer, so that he came to repose trust in the bank to advise him carefully during negotiations for a contract. The duty imposed on the bank in such circumstances required the bank to ensure that the farmer obtained independent advice and that it disclosed all the information about the transaction to the farmer. Similar relations of trust may arise from the conduct of the parties in many diverse instances, such as the dealings between shareholders in a small family firm,[79] or between the beneficiaries under a Will.[80]

Weaker duties of disclosure arise in connection with particular types of contract, perhaps on account of custom or a perception by the courts that there will otherwise arise a risk of abuse of trust. Here the duty of disclosure does not extend to all material facts, but merely certain facts which are exclusively known to one party and there is a commercial incentive to leave them undisclosed. For example, a duty is placed on a creditor to explain to a surety any terms in the contract between creditor and debtor which render the surety's obligation materially different in a potentially disadvantageous way from those which the surety might naturally expect.[81] But the duty of disclosure does not extend to the debtor's likely creditworthiness, for the surety is expected to make his or her own enquiries on that point and take the risk of default.

E. Misuse of confidential information

During negotiations for a contract, one party may reveal to the other confidential information for the purpose of inducing the other to enter into the contract with him. He may be trying to sell an invention such as a new mechanical system for automobiles,[82] or to enter into a joint venture to exploit a discovery such as a seam of gold,[83] and necessarily information about the invention or discovery will have to be disclosed before the other party will be induced to enter a binding contract. Since this information has a commercial value, the risk exists, if the contract is not concluded, that the other party, having become acquainted with the invention or discovery, will then seek to exploit it alone. As part of the duty to negotiate with care, such action will be regarded as a misuse of confidential information, and will give rise to a duty to pay compensation. This aspect of the duty serves the valuable purpose of permitting frank negotiations to take place, so that an efficient contract can be concluded.

A number of technical problems make this aspect of the duties during negotiation difficult to state with precision. Given that the parties have never formally

79 *Coleman v Myers* [1977] 2 NZLR 225, CA.
80 *Greenwood v Greenwood* (1863) 2 De GJ & Sm 28.
81 *Levett v Barclays Bank plc* [1995] 2 All ER 615, [1995] 1 WLR 1260, QB.
82 *Mechanical and General Inventions Co Ltd and Lehwess v Austin* [1935] AC 346, HL.
83 *LAC Minerals v International Corona Resources Ltd* (1989) 61 DLR (4th) 14.

entered into a contract, the cause of action must lie either in some form of implied contract or constitute an independent tort. The technique of an implied contract clearly runs directly counter to the traditional law's reluctance to impose contractual obligations during negotiations. But in fact it perhaps most closely accords with the understanding of the parties, which is usually that the information is disclosed on the basis that it will be used for the purpose of considering whether or not to enter the main contract, and not for any other purpose. An implied agreement on these terms should not be difficult to infer from the conduct of the parties and as a necessary incident of their bargaining relationship. But it is also possible to present the claim as an independent tort of breach of confidence. The disadvantage of the tort claim is that it raises the question of what information should be regarded as confidential. This question is an unnecessary diversion in the context of pre-contractual negotiations, for the point is that the information given has been used for an unauthorized purpose. It should not matter whether the information was secret, or given in confidence. The information was given for a particular purpose, the evaluation of the proposals to enter the contract, and the breach of duty arises from the unauthorized use of the information.

A second technical problem concerns the calculation of an appropriate remedy in damages. In many instances the claimant has suffered no direct loss from the misuse of the information. What has occurred rather is that the defendant has been able to take commercial advantage of the information without having to pay for it. The measure of compensation could therefore be formulated as either the commercial value of the information if it had been sold, or the actual profits which the defendant obtains through use of the information. In the Canadian case *LAC Minerals v International Corona Resources Ltd*,[84] the Supreme Court of Canada favoured the latter measure for the remedy, La Forest J arguing that only that measure would deter breach of the obligation to bargain in good faith. In this case the claimant had revealed to the defendant the likely presence of gold under a third party's land for the purpose of negotiating a joint venture to purchase the land and mine it. Negotiations broke down and the defendant purchased the land and mined it for its own benefit. The claimant succeeded in recovering the stupendous profits made from the mine, which was far greater than the value of the information about the likelihood of a gold seam at the time it was disclosed. For a similar reason of deterring the misuse of confidential information, the use of damages to require the defendant to disgorge profits for breach of a contractual duty not to disclose confidential information was approved by the House of Lords in *A-G v Blake*.[85] These cases suggest that the remedy of disgorgement of profits may be available for the unauthorised use of confidential information which was disclosed during contractual negotiations, whether or not the claim is based upon an implied contract or a breach of a duty in tort.

84 (1989) 61 DLR (4th) 14.
85 [2001] 1 AC 268, [2001] 4 All 385, HL; see Chapter 17.

F. Misleading implied promises

In stark opposition to the traditional view that during the negotiations for a contract no binding obligations may arise, it is possible for the courts to infer implied contractual undertakings from conduct and statements made during the negotiations. These undertakings differ from misrepresentations, for they involve a promise to act or refrain from acting in certain ways in the future. Liability for such undertakings may be conceived as either a contract based upon the exchange model supported by consideration, usually in the form of a unilateral contract, or as an estoppel based upon the reliance model. The difference in legal technique depends upon whether or not the court can infer a request to perform an act of detrimental reliance in exchange for the undertaking. If it can, a contract to perform the undertaking will be found; if not, then the reliance model of estoppel will found the obligation. The difference in the legal technique employed may affect the remedies available to the injured party.

1. Collateral contracts

There is nothing anomalous in the idea of a contract preceding another contract. An option to purchase an item in the future acquired for consideration is a typical instance of such a prior contractual undertaking. During negotiations for a major transaction, the parties may wish to secure their position in the meantime against various kinds of opportunism, and they can do so through express contracts. They may make an enforceable agreement to use best endeavours to negotiate an agreement, or an undertaking not to negotiate with any other person for a fixed period of time. What these 'lock-out' agreements seek to achieve is a contractual expression of a duty to bargain with care and in good faith. The validity of such contracts is in general not in doubt, and indeed the courts may imply into such agreements a term to make reasonable endeavours to reach an agreement.[86] But the courts have declined to enforce obligations which they regard as too vague to be policed, such as an undertaking to negotiate for a reasonable period of time or to negotiate in good faith.[87]

In the absence of an express agreement, the courts can also infer a prior contract from the circumstances of the case in order to support the duty to bargain with care. As an example of this contractual approach based upon a finding of consideration, we should consider *Blackpool and Fylde Aero Club Ltd v Blackpool Borough Council*.[88] The defendant owned an airport and granted the right to use

---

86 *Queensland Electricity Generating Board v New Hope Collieries Pty Ltd* [1989] 1 Lloyd's Rep 205, PC.

87 *Walford v Miles* [1992] 2 AC 128, [1992] 1 All ER 453, HL; Neil, 'A Key to Lock-Out Agreements?' (1992) 108 *Law Quarterly Review* 405.

88 [1990] 3 All ER 25, [1990] 1 WLR 1195, CA; see also *Harvela Investments Ltd v Royal Trust Co of Canada (CI) Ltd* [1986] AC 207, [1985] 2 All ER 966, HL.

the airport for a fee. The defendant invited tenders for such a concession, stating in the invitation that it was not bound to accept all or part of any tender, and that no tender submitted after noon on a specified day would be considered. The claimant submitted a tender by posting it by hand an hour before the expiry of the deadline in the defendant's letter box. Due to the defendant's oversight, the letter box was not emptied at noon, and subsequently the claimant's bid was treated as having been submitted too late for consideration. The defendant then accepted another bid which was lower than the claimant's. The claimant successfully claimed damages for breach of an implied undertaking by the defendant either that the claimant's bid would be considered along with all other bids conforming to the invitation, or that the claimant's bid would be considered if other conforming tenders were considered.

Although it is well established that an invitation to tender does not in itself create a contractual obligation, but should be regarded as an invitation to treat, the court found in the particular circumstances of the case an implied contractual obligation to conform to the terms of the invitation. The court emphasized that the implied contract arose because on the facts the defendant had invited the claimant to tender (the claimant having held the concession until that time), that the defendant was required as a public authority under its rules to conduct the tendering process fairly, and that it had specified in great detail how tenders should be made, not only as to the time, but also by the use of an official envelope to ensure secrecy. This detail in the invitation to tender entitled the claimant to go beyond the hope that its tender would be considered, the normal position in tendering cases, and to have a reasonable expectation that a conforming tender would be considered along with the others. This analysis created an implied contract: the defendant undertook to tenderers to conform to the terms of its invitation, if they in turn submitted bids in conformity with those terms.

2.   The reliance model

The alternative legal analysis of these undertakings given during the bargaining process consists of an application of the doctrine of estoppel as in the cases examined under the reliance model such as *Crabb v Arun District Council*.[89] In that case, as a result of the defendant's oral undertaking that the claimant would be granted a right of access to a road, the claimant sold a portion of his land leaving the remainder inaccessible without the point of access. Subsequently negotiations for the legal conveyance of the right of access broke down, so no formal contract was concluded. Nevertheless, the defendant was held to be bound by the oral undertaking, which had been supplemented by conduct, all of which induced the claimant to act to his detriment. The claimant's remedy was conceived as one to remedy the injustice which he had suffered, which in this case could only be achieved by granting him the right of access.

89 [1976] Ch 179, [1975] 3 All ER 865, CA.

In both kinds of legal analysis, whether it be contractual or by estoppel, the courts look for a promise, either express or implied, which induces the other party to change his position on reliance of the promise. The difference between the two analyses is simply that under the contractual analysis the change of position has been either expressly or impliedly requested by the promisor, whereas no such request can be implied in the instances of estoppel. Thus in *Blackpool and Fylde Aero Club v Blackpool Borough Council*, the court implied a request to the claimant to submit a bid in accordance with the terms of the invitation to tender. In contrast, in *Crabb v Arun District Council*, the court could not find an implied request on the part of the owner of the road for the claimant to sell a portion of his land, although certainly such a sale was foreseen as a consequence of the undertaking. But it must be admitted that the implied request which forms the basis of the contractual claim is often artificial. It stretches the facts of *Blackpool and Fylde Aero Club v Blackpool Borough Council* to say that the defendant asked the claimant to bid for the concession, rather than simply promising to consider the bids strictly according to the stated terms.

3.   Damages

The need to use the contractual analysis, and therefore to infer requests from all the circumstances of the case, derives from the limitations of the reliance model of liability considered in Chapter 5. In particular, we noted the hesitation of English courts, not shared in other jurisdictions, to extend this basis of liability beyond promises concerning interests in land. In addition, English courts betray a marked reluctance to award damages for breach of these promises under the reliance model, preferring to use traditional equitable remedies for unravelling transactions or completing them. These limitations rendered it more controversial, for example, to use the reliance model as the basis for liability in *Blackpool and Fylde Aero Club v Blackpool Borough Council*. It was difficult to describe the granting of a concession or the promise to conduct a tendering operation fairly and carefully as relating to an interest in land. Even worse, since the concession had already been granted to another organization, the only practicable remedy available was compensatory damages, a remedy which would have broken new ground under English law.

We observed in discussing the reliance model that other common law jurisdictions have dispensed with these limitations upon the use of estoppel to render promises binding when made during the negotiation process. In the Australian case of *Waltons Stores (Interstate) Ltd v Maher*,[90] the company, largely by its silence, misled the contractor into commencing demolition operations even though it had decided not to proceed with the transaction which had reached the final stage of negotiation. The High Court of Australia held the company to be

90 (1988) 164 CLR 387, Aust HC.

bound by its implied promise to complete the contract because, knowing that the contractor was incurring expenses by acting on the basis of a false assumption, it was unconscionable for the company to adopt a course of inaction which served to encourage the contractor to incur that detriment. This application of the reliance model is not confined to interests in land, and resulted in an award of damages. This approach seems preferable, because it avoids the fictitious implication of requests, yet leaves the court flexibility with respect to the remedy.

It should not be supposed, however, that the courts will lightly infer such promissory obligations arising during the course of negotiations. One party will often be put to considerable expense and trouble in preparing a bid for a contract, or incur legal expenses in negotiating the terms, but normally these expenses will not be recoverable. What distinguishes the successful claims for compensation is the presence of an express or implied undertaking which makes it reasonable for the promisee to incur those expenses in reliance upon the promise. To avoid this liability, the promisor must take care to avoid giving such a false impression, or, on realizing such an impression has been given, to act promptly to disabuse the promisee of the mistaken assumption. In this sense, this source of liability fits into the general framework of a duty of care during negotiations, the duty comprising one of disabusing the other of mistaken assumptions about intentions which foreseeably will cause the other to act to his detriment.

G.   Rationale for the duty to negotiate with care

Having drawn together all these strands in the law which govern duties during the negotiation process, it is time to consider whether these duties can be understood as resting upon some more general principles. The discussion has revealed that the law's analysis of different aspects of the negotiating process differs radically in the concepts employed. Numerous doctrines such as misrepresentation, undue influence, fiduciary duties, estoppel and implied contracts, together with extensive regulatory provisions, supply a subtle and intricate tapestry by which the law regulates behaviour during negotiations. The complexity of the law combined with the traditional English reluctance to embrace broad principles instead of narrow technical doctrines has so far prevented the emergence and recognition of any general principle which unites these diverse rules governing negotiations:

> In many civil law systems, and perhaps in most legal systems outside the common law world, the law of obligations recognizes and enforces an overriding principle that in making and carrying out contracts parties should act in good faith. This does not simply mean that they should not deceive each other, a principle which any legal system must recognize; its effect is perhaps most aptly conveyed by such metaphorical colloquialisms

as 'playing fair', 'coming clean' or 'putting one's cards face upwards on the table'. It is in essence a principle of fair and open dealing . . .

English law has, characteristically, committed itself to no such overriding principle but has developed piecemeal solutions in response to demonstrated problems of unfairness.[91]

This piecemeal approach is now under challenge from the EC as part of its policy on consumer protection. The Commission has proposed a mandatory general principle contained in a framework Directive that would prohibit 'unfair commercial practices' that cause a detriment to consumers.[92] The general principle would be described in prohibitions of various types of unfair commercial practices, including practices that are misleading or likely to mislead consumers, the failure to disclose to consumers material information which is likely to affect the consumer's decision, practices involving harassment, coercion or undue influence, and failure to provide information and adequate complaint handling in the after-sales service period. Further substance would be provided to the general duty by means of codes of conduct agreed by particular trade sectors and non-binding guidance issued by the Commission. The two principal advantages of this proposal for English law are that:

(i)   by creating a general principle, the law may be able to adapt to the rapid changes in deceptive market practices that afflict consumers; and

(ii)   by creating a principle that applies only to dealings with consumers, the law can evolve in a way that differentiates adequately between the consumer context and the commercial context.

It is, of course, possible that the enactment of a general standard governing dealings with consumers might influence the evolution of private law towards a general principle governing all pre-contractual negotiations. If such a principle were to be recognized by the courts as the underlying rationale of their decisions in the light of legislative developments, how should it be described and justified?

A justification for a general principle must commence with a reflection upon the compelling reasons for interfering with the general freedom to enter into negotiations without a binding commitment. This general freedom itself rests upon several possible justifications. In part it depends upon a conception of freedom which allows individuals to act in their own best interests without regard to others. But this is strengthened by considerations of market efficiency. The ability to enter negotiations without commitment permits traders to discover

---

91 Bingham LJ in *Interfoto Picture Library Ltd v Stiletto Visual Programmes Ltd* [1989] QB 433, [1988] 1 All ER 348, CA.

92 Commission, Green Paper on European Union Consumer Protection, COM (2001) 531 final, 2.10.2001; Commission, Follow-up Communication to the Green paper on EU Consumer Protection, COM (2002) 289 final, 11.6.2002; Council, Resolution on Community Consumer Policy Strategy 2002–2006; H Collins (ed), *The Forthcoming EC Directive on Unfair Commercial Practices* (The Hague, 2003).

which possible bargain will be the most advantageous, which in turn promotes the goal of wealth maximization. The same ability permits the parties to discuss in advance the details of their proposed relation, which should avoid misunderstandings which might generate costs and opportunistic behaviour later on. 'If the utility of contract as an instrument of self-government is not to be seriously weakened, parties must be free to break off preliminary negotiations without being held to an accounting.'[93] Finally, we have observed that self-interested behaviour must be permitted in order to protect the incentives to acquire information and expertise. Any duty of care towards the interests of the other negotiating party must be constrained so that one who has acquired at some cost or ingenuity better skills or information should be able to reap the rewards of that effort through making advantageous contracts.

But these reasons for rejecting any general principle relating to bargaining duties do not rule out all forms of regulation of negotiations. Considerations of market efficiency can be employed to justify regulation of types of negotiating behaviour which harm the efficiency of the market, as in the case of fraud which induces contracts on the basis of false information. Moreover, bargaining duties may prove necessary in order to ensure that negotiating parties retain the fruits of their efforts, as in the case of disclosure of confidential information. Thus, even on the narrow ground of enhancing the competitive properties of the market, it is possible to justify considerable regulation of the negotiating process. I suggest, however, that this combination of respect for the self-interested exercise of individual liberty, subject to considerations of preserving and enhancing market efficiency, is inadequate to justify the extent to which today the law regulates the parties to contractual negotiations.

At several points in my survey of the law, the full extent of the duties during negotiations for a contract has been explained by reference to the concept of relations of dependence. In these situations the relative skills and knowledge of one party have led to the imposition of a duty to take into account the interests of the other party. In the sale of goods, for example, a seller who is in the business of trading in certain types of goods has imposed on him the duty to warrant that the goods are of satisfactory quality or alternatively to point out the defects to the purchaser. Similarly, when discussing the terms of a contract, one party who is in a better position to understand the legal consequences of the contract will be under a duty to explain the full import of the terms, or else risk liability for misrepresentation. These, and many other instances of relations of dependence, imply that a purely self-interested exercise of freedom during the negotiating process is impermissible where one party stands in a relation of dependence to the other.

This interpretation of the law does not create a direct conflict with the ideal of freedom of contract. It merely interprets the privilege to act in a purely

---

93 F Kessler, G Gilmore and A Kronman, *Contracts* (Boston, 3rd edn, 1986), p 201.

self-interested way within narrower confines. The law never permits self-interested action where it causes direct physical harm to another. The law also protects various economic interests from deliberate or negligent harm, either through actions for breach of contract or the use of the law of torts. In employing the idea of a relation of dependence, the law governing duties during the negotiations for a contract merely expands its conception of when the economic interests of another can be said to have been harmed. The legal duties do not require unlimited altruism, but merely expand the situations when the law requires care to ensure that the economic interests of another are not harmed. In this sense the existence of a law governing negotiating duties does not conflict with the general principle of freedom of contract. Instead, it reinterprets the limits placed upon freedom, narrowing the scope of permitted self-interested action on the ground that it harms the economic interests of others.

Given this justification for the existence of duties during negotiations for a contract, I suggest that the law can best be interpreted by reference to a duty to negotiate with care. This formulation draws attention to the emphasis in the justification on the protection of the interests of the other party. At the same time, by employing the idea of care, it recognizes that carefulness is a flexible standard, so that the duty becomes stricter as the other party to the negotiations is a person in a relation of dependence, and that the required degree of care will alter between contexts. These features are superior to the alternative formulation of a duty to bargain in good faith. The latter formulation implies that the law merely requires honesty, which is plainly inaccurate in instances of negligence liability.[94] Moreover, the good faith idea suggests that the standard is constant, which fails to capture the way in which the legal duties increase in relations of dependence and may vary according to market context. Nevertheless, good faith can be understood as a requirement for an objective standard of conduct, not limited to unconscionable practices akin to fraud, but encompassing ideas of fair dealing,[95] in which case a good faith standard may effectively amount to a duty to negotiate with care.

As we have seen, the pragmatism and doctrinal complexity of English law, born of its system of piecemeal development of the law through precedent decisions, typically resists generalizations such as a duty to negotiate with care as part of the formal fabric of the law. But these generalizations serve the useful purposes of assisting an orderly exposition of the law, revealing its underlying tensions, and articulating the relevant considerations which need to be balanced in a particular case. The principle should not be understood as a rule to be applied according to its terms in each case, but as the basic justification for regulation of the bargaining process. With this justification in mind, then anomalies and inconsistencies may be avoided.

94 For a different interpretation of good faith as co-operation, see J Adams and R Brownsword, *Key Issues in Contract* (London, 1995), ch 7.
95 Mason, 'Contract, Good Faith and Equitable Standards in Fair Dealing' (2000) *Law Quarterly Review* 66.

In particular it is to be hoped that the recognition of a duty to negotiate with care will lead to the elimination of many of the anomalies resulting from the application of different conceptual analyses to similar states of facts. For example, we have noted in the context of implied undertakings during the process of negotiation, that the application of the two organizing frameworks of implied contracts and estoppel leads to inconsistencies of approach to liability and remedies. If a general principle were acknowledged, then a uniform test for liability and a coherent approach to remedies might be achieved.

Similarly, we noted the strange result in connection with the measure of damages for misrepresentation that a claimant may gain a higher measure for pre-contractual representations than claims based upon warranties contained expressly in the contract itself. The advantage of a recognition of a general duty to negotiate with care in this context would be to create a distinct species of liability, which is neither precisely contractual nor tortious, so that the courts could develop appropriate principles for the quantification of damages. The measure of damages here should include the losses incurred and the opportunity costs of entering a disadvantageous transaction, since the purpose of the general duty is both to compensate for harm caused and to promote a competitive market. But there should be no need in the context of commercial transactions, apart from perhaps in cases of fraud, for the law to extend liability to non-economic losses such as disappointment and inconvenience, or to remote and unforeseeable risks which are not normally ones which a contract seeks to reallocate.

The underlying problem here is that the failure to develop an independent legal concept of duties existing during the process of negotiation has forced the courts to borrow concepts from other branches of the law which often prove inappropriate. To discover a positive duty in these circumstances, the courts have been compelled to employ the law of tort, which often falls short in describing the kinds of misleading bargaining practices which should be the basis for censure, yet at the same time, when it does apply, suggests a measure of damages remedy which is anomalous in a commercial context. The alternative conceptual framework available to the courts is to treat all these cases as factors which vitiate consent to a contract. The disadvantage of this approach is that it makes little provision for damages beyond restitution, and often a remedy will be barred altogether as a result of the unwitting involvement of innocent third parties or subsequent transactions. The recognition of a duty to negotiate with care as part of the law of contract, yet not comprising contractual obligations based upon the terms of a contract, would solve these conceptual difficulties by filling a black hole at the heart of the common law's regulation of trading practices.

Terms

A.   The forms of agreement

For what does a person make himself contractually responsible? In fidelity to the ideal of individual liberty, which gives rise to a presumption that the parties should be free to choose the terms of their contract, the classical law answers this question by asserting that a party to a contract is bound by those obligations to which he has consented and no others. In short, the terms of the agreement determine the content of the contractual obligations.

This simple principle still provides the first indication of the content of the parties' contractual obligations, but in the modern law it must be substantially modified. In later chapters we will examine the different ways in which the modern law both supplements and controls the terms of contracts, and hence affects the content of the contractual obligations. Those chapters reveal the significant degree to which the freedom to choose the terms has been eviscerated in modern law. This chapter confines its attention to the complicated development of the principle that in the first instance the agreement determines the content of the obligations.

The terms of the contract include both express and implied terms:

- The express terms comprise written statements of the agreement and any oral agreement.
- The implied terms are those that have not been mentioned by the parties, but the court nevertheless deems the parties to have agreed to these additional terms.

This process of supplementing the express terms is usually justified by reference to the intentions of the parties. It is alleged that the parties intended to include the implied terms, although did not do so expressly either due to lack of time or because the implied terms were so obvious that it seemed unnecessary to state them formally. We shall see, however, that this conventional explanation of the source of implied terms in the intention of the parties wears thin in view of the expansive nature of these implied obligations.

Under the classical law, the express and implied terms are regarded as properly determining the content of the contractual obligations because they conform to the intentions of the parties. This reference to intention provokes a perennial difficulty. If a determination of the content of the terms rests upon the intention of the parties, what happens when there is a dispute about the content or meaning of the terms? If the parties were genuinely at cross-purposes, it seems that there was no real agreement on the terms. If that is so, how can the court find that a contract was ever reached between them? The danger is that any dispute over the terms of the contract will be elevated into a dispute about the very existence of the contract in the first place.

It will be recalled that the existence of the contract, the ascription of contractual responsibility, was determined by an objective test. The question posed by the court was not whether a party intended to enter a contract, but rather whether the other party reasonably supposed that he did so intend. The same practice of adopting an objective approach emerges in this context of determining the content of the terms of the contract. The test is not what the promisor intended, but rather what the promisee reasonably supposed that he had been promised. In the case which we used to illustrate the objective test of contractual responsibility, *Smith v Hughes*,[1] a problem of interpretation of the content of the agreement was also raised. As well as arguing that no contract had been reached, the buyer alleged that he believed that one of the terms of the contract was that the oats were warranted to be old, which the seller disputed. If the court had sought the true intentions of the parties, no doubt it would have discovered that the parties were at cross-purposes: the seller only had new oats to sell, so would not have

1   (1871) LR 6 QB 597, QB.

made such a warranty; the buyer, a horse trainer, had no use for new oats, so clearly only wanted to purchase old oats. But the court avoided the issue of intent again, and instead asked whether the buyer reasonably supposed that he had been promised that the oats were old. The reasonableness of such a supposition would depend upon evidence about the seller's statements or conduct.

Once the test for determining the content of a contract shifts to an objective approach, again we must question whether or not the connection with the intention of the parties is preserved. It is not the intention of the promisor but the reasonable expectation generated by the promise from the point of view of the promisee that determines the content of the contractual obligation. It follows inevitably from the objective test that a promisor may be bound by an obligation that he or she never intended to undertake. The reasonable expectation of the promisee must be based on the words of the promise or the text of the contractual document, but it may not correspond exactly with the intention of the promisor. These reasonable expectations of the promisee will also be informed by the nature of the proposed transaction, the normal terms for such a transaction, and any express refinements or qualifications which have been drawn to the promisee's attention. The use of the objective test for determining the content of the contractual obligations can be used to support the view that the justification for the enforcement of consensual obligations cannot be discovered in the idea that the courts enforce the will of the parties. Instead, the self-regulation created by the parties in their contract is approached as an incomplete record of their understanding, which needs to be supplemented by implied terms, for the purpose of protecting the reasonable expectations generated by the assumption of contractual responsibility.

B. Incorporation of express terms

The express terms of a contract can comprise not only the oral and written promises given at the time of the contract, but also any documents to which those promises refer as comprising additional express terms of the contract. The express agreement may refer to the business's standard terms of business, which then become part of the contract. For contracts of employment, the employer may issue a short written contract which refers as a source of further contract terms to other lengthy documents, such as a relevant collective agreement with a recognised union or a pension scheme. A short oral or written agreement can therefore incorporate a lengthy document setting out the rights and obligations of both parties.

A standard form contract is likely to become a statement of the terms of the contract either because the printed document was handed over at the time of the formation of the contract, or because it was incorporated by the express terms of the agreement.

Documents may also be incorporated as express terms of the contract by virtue of custom or a regular course of dealing between the parties. In *British Crane Hire Corpn Ltd v Ipswich Plant Hire Ltd*,[2] the owner of a crane hired it out to a contractor in the same business, without expressly mentioning the intention to enter the contract on the standard trade terms contained in a model supplied by the trade association. But the court inferred that the standard model contract had been incorporated into the contract, these being the customary terms of the trade. A standard set of terms for a contract will also be incorporated automatically into a contract, if there has been a long and consistent course of dealing on those terms between commercial parties.[3]

For a document to be incorporated into the contract as part of its express terms, however, it must be introduced at the time of the formation of the contract. An attempt to impose a further document containing additional terms after the agreement has been reached will be impermissible, unless this document amounts to an agreed variation of the contract. In order to draw this distinction, a court will often have to forge a contrast between a contractual document and a mere receipt or acknowledgment. In *Chapelton v Barry UDC*,[4] the plaintiff hired a deck-chair, and having paid his fee he was given a ticket. The court treated the ticket as a receipt rather than a document containing any express terms of the contract, so the exclusion clause contained in it could not form part of the express terms of the contract.

When both parties to the contract incorporate their standard terms of business into the agreement, there is a danger that the terms may conflict in crucial respects. In these 'battle of forms' cases, it can be argued that the parties never reached an agreement at all, so no contract has been created. In practice, however, the courts will resolve any dispute about the content of the contract by regarding one standard form as the content of the contract. This result can be achieved by interpreting the facts of the case so that one set of terms was impliedly withdrawn or only issued after the formation of the contract. As a last resort, the court will give priority to the last set of terms delivered before the other party commences performance of the contract. Under the objective approach the conduct of performing the contract is regarded as acceptance of the standard form.[5]

C. Oral agreements

Although oral agreements also determine the content of the express terms of the contract, they can provide fertile terrain for disputes about the content of the

2 [1975] QB 303, [1974] 1 All ER 1059, CA.
3 *Henry Kendall & Sons (a firm) v William Lillico & Sons Ltd* [1969] 2 AC 31, [1968] 2 All ER 444, HL.
4 [1940] 1 KB 532, [1940] 1 All ER 356, CA.
5 For comparisons with similar developments in other legal systems: see Von Mehren, 'The "Battle of Forms": A Comparative View' (1990) 38 *American Journal of Comparative Law* 265.

contract. In the absence of a written record of the terms, there can be endless disagreement about whether a particular warranty was offered or a particular disclaimer made. No doubt for this reason, written terms predominate in business transactions.

1. Informal understandings

It seems to be not an infrequent occurrence that in commercial contracts the parties will seek informal understandings between them, which go beyond the written terms of the transaction. Perhaps the lawyers are left to haggle over the details in the formal contract, and the businesses agree informally that the contract should be performed in a particular way or according to a shared understanding. This practice reveals how the parties will often rely upon standards of good faith and co-operation in commercial relations to resolve any issues between them, rather than insist upon strict performance of the contract according to its letter.

Even more frustrating for the lawyers will be the case where the parties deliberately leave the terms of the written contract ambiguous, relying on informal commercial standards to resolve any disputes which may arise.[6] Of course, if the trust reposed in the informal undertaking proves unfounded, then the question must arise whether or not the informal promises were part of the contract so that they can supplement the studied ambiguity of the express terms. In some instances the court will conclude that these informal understandings were not intended to be legally binding commitments, so they will fail the test of legal enforceability. In other instances, the informal understanding may be used to interpret the meaning of the contract, as in the case where the performance must be carried out within a reasonable time. A severe difficulty arises when the informal understanding contradicts the written contract.

Formerly the courts applied a rule which excluded such parol evidence of informal understandings which contradicted the written letter of the contract. But the courts now recognise many techniques which remove the force of this rule so that rarely, if ever, will a party to a written contract be prevented from alleging that the terms of the contract were altered by independent oral promises. For example, in *Evans & Son (Portsmouth) Ltd v Andrea Merzario Ltd*,[7] by a written agreement the defendants shipped the plaintiff's goods from Italy to England, but the goods were damaged in transit because they were carried above deck. Under the terms of the contract, the defendants benefited from an exemption clause against damage to the goods and a term which gave them freedom to control the placing of the goods on the ship unless this term was altered by express written agreement. The plaintiff proved, however, that the defendants had given an oral undertaking prior to the

---

6   Thomas, 'Legal Skills and the Use of Ambiguity' (1991) 42 *Northern Ireland Legal Quarterly* 14.
7   [1976] 2 All ER 930, [1976] 1 WLR 1078, CA.

formation of the contract that the containers would be shipped under the deck, an undertaking which had induced the plaintiff to agree to the contract. On these facts the English Court of Appeal permitted the plaintiff to claim damages for breach of the oral promise to load the goods under the deck. They held that the oral promise was intended to be legally enforceable. It was either incorporated into the written contract and overrode the contrary written terms, or it constituted a collateral contract, the consideration for which was the plaintiff's entry into the main contract of carriage. Whichever analysis is preferred, the decision in practice eliminates the parol evidence rule from English law.[8]

Even in the absence of an express agreement, a court may enforce an informal understanding about how the contract should be construed by the technique of 'estoppel by convention'. If both parties treat the terms as having a certain meaning and act on that assumption, they will be prevented from denying that the contract should be construed in that way.[9]

Informal understandings also run the risk of invalidity for failure to satisfy any statutory requirement of formalities, such as the rule that a contract for the sale of land must be in writing and that the documents must incorporate all the terms.[10] An informal understanding such as a letter may not be incorporated into the contractual documents and, therefore, becomes unenforceable under the statute. Nevertheless, if the informal understanding can be interpreted as a collateral contract, one which induced entry into the main contract of sale, it may be enforceable as an independent transaction to which the statutory requirement of formalities does not apply.[11]

The practice of the parties during the performance of a contract may also reveal that they placed a particular interpretation on the words of the contract. The courts generally resist the suggestion that evidence of subsequent conduct can be an aid to interpretation of the document.[12] Nevertheless, this conduct can be evidence of an agreement to modify the contract or waiver of breach, which achieves the same effect by a more complex reasoning process.[13]

2.   Rectification

The mirror image of the problem occurs where it is alleged that the written record of the terms of the contract does not conform to the prior oral agreement. Under an action for rectification of a written contractual document, the claim will

---

8   Law Commission, *The Parol Evidence Rule*, Report No 154 (London, 1986).
9   *Amalgamated Investment and Property Co Ltd v Texas Commerce International Bank Ltd* [1982] QB 84, [1981] 1 All ER 923; affd [1982] QB 84, [1981] 3 All ER 577, CA.
10   Law of Property (Miscellaneous Provisions) Act 1989, s 2.
11   *Record v Bell* [1991] 4 All ER 471, [1971] 1 WLR 853, Ch.
12   *Schuler AG v Wickman Machine Tool Sales Ltd* [1974] AC 235, [1973] 2 All ER 39, HL.
13   *Panoutsos v Raymond Hadley Corpn of New York* [1917] 2 KB 473, CA; see Chapter 15.

succeed when the court concludes that the document does not contain the terms which were orally agreed between the parties. This is not an exception to an objective approach to determining the content of the contract, but rather a clarification of the priorities between different sorts of evidence which satisfy the objective test. The action for rectification prevents the written contract from constituting conclusive evidence of the terms where it can be established that the document does not conform to a prior oral agreement.

The narrowness of this claim for rectification is illustrated by *Rose (Frederick E) (London) Ltd v William H Pim Jnr & Co Ltd*.[14] The plaintiff had received an order for 500 tons of Moroccan horsebeans called 'feveroles', but, not knowing what feveroles were, it asked the defendant who said that 'feveroles means just horsebeans'. The plaintiff then orally agreed to buy 'horsebeans' from the defendant, and subsequently entered a written agreement to buy 500 tons of 'Tunisian horsebeans' from the defendant. But the plaintiff's customer rejected these horsebeans on the ground that the beans were a larger, less valuable type known as 'feves', not the feveroles which had been ordered. The plaintiff then sought to have its written contract with the defendant rectified, so that the word 'feveroles' would be substituted for 'horsebeans'. If successful, this claim for rectification would have then put the defendant in breach of contract for supplying the wrong type of horsebeans, so that the plaintiff would be able to recoup its losses resulting from rejection of the goods by the customer. But the action for rectification had to fail, because the written contract with the term 'horsebeans' conformed exactly to the prior oral agreement for 'horsebeans'. As Denning LJ observed:

> Rectification is concerned with contracts and documents, not with intentions. In order to get rectification, it is necessary to show that the parties were in complete agreement on the terms of their contract, but by an error wrote them down wrongly. And in this regard, in order to ascertain the terms of their contract, you do not look into the inner minds of the parties – into their intentions – any more than you do in the formation of any other contract. You look at their outward acts, ie, at what they said or wrote to one another in coming to their agreement, and then compare it with the document which they have signed. If you can predict with certainty what their contract was, and that it is, by a common mistake, wrongly expressed in the document, then you rectify the document. But nothing less will suffice.

It follows from these principles that a unilateral mistake made by one party about the content of the agreement which is unknown to the other party will not provide the basis for an action for rectification. If, for example, one party does not

14 [1953] 2 QB 450, [1953] 2 All ER 739, CA.

intend a particular clause to be included in the written contract, but does not communicate this intention and the written contract contains the clause, an action for rectification will fail.[15]

D. Interpretation

We observed at the outset that the law employs an objective test for determining the content of the contract. But the meaning and implications of this objective test are far from certain.[16] The source of the difficulty lies in a vestigial attachment to the idea that the intentions of the parties should determine the content of the contract. It is commonly stated that for the purpose of interpretation of contracts a court should search for the intentions of the parties, but that statement is immediately qualified by the observation that the actual intentions of the parties are irrelevant under the objective test. In the words of Lord Bingham:

> In construing this provision, as any other contractual provision, the object of the court is to give effect to what the contracting parties intended. To ascertain the intention of the parties the court reads the terms of the contract as a whole, giving the words used their natural and ordinary meaning in the context of the agreement, the parties' relationship and all the relevant facts surrounding the transaction so far as known to the parties. To ascertain the parties' intentions the court does not of course inquire into the parties' subjective states of mind but makes an objective judgment based upon the materials already identified.[17]

The reason for not searching for the actual or subjective intentions of the parties is that it would always be open to either party to declare that any written agreement did not conform to their true wishes, or that a promise was not intended to be taken literally. These arguments would provide a simple escape route from any contractual obligation that turned out to be unpalatable or inconvenient. An objective test is necessary so that the parties are bound by the terms of their ostensible agreement. Their actual intentions in agreeing to the contract, perhaps supported by evidence of motives, will be regarded as irrelevant.

It can be argued further that the objective test implies that a court should in principle not be concerned with an inquiry into intention at all. The issue is rather

---

15 *Riverlate Properties Ltd v Paul* [1975] Ch 133, [1974] 2 All ER 656, CA.
16 Howarth, 'The Meaning of Objectivity in Contract' (1984) 100 *Law Quarterly Review* 265; Vorster, 'A Comment on the Meaning of Objectivity in Contract' (1987) 103 *Law Quarterly Review* 276; Farnsworth, 'Meaning in the Law of Contract' (1967) 76 *Yale Law Journal* 939.
17 *Bank of Credit and Commerce International SA v Ali* [2001] UKHL 8 at [8], [2002] 1 AC 251, [2001] 1 All ER 961.

what a reasonable promisee would have understood by the promises being made in the contract, not what the promisor intended nor what the promisee had hoped for at the outset. Support for an objective test that excludes any reference to the intention of the parties can be found in a well-known judgment by Lord Hoffmann:

> Interpretation is the ascertainment of the meaning which the document would convey to a reasonable person having all the background knowledge which would reasonably have been available to the parties in the situation in which they were at the time of the contract.[18]

The different implications of these two versions of the objective test can be illustrated by the problem raised in *Bank of Credit and Commerce International v Ali*.[19] An employee of the bank was dismissed as part of a reorganisation in 1990. He was offered substantial compensation, and additional compensation if he signed a release form in which he agreed to accept the compensation 'in full and final settlement of all or any claims whether under statute, common law or in equity of whatsoever nature that exist or may exist . . .' The following year the bank was wound up amidst the discovery that its senior officials had carried on the business in a corrupt and dishonest manner and that the bank had been for some years seriously insolvent. Employees who had lost their jobs during the collapse brought claims for compensation, and in particular won a claim that in principle they should be able to recover the economic losses caused to them by the damage to their reputation resulting from their unwitting association with the corrupt bank.[20] The claimant, who had been dismissed earlier, now sought to claim those 'stigma damages' himself, but the liquidator rejected the claim on the basis of the release clause. Before the House of Lords the claimant argued that the release did not include a claim which was unknown and not recognised by the law at the time. Neither party could have intended the release to include this novel claim for stigma damages. Lord Bingham, with the approval of the majority of the House of Lords, applied his statement of principle recited above, and reached the conclusion that the release did not apply to such a claim because neither party could have supposed that such a claim was available. Lord Hoffmann dissented, arguing that the reasonable employee would have understood in the circum-stances that the release given for an additional payment beyond full compensation of all his known claims was to govern any kind of claim, no matter how improbable. Although the members of the House of Lords did not articulate this difference in approach, it seems clear that the majority regarded the search for the intention of the parties as the main aim of interpretation, whereas Lord Hoffmann stressed what the reasonable promisee would have expected to result

18 *Investors Compensation Scheme Ltd v West Bromwich Building Society* [1998] 1 WLR 896 at 912.

19 *Bank of Credit and Commerce International SA v Ali* [2001] UKHL 8, [2002] 1 AC 251, [2001] 1 All ER 961.

20 *Mahmud (and Malik) v Bank of Credit and Commerce International SA* [1998] AC 20, [1997] 3 All ER 1, HL.

from the agreement. In short, is the objective test a method for attributing intention to the parties from observable evidence, or is it really an enquiry into the reasonable expectations generated by the promise? These two views seem to jostle for supremacy in the common law.

For the interpretation of terms in contracts, the objective test commences with the principle that the meaning of a promise should depend on how it was reasonably understood by the promisee. This interpretation should usually follow the ordinary meaning of the words used by the promisor. But of course the meaning of words can prove indeterminate, and to resolve ambiguity or vagueness the courts are likely to appeal to the reasonableness of the outcome, and to resist a construction which favours the party which is relying on its own standard form contract:

> The principles governing the construction of commercial contracts are not in doubt: the more unreasonable the result of a given construction, the readier should the court be to adopt some less obvious construction of the words.[21]

In the last resort, the court must endorse the interpretation placed on the words by the reasonable promisee. The reasonable understanding must be based upon the documents and written terms of the contract. In a case where the defendant purchased a public house at an auction under the mistaken belief that the lot included a field, the defendant was bound by the contract since the specification of the scope of the property for sale was stated clearly in the particulars which were available for inspection.[22] The reasonable understanding must also take into account the actual knowledge of the promisee about the circumstances of the transaction and the likely objectives of the promisor.

The objective approach to interpretation affords some protection to consumers. When they are confronted with a standard form document which is couched in technical and confusing language, they can rely upon their reasonable understanding of the meaning of the terms. But this protection is overtaken by the Unfair Terms in Consumer Contracts Regulations 1999, which provide in reg 7:

(1) A seller or supplier shall ensure that any written term of a contract is expressed in plain, intelligible language.

(2) If there is doubt about the meaning of a written term, the interpretation most favourable to the consumer shall prevail . . .[23]

If a standard form contract is riddled with technical language and subordinate clauses, therefore, its literal or technical meaning may not be enforceable against the consumer, if the consumer alleges that he or she understood the terms differently.

---

21 Simon Brown LJ, *Lancashire County Council v Municipal Mutual Insurance Ltd* [1996] 3 All ER 545 at 552, CA.
22 *Tamplin v James* (1880) 15 Ch D 215, CA.
23 SI 1999/2083.

Although the objective test provides the general guide to the courts' resolution of disputes over the terms of the contract, a number of decisions fit uneasily into this framework. These are cases where it appears that one party to a contract has been able to persuade the court that the ostensible words or conduct did not conform to the true intent, and that as a result either the ostensible contract should not be enforced, or a contract should be enforced on terms corresponding to the true intent. One interpretation of these cases suggests that the courts invoke an exception to the objective test that permits an examination of the actual intentions of the parties. The interpretation preferred here, however, suggests that these cases merely display some particular ramifications of the objective approach.

I.   'Snapping up' the offer

One type of case occurs where the promisee realises that the promisor's offer does not represent his true intention, but nevertheless purports to accept it. In *Hartog v Colin and Shields*,[24] the defendant offered to sell 3,000 Argentinian hare skins at a fixed price per pound, and the offer was accepted by the plaintiff. The defendant in fact intended to offer the hare skins at the same fixed price per piece, a rather different offer because there are about three pieces to a pound. A crude application of the objective test would have led inexorably to the conclusion that the original contract was binding, because the defendant had not communicated his true intention. But the court rejected the plaintiff's claim for damages for breach of contract, holding that because the plaintiff must have realized, and in fact knew, that the defendant's offer was a mistake, the plaintiff should not be permitted to enforce the ostensible contract. The plaintiff's knowledge of the mistake, although not admitted, was inferred from the prior verbal negotiations and written letters during which prices had always been discussed per piece. Proof of actual knowledge of the mistake in the terms of the offer is unnecessary. It suffices to show that the mistake in the terms 'would have been obvious to a reasonable person in the light of the surrounding circumstances',[25] or that it was one which the promisee 'could reasonably have known at the time when he accepted it'.[26] This actual or constructive knowledge of the mistake in the terms of the offer prevents the plaintiff from 'snapping it up'.

What is the legal effect of the finding that an offer has been snapped up? The remedy in *Hartog v Colin & Shields* was merely a rejection of the promisee's action

---

24 [1939] 3 All ER 566.

25 Thompson J, *McMaster University v Wilchar Construction Ltd* (1971) 22 DLR (3d) 9; affd (1973) 69 DLR (3d) 400.

26 Slade LJ, *Centrovincial Estates plc v Merchant Investors Assurance Co Ltd* [1983] Com LR 158, CA. Decisions in cases involving applications for rectification appear to require actual knowledge of the mistake: *Thomas Bates & Son Ltd v Wyndham's (Lingerie) Ltd* [1981] 1 All ER 1077, [1981] 1 WLR 505, CA; although probably suspicion of mistake combined with intention to deceive suffice as unconscionable conduct: *Commission for the New Towns v Cooper (GB) Ltd* [1995] Ch 259, [1995] 2 All ER 929, CA.

to enforce the apparent contract. When the issue was raised in *Smith v Hughes*, the case concerning the purchase of new oats, the court merely concluded that the seller would not be able to enforce the contract if he knew that the buyer was purchasing under a mistake that the seller had warranted the oats to be old. This remedy appears to imply that no contract had been formed at all, a conclusion which might flow from a fidelity to the idea of consent resting on the actual intentions of the parties. But the remedy is also consistent with the possibility that a contract existed on the terms which the promisor intended and of which the promisee was aware. This latter view avoids any exception to the objective approach.

2. Confusing or ambiguous offers

A second type of case which apparently qualifies the objective test of the terms of the contract concerns confusing and ambiguous offers. Where an offer is susceptible to different interpretations, and the parties choose different interpretations, which version of the meaning of the terms should govern the case? Where the confusion results from the negligence of one party, then the courts will refuse to enforce the contract according to that party's interpretation. In *Scriven Bros & Co v Hindley & Co*,[27] an auctioneer, acting for the plaintiff, put up for sale lots of hemp and tow, the latter being a less valuable commodity. The defendant bid for one lot, believing it contained hemp, whereas in fact it was tow, offering a high price so his bid was accepted. The reason for the defendant's mistake was that the shipping marks on the lots were all the same, which witnesses explained never happened for different commodities from the same ship. The auctioneer had failed to alert bidders to this unusual circumstance, which had contributed to the defendant's mistake. When sued for the price of the goods, the defendant sought to extricate himself from the apparent contract concluded at the auction. His first argument, that the auctioneer had 'snapped up' the offer failed, for the jury found that the auctioneer did not think that the defendant had made a mistake about the terms of the contract, but merely a mistake about the value of tow. But a second line of defence succeeded. The court decided that the plaintiff could not enforce the contract when his own negligence, or that of his agents, caused, or contributed to cause, the mistake. Thus the auctioneer's failure to alert the defendant to the confusing shipping marks prevented the enforcement of the contract.

Similarly, a court will not enforce a contract which has ambiguous terms at the request of the party who put forward those terms, if the other party reasonably understood the terms to mean something else. In *Raffles v Wichelhaus*,[28] the seller tried to enforce a contract for the sale of cotton to arrive on a ship called *'Peerless'*

---

27 [1913] 3 KB 564.
28 (1864) 2 H & C 906, 159 ER 375, Exch.

from Bombay. Unfortunately, there were two ships coming from Bombay with the same name, and the defendants claimed that they intended the contract to apply to the ship which arrived three months earlier. Because the plaintiff seller had not been specific about which ship was intended, he was unable to enforce the contract. As we have seen, this principle is extended in the context of consumer standard form contracts by the Unfair Terms in Consumer Contracts Regulations 1999, reg 7 to include terms which, although perhaps precise in their legal meaning, are expressed in language which is not plain and intelligible to the consumer.

Although it is clear that carelessness in formulating the offer will prevent enforcement of it by the offeror if it was reasonably understood by the offeree in a different sense, the full legal effect of this misunderstanding remains in doubt. It could be argued in such cases that there never was a coincidence of offer and acceptance, once the terms are viewed according to the actual intentions of the parties, so that the parties never reached agreement on the same terms. This would result in the contract being void, or rather that it never was concluded. The decisions in *Scriven Bros v Hindley* and *Raffles v Wichelhaus* have often been understood to have decided that no contract existed. The effect would be to prevent the other party from enforcing the contract as well. But it is possible to read the cases as merely preventing enforcement by the party who has negligently caused the mistake, with the effect that the contract is preserved but construed against the negligent party in resolving disputes over the content and meaning of the terms.

3.   Unusual and onerous terms

A third illustration of an apparent exception to an objective approach to interpretation concerns contracts containing unexpected terms in small print. Assuming that the printed document has become incorporated into the contract and therefore represents all or part of its express terms, the question arises whether unexpected clauses which the promisee did not intend or expect to be included should be part of the terms of the contract?

In this scenario, courts have confirmed an exception to the objective approach such that where a condition of a contract is particularly onerous or unusual that term will not form part of the terms of the contract, unless the party seeking to enforce can demonstrate that the condition was fairly brought to the notice of the other party. In *Interfoto Picture Library Ltd v Stiletto Visual Programmes Ltd*,[29] the defendant advertising agency arranged to hire some photographs from the plaintiff library. The pictures arrived with a delivery note containing the standard terms of hire. It included a term under which the defendants were bound to pay a set fee per day per picture hired after the agreed period of hire was over. The

29 [1989] QB 433, [1988] 1 All ER 348, CA.

defendants did not read the conditions and forgot to return the pictures until they were two weeks overdue. On the basis of the condition, the plaintiff sued for the holding charge which they calculated at £3,783. Although the Court of Appeal found that the delivery note was incorporated as the terms of the contract, it declined to enforce the holding charge on the ground that the plaintiff had not taken all the steps reasonably necessary to draw the condition to the defendant's attention. This approach to onerous conditions apparently qualifies the normal objective test for interpretation, for it permits one party's reasonable expectations to override the express and ostensible terms of the contract unless reasonable steps were taken to disabuse him of that expectation.

It is unclear whether this qualification applies to contracts which have been signed. There is old authority from Scrutton LJ in *L'Estrange v Graucob*[30] to the effect that:

> When a document containing contractual terms is signed, then, in the absence of fraud, or, I will add, misrepresentation, the party signing it is bound, and it is wholly immaterial whether he has read the document or not.

This statement suggests that a signature functions to make the written document a conclusive proof of the content of the contract. But such a principle contradicts the idea that reasonable steps should be taken to draw unusual and onerous terms to the attention of the promisee. Perhaps the two doctrines can be reconciled by limiting the effect of a signature to the ascription of contractual responsibility, rather than to determining the content of the contract as well.

4. Exceptions to the objective approach?

The types of case described above pose a difficulty for the objective approach to interpretation. They display an apparent disposition on the part of the court to permit the actual intention of a party to override the ostensible agreement, at least to the extent of declining to enforce the agreement against him. Do these doctrines reveal exceptions to the objective approach, or even reveal that the objective approach is not the underlying method of interpretation?

If the illustrations are regarded as exceptional instances when actual or subjective intent is permitted to determine the content of the contract, the crucial issue becomes one of identifying how to define the exceptions, which in turn depends on their justification. It is, of course, possible to provide a list of the exceptions, such as 'snapping up', 'confusing offers', and so forth. But this approach cannot tell us whether the list is complete without explaining the justification for the

30 [1934] 2 KB 394, DC.

exceptions. The inadequacy of this analysis becomes plain when the textbooks offer lists of exceptions that differ from one another both in their number and character.

The justification proffered for the exceptions is typically grounded in mistake, although sometimes the exceptions are explained as an aspect of the law of offer and acceptance. It is suggested that the mistake negatives the intent to agree to the objectively established terms. The problem with this explanation is that it cannot distinguish between those mistakes which count from those which do not. For example, why did the mistake about the sale of the public house and the inclusion of the field not count, whereas the mistake about hemp and tow managed to defeat the claim for breach of contract? The justification based upon mistake is lacking a crucial ingredient which would explain why some mistakes are effective whereas others are not. The answer plainly lies in the conduct of the parties, ie whether they have acted reasonably and in good faith. But the theory of mistake (or offer and acceptance) provides no criteria for determining when conduct should deprive a party from insisting upon the objectively interpreted agreement.

The underlying error of these explanations is to attempt to resuscitate the vestigial attachment to definition of the content of contracts by reference to the intention of the parties. It is better to recognize that the objective approach to interpretation always rejected actual intent as the key to determining the meaning of the terms of a contract. But the objective approach proves insufficient to handle all disputes about the content of contracts.

5.   The duty to negotiate with care

The objective approach to interpretation tackles certain types of deceptive practices, such as making a vague promise which could be understood in different ways. But the objective approach needs to be supplemented by aspects of the duty to negotiate with care in order to prevent one party from taking advantage of a misunderstanding which it has induced. On this analysis, the justification for any departure from the objective approach depends upon a breach of a duty to negotiate with care, for which the remedy is to deprive the guilty party of the right to enforce the contract according to the objective approach to interpretation.

Under the objective approach to interpretation, the test is what a reasonable promisee understands to be the terms of the promise. The content of the contract thus turns on what obligations each party reasonably supposed the other had undertaken. The cases on 'snapping up' should be regarded as an application of the objective approach. For example, in *Hartog v Colin and Shields*, the buyer of the hare skins could not reasonably suppose that they were offered per pound in the light of the previous negotiations, so he could not enforce that version of the contract. The difficulty which the objective approach encounters is that if each promise is interpreted objectively from the point of view of the reasonable promisee, we may discover that the parties have been at cross-purposes all along. In *Scriven Bros v Hindley*, the bidder at the auction acted reasonably in believing that the content of the lot (the promise) was hemp rather than tow, yet the auctioneer reasonably believed that he had received a high offer to buy tow. Similarly, the reasonable beliefs of the parties in *Interfoto Picture Library Ltd v Stiletto Visual Programmes Ltd* were almost certainly at cross-purposes. If we allow both parties to rely upon their reasonable beliefs as to the content of the other's promise, we end up with no agreed terms at all. Instead of declaring that they have failed to reach an agreement, however, the courts investigate the relative fault of the parties in order to determine who is entitled to insist upon their version of the meaning of the contract.

A party to a contract cannot rely upon the objectively interpreted terms, if he has violated the duty to negotiate with care. As we saw in Chapter 10, this duty comprises a set of standards of behaviour which proscribe sharp practice and misleading sales talk during the bargaining process. Since human imagination constantly expands the range of tricks and manoeuvres, no simple rule can encompass the relevant legal regulations. Instead, the general duty to negotiate with care constantly finds new applications and so the precise content of the duty cannot be pinned down. It requires contracting parties to act fairly and reasonably towards each other, but the precise scope of the duty depends upon the kind of abuse which the law seeks to prevent. Once the legal analysis is restated as the application of the set of public standards comprising the duty to negotiate with care, we are not driven to the conclusion that since the parties were at cross-purposes there was no agreement and therefore no contract. The appropriate remedy becomes one to rectify the breach of duty to negotiate with care, which may include a refusal to enforce the contract, the deletion of particular terms, the rectification of a written document, or an award of damages for breach of the duty to negotiate with care. An alternative remedy often makes even better sense: namely to permit the innocent party to enforce a contract on the terms which he supposed constituted the contract.

Where one party misrepresents the content or meaning of the agreement, the other may rely upon that representation to modify the content of the obligations. For example, in *Curtis v Chemical Cleaning and Dyeing Co*,[31] the plaintiff took her wedding dress to the defendant's shop to be cleaned. She was required to sign a contract, which, she was told by an assistant, disclaimed liability for certain specified risks to the beads and sequins which adorned the dress. In fact, the contract contained a clause which exempted the defendant from any damage to the dress whatsoever. The plaintiff subsequently sued for damage to her dress comprising a stain of uncertain origin. The English Court of Appeal held that the defendant could not rely upon the full width of the exemption clause on account

---

31 [1951] 1 KB 805, [1951] 1 All ER 631, CA.

of the misrepresentation of their employee and permitted the plaintiff's claim for damages. This decision may be explained by stating that, although the ostensible agreement was the signed contract, the defendant could not rely upon the exclusion clause because it broke the duty to negotiate with care by giving misleading information about the content of the terms.

Short of an actual misrepresentation, a party may break the duty to negotiate with care by inducing a mistake as to the consequences of a transaction by representing the terms in a confusing or ambiguous fashion. This breach of duty explains why the seller at the auction in *Scriven Bros & Co v Hindley & Co*, and the seller of cotton off the ship *Peerless* in *Raffles v Wichelhaus*, were unable to enforce the ostensible agreement. The duty to negotiate with care requires that the offeror presents the terms of his offer in a manner which will be properly understood and which avoids ambiguity. The duty can also be expressed as one to refrain from unconscionable conduct, which might include distracting the other party from noting new adverse provisions.[32]

The common law imposes a duty upon the offeror to take reasonable steps to acquaint the offeree with all the terms of the contract, especially those which are unusual or oppressive, as in *Interfoto Picture Library Ltd v Stiletto Visual Programmes Ltd*. This principle has a long ancestry, but the duty to negotiate with care has increased the steps necessary to give reasonable notice of the terms in those cases where the offeree is a consumer or for some other reason is unlikely to be familiar with the normal terms of the trade. For consumer standard form contracts, the principle has been modified by the Unfair Terms in Consumer Contracts Regulations 1999, which suggest that unless the consumer has a real opportunity to become acquainted with the terms of the contract prior to its formation, the terms will be unenforceable against the consumer.[33] An alternative mode for expressing this duty embodied in the American Restatement (Second) of Contracts, s 211(3), disallows any term where the profferor has reason to believe that the other party would not agree to the term if he became aware of it. The obvious disadvantage of this technique for imposing a duty to take reasonable steps to communicate the terms lies in cases where an entire trade or profession employs similar harsh terms, so that the profferor has no reason to believe that the other party would reject the contract and seek an alternative. This approach of American law suffers from the further disadvantage that it tries to present this aspect of the duty to negotiate with care as merely an interpretative technique, which always runs the risk of permitting skillful draftsmen to eviscerate the public duty by comprehensive standard forms. In practice, however, the American courts seem to follow closely the approach of the English.[34]

---

32 *Commission for the New Towns v Cooper (GB) Ltd* [1995] Ch 259, [1995] 2 All ER 929, CA.
33 SI 1999/2083, Sch 2, para 1(i).
34 *Weisz v Parke-Benet Galleries, Inc* 67 Misc 2d 1077, 325 NYS 2d 576 (1971).

The duty to negotiate with care also places obligations on the offeree. He or she is not permitted to snap up offers which are obviously presented with mistaken terms. This analysis explains why the test does not require actual knowledge of the mistake. The duty to negotiate with care can also encompass those cases such as *Hartog v Colin and Shields*, where it is reasonable to infer that a mistake has been made. In other instances, such as the facts of *Scriven Bros v Hindley* where the terms of an offer are less surprising, only actual knowledge of the mistake would be sufficient to support a finding of a breach of the duty to bargain with care.

Finally, a duty to negotiate with care explains the existence of those cases in which it is suggested that, where one party knows that the other's acceptance of the ostensible terms of the contract is the result of a mistake as to their content, then the ostensible contract cannot be enforced by the party aware of the other's mistake. The duty to negotiate with care extends to this case, because it would be wrong to permit the offeror to take advantage of the objective test when he knows that the other party does not intend to make a contract on those terms. But this breach of the duty to negotiate with care does not necessarily mean that the mistaken party cannot enforce the contract on the terms which he intended. Since the mistaken party has not broken the duty to negotiate with care, in the absence of negligence, it should be possible for the mistaken party to obtain some remedy, if not rectification, at least to cover any loss arising from the breach of duty.

E.   Implied terms

As well as the express terms of a contract, the primary obligations undertaken will be supplemented by terms implied into the contract by the courts. This power to imply terms into contracts is exercised cautiously, for it threatens to interfere with the freedom of the parties to select their own contractual obligations. This caution results in two governing principles for the implication of terms into contracts.

Firstly, terms will not be implied which contradict the express agreement of the parties. This principle reflects the priority attached to the choice of the parties in determining the content of their contractual obligations. But disputes may arise whether or not a proposed implied term contradicts an express term of the contract. In *Johnstone v Bloomsbury Health Authority*,[35] the contract of employment of a junior hospital doctor provided that the employer could require the doctor to work up to 88 hours per week. The doctor contended that this power was subject to an implied term which limited the exercise of the power for the sake of the health and safety of the doctor and his patients. Although no such limitation was mentioned in the express terms of the contract, the Court of Appeal accepted that the implied term was part of the contract. Browne-

---

35 [1992] QB 333, [1991] 2 All ER 293, CA.

Wilkinson LJ avoided the apparent contradiction by stating that the employer's discretionary power to determine overtime hours of work did not expressly state that it was without any limitation, so that the implied term did not formally contradict the employer's contractual rights.

Secondly, the grounds on which the courts will imply terms into contracts have been circumscribed within three principal categories, discussed below. The purpose of this limitation of the acceptable grounds for the implication of terms is to avoid the use of a more general power to imply terms into contracts which the courts regard as fair and reasonable, for this power might contradict too directly the freedom of the parties to choose the content of the contract. But in truth the three accepted grounds for implication of terms confer ample discretion upon the courts to shape the terms of contracts, which can be exercised in a way such that the terms of a contract reflect considerations of fairness and reasonableness.

The three grounds for the implication of terms will be considered in turn before a concluding examination of the justification for the practice of implying terms into contracts.

1. Unexpressed intentions

The first ground for the implication of terms into contracts is that the term represents the unexpressed joint intention of the parties. When articulating the terms of a contract, whether it is concluded orally or in writing, the parties may not state fully all aspects of their agreement. This failure may have a number of causes. The term may be so obvious and essential to the agreement that it was never stated explicitly. Alternatively, the term may be omitted because of shortage of time and the expense of reciting every detail of the proposed agreement. If a court is persuaded that a proposed term does represent the unexpressed joint intention of the parties, it will imply the obligation as a term of the contract:

> Prima facie that which in any contract is left to be implied and need not be expressed is something so obvious that it goes without saying; so that, if, while the parties were making their bargain, an officious bystander were to suggest some express provision for it in their agreement, they would testily suppress him with a common 'Oh, of course!'.[36]

This colourful 'officious bystander' test leaves unresolved the question of how the courts should infer the intent of the parties. Given that the 'officious bystander' has not in fact intervened, the courts must resort to other evidence from which to infer the intent of the parties. One possibility will comprise the claim that the words used by the parties included, as part of their meaning, the implied term in question. In a contract for the sale of a boat, for example, the use of the word

36 Mackinnon LJ, *Shirlaw v Southern Foundries (1926) Ltd* [1939] 2 KB 206, [1939] 2 All ER 113, CA.

'boat' by the parties might be held to imply that the object in question floats upon water, for the ordinary usage of the word boat usually refers to something capable of floating.

A more significant source of evidence of intent employed by the courts, however, involves references to the business efficacy of the contract.[37] By the term 'business efficacy' the courts mean to refer to the commercial purpose of the transaction. They examine the objectives of the parties in entering the transaction, and infer their intent about the terms of the contract in the light of those supposed objectives. The courts will imply terms which give effect to those objectives, or at least imply terms so that those objectives are not frustrated. In a contract for the sale of a door lock, for instance, a court could easily imply a term to the effect that the seller will also supply a key, for without a key the lock would not serve the purchaser's objective in entering the transaction. This process of inferring the intent of the parties from the supposed business objectives of the parties is not without difficulty, for the parties may be in dispute about the nature of the business objective.

Indeed, we must suspect that if the parties were asked by the officious bystander about a particular provision, in most instances they would not be in agreement at all due to their differing commercial interests. Implied terms are often presented as default rules, ie rules which the parties would agree were the costs of negotiation low or absent.[38] Yet in all probability the parties have not failed to reach agreement on this point because of shortage of time and resources, but have simply not wished to enter into such detailed specification for fear of failure to reach agreement.[39] The attempt to resolve this problem by means of a reification of the purpose of the contract in the business efficacy test only serves to obscure the problem. If the commercial motives of the parties for entering into the contract diverge, as they usually will outside the realm of symbiotic contracts such as partnerships and joint ventures, the performance of the contract without the implied term might easily satisfy the commercial objective of one party whilst simultaneously frustrating the objective of the other. Although these tests have been hallowed by constant judicial use for over a century, we must doubt whether they always provide a convincing justification for the insertion of additional obligations.

37 The source of this criterion is the judgment of Bowen LJ in *The Moorcock* (1889) 14 PD 64, CA.
38 Goetz and Scott, 'The Limits of Expanded Choice: An Analysis of the Interactions Between Express and Implied Terms' (1985) 73 *California Law Review* 261; Ayres and Gertner, 'Filling Gaps in Incomplete Contracts: An Economic Theory of Default Rules' (1989) 99 *Yale Law Journal* 87.
39 Johnston, 'Strategic Bargaining and the Economic Theory of Contract Default Rules' (1990) 100 *Yale Law Journal* 615.

2. Importation of general civil obligations

The second ground for the implication of terms into contracts involves the application of general civil obligations arising under the law of tort and unjust enrichment to the obligations of the contracting parties. These obligations could be handled as distinct legal duties arising by operation of law outside the contract. But it has become customary to regard them as implied terms of the contract whenever the parties have entered into a contractual relation. This incorporation of general legal obligations serves the purpose of ensuring the priority or hierarchy of the express contractual obligations over the residual legal obligations, for under the first principle governing implied terms, they must always give way to contrary express terms.

Under the law of tort the parties to a contract will owe each other a duty of care in various respects. In a contract for services, for example, there is a duty to use reasonable care in the performance of the service. This duty arises even in the absence of a contract for the service under the law of tort, but in the case of contractual services the duty is conceived as an implied term to use reasonable care in the performance of the contractual undertaking. This particular duty has been given statutory force under the Supply of Goods and Services Act 1982, s 13, which provides that:

> In a contract for the supply of a service where the supplier is acting in the course of a business, there is an implied term that the supplier will carry out the service with reasonable care and skill.

Although the precise content of this duty must depend upon the normal complex balancing of the degree of risk against the cost of precautions applicable to the standard of care in tort,[40] it should normally require conformity to any applicable regulations governing safety standards and practices.[41]

Under the law of unjust enrichment or restitution, one person who has unofficiously conferred a benefit upon another may usually demand compensation for the goods or services provided. In the context of a contractual agreement, this restitutionary duty becomes an implied term to make a reasonable payment for goods or services if no price has been expressly agreed. Again this implied term based upon a restitutionary duty has received statutory backing.[42]

3. Model contracts

The third ground for the implication of terms is both more controversial and uncertain in its scope. Here the courts take notice of the fact that many types of

---

40 *Bolton v Stone* [1951] AC 850, [1951] 1 All ER 1078, HL; *Haley v London Electricity Board* [1965] AC 778, [1964] 3 All ER 185, HL.
41 *Wilson v Best Travel Ltd* [1993] 1 All ER 353, QB.
42 Sale of Goods Act 1979, s 8; Supply of Goods and Services Act 1982, s 15.

contracts have become routine and commonplace. These standard types of transaction, such as contracts of sale, employment and tenancy, normally share many of the same terms. In the absence of a full expression of these terms by the parties, the courts will imply into the contract the standard incidents of such a transaction. These implied terms cannot be justified on either of the previous two grounds, for they are neither essential to the business purpose of the transaction nor a normal obligation arising under the general law of civil obligations. For example, the contract of sale contains an implied term that the goods sold are of satisfactory quality and fit for their normal use, an implication now required by statute.[43] The satisfactory quality is defined as the standard that a reasonable person would regard as satisfactory, taking into account any description of the goods, the price, and other relevant circumstances. There is a broad conception of quality, so that it includes not only fitness for all the purposes for which goods of the kind in question are commonly supplied, but also their appearance, freedom from minor defects, safety and durability.[44] With respect to descriptions that enhance the expectations of a reasonable person about the quality of the goods, a consumer can rely not only on statements made by the seller but also on those made by the producer or manufacturer in advertising and labelling.[45] That the goods should satisfy this quality standard is neither essential to the efficacy of a transaction designed to transfer ownership of goods, nor required by the ordinary law of tort and restitution.

This broader power to imply terms involves the court in determining the standard incidents or duties of the respective parties of particular types of contract. The courts select these terms in the light of practical experience, views about the fair allocation of risks between the parties, and customary practices in the trade or business. These implied terms complete the fabric of the contract in the absence of express agreement. This practice enhances the utility and efficiency of contracts as an economic mechanism, for it saves the parties from having to spend time discussing and agreeing the details of the transaction, provided that it fits into a standard pattern of contractual relation.

A typical example of the way the courts shape the content of contractual relations through the use of implied terms and model contracts is provided by the contract of employment. Since these contracts were in the past often concluded informally with a brief oral description of the nature of the job and the wages paid, the courts were often called upon to fill out the terms of the agreement. Under these implied terms an employee agrees impliedly to refrain from misconduct, to avoid neglect of the business, to eschew intemperance and insobriety, and to perform the work

---

43 Sale of Goods Act 1979, s 14(2).
44 Sale of Goods Act, s 14(2A), (2B).
45 Sale of Goods Act, s 14(2D), as amended by the Sale and Supply of Goods to Consumers Regulations 2002, SI 2002/3045, implementing EC Directive 1999/44/EC on the Sale of Consumer Goods; M Bianca and S Grundmann (eds), *EU Sales Directive: Commentary* (Antwerp, 2002).

honestly, obediently, with due diligence and in a manner loyal to the employer's interests.[46] In recent years the courts have developed commensurate duties upon employers to be implied as terms in contracts, such as the duty not to treat employees arbitrarily, capriciously, or inequitably, to take reasonable care to ensure the safety of employees, and to refrain from acting in a way calculated to destroy mutual trust and confidence.[47] This list of implied terms in the contract of employment is far from complete, but it suffices to illustrate how through the idea of model contracts the courts develop a complete set of terms for a typical contract. These terms will apply to any transaction which the court regards as fitting into a type of employment relation, and in the absence of express terms to the contrary will provide the applicable terms of the contract.

This broader power to imply terms is confined in two ways. In the first place, the transaction has to approximate to a standard type of contract. If, on the contrary, the court is confronted with a unique type of contractual relation, one which is not a matter of settled legal practice, the court will confine its intervention to the first and second grounds for the implication of terms.[48] It is important to notice, however, that standard types of transactions need not be commonplace. In commercial relations there may be a settled way of doing business, and, although few people may be involved in the trade, the court will imply the customary terms of the trade into this type of contract. Secondly, the use of the power will be limited to terms which would be generally applicable to this standard type of transaction or 'necessary' for this sort of transaction. A court will not exercise the power to introduce terms which could only apply to a particular instance of this type of contractual relation. In other words, the nature of the terms which a court will imply are only those of general application to the class of contracts, and the power will not be exercised to introduce detailed particularistic terms.[49] In a sale of goods, for example, the general term requiring the goods to be of satisfactory quality is permissible, but the courts would not introduce an implied term which could only apply to a particular type of goods, such as a term that a car should use fuel efficiently.

In truth, however, these two limitations do not place a significant brake on the courts should they wish to insert an implied obligation. It is always possible to assert that the agreement represents a standard type of contract, and having defined the type of contract in a suitably narrow manner, insert a term which could be applicable to every contract of this type. For example, in *Scally v Southern Health and Social Services Board*,[50] the issue was whether the employer had broken an implied term to alert their doctors of a potential benefit under a pension scheme that could only be acquired by following a particular procedure. In

46 *Lister v Romford Ice and Cold Storage Co Ltd* [1957] AC 555, HL.
47 *Mahmud v Bank of Credit and Commerce International SA* [1998] AC 20, [1997] 3 All ER 1, HL.
48 *Shell UK Ltd v Lostock Garage Ltd* [1977] 1 All ER 481, [1976] 1 WLR 1187, CA.
49 *Reid v Rush & Tompkins plc* [1989] 3 All ER 228, [1990] 1 WLR 212, CA
50 [1992] 1 AC 294, [1991] 4 All ER 563, HL.

deciding in favour of the doctors, the House of Lords imposed a duty of notification of potential benefits because this duty was necessary, not for all contracts of employment, but for this type of contract of employment, namely one where the terms were partly included in a complex pension scheme, negotiated by other parties, and where the employee had inevitably to rely upon the employer to inform him about the scheme. One suspects that if the type of contract is defined sufficiently narrowly, any implied term might be regarded as necessary.

It should be noted that all three grounds for the implication of terms can operate simultaneously and cumulatively in a particular instance. In *Liverpool City Council v Irwin*,[51] the council owned a tower block of flats which were let to the tenants. The standard form contract contained extensive provisions regarding the obligations of tenants, but said little about the landlord's obligations. The tenants refused to pay rent by way of a protest against the dilapidation of the premises, and in particular about the failure of the landlord to maintain the common parts of the block of flats, such as the lifts, staircases and corridors. In the landlord's action for possession resulting from the failure to pay rent, the question was raised whether the landlord was in breach of an implied term of the contract for failure to maintain the common parts of the premises.

What terms could be implied into this transaction? Under the first ground for implication, the House of Lords implied an easement under which the tenants could use the common parts for access, for without such a right of access the lease of a flat would be futile. The landlord itself conceded that under the second ground for the implication of terms, it was under the duty imposed on all occupiers of the premises to take reasonable care with regard to the safety of persons entering the premises. The crucial point of the case, however, fell under the third ground for the implication of terms. The court found that in such leases for buildings with multiple occupation, it was an implied term that the landlord owed a duty to take reasonable care to keep in reasonable repair and useability the common parts of the premises. This provision placed the cost of maintenance on the landlord, subject to any contrary term in the contract. On the facts of the case, however, the House of Lords concluded that the landlord was not in breach of this obligation.

Notice that this implied term could not be justified on either of the two other grounds for the implication of terms. It could not satisfy the business efficacy test, for, although it was necessary for either landlord or tenant to maintain the common parts in reasonable repair, it could not be said that it was necessary for this duty to fall on the landlord. Similarly, the duty of care in tort could only extend to items which imperilled the safety of the occupants, and would not include such items as keeping the lifts in working order. The implication of the term into the lease in this case therefore depended upon the reasoning that in this

51 [1977] AC 239, [1976] 2 All ER 39, HL.

class of contract the model should place the cost of reasonable repairs on the landlord. The court perhaps preferred this solution because this seemed to be the most practical and efficient result, since it may have been difficult and expensive for the tenants to organize themselves into an effective management company for the premises.

4. Justifications for implied terms

How can we explain and justify the above use of implied terms to supplement contractual obligations?[52] In some instances it is apparent that the reference to the joint intention of the parties, as evidenced by the need to give business efficacy to their transaction, supports the implication of terms on grounds which merely complement the traditional justification of contractual obligations based upon the will of the parties. It is true that the will of the parties was never expressed, but the evidence supporting the claim that the term represents a presupposition or necessary implication of the words used can be so overwhelming that few could doubt that the term represents their original intention. But it is clear that the use of implied terms extends beyond any sort of justification of the type that the term merely states expressly what was silently understood by the parties.

Economic analysis of law suggests a good reason why the courts should provide a set of default rules to govern contractual relations in the absence of express terms. Default rules save transaction costs by permitting the parties to avoid the costs of negotiating every detail of their arrangement every time they make a contract, because they know that the courts will fill in the gaps in the usual way. This makes good sense, but it is arguable whether or not participants in the market deliberately avail themselves of this opportunity to save transaction costs. On the contrary, the proliferation of the standard form contract suggests that any party with sufficient resources is likely to devise a standard set of express terms to suit his or her purposes exactly. Many cases we have discussed so far concerning implied terms, such as *Johnstone v Bloomsbury Health Authority*[53] and *Liverpool City Council v Irwin*, comprise instances where the claim that an implied term exists is used to combat the one-sided standard form contract of the other party.

Nor does the economic analysis suggest a satisfactory account of the grounds for the selection of terms by the courts. Under the efficiency analysis, the court should select those implied terms to which the parties would have agreed but for the presence of transaction costs. Although this criterion makes sense for terms which give a contract business efficacy, it is far from clear that it provides an intelligible guide in other cases. Consider the bargaining situation in *Liverpool City Council v Irwin*. The council was presumably reluctant to agree to an

---

52 Peden, 'Policy Concerns Behind Implication of Terms in Law' (2001) 117 *Law Quarterly Review* 459.
53 [1992] QB 333, [1991] 2 All ER 293, CA.

obligation to maintain the common premises, so it would have held out against such an obligation, and, depending upon the local forces of supply and demand for tower block local authority housing, it might or might not have been successful. But even if it had agreed to the obligation, it could have insisted upon an increased rent to cover those costs, so to imply a term requiring a maintenance obligation without adjusting the rent produces a contract to which the parties never would have agreed.

Further, this economic analysis does not appear to correspond to the reasons ventured by the courts for the selection of implied terms. What seems to be at the heart of the model reasoning surrounding the implication of terms is the courts' endeavour to structure contracts so that they incorporate a fair and practical allocation of risks. The court imposed the duty to maintain the premises upon Liverpool City Council almost certainly because this was the most practical and efficient means of achieving the result. In the context of the employment relation, the recent introduction of implied terms which impose obligations upon employers surely reflects changing views about the fair treatment of employees and the risk of losing a job. Similarly, the duty imposed upon professional sellers of goods to ensure that they are of satisfactory quality cannot be justified as the term which would have been agreed in the absence of transaction costs, for sellers would almost certainly seek to avoid such liability for latent defects. The reason for this allocation of risk is surely that it fits both the purpose of consumer protection and it places the risk of defects on the person in a better position to avoid the advent of such risks occurring.

The notion of a default rule is, therefore, a misleading description of the use of implied terms. Through the implication of terms the courts can achieve what they regard as a fair and practical allocation of risks between the contracting parties, a view which may alter over time as illustrated by the changing implied terms inserted into the contract of employment. In this process the courts can seek to equalize the obligations of the parties, even in the teeth of express terms of standard form contracts, and so pursue ideas of fairness. The justification for implied terms therefore rests ultimately not on the intentions of the parties but rather the court's view of the reasonable expectations of the parties to the transaction.

Chapter 12

Mandatory obligations

A. The social dimension of markets

The virtue and danger of markets lies in their delegation of power to individuals. The virtue consists in the capacity of individuals to use markets to make choices which contribute to their chosen way of life. Through contracts of employment, sale, hire and so forth, individuals may realize many aspects of a way of life which has meaning for them. The availability of such choices is ensured by a free market in goods and services. The market therefore augments the autonomy of individuals and compares favourably in this respect with the selection of goals for life by political authorities. But this virtue of markets carries with it the danger of subversion of important social goals.

Consider, for example, the problem of the sale of dangerous and defective products to consumers. Under a free market regime such sales would be permitted, with the consumer left to bargain for warranties of quality and compensation for injuries. Under the classical law the seller of such goods would be equally free to insist upon terms in the contract which prevented any liability from arising. Important social policies lead the modern law to reject this type of market. We seek to eliminate dangerous and defective products from markets in order to reduce injuries to consumers. Furthermore, in the event of injuries occurring, we seek to ensure that the consumer receives adequate compensation. More fundamentally, legal guarantees are calculated to augment the confidence of consumers that market transactions will serve to realise their expectations and goals: they increase trust in the market mechanism for the production and distribution of goods and services. These social policies can only be achieved by regulation of the market in ways designed to compel traders to sell only safe and reliable products, and to impose sanctions if they fail to do so. In effect, the modern law imposes a mandatory obligation on businesses to supply safe products free from defects to consumers.

From an economic perspective, these social policies can be described as responses to 'market failures' and a concern for 'externalities'.[1] The market failure problem with dangerous and defective goods arises because the consumer lacks the expertise to determine by inspection whether or not the goods conform to a satisfactory quality. The risk arises that traders lack an incentive to supply good quality products, for the consumer cannot easily distinguish those products and is therefore likely to select on the basis of price.[2] The concern for externalities consists in the observation that the incentives in individual transactions may not take into account the costs which may be imposed on others. For example, the cost of accidents arising from dangerous products may be borne by others through the insurance system or health care system, so that neither the trader nor the individual consumer will be influenced by those costs when entering particular market transactions. One way to address both market failure and externalities is to impose a compulsory obligation on the trader to supply goods of satisfactory quality. This obligation reduces the trader's incentive to skimp on quality, and forces the trader to include in the price of the goods an allowance to pay for insurance against the risk of accidents.

A wide range of social policies might justify the imposition of compulsory obligations. The protection of consumers' health and safety and their economic interests, which is regarded as a general goal of European Community law,[3] explains the imposition of compulsory obligations in many types of contract, from sales and services, to consumer credit agreements and package holidays. The protection of the environment, the cost of which is frequently treated as an externality, can occasionally be the justification for compulsory obligations, as in

1 MJ Trebilcock, *The Limits of Freedom of Contract* (Cambridge, Mass, 1993).
2 Ackerlof, 'The Market for "Lemons": Qualitative Uncertainty and the Market Mechanism' (1970) 84 *Quarterly Journal of Economics* 488.
3 Council declaration, OJ C92 of 25 April 1975, 1; Reich, 'Protection of Consumers' Economic Interests by the EC' (1992) 14 *Sydney Law Review* 23.

the requirement that new cars should use lead-free petrol. A concern for the rights of citizens can lead to compulsory obligations against discrimination in contracts, such as the requirement for an equality clause in every contract of employment which ensures that women receive equal pay for work of equal value. Similarly, a concern to redress the element of subordination inherent in every employment relation leads to the introduction of an inalienable right not to be unfairly dismissed.[4]

As well as these measures designed to protect particular interest groups or to reduce harmful side effects of markets, mandatory obligations may serve to enhance the reliability and calculability of the market itself. Here the argument for a compulsory obligation suggests that under certain conditions it will be advantageous for all parties to eliminate a free market and choice over terms in favour of a non-negotiable standard package with a recognized meaning. These conditions may arise when the cost of negotiating terms deters entry into contracts, or when the uncertainty about the meaning of negotiated terms discourages the formation of agreements. These conditions may be satisfied, for example, in cross-border trade, where the consumer or small business may be reluctant to make purchases under contracts whose meaning and implications may be unclear. Here a solution may be to remove the freedom to select the terms in favour of a set of compulsory standard obligations. This argument has been used, for example, to justify the development of common rules for consumer contracts in the European Community.[5]

The common theme behind these mandatory obligations consists of a concern to promote a social policy, either in the form of the protection of a group as a class such as consumers, or to protect a social institution such as the market. This theme is distinguishable from a concern about the unfairness of the terms of a particular contract, which might also justify an interference with freedom of contract. In the case of defective and dangerous products, for instance, although it may be the case that a consumer who has purchased an unsafe product has made a poor bargain, the content of the contract would be objectionable no matter how low the price paid by the consumer might have been. Moreover, these compulsory obligations are not necessarily tied to any redistributive aims.[6] If a seller of goods is compelled to give a warranty as to the quality of the goods, the supplier is likely to charge a higher price, so there may be no net benefit to consumers. There may be distributional effects if the costs of the social policy cannot be redistributed through the market, but this is not the principal objective

---

4 Employment Rights Act 1996, s 94.
5 Preamble to EC Directive 93/13/EEC on Unfair Terms in Consumer Contracts; Collins, 'Good Faith in European Contract Law' (1994) 14 *Oxford Journal of Legal Studies* 229.
6 Kennedy, 'Distributive and Paternalist Motives in Contract and Tort Law, with Special Reference to Compulsory Terms and Unequal Bargaining Power' (1982) 41 *Maryland Law Review* 563.

of the imposition of mandatory obligations. Interventions on the ground of fairness and for redistributional purposes will be considered in Chapter 13.

B.   The use of compulsory obligations

Although mandatory obligations may achieve the goals which they are designed to serve, there is a danger that such a blunt interference with the operation of a competitive market will provoke deleterious side-effects. Increased obligations on businesses selling to consumers will presumably drive up the price of the products, which may have the effect of excluding some consumers from the market altogether. If landlords fall under a duty to provide rented accommodation of a minimum standard of habitability, they may opt to increase rents or invest in some other project, with the consequence of a shortage of rented accommodation and a corresponding price increase. Similarly, if workers are awarded an inalienable right not to be unfairly dismissed, they lose the chance to negotiate with an employer for a higher wage without job security. These arguments share the pattern that from an economic perspective the social goods obtained by compulsory obligations can only be obtained at a price, and that the market will adjust prices to a new equilibrium which may not be in the best interests of those groups for whom the protection was initially introduced.

Of course, the market may not work perfectly due to inelasticities of supply and demand, so that the deleterious consequences may not occur. The market for consumer products may prove so competitive that businesses cannot increase prices; landlords may be unable to sell property and reinvest their capital elsewhere; the employer may not be prepared to increase wage costs even to obtain numerical flexibility of labour. Nevertheless, the simple economic model suggests the advisability of caution before imposing compulsory obligations.

This concern leads to a preference in economic analysis of contract law for less interventionist measures. The preferred remedy for market failure, for example, is to increase the information available, so that the purchaser can make an informed choice. On this view there should be no obligation to supply safe products free from defects, but simply a duty to inform the purchaser of the exact details of the product, faults and all. Similarly, the landlord should point out the leaking roof and the broken boiler, draw the prospective tenant's attention to the clause in the contract which absolves the landlord from any duty to make repairs, and then let the tenant bargain for the lowest rent obtainable. This remedy for market failure can never be complete, of course, for the supply of vast amounts of detailed information creates the problem of processing and evaluating this information. Methods for remedying market failure by controlling bargaining practices were considered in the context of the control over coercion and the duty to negotiate with care in Chapters 8 and 10. These methods can certainly be employed to help to achieve the social goals considered in this chapter, but mandatory obligations comprise a distinctive and more effective technique.

As an alternative to compulsory terms or information requirements, the economic perspective suggests that the law should merely provide a set of 'default rules' or implied terms, which the parties to a contract should be free to exclude. The process of negotiating the exclusion of the implied term should then put the parties on notice of the allocation of risks, thereby averting market failure. The flaw in this argument arises from the fact that the process of negotiation is typically truncated by the provision of a standard form contract, so that the reallocation of risks passes unnoticed. The purchaser of goods is asked to sign a document which excludes the implied terms; the tenant signs a lease which absolves the landlord from any responsibilities in technical legal jargon; and the employee is issued with the standard terms of employment.

Against these economic arguments for resisting compulsory obligations, we should place two considerations. First, in the conception of the social market articulated in Chapter 2, we regarded the market not merely as a source of preference satisfaction, but as an opportunity to augment and contribute to the meaning of a person's life. The creation of this opportunity leads to the view that the law of contract, in regulating and constituting the market order, should channel market opportunities towards those which possess the potential for a genuine contribution to the construction of meaning. Although this policy involves some difficult subjective judgments, which run the risk of being labelled a form of authoritarian paternalism,[7] we can point to certain types of transactions which seem unlikely to make any worthwhile contribution. The purchase of a dangerous product which is likely to maim or kill the consumer looks unlikely to satisfy the test of making a contribution to the construction of meaning in a person's life. Similarly, the acquisition of a lease on an uninhabitable dwelling will not except in the most extreme circumstances of necessity make a useful contribution towards the establishment of a home. Finally, employment in circumstances where the employer has an unfettered discretion to dismiss at will for any reason creates a degree of subjugation to arbitrary power which presents such a severe sacrifice of autonomy and dignity for the worker that it is likely to impede any endeavour to find meaning through work.

A second consideration which favours the use of compulsory obligations returns to the problem of externalities. Neither a greater disclosure of information nor the provision of suitable default rules in contracts will tackle the problem of deleterious effects on third parties, for the economic incentive to ignore those interests remains the same. The solution to the problem must lie in regulation by the state, although not necessarily by means of compulsory obligations inserted into contractual relations. In some instances, for example, differential taxation can alter incentives, as in the case of lower taxation on lead-free petrol, with the

---

7   Kronman, 'Paternalism and the Law of Contracts' (1983) 92 *Yale Law Journal* 763.

effect of steering behaviour in directions which respect externalities. Other cases may require more elaborate international regulatory agencies which effectively exclude any scope for the negotiation of terms. Nevertheless, for some problems of externalities, the use of compulsory terms in contracts may prove a simple and effective solution.

What seems to be common to the examples of mandatory obligations arising in contractual relations is, first, a sense that criminal sanctions would be inappropriate to these commercial relations; secondly, a belief that control over bargaining practices would not be sufficient to achieve the social purpose, because of the typical inequality of the bargaining power between the parties; and finally, a belief that the compulsory term would function to achieve the social goal, because private enforcement would suffice.

C.   Compulsory terms

Mandatory obligations remove from the parties to a contract the freedom to choose some of the terms for their transaction. The most straightforward example comprises legislation which determines that every contract of a particular type is deemed to include a particular term, regardless of the express terms of the contract and overriding any contrary terms. Under the Equal Pay Act 1970, s 1, for instance, every contract of employment contains an equality clause under which the employer promises to pay a woman employee equal pay to that paid to men in like work or work of equal value. The same effect can be achieved by granting a statutory right which cannot be excluded or qualified by contrary agreement, as in the case of the right of an employee to claim unfair dismissal against an employer.[8]

Statutes do not always contain express prohibitions against terms of contracts designed to subvert rights which the statutes purport to grant. Courts may infer such prohibitions, however, as a necessary concomitant to the statutory scheme of protection. The issue in *Johnson v Moreton*[9] concerned the collective interest in ensuring long-term investment in farming land, such as mechanization and fertilization of soil. Under the Agricultural Holdings Act 1948 Parliament had sought to protect the security of tenure of tenant farmers, so that they had the incentive to make such investments knowing that they could reap the benefits later. The statutory scheme provides that when a landlord serves a notice to quit upon the termination of a lease, the tenant may serve a counter-notice which entitles the tenant to a hearing before a tribunal. The tribunal normally awards the tenant another lease, for it is governed by a presumption in favour of

8   Employment Rights Act 1996, s 203; *Igbo v Johnson Matthey Chemicals Ltd* [1986] ICR 505, CA; *Birch v University of Liverpool* [1985] ICR 470, CA.
9   [1980] AC 37, [1978] 3 All ER 37, HL.

preserving security of tenure. It would have been possible, of course, for the landlord and tenant to have agreed in their contract that a similar option to renew a lease should prevail. Parliament must have determined, however, that tenants were unable to bargain for such terms in the open market, either through ignorance of this possibility, or more likely because of their weak bargaining power. The question in this particular case was whether a term in the contract could provide that the tenant relinquished the right to serve a counter-notice. Although the statute did not expressly preclude such terms, the House of Lords was able to conclude that such a term, if permitted, would quickly subvert the purpose of the statute. Lord Hailsham explained that freedom of contract only permits a person to renounce a right which exists solely for his benefit, but not where a public interest is at stake. The public interest here was the collective interest in investment in farming:

> The truth is that it can no longer be treated as axiomatic that, in the absence of explicit language, the courts will permit contracting out of the provision of an Act of Parliament where that Act, though silent as to the possibility of contracting out, nevertheless is manifestly passed for the protection of a class of persons who do not negotiate from a position of equal strength, but in whose well-being there is a public as well as a private interest.

The granting of statutory rights and the insertion of compulsory terms as methods of supporting and protecting social goals have the advantage that they minimize collective enforcement costs. If every contract of a particular kind has to include a particular term, then this rule will be largely self-applying by the parties to contracts. At the same time, of course, it shares the endemic weakness which we have already observed in private law remedies, that the term may not be rigorously enforced by private contracting parties because of the costs and uncertainties of litigation.

Under English law the courts have not claimed the power to insist upon compulsory terms without statutory authority. In the absence of a statutory power to declare an exclusion clause invalid, the express term will override implied obligations. In the United States, however, some courts have developed compulsory obligations in contracts by describing them as tort obligations which arise in contracts in certain types of relationships. These tort obligations cannot usually be excluded by the terms of the contract, so in effect they become mandatory obligations. Examples include the warranty of habitability for new dwellings,[10] and discharge from employment contrary to public policy.[11]

D.   Statutory invalidity

Certain statutes prohibit the use of particular terms in contracts. The purpose of such prohibitions is usually to ensure that the obligations which would otherwise

---

10 *Melody Home Manufacturing Co v Barnes* 741 SW 2d 349 (Tex 1987).
11 *Palmateer v International Harvester Co* 421 NE 2d 876 (Ill 1981).

govern the relation between the parties to a contract cannot be excluded or qualified. The statute normally states that a particular type of term shall be invalid, ineffective or void.

One important provision of this kind in English law is the Unfair Contract Terms Act 1977, s 2(1) which provides that:

> A person cannot by reference to any contract term or to a notice given to persons generally or to particular persons exclude or restrict his liability for death or personal injury resulting from negligence.

The effect of this prohibition is twofold. It prevents a term in a contract from excluding liability in tort for negligence in causing personal injuries or death. It also prevents the exclusion of implied terms in contracts which would also impose liability for negligently caused personal injuries and death. As an example of this latter kind of case, in *Johnstone v Bloomsbury Health Authority*,[12] a junior hospital doctor persuaded the court that his contract of employment contained an implied term that he would not be required to work such long hours as would foreseeably damage his health. The defendant employer sought to rely upon an express term which granted it the discretion to require up to 88 hours of work a week, but this term was regarded as one which potentially contradicted the implied term and could therefore be invalid under s 2(1). In effect this statutory provision ensures that a duty to take reasonable care for the safety of the other party to the contract becomes a compulsory term of contracts where it is appropriate.

The main social objective of this provision is to ensure that the standard of reasonable care is always required with respect to the safety of persons, there being a collective interest in requiring this standard, an externality, which cannot be bargained away by individual contracts. The prohibition also serves the goal of providing compensation to those suffering personal injuries through the negligence of others. But these objectives do not rule out the possibility of contractual terms which allocate the risk of loss through indemnities between the wrongdoer and others, provided that these terms do not prevent the injured party from suing the wrongdoer.[13]

The technique of invalidating particular types of terms in contracts applies especially to consumer transactions. In sales by a business to a consumer, for instance, under the Unfair Contract Terms Act 1977, s 6, the contract cannot exclude the obligation implied by the Sale of Goods Act 1979, s 14 to supply goods of 'satisfactory quality'. This statutory prohibition therefore has the effect that the duty to supply goods of a 'satisfactory quality' becomes a compulsory term of every consumer sales contract.

The social objective of protecting consumers requires the legislation to classify the nature of the parties to the contracts. The paradigm case consists of a shopper

12 [1992] QB 333, [1991] 2 All ER 293, CA.
13 *Thompson v T Lohan (Plant Hire)* [1987] 2 All ER 631, [1987] 1 WLR 649, CA.

purchasing goods from a retailer in the high street, but the concepts of the seller or supplier acting 'in the course of business',[14] and the purchaser being a 'consumer' pose difficulties of application at the boundaries. In order to identify the seller or supplier as a business, the courts typically look for a degree of regularity in making transactions of this type.[15] The concept of a consumer is normally defined more closely by the relevant legislation, as in the Unfair Contract Terms Act 1977, s 12(1):

A party to a contract 'deals as consumer' in relation to another party if—
(a)   he neither makes the contract in the course of a business nor holds himself out as doing so; and
(b)   the other party does make the contract in the course of a business; and
(c)   in the case of a contract governed by the law of sale of goods . . . the goods passing under or in pursuance of the contract are of a type ordinarily supplied for private use or consumption.

Under this definition of a consumer, the purchaser can be a private individual, but not count as a consumer, if the item purchased is a business machine or a heavy goods vehicle. On the other hand, a business company may count as a consumer if it purchases an item which is ordinarily for private use, such as a saloon car, and it does not trade in cars as part of its normal business operations.[16]

In contrast, in European legislation, such as the EC Directive on Unfair Terms in Consumer Contracts, only a natural person may count as a consumer, and only if he or she is acting outside his trade, business or profession.[17] This latter definition of a consumer differs because it identifies a consumer by reference to the scope of a person's normal trade rather than the nature of the goods involved. This difference creates the possibility under the European concept of consumer that a small business, trading as a natural person or a partnership, can count as a consumer if the goods purchased, although normally used only in business, are not the kind of goods usually purchased by that particular business.

These differences in statutory concepts of a consumer pose the issue of whether the concept should reflect the actual level of expertise of the purchaser, or whether it should be assumed that all businesses have sufficient resources to acquire expertise whenever necessary. Given that many small businesses lack those resources, European law assumes that the adoption of the corporate form signals the availability of those resources, but in England, where the corporate form is cheaper and more common for small businesses, such a proxy seems unsatisfactory.

14 This is the term used in the Sale of Goods Act 1979, s 14, and for the criminal regulation of misleading trading practices: Trade Descriptions Act 1968, s 1.
15 *Davies v Sumner* [1984] 3 All ER 831, [1984] 1 WLR 1301, HL.
16 *R & B Customs Brokers Co Ltd v United Dominions Trust Ltd* [1988] 1 All ER 847, [1988] 1 WLR 321, CA.
17 EC Directive 93/13/EEC, Art 2; implemented by the Unfair Terms in Consumer Contracts Regulations 1999, SI 1999/2083.

E.   Judicial discretion over exclusion clauses

In relation to many types of contractual obligations, however, it is difficult to determine in advance whether a particular term will subvert a social policy and thereby merit statutory prohibition. Short of leaving the matter alone for the sake of achieving certainty with respect to the validity of contractual terms, the legislature must delegate a discretion to the courts or some other agency to distinguish between those cases where a compulsory term is required and those where it is not. The major example of the use of judicial discretion for this purpose in English law is the employment of the test of fairness and reasonableness to govern exclusion clauses in some types of contracts under the Unfair Contract Terms Act 1977. A similar jurisdiction emerges in US law with the test of unconscionability under the Uniform Commercial Code.[18] Although these broad tests do not identify with precision any compulsory term which must be included in contracts, their effect in particular instances is to prevent the express exclusion of certain types of liability which would otherwise arise, and so for the parties concerned with this particular contract the law has the effect of compelling them to contract on particular terms. In *Smith v Eric S Bush*,[19] for instance, the question was whether a surveyor could exclude liability to the purchaser of the house for negligence in making a survey and valuation of a house. The House of Lords concluded that such exemption clauses were unreasonable in the context of ordinary home purchases. The effect of this judgment is that it becomes a compulsory term of every home survey and valuation that the surveyor accepts liability for professional negligence.

In exercising their discretionary power, the courts have to balance the collective interest in a competitive market achieved by freedom of contract against the potential danger to other social values. In balancing these competing interests the question whether or not a particular term which excludes liability offends too greatly against social values may depend upon the weighing of a variety of factors, such as the nature of the parties to the contract, the importance of the social value at stake and the extent to which the contract term qualifies the obligation. In the case of *Smith v Eric S Bush* no doubt important considerations at stake were the protection of the consumer when making a major investment and the concern to ensure that professions comply with a reasonable standard of care when delivering services. In some cases, the factor of the unfairness or imbalance of the terms of the contract also plays a role in influencing the court's exercise of discretion, so that it becomes impossible to draw a sharp distinction between the social policies being pursued and the court's perception of the unfairness of the particular contract under consideration.

The technique of judicial control obviously suffers from several disadvantages:

18 Art 2-302; Leff, 'Unconscionability and the Code – The Emperor's New Clause' (1967) *University of Pennsylvania Law Review* 485.
19 [1990] 1 AC 831, [1989] 2 All ER 514, HL.

(i)   It inhibits contract planning, for the parties will be uncertain whether or not a chosen clause will be regarded as acceptable by a court.

(ii) It operates retrospectively, so that the parties cannot ascertain the validity of the terms of their contract until the final outcome of litigation is known.

(iii) There is also a danger of inconsistent judicial decisions, for in the exercise of a broad discretion particular judges may place greater weight on some factors than others.

For these reasons the technique of judicial control for the introduction of compulsory terms often proves the least satisfactory.

Some of these objections to judicial control can be addressed in part by the development of clear principles for application of the discretion. As the courts consider numerous cases, they can develop principles which guide their decisions, and those principles together with reasoning by analogy from decided cases can permit parties to a contract to predict with considerable accuracy the validity of terms which seek to exclude obligations. Another technique for reducing the harmful effects of judicial discretion involves what may be called 'grey lists'. Here the legislation indicates to the courts a presumption of how their discretion ought to be exercised in relation to a list of examples of contract terms. The EC Directive on Unfair Terms in Consumer Contracts adopts such a list.[20] If a contract term fits into this list, it is likely to be held to be unfair, but it remains open to a court to conclude from looking at all the terms of the contract and the circumstances in which it was made that the general test of unfairness is not satisfied, so the potential uncertainty provoked by judicial discretion remains.

1. The scope of judicial discretion

Despite these concerns about contract planning, the technique of judicial control has been given a prominent position in English law by the Unfair Contract Terms Act 1977. Its key provisions introduce compulsory terms subject to a test of reasonableness. The Act is confined to exemption clauses, ie terms which purport to exclude, restrict or limit liability which would otherwise arise under the contract either by express or implied terms.[21] By rendering an exemption clause invalid due to its unreasonableness, the effect is to make the obligation which would otherwise have been excluded a mandatory obligation. Moreover, this mandatory obligation is contrary to the intention of the parties as it is recorded in their written contract.

The test of reasonableness applies in several circumstances, of which the most important are the following:

20 EC Directive 93/13/EEC, Art 3(3), Annex; this is replicated in the Unfair Terms in Consumer Contracts Regulations 1999, SI 1999/2083, Sch 2.

21 Unfair Contract Terms Act 1977, s 13 gives an extended meaning to exemption clause to include making legal liability subject to onerous conditions, and limiting the amount or kinds of remedies that may be claimed.

(i)   Section 2(2) brings under the test of reasonableness terms which exclude or restrict liability for damage to property where liability arises from negligence, that is an express or implied term of the contract which requires the exercise of reasonable care with respect to property.

(ii)   Section 3 addresses principally the situation where an exclusion clause seeks to exclude liability for breach of an express term in a standard form contract, and again this is subject to a test of reasonableness. A typical case under this section would consist of an express promise or guarantee in the standard form contract being subject to other provisions which substantially undermine the extent and worth of the guarantee.

(iii) Section 6 states that in contracts for the sale of goods where the purchaser is not dealing as a consumer the implied terms of such contracts required by the Sale of Goods Act 1979, ss 13–15, such as the requirement that the goods be of satisfactory quality, cannot be excluded unless the exemption clause satisfies the test of reasonableness.

The Unfair Terms in Consumer Contracts Regulations 1999[22] also empower courts to review the fairness of exclusion clauses (and other clauses) in consumer contracts. These Regulations are much broader in scope, applying to a broad range of terms in standard form contracts, and employ a range of legal procedures. Although detailed consideration of these Regulations will be deferred until Chapter 13, it is certainly possible that an attempt in a standard form consumer contract to exclude potential liabilities may be ineffective either under the 1977 Act or the 1999 Regulations. The overlap in coverage by these two pieces of legislation and the confusion which this provokes has induced proposals to produce one single piece of legislation.[23]

2.   The test of reasonableness

The courts receive little guidance from the legislation on how the test of reasonableness should be applied. The Unfair Contract Terms Act 1977, s 11(1) explains that the test of reasonableness is that:

> the term shall have been a fair and reasonable one to be included having regard to the circumstances which were, or ought reasonably to have been, known to or in the contemplation of the parties when the contract was made.

The statute emphasizes that the court should not use the benefit of hindsight, but must consider what was 'fair and reasonable' according to the circumstances known at the time of the formation of the contract. Section 11(4) indicates that the courts should consider in cases where liability is limited to a specified sum of

---

22 SI 1999/2083.
23 Law Commission, *Unfair Terms in Contracts*, Consultation Paper No 166 (London, 2002).

money whether or not the person liable could have covered his full liability through insurance. If not, the court may regard the limitation as more reasonable.[24] Finally, Sch 2 of the Act provides some guidelines for the courts, which must be considered in relation to s 6, but in practice will be taken into account in all cases involving a question of reasonableness. Of particular interest in these guidelines is the stress upon two factors:

(i) The courts are advised to consider the bargaining positions of the parties relative to each other and to consider whether in fact some alternative arrangement was available which would not have avoided liability. If such an alternative was available and practicable in the circumstances, then the courts are likely to consider the exemption more reasonable.

(ii) The guidelines stress the significance of the customer's knowledge of the terms; if the customer knew or ought to have known of the term, then this fact argues in favour of the reasonableness of the exemption clause.

The statute therefore confines the discretion to be exercised by the courts in invalidating contract terms on the ground of unreasonableness, but it does not eliminate it entirely. The court must weigh up the factors mentioned explicitly in the legislation, together with any other factors which it regards as relevant, before reaching a conclusion. In borderline cases, it will be far from predictable which factors the courts will regard as possessing considerable weight and which way a court will eventually jump. In reviewing the existing cases which have dealt with this issue, however, I suggest that the social policies pursued by the courts in the course of determinations of reasonableness have become clear, even if their relative weight in a particular instance remains indeterminate. The following considerations constitute the recurrent significant social policies pursued by the courts when assessing questions of reasonableness.

(a) ENFORCEMENT OF DUTIES OF CARE

When the law would normally imply a duty to take reasonable care between the contracting parties, the courts can use the test of reasonableness to prevent derogations from this duty. This liability for negligence itself rests on the proposition that liability will normally be imposed upon the person in the position to avoid the risk at the least cost. The social policy behind negligence liability is therefore to reduce the cost of accidents. The courts accord this policy considerable weight and are reluctant to permit contractual terms to defeat it. Thus in *Smith v Eric S Bush*, Lord Templeman regarded a notice which sought to exempt a surveyor for liability in negligence for an inaccurate valuation of a house as unreasonable primarily on the ground that it would defeat the useful purpose of

---

24 Adams and Brownsword, 'The Unfair Contract Terms Act: A Decade of Discretion' (1988) 104 *Law Quarterly Review* 94; Beale, 'Unfair Contracts in Britain and Europe' (1990) *Current Legal Problems* 197.

the general rule imposing negligence liability. For the same reason, a court is unlikely to approve a clause which seeks to exclude liability for both negligence and default for other reasons.[25] Attempts to limit the quantity of liability for negligence may be reasonable if full insurance cover is unobtainable or very expensive, but otherwise limitations of damages for negligence also receive a hostile treatment in consumer transactions. When, in *Waldron-Kelly v British Rlys Board*,[26] the railway lost a customer's suitcase through negligence, the limitation of damages clause was held to be unreasonable because it would have effectively permitted the railway to escape the consequences of its own negligence.

An exclusion clause that restricts liability for negligence may prove reasonable and valid in a commercial context where the parties have used the terms to plan risk, allocate liabilities and distribute the burden of taking out insurance. In the case of construction work, for instance, the owner of the building may have insurance against fire damage, so that it is reasonable for the building contractor to exclude liability for fire damage, thereby saving the costs of taking out duplicate insurance. In the case of contracts of carriage, the owner of the goods usually is in the best position to take out insurance given its superior knowledge of the value of the goods compared to the carrier, so that a carrier's exclusion clause may be regarded as reasonable. In practice, in order to preserve an incentive to be careful, the risk is likely to be shared between the parties: the carrier accepts limited liability for negligence, but requires the owner of the goods to take out insurance against loss to any greater extent.

(b) REMEDYING MARKET FAILURE

Of almost equal importance in assessing the reasonableness of exclusion clauses, the courts are concerned to remedy market failure. Here the courts are concerned to challenge uncompetitive markets in an attempt to force traders to offer different and competing terms. Market failures may arise from a number of causes.

One source is consumer ignorance of the terms of contracts apart from key items such as price, so that there is no incentive for traders to compete with respect to the other terms on offer. The Unfair Contract Terms Act 1977 expressly makes the issue of whether the customer knew or ought reasonably to have known of the existence and extent of the term relevant to the question of reasonableness.[27] The courts can deter the use of small print in standard forms and reliance upon incorporated documents which are hard to obtain. But if the trader takes steps to

25 *George Mitchell (Chesterhall) Ltd v Finney Lock Seeds Ltd* [1983] 2 AC 803, [1983] 2 All ER 737, HL.

26 [1981] CLY 303, in C Miller and B Harvey, *Consumer and Trading Law Cases and Materials* (London, 1985), p 250.

27 Unfair Contract Terms Act 1977, Sch 2.

draw the customer's attention to the clause,[28] or if it can be shown that the customer was aware of the clause, perhaps as a result of previous dealings,[29] this knowledge will direct the court towards a finding that the term is reasonable.

Another source of market failure is an effective cartel in a particular trade, so that all traders offer identical or very similar terms. Where the courts detect such a source of market failure, they will normally regard exclusion clauses as unreasonable, with the intended effect of compelling traders to engage in more competitive offers of terms. In *George Mitchell (Chesterhall) Ltd v Finney Lock Seeds Ltd*,[30] for instance, a farmer purchased cabbage seeds from merchants, who limited their liability for supplying the wrong sort of seeds to the cost of the seeds. One important consideration against the validity of the limitation of damages clause was the finding that 'a similar limitation of liability was universally embodied in the terms of trade between seedsmen and farmers and had been so for many years.'[31] This indicated a market failure caused by an effective cartel. Similarly, there was evidence in *Waldron-Kelly v British Rlys Board* that other potential carriers for the suitcase used similar but not identical exemption clauses, so there was no advantage to be gained in 'shopping around'.

The remedy for this market failure which is normally favoured by the courts is that, in the absence of any realistic possibility of renegotiation of terms, traders should offer different sets of terms at different prices which involve different levels of responsibility. In *Woodman v Photo Trade Processing Ltd*,[32] the claimaint's photographs were lost during processing by the defendant, who sought to limit his liability to the cost of the film as indicated in a notice at the retailers. Such a limitation of liability was standard practice throughout the trade, and of course it helped to keep costs down for the mass of consumers. Nevertheless, the court regarded the limitation of liability as unreasonable. It insisted that the trade should offer two sets of terms to customers, one cheap service with limited liability, and the other option with increased liability which consumers with particularly valuable photographs would choose. The court accepted that it would be reasonable for a trader not to offer the more expensive service itself, provided that it notified customers of the availability of such a service elsewhere.

(c) Fairness

Under the test of fairness and reasonableness contained in the Unfair Contract Terms Act 1977, s 11, the courts assess the equivalence of the obligations

28 *Woodman v Photo Trade Processing Ltd* (7 May 1981, unreported), in I Ramsay, *Consumer Protection* (London, 1989), p 107.
29 *Waldron-Kelly v British Rlys Board* [1981] CLY 303, in C Miller and B Harvey, *Consumer and Trading Law Cases and Materials* (London, 1985), p 250.
30 [1983] 2 AC 803, [1983] 2 All ER 737, HL.
31 Lord Bridge, [1983] 2 AC 803, [1983] 2 All ER 737, HL.
32 (7 May 1981, unreported), in I Ramsay, *Consumer Protection* (London, 1989), p 107.

undertaken by the parties. Where the exclusion clause has the effect of substantially devaluing the promise given by one party with no commensurate reduction in the price paid by the other, the court is likely to invalidate it. This consideration influenced the court in *Woodman v Photo Trade Processing Ltd* in recommending that a two-tier service be offered: an expensive service offering full guarantees, and a cheap service with limited compensation for loss of photographs. But this alternative will not itself satisfy the test of fairness, if the increased cost of full protection is too substantial and in practice prohibitively expensive. A similar set of alternative terms was recognized in *Smith v Eric S Bush* as a possible reasonable market practice, but the alternative offer of a full survey with guarantees was not regarded by Lord Griffith as practicable in that case, because it was prohibitively expensive.

Under this consideration of fairness, the courts have also been impressed by the difference between an agreed limitation of damages clause and the actual loss incurred. In *George Mitchell (Chesterhall) Ltd v Finney Lock Seeds Ltd* for instance, the contract fixed liability at the price of the seeds worth £192, but the actual losses of the farmer for losing a year's harvest were claimed to be £61,000. Similarly in *Waldron-Kelly v British Rlys Board* the value of the lost suitcase was £302, but the limitation of damages clause fixed the loss at £27. These disparities are impressive, but I doubt whether they should be relevant in themselves to the question of reasonableness or fairness. The real question is whether, in view of the price paid for the goods or services and the size and likelihood of the risk of loss, the limitation clause was unfair in restricting liability to such an extent. The court should balance the respective obligations of the parties, so that it may be reasonable to restrict liability severely where either the price paid is low or the risks of great loss so high that, for the price paid, it could not be reasonably expected that full liability had been undertaken. Customary business practice in a particular trade may prove a useful guide in this respect, provided that there is no suspicion of market failure.

(d)   EFFICIENT ALLOCATION OF THE BURDEN OF INSURANCE

Most of the losses arising from breach of contract can be insured against, and the costs of this insurance incorporated into the price of the contract. But it may be cheaper for one party to insure against the risk of loss than the other, and the courts will support exclusion clauses where they reflect an agreed and efficient distribution of the burden of insurance. One saving in insurance costs can be achieved by reducing the number of policies taken out. For this reason it was more efficient for the few firms of seedsmen in *George Mitchell (Chesterhall) Ltd v Finney Lock Seeds Ltd* to take out insurance than for the burden to fall on their thousands of customers. On the other hand, the risks at stake may be peculiarly within the knowledge of one party, and this will tend to make it more efficient for that party to insure against loss. In *Waldron-Kelly v British Rlys Board* the railway company argued that only customers knew the exact value of their goods, so that it was reasonable for them to limit their liability to a fixed amount, leaving it to the customer to take out any additional insurance necessary. This argument was not regarded as persuasive in the end, however, perhaps because it would have been more efficient for the railway to take out a single insurance policy and pass on the costs to all customers. It must be admitted that although the courts do pay attention to this factor of the efficiency of insurance arrangements, they have not so far investigated this issue with care, no doubt being hesitant to conduct the complex economic and empirical investigations which this factor really requires. Instead, the courts are likely to assume, in a contract between commercial parties which apparently apportions risk carefully, that the exemption clause should be enforced as appropriate insurance arrangements will have been constructed around it.[33]

(e)   SUPPORT FOR COLLECTIVE AGREEMENT OF TERMS

The reasonableness test is likely to be satisfied if the terms of the contract have been the product of negotiation between the relevant interest groups. In these circumstances the fears of market failure and the consequent misuse of standard form contracts to achieve unfair bargains disappears, and the courts are likely to find any agreed terms reasonable. Similarly, if there are agreed trading standards set with the approval of the Director General of Fair Trading, a contract which complies with those terms is likely to be held to be reasonable. If, however, the contract departs from such collectively agreed terms, or fails to conform to standard approved trade terms, then the court is likely to find an exemption clause unreasonable. In *Woodman v Photo Trade Processing Ltd*, for example, the court paid special attention to the Code of Practice for the Photographic Industry which had been promulgated with the approval of the Director General. This code clearly envisaged that traders would offer a two-tier service, and the failure to conform to this model was probably decisive in the finding that the limitation of liability was unreasonable. Similarly, in *George Mitchell (Chesterhall) Ltd v Finney Lock Seeds Ltd*, the House of Lords indicated that it would have accepted the seedsmen's limitation of liability, if it had been negotiated with a powerful representative of the customers such as the National Farmers' Union. This is an unexpected but welcome recognition by the courts of the desirability of encouraging this form of negotiated regulatory control over contract terms.

(f)   CONTROL OVER REMEDIAL DISCRETION

One objective of exclusion clauses may be to give the party in breach a range of choices with respect to the redress afforded. By inserting a clause which severely

33 *Photo Production Ltd v Securicor Transport Ltd* [1980] AC 827, [1980] 1 All ER 556, HL.

limits remedies for breach, this gives an option to grant greater compensation on an 'ex gratia' basis where commercial considerations may indicate this is advisable. If the dissatisfied customer is a business which frequently purchases the product or requires the service, then, in the interests of preserving this good business relation, it may be desirable for the party in breach to waive the exclusion clause and offer a better remedy in settlement of the claim. The courts have exhibited a hostility to this exhibition of contract power. The House of Lords in *George Mitchell (Chesterhall) Ltd v Finney Lock Seeds Ltd* relied upon evidence which revealed that the seedsmen often gave greater compensation than provided by the limitation clause in the contract in order to justify its conclusion that the limitation was unreasonable.

(g)   UNDIFFERENTIATED STANDARD FORMS

Finally, we can discern signs in the cases that the courts view with suspicion the practice of using an identical standard form contract regardless of the nature of the customer. Evidence which shows that the same terms are proffered regardless of whether the customer is a consumer or a substantial business may indicate that the term is unreasonable in the context of a consumer transaction.[34] Here the policy of support for a social market which differentiates between the types of traders in the market can be realized by insisting upon more flexible contracting practices.

F.   Agency discretion

The great potential advantage of the use of an agency to police the use of exclusion clauses over the court system comprises the potential to regulate in advance the use of terms in contracts. Instead of the parties waiting until trial to discover whether or not a clause is unreasonable and therefore invalid, the issue can be tested in advance by reference to an independent agency. Many other advantages of agencies exercising this type of discretion should also be noted. The process is usually cheaper and quicker for interested parties. The agency can look at all the contracts used in a particular trade or business and set publicized standards applicable to all traders. The judicial process, in contrast, usually results in an unreported and undiscoverable determination about a particular contract, which is unlikely to have any impact on any other traders' contracting practices.

Under the requirement of the EC Directive on Unfair Terms in Consumer Contracts, the English Regulations establish a duty on the Director General of

---

34 *Waldron-Kelly v British Rlys Board* [1981] CLY 303, in C Miller and B Harvey, *Consumer and Trading Law Cases and Materials* (London, 1985), p 250.

Fair Trading to consider complaints about unfair terms in consumer contracts.[35] If the Director General considers a complaint to be well founded, then he is empowered to negotiate with the business informally for the withdrawal of the unfair terms, and to accept an undertaking from the business to withdraw the clause, or, if no such undertaking is given, to apply to a court for an injunction against any person using or recommending use of such a term. The Unfair Contract Terms Unit established by the Director General to process this new power received 817 cases in its first year of operation.[36] Many of these cases concern instances of unfairness between the parties and will be considered in Chapter 13. Here what is relevant is the way in which the Unit has effectively rendered some obligations compulsory in consumer contracts by regarding attempts to exclude or modify the obligations unfair and invalid.

Many of the clauses which the Unit has insisted should be withdrawn comprise prohibited clauses under the Unfair Contract Terms Act 1977. The need for this intervention tends to confirm the hypothesis that a private law remedy backed solely by the judicial sanction of invalidity is unlikely to be effective. The Unit has dealt with clauses in contracts which purport to exclude liability for negligently caused personal injuries, as in this typical notice in a car park:

> Vehicles and their contents are parked at the owner's risk and no liability is accepted for any loss or damage to the vehicle or contents or persons, however caused.

The effect of the Unit's decision in that instance and others like it is that gradually these notices are being taken down across the country. Similarly, the Unit has had to reject as unfair terms which remove the consumer's basic warranty that goods sold in the course of business are of satisfactory quality, an exclusion which is again prohibited by the Unfair Contract Terms Act 1977. An example comes from the terms of a second-hand car dealer:

> No responsibility can be taken by ourselves if the vehicle is not in a roadworthy condition.

Other clauses which the Unit has caused to be withdrawn comprise terms which would have been subject to the test of reasonableness under the Unfair Contract Terms Act 1977. For example, terms which exclude liability for negligently caused damage to property must pass the test of being fair and reasonable in the circumstances. Here the underlying issue is when, if ever, will it be appropriate for a business to avoid the liability which would otherwise arise in tort or under an implied term of the contract to perform work with reasonable care so that no damage is caused to the purchaser's property. In a typical example, the terms of

---

35 Unfair Terms in Consumer Contracts Regulations 1999, SI 1999/2083, reg 10, implementing EC Directive 93/13/EEC.
36 Office of Fair Trading, *Unfair Contract Terms Bulletin*, No 2, September (London, 1996).

the standard contract used by a company which stripped and re-roofed houses excluded liability for damage to the building or its contents however caused.

The scope of the Unit's powers is unfortunately limited to the investigation of the unfairness of the terms of the particular contract which is the subject of complaint. It lacks the power to issue general regulations applicable to a trade or industry, or to a particular type of standard form contract in common use. The final determination of whether or not a term is unfair is left to judicial decision, so that the Unit's opinions remain advisory and limited to the particular contract. This regulatory framework misses the opportunity to create an agency which might be empowered to approve in advance particular standard form contracts, which could then be used by businesses with the assurance that they are valid and, therefore, a safe basis for contract planning. This limitation on the Unit's powers reflects a deference to the judicial process for determining contractual rights and the continuation of an assumption that ultimately it must be left to the parties to decide the terms of their contract. Yet this absence of the regulatory power to determine the validity of contracts in advance has the deleterious effect on contract planning that it continues the uncertainty as to the validity of the terms in consumer contracts. Even if the Unit has approved a term in a particular contract, it remains possible that a court will strike it down as unfair under the Regulations.

G.   Negotiated regulation

The obvious remedy for the inefficiency and unpredictability of judicial discretion to introduce compulsory terms consists of increasing the number and specificity of the compulsory terms by means of administrative regulation or delegated legislation. But detailed regulation often shares the same defects, for the sheer quantity of regulatory measures ensures widespread ignorance of their requirements, which makes the law appear unpredictable, and increases the cost of legal advice and other measures to ensure compliance. To compound these problems for the effectiveness of regulation, we must suspect that the law, by seeking to regulate economic activity, may be treated as a cost incorporated into a broader economic calculus guided by the pursuit of profits. If so, the cost of compliance with detailed regulations may be regarded as too expensive compared to the risk of invalidity of contracts, so that we reach the point of efficient breach of regulations. In the case of a minimum wage law for employees, for instance, employers may regard the risks arising from failure to comply as less costly than the increase in labour costs required by the law, so the rational economic calculus will lead to widespread flouting of the law.

Moreover, detailed regulation of contract terms may create harmful effects on the market. Legal regulation presents the danger that, by neutralizing competitive advantages, it will create disincentives to the provision of an efficient supply of goods and services to the public. Although some regulatory measures can be justified on the ground of their improvements to the efficiency of the market, such as duties of disclosure which supply consumers with sufficient information in order to judge intelligently between products, detailed legal regulation for compulsory terms in pursuit of collective interests may often stifle economic growth and frustrate consumer demand.

In addition, government measures run the risk of merely replacing one set of injustices by another. By replacing the market mechanism for the selection of terms, the legal regulation may achieve priority for one set of collective interests whilst ignoring or devaluing others. The recurring advantage of the market mechanism over legal regulation for determining terms consists in its responsiveness to the choices of all individuals involved in the economic activity. Legal regulation achieved by one pressure group through the political process may exclude the interests of other groups. The regulation simply replaces economic power with political power in the determination of contract terms.

Many of these disadvantages of legal regulation can be relieved by a final technique of regulation for compulsory terms. This method comprises a negotiation between representatives of collective interests resulting in a model set of terms for contracts of a particular type, and prescribed Codes of Practice which govern bargaining practices and avenues for redress of grievances. The model contract then becomes the mandatory standard form contract for transactions made by members of this trading group. The groups involved in negotiation often provide for arbitration of grievances, as opposed to judicial decisions, both because of the greater efficiency of arbitration, and because specialized arbitrators can often supplement negotiated agreements more intelligently in the light of their knowledge of the relevant conflicting interests. The state recognizes the authority of these negotiated model contracts through systems of licensing, provisions encouraging self-regulation and informal adjudication, and ultimately by backing up the codes of conduct and model contracts with legal sanctions including criminal penalties. Within this corporatist pattern, the typical role for the judiciary lies in review of the conduct of groups and bureaucratic administrators rather than adjudication of individual grievances. The purposes of review include checking that groups and administrators do not exceed or abuse their powers, ensuring that the proper level of consultation takes place with affected groups, and guaranteeing that arbitrators conform with the established regulations.[37] These four features of the modern law – negotiated standards, arbitration, state recognition, and judicial review – compose the corporatist or negotiated regulation pattern to which the law of contract increasingly turns.

We discover important examples of this technique in the regulation of many trades. Statutes aimed primarily at consumer protection encourage traders to

---

37 Stewart, 'The Reformation of American Administrative Law', (1975) 88 *Harvard Law Review* 1667.

establish binding Codes of Practice,[38] which sometimes receive legal support through sanctions, including criminal penalties and removal of a licence to trade. International conventions agreed between the relevant countries govern frequent international transactions, such as carriage of goods by air or sea.[39] Professions such as medicine and the law often prescribe a code of conduct which is enforced through occupational licensing and some criminal penalties. Special agencies including Ombudsmen also protect investors in banks, company shares and other securities. Occupational licensing schemes apply to many trades and professions, so that breach of approved standards of conduct leads to forfeiture of the licence to trade.

This corporatist pattern alters slightly in the context of consumer protection, because consumers often lack a representative body with which traders should negotiate. State officials such as the English Director General of Fair Trading assume the burden of negotiating the appropriate standards on behalf of consumers. The final agreement can result in the imposition of delegated legislation, which prohibits in advance certain kinds of terms in standard form contracts or other unsavoury market practices. Moreover, some agencies enjoy the power to use the criminal law process to punish traders who violate the required standards. Together these powers of regulation and enforcement through the criminal law process serve to make up for the weakness of consumers in pursuing their ordinary civil remedies against unscrupulous traders. Indubitably, in some cases the state officials betray the trust reposed in them by failing to represent the interests of consumers forcefully, but this inherent defect in the institutional design of corporatist controls in the context of consumer protection has not prevented it from becoming the prevailing pattern of control.

For similar reasons, self-regulation by business sectors without effective legal supervision and sanctions should be regarded with suspicion. The regulations are unlikely to be very restrictive and the sanctions against members of the trade association who break the rules often prove illusory in practice. Nevertheless, self-regulation by a trade or profession has become frequent in England. For example, the Advertising Standards Authority sets regulations against misleading advertisements, backed up by the threat of adverse publicity and, if the media co-operate, elimination of the offending advertisement. Insurance companies have also agreed not to take unreasonable advantage of the doctrine of 'uberrimae fidei' and the harsh provisions of their standard form contracts. In the absence of serious penalties, however, these initiatives have a minimal impact on those inclined to be unscrupulous.

---

38 Fair Trading Act 1973, s 124; R Cranston, *Consumers and the Law* (London, 2nd edn, 1984), ch 2.

39 Merchant Shipping Act 1995, s 183 incorporates the Athens Convention Relating to the Carriage of Passengers and their Luggage by Sea; Carriage by Air Act 1961, Sch 1 incorporates the Warsaw Convention; these separate regimes are insulated from attack under the Unfair Contract Terms Act 1977 and other consumer protection legislation.

Gathering together these trends in legislation and legal doctrine, we can discern the principal features of this pattern of law for market transactions. Corporatism or co-regulation replaces the old dichotomy of public and private law – that metaphor for a clash between the Welfare State and the free market – with an institutional framework of compulsory associations loosely supervised by bureaucratic and judicial organs of government. Individual traders are bound to observe the approved standards of their compulsory association on threat of criminal penalty or being driven out of business, yet they receive protection against abuse of organizational power through the application of administrative law by the courts. Through this institutional arrangement, a corporatist system counters the danger of an oppressive and inefficient public bureaucratic strangle-hold over market transactions. Its participatory and devolved style of government, which encourages the participation of stakeholders in the formation of standards and the policing of compliance, ushers in a procedural transformation in regulatory activities. At the same time, in the interests of efficiency and securing compliance, each trade association is permitted considerable latitude in devising its regulations and techniques of enforcement. In the light of these advantages of corporatism or co-regulation for the promotion of the social market, deviations from the pattern of negotiated regulation begin to appear suspect. Bodies which claim the power of regulation without being subject to external review, such as the Law Society or the Stock Exchange, experience considerable pressure to submit to some species of state control. Similarly, as we noted above, when courts examine the fairness of the terms of contracts under broad discretionary powers, if a standard form has not been approved by a representative body on both sides of the transaction, it becomes increasingly likely that the court will invalidate the harsher terms.[40] But vice versa, if the standard form contract, or a particular term in it, has been approved through a process of co-regulation, there should be a strong presumption in favour of its reasonableness and fairness, even if it reconfigures the standard incidents of private law obligations.[41]

---

40 Eg *Walker v Boyle* [1982] 1 All ER 634, [1982] 1 WLR 495 (standard conditions for sale of property unreasonable because not the product of negotiations between representative bodies).
41 Unfair Contract Terms Act 1977, s 29(2) exempts terms approved by an industry regulator from judicial review.

Fairness

A.   Substantive fairness

A system of contract law committed to freedom of contract must reject controls over the fairness of contracts. No matter that the purchaser has paid an excessive price or the seller received gross undervalue, the principle of freedom to select the terms must prohibit intervention designed to redress the balance of the obligations. At most the law can scrutinize minutely the procedures leading up to the contract to ensure that the freedom of the parties was not restricted by pressure, fraud, abuse of positions of trust, and other factors which interfered with the voluntariness of consent. Tests of procedural propriety are both compatible with and required by the principle of freedom of contract, but any examination of the fairness of the substance of the contract must be forbidden. Accordingly, texts describing the classical law of contract offered no place for a discussion of a requirement of fairness in contracts.

A reluctance to acknowledge the significance of substantive unfairness in contracts as a ground for intervention still characterizes judicial decisions in the common law. A court will prefer to stress any elements of procedural impropriety that it can discover rather than address directly the unfairness of the bargain. The substantive unfairness may provide the motive for intervention, but the formal legal reason given for upsetting the contract will be couched in terms of a procedural defect, such as deception, manipulation, or unfair surprise. This approach receives further support from economic analysis of law, since these procedural defects can be regarded as evidence of a market failure which prevented the operation of a competitive and efficient market. To discover the real significance of substantive unfairness in the common law of contract therefore requires an investigation which digs behind the formal reasons given for decisions.

On its own such an investigation could produce ambiguous results. Although it might seem plausible that the courts were concerned about substantive unfairness in a particular case, since their formal reasons for the decision invariably latch onto a procedural impropriety, the case for believing that substantive unfairness was crucial to the decision might be regarded as unproven. The argument is strengthened, however, by reference to a batch of statutory provisions which permit the courts to discuss substantive unfairness openly. Although few common law jurisdictions grant the courts a general oversight of fairness in contracts,[1] a patchwork of legislation governing particular types of contracts provides an impressive array of instruments. The most important example of this legislation derives from Article 3 of the EC Directive on Unfair Terms in Consumer Contracts, enacted as reg 5(1) of the Unfair Terms in Consumer Contracts Regulations 1999:

> A contractual term which has not been individually negotiated shall be regarded as unfair if, contrary to the requirement of good faith, it causes a significant imbalance in the parties' rights and obligations arising under the contract, to the detriment of the consumer.[2]

---

1 An exception is the Contracts Review Act 1980, NSW; *West v AGC (Advances) Ltd* (1986) 5 NSWLR 610, CA; *Dillon v Baltic Shipping Co (The Mikhail Lermontov)* [1991] 2 Lloyd's Rep 155, CA.

2 SI 1999/2083, implementing EC Directive 93/13/EEC.

When legislation of this kind is combined with the circumstantial evidence from the common law of a concern for substantive fairness, the significance of intervention on this ground emerges as a major concern of the law of contract.

In examining the extent to which the law intervenes on the ground of fairness we should be sensitive to the point that the meaning of fairness shifts according to the context in which it is raised. When the allegation is simply that a price is too high or derisory, it is likely that a comparison is being drawn between the contract price and the normal market price or perhaps some statutory rate. When the allegation is that the terms of the contract are unfair because buried in the details of the contract are ancillary terms that give one party a significant advantage, the idea of fairness may include the idea that such a benefit should have been paid for in a lower price, but it is also likely to include the idea that the ancillary term obtains an advantage that is not matched by some commensurate benefit to the other party and that it defeats the reasonable expectations of the other party. In a third context, the terms of the contract may have appeared fair at the outset, but subsequent unforeseen events have rendered the contract in its operation unexpectedly onerous to one of the parties. Here the idea of fairness commonly employed is that the balance of advantage under the contract has been disturbed by external events, and that somehow this balance should be restored.

This chapter first examines the extent to which the common law takes considerations of fairness into account through the legal doctrines which, for the most part, we have already considered. The second section examines the scope of statutory controls over unfair terms in contract, and the third investigates the extent to which the courts respond to a change in circumstances that upsets the balance of the bargain. The topic of controls over contractual terms that fix the remedies available for breach of contract will be deferred until Chapter 16.

B.   Fairness in the common law

Under the classical conception of contract law, lawyers both asserted the fairness of agreements which satisfied the conditions for the formation of valid contracts, and refused to adopt any explicit measures designed to invalidate unfair transactions. The central rule remains that a court will refuse to test the adequacy of consideration. Even a peppercorn can provide the consideration for a major capital transaction.

This rule endorses the fairness of voluntary transactions and demonstrates a faith in the ability of individuals to take care of their own interests and to make informed and rational judgements. This faith in individual autonomy and rationality leads to a belief in the fairness of the distributive outcomes of a relatively uninhibited market. Far from refusing to develop a theory of distributive justice and fairness in contracts, the classical conception of contract law states a clear preference for the distributive outcome of a largely uninhibited market.

Behind this facade, however, there lurked an understandable reluctance on the part of the courts to be used as instruments of exploitation. When confronted by a manifestly disadvantageous transaction, they could deploy a host of legal doctrines in order to avoid enforcement. Although the doctrines themselves rarely refer to fairness as a relevant consideration, they could be used instrumentally to achieve the outcome of invalidating the contract or a noxious term. Indeed, most of the rules governing the formation of contracts could be used instrumentally for this purpose.

1. Consideration

Although the courts decline to test the adequacy of consideration, the issue of whether or not any consideration existed at all to support the transaction provides fertile territory for instrumental decisions. If an apparent exchange can be described as two unconnected donative promises, because the promises were not given in response to a request from the other party, a court can declare that no contract was established. A court might follow this line of reasoning where the promises have a marked imbalance of value.

For example, the legal issue in _Combe v Combe_[3] was whether a husband's promise to his wife during divorce proceedings to pay her £100 maintenance a year was supported by consideration. The Court of Appeal concluded that it was a donative promise because the husband had not requested any action in return for the promise. It would not have been impossible for the court, if it had so wished, to have inferred from the facts of the case an implied request from the husband to the wife to refrain from applying to a court for maintenance. But the court clearly regarded the denial of a remedy to the wife as a just result in this case. Denning LJ observed, 'I do not think it would be right for this wife, who is better off than her husband, to take no action for six or seven years and then come down on him for the whole £600.' This remark reveals that the court regarded the alleged transaction as unfair, for the consideration for the husband's promise would be the sacrifice of a right to maintenance in circumstances where it was unlikely that a court would order maintenance owing to the wife's superior income. One may surmise that, if the wife had shown urgent financial need, the court would have used its ingenuity to imply a request in order to satisfy the doctrine of consideration.

We noted in Chapter 4 when examining the concept of consideration that in fact the courts switch from an abstract exchange model to a concept of benefit and

3   [1951] 2 KB 215, [1951] 1 All ER 767, CA.

detriment. The move to an evaluation of whether the promise involved a real detriment to the promisor marks a surreptitious deviation from the principle that the court will not test the adequacy of consideration. The reason for switching the concept of consideration is plainly to avoid the enforcement of agreements where the court regards the promise as illusory or without value. Similarly where a court insists that an agreement is supported by consideration because it conferred a real commercial benefit it seems likely that the court has formed a view that the contract produced a fair outcome. In *Williams v Roffey Bros and Nicholls (Contractors) Ltd*,[4] a builder offered a carpenter an additional payment as an inducement to complete performance of an existing contract on time. Although it was hard to discern what fresh consideration the carpenter had supplied to support the additional payment, since the carpenter had merely agreed not to breach the existing contract, the court upheld the modification as legally enforceable. The consideration was found in the commercial benefits to the builder in completing the job on time, such as the avoidance of damages payable to the owner for delay. But the court was surely also influenced by the reason that the builder had offered a price increase in the first place, namely that it appreciated that the carpenter had originally under-priced the job. If, on the contrary, the carpenter had acted opportunistically to extract a higher price in an emergency, the court may not have been so willing to discover any fresh consideration, or alternatively, the court might have applied the doctrine of economic duress to avoid the modification.

2. Incorporation of terms

In the context of disputes over the terms of the contract, the unfairness of the terms may indicate that advantage was taken of the opportunity to sneak oppressive terms into a standard form contract small print. What the law requires in such cases, as in *Interfoto Picture Library Ltd v Stiletto Visual Programmes Ltd*,[5] is that the more unusual and onerous the terms, the greater the steps required to bring these terms to the actual notice of the disadvantaged party. The logic of this rule is that a party should not be permitted to take undue advantage of the bargaining position gained by insisting upon a standard form contract. The unfairness of the terms and the absence of specific notice of these terms suggests that the opportunity to take advantage of this bargaining position was seized upon. The fact that the terms were unfair merely tends to show that the risk to the competitive market presented by small print in long contracts materialized in this instance.

3. Undue influence and 'unconscionability'

In principle, the issue of whether or not consent was given to a transaction should depend upon the conduct of the parties during the negotiations and not on the

---

4 [1991] 1 QB 1, [1990] 1 All ER 512, CA; see Chapter 15.
5 [1989] QB 433, [1988] 1 All ER 348, CA.

content of the contract. The absence of agreement or the presence of coercion will negative consent to the contract. Nevertheless, many cases come before the courts where the argument presented suggests that the ostensible consent provided perhaps by a signature on a document was not given voluntarily due to subtle forms of pressure and influence which may or may not be regarded as having negatived consent. These cases are usually considered under the doctrine of undue influence, although the term 'unconscionability' is also used, particularly in connection with cases where the victim has a special disability, such as mental infirmity or illiteracy.

In our earlier discussion of these doctrines in Chapter 8, we observed that although the unfairness of the contract was not a requirement to avoid a contract, the courts require evidence that undue influence was in fact exercised. The best evidence that advantage was taken of the weaker party is likely to be found in the unfairness or imprudence of the transaction for the weaker party. The greater the disadvantage to the vulnerable person, the stronger the presumption that unfair advantage was taken, and the more cogent must be the explanation of why undue influence was not in fact exercised in order to rebut the presumption. In this equitable jurisdiction, the courts insist that their reason for invalidating the contract is ultimately that there was a defect in consent caused by the unconscionable behaviour of the dominant party. But it is plain that this emphasis on the procedure leading up to the contract leans heavily on a determination that the weaker party has suffered a manifest disadvantage from the contract. As Lord Scarman once observed, 'I know of no reported authority where the transaction set aside was not the manifest disadvantage of the person influenced.'[6]

4. Interpretation and implied terms

In the course of interpreting contracts, the courts have many opportunities to construct the obligations so that they conform to the reasonable expectations of the parties. During this process the courts do not simply rewrite the terms of the agreement so that they comply with a latent standard of fairness, but they can interpret vague terms and insert implied terms in order to bring the contractual obligations more into balance and to protect reasonable expectations. The idea of reasonable expectations differs from a simple fairness criterion, for its reference is not to an independent standard of a fair price, but rather to the unexpressed intentions of the parties. But the circle becomes almost closed once it is accepted that those intentions are likely to be construed as a desire to enter a contract with a reasonable balance of obligations on both sides.

The criterion of fairness influences, but is not determinative of, the decision to imply a term into a contract. The courts are engaged in seeking a fair and

6 *National Westminster Bank plc v Morgan* [1985] AC 686, [1985] 1 All ER 821, HL.

practicable allocation of risks. In *Liverpool City Council v Irwin*,[7] it will be recalled that the court inserted an implied term into a lease for an apartment in a high-rise block that the landlord should take reasonable steps to keep the common parts of the premises in good repair and usable. I suggested that the court preferred this solution because it appeared the most practical and efficient solution, since it may have been difficult and expensive for the tenants to manage this task themselves. If the criterion of fairness had been used, the court should have considered the level of the rent compared to the services offered by the landlord. But fairness in the sense of balance of obligations and reasonable expectations is relevant here, for no doubt the tenants held the reasonable expectation that the landlord would look after the lifts, corridors and staircases in the absence of express contrary provision. When this reasonable expectation coincides with a practicable and efficient solution to the handling of a risk, the implied term can be asserted with confidence.

During the interpretation of terms of contracts, there is also considerable opportunity for the courts to mould the contract to conform with the reasonable expectations of the parties. A court can construe exclusion clauses narrowly, so that the normal obligations arising, such as the duty of care, can be protected. It can insist that express discretionary powers are subject to a requirement of honesty and rationality, so that use of the power for an unexpected purpose to gain an opportunistic advantage can be regarded as a breach of contract. Vague terms, such as the requirement of satisfactory quality for goods which are sold, or duties to take reasonable care in the performance of services, also provide the courts with an opportunity to satisfy reasonable expectations and maintain the balance of the obligations. What counts as satisfactory quality will depend upon the price. The buyer is entitled to receive value for money, ie goods of a quality which reflects the price paid for them,[8] unless the buyer is consciously taking a risk that the goods may not be as valuable as he or she hopes. The purchaser of a new car for a high price can reasonably expect a car without any faults and blemishes, whereas the purchaser of an 'old banger' for £100 can only reasonably expect conformity with basic safety standards. Similarly, what counts as reasonable care will depend in part upon the price being paid for the service.

5. Mistake

We observed in the discussion of consent in Chapter 7 that the doctrine of mistake occupies an uncertain position. Although there is a superficial logic in regarding a mistake as negativing the intention to enter into a particular contract, this logic cannot be permitted to govern contracts because it could provide an

---

7 [1977] AC 239, [1976] 2 All ER 39, HL.
8 Sale of Goods Act 1979, s 14(2A); *Rogers v Parish (Scarborough) Ltd* [1987] QB 933, [1987] 2 All ER 232, CA; Willett, 'Fairness in Sale of Goods Act Quality Obligations and Remedies', in C Willett (ed), *Aspects of Fairness in Contract* (London, 1996), p 123.

open-ended excuse to avoid any transaction which turns out to be unpalatable. A better understanding of the doctrine of mistake places it in the context of interpretation of contracts. On this view, certain facts could be regarded as a condition precedent to the obligations arising under the contract. If as a result of a mistake these conditions did not exist, the contractual obligations should be unenforceable because the condition precedent has not been satisfied. Nevertheless, the courts appear to accept the existence of a doctrine of mistake that renders a contract void, and it provides fertile terrain for a party seeking to escape from a disadvantageous contract. In *Bell v Lever Bros*,[9] the decision of the House of Lords that appears to confirm the existence of the doctrine of mistake at common law, the employers were seeking unsuccessfully to renege on an agreement to pay directors compensation for dismissal. Having failed to establish fraud, the employers argued that the agreement was void for mistake. Although the directors may have been in breach of contract, which would have entitled the employer to dismiss them without paying compensation, the contract to pay compensation was binding. The identity of the subject matter of the contract, namely a release from any claims that the directors may have had against the employer, had not altered merely because it turned out that in fact the directors had no valid claims.

Despite this unpromising start for the use of mistake to avoid contracts that, owing to facts unknown at the time of the contract, seem to one party to be unfair, the argument has been successful in a few instances. In *Grist v Bailey*[10], for example, the vendor of a house sold it for £850, rather less than its probable market value of £2,250, under the influence of a mistake that it was occupied by a tenant with tenure protected by statute, whereas in fact the tenant was dead. The English Court of Chancery permitted rescission of the contract on the ground that the parties had made a fundamental mistake, but the court attached a condition to its order which required the parties to make a new contract at the market price for such a house with vacant possession. One cannot doubt that the crucial factor that determined whether or not this mistake was sufficiently fundamental to warrant rescission of the contract was the substantial difference in price between the property with and without vacant possession.

The practice of applying the doctrine of mistake to invalidate unfair transactions appears more common in some jurisdictions in the USA.[11] In *Sherwood v Walker*,[12] the plaintiff demanded possession of a cow named 'Rose 2d', which he had agreed to purchase for $80. The defendants refused to deliver the cow for that price, on the ground that they had agreed the price on the mistaken assumption that she was barren, whereas she was with calf and worth between $750 and $1,000. The Michigan Court of Appeals reversed the trial court which had

9 [1931] All ER Rep 1, HL.
10 [1967] Ch 532, [1966] 2 All ER 875, Ch.
11 *Patterson*, 'Equitable Relief for Unilateral Mistake' (1928) 28 *Columbia Law Review* 859.
12 66 Mich 568, 33 NW 919 (1887).

enforced the action for possession of the cow. It held that the defendants were entitled to rescission of the contract if the mistake went to the root of the matter, the very nature of the thing. The court held that a barren cow is a substantially different thing from a breeding one, but who can doubt that this judgment was influenced largely by the commercial value of the two kinds of animal rather than their external appearance?

The existence of any comparable wide equitable jurisdiction in England to rescind contracts on the ground of mistake was rejected in *Great Peace Shipping Ltd v Tsavliris Salvage (International) Ltd*.[13] The defendants had agreed to rescue a ship that had suffered serious damage in the South Indian Ocean. In order to fulfil that obligation, they hired the claimant's vessel to tow the damaged vessel to safety. At that time both parties believed the claimant's vessel to be 35 miles from the stricken ship, but it quickly emerged that it was 410 miles distant. The defendants hired another ship for the purpose and purported to cancel the agreement with the claimant. In response to the claim for breach of the hire contract, the defendants argued that the common mistake about the location of the ship rendered the contract void or voidable. Whilst the Court of Appeal accepted the existence of a doctrine of mistake, the court insisted upon its narrow application, and rejected the existence of the looser equitable approach as had been used in *Grist v Bailey*. For a contract to be avoided by common mistake, there had to be a common assumption as to a state of affairs, no warranty by either party that the state of affairs in fact existed, and the non-existence of the state of affairs had not to be caused by the fault of either party. In addition, the inaccuracy of the common assumption had to render performance of the contract impossible or something essentially different from that which the parties had agreed. These conditions had not been satisfied since the claimant's ship could have been used for the intended purpose, albeit after a delay, and would have been used if it had not happened that the defendants had discovered a more proximate vessel. The defendants therefore had to pay the minimum hire charge under the contract of US$82,000 even though in the event they had no use for the vessel. But the court thought there was, in the circumstances, no injustice in that result because the defendants had acquired the use of the vessel, which, in the absence of finding another, might have been vital to save lives and to fulfil their contract to rescue the ship.

The effect of this decision is to reduce the potential of the doctrine of mistake to assist parties who have made a bad bargain. In most cases, the contract in its express or implied terms, when properly interpreted, has allocated the risk that the circumstances will turn out to be different from those assumed by the parties to exist at the time of the formation of the contract. The courts accept, however, that occasionally the shared mistake of fact is so significant that the contract cannot be construed as having allocated the risk. In such cases, performance of the

13 [2002] EWCA Civ 1407, [2003] QB 679, [2002] 4 All ER 689.

contract must become essentially different or impossible for the court to apply the doctrine of mistake to declare the contract void. Apart from fanciful examples, such as the sale of an animal where both parties believe it to be a pig but in fact it is a cow, it is hard to conceive when these narrow criteria might be satisfied. The most likely instances concern transactions which assume the existence of certain goods, and in fact those goods never existed or were destroyed before the contract was made, although even in such cases it is likely that the contract can be construed easily to allocate the risk of the non-existence of the goods between the parties.[14]

6. Restraint of trade

Terms in contracts designed to restrict freedom of trade, such as restrictions on setting up a business or seeking employment, are void under the common law doctrine of restraint of trade unless the term can be justified as reasonable. Although the ostensible purpose of the doctrine is plainly to protect freedom of competition in the market, it can be used instrumentally to invalidate contracts which a court perceives to be unbalanced in its obligations. For example, in *Schroeder Music Publishing Co Ltd v Macaulay*,[15] a composer agreed to give all his song compositions to a publisher for a period of five years, renewable at the option of the publisher, in return for low royalties but no promise to publish the work. The composer enjoyed considerable success and sought to extract himself from this unfavourable agreement. The House of Lords invalidated the contract on the ground that the weak bargaining position of the composer had led to an unfair agreement under which the publisher undertook minimal obligations in return for total commitment by the composer. Trebilcock correctly observes that this transaction was produced within a competitive market, so that there could be no market failure justification for upsetting the terms of the contract nor any alternative set of terms to be discovered as a different going rate for royalties in the market.[16] Nevertheless, the court clearly regarded the obligations as out of balance, and so was prepared to extend the doctrine of restraint of trade to avoid the contract.

7. Instrumentalism in the common law

Few students of the law of contract doubt that the doctrines of the common law can be used for instrumental purposes beyond those for which they were created. It has also struck many students that judicial perceptions of the fairness or

14 Eg *Associated Japanese Bank (International) Ltd v Credit du Nord SA* [1988] 3 All ER 902, [1989] 1 WLR 255, QB.
15 [1974] 3 All ER 616, [1974] 1 WLR 1308, HL
16 Trebilcock, 'An Economic Approach to the Doctrine of Unconscionability', in B Reiter and J Swan (eds), *Studies in Contract Law* (Toronto, 1980), p 381.

unfairness of a particular transaction is likely to influence the result and to encourage a court to use a doctrine instrumentally to avoid the position of being required to enforce a grossly unfair contract. The foregoing examples of doctrines that have perhaps been used for the purpose of invalidating or blocking the enforcement of contracts perceived to be unfair could no doubt be multiplied by other examples. Although the courts reject any formal statement of a substantive test of fairness for the enforceability of contracts, it is equally hard to find instances where the court, having analysed the allocation of the risks in the contract, enforces a contract which it believes causes unfairly a manifest disadvantage to one party. How should this legal position be interpreted?

Can we assert, despite the formal rhetorical support for freedom of contract and an uninhibited market, that the courts are in fact operating covertly a criterion of fairness for judging the validity and meaning of contracts?[17] Or should we accept the rationalizations presented by classical lawyers of this practice, that the legal doctrine achieved consistency and integrity, because the rules governing consent merely articulated the necessary conditions for freedom of contract to be exercised, and the rules governing interpretation merely ensured that the terms of the contract represented the true intentions of the parties? Or should we accept the contention of economic analysis of law that every instance of intervention can be justified on the ground of market failure, so that the purpose of the intervention is to restore competition, not to ensure fairness? The legal position is probably more complex than is suggested by any of these rival interpretations.

The freedom of contract ideal necessarily depends upon a conception of what should count as a competitive market. In describing the situations where a competitive market ceases to exist, the courts must examine all the circumstances which point both to the opportunity to abuse an advantageous market position and to the fact that abuse has taken place. The unfairness of the terms of the contract will inevitably provide crucial evidence of abuse of market position. The rival 'freedom of contract' and 'fairness' interpretations of the common law are therefore much closer than they typically suppose. In articulating a concept of freedom of contract, the courts must be driven to examine the unfairness of the terms of particular contracts. The mistake made by the classical lawyers was to suppose that an examination of the terms of the contract was irrelevant to the protection of freedom of contract.

This mistake seems to have arisen from a number of sources. It was not recognized that the idea of voluntary consent was insufficient on its own to describe the conditions for valid consent without some further specification of the necessary conditions for competitive markets. But when the courts were compelled to describe the conditions for a competitive market through doctrines such as undue influence and the objective test of agreement, they found themselves driven to consider whether or not an abuse of bargaining power had

17 P Atiyah, *Essays on Contract* (Oxford, 1988), ch 11.

taken place, and the unfairness of the terms proved the determinative evidence on this point. Thus the practical application of the idea of voluntary consent necessarily entails an examination of the fairness of the terms of the contract.

A second mistake of the classical lawyers was to infer from their commitment to the economic analysis of the subjectivity of values, as embodied in the rule against testing the adequacy of consideration, that it was impossible to judge the fairness of terms.[18] This mistake led classical lawyers to suppose that not only was a consideration of the fairness of contracts undesirable but that it was also impossible. A theory of contractual fairness needs both a system of evaluating the obligations undertaken by the parties, and a calculus to determine when the disproportion in value is sufficiently great to justify legal control, for otherwise even the slightest disequilibrium would upset a contract. Classical lawyers assert that it is impossible to devise a suitable two-part theory of valuation. The subjective nature of values prevents the general acceptance of any objective criterion of value by which courts may assess unfairness. As Chief Baron Eyre remarked:

> The value of a thing is what it will produce, and admits of no precise standard. It must be in its nature fluctuating, and will depend upon ten thousand circumstances. One man in the disposal of his property may sell it for less than another would; he may sell it under pressure of circumstances, which may induce him to sell it at a particular time. Now, if Courts of Equity are to unravel all these transactions, they would throw everything into confusion, and set afloat all the Contracts of mankind.[19]

By accepting the theory of marginal utility, under which prices are set according to the impulses of supply and demand, the classical lawyers concluded that no objective tests of value exist by which prices can be substituted for what the parties have in fact agreed. Each contract represents a moment in the flow of supply and demand, and, therefore, to hold a contract to be unfair would be merely to substitute another moment in time or another market. Although this might be possible, it would be difficult to imitate the exact conditions under which the contract was made, and furthermore there is no reason to think that a price determined at a later moment or in another context would be any fairer.

The practical objection to a test of fairness has been shown to be false by experience. Whilst it is true that no objective standards of value exist, we can certainly devise mechanisms for determining a fair price which are perfectly rational. Legislation often employs a substitute for a market price, devised according to a calculus which reflects competing policy considerations. Although the ordinary market inhibits intervention, because major adjustments of price may seriously damage supply or demand, mechanisms for setting prices are

18 Gordley, 'Equality in Exchange' (1981) 69 *California Law Review* 1587.
19 *Griffith v Spratley* (1787) 1 Cox Eq Cas 383.

frequently constructed which introduce marginal adjustments in order to serve distributive goals. For example, rent controls help the position of tenants by reducing the price of accommodation, but the price must be set at a sufficiently high level in order to ensure the continuing supply of adequate quantities of housing. Similarly, the fairness of a price for consumer goods charged by a door-to-door salesperson can be measured against the market price in retail stores. This device involves a transference of the contract from one market – door-to-door sales – to another – retail stores – and, provided this shift is justifiable and makes allowance for the greater convenience, it provides an adequate criterion of fairness for the courts to use. In *Toker v Westerman*,[20] for example, a door-to-door salesman sold a refrigerator-freezer to the defendants at a total price of $1,229, payable in 36 monthly instalments. On a claim for an unpaid balance on the account of $574, the defendants proved that the normal retail price in shops for an identical appliance was about $400. The New Jersey Superior Court refused to give judgment for the outstanding balance on the ground that the price was unconscionably high compared to the ordinary retail value. The court's jurisdiction to intervene rested upon the provision concerning unconscionability in the Uniform Commercial Code. In England the jurisdiction might rely upon the special provisions regarding door-step sales, or the equitable jurisdiction of undue influence with the facts indicating a combination of taking advantage of an effective monopoly and the business ignorance of the consumer. In this case the court used the comparable market of retail sales to demonstrate the unfairness of the terms achieved by door-to-door sales.

These two mistakes of the classical lawyers' rationalizations of the law governing the fairness of contracts persisted because they fitted so closely into the ideal of autonomy celebrated in the slogan 'freedom of contract'. Under the influence of the competitive model of human life derived from evolutionism, and reflecting a concern for the protection of rights of private property, the classical law was drawn to doctrines which insisted that individual freedom could only be realized by an uninhibited market. Any control over the fairness of the terms was regarded as a dangerous distortion of its operation as a competitive system for the distribution of goods and services, and ultimately as a threat to the private property system on which markets were based.

In the modern law of contract, however, it is recognized that we require a more complex idea of the relation between individual freedom and markets. The purpose of markets is to provide worthwhile opportunities to pursue individual goals. Competition in markets is essential for this purpose, but the mere existence of a competitive market does not ensure that any particular transaction has been entered into under conditions of fair competition without an abuse of bargaining position. Similarly, although freedom to select the terms of a transaction usually assists in the process of ensuring that the market provides worthwhile

20 13 NJ Super 452, 274 A 2d 78 (1970).

opportunities, we must introduce safeguards so that the terms reflect the reasonable expectations of the parties when there is a danger that the express terms surreptitiously deviate from those expectations. Although this modern interpretation of the connection between individual freedom and contracts, which I have described as the social market, does not require any general rule which invalidates unfair contracts,[21] it does demand that the courts should eliminate instances where abuse of bargaining position has obtained terms which are out of line with comparable market transactions or where the terms defeat the reasonable expectations engendered by the proposed transaction. Such justifications for intervention and control over freedom of contract, although not amounting to a simple test of fairness in contracts, provide reasons for using and evolving doctrines that might serve such goals more completely.

C. Statutory controls

These modern ideas on the connection between individual freedom and markets have had a much clearer impact on legislation governing contracts. Because legislation lacks the commitment to general principles, but can demarcate interventions by reference to types of transaction and the character of the parties, it can introduce tests of fairness within narrow confines without seeking to impose a general test of the fairness of terms on all contracts. The purpose of these controls over the fairness of terms may imitate the common law's concern for the protection of competitive markets and reasonable expectations. Legislation can introduce tests of fairness of contract terms for quite different purposes as well. The statutes may be concerned with the stabilization of markets or the distributive effects of certain kinds of transactions. For instance, controls over the price of agricultural products may serve the purpose of stabilising the markets for farm produce, thereby insulating farmers from short-term fluctuations in prices. The adoption of minimum wage laws serves several purposes including the reduction of poverty, promoting social inclusion through work, and savings to the taxpayer in providing welfare benefits to the low paid.

I. Price regulation

Attempts by legislation to regulate market prices always sparks controversy. Although the aims of such regulation may be regarded as praiseworthy, critics object that the regulation is likely to prove ineffective or harm those groups which are intended to benefit. A minimum wage law, for instance, may reduce the number of jobs available because it may diminish an employer's demand for labour in response to the price increase. Similarly, the establishment of fair rents

---

21 For the contrary argument, Smith, 'In Defence of Substantive Fairness' (1996) *Law Quarterly Review* 138.

may induce landlords to reduce the supply or quality of tenancies if their profits are reduced.[22] The danger of intervention in contract terms for the purpose of fairer distributive justice may therefore be to create disequilibrium in markets, with resulting undesirable side-effects such as higher unemployment or poor quality housing. In some cases the harmful side-effects may even worsen in the long run the position of those classes of people which the intervention was intended to help, by for example creating a shortage of accommodation. For these reasons, any attempt to meddle with freedom of contract through regulation, and especially regulation of prices, is often heavily criticised. The goals of distributive justice, it is suggested, should be pursued through progressive taxation and welfare benefits, which do not directly disrupt the operations of a competitive market and which may more accurately pin-point instances of hardship.

Although these objections to control over the fairness of contracts are powerful, they are frequently overstated. To begin with, the costs of implementation of controls must be considered on a comparative basis.[23] In some cases it is cheaper to regulate contracts than to redistribute wealth through taxation. After all, taxation involves administrative costs just as much as price regulation. In attempts to redistribute wealth, we may discover, for example, that a minimum wage law more efficiently fills the pockets of the poor than does a complex redistributive tax mechanism, because the former is largely self-enforcing. Furthermore, given that the precise effects of any regulation of markets is always difficult to predict because of varying elasticities of supply and demand, it may make sense to chance direct regulation of contracts for distributive ends and test the effects by experience.[24]

A deeper argument in favour of permitting control over the fairness of terms for distributive motives concerns the degree of risk which citizens should encounter when entering markets.[25] Because of shortage of time and information most contracts occur in imperfect markets. It is likely, however, that contracts will gravitate towards an equilibrium market price due to the cumulative effect of many different transactions taking place after a perfunctory search for market opportunities. But there remains a residual risk that a transaction will be isolated from these market forces, so that a party may pay an excessive price or receives derisory consideration. This risk is both inescapable and to some extent desirable. The risk encourages care in comparing market opportunities, which in turn assists the operation of a competitive market. But it is not inconsistent with the

---

22 K Hartley, *Problems in Economic Policy* (London, 1977), ch 8, also in A Ogus and C Veljanovski (eds), *Readings in the Economics of Law and Regulation* (Oxford, 1984), p 275.
23 Kronman, 'Contract Law and Distributive Justice' (1980) 89 *Yale Law Journal* 472.
24 Kennedy, 'Distributive and Paternalist Motives in Contract and Tort Law, with Special Reference to Compulsory Terms and Unequal Bargaining Power' (1982) 41 *Maryland Law Review* 563; Leff, 'Economic Analysis of Law: Some Realism about Nominalism' (1974) 60 *Virginia Law Review* 451.
25 Collins, 'Distributive Justice Through Contracts' (1992) 45(2) *Current Legal Problems* 49.

acceptance of this risk to recognize that contracting parties should be given, through the law, some limited degree of insurance, so that if a transaction turns out to be significantly disadvantageous compared to alternative market transactions which were available, this harmful transaction should not be permitted to determine the distribution of wealth. In other words, although it is desirable that contracts should be permitted to distribute wealth, it is far less clear that the law should provide no insurance at all against the possibility that the outcome unexpectedly proves seriously disadvantageous to one party to the benefit of the other.

The common law takes some steps in this direction through its doctrines of duress and undue influence, but these controls invariably require proof of abuse of market position. Legislation may go further, either by creating a presumption that some markets work so imperfectly as to justify intervention simply on the ground of unfairness, or by providing an insurance against severely disadvantageous contracts even without evidence or suspicion of abuse of bargaining power. The Law Society's control over the prices charged by solicitors to clients may illustrate the former case, where the market for a solicitor's services may be extremely imperfect and the client may not be able to judge the fairness of the charges.

Statutes against usury have proved one intensely controversial site for these debates about the desirability of price regulation. Although the common law traditionally permitted interest charges on loans, the courts viewed high interest rates with suspicion. In particular, in secured loans such as mortgages the courts protected the possession of property against high interest rates by reserving a residual power to declare the invalidity of terms providing for excessive interest rates in mortgages on the ground of unconscionability.[26] In the past, legislation attempted to impose ceilings on the rate of interest which may be charged for loans, but this method has been abandoned in the UK on the ground that the regulation proves too complex and seems to back-fire against poor consumers. This method of regulation is necessarily intricate, because the ceilings must vary according to the type of transaction, the prevailing market rates and the technique of computing the rate. For example, in the case of a simple loan of money from a bank, the permissible rate of interest may be calculated either by adding up the total finance charges over the period of the loan and analysing them as a percentage of the capital sum, or by the actuarial method of judging the interest payments as a percentage of a declining unpaid balance. In addition, there is a danger that consumers with poor credit ratings will not be able to obtain a loan at all with fixed rate ceilings.[27] Of course, this paternalistic limitation on the market for credit may not be objectionable if it prevents individuals from taking

26 *Cityland and Property (Holdings) Ltd v Dabrah* [1968] Ch 166, Ch.
27 Cayne and Trebilcock, 'Market Considerations in the Formulation of Consumer Protection Policy' (1973) 23 *University of Toronto Law Journal* 396.

on loans which they could never afford to repay.[28] Furthermore, by helping to keep interest rates low, the regulation improves the potential of the market to provide access to worthwhile opportunities for purchases to a wider sector of the population, and by reducing the chances of default the regulation may protect family stability.[29]

Instead of price controls, the Consumer Credit Act 1974 requires all interest rates to be stated prominently in the same form, the annual percentage rate (APR), and provides a broad judicial discretion to reopen credit agreements which are extortionate.[30] If the bargain is found to be extortionate, a court may order a range of remedies for the purpose of relieving the debtor from payment of any sum in excess of that fairly due and reasonable.[31] In determining whether the bargain is extortionate, a court has to find that the payments due are grossly exorbitant or grossly contravene ordinary principles of fair dealing.[32] But in applying this standard, the courts are instructed to examine all the circumstances of the transaction, and in particular to be sensitive to the point that the debtor offered such a poor risk to the creditor that the high interest rate was justified. It is quite possible therefore, as illustrated in *Ketley Ltd v Scott*,[33] for a credit agreement in which the interest rate appears well above ordinary market rates, in this case 48% per annum, to be a valid agreement, provided that the creditor can persuade the court that such a high degree of risk of default was attached to the loan that the interest rate was justifiable. The courts occasionally place limits on interest rates, however, as provided for under the Act. Where a woman in need of a loan for £5,000 for six months agreed to give her car as security and to pay interest at an APR of 94.98%, a court reduced the interest rate by about one-third.[34] Even so this decision preserves a high interest rate, and the effect of such interpretations of the legislation is to remove its potential as an instrument of redistribution.[35] It cannot protect poor borrowers from high interest rates as long as the risk of default remains high, so the position that poor people pay more for credit is preserved.[36]

2.   Unfair terms in consumer contracts

Legislation designed to protect consumers has the general aims of preserving competitive markets and ensuring that contracts fulfil the reasonable expecta-

---

28 Report of the Committee on Consumer Credit (Crowther Committee), Cmnd 4596 (1971), para 6.6.6.

29 Ramsay, 'Consumer Credit Law, Distributive Justice and the Welfare State' (1995) 15 *Oxford Journal of Legal Studies* 177, at p 192.

30 Consumer Credit Act 1974, ss 137–138.

31 Consumer Credit Act 1974, s 139(2).

32 Consumer Credit Act 1974, s 138(1).

33 [1981] ICR 241.

34 *Wilson v First County Trust Ltd* [2001] QB 407, CA.

35 Bentley and Howells, 'Extortionate Credit Bargains' (1989) *Conveyancer* 164, at p 234; Wilkinson, 'Unjust Credit Transactions' (1992) (Jan 24) *New Law Journal* 98.

36 I Ramsay, *Consumer Protection* (London, 1989), pp 340–348.

tions of the parties. The relevance of this legislation to the issue of fairness in contracts lies in the attempts to ensure that contractual obligations conform to the reasonable expectations of consumers. For example, the compulsory term in contracts of sale to consumers that the goods should be of satisfactory quality tries to ensure that consumers receive value for money, so that the balance of the obligations is roughly equivalent. Similarly, we noted in the discussion of the test for the validity of exclusion clauses under the Unfair Contract Terms Act 1977, in Chapter 12, that the courts use as one criterion of reasonableness the equivalence of the obligations undertaken by the parties in the light of the exclusion clause. The extent to which this Act introduces a general requirement of equivalence of obligations depends upon the scope of its coverage. Although its central objective is to tackle the exclusion of obligations which would otherwise arise by implied terms and duties of care in tort, the scope of the Act is broadened in some instances beyond conventional exclusion clauses.[37]

(a) THE UNFAIR CONTRACT TERMS ACT 1977

In particular, the Unfair Contract Terms Act 1977, s 3(2)(b), which applies to claims under other consumer and standard form contracts, extends the notion of an exclusion clause to encompass terms which permit the defendant to:

> claim to be entitled—
> (i)   to render a contractual performance substantially different from that which was reasonably expected of him, or
> (ii)   in respect of the whole or any part of his contractual obligations, to render no performance at all.

The purpose of these provisions is to prevent evasion of judicial control by means of careful drafting of contracts. To evade the Act, a standard form contract might eschew express exclusions of liability, and merely state that the positive obligations are extremely limited. In a contract for carriage of goods, for example, the contract may not promise to convey the goods, but merely state that the promisor undertakes to convey the goods to the selected destination if he so wishes. Such a discretionary power not to perform or to alter performance will be subject to a test of reasonableness.[38] Once the meaning of exclusion clauses is extended in this way, the Act necessarily introduces the idea that the contract should conform to the reasonable expectations of the consumer regardless of the express provisions of the contract in the small print. This measure provides the opportunity to introduce a standard of fairness, so that the obligations of the trader should conform to what service the consumer reasonably expects in the light of the price being paid.

37 Macdonald, 'Exclusion Clauses: the Ambit of s 13(1) of the Unfair Contract Terms Act 1977' (1992) 12 *Legal Studies* 277.
38 See Chapter 15.

This objective becomes more clearly realized under the Unfair Terms in Consumer Contracts Regulations 1999, which implement the EC Directive on Unfair Terms in Consumer Contracts.[39] Under these Regulations a court can consider the fairness of a wide range of terms in contracts made by consumers, provided that the term has not been individually negotiated by the consumer. In addition, consumers can complain to the Director General of Fair Trading, an administrative authority, which can use legal proceedings to challenge the use of a term in standard form contract.[40] The Regulations do not implement a system of price control, but try to draw a distinction between terms about price and ancillary terms, so that only the latter are subject to judicial control on grounds of fairness.

(b)   Unfair Terms in Consumer Contracts Regulations 1999, Reg 6(2)

In so far as it is in plain intelligible language, the assessment of fairness of a term shall not relate (a) to the definition of the main subject matter of the contract, or (b) to the adequacy of the price or remuneration, as against the goods or services supplied in exchange.

The objective of reg 6(2) is to preclude courts from examining claims by consumers that they paid too much, or that the price was high in view of the quality of the goods. This exclusion may prove troublesome in borderline cases. In contracts of insurance, for instance, the limitations on the coverage provided by the insurer could be regarded as the 'main subject matter of the contract', even though the limitations may dash the reasonable expectations of the consumer about the coverage of the policy. In such instances, perhaps the protection of the consumer may be derived from the requirement that such limitations should be stated in plain intelligible language. In a contract for a loan, it is clear that the interest rate comprises part of the main subject matter of the contract. Yet if the small print in the contract creates contingencies under which the rate of interest increases substantially, such a condition might be considered not as the definition of a core term that sets the price but as an ancillary terms subject to judicial control. The House of Lords accepted in *Director General of Fair Trading v First National Bank plc*,[41] that terms governing the interest rate payable after default by the consumer fell outside the exclusion.

In that case, the term in question provided for the interest rate payable after any judgment against the debtor. The term stated:

Interest on the amount which becomes payable shall be charged in accordance with condition 4, at the rate stated in paragraph D overleaf

39 SI 1999/2083; EC Directive 93/13/EEC.
40 SI 1999/2083, regs 10–15.
41 [2001] UKHL 52, [2002] 1 AC 481, [2002] 1 All ER 97.

(subject to variation) until payment after as well as before any judgment (such obligation to be independent of and not to merge with the judgment).

The purpose of this clause was to ensure that after judgment had been given against the debtor, interest would continue to be payable at the rate specified by this clause on the amounts outstanding. Without this clause, the lender would be confined to claiming an interest rate fixed by statute, and in cases where the court had exercised its power under the Consumer Credit Act 1974 to order repayment of the debt by instalments, no further interest would be recoverable at all. The effect of the clause was to produce a nasty surprise for debtors: having paid off all the instalments required by the court order, they would be notified by the lender that large sums were still outstanding based upon the contractual interest rate on the declining sum owed as the judgment debt was slowly paid off. Given a lengthy period of instalments, it was possible that the consumer would owe a larger sum than the original judgment. Although this contractual provision was clearly concerned with payment of interest, the House of Lords accepted that since the term only governed the position after default, it was not concerned with the main subject matter of the contract. Even if the court had viewed the term as concerned with the main subject matter of the contract, it is possible that its obscurity might have permitted control to be exercised on the ground that it was not written in plain intelligible language. The purpose of reg 6(2) should perhaps not be understood as precluding an assessment of fairness of contracts, but rather as one to exclude a judicial assessment of those terms of which the consumer was fully aware and had appreciated, ie the basic price and the main features of the product being purchased, on the ground that there was no danger of market failure caused by the complexity of standard form contracts in such a case.[42]

(c) Unfair Terms in Consumer Contracts Regulations 1999, reg 5(1)

A contractual term which has not been individually negotiated shall be regarded as unfair if, contrary to the requirement of good faith, it causes a significant imbalance in the parties' rights and obligations arising under the contract, to the detriment of the consumer.

For terms that fall within the scope of the Regulations, a court must apply this test of fairness, and this duty arises even without the point being raised by either party.[43] The Regulations also instruct the court to consider as part of the assessment of fairness all the circumstances attending the conclusion of the

---

42 Law Commission, *Unfair Terms in Contracts*, Consultation Paper No 166 (London, 2002) paras 3.27–3.34.

43 Joined Cases C 240-244/98 *Oceano Grupo Editorial SA v Quintero*, [2000] ECR 1-4941, ECJ; Whittaker, 'Judicial Interventionism and Consumer Contracts' (2001) 117 *Law Quarterly Review* 215.

contract and all the other terms of the contract.[44] Within this broad judicial discretion, the key concepts of the test of fairness are the terms 'good faith' and 'significant imbalance'. In addition, Sch 2 of the Regulations provides a 'grey list' of terms which may be regarded as unfair.

The idea of 'good faith' is familiar to civil law systems, but as we have noted it is a relative novelty in English law since its meaning clearly extends beyond fraud. The concept of good faith certainly includes procedural elements such as those concerned with misrepresentation, misleading trade practices, undue influence and other forms of coercion. As the concept derives from European law, it is probable that the European Court of Justice will acknowledge the relevance of the construction placed on the concept of good faith in the various national legal systems. In some jurisdictions, such as Germany and Italy, the idea combines procedural and substantive elements in a way which is similar to the idea of unconscionability deployed in some equity cases in English law. In the context of ancillary terms in consumer contracts, the criterion of reasonable expectation may prove the most useful guide to the interpretation of the concept of good faith, for it describes what the consumer might reasonably expect to be contained in the small print of the contract: if the terms differ significantly in favour of the supplier, this could be described as inflicting an unfair surprise on the consumer and evidence a lack of good faith on the part of the supplier. The idea of reasonable expectation is not so alien to English law, although it has never functioned directly as a legal principle. As Lord Steyn has observed:

> A theme that runs through our law of contract is that the reasonable expectations of honest men must be protected. It is not a rule or principle of law. It is the objective which has been and still is the principal moulding force of our law of contract.[45]

In *Director General of Fair Trading v First National Bank plc* Lord Bingham offered a definition of good faith in this context, which he thought was a sufficiently transparent concept not to require any reference to the European Court of Justice for further clarification:

> The requirement of good faith in this context is one of fair and open dealing. Openness requires that the terms should be expressed fully, clearly and legibly, containing no concealed pitfalls or traps. Appropriate prominence should be given to terms which might operate disadvantageously to the customer. Fair dealing requires that a supplier should not, whether deliberately or unconsciously, take advantage of the consumer's necessity, indigence, lack of experience, unfamiliarity with the subject matter of the contract, weak bargaining position or any other factor listed in [the Recitals in the Preamble to EC Directive 93/13/EEC].

---

44 SI 1999/2083, reg 6(1).
45 Steyn LJ, *First Energy (UK) Ltd v Hungarian International Bank Ltd* [1993] 2 Lloyd's Rep 194, CA; cf W D Slawson, *Binding Promises* (Princeton, 1996), ch 3.

The emphasis in this description of the concept of good faith lies upon unfair procedures leading up to the contract, especially those matters covered by the doctrine of undue influence. It seems broader than the controls supplied by the law of undue influence, however, because it does not require the supplier to be aware of the weakness of the consumer. But it seems wrong to confine the idea of good faith merely to procedural matters, since the Regulation refers to the idea that the term is contrary to good faith. 'Any purely procedural or even predominantly procedural interpretation of the requirement of good faith must be rejected.'[46]

The second concept of significant imbalance implies a 'mirror image' rule for ancillary terms.[47] This principle suggests that if a supplier inserts into the standard form contract a particular protection or advantage, then a similar or equivalent protection should be afforded to the consumer. The 'grey list' of presumptively unfair terms in Sch 2 is replete with illustrations of this mirror image rule. For instance, example (f) suggests that a term which authorises the seller or supplier to dissolve the contract on a discretionary basis will be unfair unless the consumer is granted a similar right. Similarly, example (i) concerns clauses which permit the seller to determine the price of goods at the time of delivery are presumptively unfair unless the consumer is given the corresponding right to cancel the contract if the consumer regards the price as too high. In its practical application of the Regulations, the Office of Fair Trading has insisted that simple price variation terms should be deleted, or they have permitted the variation clause subject to a clause which grants the buyer the right to cancel the contract and receive a full refund if the increase is not acceptable to him.[48]

This last example reveals how close the Regulations come to empowering the courts to upset unfair consumer contracts. Although they are not permitted to declare the contract unfair on the ground of price alone, an ancillary clause which affects the price to be charged is subject to control and will be unfair unless the consumer is granted a discretion to cancel. Similarly, the courts are not permitted to challenge the fairness of a contract on the ground that the main subject matter of the contract represented a poor bargain, but an ancillary term which permits the seller to alter the specifications of the product unilaterally will be regarded as invalid under illustration (k) in the grey list.[49] The reasonable expectation of the consumer will be that the price charged and goods supplied will be those which were stated in the main terms of the contract, and terms which permit deviation will be regarded as contrary to the requirement of good faith unless the consumer is given corresponding rights under the mirror image rule. Hence, these

46 Lord Steyn, *Director General of Fair Trading v First National Bank plc* [2001] UKHL 52 at [36], [2002] 1 AC 481, [2002] 1 All ER 97.
47 Hondius, 'European Approaches to Fairness in Contracts' in C Willett (ed), *Aspects of Fairness in Contract* (London, 1996) p 61, at p 70.
48 Office of Fair Trading, *Unfair Contract Terms*, Bulletin No 2 (London, 1996), p 58.
49 Office of Fair Trading, *Unfair Contract Terms*, Bulletin No 2 (London, 1996), p 57.

Regulations pose a challenge to the continued use of standard form contracts which seek in their detailed provisions to defeat the reasonable expectations of consumers through ancillary clauses.

Nevertheless, the courts may not wish to proceed so far as to upset detailed contract planning in standard form contracts. In *Director General of Fair Trading v First National Bank plc, discussed above,* the court concluded unanimously that the term in question was fair, albeit that the effect of the clause often came as a nasty surprise to debtors. Under the Consumer Credit Act 1974, a court has a power to revise the contract to prevent such a surprise from occurring by determining that a revised payment schedule should extinguish the debt completely, but this power is only exercised on the request of the borrower, and of course borrowers rarely know of its existence. The court held that the term was fair because ultimately all that it required from the consumer was payment of interest on sums of money that had been borrowed, which preserved the balance of the obligations under a loan. There was therefore no significant imbalance to the detriment of the consumer, and the disagreeable surprise, which might amount to a violation of the good faith standard, was caused not by the term of the contract but by the procedures surrounding the rescheduling of consumer debt that failed adequately to warn the consumer of potential pitfalls. The finding that there was no imbalance depends on pointing to the advantage to the borrower of continuing the loan, an advantage that the debtor may not have appreciated in fact existed once the court judgment had ordered a reschedule of repayments. Yet it is also true that the disagreeable surprise to the reasonable expectations of the consumer was caused rather more by the court's procedure than the term itself, so that the term itself may not have been contrary to the requirement of good faith.

(d) INJUNCTIONS PROCEDURE

It is important to appreciate, however, that the practical effect of the Unfair Terms in Consumer Contracts Regulations 1999 is likely to be determined not by the occasional judgment of a court but by the administrative procedures for policing the use of unfair terms. The impact of the Regulations depends heavily on the extent to which the Office of Fair Trading can persuade businesses to modify the terms of their contracts, and, owing to the expense of litigation, the view of the Office about the meaning of unfairness is likely to be challenged only occasionally in the courts. This power to consider complaints from consumers about unfair terms and to negotiate changes with businesses has been extended to other specified bodies including the Consumers' Association and regulators of utilities.[50] If a satisfactory change cannot be negotiated, the Office of Fair Trading or the other specified bodies can seek an injunction to prevent further use of the

---

50 SI 1999/2083, reg 11, Sch 1. The Financial Services Authority is included as a qualified regulator, but it also has independent powers to control terms in contracts for financial services: Financial Services and Markets Act 2000, ss 157, 158.

term in standard form contracts. Usually, the implicit threat of this injunction procedure is sufficient to secure the amendment or withdrawal of the term.

Furthermore, the Office of Fair Trading sometimes examines the standard terms used in a whole business sector, such as contracts for the use of mobile phones. The whole package of terms used in the trade can be inspected for allocations of the balance of advantage in order to ensure that they do not impose a significant detriment on consumers.

The Office of Fair Trading also produces reports and guidance to businesses on what terms it is likely to regard as unfair, which in effect amounts to a gradual extension of the list of indicative clauses that are likely to be regarded as unfair. Examples of such terms include terms that permit a supplier to impose an unfair financial burden, such as a demand for an advance payment at its discretion, terms which give the supplier the power to determine unilaterally whether it has performed some aspect of its obligations or whether the consumer is in breach of contract in some respect, and exclusions or limitations of the consumers non-contractual rights under data protection legislation.[51]

D. Judicial revision

During the performance of a contract, the classical rule holds the parties strictly liable for failure to fulfil their obligations. No matter that unexpected events have dramatically altered the costs of one party's performance, the courts have generally insisted upon a principle of strict enforcement of the terms of the contract. In *Blackburn Bobbin Co Ltd v TW Allen & Sons*,[52] for example, the seller of Finland birch timber found it impossible to import the commodity from Finland as he had intended because of the outbreak of war. Even so, he remained liable to the buyer for breach of contract. He had agreed to deliver the timber, and it was of no concern to the buyer where he acquired the timber.

This rule of strict enforcement of the contract is not as harsh as it first appears. It provides an incentive for the parties to plan for risks and contingencies, so that if performance becomes more onerous, the contract will provide for some exception or adjustment of the obligations. The price of the contract may be fixed on a 'costs plus' basis, which insulates a contractor against rising prices in materials and secures a fixed percentage rate of profit, or by a formula for tracking market prices.[53] The contract may make provision for price adjustment by means of a neutral arbitrator. Exclusion clauses may absolve one party from his

---

51 Office of Fair Trading, *Unfair Contract Terms*, Bulletin No 13 (London, 2000); Office of Fair Trading, *Unfair Contract Terms Guidance* (London, 2001).
52 [1918] 2 KB 467, CA.
53 Jaskow, 'Price Adjustment in Long-term Contracts: The Case of Coal' (1988) 31 *Journal of Law and Economics* 47.

contractual obligations in the event of certain risks materializing, such as bad weather, industrial conflict and war. Many commercial contracts include a 'force majeure' clause, which excludes liability in the event of performance becoming impossible or unlawful. The contract may also provide that a party should only be responsible for due care or best efforts, and not be understood to be guaranteeing a result. We can expect, therefore, that in carefully planned commercial transactions the rule of strict enforcement will not lead to severe imbalances in the contractual obligations between the parties, since the contract will make careful provision for contingencies and risks.

Even so, not every contract makes careful provision for contingencies. The events which render the contract more onerous for one party may not have been foreseen, or, if foreseen, the parties may not have been able to reach agreement on an appropriate provision in the contract because of the time and expense involved in negotiations. Here the question arises whether or not the courts should revise the terms of the agreement, in order to restore the balance of advantage under the contract, or, if that is impossible, terminate the contract altogether. The objective of such judicial intervention would be to prevent the enforcement of a contract which had become unfair in its operation as a result of a change of circumstances which had not been provided for in the terms of the contract and was outside the control of either party.

1.   Objections to judicial revision

By stating the implications of judicial revision of contracts in this stark fashion, we can appreciate immediately why most judges and commentators fervently reject it.[54] In the first place, judicial revision undermines the role of the uninhibited market in determining the distribution of wealth. The classical conception of the market imagines a place where individuals use their resources and judgement to strike advantageous bargains. The strict enforcement of contracts provides incentives for the shrewd and calculating to enter the market to increase their wealth, and so to remove those incentives by judicial revision of terms to adjust prices and obligations in the light of changing market conditions would tend to undo the market system itself. Contracts can also be used as a type of insurance against risks such as a shortage of supply. To revise the contract when the risk materialises would deprive the social practice of making contracts of this useful function.

A second defence of strict enforcement of contracts reminds us that the legitimacy of contractual relations depends in classical law upon the agreement of the parties. On this view, the parties have deliberately allocated the risks of

---

54 Dawson, 'Judicial Revision of Frustrated Contracts: The United States' (1984) 64 *Boston University Law Review* 1; Gillette, 'Commercial Rationality and the Duty to Adjust Long-Term Contracts' (1985) 69 *Minnesota Law Review* 521.

misadventure between themselves in advance. Where the parties remain silent about a particular risk, the law infers that the party on whom the loss will naturally fall has assumed that risk as well. This inference is not unreasonable in most commercial transactions, for the risk is likely to be foreseeable, and any concern that the risk may materialise can be dealt with either by inserting a suitable exclusion clause in the contract or by taking out insurance.[55] In the case concerning the sale of Finnish timber, if there is a risk that war will disrupt supplies, the seller can exclude liability in that eventuality. If the contract remains silent on this point, however, the court is likely to infer that this risk was accepted by the seller. Judicial revision of contracts can be presented as involving the rewriting of the contract by a court, contrary to the implicit agreement between the parties with respect to a particular risk. This intervention can be viewed as an illegitimate interference with the joint wishes of the parties.

One last objection to judicial revision of contracts predictably raises the issue of the practicability of the exercise. In its simplest form, this objection relies upon the subjectivity of values again, in order to claim that judges cannot impose their own valuation of the obligations upon the parties. But usually the argument more subtly stresses the interdependence of the obligations and objects to piecemeal reform on the ground of fairness. For instance, in our example, the contract price for the timber may be higher than normal because the seller has assumed the risk of war and has used his expected profits in part to insure against this eventuality. In these circumstances, to revise the price upwards to compensate the seller for his increased costs would distort the original fairness of the contract. The practical objection to judicial revision states, therefore, that a court should not meddle with the terms because they may already reflect the risks assumed and lead to a fair result.[56]

Despite these powerful objections to judicial revision of contracts, which have plainly steered the direction of the common law, a few statutory interventions grant this power to judges. We have already encountered perhaps the most significant example in the Consumer Credit Act 1974, which gives a court considerable powers to revise a consumer credit agreement. If a court regards it as just to do so, it can reschedule debts or payments of interest in the light of the debtor's likely ability to pay, so that the consumer may receive a breathing space.[57] In a comparative study of consumer protection law, Wilhelmsson suggests that in Nordic law there is a unifying thread in statutory interventions and judicial

---

55 Narasimhan, 'Of Expectations, Incomplete Contracting, and the Bargain Principle' (1986) 74 *California Law Review* 1123.

56 For contrary arguments see: Coons, 'Approaches to Court Imposed Compromise : The Uses of Doubt and Reasons' (1964) 58 *Northwestern University Law Review* 750; C Fried, *Contract as Promise* (Cambridge, Mass, 1981), ch 5; Speidel, 'Court-Imposed Price Adjustments Under Long-Term Supply Contracts' (1981) *Northwestern University Law Review* 369.

57 Consumer Credit Act 1974, s 129. The court is unlikely to make a time order if there is no reasonable prospect of repayment in the future: *First National Bank plc v Syed* [1991] 2 All ER 250, CA.

interpretation of contracts which relieves a consumer from contracts when they prove oppressive as a result of a serious change in the consumer's fortunes, due perhaps to illness or unemployment.[58] The costs of such deferrals of payments will raise the cost of credit to consumers in general, so that the risks of temporary inability to repay loans will be dispersed. Increasingly, creditors also offer consumers an insurance policy against the risk of inability to repay a debt through illness or unemployment, which has the same effect of dispersing the costs. Insurance is perhaps a more efficient way of handling the problem of what Wilhelmsson calls 'social force majeure', although it has the flaw that the insurance policy is not compulsory.

2. Unplanned contingencies

Although these objections to judicial revision suffice to deter the courts from engaging directly in judicial revision of contracts, there are a number of techniques which can be employed for this purpose covertly. The most important technique consists of construction of the contract so that its apparent harsh effects can be modified by implication. In some cases, the methods of judicial intervention have been described as rules of law, namely frustration and sometimes mistake, doctrines which are occasionally used to relieve the parties of their obligations under the contract. Whilst the courts do not usually acknowledge that they are operating a fairness criterion to handle unplanned contingencies under these techniques of intervention, it is hard to believe that the balance of the reciprocal obligations is not the determinative criterion.

(a) CONSTRUCTION OF THE CONTRACT

Construction of a contract amounts to no more than elaborate interpretation of its content. It avoids in a formal way any direct conflict with the objections to judicial revision. Yet, clearly, an elaborate construction of terms that the court claims were implicit in the contract opens the door to reconstruction or revision.

Under the oldest method of construction of the contract in the face of unplanned contingencies, the courts depart from their normal practice of ascribing risks to one party or the other according to the principle that the risk is assumed by the person on whom the loss will naturally fall. The courts discover instead that some risks are covered by an implied condition which automatically terminates the contract, thereby relieving the parties from any future obligations. Such a condition was regularly implied into contracts of employment, so that in the event of the employee's death or imprisonment, the contract was terminated

---

58 Wilhelmsson, 'Social Force Majeure – A New Concept in Nordic Consumer Law' (1990) 13 *Journal of Consumer Policy* 1, also in T Wilhelmsson, *Twelve Essays On Consumer Law and Policy* (Helsinki, 1996), p 226; T Wilhelmsson, *Critical Studies in Private Law* (Dordrecht, 1992), ch 8.

leaving neither party under any obligations towards the other. Similarly, in *Taylor v Caldwell*,[59] the court terminated a contract for the lease of a music hall when it burnt down, on the ground that the contract contained an implied condition that the hall should continue to exist. Similar reasoning which invokes an implied condition can be employed in cases of mistakes about the facts that existed prior to the formation of a contract.[60]

A second, rather metaphysical, style of construction argues that the scope of the contract's allocation of risk does not include the events which have arisen. In other words, the courts place limits upon the silent assumption of risk arising from a failure to make express provision for unexpected events. The House of Lords favoured this method in *Davis Contractors Ltd v Fareham UDC*,[61] where, because of labour shortages leading to higher wages and shortages of building materials, a contractor found the job of building a number of houses much more expensive than anticipated. The court reasoned that the contractor was bound by the contract price unless, on its true construction, the contract did not apply to the circumstances which had arisen. On this basis, the court rejected the contractor's appeal, for it regarded the price of labour and the availability of building supplies as one of the risks which had been allocated between the parties in determining the price of the contract. The change of circumstances had not altered the significance of the contractor's obligation, but had merely rendered it more onerous. Although the argument failed in this case, it is clearly possible for a court to argue that some unforeseeable event or remote contingency had not been allocated implicitly by the contract, and that the court should regard such a risk as not being governed by the contract at all.

The third technique of construction which places limits upon the apparent strictness of contractual liability invokes the metaphor of base and superstructure. Every contract rests upon fundamental assumptions of fact shared by the parties. If these assumptions turn out to be false, the court may conclude that the contract should fall like a building without foundations. For example, in *Krell v Henry*,[62] the defendant rented a room for two days at an inflated price of £75, paying £25 in advance, in order to view the Coronation procession of Edward VII. When the Coronation was postponed due to the king's illness, the defendant defeated a claim for the balance of £50, because the occurrence of the Coronation was a foundation of the contract, a state of facts without which the contract could not exist. Similar reasoning pervades cases of mistake such as *Sherwood v Walker*.[63] In that case, it will be recalled, the court ruled that it was possible to set aside a

59 (1863) 3 B & S 826.
60 *Associated Japanese Bank (International) Ltd v Crédit du Nord* [1988] 3 All ER 902, [1989] 1 WLR 255, QB.
61 [1956] AC 696, [1956] 2 All ER 145, HL.
62 [1903] 2 KB 740, CA.
63 66 Mich 568, 33 NW 919 (1887).

contract for the sale of a cow on the ground that both parties mistakenly believed the cow to be barren, a factual assumption at the foundation of the agreement.

Although we have distinguished these three techniques of construction, courts rely upon them cumulatively in many cases and they blend into each other. The need for these elaborate techniques of construction arises because the contingencies which may justify the refusal to enforce the contract must be so unexpected and outside the risks allocated by the contract that the courts are reluctant to assert simply that the exception depends upon an implied term which represents the unexpressed intentions of the parties. Since the contingency was probably never contemplated and was perhaps unforeseeable, to assert that the parties shared any intentions on the matter strikes the courts as an odd and improbable claim. But an elaborate technique of construction of the contract is ultimately vulnerable to the same criticism that it seeks artificially to justify refusal to enforce the contract by reference to the intentions of the parties.

(b)   FRUSTRATION OF CONTRACTS

The legal reasoning that uses construction to handle unplanned contingencies not only encounters the difficulty that it fits uneasily with the idea that implied terms represent the implicit intentions of the parties but also leaves unclear how the dispute should be resolved. If the court should invent a term to deal with the contingency, how should it be formulated? The loss caused by the unexpected contingency will have to fall on one party or the other. Which party should bear the loss, given that in reality the losses have not been allocated by the contract? To answer these questions, the courts began to use a legal rule, the doctrine of 'frustration of contracts', which stated that in the event of some unplanned contingencies the court would regard the contract has having been terminated. Lord Radcliffe suggested as a definition of the doctrine of frustration in *Davis Contractors Ltd v Fareham UDC* that:

> frustration occurs whenever the law recognizes that, without default of either party, a contractual obligation has become incapable of being performed because the circumstances in which performance is called for would render it a thing radically different from that which was undertaken by the contract.[64]

This view of the doctrine permits frustration of contracts when performance becomes impossible, unlawful, or completely different from what was originally contemplated. If frustration of the contract occurs, the obligations of both parties are automatically terminated, so that neither is obliged to continue performance

---

64 [1956] AC 696, [1956] 2 All ER 145, HL.

of the contract, and no liability for breach of contract after the frustrating event can arise. In a similar vein, the statutory law of sales cancels further performance of the contract if the goods perish without fault of either party before ownership has passed to the buyer.[65]

In theory there is a profound difference between, on the one hand, legal rules which permit judicial revision of contracts on the ground of frustration, and, on the other, techniques of construction of contracts which aim to secure the implied intentions of the parties. In practice the rival analyses are hard to distinguish, for elaborate methods of construction of contracts must look suspiciously like legal rules permitting judicial intervention.[66] Similarly, the determination that the contract has been frustrated requires meticulous construction of the contract. For example, the rule that for a contract to be frustrated the performance of one party must have become impossible or impracticable looks like an independent test irrespective of the content of the particular contract. Yet in practice it depends for its application upon the terms of the contract. A contract for the supply of timber is not frustrated by the outbreak of war; but a contract that specifies that the timber to be supplied will come from a particular source in Finland at a particular time will be rendered impossible by the outbreak of war. Impossibility depends on what the contract promise stated. In *Krell v Henry*, the court's conclusion that performance of the contract was no longer possible depended crucially on the interpretation of the contract that it was not simply for the hire of a room, but for hire of a room to watch the Coronation procession. Indubitably, the courts are tempted to reify the concept of an event rendering performance impossible in order to distinguish frustration from techniques of construction, but in practice a determination that performance has become impossible depends upon the construction of the terms of the contract to discover what performance is actually required.

The invocation of the doctrine of frustration apparently relieves the court from having to choose which party should carry the loss caused by the unplanned contingency. By asserting that the frustrating event terminates the contract automatically, it appears as if neither party has to bear the loss: the contract is simply over. But that appearance is deceptive. If no obligation to perform persists, the party who relied upon performance (or compensation in lieu) is deprived of a remedy. Once it is determined that the cancellation of the Coronation terminates the hire of the room, the landlord loses the expected rent or a financial equivalent. It is unclear why this result should be regarded as any fairer than the opposite of upholding the contract and making the tenant pay.

65 Sale of Goods Act 1979, s 7; Uniform Commercial Code, s 2-615.
66 Atiyah and Bennion, 'Mistake in the Construction of Contracts' (1961) 24 *Modern Law Review* 42; Slade, 'The Myth of Mistake in the English Law of Contract' (1954) 70 *Law Quarterly Review* 385.

(c) THE RELEVANCE OF FAIRNESS

Although the courts prefer to describe their practices that are analogous to judicial revision as either construction of the contract in order to fulfil the intentions of the parties or as independent rules of law concerned with impossibility, neither of these accounts appears strongly persuasive. If the intervention is described as merely construction of the contract, given that the parties did not foresee and have any clear intentions towards the events which have occurred, we must suspect that the courts use a further criterion for determining the intent of the parties. This criterion may be one which takes fairness in the sense of the preservation of the balance of advantage of the contract as the unacknowledged but vital guide to interpretation. Alternatively, if the intervention is described as the application of a rule about impossibility, again the decision whether an unexpected event renders an obligation impossible seems likely to depend upon a judgment as to whether to continue to insist upon performance would upset the balance of advantage contained in the contract. On this interpretation, the real issue in *Blackburn Bobbin Co Ltd v TW Allen & Sons Ltd*[67] was not whether supplies of Finnish timber could be obtained any longer, but rather whether to impose this obligation upon the seller after the outbreak of war would upset the balance of advantage of the contract. Here the court took the view that the parties to a commercial agreement had allocated the risk of this eventuality in their contract, and that the materialization of the risk did not upset the balance of the obligations.

The relevance of fairness is often betrayed when a court finds an excuse to deny that a contract has been frustrated on the ground either of attributing the insuperable difficulty to the fault of the party in breach or by denying that performance has become impossible. For example, in *Tamplin Steamship Co Ltd v Anglo-Mexican Petroleum Co*,[68] a ship hired under a five-year time charter was requisitioned by the government during the war in 1915 after three years of the charter. Normally a court would find that the requisitioning of a ship would frustrate a time charter, but in this case the House of Lords declined to hold that the contract had been frustrated on the dubious ground that the war might be over in time to permit further use of the charter. In reality, by this decision the court tried to achieve fairness between the parties, for the person entitled to use the ship would benefit from government compensation which was higher than the charge under the agreed hire. In this case the owner of the ship was attempting unsuccessfully to escape from his contract, so that he would receive the superior level of income from the government.

Although many judges deny that fairness is relevant to the question of whether or not a contract is frustrated, they frequently acknowledge that their interventions

---

67 [1918] 2 KB 467, CA.
68 [1916] 2 AC 397, HL.

are required by the need to do justice between the parties. In a representative description of the doctrine of frustration, Bingham LJ states:

> The object of the doctrine was to give effect to the demands of justice, to achieve a just and reasonable result, to do what is reasonable and fair, as an expedient to escape from injustice where such would result from enforcement of a contract in its literal terms after a significant change in circumstances . . . [69]

These references to injustice, or as we prefer to say unfairness, require further elucidation.

The process of judicial revision is not so simple as to compare the obligation of one party before and after the unexpected event in order to discover whether the event has substantially increased the cost of performance of his obligation. The criterion of fairness must also be sensitive both to the sophistication of the parties when they established their contract and the precise allocation of risks by the contract. Where the parties enjoyed comparable resources for devising a complex commercial transaction and exercised those resources in order to create a contract which attempted to allocate all the risks between the parties, it is unlikely except in calamitous circumstances that the courts will be prepared to accept that unexpected events have created any imbalance in the obligations. If, on the other hand, either one or both parties lack these skills, the terms of the contract are less likely to be regarded as a presumptively fair allocation of the burdens of unforeseen eventualities. In these cases, the courts are more likely to use the techniques of judicial revision such as construction or frustration in order to restore the expectations of the parties with respect to the balance of advantage contained in the contract. But intervention may be rejected, of course, if the court finds that a reconstruction of the contract or the application of the doctrine of frustration would not produce a fairer result. Frustration of the contract is, in truth, a crude device, which is rarely applied by the courts, because it fails usually to satisfy the criterion of restoring the balance of advantage between the parties. Better results can often be achieved by techniques aimed at restoring the viability of the contract for both parties, which will be considered in Chapter 15.

---

69 *J Lauritzen AS v Wijsmuller BV, The Super Servant Two* [1990] 1 Lloyd's Rep 1, CA.

The range of liability

A. Privity of contract

A contract can neither impose additional obligations on nor give any enforceable rights to a person who was not a party to the contract. Lawyers call this rule governing the range of liability the doctrine of privity of contract. Under the traditional law of contract, the principle of privity was believed to follow logically from the principle that contractual responsibility arises only from agreement or voluntary consent: a contract could not affect the rights and obligations of those who had not consented to the agreement. Even if Peter and John agree under a legally enforceable contract that Peter should hand money over to Mavis, under the doctrine of privity Mavis possesses no legal right to sue Peter for the money unless she is a party to the contract.

This severe limit on the range of contractual liability does not apply to other branches of the law of obligations. Claims based upon ownership interests in property do not depend upon the establishment of a contract between claimant and defendant. If Mavis could establish a proprietary interest in the money, perhaps because Peter and John had established a trust in her favour, then Mavis could assert her right to the money without the need to claim rights under the contract. Similarly, under the tort of negligence, a claim for personal injury or damage to property may arise without any contractual link between claimant and defendant. When a house-owner contracts with a builder to construct an extension, and the builder sub-contracts the electrical work to an electrician, if through negligence the electrician causes the whole house to burn down, the house-owner may sue the electrician in the tort of negligence for the damage to his property even though the house-owner had no direct contract with the electrician. But the tort of negligence does not normally permit recovery for pure economic loss as opposed to damage to property, so if the house-owner's grievance against the electrician is merely that the electrical work was done poorly so that rewiring is required, the house-owner probably has no claim against the electrician either in contract or tort for the cost of rewiring. Since the different branches of the law of obligations may overlap and apply simultaneously to particular cases, the effect of the doctrine of privity of contract can be that the third person possesses non-contractual rights based on tort or proprietary interests which supplement or even subvert the contractual arrangements.

The doctrine of privity of contract restricts four different kinds of claims referable to a contract.

1. Burden of positive obligations

A person who is not a party to the contract cannot have obligations to perform acts imposed upon him by the contract without his consent. It would plainly be a serious invasion of the liberty of the individual if a person could be subject to additional obligations merely by virtue of an agreement between other people without his consent. Such an invasion of liberty would occur, for instance, if the parties to a contract agreed that a third person should run a marathon. The doctrine of privity of contract wisely denies the parties to the contract the right to sue the third person for refusing to run the race.

2. Burden of disability

A person who is not a party to the contract cannot have his rights arising under other branches of the law of obligations reduced or eliminated by the contract without his consent. A contract which purports to appropriate a third person's proprietary rights or to exclude a third person's rights to claim compensation for injury in tort is ineffective in imposing a disability on the third person.

We observed in Chapter 7, however, a third part's consent may be inferred from conduct. Although the courts will rarely infer consent to positive obligations without express indications, the inference may be more quickly drawn in respect of disabilities within networks of contracts. The case of *Morris v CW Martin & Sons*[1] illustrates how consent to a disability contained in a contract to which the claimant was not a party can be inferred from the claimant's conduct. It will be recalled that the claimant agreed with a furrier that her mink stole should be sent to the defendant specialists for cleaning, but her claim against the defendant for the loss of the stole was obstructed by a term in the furrier's contract with the defendant. Although the claimant was not a party to the agreement between the furrier and the defendant, she was held bound by its terms when she brought a claim in tort against the defendant. Lord Denning MR inferred her consent to this disability from her agreement that the stole should be sent to the cleaner on the normal terms of the trade. In effect this reasoning discovers a direct contractual link between claimant and defendant, a collateral contract which includes the term limiting the defendant's liability.

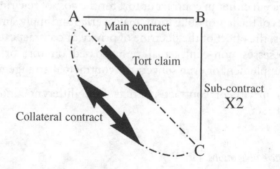

In the diagram, the claimant (A) has an implied collateral contract with the defendant (C), which includes the exclusion of liability (X2) contained in the sub-contract between the furrier (B) and C. The case does not contradict this aspect of the doctrine of privity of contract, but it reveals how easily the courts may infer consent to a disability.

3.   Beneficial positive rights

The doctrine of privity prevents a third person from being able to sue upon a contract made for his or her benefit. In a simple illustration, if a father contracts for renovations to be carried out to his son's home by a builder, the son cannot bring a claim against the builder for failure to carry out the renovations. In *Beswick*

---

1   [1966] 1 QB 716, [1965] 2 All ER 725, CA.

v Beswick,[2] a nephew promised his uncle that in return for transfer of the uncle's coal business, the nephew would pay his aunt an annuity after his uncle's decease. The nephew failed to keep his promise, but his aunt had no legal right to claim the annuity. Similarly, in an English case, *Jackson v Horizon Holidays Ltd*,[3] where a man bought a package holiday for himself and his family from a tour operator, and the tour operator broke the contract by providing an unpleasant holiday, by virtue of the doctrine of privity, his wife and children were unable to sue the tour operator directly for damages, since they were not parties to the agreement, but merely third persons intended to benefit from the contract.

This limitation on the rights of third parties intended to benefit under contracts would perhaps not matter much but for the normal rule in the law of damages that a claimant may only recover for his or her own losses. If the losses arising from a breach of contract fall on a third party, as a general rule the promisee cannot recover compensation for those losses. Under this rule, for instance, it seems unlikely that the uncle's estate in *Beswick v Beswick* could have obtained more than nominal damages, since only the aunt suffered loss resulting from failure to pay the annuity. This general rule has been qualified in several instances, including *Jackson v Horizon Holidays Ltd*, the scope of which need to be examined below. Similarly, the privity rule would matter rather less if the parties to the contract could obtain specific performance, ie an order from a court to perform the contract. In general, however, the courts are reluctant to order specific performance of contracts except those involving interests in land. Nevertheless, this approach was successful in *Beswick v Beswick*. The estate of the deceased uncle succeeded in obtaining an order of specific performance which required the nephew to pay the annuity to his aunt. In order for this technique to circumvent this aspect of the doctrine of privity of contract more widely, however, it would be necessary to follow the Australian law that contracts for the benefit of third parties are normally ones for which damages will be an inadequate remedy and where justice requires an order for specific performance.[4] There are signs that the interests of third parties may possibly influence the exercise of the discretion to award specific performance in England.[5]

4. Beneficial immunities

When a contract purports to give a third person a legal immunity, such as a defence against claims brought in tort by a party to the contract, the third person cannot rely upon that exclusion of liability. The doctrine of privity indicates that the third person should not be able to enforce the promised immunity by way of a

---

2 [1968] AC 58, [1967] 2 All ER 1197, HL.
3 [1975] 3 All ER 92, [1975] 1 WLR 1468, CA.
4 *Coulls v Bagot's Executor and Trustee Co Ltd* (1967) 119 CLR 460, Aust HC.
5 *Co-operative Insurance Society Ltd v Argyll Stores (Holdings) Ltd* [1996] Ch 286, [1996] 3 All ER 934, CA; revsd [1998] AC 1, [1997] 3 All ER 297, HL.

defence to the claim by the promisor, since the third person cannot obtain any rights from a contract to which he is a stranger. *Scruttons v Midland Silicones Ltd*,[6] illustrates this rule. Under a contract for the carriage of goods in the form of a bill of lading, the owner of the goods agreed to a limitation of liability for damage to the goods which purported to cover not only the other party to the contract, the carrier, but also any bailee, ie a person entrusted with the goods. When one company which was arguably a bailee, the stevedores, damaged the goods whilst unloading them from the ship, the company was unable to rely upon the promised immunity as a defence to the claim in the tort of negligence from the owners of the goods, since the company was not a party to the bill of lading.

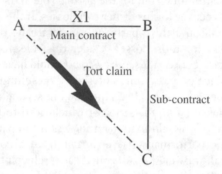

In the diagram, the owners of the goods (A) were able to sue the stevedores (C) in the tort of negligence for damaging the goods, and the stevedores were unable to set up as a defence the exclusion clause (X1) in the contract between A and the carrier (B) since the stevedores were not a party to that contract.

Although the doctrine of privity prevents a defendant third person from relying on the benefit of an immunity directly by enforcing the contract, the immunity in the contract may affect the main cause of action of the third party. In the tort of negligence, for instance, a claim depends upon the court discovering that the defendant owed the claimant a duty of care to avoid the harm which occurred. A duty of care may be negatived or modified by reference to the claimant's conduct, including consent to a restriction of liability. A court may conclude in cases where the claimant has consented in a contract to a restriction upon the duty of care owed by a third party defendant that in the circumstances it would not be 'just and reasonable' to impose a duty of care on the defendant.[7] This policy argument for restricting the duty of care by reference to the surrounding network of contracts succeeded in *Norwich City Council v Harvey*.[8] Under a construction contract for a

---

6 *Scruttons Ltd v Midland Silicones Ltd* [1962] AC 446, [1962] 1 All ER 1, HL; for criticism of this logic, see Andrews, 'Does a Third Party Beneficiary have a Right in English Law?' (1988) 8 *Legal Studies* 14.
7 *Caparo Industries plc v Dickman* [1990] 2 AC 605, [1990] 1 All ER 568, HL.
8 [1989] 1 All ER 1180, [1989] 1 WLR 828, CA.

swimming pool, the claimant had agreed with the main contractors to accept any risk of loss or damage by fire to the building. Unfortunately the defendant sub-contractors set fire to the building while using a blowtorch. But the claimant's action for negligent damage to the building against the defendant failed. Although the defendant would normally owe the claimant a duty of care to avoid burning down the building, the court regarded the contractual arrangement governing the allocation of the risk of fire between the claimant and the main contractor as demonstrating that it would not be just and reasonable to impose the duty in this case. The underlying argument in favour of this result is that the claimant undertook to accept the risk of fire and obtained suitable insurance cover, and that the defendant sub-contractor when accepting the work reasonably relied upon this arrangement.

A similar argument defeated a claim of negligence in *Marc Rich & Co AG v Bishop Rock Marine Co Ltd, The Nicholas H.*[9] The owners of goods which had been destroyed when a ship sank claimed compensation against a surveyor who had certified negligently that the ship was seaworthy. The owners of the goods had no direct contract with the surveyor, but in their contract with the carrier had accepted a limitation of the carrier's liability for damage to the goods. The claim in negligence against the surveyor was defeated on the ground that the contractual arrangements between the owners of the goods and the carrier, which included insurance arrangements against the loss of the goods, negatived a duty of care owed by the surveyor to the owners of the goods. The House of Lords prevented the law of tort from upsetting the careful contractual allocation of risk by acceding to the argument that the contract had effectively conferred an immunity on the surveyor from direct claims by the owners of the goods. The sole claim available to the owners of the goods was the one created and controlled by their contract with the carrier.

Where the promisor brings a contractual claim against the third person, despite having agreed in a contract with another party not to make the claim, again in principle the doctrine of privity of contract prevents the third person from claiming an immunity. In a simple case a father pays off the debts of his son owed to the claimant in return for the claimant's promise not to pursue his claim in debt against the son. If the claimant nevertheless brings his claim against the son, the doctrine of privity of contract appears to prevent the son from taking advantage of the defence offered by his father's contract. Such a result appears unjust, both because it practises a deceit on the father and because it may permit the claimant double recovery. The courts are likely to reject the claimant's claim in the circumstances, either on the ground that the debt has been extinguished, or that the action represents a type of equitable fraud against the father which a court should prevent.[10]

9   [1996] AC 211, [1995] 3 All ER 307, HL.
10 *Hirachand Punamchand v Temple* [1911] 2 KB 330, CA.

B.　Parties to the contract

Since the doctrine of privity of contract restricts the rights and obligations arising from the contract to the parties, it becomes vital to know whom the courts will regard as parties to the contract. As well as the general principles determining who are parties to a contract, special rules such as agency can extend who will be deemed to be parties.

1.　The general principle

Perhaps surprisingly English law remains confused on the question of the determination of the parties to the contract. One view suggests that all persons expressly named as parties will enjoy the rights and obligations arising under the contract. An alternative theory suggests that the doctrine of consideration applies to this issue, so that only persons who have supplied some consideration under the contract count as parties. The difference between the views arises when two persons, perhaps a husband and wife, both promise to sell property which is in fact owned by the husband alone, and then the question arises whether the wife can bring a claim against the promisee for the agreed payment. On the former view, the wife can claim the sum due as an express party to the contract, whereas on the latter only the husband can sue because he alone provided consideration.

The second view that the doctrine of consideration provides the test of who are parties to the contract receives considerable support from the frequent repetition of the adage 'consideration must move from the promisee'. Unfortunately this phrase is ambiguous, for it usually means no more than the proposition that an enforceable promise requires consideration, but it can be understood as determining the range of persons who may sue upon the promise, in other words it defines who are the parties to the contract.

It is surely a mistake, however, to confound the question of which promises are legally enforceable with the issue of who are parties to the contract with the right to sue upon it. Furthermore, it is surely undesirable to introduce a complication into the determination of the parties to a contract by searching behind the formal document in order to check that both promisees provided consideration.

Despite frequent reference to the adage that 'consideration must move from the promisee', the courts appear to determine the question of the parties to the contract by a careful examination of the facts of the case and the intentions of the parties. In some instances, although a person may be named in a contract, the court regards that person as a third person who cannot enforce the contract. In other cases, the court interprets the arrangement as one where the third person is a joint promisee, so that the parties intended all three to be parties to the contract, with the effect that all three obtain rights under the contract.[11]

2. The extension of parties

Many rules permit the extension of the parties to a contract. On the death of a party to a contract, the contractual rights pass to the executors or administrators of the deceased's estate. Negotiable instruments, such as cheques and bills of exchange, provide commonplace instances where a third party may claim rights under a contract, for the rights created by these instruments can usually be transferred to third parties by means of a simple endorsement. Similarly, under many types of contracts, such as leases and money debts, the original parties frequently assign their rights to third parties, and, with certain safeguards, the law recognizes that a written or verbal transfer of rights effectively substitutes the third party as a party to the contract.[12] In addition, the common law permits wide relations of agency where a principal may gain rights under a contract made on his behalf by his agent.

In each of these examples, the legal reasoning shares an identical pattern: by virtue of a legally recognized technique, such as endorsement or written assignment, a third party is added or substituted as the holder of the rights under a contract. This reasoning deftly avoids a direct challenge to the doctrine of privity, whilst creating simple legal methods for providing third parties with benefits under a contract. It is therefore unusual these days for the doctrine of privity to lead to much injustice and frustrated expectations, for often with no more than trivial precautions the original parties can make certain that the third party gains rights under the contract.

3. Agency

The principles of agency apply to many routine transactions. If a consumer purchases goods in a supermarket, although the transaction takes place superficially between the sales assistant and the consumer, the legal analysis describes the sales assistant as an agent for the supermarket, so that the only parties to the contract are the consumer and the supermarket. The supermarket is the principal which makes the contract through its agent the sales assistant. The agent is not a party to the contract at all, although the agent may owe other duties to both parties, such as a duty to refrain from fraudulent conduct. The formation of contracts through agents provides a method for circumventing the doctrine of privity of contract.

---

11 *Coulls v Bagot's Executor & Trustee Co Ltd* (1967) 119 CLR 460, Aust HC; Law Commission, *Privity of Contract: Contracts for the Benefit of Third Parties*, Report 242 (London, 1996), p 70.

12 The common law principles are supplemented by statute to achieve this effect: Landlord and Tenant (Covenants) Act 1995.

It is even possible for a person to enter a contract simultaneously as a party and as an agent for a third person, provided that this dual status is clearly expressed. When one of the parties to the main contract simultaneously enters into a collateral contract acting as an agent for a third person, then two contracts have been created, one of which gives the third person legal rights. This analysis applied in *New Zealand Shipping Co Ltd v Satterthwaite & Co Ltd (The Eurymedon)*.[13] The claimant's goods were damaged due to the defendant stevedores' negligence during unloading from a ship. Under the claimant's contract of carriage with the carrier in the form of a bill of lading, the claimant had agreed that liability for damage to the goods should be limited. The contract recited that this promise was made not only to the carrier, but also that for this purpose the carrier acted as an agent for any employees, agents or independent contractors. The Privy Council accepted that this agency clause permitted the stevedores, as independent contractors of the carrier, to rely upon the immunity conferred by the bill of lading.

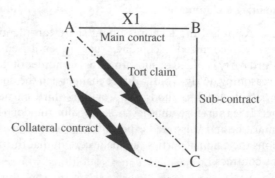

In the diagram, the claimant (A) has agreed with the carrier (B) to a limitation of liability (X1), which defeats the claimant's claim in tort against the stevedores (C) by virtue of the collateral contract created between A and C by means of B acting as C's agent for this purpose. Although similar on its facts to *Scruttons Ltd v Midland Silicones Ltd*, the creation of an express agency relation in the terms of the bill of lading permitted the court to discover a collateral contract between the claimant and the stevedores under which the stevedores benefited from an exclusion of liability. This method for circumventing the doctrine of privity only works when the technical agency relation between the promisee and the third person can be established, although by relying on the ostensible authority of an agent and subsequent ratification by a principal the method has a potentially wide field of application.[14]

---

13 [1975] AC 154, [1974] 1 All ER 1015, PC.
14 *Port Jackson Stevedoring Pty Ltd v Salmond and Spraggon (Australia) Pty Ltd (The New York Star)* [1980] 3 All ER 257, [1981] 1 WLR 138, PC; see also Lord Goff, *The Mahkutai* [1996] AC 650, [1996] 3 All ER 502 at 512, PC.

4. Remedies for the parties

The doctrine of privity of contract presents no obstacle to the parties to the contract from vindicating their rights. They can claim for breach of contract in the normal way. But the difficulty arises that if the benefit of performance under the contract was supposed to have been conferred on a third party, it is unclear whether the promisee should be entitled to recover any compensation. This result is produced by the ordinary principles of the law of compensatory damages, considered in Chapter 17, which limits the claimant's remedy to the claimant's losses. For example, in the case of the disappointing family holiday, *Jackson v Horizon Holidays Ltd*, under the ordinary principles of the law of damages, the husband, as the party to the contract with the travel company, was able to claim compensation for all his losses, but in principle he should not have been able to claim compensation for the losses incurred by his wife and family.

Some of the harsher effects of this rule may be avoided by taking a broad view of the claimant's loss. In the case of a family holiday, for instance, the husband's loss may be described as including his inconvenience and disappointment resulting from his family's unpleasant experience. On this basis the majority of the court in *Jackson v Horizon Holidays Ltd* determined that the husband's loss included the suffering of his family, and so awarded an augmented measure of damages.

But some doubt has been cast on the general rule prohibiting the recovery of substantial damages where the claimant has suffered no personal loss. Consider the example where a father enters a contract with a builder to make renovation's to his son's home. If the builder performs the work poorly in breach of contract, the father can sue the builder for breach of contract, but what loss has the father suffered? It is the son's house which requires additional work, so the loss or the need to recover the cost of remedial work falls on the son. But the son is not a party to the contract and so, under the doctrine of privity, has no claim against the builder at all. Can the father recover compensation from the builder to cover the cost of the renovations to the son's house? It seems likely that the father would be permitted to recover substantial damages in this hypothetical case, but the principle on which recovery may be based remains unclear.

One possibility is that the principle permits recovery where one party has entered into a contract on behalf of himself and others and on the footing that he will be able to sue for the losses of the third parties. This principle may explain the decision in *Jackson v Horizon Holidays Ltd*, where it could be argued that the husband entered into the contract to benefit his family on the footing that if the holiday went wrong he would be able to claim compensation for all their losses. It may also explain the result in *The Albazero*,[15] where under an international contract of carriage by sea, the promisee and original owner of the goods successfully claimed full compensation for damage to the goods against the

---

15 [1977] AC 774, [1976] 3 All ER 129, HL.

carrier even though by the time the damage occurred the owner had transferred his interest in the goods to a third party. Such a result may be justified by arguing that when the original owner of the goods entered the contract of carriage the owner was expecting to sell the goods whilst they were in transit and, therefore, the owner entered into the contract on the footing that if any damage occurred to goods in transit the owner would be able to claim compensation on its own behalf or on behalf of subsequent owners.

This principle may also explain the result in *Linden Gardens Trust Ltd v Lenesta Sludge Disposals Ltd*.[16] In this case the owner of a building had transferred it to a purchaser and at the same time had purported to assign its rights under a contract with a builder to the purchaser as well. Unfortunately, the assignment of the rights against the builder was ineffective, because the building contract expressly forbade assignment without the builder's consent. After the sale of the building had been completed, the builder broke the contract. The original owner sought substantial damages against the builder even though the original owner had suffered no direct loss from the builder's breach of contract. This claim was also successful, and was possibly based on the same principle that the owner had entered the contract on the footing that it would be able to claim full compensation against the builder on behalf of subsequent owners. That interpretation of the case, however, appears improbable on the facts, given that the original owner had purported to assign its rights against the builder under the building contract. Nor does it seem important to the decision in the case whether or not the original owner was contemplating a sale at the time of entering the building contract. This case could therefore be understood as representing a broader principle. One possibility is that if the claimant under the contract actually incurs or will necessarily incur the cost of curing the defect, the claimant should be entitled to recover those costs. Under this interpretation, it is important that the claimant should be able to show that it actually intends to use the compensation to pay for the cost of curing the defect. In the example of the father's contract with the builder to perform work on his son's house, this principle would permit the father to recover the cost of remedying the defects provided that the father intended to pay for the repairs.

A further possible interpretation of the decision in the *Linden Gardens* case is that the original owner of the building was entitled to claim substantial compensation, even though it suffered no loss, simply on the ground that it did not receive what it had bargained for under the contract. In short, the owner should be entitled to proper performance of the contract or its financial equivalent regardless of its loss.

This broad principle, sometimes referred to as 'the performance interest', was not accepted by the majority of the House of Lords in *McAlpine Construction Ltd v*

16 [1994] 1 AC 85, [1993] 3 All ER 417, HL.

Panatown.[17] In this building contract, the employer entered a contract with the builder to construct an office building and car park in Cambridge on a site owned by another company in the same group of companies as the employer. When serious defects in the building were discovered, the employer's claim for compensation was resisted by the defendant builder on the ground that the employer had suffered no loss. The majority of the House of Lords were unwilling to accept the broad principle of recovery for the performance interest, although they accepted that the claim could succeed in principle either on the ground that the building contract had been entered into on the footing that the employer could recover on behalf of the owner or that the employer could recover substantial damages if it intended to use the compensation to pay for the repairs. But the majority also upheld an exception that defeated the claim in this case. Where the third party, in this case the owner of the building, had entered into a direct contractual relation with the builder, the employer could not claim substantial compensation: the owner of the building had to recover its losses under the direct contract with the builder. The reason for this restriction is that the additional direct contract should be regarded as deliberate planning for the eventuality of defects in the building, and the court should not upset this contractual allocation of risk. In this case, the direct contract (made by a deed that was assignable to subsequent owners) between the owner and the builder rendered the builder liable for any failure to exercise reasonable skill, care and attention, and any claim against the builder had to be based on this contractual agreement.

Given the disagreements in the court about how far the promisee may recover for losses of third parties, it is possible that the law will further evolve to expand the situations when the promisee can recover substantial compensation when the contract was intended to benefit the third party. It seems likely, for instance, that were the facts in *Beswick v Beswick* considered today, the husband's estate would be permitted to recover substantial damages on behalf of the widow for her nephew's refusal to pay her annuity. What perhaps makes the courts cautious in their acceptance of the broad principle of protecting the performance interest is that there seems to be no safeguard against the promisee obtaining substantial damages and then not devoting them to the benefit of the third party by, for example, curing the defect in the building. Furthermore, it should be noted that the third party has no means of compelling the promisee to bring a claim for damages, except in fiduciary or trust relations, so that a claim by a promisee for substantial compensation on behalf of the third party provides an unreliable method for circumventing the doctrine of privity of contract.

17 [2001] 1 AC 518, sub nom *Panatown Ltd v Alfred McAlpine Construction Ltd* [2000] 4 All ER 97, HL.

C.   Rationale of privity

Numerous justifications have been advanced for the doctrine of privity. None of them entirely succeed in justifying the current legal rules that exclude third parties from taking the benefit under contract. But they do reveal that some constraints upon actions brought by third parties are necessary. We should consider three of the principal justifications for the doctrine.

1.   Autonomy

Under the principles governing the ascription of contractual responsibility, only consent to an agreement engenders contractual responsibility. Without consent to the agreement, the third party should not obtain rights and obligations under it. In other words, contractual rights and duties remain personal to those who create them: all contracts resemble a marriage in so far as no third party can claim the right to share the intimate relations established between the spouses. This argument justifies the restriction of the range of responsibility to the parties to the contract.

The same argument, however, overlooks the distinction between the issue of how a person becomes bound by contractual obligations and the separate question of who may obtain rights under a contract. It is perfectly consistent to say out of respect for the autonomy of individuals that only persons who have consented to an agreement should be bound by the contract, but at the same time permit another to claim rights under the contract if the contract purports to confer a benefit on this third party. The purpose of entering contracts is to restrict the freedom of the parties in certain ways for their mutual advantage, and if they choose to give a legal right to a third person this is no greater interference with their autonomy than any other term of the contract.

This rebuttal of the argument based on respect for autonomy must be qualified in one respect. In some circumstances, to permit third parties to sue upon a contract would interfere with the autonomy of the original parties to the contract by preventing them from terminating or modifying it by agreement. But this consequence does not follow automatically. The parties to the contract could be permitted to terminate or modify it, in which event the third party would lose any rights under it, except perhaps the right to claim damages for any detrimental reliance on the basis of a claim under the reliance model. Alternatively, sufficient protection for the autonomy of the contracting parties could be achieved by declaring that the right to modify or vary the agreement is lost when either the third party materially changes his position in justifiable reliance on the promise or when the third party manifests his assent to the contract at the request of the promisor or promisee.[18]

2. Mutuality of rights

The doctrine of privity is also justified by the argument that since the third party provides nothing in return for the promised benefit and cannot be liable for breach of contract, it is inequitable to give the third party the right to sue upon the contract. This moral argument that the law of contract should always insist upon a mutuality of rights and liabilities became confused with the doctrine of consideration. It was suggested that the rule was that only a person who has provided consideration may enforce a promise.[19] Of course, the doctrine of consideration deals with the quite separate question of what types of agreement should be enforced by the state: it should have no application to the different question of which persons should be entitled to claim rights under a contract.[20]

Yet the moral argument in favour of privity based upon mutuality of rights, unencumbered by references to the doctrine of consideration, has greater substance. If third parties were granted rights to sue upon a contract, but not being parties themselves could not be sued, this position would create an imbalance of rights. This argument only works, however, on a superficial analysis of the situation. In a typical case, the promisor ensures that his remedies against the promisee under the contract are adequate so that there is no need to acquire additional rights against the third party. If such additional rights are required, they can be sought through such devices as guarantees and indemnities.

Indeed the promisor often has obtained full performance of the contract from the promisee already, so that the equity of rights idea in fact points to the opposite conclusion. In *Beswick v Beswick*,[21] for instance, the uncle had transferred his business to his nephew, so that the protection of mutuality of rights suggests that the nephew should now be required to fulfil his side of the bargain, namely to pay his aunt an annuity. Although it may be said of this case that, since the nephew could not sue his aunt, it would be wrong to grant her a cause of action, this argument ignores the point that the nephew had already received in full his expected benefit under the contract, so he has no need of any remedy. On the contrary, to deny the aunt a remedy must promote unjust enrichment of the

---

18 See Restatement (Second) of Contracts, s 311(3); *Wiley v Berg* 282 Or 9, 578 P 2d 384 (1978).

19 This history is described in: Flannigan, 'Privity – The End of an Era (Error)' (1987) 103 *Law Quarterly Review* 564.

20 This view of the separation of consideration and privity has often been questioned: Coote, 'Consideration and the Joint Promisee' (1978) *Cambridge Law Journal* 301; Law Revision Committee, Sixth Interim Report (Statute of Frauds and the Doctrine of Consideration), Cmd 5549, paras 37, 41.

21 [1968] AC 58, [1967] 2 All ER 1197, HL.

nephew, in the sense that he has acquired the coal business without having had to pay the agreed price for it. Similarly, in *Jackson v Horizon Holidays Ltd*, it is true that the tour operator cannot sue the man's family for the price of the holiday, but it can sue the husband directly, and has almost certainly required payment in advance. In these circumstances, the tour operator enjoys full protection, but the law of privity prevents third party beneficiaries from gaining a corresponding level of security.

On closer inspection, therefore, the moral argument concerning the equity of rights rarely carries any weight, for promisor and third party are not in equivalent positions. The moral argument concerning equity between the parties often in fact points in the opposite direction: since the promisor's rights have been fully vindicated, either a contracting party should be entitled to claim damages on behalf of intended beneficiaries or, more simply, third parties should receive equivalent rights, for otherwise there is a risk of unjust enrichment to the promisor.

The moral argument concerning the mutuality of rights can also be weakened by reference to the intentions of the promisor. If the promisor has agreed to an arrangement under which he accepts liability to perform a promise, even though the beneficiary of the promise will incur no obligation, it could be insisted that for the promisor to go back on his word would be to undermine the intentions of the parties to the contract. The promisor no doubt took the opportunity to secure his interests in other ways, and this denial of a right vested in the third party is in reality an attempt to revise the contract without the consent of the promisee.

3.   Indeterminate range of liability

A much more substantial objection to an abolition of the rule that third parties cannot sue upon a contract points out that the numbers of third parties interested in suing may be considerable and engender unexpectedly enormous liabilities. The ever present danger of introducing third party rights is the possibility of exposing the promisor 'to a liability in an indeterminate amount for an indeterminate time to an indeterminate class'.[22] If such broad liability to third parties could be created by contracts, then this would certainly discourage entry into transactions, with the consequence of serious harm to the whole market system for the creation of wealth.

The American case, *Martinez v Socoma Co Inc*,[23] illustrates this problem well. Under the Economic Opportunity Act of 1964 (as amended) the US Congress designated certain neighbourhoods which had high concentrations of low income persons and unemployment as Special Impact Areas and made federal funds

22 *Cardozo CJ, Ultramares Corpn v Touche* 174 NE 441 (1931) at 444.
23 11 Cal 3d 394, 521 P 2d 841 (1974).

available for government contracts with local private industry. The defendants entered into such a contract with the government and undertook to train and employ a specified number of local residents. The plaintiffs were members of the class intended to benefit from legislative aid who alleged that the company had failed to comply with its contractual obligation to hire and train the required number of local residents. The plaintiffs claimed a right to sue the company as intended beneficiaries under the contract. The California Supreme Court denied their claim on the ground that, from the terms of the contract, it did not appear that the government intended to make a gift to the plaintiffs or to confer on them a legal right against the defendants. The plaintiffs were simply incidental beneficiaries of the contract, and the company's responsibility did not extend so far. It is evident that the court feared to extend rights to such a wide class of beneficiaries, ie, all the poor and unemployed persons in the Special Impact Area, and that this fear provided the reason for preserving a modified privity rule. To make the company liable to the poor and unemployed persons in the neighbourhood certainly would have provided a vigorous incentive for the company to comply with the terms of the government contract and the policy of the legislation, but, in the long run, to impose such liability might deter companies from accepting federal aid and ultimately thwart the purpose of the law. Thus even in jurisdictions which do not follow the strict doctrine of privity, the courts must balance the interests of third parties who indirectly depend upon proper performance of the contract against the danger that worthwhile transactions will be discouraged by the threat of liability to a wide range of persons.

The law of tort encounters the same problem of limiting the range of liability. Suppose that under a contract for the carriage of goods by road the driver of the lorry negligently crashes and destroys the load. The driver or his employer will be liable for breach of contract, but there is also the prospect of potential liability to anyone affected by the damage to the goods. We may imagine that the intended recipient of the goods is a factory which is forced to shut down temporarily until fresh supplies can be obtained, which in turn leads to loss of wages for employees at the factory, which in a further ricochet effect reduces the turnover of local shops. The law of tort shrinks from the prospect of rendering the driver liable to all these potential claimants, even though it is possible to trace a causal link between the negligent driving and these losses. For this reason, the law of negligence generally prohibits claims for pure economic loss, ie claims not based on damage to the claimant's property. This restricts claims in tort in the example to the owner of the goods at the time when they are damaged. Here the law of tort responds to the same problem that liability to an indeterminate number of claimants would discourage any market transactions.

The most significant justification for the doctrine of privity thus boils down to the simple point that the law of contract must draw a line at some point to set limits to the range of liability to third parties. English law established the line firmly at the point where a person was a party to the agreement. But many other possibilities could have been recognized. These possibilities can be illustrated by a series of circles that progressively expand the range of liability from the smallest group of potential claimants – the parties to the contract, as in the rule governing privity of contract – to the widest group – which might be anyone whose economic loss was caused as a result of justifiable reliance upon the defendant.

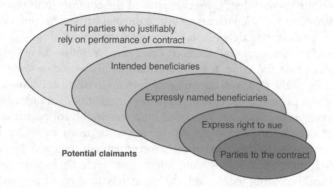

The test for the range of liability could have been any person explicitly named as an intended beneficiary of the contract. A slightly broader circumference of liability would have included all those persons intended to benefit from performance of the contract. For instance, American courts recognize an exception which provides that, where the contract expressly mentions third parties as intended beneficiaries of the contract, they will be permitted to claim the envisaged benefits. The facts of the previous examples concerning the rights of beneficiaries of a contract for a package holiday and of the intended recipient of a sum of money probably fit within the exception. Furthermore some American courts proceed so far as to permit intended beneficiaries who were not expressly mentioned in the contract to claim rights under it. For example, a downstream landowner successfully sued a chicken processor for breach of its contract with the local city not to over-saturate its sewage treatment facilities, since the purpose of the agreement plainly included the protection of those drawing water from the creek.[24] These results indicate that the doctrine of privity enjoys a precarious existence in modern American law.

All of these tests have been used in different jurisdictions, so the question which must be addressed in English law is whether or not there is a good justification for setting the range of liability so narrowly? Although the problem of remote third parties requires a limitation upon the range of liability, it is far from clear that the line drawn by the English law of contract by reference to consent to the contract achieves satisfactory results.

24 *Ratzlaff v Franz Foods* 250 Ark 1003, 468 SW 2d 239 (1971).

D.   Objections to privity

Does the law of privity cause injustice? Certainly, it can be criticized on three grounds. One concerns the frustration of the intentions of the contracting parties; another seeks to provide relief from justifiable detrimental reliance incurred by the third party resulting from reliance upon the contract; and the third concerns the possibility of unjust enrichment to the promisor. We will consider these objections in turn.

1.   Intentions of the parties

The doctrine of privity of contract may defeat the intentions of the parties to the contract. Under their contract it may have been their joint intent to confer a benefit on the third party, either by way of a gift of property or the conferral of an immunity from suit by the promisee. If the third party cannot vindicate this right, the intention of the parties may be defeated, and the utility of the law of contract in supporting transactions may be undermined.

The strength of this argument depends considerably on the ease with which the parties to the contract can evade the doctrine of privity by invoking some legal mechanism through which the third party can acquire enforceable rights. We have noted how this may be done, either through the establishment of an agency relation between promisee and the third party, or the assignment of rights to the third party. More complex legal arrangements such as trusts can also achieve the same effect. But these techniques all require a degree of legal skill, and it must be questioned whether the law of contract serves its purpose of buttressing market transactions adequately when it requires traders to secure the services of a lawyer before they can give effect to their joint intentions. It would have been possible, for example, for the uncle in *Beswick v Beswick* to have achieved the desired result of conferring the benefit of an enforceable annuity upon his wife by means of a trust or an assignment, but it is doubtful whether the law should erect such hurdles to simple transactions.

Even in those cases where the parties are guided by lawyers, it may not always be possible to devise a contract which secures the interests of third parties adequately. This problem arises where the identity of the third parties cannot yet be known at the time of the formation of the contract. In the case of construction contracts, for instance, the main contractor may not have fixed upon all the sub-contractors for the work, and indeed their identity may depend upon subsequent nomination by the promisor. If the main contractor seeks to confer any benefit upon these sub-contractors, such as protection under an insurance policy, then without being able to name the sub-contractors as insured persons under the contract, it may not be possible to give the sub-contractors enforceable rights against the insurance company.[25]

This objection to the doctrine of privity points to the need for modest reform. The intentions of the parties could be fulfilled in two ways:

(i)   Third parties could be granted the right to sue for a benefit or to claim an immunity if the contract intended to benefit them in this way and identified them clearly either by name or by intended function, as in the case of sub-contractors.

(ii)   Alternatively, the promisee could be granted the right to sue upon the contract in order to obtain the benefit intended to be conferred upon the third party, but then be under an obligation to transfer that benefit to the third party.

2.   Justifiable reliance

A broader objection to the doctrine of privity insists that the law of contract should seek to protect persons engaged in commerce from incurring losses resulting from justifiable reliance upon the words and conduct of others. We have already noted the significance of this principle both under the reliance model of the test of enforceability, and as part of the duty to bargain with care. Here the principle suggests that those third parties who have acted in reliance upon the proper performance of the contract by the promisor, either by incurring expense or by failing to take steps to safeguard their position, should be protected if that reliance was justifiable.[26] Although this principle, if adopted, would deal a lethal blow to the doctrine of privity of contract, we should observe that the elements of this idea have provided a crucial theme in pushing the courts towards circumventing the doctrine of privity by alternative legal techniques.

One example of how the idea of justifiable reliance influences the development of routes around the doctrine of privity concerns the device of collateral contracts. In the leading example of this device, *New Zealand Shipping Co Ltd v AM Satterthwaite & Co Ltd (The Eurymedon)*,[27] the Privy Council found a collateral contract between the owners of goods and stevedores who unloaded the goods under a contract with a carrier. The terms of this collateral contract provided that in return for unloading the goods the owner would accept certain limitations upon his rights to sue the stevedores in tort for negligent performance of their

25 *Trident General Insurance Co Ltd v McNiece Bros Pty Ltd* (1988) 165 CLR 107, Aust HC.
26 G Gilmore, *The Death of Contract* (Columbus, Ohio, 1974), pp 87–96; Reiter, 'Contracts, Torts, Relations and Reliance' in B Reiter and J Swan (eds), *Studies in Contract Law* (Toronto, 1980), pp 288–310.
27 [1975] AC 154, [1974] 1 All ER 1015, PC.

work. The court found its justification for the imposition of a collateral contract from the fact that, in the contract between owner and carrier, the owner expressly promised to respect certain limitations of his rights against the sub-contractors of the carrier. The strength of the stevedores' claim to be protected by the exemption clause surely stems in part from the fact that it was eminently foreseeable that stevedores would rely upon the exemption clause when unloading the goods. Suppose, for instance, that the damage to the goods had been committed not by the stevedores but by a building contractor who happened to be working for the carrier on the dock. Although the terms of the owner's promise encompassed all independent contractors of the carrier, surely the court would have been much less willing to allow the builder to take advantage of this clause, because such reliance would not be justifiable.

In the USA, where the reliance model for the test of enforceability is more firmly established, the courts can use the idea of promissory estoppel to protect third parties under this principle. In *Hoffman v Red Owl Stores Inc*[28] the liability of the franchise company extended not only to the man whom they had strung along during their negotiations, but also to his wife, who, as joint owner of their assets, foreseeably acted on the faith of the representations made to her husband. Similarly, a bank's promise to a businessman to approve a loan could lead to foreseeable reliance by other creditors of the businessman, who might extend credit in the expectation of repayment out of the bank's loan. If the bank then failed to produce the loan, the creditors might be able to claim compensation for their misplaced reliance upon the bank's promise to grant a loan, even though the promise was not made to them.[29]

In English law, the development of this principle of justifiable reliance has been undertaken primarily by the law of tort. Because the duty of care is not confined to contractual relations, it is open to the courts to discover a duty of care between the promisor and the third party. When the third party has suffered physical damage or personal injuries, normally such a duty of care will be discovered provided that the parties were in a proximate relation. The law of tort developed this protection in the context of consumers who purchased defective products which caused personal injuries or damage to property. For the sake of consumer protection and to improve the safety of products put on the market by manufacturers, the courts permitted the consumer to sue the manufacturer directly for negligence. This jurisdiction has now been largely overtaken by a statutory regime of strict liability in the Consumer Protection Act 1987, Part 1, which gives effect to the EC uniform regime throughout the single market area of

---

28 26 Wis 2d 683, 133 NW 2d 267 (1965).

29 *Alaska v First National Bank of Ketchikan* 629 P 2d 78 (1981), where the argument failed on the facts.

Europe.[30] Under these rules, a consumer who suffers personal injury or minor property damage due to a defective product may claim compensation directly from the manufacturer or producer.

The principle of protecting justifiable reliance runs headlong into the worry that indeterminate numbers of remote claimants may claim compensation for their economic losses. Here the law of tort restricts the potential range of liability by excluding claims for pure economic loss except within relations of close proximity. The relevant principles in English law may be gleaned from inspecting two leading decisions. The defendants in *Caparo Industries plc v Dickman*[31] were auditors of a company under a contract with the company. It was alleged that the defendants were negligent in certifying that the accounts showed a true and fair view of the company's financial position. If this allegation were true, clearly the auditors would be liable for breach of contract to the company for failure to provide the service with reasonable care, subject to any exclusion of liability in the contract. The question addressed by the court was whether other groups of people who had relied upon the auditors performing the service carefully could also claim damages for the losses which they had incurred when the accounts proved misleading under an action for negligence in tort. Since the audited accounts become a published document available for anyone to inspect, the court regarded the problem of remoteness as severe, and so ruled out any possibility of general liability towards third parties. But the court did consider that some classes of third parties might have a sufficiently proximate relation to be entitled to claim in tort. The test for the existence of this proximate relation required that the defendant should know that the accounts would be communicated to the claimant, and that to the defendant's knowledge the claimant would use those accounts for the purpose of deciding whether or not to enter a transaction of a particular kind or adopt some other particular course of action to the claimant's detriment. Under this test the court regarded it as possible that the shareholders as a group could sue the accountants, if the shareholders could demonstrate that the false accounts had failed to alert them to the need to exert their powers to replace the directors of the company. The shareholders' claim to fall within a proximate relation was strengthened by the point that the company's statutory duty to submit to audit was designed for the protection and information of shareholders in the running of the company. But the claimant in this case, who had relied on the accounts to purchase shares in the company and to mount a successful takeover bid, was found not to be in the requisite proximate relation. The auditors owed no duty of care to potential investors in the company in the

---

30 Under EC Directive 85/374/EEC on Liability for Defective Products. See Stapleton, 'Products Liability Reform – Real or Illusory?' (1986) 6 *Oxford Journal of Legal Studies* 392; Clarke, 'The Consumer Protection Act 1987' (1987) 50 *Modern Law Review* 614. Compare, J White and R Summers, *Handbook of the Law under the Uniform Commercial Code* (St Paul, Minn, 2nd edn, 1980), pp 398–411.

31 [1990] 2 AC 605, [1990] 1 All ER 568, HL.

absence of direct communication between the parties with the intended investment expressly drawn to the auditor's attention.[32] This test of proximity was satisfied, however, in *Smith v Eric S Bush*,[33] where the purchaser of a house relied upon an inaccurate survey and valuation which was arranged under a contract between the surveyor and the mortgage lender. Not only was the surveyor aware in this case that the survey would be given to and relied upon by the intended purchaser, but also the purchaser had in effect paid for the survey in her contract with the mortgage lender.

A second leading authority, *White v Jones*,[34] appears to take the protection of justifiable reliance much further when no problem of indeterminate liability is present. Here a solicitor who had undertaken to draw up a Will failed to do so prior to the client's death, with the result that the claimants who were intended to benefit under the Will did not receive their expected bequest. The claimants successfully sued the solicitor for negligence. This claim differs from the case of *Caparo Industries plc v Dickman*, since the solicitor had not made representations which he knew would be relied upon by the claimants. One way of explaining the decision is to say that in undertaking the work the solicitor assumed an obligation of responsibility not only to the client but also to the intended beneficiaries. Such a broad principle would, however, permit the law of tort to be employed to protect the justifiable reliance of many third parties. It might revive the principle in the earlier discredited case of *Junior Books Ltd v Veitchi Co Ltd*,[35] where, under a contract with a building contractor, a sub-contractor produced faulty work in laying a floor. The owner of the building successfully sued the sub-contractor directly for the negligent performance of the contract, even though he was not a party to a contract with the sub-contractor.

The underlying difficulty for the courts in developing protection for justifiable reliance through the law of tort is that whether or not reliance is justifiable depends on several crucial considerations. Not only is it relevant that the defendant was aware of the degree and type of reliance, and not only is there the concern to avoid the deterrence to commerce from the potential risk of indeterminate liabilities, but also the agreed allocations of risk will be pertinent. Reliance should not be regarded as justifiable if it in effect renders nugatory a contractual provision designed to allocate risks in other ways. If, for example, the owner of the building in *Junior Books Ltd v Veitchi Co Ltd* had agreed with the main contractor not to make any claims against the sub-contractor for negligent work, this agreement should count against any claim based upon reliance.

32 *Morgan Crucible Co plc v Hill Samuel & Co Ltd* [1991] Ch 295, sub nom *Morgan Crucible Co plc v Hill Samuel Bank* [1991] 1 All ER 148, CA.
33 [1990] 1 AC 831, [1989] 2 All ER 514, HL.
34 [1995] 2 AC 207, [1995] 1 All ER 691, HL; McBride and Hughes, 'Hedley Byrne in the House of Lords: an Interpretation' (1995) 15 *Legal Studies* 376.
35 [1983] 1 AC 520, [1982] 3 All ER 201, HL; cp *Sears, Roebuck & Co v Jardel* 421 F 2d 1048 (3d Cir 1970).

The test for existence of a duty of care includes the element that the duty must be just and reasonable in the circumstances. Increasingly courts refer to the contractual allocations of risk pertinent to the case in order to determine whether either that the imposition of a duty of care would upset the contractual allocation of risk, or that it would in fact fill in a gap in the economic arrangements between the parties. It was this kind of reasoning which led the court in *Norwich City Council v Harvey*[36] to deny the existence of a duty of care, even in a case where the defendant had seriously damaged the claimant's property by fire, on the ground that it was not just and reasonable in view of the contractual allocation of risk of fire agreed by the promisor to absolve the defendant from a duty of care.

3. Unjust enrichment

The third objection to the doctrine of privity is that it can lead to unjust enrichment. By the phrase 'unjust enrichment', it is not intended to refer to the precise rules governing restitutionary claims, but rather the general concept that one person has unjustifiably obtained a benefit at another's expense. This defect of the doctrine of privity emerges clearly in those cases such as *Beswick v Beswick*, where the promisor receives valuable property in return for an unenforceable promise to benefit a third party. But the problem of unjust enrichment will occur whenever the promisor has received the consideration under the contract and is seeking to avoid the reciprocal obligation to confer a benefit on the third party. Here the promisee under the contract has suffered no loss, so cannot claim substantial damages, but the third party cannot claim the intended benefit.

An analogous problem arose in the Australian case *Trident General Insurance Co Ltd v McNiece Bros Pty Ltd*.[37] The insurance company had agreed to provide liability insurance against claims for personal injuries to the owner of a site, and under the policy the insured person was defined to include not only the owner but also its independent contractors and their sub-contractors engaged on the construction project. An employee of a sub-contractor was injured on the site and successfully claimed damages for personal injuries against the main contractor. The main contractor then sought an indemnity under the owner's insurance policy. The doctrine of privity blocked this claim, because the main contractor was not a party to the contract of insurance, and nor had the owner contracted as an agent for the main contractor. Nevertheless the claim succeeded, although the High Court of Australia gave different reasons for its decision, ranging from direct assaults on the doctrine of privity to a more limited exception governing insurance policies. Under English law, apart from special rules governing liability insurance,[38] the claim would fail for want of privity of

36 [1989] 1 All ER 1180, [1989] 1 WLR 828, CA.
37 (1988) 165 CLR 107, Aust HC.
38 Road Traffic Act 1988, s 148(7); Third Parties (Rights Against Insurers) Act 1930.

contract.[39] The underlying objection to the application of the doctrine of privity in this case is surely that the insurance company had received the premiums under a policy the risks for which had been calculated on the basis of having to indemnify all contractors on the site, yet now it was seeking to keep those premiums and to not pay out under the policy when a claim contemplated by the contract of insurance was brought.

Of the three arguments for reform of the law of privity of contract, this concern with the unjust enrichment of the promisee is surely the most compelling. But it would not address all the problems created by the doctrine of privity, such as the creation of immunities for third parties.

E. Statutory reform

There has been widespread acceptance of the need for reform of the English law of privity of contract in order to remove the injustice which it occasions. In addition, proponents of reform suggest that it would have the advantages of reducing the need for complex contractual arrangements to circumvent its unwanted effects, and would also bring English law into harmony with other European legal systems. Given the unwillingness of the courts to reform the common law, the question for a statute was whether it would try to address all the objections to privity of contract – namely that it thwarts the intentions of the parties; it leaves justifiable reliance unprotected; and that it leads to unjust enrichment of the promisor. The English Law Commission proposed a reform that addressed primarily the problem that privity of contract may thwart the intentions of the parties.[40] This reform proposal was enacted in the Contracts (Rights of Third Parties) Act 1999.

Under s 1 of the Act a third party intended to benefit under a contract may bring a claim for damages or other remedies for breach of contract:

1(1) Subject to the provisions of this Act, a person who is not a party to a contract (a 'third party') may in his own right enforce a term of the contract if—
   (a)   the contract expressly provides that he may, or
   (b)   subject to subsection (2), the term purports to confer a benefit on him.
(2) Subsection 1(b) does not apply if on a proper construction of the contract it appears that the parties did not intend the term to be enforceable by the third party.
(3) The third party must be expressly identified in the contract by name,

39 *Vandepitte v Preferred Accident Insurance Corpn of New York* [1933] AC 70, PC.
40 Law Commission, *Privity of Contract: Contracts for the Benefit of Third Parties*, Report No 242, Cm 3329 (London, 1996).

as a member of a class or as answering a particular description but need not be in existence when the contract is entered into.

The effect of the Act is to enable third parties who expect to receive a benefit or an immunity under a contract to assert their rights or defences provided by the contract. In effect the legislation creates a presumption that contracts designed to confer a benefit on third parties will afford the third party the right to enforce it subject to contrary indications in the contract. For example, the aunt in *Beswick v Beswick* could now claim in her personal right the annuity from her nephew, since she was almost certainly named in the contract that provided for her benefit. Similarly, in *New Zealand Shipping Co Ltd v Satterthwaite & Co Ltd (The Eurymedon)*, the stevedores unloading the goods could avail themselves of the limitation of liability provided for them as sub-contractors or bailees under the contract of carriage.[41]

Under the statute, the promisor can rely on any defence provided by the contract as against the promisee to also protect him against the third party.[42] For example, if the contract is for the supply of goods to the promisor in return for payment to a third party, neither the third party nor the promisee can claim the price if the promisor lawfully rejected the goods for their failure to conform to the contractual standard of quality.

In order to deal with the problem that to give third parties rights under the contract may restrict the ability of the parties to the contract to vary it, a further provision allows variation or termination of the contract subject to protection of any reliance by the third party:

2(1)   Subject to the provisions of this section, where a third party has a right under section 1 to enforce a term of the contract, the parties to the contract may not, by agreement, rescind the contract, or vary it in such a way as to extinguish or alter his entitlement under that right, without his consent if—

(a)   the third party has communicated his assent to the term to the promisor

(b)   the promisor is aware that the third party has relied on the term, or

(c)   the promisor can reasonably be expected to have foreseen that the third party would rely on the term and the third party has in fact relied on it.

The parties to the contract can expressly exclude the protection afforded to the third party by this provision.[43]

---

41   Although the statute does not apply to a contract of carriage of goods, an exception applies to immunities conferred on third parties: Contracts (Rights of Third Parties) Act 1999, s 6(5).

42   Contracts (Rights of Third Parties) Act 1999, s 3. Section 5 also protects the promisor against double liability.

43   Contracts (Rights of Third Parties) Act 1999, s 2(3).

The reform addresses directly the criticism of the doctrine of privity that it is liable to defeat the intentions of the parties. Even where that intention is not explicitly stated, the arrangement by which a benefit will be conferred on a third party under a contract creates a presumption that the third party is entitled to claim under the contract, subject always to the court's construction of the contract which may evidence a contrary intention. This formulation permits the courts to use the statute to extend the range of liability beyond the parties to the contract in the light of their interpretation of the contract in its commercial context.

To some extent the reform may also be used to counter the other objections to privity of contract. Where the third party has foreseeably relied upon the contract and the expectation of receiving a benefit or an immunity, the parties will normally require the third party's consent to vary or terminate the contract. It is possible, for instance, that on facts similar to those in *Junior Books v Veitchi Ltd*, a sub-contractor on a construction project will enter a contract for work which will benefit the owner of the building, and if the main contract contains an immunity to benefit the sub-contractor, that immunity is likely to be binding unless the sub-contractor agrees to a release. It is unclear, however, whether such contracts fall within the statute, because the sub-contract may not be framed in term of conferring a benefit on the owner of the building as opposed to providing a service for the main contractor. Similarly, on the facts of *White v Jones*, the contract with the solicitor to draft a Will was likely to result in benefits to the beneficiaries, but it would be difficult to argue that the contract itself purported to confer a benefit on them. The same reasoning might prevent the application of the statute to the case where the promisee employs a builder to construct a building on a third party's land: on its face the contract may not purport to confer a benefit on the third party, although it will necessarily in fact do so, and a court may infer from the absence of reference to the owner of the land that the contract, properly construed, rebuts the third party's claim to be able to claim damages against the builder directly. The extent to which the proposed reform tackles instances of justifiable reliance by third parties will depend crucially on how the idea that the contract purports to confer a benefit on the third party will be interpreted.

The statute does not interfere with or replace other possible claims of third parties based on tort, proprietary interests, and other branches of the law.[44] It is perhaps understandable that these instances of justifiable reliance should be left mostly to the common law of tort, because the issue of when reliance is justifiable depends upon numerous factors which have to be weighed. It is not possible to create a simple rule which grants enforceable rights to third parties when such rights may turn on such issues as whether the right might upset the allocation of risks in a network of contracts or the right might extend to an indeterminate number of third parties. Yet the failure to tackle these issues as part of the law of

---

44 Contracts (Rights of Third Parties) Act 1999, s 7(1).

contract merely displaces them into tort, where further irrelevant considerations such as proof of negligence serve merely to complicate matters. The simple issue at the heart of both *White v Jones* and *Junior Books v Veitchi Ltd* was whether a third party who had relied upon proper performance of a contract could sue for its breach by incompetent performance? The answer to that question should not depend upon proof of negligence, but whether or not the contract had been broken, and whether the third party had justifiably relied upon performance. In turn the issue of justifiable reliance should not depend on whether or not the contract purported to confer a benefit on the third party, but rather on whether the contract would foreseeably benefit the third party, whether the third party had in fact relied upon performance, and whether the reliance was justifiable in the light of the potential range of liability and the surrounding contractual allocations of risk. These considerations are relevant under the legislation when removing the right of the parties to vary or cancel the contract, but the legislation does not make them a possible basis for a third party claim under the contract.

This statutory reform of the doctrine of privity of contract only proceeds some way towards dealing with the objections to the doctrine. In particular, it does not systematically address the problems created by the doctrine of privity for the organization of relations of production through networks of contractual relations.[45] Here, three or more parties are engaged in a productive enterprise. It is time-consuming and expensive to ensure that all parties enter into direct contractual relations with each other. Normally the absence of direct contracts provokes few problems, for if the parties foresee difficulties they will seek contractual arrangements to govern them. Nevertheless, it always remains possible for an economic relation not governed by contract to cause loss to one of the parties. What the courts need to achieve here is to fill in the gaps in the economic relations constituting a network, so that the business relations provide a coherent pattern of incentives and risks between the parties. The underlying strength of the stevedores' claim in *New Zealand Shipping Co Ltd v AM Satterthwaite & Co Ltd (The Eurymedon)* rests upon the good sense of the business practice that the owner of the goods should insure against loss or damage, because that person knows best the value of the goods and thus insures efficiently. It therefore made sense for the Privy Council to supplement the arrangements of this network for the transportation of goods by discovering a collateral contract in order to protect the stevedores' justifiable reliance upon the promised immunity. The principle of justifiable reliance has sufficient flexibility to be used in this role: it can supplement these economic relations, and has additional duties to protect the economic interests of members of the network who lack direct contractual claims, in particular employees of contractors, whilst at the same time suppressing potential liability where this would subvert the scheme of risk allocation implicit in the network.

45 Adams and Brownsword, 'Privity and the Concept of a Network Contract' (1990) 10 *Legal Studies* 12.

Co-operation

A.   Supporting co-operation

In most transactions, co-operation simply requires performance according to the terms of the contract. A shopkeeper hands over the goods in return for payment by the customer, or a solicitor drafts a Will and then is paid for the service by the client when it has been completed. This co-operation takes place largely as a result of the economic self-interest which led the parties to enter the transaction in the first place. The incentive for co-operation is strengthened in competitive markets by the recognition that each party has the opportunity to enter similar transactions with others for the goods or services. These incentives ensure that most contracts are self-enforcing without the need to invoke the law.

In accordance with this model of co-operation in contracts, the classical law limited its regulation to two principles. The first involved a commitment to support co-operation by enforcement of the terms of contract agreed by the parties. The second set the conditions under which one party might terminate the contract in the face of breach by the other. The right to terminate the contract was essential, so that the injured party could take up the opportunity to acquire the goods and services elsewhere. Under the classical law, there was no further general obligation to co-operate, to assist each other, to perform in good faith, or to make the contract a success for both parties. Such additional mandatory duties not only appeared unnecessary to secure co-operation, but also they threatened to breach the principle that the parties must consent to contractual obligations.

The flaw in the classical law's approach to co-operation consists in its assumption that all contracts fit into the pattern set by an isolated sale of goods or the performance of a finite service. As soon as the context shifts to long-term commercial relations, such as a business partnership, it becomes readily apparent that co-operation requires considerable obligations of loyalty and mutual assistance in order to make the transaction a success. Indeed, a strict insistence upon the terms of the contract or a threat to terminate the contract for a minor breach would almost certainly destroy co-operation between the parties and lead to dissolution of a long-term business relation. For some categories of business relation, such as partnership and agency, the classical law responded to this context by supporting co-operation through the imposition of equitable fiduciary duties of good faith and loyalty. Outside these special categories of business relation, however, the traditional approach persisted.

In the modern law, however, we can detect an increasing willingness of the courts to recognize that for many transactions support for co-operation between the parties requires the recognition of supplementary obligations. Consider the case of an employment contract, where the employee insists upon a 'work to rule', ie strict performance of the contract according to its terms. Unless the employer has foreseen every eventuality, and so tightly constrained the discretion of workers that they must perform as automatons under the terms of the contract, the employees will necessarily enjoy a degree of discretion in how they carry out their tasks. They could quickly frustrate the employer's business objectives by a 'work to rule' in which they withdraw goodwill, that is fail to act in a co-operative manner, taking into account the interests of the employer. Performance according to the strict terms of the contract would render the contract unworkable and destroy its commercial purpose for the employer.

Contracts of employment illustrate a type of contract which is incomplete by design. The terms of the contract do not seek to fix in detail the obligations of each party. Instead, the contract gives a degree of discretion to both parties as to how performance should be achieved: the employer retains a discretion to direct or manage employees, and the employee retains a discretion over the details of how the work is to be completed. Contracts which are incomplete by design often contain their own dispute resolution mechanism, so that minor disagreements about how discretion should be exercised can be resolved by arbitration or further negotiation. Neither party wishes disagreement to escalate into termination of the economic relation. Similarly, business format franchises and the relation between manufacturer and distributor are incomplete by design, for they leave discretion to the parties to determine the details of performance.[1] For example, the franchisor or the manufacturer will commit themselves to advertising the product, but the manner and extent of advertising will be left to their discretion. At most, the contract may specify that the discretion should be exercised in good faith or that 'best efforts' should be employed.

There are many reasons why contracts are left incomplete by design.[2] The parties recognise that adjustments to their obligations will have to be made in order to respond to changing market conditions. By leaving the details indeterminate, these adjustments can be effectuated without the cost and delay of a renegotiation of the contract. Another important reason for incompleteness is that this type of contract can take better advantage of the division of labour by granting to each party the discretion to utilise its skills and knowledge in the best way to achieve performance of the objective of the contract.[3] This discretion can also tap into the potential of both parties for innovation and creativity, which may lead to greater profits for both parties. In a business format franchise for a restaurant, for instance, the franchisee may discover that the local market favours a particular variation of the product such as a fishburger, and this innovation may then be disseminated by the franchisor throughout the franchise operation to the mutual benefit of franchisor and other franchisees.

These potential advantages of contracts incomplete by design will only be realized if the parties co-operate in ways which go beyond performance according to the strict terms of the contract. The parties must display trust towards each other, both in the sense of respecting the exercise of discretion and more fundamentally in assisting each other as far as possible in the effective use of that discretion. Where such a relation of trust permeates the business relation, the

1 Beale, Harris, and Sharpe, 'The Distribution of Cars: A Complex Contractual Technique', in D Harris and D Tallon (eds), *Contract Law Today* (Oxford, 1991); Hadfield, 'Problematic Relations: Franchising and the Law of Incomplete Contracts' (1990) 42 *Stanford Law Review* 927.
2 H Collins, *Regulating Contracts* (Oxford, 1999), ch 10.
3 Schanze, 'Symbiotic Contracts: Exploring Long-Term Agency Structures between Contract and Corporation', in C Joerges (ed), *Franchising and the Law* (Baden-Baden, 1991), p 67.

contract can be left radically incomplete as merely a framework document, thereby permitting adjustment to cope with shifts in demand; the parties can dispense with detailed monitoring of each other's performance; and the parties can exchange knowledge and expertise in order to improve the competitiveness of the product.[4] The normative standards will be supplied by the more general sense of good faith dealing and customary standards in the trade or business. This style of business relation based upon trust has been constructed in many business contexts, as in the example of 'supplier partnerships' between automobile assemblers and their component suppliers.

The problem which the law must address is how to differentiate between types of contracts in order to respond appropriately to the unwritten expectations of co-operation. In some contexts, such as an isolated sale of goods, the appropriate response will normally be to insist upon strict observance of the terms of the contract. In other contexts, however, an insistence upon the strict terms of the contract will undermine the trust required for achievement of the objectives of the contract. In order to achieve this differentiation, the key insight is to recognise that the long-term business interests of the parties may be at variance with a short-term insistence upon performance of the contract according to its letter.[5] These long-term business interests may be used as a criterion to interpret the obligations under the contract, to constrain the discretion in contracts incomplete by design, and to validate informal adjustments to the obligations contained in the contract.

Respect for the requirements of co-operation does not therefore require the courts to believe that the parties have suddenly been overcome by altruistic concerns. Nor does the idea suppose that the parties share a common interest in performance of the contract which differs from their individual interests.[6] It is no doubt likely that their co-operation will be guided in part by standards other than those of their strict economic interests, such as a desire to remain on friendly terms with the other party in order to sustain personal relationships of trust.[7] But a court can focus on the criterion of long-term economic interest as a guide to the requirements of co-operation in each particular contract. This approach is compatible with a commitment within a social market of fostering worthwhile economic opportunities. If such opportunities can only be realized by the law

4 Deakin and Wilkinson, 'Contracts, Co-operation and Trust: The Role of the Institutional Framework', in D Campbell and P Vincent-Jones, *Contract and Economic Organisation* (Aldershot, 1996), p 95.
5 Campbell and Harris, 'Flexibility in Long-term Contractual Relationships: The Role of Co-operation' (1993) 20 *Journal of Law and Society* 166.
6 For this suggestion, see Brownsword, 'From Co-operative Contracting to a Contract of Co-operation', in D Campbell and P Vincent-Jones, *Contract and Economic Organisation* (Aldershot, 1996), p 14.
7 Collins, 'Competing Norms of Contractual Behaviour', in D Campbell and P Vincent-Jones, *Contract and Economic Organisation* (Aldershot, 1996), p 67.

respecting unwritten expectations of co-operation, then the law must construe the obligations of the parties so that those expectations can be protected.[8]

This chapter examines how the law supports co-operation between the parties. The discussion is divided into three parts: we examine obligations arising during performance of the contract; the handling of adjustments and modifications to the contract; and finally, the rules governing the right to terminate performance of the contract in response to breach of contract.

B.   Performance of the contract

Duties of co-operation can be introduced into contracts through processes of construction of the terms and the development of implied terms. The interpretation of the contract can supplement the express terms with further implied obligations which support co-operation, such as the requirement in contracts for services that the service will be provided with reasonable care and skill.[9] Implied terms may qualify the express contract terms in such a way that strict insistence upon those express rights will itself amount to a breach of contract. The construction of the contract can also emphasize the incentives for the parties to perform their obligations in full and in good time.

1.   Implied terms supporting co-operation

These techniques of construction and interpretation remain faithful to the basic tenets of the classical law of contract, by justifying the imposition of obligations by reference to the implied intentions of the parties. English law lacks a more general principle of law that the parties should perform the contract in good faith, which is common in many other European and common law systems. In the USA, for instance, the Uniform Commercial Code, s 1-203 decrees that, 'Every contract or duty within this act imposes an obligation of good faith in its performance or enforcement'.[10] The apparent contrast is misleading, however, since English courts can achieve similar results on the basis of the interpretation of particular contracts.

The most common justification for implied terms, that they are necessary to give business efficacy to a contract, illustrates this process well. We can understand the idea of business efficacy to mean that, without the supposed implied duty, one party would be prevented from obtaining the full value of his expectation under

8   Macneil, 'The Many Futures of Contracts' (1974) 47 *Southern California Law Review* 691.
9   Supply of Goods and Services Act 1982, s 13; Farnsworth, 'On Trying to Keep One's Promises: The Duty of Best Efforts in Contract Law' (1984) 46 *University Pittsburgh Law Review* 1.
10 Summers, 'Good Faith in General Contract Law and the Sales Provisions of the Uniform Commercial Code' (1968) 54 *Virginia Law Review* 195.

the contract, because the other party is insisting upon limiting his obligations to a strict interpretation of the express terms of the contract. In Chapter 9 we illustrated this style of interpretation of contracts by the decision in *Liverpool City Council v Irwin*.[11] In that contract for the tenancy of a flat in a high-rise apartment building, the landlord resisted the implication of a term requiring it to take reasonable steps to keep the common parts such as staircases and lifts in good repair. The court's acceptance of this term as reasonably necessary to give business efficacy to the contract reveals a disposition to introduce a duty of co-operation. In theory either the landlord or tenant could have arranged for the repair of common parts, but it would obviously be simpler and more efficient (by saving transaction costs) for the landlord to undertake the burden.

As well as the business efficacy test, other implied terms reflect a concern to promote a duty to co-operate during performance of a contract. If, for example, an employee insists upon a 'work to rule', a court will discover that, far from this constituting performance according to the terms of the contract, it in fact constitutes a breach of an implied term of the contract. The implied term will require the employee at least not to frustrate the business objectives of the employer, and perhaps go further to require the exercise of good faith in deploying any discretion in the performance of work.[12] The introduction of the implied term supports the duty to co-operate, which in turn ensures that the contract itself does not become an obstacle to the maximization of the joint values of the parties to it. Similarly, in another type of incomplete contract, the requirements contract under which the purchaser agrees to buy all requirements for a particular product from the other party, the courts interpret the buyer's duty to include a determination of its requirements in good faith, ie honestly, for that was the expectation of how the discretion would be exercised.

2.   Incentives and the order of performance

Where the performance required from each party to a contract takes place on different occasions or over a period of time, in the absence of explicit contractual provisions, the courts must determine the order in which each party should perform, and the duties impliedly undertaken. In a contract of employment, for example, as a rule the employee must carry out his work before the employer's duty to pay wages arises, which obviously encourages an employee to perform his obligations under the contract of employment. At the same time, however, the modern law balances this duty upon the employee to perform first by placing obligations upon the employer to avoid interference with performance of the contract by, for example, failing to supply the employee with work and suitable tools. In this case, provided that the employee is ready and able to work, he is

11 [1977] AC 239, [1976] 2 All ER 39, HL.
12 *Secretary of State for Employment v Associated Society of Locomotive Engineers and Firemen (No 2)* [1972] ICR 19, CA; *British Telecommunications plc v Ticehurst* [1992] ICR 383, CA.

entitled to payment of wages. Through this interplay of ordering performance and implied duties, the modern law reinforces the incentives created by the contract for performance and thereby establishes a co-operative spirit in which each party assists the other's aims and helps to satisfy expectations.

In determining the order of performance, the courts employ a bewildering variety of conceptual distinctions including the division between unilateral and bilateral contracts, the implication of conditions precedent, and the distinction between entire and severable obligations. Whatever the terminology, at bottom a court strives to establish duties of co-operation appropriate to the needs of the parties and the nature of the transaction. By insisting that one party's performance should be completed substantially before the other party falls under a duty to commence performance, the court can ensure that full performance is effected by both sides to the transaction.

(a) UNILATERAL CONTRACTS

In a unilateral contract, by definition the promisee must perform his duties first before payment becomes due. In contrast, no set rule governs the ordering of performance in bilateral contracts. Hence judicial classification of contracts into unilateral and bilateral categories often conceals instrumental reasoning aimed towards establishing principles for the timing of performance conducive to completion of the obligations. In the case of commercial agents working for a commission on sales of a product, for example, the classification of the contract as unilateral relieves the agent from any duty to seek a purchaser, for his entitlement to a commission arises only if he chooses to achieve a sale. Yet at the same time, the agent knows that no payment falls due until a sale has been achieved,[13] which provides the agent with a strong incentive to solicit customers. The incentive becomes even stronger if the employer is entitled to cancel the agency at any time, which is the effect of classifying the contract as unilateral, for until the agent has performed by finding a customer, the agent has not provided consideration for the seller's promise. A similar result can be achieved by a bilateral contract in which the agent is placed under an express or implied obligation to use his best efforts to achieve sales, but the seller may find the threat of complaining about breach of this term less efficacious in achieving full co-operation from the agent than the threat of withholding any remuneration.

(b) CONDITIONS PRECEDENT AND ENTIRE OBLIGATIONS

In bilateral contracts, the courts represent their determinations of the order of performance as a process of construction. They purport to search for conditions precedent, ie express or implied terms which make it clear that the performance

---

13 *Luxor (Eastbourne) Ltd v Cooper* [1941] AC 108, [1941] 1 All ER 33, HL.

by one party is a condition precedent to the duty upon the other to perform. Another way of describing the process of construction uses the classification of entire and severable obligations. When a court concludes that in order to achieve the necessary incentives for co-operation one party ought to complete his performance before obligations on the other party fall due, then the court describes his obligation as entire. Under either classification, until the promisor satisfies the condition precedent or completes his entire performance, the promisor is entitled to neither payment nor damages.

The instrumental character of this conceptual reasoning reveals itself in cases where the courts employ it in order to protect consumers from defective performance. For example, following a credit agreement for the purchase of a car, a buyer avoided liability for default upon his repayments on the ground that the seller's duty to supply the legal documents evidencing change of ownership was a condition precedent to the buyer's performance of his obligations under the credit agreement.[14] Similarly, a contractor who had agreed to install central heating into the defendant's house failed to recover the agreed price on the ground that his work was so unsatisfactory that in reality he had failed to complete the contract, and that fulfilment of the entire obligation was essential before any payment fell due.[15] In both instances, the court manipulates the order of performance to strengthen the position of a consumer/purchaser and to ensure proper performance of the contract.

3. Disclosure of information

In order to obtain the full benefits of a long-term business relation, the parties will often need to exchange information, ideas for innovation, insights of fresh market opportunities, suggestions for improvements in efficiency and so on. Early disclosure of information about risks to the joint enterprise can also avoid or reduce the effects of adverse changes in circumstances. In Chapter 8 we observed that the law is reluctant to impose obligations to disclose information during the formation of contracts. This general stance can be justified by the need to provide incentives for the discovery of commercially valuable information. Unfortunately, this reluctance to require disclosure of information seems to extend to the performance of contracts, when the efficiency considerations point in the opposite direction, especially in contracts incomplete by design.

It is possible that the disclosure of information acquired during performance of a contract might prevent the party in possession of the information from taking commercial advantage of it in another transaction, thereby reducing the incentive to acquire the information. Yet if the sharing of the information improves the return on the investment in the long-term business relation, then efficiency

14 *Bentworth Finance Ltd v Lubert* [1968] 1 QB 680, [1967] 2 All ER 810, CA.
15 *Bolton v Mahadeva* [1972] 2 All ER 1322, [1972] 1 WLR 1009, CA.

considerations indicate that disclosure should be required. For this reason, some contracts such as partnership and agency will be classified for this purpose as fiduciary in character, so that information pertinent to the success of the project must be disclosed. The problem for the courts is to differentiate other types of business relation where a duty to disclose information would enhance the joint value of the venture without removing the incentive to acquire the information.

The classical law of contract normally rejected any duty of disclosure. The courts viewed such a term as in conflict with a more basic right of every individual to go about his business as he chooses, even where the exercise of that right obstructs successful performance of existing contracts.[16] In addition, the courts rejected a duty of disclosure where the information could only be obtained at considerable cost.[17] At most, the courts were prepared to imply a duty to disclose information where that information was exclusively in the possession of one party and, without it, the other party could not perform a central obligation under the contract. If a seller of goods has to acquire an export licence, for instance, it will be an implied term that the buyer must co-operate by telling him the destination of the goods and other information which is required to obtain the licence.[18]

Where the express terms of the contract create an obligation to disclose information, the courts give full effect to the provisions. Express terms of this kind will be inserted into contracts where one party is likely to acquire information which substantially alters the risk undertaken by the other. In a contract of insurance, for instance, the insured may become aware of a new serious risk, and under the policy the insured will be under a duty to disclose the information. Similarly, where security is given for a loan, the contract may require the lender to be notified of risks to the value of the security.[19]

There are recent signs that the courts are reconsidering their restrictive attitude towards implied duties of disclosure of information.[20] In contracts of employment, for instance, both employer and employee owe limited duties of disclosure. An employer must advise employees on safety matters and give proper instructions on how to adopt safe methods of work.[21] The employer must also keep employees informed of any changes in the terms of the contract of employment, such as alterations in the occupational pension scheme.[22] The

16 *Mona Oil Equipment Co v Rhodesian Rlys Ltd* [1949] 2 All ER 1014, QB; *Luxor (Eastbourne) Ltd v Cooper* [1941] AC 108, HL; Burrows, 'Contractual Co-operation and the Implied Term' (1968) 31 *Modern Law Review* 390.
17 *Reid v Rush & Tompkins Group plc* [1989] 3 All ER 228, [1990] 1 WLR 212, CA.
18 *Pound & Co Ltd v Hardy & Co Inc* [1956] AC 588, [1956] 1 All ER 639, HL.
19 Both examples are illustrated in *Bank of Nova Scotia v Hellenic Mutual War Risks Association (Bermuda) Ltd (The Good Luck)* [1992] 1 AC 233, [1991] 3 All ER 1, HL.
20 Collins, 'Implied Duty to Give Information During Performance of Contracts' (1992) 55 *Modern Law Review* 561.
21 *General Cleaning Contractors Ltd v Christmas* [1953] AC 180, [1952] 2 All ER 1110, HL
22 *Scally v Southern Health and Social Services Board* [1992] 1 AC 294, [1991] 4 All ER 563, HL.

employee has a duty to disclose information concerning breaches of contract by subordinate employees,[23] although the implied duty of loyalty does not extend to a duty to disclose information about the employee's own breach of contract.[24] Similarly, if there is a contractual relation between doctor and patient, the doctor will be required to disclose to the patient information concerning treatment such as surgery and its likely effects.[25] In a contract of insurance the pre-contractual duty of disclosure, which arises because this is classified as a contract requiring the utmost good faith during negotiation, can persist by implication during the performance of the contract.[26] These duties of disclosure of information have been developed so far in particular contexts often for the purpose of buttressing other statutory safeguards such as safety standards at work, but their proliferation suggests that the courts will be disposed to recognize implied duties of disclosure in a wide range of contractual relations.

One interesting feature of the developing duty of disclosure during performance of contracts is that it reveals the courts trying to grasp the nature and dynamics of contracts which are incomplete by design. The imposition of a duty of disclosure may be regarded as a legal response to the perception that for such business relations to work successfully both parties must co-operate and build up reciprocal trust. A duty of disclosure in performance is an elementary ingredient in such relationships, one which will be expected according to the informal norms of that business relation, which the law can then endorse in the event of disputes.

Where a court finds that there has been a breach of a duty of disclosure during performance of a contract, the available remedy depends upon the source of the obligation. If the obligation arises from the breach of an implied term of the contract, a breach should permit an award of damages for the resulting losses, and in serious cases may permit termination of the contract. If the failure to disclose information amounts to a breach of the duty of care in tort, again this will permit a remedy in damages. But if the duty to disclose information during performance of the contract arises because the parties are held to be in a fiduciary relation, or because the contract is one like insurance which requires utmost good faith, then breach of the duty merely entitles the injured party to avoid the contract and seek restitution for any benefits conferred under the contract.[27] The duty to disclose information may also arise where one party seeks to rely upon the other's breach of contract to terminate the contract, whilst being aware that the breach of

---

23 *Sybron Corpn v Rochem Ltd* [1984] Ch 112, [1983] 2 All ER 707, CA.

24 *Bell v Lever Bros Ltd* [1932] AC 161, HL; *Horcal Ltd v Gatland* [1984] IRLR 288, CA; Freedland, 'High Trust, Pensions and the Contract of Employment' (1984) 13 *Industrial Law Journal* 25.

25 *Sidaway v Bethlem Royal Hospital* [1985] AC 871, [1985] 1 All ER 643, HL; *Thake v Maurice* [1986] QB 644, [1986] 1 All ER 497, CA

26 *Black King Shipping Corpn v Massie (The Litsion Pride)* [1985] 1 Lloyd's Rep 437; *Banque Keyser Ullmann SA v Skandia (UK) Insurance Co Ltd* [1990] 1 QB 665, sub nom *Banque Financière de la Cité SA v Westgate Insurance Co Ltd* [1989] 2 All ER 952, CA.

27 *Banque Keyser Ullmann SA v Skandia (UK) Insurance Co Ltd* [1990] 1 QB 665, sub nom *Banque Financière de la Cité SA v Westgate Insurance Co Ltd* [1989] 2 All ER 952, CA.

contract is unknown to the party in breach, with the effect that the failure to disclose this information prevents a remedying of the breach. Here the remedy will lie in disallowing termination of the contract on the ground of estoppel or waiver.[28]

4. Control of discretionary powers

To permit adaptation to changing circumstances and to secure the necessary co-operation, the terms of the contract may expressly confer on one or both parties a broad discretionary power to determine the content of performance. In contracts of employment, for instance, a flexibility clause may allow the employer to deploy the worker to any task and to vary hours of work at will. In a contract for a loan, the interest rate may be variable and fixed by the lender at its complete discretion. Although these discretionary powers facilitate the successful performance of the contract over a period of time, such terms create the risk that they may be used opportunistically, in the short-term interest of the power-holder, rather than for the purpose of ensuring that the transaction is wealth-enhancing for both parties. In jurisdictions that observe a general obligation to perform in good faith, the misuse of discretionary powers during performance of contracts can be controlled by the courts. In English law, in the absence of a general good faith standard, the courts have to rely principally on implied terms as the basis for intervention.[29]

In some instances of the misuse of discretionary powers, however, control by the courts may be assisted by statute. For terms that confer a discretion on the promisor to vary its own obligations under the contract, the fairness of the discretionary power itself can be examined by a court. The Unfair Contract Terms Act 1977, s 3(2) includes, under a test of reasonableness, a standard form contract in which a term purports to give one party the right 'to render a contractual performance substantially different from that which was reasonably expected of him'. In *Timeload Ltd v British Telecommunications plc*,[30] a contract for the supply of a telephone service, the main terms of the contract indicated that the service would not be terminated without good reason, but another clause authorised the supplier to withdraw the service on giving one month's notice at its complete discretion. The Court of Appeal accepted that it was at least arguable that s 3(2) applied to the termination clause, because it undermined the reasonable expectations created by the remainder of the contract, which also reflected the regulatory regime governing telecommunication services.

---

28 *Tradax Export SA v Dorada Cia Naviera SA (The Lutetian)* [1982] 2 Lloyd's Rep 140.

29 Beatson, 'Public Law Influences in Contract Law', in J Beatson and D Friedmann (eds), *Good Faith and Fault in Contract Law* (Oxford, 1995), p 263; Collins, 'Discretionary Powers in Contracts', in D Campbell, H Collins, J Wightman (eds), *Implicit Dimensions of Contracts* (Oxford, 2003), ch 8.

30 *Timeload Ltd v British Telecommunications plc* [1995] EMLR 459, CA; C Scott, 'The Juridification of Regulatory Relations in the UK Utilities Sectors', in J Black, P Mulchinski, P Walker (eds), *Commercial Regulation and Judicial Review* (Oxford, 1998), p 19, at p 42.

Clauses in standard form consumer contracts that confer a broad discretion on the supplier to vary its own obligations are likely to be caught by the test of fairness in the Unfair Terms in Consumer Contracts Regulations 1999.[31] In particular, Sch 2, para 1(k) describes as probably unfair a term which enables the supplier 'to alter unilaterally without a valid reason any characteristic of the product or service to be provided.'

For terms that confer a power on one party to vary the obligations of the other, the 1977 Act probably does not apply, since it is concerned with exclusion clauses and analogous provisions that limit the power-holder's obligations. The Regulations may apply, however, to consumer standard form contracts that enable the supplier to vary the consumer's obligations. Schedule 2, para 1(j) lists as potentially unfair a contractual power that enables the supplier to alter unilaterally without a reason specified in the contract any terms of the contract, and para 1(l) invalidates clauses that permit price increases after the contract has been concluded without granting the consumer the right to cancel the order.

In the absence of relevant statutory provisions, the courts use implied terms to control the misuse of contractual powers during the performance of the contract. These implied terms are usually based upon a construction of the contract as a whole, so that where a particular exercise of discretion seems to conflict with the scheme envisaged in the contract, even though the discretion is expressed as unfettered in the contract, an implied limitation on its use can be inferred in order to protect the reasonable expectation of the subject of the power.[32] In *Mallone v BPB Industries plc*,[33] a managing director received substantial compensation on being dismissed for under-performance, but claimed to be entitled in addition to some share options. The company had purported to deny any share options under a term of the contract which, having conferred on the directors the power to grant an employee an appropriate proportion of share options in view of the employee's length of service and taking into account any misconduct, also stated that the amount of share options should depend on whatever grant 'the directors in their absolute discretion determine'. The claimant succeeded in a claim for compensation against the company's decision to award no share options. The Court of Appeal held that the apparently absolute discretion was limited by an implied term that required the power to be exercised honestly, not capriciously or for an improper motive, and not irrationally in the sense that no reasonable employer would have exercised the power in this way. The decision to award no stock options was held to be irrational because the option scheme implied that this deferred remuneration would be assessed by reference to good performance and loyalty.

---

31 SI 1999/2083; see also the Package Travel, Package Holidays and Package Tours Regulations 1992, SI 1992/3288, regs 12, 14.
32 *Equitable Life Assurance Society v Hyman* [2002] 1 AC 408, [2000] 3 All ER 961, HL
33 [2002] EWCA Civ 126, [2002] ICR 1045, CA.

A similar test of good faith and irrationality has also been applied to the exercise of powers that permit the power-holder to vary the other party's obligations. It is common practice in long-term loans to agree to variable rates of interest, which protect both parties against major fluctuations in the market. The contracts typically confer the power to vary the interest rate exclusively on the creditor bank, at its unfettered discretion, on short notice. In *Paragon Finance plc v Nash*, the claimants argued that this power had been misused, so that they had been required for a long time to pay substantially above the market rates of interest for secured loans, and that they were unable to find a different lender owing to the fact that their repayments had fallen into arrears. The Court of Appeal applied the tests of dishonesty and irrationality: in order to be a breach of contract the exercise of the discretion to vary the interest rates had to be perverse, arbitrary or capricious, not simply unreasonable or unfair. Dyson LJ justified the application of this test of irrationality on the ground that it was 'necessary in order to give effect to the reasonable expectations of the parties.'[34] The claim failed, however, because the bank had acted reasonably to protect its own business interests.

Taken together, these statutory protections and implied terms indicate that, although English law lacks a general requirement of good faith in performance, a similar protection for the reasonable expectations of the subject of a discretionary power can be constructed by the courts. The common law test is not whether the power-holder acted reasonably, but whether it acted dishonestly, capriciously or irrationally, and in that sense not in good faith.

C. Modifications to the contract

In the light of changing market conditions or fresh information, the parties to a contract may wish to vary their obligations under it. One party should not be permitted to make changes in the terms unilaterally, for this action would permit opportunistic variations in its favour. For example, an employer is not permitted to reduce the wages of employees unilaterally.[35] But there is no objection in principle to consensual variation. On the contrary, in a long-term business relation mutual adjustments of obligations will almost certainly be necessary in order to maximize the opportunities presented by the business relation.[36] Indeed, a refusal to renegotiate prices in the light of altered market circumstances might

---

34 [2001] EWCA Civ 1466, [2002] 1 WLR 685 at 703. There is a specific exception for variable interest rates in Sch 3, para 2(b) of the Unfair Terms in Consumer Contracts Regulations 1999, SI 1999/2083, and under the Consumer Credit (Total Charge for Credit) Regulations 1980, SI 1980/51.

35 *Rigby v Ferodo Ltd* [1988] ICR 29, HL.

36 Macneil, 'Contracts: Adjustment of Long-Term Economic Relations under Classical, Neoclassical, and Relational Contract Law' (1978) 72 *Northwestern University Law Review* 854; Goldberg, 'Relational Exchange' (1980) 23 *American Behavioral Scientist* 337.

be regarded by the party who made the request to modify the terms as a breach of trust and could lead subsequently to a damaging decision to terminate all future business dealings.[37]

The classical law, however, placed considerable obstacles in the way of modification of contracts. It viewed with suspicion any claim that the original contractual agreement was not binding on the parties. The ground for this suspicion was the observation that debtors are frequently inclined to avoid their contractual obligations by suggesting that some understanding or accommodation has been reached which exculpates them from strict performance of the original contract. Moreover, even if the debtor could prove the existence of such an agreement to modify the original contract, there remained the doubt whether the creditor had truly consented to the variation, or, as often proved the case, the creditor had been forced to consent because of commercial pressure or concern about the debtor's creditworthiness. In response to these justified concerns about modifications of contracts, the classical law developed a test for their validity which proved unnecessarily obstructive to genuine consensual variations of contracts.

1.   Obstructions to modification

The classical law decided to judge the validity of modifications of contracts by reference to the same rules as those governing formation of contracts.[38] It insisted that variations could only be binding if they satisfied the requirements of agreement and consideration, and, if necessary, they complied with any requirements of formalities for the formation of contracts, such as the need for the contract to be in writing. In addition, any further grounds for the invalidity of contracts such as misrepresentation, duress and undue influence, were also applied to modifications of existing contracts. Although these strict requirements for the enforceability of modifications of contracts could be complied with, so that variation was possible, they set a series of traps for the unwary, which often served merely to frustrate the intentions of the parties to the contract. Even worse, the legal rules could become the instrument of fraud in the sense that one party might employ the rules opportunistically in order to invalidate a perfectly consensual adjustment.

(a)   AGREEMENT

The classical law normally requires an express agreement for any modification of contractual obligations. This serves as an important bulwark against unilateral

---

37 Goldberg and Erickson, 'Quantity and Price Adjustment in Long-term Contracts: A Case Study of Petroleum Coke' (1987) 30 *Journal of Law and Economics* 369, at p 396.

38 Stoljar, 'The Modification of Contracts' (1957) 35 *Canadian Bar Review* 485.

variations which detrimentally affect the other party to the contract. The problem which occurs with the requirement of an express agreement between the parties to modify their obligations is that often there will be a degree of informality and paucity of communication between the parties, so that it becomes impossible to say that agreement was reached, even though both parties acted as if an understanding were in place.

This informality will often occur when one party commits a technical breach of the contract, but the other, knowing of breach, does not object, but rather continues to act as if the contract was being properly performed. For example, in *Panoutsos v Raymond Hadley Corpn of New York*,[39] the seller agreed to make several deliveries of flour in return for the buyer paying for each shipment by a confirmed banker's credit (ie an irrevocable credit arrangement which the seller can draw upon at the buyer's bank). The buyer in fact paid for each shipment, but failed, to the seller's knowledge, to open the necessary credit arrangement. The seller continued to perform the contract for a time, but subsequently purported to terminate the contract on the ground of the buyer's breach of the requirement to open a credit facility. The court was unable to find that any modification of the contract had been expressly agreed, so it was compelled to conclude that the original contract stood. Fortunately the court prevented this opportunistic reliance upon the legal requirement of an express agreement by drawing upon the doctrine of waiver of breach or affirmation of the contract. The court implied from the seller's conduct a promise not to rely upon the breach, on which promise the buyer had acted, so that in conclusion the court could deny the seller's right to terminate the contract for breach. But this instrumental use of the doctrine of waiver of breach should not disguise the point that in effect the court modified the contract on the basis of an informal understanding which was little more than an implied promise that had been acted upon.

(b) CONSIDERATION

A similar pattern emerges in connection with the requirement of fresh consideration to support the variation. Although in many instances a modification of a contract will result in a mutual adjustment of obligations, with the consequence that the doctrine of consideration is satisfied because each party expects to gain something from the alteration, this beneficial result will not always be the case. In some instances, one party may agree to pay more for what he or she is already entitled to under the contract. In another scenario, one party may agree to receive less than full contractual performance. In either case, it will be difficult to satisfy the benefit and detriment concept of the doctrine of consideration, for it appears that the party whose rights have been altered has received nothing in return: he or she either receives less for the same price, or the same performance for an increased price.

39 [1917] 2 KB 473, CA.

No doubt with the aim of creditor protection in mind, the courts usually concluded in such cases that the modification of the contract was unenforceable because of the absence of fresh consideration. In *Stilk v Myrick*,[40] which involved a claim by a sailor for extra wages on the faith of a promise by the captain during the ship's voyage, Campbell's report of the case, which has since been treated as authoritative, states that the court rejected the claim on the ground that the captain's promise to pay more was unsupported by fresh consideration in the form of additional duties to be performed by the sailor. Similarly, with respect to a promise to accept less, the case of *Foakes v Beer*[41] has been treated as firm authority that a creditor's promise to accept less money than is due will also be unenforceable for want of consideration.

These decisions frustrate the intentions of the parties in cases of genuine adjustments of obligations. The promise to pay more may reflect a recognition that the original contract price was based upon a mistake about the burdens entailed, or an error in drafting the terms of the contract so that they do not fully accord with the intentions of the parties, or it may be a response to changing circumstances which render performance more onerous. A disadvantageous promise may be given by the promisor in anticipation of future advantageous transactions that may come his way, especially if the variation serves to keep a valued customer. The agreement to modify the contract may also reflect a reluctance to harm the promisor's business in the long run, such that it might drive the other party out of business, as in the case where the contract envisages a long-term production relation such as a franchise or a requirements contract. Moreover, if the promisor is in a position to pass on increased costs, the variation in the contract price may not cause any significant disadvantage; this facility may explain a disposition to be flexible about the price, provided that due performance is completed on time. Similarly, the decision to accept a lesser payment may be the result of a wise commercial calculation of long-term business interests and business reputation, combined with a realistic assessment of the chances of being paid in full without considerable legal costs. For all these reasons, even disadvantageous variations may be perfectly fair and sensible within the context commercial transactions.

Some techniques were available for avoiding the potential for opportunism presented by the requirement of fresh consideration. Trivial alterations in the contractual obligations could be regarded as amounting to fresh consideration. A valid modification could be effected by an alteration in the time or place of payment, or the mode of payment such as by cheque rather than cash. But the courts will not always be drawn into such absurdities except for the purpose of

---

40 (1809) 2 Camp 317, 6 Esp 129. Halson, 'The Modification of Contractual Obligations' (1989) *Current Legal Problems* 111.
41 (1884) 9 App Cas 605, HL.

defeating opportunism. In *D & C Builders Ltd v Rees*,[42] the Court of Appeal was not persuaded that the plaintiff builder's agreement to accept a cheque for a lesser sum than the debt owed, instead of payment in cash, could be described as fresh consideration to support a promise to accept less, no doubt because the facts of the case revealed a degree of coercion rather than a consensual agreement.

A more complicated technique for discovering fresh consideration asserts that the original contract has been terminated by agreement, and that a completely new contract with different terms has replaced it. Although this analysis overcomes any problems of consideration, it often amounts to an improbable interpretation of the simple facts of the case, where all that has happened is that one party has agreed to a disadvantageous modification of one of the terms of the original contract. The doctrine of consideration as a test for the enforceability of modifications proved a blunt instrument by which to distinguish between instances where the debtor was compelling the creditor reluctantly to agree to an inferior deal, and those where the creditor was genuinely willing to arrange some accommodation.

(c) FORMALITIES

The classical law also insisted upon the application of the requirements of formalities to modifications, as well as to formation, of contracts. This presented a serious trap for the unwary, for if the law required a contract to be in writing, then an orally agreed modification could have no effect. The only exception to this rule which the courts endorsed was that an oral agreement could terminate or rescind a contract entirely. An example of this trap and the absurd consequences which it produced is found in *Morris v Baron*.[43] This case concerned a contract for a sale of goods which at that time had to be evidenced in writing. Following a dispute between the parties, they reached an oral settlement on slightly different terms. But the court declared that this oral modification was unenforceable. Either the oral variation was ineffective to change the original contract because of the absence of writing, or the oral agreement was effective to rescind the original contract, but it could not create any new binding agreement because of the absence of formalities. Thus, the court concluded that either the original contract was binding still, or, and this was the final outcome in the House of Lords, there was no contract at all.

This astonishing result exemplifies the problem of the application of the rules requiring formalities in the formation of contracts to subsequent modifications: because these modifications will often be agreed informally, without regard to legal niceties, the parties may end up with their whole transaction confounded and invalidated by the courts.

42 [1966] 2 QB 617, [1965] 3 All ER 837, CA.
43 [1918] AC 1, HL.

2.   Modern flexibility

The classical law governing modification reveals a series of obstructions calculated to defeat the genuine intentions of the parties and to create the potential for opportunism. The underlying mistake of the classical law was the failure to realize that long-term business interests could lead rational self-interested parties to agree informally to disadvantageous adjustments. Commercial contractors expect a degree of 'give and take' during performance. They will offer indulgences, refrain from pedantic insistence upon strict contractual rights, and seek genuine accommodations in cases of difficulty. They do so in order to co-operate, so that the contract is performed, and to preserve goodwill in long-term informal commercial relations. This mistake of the classical law then led to the insistence that any modification should comply with the rules governing formation of contracts, which were designed to ensure that the variation complied with short-term economic interest.

In the modern law, however, we can observe a series of adjustments to the rules which permit the courts to differentiate between cases where the requirement of co-operation demands strict observance of the original contractual rights and those where the parties have modified their agreement with a view to long-term business interests. The traditional obstacles to modification have been evaded or diluted in these latter cases. The law appears complex and even inconsistent until it is appreciated that this process of differentiation requires divergent handling of cases of modification.

(a)   CONSENT AND CHANGE OF POSITION

In a business relation which is sustained by trust, where the parties undertake incomplete obligations, they expect minor adjustments to obligations. In some instances the variation will be the result of a deliberate agreement, but in others it may be arranged casually or even evolve out of an alteration of practice without either party being aware that it involves a breach of the original contract. A seller may be lulled into believing that the buyer does not object to a minor alteration in the type of goods or method of delivery, especially if this practice continues for some time without objection. Similarly, a unilateral increase of wages by an employer is unlikely to be met by a formal letter of acceptance by the employee, but rather the employee indicates assent by the conduct of continuing to work without raising objection. Instead of seeking an express agreement to the variation, the modern law can be satisfied by either an express promise which is acted upon or conduct which can reasonably be interpreted to indicate an implied promise and a corresponding acceptance of a change in the contractual relation through conduct involving a change of position. This flexibility in detecting consent to a variation is achieved either by a dilution of the traditional requirements of offer and acceptance, or by the use of the doctrine of equitable estoppel.

For express promises to vary the contract which are then acted upon, the courts can either find agreement through conduct or determine the case under the principles of equitable estoppel. The latter principles were adopted by Denning J in *Central London Property Trust Ltd v High Trees House Ltd*.[44] The landlord made an express promise to accept a reduced rent for a period of time, and, since this was acted upon by the tenant by paying the reduced rent, it was unnecessary to point to an express acceptance of the landlord's offer.

In the absence of an express promise, the courts may still with difficulty infer agreement from the conduct of the parties or seek to vindicate the modification through estoppel. The danger here is that the construction of implied modifications runs the risk of unilateral imposition of opportunistic variations. In the leading case on implied agreements, *Paal Wilson & Co A/S v Partenreederei Hannah Blumenthal (The Hannah Blumenthal)*,[45] the contract for the sale of a ship contained an arbitration clause which governed any disputes. The buyers, dissatisfied in some respects with the ship, initiated arbitration proceedings in 1972. Apart from some exchanges of letters, however, little happened until 1980 when the buyers purported to fix a date for the arbitration proceedings. The sellers then sought to establish before the court that (amongst other points) the contract had been modified to the extent that the buyers had agreed to abandon their claim and the arbitration proceedings. The obstacle to this argument was the absence of any express agreement to abandon the claim. The sellers had to rely upon the conduct of the buyers, or more precisely their inactivity for eight years, in order to establish the modification. The sellers failed to establish the modification on the facts of the case, because there was evidence indicating that the sellers knew that the buyers were still intending to proceed with the claim. But the tests of modification employed by the House of Lords indicate an acceptance of a less formal test of agreement. It was sufficient, said Lord Brandon, that:

> the conduct of B, as evinced towards A, has been such as to lead A reasonably to believe that B has abandoned the contract, even though it has not in fact been B's intention to do so, and that A has significantly altered his position in reliance on that belief.

The emphasis in this judgment lies upon the three elements of (i) conduct which implies a promise to modify; and (ii) which induces a reasonable belief in such a promise to modify; and (iii) which is acted upon by the promisee. The conduct may consist almost entirely in a failure to act, as in the case of a failure to complain

---

44 [1947] KB 130, KB.
45 [1983] 1 AC 854, [1983] 1 All ER 34, HL.

within a reasonable time about late deliveries or minor defects,[46] although mere silence alone can only be treated as equivocal.[47]

Similar principles apply to cases such as *Hughes v Metropolitan Rly Co*,[48] which have been decided on the basis of equitable estoppel. Here a landlord gave the tenant of his property six months' notice to effect repairs as he was entitled to do under the lease. The parties then entered into negotiations for sale of the property. But when these negotiations failed, the landlord purported to exercise a forfeiture clause under the lease to evict the tenant on the ground that the repairs had not been carried out in the six-month period. The House of Lords gave relief from forfeiture on the ground that the negotiations for sale of the property led the tenant reasonably to believe that the contractual right to forfeiture would not be enforced. In effect the court found that the landlord had made an implied promise which had been acted upon by the tenant failing to complete repairs pending negotiation of the sale. By negotiating for the sale of the land to the tenant, the court was able to infer from this conduct that the strict contractual rights of the landlord and tenant relation were temporarily suspended, for there was no point in the tenant effecting the repairs if he was shortly to acquire the property himself.

The reasonable belief criterion makes it clear that the conduct need not in fact be based upon an intention to modify the contract. What is necessary is that it is reasonable for the other contracting party to interpret that conduct as amounting to an implied promise to modify the agreement. It did not matter, therefore, that neither the landlord in *Hughes v Metropolitan Rly Co*, nor the buyer in *Paal Wilson & Co A/S v Parten-reederei Hannah Blumenthal (The Hannah Blumenthal)*, intended to modify the contract; the crucial issue was whether the other party had formed a reasonable belief that such an implied promise was being made. In the former case, the tenant did have reasonable grounds for belief in the implied promise, but in the latter case the buyer had sufficient indication from the intermittent correspondence that the claim was not abandoned to prevent it from reasonably supposing that an implied promise of abandonment had been made.

(b) A TEST OF ENFORCEABILITY?

A question which remains unsettled in the development of the modern law governing modification concerns the extent to which it requires a test of enforceability in addition to the diluted requirement of agreement described above. In other words, is there still a requirement of consideration before a

---

46 *Société Italo-Belge pour le Commerce et l'Industrie SA v Palm and Vegetable Oils (Malaysia) Sdn Bhd (The Post Chaser)* [1982] 1 All ER 19, [1981] 2 Lloyd's Rep 695, QB.

47 *Allied Marine Transport Ltd v Vale do Rio Navegacao SA (The Leonidas D)* [1983] 3 All ER 737, [1984] 1 WLR 1.

48 (1877) 2 App Cas 439, HL.

modification will be enforceable?[49] The importance of the question in practice should not be exaggerated. In most instances the test of consideration will be satisfied, because both parties give up or gain some rights. In addition, some modifications amount to a rescission of the original contract and its replacement or abandonment, and here again no doubts arise about consideration. But in the cases highlighted earlier of promises to pay more for the same performance, and promises to accept a lesser sum for the same contractual obligations, the difficulty created by the classical law of finding consideration persists. The legal doctrine seems to have taken an unnecessarily complex and even absurd turn in these contexts. It divides the problem into two parts and deals with them quite separately.

With respect to promises to pay more for the same contractual performance, the cases stick to the test of consideration in order to determine the enforceability of the modification. But the definition of consideration has become subtly altered in order to take into account the long-term commercial advantages of superficially adverse variations. In *Williams v Roffey Bros and Nicholls (Contractors) Ltd*,[50] the plaintiff carpenter agreed with the defendant building contractor to perform work on the refurbishment of 27 flats in return for a fixed sum of £20,000. The plaintiff fell behind schedule in the work, which concerned the defendant because under the main contract for the building works a clause reduced payment for late completion. The defendant, partly out of recognition that the original price was too low for the plaintiff to be commercially viable, and partly as an inducement to speed up the work, promised to pay the plaintiff an extra amount of £10,300, at the rate of £575 per completed flat. The plaintiff completed work on eight flats, but the defendant only paid £1,500 more, so the plaintiff sued for the balance under the modified contract. The Court of Appeal overcame the objection that the promise to pay the additional sum was not supported by consideration because the plaintiff did not undertake any new obligations, by arguing that the defendant had secured other commercial benefits through the promise. These benefits included changing work practices so that at least some of the flats were completed, avoiding or reducing the penalty for delay, and avoiding the expense and difficulty of having to make alternative contractual arrangements. Once the courts acknowledge these commercial factors as constituting consideration, the doctrine ceases to be a bar to enforceability in those cases where the promisor has good commercial reasons for agreeing to a modification. But it is important to notice how the doctrine of consideration has been manipulated to achieve that aim. The commercial benefits obtained by the contractor were not actions requested by the carpenter in return for the payment of a higher price. Nor were

49 Hillman, 'Contract Modification under the Restatement (Second) of Contracts' (1982) 67 *Cornell Law Review* 680; Uniform Commercial Code, s 2-209 dispenses with the requirement of consideration.
50 [1991] 1 QB 1, [1990] 1 All ER 512, CA.

the benefits ones which would not have been obtained by the contractor in any case if the carpenter had performed his original agreement properly.

The courts have treated promises to accept less in return for the same performance rather differently. Since the decision in *Central London Property Trust Ltd v High Trees House Ltd*,[51] it has been accepted that a promise to make such an indulgence will be enforceable if acted upon. Thus the doctrine of consideration seems to be regarded as irrelevant in such cases. The promise by the landlord to accept a reduced rent for a period of time was binding, Denning J suggested in that case, because the tenants had acted upon it, not because they had provided consideration for it. By the time the action was brought, however, the flats were full and the condition of the promise was satisfied, so that the landlords could insist upon reversion to the original higher rent on reasonable notice. To justify this evasion of the requirement of consideration for modifications of contracts, Denning J relied upon the doctrine of equitable or promissory estoppel. But in so doing he stretched that doctrine considerably. In particular, estoppel had usually been confined to statements of fact which were relied upon rather than promises with respect to the future. In addition, estoppels are normally binding only if they induce detrimental reliance, but in this case the tenants could not realistically claim they had suffered any detriment from being permitted to pay a lower rent. But Denning J was content to brush these difficulties aside in order to circumvent the application of the doctrine of consideration to modifications of contracts, where such application would clearly defeat the intentions of the parties in the pursuit of their long-term business interests.

This bifurcation of approach apparently requires a radically different treatment of the two kinds of modification: promises to pay more on the one hand, which require consideration; and on the other promises to accept less, which do not. One justification for this complexity claims that the idea of promissory estoppel in the *High Trees* case must be confined to defences to claims rather than itself constitute a new cause of action. This limitation is insisted upon, for otherwise the principle of promissory estoppel might indirectly abolish the requirement of consideration in the formation of contracts. The limitation is often described metaphorically by stating that promissory estoppel only functions 'as a shield and not a sword'.[52] Accordingly, it is suggested that, whereas in the context of promises to accept less, the enforcement of the promise merely functions as a defence to a claim under the original contract, in the case of promises to pay more, promissory estoppel is not available, for this use would amount to the employment of a sword to enforce a new claim for money or additional performance.

51 [1947] KB 130, KB.
52 Birkett LJ, *Combe v Combe* [1951] 2 KB 215, [1951] 1 All ER 767, CA.

In my view, however, this justification lacks any real merit. We should recognize that in both instances, the issue is one of the modification of contracts, for which the doctrine of consideration is not properly suited. In an important sense all cases of contractual modification concern defences to a cause of action, ie enforcement of the original contract, so that to distinguish between the different types of modification as if there is some principle at stake is wholly misleading. If any test of enforceability is required other than the presence of an express or implied agreement, this test should reflect the reasons why such modifications are agreed and should be binding. We have noted that collateral commercial advantages lie at the heart of the reasons for agreeing to these modifications. The test should look for advantages, such as the preservation of a commercial relationship because of mutual economic dependence, the possibility of continuing contractual relations with a valued customer, the avoidance of possible harms such as loss of confidence or reputation and contingent financial penalties under other contracts. The revised doctrine of consideration in *Williams v Roffey Bros and Nicholls (Contractors) Ltd* examines these matters and so should be preferred and applied to all modifications, if a test of enforceability is required at all. It is certainly more appropriate than the approach contained in the *High Trees* case, which looks for action in reliance upon the promise. This idea of reliance, I argued above, is in fact an element of the test of an informal agreement rather than an independent test of enforceability. The action in reliance confirms that the promisee accepts the modification, for it is important to prevent unilateral alteration of terms of contracts.

It might be better, however, to drop this requirement of a test of enforceability altogether and concentrate instead on the questions of whether there was an express or implied agreement, and if so, was it invalidated on the ground of economic duress? The essential question posed for the courts is not whether there is a binding contract, but what are its current terms in the light of purported subsequent modifications? The question of content should be judged by reference to the express or implied agreement, and the question of the validity of this agreement should be considered in the light of the normal factors which vitiate consent such as fraud and duress.

(c) ECONOMIC DURESS

The reason why it may be possible to drop a test of enforceability for modifications altogether is that the law of duress has evolved to handle the difficult issues of coercion and opportunism in the context of variations of contract. The doctrine of economic duress, as it has been developed, examines the question of whether collateral benefits or long-term business interests motivated the agreement to vary the contract much more closely than the doctrine of consideration, and infers from their absence that the modification was coerced. Any further test of enforceability seems to be an unnecessary duplication in the context of modifications.

Although the doctrine of economic duress applies in principle to the formation of contracts as well, the potential for opportunism is greatly enhanced in the context of modifications, since there is often a real danger of exploitation of a bilateral monopoly. Once a party has become locked into a particular agreement, and perhaps performed a substantial part of the contractual undertaking, he or she may be vulnerable to coercive claims for additional advantages because the costs of terminating the contract far exceed the additional demands. This predicament will occur especially when the character of performance requires a particular kind of investment unique to the customer, so that the only way in which these 'sunk costs' can be recovered is through performance by the customer. Similarly, the customer may become peculiarly dependent upon the supplier where no other sources of supply are available in the time available. For example, in *North Ocean Shipping Co v Hyundai Construction Co (The Atlantic Baron)*,[53] the buyers under a shipbuilding contract had in anticipation of performance leased the ship from a certain date, so that, when the shipbuilders demanded additional payment before delivery (in order to compensate them for devaluation in the currency of payment), the buyers were compelled to agree to the higher price since they could not find a substitute ship of the same specifications in the short time available. Another example occurs when a consumer has a valid claim for payment against a business, as in the case of a claim on an insurance policy, and the insurer uses its advantage of business skills to compel a disadvantageous settlement.[54] These examples indicate that apparent modifications of contracts need to be invalidated where these characteristics of a bilateral monopoly exist, in order to prevent opportunistic advantage-taking, but in the absence of such factors, there should be no reason to doubt the validity of the agreed modification.

The task confronting the courts is to distinguish between genuine, co-operative accommodations during the lifetime of an agreement, and coerced modifications which seek to exploit a strong bargaining position. The law of economic duress has developed rapidly in recent years, yet it still remains unequal to this task, because it has failed to make explicit all the relevant considerations to making this distinction.

The leading case, *Pao On v Lau Yiu Long*,[55] however, makes a useful start in the right direction. The plaintiffs sold their company to the defendants' company in exchange for shares in the defendants' company, but the plaintiffs agreed not to sell 60% of those shares for a year in order to avoid causing a sudden drop in value of those shares. In a collateral agreement the defendants in person agreed to buy back 60% of the shares at or before the end of the year for a fixed price, so that the plaintiffs would not suffer from any drop in the value of the shares. Subsequently

---

53 [1979] QB 705, [1978] 3 All ER 1170, QB; cf *Atlas Express Ltd v Kafco Ltd* [1989] QB 833, [1989] 1 All ER 641, QB.
54 *Dillon v Baltic Shipping Co (The Mikhail Lermontov)* [1991] 2 Lloyd's Rep 155, CA.
55 [1980] AC 614, [1979] 3 All ER 65, PC; cf *Atlas Express Ltd v Kafco Ltd* [1989] QB 833, [1989] 1 All ER 641, QB.

the plaintiffs realized that, if the shares rose in price, they would not be able to take advantage of this increase, because the collateral agreement was effectively a future sale at a fixed price. So the plaintiffs refused to proceed with the main contract, unless the collateral agreement was cancelled and replaced by a promise of an indemnity if, at the end of the year, the shares were sold below a fixed price. The question before the court was whether the indemnity, which was agreed, was a binding contract. The Privy Council made extraordinarily heavy weather over the difficulty of finding consideration, apparently missing the point that the consideration supporting the indemnity could be found in the agreement to cancel the collateral contract, a common technique in cases of modification as we have noted. But then came the crucial question of whether the plaintiffs had only secured the indemnity by means of impermissible economic duress by threatening not to proceed with the main contract for the sale of their company. In deciding that no economic duress had occurred, Lord Scarman stated the doctrine of economic duress in the following terms:

> Duress, whatever form it takes, is a coercion of the will so as to vitiate consent . . . In determining whether there was a coercion of the will such that there was no true consent, it is material to inquire whether the person alleged to have been coerced did or did not protest; whether, at the time he was allegedly coerced into making the contract, he did or did not have an alternative course open to him such as an adequate legal remedy; whether he was independently advised; and whether after entering the contract he took steps to avoid it.

We must doubt, for reasons discussed in Chapter 8, whether it is helpful to conceive of duress as causing an involuntary act rather than forcing a choice between two unpalatable courses of action. But it is clear that Lord Scarman does not take the idea of an involuntary act too seriously, for the factors which he lists as relevant, such as the absence of an adequate legal remedy, merely highlight the extent to which the choice was constrained.

What I suggest is the crucial factor in this case, and one which can be defended in principle, is a situation equivalent to a bilateral monopoly, combined with evidence of advantage being taken of this superior bargaining position.[56] The failure of the claim of economic duress in this case can be accounted for in part because of the absence of a strong degree of bilateral monopoly, but mostly because the plaintiffs did not seek to take undue advantage of their position. To some extent the defendants were constrained in their bargaining position, for they were worried that if the main contract was cancelled or broken then there might be a loss of business confidence in their company. But even if this concern was enough to provide the plaintiffs with the occasion for opportunism, it could

---

56 This is a way of describing what is called in economic analysis opportunism or strategic behaviour: Aivazian, Trebilcock, Penny, 'The Law of Contract Modifications: The Uncertain Quest for a Benchmark of Enforceability' (1984) 22 *Osgoode Hall Law Journal* 173.

not seriously be argued that they had sought to take advantage of it. In reality they had made a mistake about the initial form of the collateral contract, which did not accord with their intentions. The replacement indemnity contract fitted their original intentions, and at the same time did not expose the defendants to any greater risk of loss. Indeed, as events turned out, the shares did drop in price, so that ironically the original collateral agreement would have satisfied the plaintiffs' interests, and so they need not have created all the legal problems which their simple modification engendered. What influenced the Privy Council decisively against a finding of economic duress was, I suggest, the simple fact that the modification did not impose any additional losses on the defendants and so no advantage had been taken of them.

I am suggesting, therefore, that, for economic duress to invalidate modifications of contracts, the court should, and probably does without stating so explicitly, ascertain first, whether the situation amounts to a bilateral monopoly in effect, and, secondly, whether or not that bargaining position was exploited opportunistically for gain at the expense of the other party. These criteria will explain how in other cases the court reached the different conclusion that economic duress had been exercised.

For example, it will be recalled that in *North Ocean Shipping Co v Hyundai Construction Co (The Atlantic Baron)*,[57] the shipbuilders demanded an extra 10% payment to compensate them for devaluation of the currency of payment. Because ships take a considerable time to build and they may not be readily available on the open market with the right specifications, there was certainly a possibility that the shipbuilders were in a strong bargaining position. On the other hand, the buyers might have had good reason to agree to a higher price in order to keep the favourable charter which they had arranged for the vessel, and in order to preserve amicable relations for future dealings, much like the main contractors in *Williams v Roffey Bros and Nicholls (Contractors) Ltd*,[58] where no economic duress was established. But what was decisive against the shipbuilders was the clear gain which they had seized against the buyers by increasing the price. They transferred the risk of currency fluctuations onto the buyer, despite having agreed initially to accept this risk by a fixed price contract in a particular currency. This fact distinguishes *The Atlantic Baron* from *Williams v Roffey Bros and Nicholls (Contractors) Ltd*, for in the latter case there was evidence that the main contractors realized that the original price was unrealistically low, and that they were prepared to make some accommodation to avoid driving the sub-contractor out of business.

Similarly, an agreement to accept lesser payment will not necessarily be evidence of economic duress, for there may be good reason to reduce the price. In the *High Trees* case, for example, the landlord's motive for reducing the rent was

57 [1979] QB 705, [1978] 3 All ER 1170, QB.
58 [1991] 1 QB 1, [1990] 1 All ER 512, CA.

inextricably tied up with the fact that the tenant was a wholly-owned subsidiary company of the landlord company, so there would be no commercial advantage to the group of companies to insist upon the original rent. But it will often be the case that an agreement to accept a lesser sum will have been extracted through exploitation of a strong bargaining position. Hence in *D & C Builders Ltd v Rees*,[59] the English Court of Appeal declined to enforce an agreement between a small firm of builders in financial straits and a wealthy creditor for whom they had done work to accept £300 instead of the £480 due under the original contract in the face of a threat of being paid nothing at all, which would have forced them into insolvency. Lord Denning MR justified this decision on the ground that it would be inequitable to enforce the modification. The result might have been different, however, if the court found evidence that the original agreement was overpriced, or that the builders had good commercial reasons to wish to benefit the creditor.

To conclude this discussion of economic duress, we must recognize its central importance to the law of modifications. Without it, the flexibility of the modern law would run the risk of permitting opportunistic gains during the performance of contracts. Although it is correct in a sense to view economic duress as a factor which vitiates consent, for we have seen that express or implied consent by both parties is the essential requirement for effective modification, it is wrong to confine economic duress to instances of involuntary acts as Lord Scarman seems to suggest. Behind this rhetoric of the 'coercion of the will' lies in fact a flexible analysis of the situation in which the modification was agreed. The crucial issues are whether the agreement was both coerced in the sense that one party had an effective bilateral monopoly and that this position was exploited to the detriment of the other party. It is only these factors which can account for the different results in the cases we have considered.

3. Incentives to modify contracts

The preceding discussion highlights the way the modern law facilitates modifications of contracts by removing many of the obstacles imposed by the classical law. The necessary safeguards against unilaterally imposed variations and opportunistic advantage-taking have been established despite more relaxed tests of agreement and the effective abandonment of the traditional doctrine of consideration in this context. This flexibility of the modern law encourages co-operation between the parties, recognizing that often a measure of 'give and take' will be expected and appropriate in contractual relations during performance. But the modern law goes further than simply recognizing the effectiveness of the parties' intentions and reasonable expectations with regard to co-operation during performance. To some extent, it also provides incentives to renegotiate contracts. We noted above the special advantages of such incentives

59 [1966] 2 QB 617, [1965] 3 All ER 837, CA.

in the case of long-term contracts where it is often difficult to plan for all eventualities, and so the parties may expect to alter and give greater specificity to their agreement over time.

One incentive for adjustment derives from the courts' practice of inserting an implied term into long-term contracts that they can be terminated on reasonable notice. The courts have even been prepared to do so in the teeth of apparently contrary express terms, as in *Staffordshire Area Health Authority v South Staffordshire Waterworks Co*,[60] where under a contract for the supply of water, the price was fixed 'at all times hereafter', but the court construed the contract to contain an implied term permitting termination on reasonable notice. The possibility of such an implied term then reduces the chance that the parties to the contract will be able to insist upon its original terms. Instead, in order to combat the threat to terminate the contract on reasonable notice, the other party will have an incentive to consider the option of renegotiating the terms of the agreement so that it may continue.

Another incentive to adjust the contract springs from the duty to mitigate loss arising from breach of contract.[61] A party to a contract who refuses to accept a modification may of course claim damages if the original contract is imperfectly performed, but this tactic encounters the risk that a court may reduce the measure of damages in the light of his failure to co-operate on the ground of failure to mitigate loss. If a purchaser of a ship refuses to accept late delivery, as for example in *The Solholt*,[62] its damages may be reduced to nil where the cheapest and most reasonable method for reducing his losses resulting from the breach of contract would have been to accept late delivery with some alteration in the price to reflect the costs of delay and changes in market conditions. In effect, the doctrine of mitigation, which requires the injured party to take reasonable steps to reduce losses resulting from breach, also creates an incentive in many instances to renegotiate a contract if this is the most cost-effective means of reducing loss.

D.   Termination for breach of contract

Apart from the anomalous doctrine of frustration, even a serious breach of contract does not terminate it.[63] The common law insists that the injured party should enjoy the choice of either terminating the contract or affirming it. The language of choice reflects the classical law's attempt to attribute every legal consequence to the agreement of the parties,[64] but more pressing considerations

---

60 [1978] 3 All ER 769, [1978] 1 WLR 1387, CA.
61 See Chapter 17.
62 [1983] 1 Lloyd's Rep 605, CA.
63 *Decro-Wall International SA v Practitioners in Marketing Ltd* [1971] 2 All ER 216, [1971] 1 WLR 361, CA; *Photo Production Ltd v Securicor Transport Ltd* [1980] AC 827, [1980] 1 All ER 556, HL.
64 Williston, 'Freedom of Contract' (1921) 6 *Cornell Law Review* 364.

dictate this approach. In part this choice protects the injured party from an attempt by the party in breach to rely upon his own wrongful breach of contract to escape from his remaining obligations. At the same time, this right preserves the contract intact so that the parties might be encouraged to find a compromise. It expresses the duty of co-operation by requiring the party in breach to fulfil his obligations whenever the injured party desires it.[65] In reality, no doubt, the injured party frequently has little choice but to terminate the contract in the face of a serious breach or an absolute refusal to proceed. Yet this right aids the injured party where he perceives some ancillary benefits from prolonging the life of the contract. For example, when employees go on strike in breach of contract, the employer is entitled to terminate their contracts, but he or she is unlikely to do so in the interests of promoting a quick settlement, reducing the damage to harmonious industrial relations, and retaining his or her skilled labour force.

We noted at the outset that the right to terminate the contract in response to a breach provides a powerful incentive to perform the obligations. If minor breaches can be punished by termination of the contract, so that the party in breach loses the whole commercial benefit of the transaction, there is a strong incentive to comply with the contractual obligations. Yet a right to terminate the contract even for trivial breaches may put the injured party in a position to take opportunistic advantage of changes in market conditions.[66] Where a fixed price contract becomes unattractive due to a change in the ordinary market rates, the injured party may be tempted to point to a minor breach in order to escape the transaction and make a better deal either by renegotiation or by seeking a new contractual partner. In order to promote co-operation and to discourage opportunism, the courts must in general support the right to terminate the contract for breach, but qualify this stance in cases of minor breaches.

1. Grounds for granting termination

The general test for determining whether the right to terminate the contract exists was stated by Diplock LJ:

> does the occurrence of the event deprive the party who has further undertakings still to perform of substantially the whole benefit which it was the intention of the parties as expressed in the contract that he should obtain as the consideration for performing those undertakings?[67]

In short, to justify termination the party in breach must have substantially deprived the injured party of the benefits of performance of the contract. This

---

65 Gabel, 'Intention and Structure in Contractual Conditions: Outline of a Method for Critical Legal Theory' (1977) 61 *Minnesota Law Review* 601.
66 Reynolds, 'Discharge by Breach as a Remedy' in P Finn (ed), *Essays on Contract* (Sydney, 1987), ch 6.
67 *Hong Kong Fir Shipping Co Ltd v Kawasaki Kisen Kaisha Ltd* [1962] 2 QB 26, [1962] 1 All ER 474, CA.

principle invokes a test of degree, which requires the court to examine the facts in order to determine what the effects of the breach have been and how much less than proper performance of the contract has been received by the injured party. In order to give greater specificity to this underlying principle, the courts developed further doctrines. We will consider in particular the concept of repudiation; express termination clauses; and the distinction between conditions and warranties.

(a)   REPUDIATION

One set of facts which normally satisfies this test of substantial failure of performance occurs when one party indicates through his words or conduct that he no longer intends to be bound by the contract. In this instance, the injured party may respond to a complete repudiation of the contract by terminating it. When the refusal to perform relates to one aspect of the contract, however, the court cannot escape from making a discretionary judgment concerning the degree to which the injured party will be deprived of the benefit of correct performance. A repudiation may take place even before any performance under the contract has become due, a situation often given the confusing name of 'anticipatory breach'. Whatever form the repudiation takes, the other party to the contract enjoys the normal choice of either accepting the repudiation, thereby terminating the contract, or affirming the contract by his words or conduct and awaiting further negotiations.

(b)   EXPRESS TERMINATION CLAUSES

In order to avoid the uncertainty surrounding the exercise of judicial discretion in cases of partial breach of contract, in commercial transactions the parties usually agree express provisions governing minor breaches. The contract states that breach of a particular provision or the occurrence of a particular event will entitle one party to terminate the contract. These clauses will normally be valid, subject to specific statutory prohibitions. When a party has the right to terminate under the contract, the action of declaring the contract terminated will not count as a repudiation, but rather a permitted form of performance. If, however, one party exercises the contractual right to rescind improperly and in bad faith, the purported termination is regarded as repudiation.[68] But this inference will not be drawn lightly. The power to terminate the contract provides a valuable protection against opportunism, by providing the option of quitting the contract in response. For this reason the courts tend to reject any implied terms that might

---

68 *Woodar Investment Development Ltd v Wimpey Construction (UK) Ltd* [1980] 1 All ER 571, [1980] 1 WLR 277, HL.

constrain the exercise of an express power to terminate the contract: 'an express and unrestricted power cannot in the ordinary way be circumscribed by an implied qualification.'[69]

(c) CONDITIONS AND WARRANTIES

As well as explicit termination clauses, it became established through precedent that certain phrases used in contracts signalled that breach of that term would give rise to the right to terminate the contract. A common phrase of this kind is 'time is of the essence', which has the effect that lateness, no matter how trivial, entitles the other party to terminate for delay.[70] The most important phrase was to describe a term as a 'condition', in contrast to a 'warranty', for it became established that breach of a condition gave the right to terminate the contract. Indeed, the courts tended to classify all terms of contracts into either conditions and warranties. Once a particular term had been classified as a condition, or a similar code phrase signalling that breach would entitle the injured party to terminate the contract, the precedent force of the decision would mean that in subsequent disputes involving the same term in a different contract the court would be bound to give it the same effect. Draftsmen of contracts found it a convenient technique to pre-determine the results of breach by carefully labelling each term in the contract as either a condition or a warranty.[71] Similarly, the Sale of Goods Act 1893 (now 1979) adopted the terminology of conditions and warranties, in order to express the effects of the statute as precisely as possible. The implied terms as to the quality, quantity and conformity to sample or to descriptive terms were earmarked as conditions, so that any breach entitled the buyer to reject the goods and terminate the contract.

The advantages of the classification of terms in this way go beyond the benefits of certainty and the avoidance of disputes and delays. By characterizing obligations as conditions, the parties provide a strong incentive to perform the contract according to its terms, thereby promoting co-operation. Moreover, the seller of goods will usually be in a better position than the buyer to dispose of them at the least cost in the market, especially when the buyer is a consumer, so that the costs of breach can be reduced by permitting the buyer to reject the goods for breach of the implied terms.[72]

At the same time, however, the classification of terms may permit opportunism. A buyer may be able to point to a trivial defect in order to escape the transaction in a falling market. In a contract for services, the purchaser can effectively enjoy the

---

69 Lord Millet, *Reda v Flag Ltd* [2002] UKPC 38, [2002] IRLR 747 at 753, PC.

70 *Bunge Corpn v Tradax SA* [1981] 2 All ER 513, [1981] 1 WLR 711, HL.

71 *Bentsen v Taylor, Sons & Co (No 2)* [1893] 2 QB 274, CA.

72 Priest, 'Breach and Remedy for the Tender of Non-conforming Goods' (1978) 91 *Harvard Law Review* 960.

right to terminate the contract at will if the contract specifies that even trivial deviations from the contract count as breach of condition. For example, in *Schuler AG v Wickman Machine Tool Sales Ltd*,[73] a company of sales representatives agreed to market a German product in Britain, and, as a condition of the contract, undertook to pay weekly visits to the major regular customers, the six largest motor manufacturers, during the four-and-a-half-year lifetime of the contract. On a literal reading of the contract, a single failure to visit a customer out of the contemplated 1,400 visits would have entitled the German producers to terminate the contract. The value of co-operation, therefore, points to the introduction of a limitation on the right to terminate the contract for breach of conditions in order to discourage opportunism that might prevent either party from committing themselves to the contract.

The courts, and then the legislature, have responded to the problem by reintroducing the criterion of the seriousness of the breach. In some cases, the courts argue that the parties could not have intended by their use of the term condition that even trivial breaches should trigger the right to terminate the contract. As an interpretation of the facts in a case such as *Schuler AG v Wickman Machine Tool Sales Ltd*, this may appear unconvincing, for the producers no doubt wanted to have the clause in reserve in order to keep the sales representatives on their toes. Nevertheless, this interpretation does reinsert the value of co-operation into the contract by forbidding reliance on the term as a pretext. Another approach used by the courts is to claim that some terms which have not been expressly labelled will be regarded as neither warranties nor conditions, but rather as falling into a third category of innominate terms. In this category the test for the entitlement to terminate depends upon whether or not the breach is fundamental,[74] which permits a reinsertion of the test of the seriousness of the breach.

In exercising this discretion, the courts take into consideration a variety of factors. The difference between the performance contemplated in the contract and the actual performance provides the main criterion. For example, where one party delivers defective goods as a result of unsuitable conditions during carriage, the court examines the difference in market value between the goods delivered and those specified in the contract and whether the goods are still fit for their intended purpose, in order to determine whether there has been a fundamental breach of the contract of carriage. In addition, the courts examine the position in which the injured party has been placed as a result of the breach. They ask whether damages would be an adequate remedy or whether the injured party needs to be able to terminate the contract in order to safeguard his economic position. In some cases, the injured party may be so short of time that he has no option but to terminate the contract, for otherwise he will be left with goods on a

---

73 [1974] AC 235, [1973] 2 All ER 39, HL; cf *Arcos Ltd v Ronaasen* [1933] AC 470, HL.
74 *Cehave NV v Bremer Handelsgesellschaft mbH (The Hansa Nord)* [1976] QB 44, [1975] 3 All ER 739, CA.

falling market or miss other profitable opportunities or suffer severe losses as a result of an adverse financial predicament. Here a court is likely to decide that timing was of the essence to the contract, and that even a short delay will entitle the injured party to terminate the contract. Where those factors are absent, on the other hand, a court may find that any attempt to terminate the contract is premature.

An alteration in the Sale of Goods Act 1979 has now applied this more flexible approach to the breach of the implied terms regarding quality and quantity in the sale of goods. Where the breach of one of these conditions is 'so slight that it would be unreasonable' to reject them, a court may regard the breach as only giving rise to a right to damages.[75] Following the recommendation of the Law Commission,[76] this flexibility does not apply to purchases by consumers, who remain entitled to reject goods for minor breaches of quality standards and non-conformity with express contractual descriptions of the goods.

2. Loss of the right to terminate

The right to terminate a contract for breach supplies a key incentive for performance and co-operation. The right may be lost, however, where the injured party has indicated by words or conduct that it wishes to continue with performance of the contract. This conduct is described as 'affirmation of the contract' or 'waiver of breach'. The principles applicable here mirror the modern rules used in relation to informal modifications, since they are designed to prevent the kind of opportunism where a party first indicates that a variation has been agreed and subsequently seeks to renege on that commitment.

Clear cases of the loss of the right to terminate include a demand of the injured party for further performance or for specific performance. Short of express demands or unambiguous legal action, however, the courts must look at the conduct of the injured party to discover whether he has acted in such a way as to evidence either that he has resigned himself to the termination of the contract, or that he continues to await and expect further performance. For example, if an employer imposes a wage cut on employees without their consent but the employees continue to work as normal, their conduct has to be construed as either acceptance of the breach resulting in termination and the formation of a new contract, or alternatively the employees' conduct may be construed simply as an affirmation of the original contract so that they can continue to claim the original wage rates.[77] The election to terminate the contract is likely to be found from any change of position which indicates that the injured party does not expect to

75 Sale of Goods Act 1979, s 15A(1), as amended by the Sale and Supply of Goods Act 1994, s 4.
76 Law Commission, *Sale and Supply of Goods*, Report No 160, Cm 137 (London, 1987).
77 *Rigby v Ferodo Ltd* [1988] ICR 29, [1987] IRLR 516, HL.

proceed with the transaction.[78] A special rule applies to consumer sales and analogous transactions. Where the consumer exercises the statutory right to ask the supplier to replace or repair the goods, the right to terminate the contract is not lost if the supplier fails to act within a reasonable time.[79]

3.   Incentives to renegotiate

The right to terminate not only provides an incentive to perform the contract, but also it can give the parties an incentive to renegotiate the terms of the contract in the light of changed circumstances and unplanned contingencies. The long-term business interests of the parties may dictate a renegotiation rather than the conclusion of business relations. For instance, in *Staffordshire Area Health Authority v South Staffordshire Waterworks Co*,[80] these two government agencies, a water supplier and a hospital, made a long-term contract for the supply of water at a fixed price. After more than 60 years had passed, the price was plainly unrealistic due to inflation. Although the terms provided that the contract was to be binding 'at all times hereafter', the English Court of Appeal implied a term permitting the supplier to terminate the contract upon reasonable notice. The effect of the implied term was to force the hospital authority back to the bargaining table to renegotiate the cost of water supplies up to a more economic price.

The difficult question is whether a right to terminate the contract best serves the purpose of encouraging co-operation in the form of renegotiation to handle unexpected contingencies.[81] An alternative consists in permitting the courts to revise contracts in the manner of judicial revision to secure fairness considered in Chapter 13. Were the courts to possess such a power, there would be an incentive to renegotiate the contract on terms comparable to those likely to be imposed by the court. This approach has the advantage over the right to terminate the contract in that neither party is given the option to walk away from the contract altogether, which avoids the possibility of opportunism in the light of changed circumstances. As we have seen, English law does not grant the courts an express power to revise contracts, although techniques of construction can achieve comparable results in some cases. In the USA, some courts have experimented with judicial revision, most famously in *Aluminum Co of America v Essex Group*.[82] Under a 16-year contract with an option to renew for an additional five years, the claimant company ('ALCOA') agreed to convert alumina supplied by Essex into

---

78 *Société Italo-Belge pour le Commerce et l'Industrie SA v Palm and Vegetable Oils (Malaysia) Sdn Bhd (The Post Chaser)* [1982] 1 All ER 19, [1981] 2 Lloyd's Rep 695, QB.
79 Sale of Goods Act 1979, s 48D, as amended by the Sale and Supply of Goods to Consumers Regulations 2002, SI 2002/3045, reg 5.
80 [1978] 3 All ER 769; [1978] 1 WLR 1387, CA.
81 J Bell, 'The Effect of Changes in Circumstances on Long-Term Contracts' in D Harris and D Tallon (eds), *Contract Law Today* (Oxford, 1989), ch 5.
82 499 F Supp 53 (WD Pa 1980).

molten aluminium. The contract contained detailed provisions designed to raise the price in line with the wholesale price index, but this index failed to account for the sharp rise in the cost of energy to ALCOA, so the contract became increasingly unprofitable to them. The Federal District Court declared that the contract had gone awry because of a mistake in formulating the pricing mechanism to account for inflation. So the court set aside the contract and imposed a new pricing formula. The parties subsequently renegotiated the contract in the light of this judicial revision of the contract.[83]

---

83 Campbell and Harris, 'Flexibility in Long-term Contractual Relationships: The Role of Co-operation' (1993) 20 *Journal of Law and Society* 166.

Agreed remedies

A. The normal remedy for breach

The terms of written contracts normally make provision for the remedies available to the parties in the event of breach of contract. The terms may specify the amount of compensation payable, or arrange for some guarantee of payments due under the contract, or even determine that any disputes be resolved outside the ordinary courts by an arbitrator. If no such provisions have been agreed, then the courts supply judicial remedies such as an order for compulsory performance (specific performance or injunctions) or an order to pay compensation (damages). These judicial remedies will be considered in Chapter 17. Most written contracts, however, pay considerable attention to agreed remedies. A majority of the terms of a standard form contract will in all likelihood seek to augment, structure, and confine the claims available to each party in relation to the breach of contract. In short, the normal remedy for breach of contract is that provided in the contract itself.

Indeed, the whole nature of a transaction may be devised with the remedial aspect in mind. A hire-purchase contract (or conditional sales contract), for example, can only be understood from this perspective. Instead of a finance company making a loan to a consumer who wishes to purchase some goods, such as a car, the finance company purchases the car itself and then rents it out to the consumer for a period of time in return for hire charges. At the end of the period of hire the consumer has a contractual right to purchase the car for a nominal sum. The major purpose of this elaborate arrangement is to give the finance company a security for repayment of the loan by distributing property rights in a particular way. By retaining ownership of the car, in the event of the consumer's default on payments, the finance company can bring the hire arrangement to a close, sell the car, and recoup its money, without having to rely upon the consumer's ability to pay damages. The agreed remedy of the finance company, namely the right to sell the goods in order to satisfy the consumer's debt, is central to the whole structure of this artificial contractual edifice.

The reasons for the deployment of agreed remedies are not hard to seek. Lawyers can create an advantage to their client by improving on the normal judicial remedy for breach of contract, which comprises compensatory damages. By devising a more reliable remedy, such as a security interest or a guarantee from a bank, the lawyer greatly increases the chances of the legal system providing an effective remedy against breach. This increases the threat available to the injured party, which is important both in the discouragement of breach and in obtaining beneficial settlements of claims.

The significance of agreed remedies is therefore not merely that they represent the normal remedy for breach of contract, but also that they often provide a different kind of remedy by changing the nature of the right being claimed from a personal right to a proprietary right. This aspect of contractual practice greatly facilitates the use of 'self-help' as a sanction for breach of contract.

B.   Freedom and control

These contractual practices rely on the general rule that agreed remedies will be enforced by the courts. An agreed measure of compensation, for instance, will be regarded as a debt which is owed, which can be claimed quickly through the courts' procedures for seizure of goods to the value of the debt. Similarly, the courts will decline jurisdiction over a contractual dispute governed by an arbitration clause. This support for contractual determination of remedies rests on cogent policy considerations.

In the first place, agreed remedies may considerably reduce the costs and uncertainties arising from contractual disputes. Instead of the parties engaging in prolonged debates about the measure of loss arising from the dispute, the fixed measure of compensation will be payable. Similarly, where a creditor has taken security against a debt, such as a deposit, the creditor can simply retain the deposit rather than seeking compensation in the courts. This first advantage of agreed remedies brings with it another: it reduces the cost to the public purse of the administration of justice. At a deeper level, the power to agree remedies for breach facilitates a whole range of market transactions which otherwise might be stifled. For example, few would be prepared to loan another a large sum of money without some kind of guarantee or security for repayment. Otherwise lenders naturally fear that their money will disappear without trace, or that the borrower will become insolvent and be unable to repay the loan. A hire-purchase agreement, despite the considerable advantages gained for the finance company, may be socially beneficial if it provides the necessary mechanism for consumer purchases to be bought on credit. Yet these crucial benefits deriving from respect for the agreed remedies in the contract do not rule out all regulation and control, for these terms, like other aspects of freedom of contract, pose the danger of the abuse of contractual power and can threaten the integrity of other valuable institutions of the market economy.

Complete freedom of contract with respect to remedies for breach could never be tolerated. It might permit terms granting the creditor the right to imprison, beat, or commit immoral acts against the debtor. Any agreed remedy of this type would certainly be unenforceable as immoral or contrary to public policy. However, the dangers of abuse of contractual power need not be as obvious as Shylock's demand for a pound of flesh. More commonly we find attempts to secure a scale of financial compensation for breach of contract which exceeds any loss incurred by the injured party. Alternatively, the party in breach will have used a standard form contract to minimize any compensation payable by reference to a fixed sum or a limitation of damages clause. As well as fixing the quantity of compensation payable to their advantage, purveyors of standard form contracts will often seek to enhance the reliability of their remedy by the acquisition of property rights In what is known as a 'catching bargain', for instance, the lender of money may arrange, in the event of a failure to repay instalments on time, that the lender acquires title not only to the goods purchased by the debtor with the loan, but also all the other goods of the debtor. Not only will this provide the debtor with a strong incentive to repay, but also it improves the reliability of any remedy on default. To gain such proprietary rights over all the debtor's assets as a result of failure to pay a small sum of money may be regarded, however, as an abuse of bargaining power and an unconscionable transaction.

Agreed remedies can also pose an indirect threat to the institution of the market as a whole. Two dangers should be highlighted at this point. First, there is the danger that an agreed choice of forum will prevent a fair and impartial determination of disputes. This will be an affront to the public system of justice and the civil rights of individuals, as well as perhaps leading to unfair results. We consider how this problem has been addressed in the final section of this chapter.

Secondly, many agreed remedies distribute property entitlements, not only in order to provide a security for performance, but also to ensure priority over other creditors, so that even in the event of the debtor's insolvency a substantial remedy will be available to the creditor.[1] The danger which this practice poses to the market is that it often leads to confusion and uncertainty over the exact allocation of proprietary rights. The apparent owner of a television under a hire-purchase agreement is of course the consumer, although in reality title remains vested in the finance company. Third parties may assume that the apparent owner is the true owner, enter contracts with the consumer on that false assumption, and incur loss as a result.[2] Public systems of registration of proprietary interests can reduce this problem, by making it possible to ascertain ownership of proprietary interests before entering into transactions. But not every kind of proprietary interest need be registered, so there remains the risk that the widespread divergence between ostensible ownership and legal ownership will deter entry into market transactions. For this reason the law may not give full effect to unregistered proprietary interests, particularly when they are used against third parties who are justifiably ignorant of those rights.

The legal regulation of agreed remedies therefore consists of a balance between respect for freedom of contract and controls against abuse of contractual power. We will consider how this balance is struck in relation to the principal types of remedial provisions, namely, fixed measures of compensation, security interests in property, guarantees, and arbitration clauses.

C. Fixed measure of compensation

A common agreed remedy fixes the measure of compensation payable for breach of contract. A variety of terms achieve this effect. The term may state the sum due either as an expression of the price of the contract or as damages. The term may

---

1   The question of the fairness of creditors' priorities is beyond the scope of the discussion here: V Finch, *Corporate Insolvency Law* (Cambridge, 2002), ch 14.

2   This particular problem is governed by the Hire-Purchase Act 1964, s 27 (as amended by the Consumer Credit Act 1974, s 192(3)) and protects the innocent private purchaser by giving him or her title to the television.

seek to augment or restrict the measure of damages. The fixed measure of compensation may be combined with a security interest, as in the case of a deposit, which both determines the amount of compensation and gives the creditor a proprietary right over a sum of money. The general purpose of legal controls over these terms is to frustrate attempts to secure greater compensation for breach of contract than might be obtained from judicial remedies.[3] This purpose contains a conception of fairness, one which is not concerned with the fairness of the bargain, but one which insists that the remedial arrangements should not cause a redistribution of wealth which provides the injured party with either greater or lesser compensation than his actual losses. But the incidence and tightness of these legal controls over fixed measures of compensation varies according to the form of the term and the nature of the parties to the contract.

1. Agreed price

Under an action for debt or an agreed sum of money, the plaintiff relies upon the term fixing the price of the goods or services to set the measure of compensation payable. The rules of civil procedure of the courts enable the plaintiff to adopt a quick and truncated legal process by which the claim for the price may be pursued. Unless the defendant offers a defence that the sum is not due, the plaintiff can proceed to enforce the claim by using the court's process of seizure and sale of goods to the value of the debt. There is no requirement that the plaintiff should prove the amount of the loss suffered provided that the debt has fallen due. Nor is there in general any duty to mitigate any losses resulting from the breach of contract. On the other hand, no claim can be made for additional losses such as interest on the money while awaiting payment. Because of the simplicity of the action for debt, whenever the breach of contract consists of a failure to pay an agreed sum of money, this will be the most common means of pursuing a remedy.

In this action for debt, the primary obligation which determines the price also fixes the scale of compensation. This coincidence explains why the courts are unwilling to control actions for debt. To do so would inevitably clash with their stance against testing the adequacy of consideration and their general unwillingness to intervene to invalidate or rewrite harsh bargains. Although direct controls on grounds of the unfairness of the price are not generally available, the courts have devised a number of protections for the debtor in such cases.

---

3   Macneil, 'Power of Contract and Agreed Remedies' (1962) 47 *Cornell Law Quarterly* 495.

(a) Due date of payment

The main protection consists of an insistence that the payment should have fallen due. The due date may be set by the contract itself, as in the case of an advance payment.[4] In consumer contracts, express terms which seek to order performance so that the consumer has to pay in full in advance may be regarded as unfair and invalid under the Unfair Terms in Consumer Contracts Regulations 1999.[5] In the absence of express provision fixing the due date, the courts must construe the agreement. In a sale of goods, for instance, payment will not generally fall due until the vendor has transferred ownership of the goods under the contract and is ready and willing to tender delivery of them in exchange for the price.[6] In the case of provision of services, the contract will normally be interpreted to require full or substantial performance of the service to a reasonable standard before the debt falls due.[7] In a long-term service contract, such as a contract of employment, payments of wages will fall due periodically according to the terms of the contract, as in the case of wages payable monthly in arrears.

The courts have been able to construe the contract in order to fix the due date for payment in ways to protect consumers from claims for money where the performance of the contract has proven unsatisfactory. In *Bolton v Mahadeva*,[8] the plaintiff agreed to install a central heating system into the defendant's home for £560. The system proved defective in several respects, including inadequate heat in some rooms and noxious fumes in others, and required £174 of repairs. The defendant successfully resisted an action for the full price of the work under the original contract (subject to a set-off for the defects), on the ground that payment did not fall due until the plaintiff had substantially fulfilled his obligation. This is described as an 'entire obligation', ie one which must be substantially performed before payment falls due. The test of whether substantial performance has been provided depends for its application upon the nature of the defects and the proportion between the cost of rectifying them and the original contract price. In *Bolton v Mahadeva*, there was no substantial performance since the cost of repairs amounted to nearly a third of the contract price, but the result would probably be different if the repairs cost less than 10% of the contract price.[9]

(b) Set-off

Another escape route from an action for an agreed price is to claim the right to set off against the price any sums due to the debtor from the creditor. This is a

---

4   Sale of Goods Act 1979, s 49(2).
5   SI 1999/2083, Sch 2, para 1(o) 'obliging the consumer to fulfil all his obligations where the seller or supplier does not perform his'.
6   Sale of Goods Act 1979, ss 28, 49(1). R Goode, *Commercial Law* (London, 2nd edn, 1995) pp 423–425.
7   *Hoenig v Isaacs* [1952] 2 All ER 176, CA.
8   [1972] 2 All ER 1322, [1972] 1 WLR 1009, CA.
9   For example *Hoenig v Isaacs* [1952] 2 All ER 176, CA.

common express provision in commercial contracts,[10] but the right to set-off exists in equity without the need for an express term. Thus in *Bolton v Mahadeva* the defendant offered the full price minus the cost of repairs to the plaintiff in full satisfaction of the debt. Equally a debtor may set off against an action for an agreed price debts owed by the creditor to him under other contracts,[11] provided that it would be manifestly unjust to enforce the debt without taking into account the debtor's counter-claim.[12] Courts tend to regard the right to set-off as a fundamental principle of fairness with respect to agreed remedies, so they have little hesitation in regarding attempts to exclude the right as unreasonable and therefore void under the Unfair Contract Terms Act 1977.[13] This control is strengthened in relation to consumer contracts, where the Unfair Terms in Consumer Contracts Regulations 1999 cite as a probable unfair term one which prevents consumers from exercising a right of set-off against a seller.[14]

(c) ANTICIPATORY BREACH

If a debtor repudiates the contract before performance has commenced, can the creditor nevertheless perform the contract and claim the price? Suppose that the debtor agrees to purchase some goods at a future date, but before that date states that he no longer wishes to be bound by the contract. Can the vendor nevertheless offer to deliver the goods on the due date and then claim full payment? The traditional rule of English law laid down in *White and Carter (Councils) Ltd v McGregor*[15] permits the vendor to complete performance, if this can be done without the co-operation of the debtor, and to succeed in a claim for the price in these circumstances. In that case the defendant agreed to pay a fixed price to have his business advertised by the plaintiff on litterbins for three years, but later the same day repudiated the contract. The plaintiff nevertheless carried the advertisements for three years and successfully claimed the agreed price. Here the defendant received the benefit of the advertisements for the price, but perhaps he placed no value on them, and indeed perhaps they served no useful purpose, so considerations of efficiency might have pointed against enforcing the agreed price.

This traditional rule may rest on the assumption that the debtor can dispose of unwanted goods as efficiently as the vendor, although this seems unlikely to be true for consumer purchasers. The rule may also be influenced by the principle

---

10 R Goode, *Commercial Law* (London, 2nd edn, 1995), p 657.

11 But the right to set-off may not be available against an insolvent creditor, for this might subvert the rules ensuring fairness between unsecured creditors.

12 *Federal Commerce & Navigation Co Ltd v Molena Alpha Inc* [1978] QB 927, [1978] 3 All ER 1066 CA; SR Derham, *Set-Off* (Oxford, 1987), pp 11–20.

13 *Stewart Gill Ltd v Horatio Myer & Co Ltd* [1992] QB 600, [1992] 2 All ER 257, CA.

14 SI 1999/2083, Sch 2, para 1(b).

15 [1962] AC 413, [1961] 3 All ER 1178, HL. Compare *Clark v Marsiglia* 1 Denio 317 (NY 1845).

that the debtor acquires ownership of the goods on the due date of performance, since the repudiation has not been accepted by the vendor, which has the effect that the vendor may not be able to give good title to a third party.[16] The rule may be criticised because it appears to lead to inefficient results when the goods or services have no commercial value either to the debtor or a third party, as in *White and Carter (Councils) Ltd v McGregor*. Suppose that a fixed price is agreed for the painting of a portrait by using photographs. If the debtor announces before the artist has begun work that he no longer wants the portrait, should the artist be entitled to proceed and sue for the price when the picture has been completed? Assuming that the picture has little or no value to anyone else, the debtor has little chance of recouping his loss if he has to pay the price. On the other hand, the artist could have reduced her loss by seeking alternative employment.

English courts have qualified the rule, however, in cases where the creditor is behaving wholly unreasonably and has no legitimate interest in performing the contract. The scope of this qualification remains uncertain, since it is difficult to foresee how it can ever be 'wholly unreasonable' to perform a contract and ask for the agreed price. Given the uncertainties and additional expense of claiming damages, a claim for the agreed price will almost invariably represent a sensible choice. Nevertheless, this exception has been applied in *Clea Shipping Corpn v Bulk Oil International Ltd (The Alaskan Trader).*[17] Under a time charter for hire of a ship for two years, engine failure took the ship off-hire for several months and the charterers indicated that they wished to repudiate the contract since the cost of chartering ships had fallen. Nevertheless, the owners had the ship repaired and then anchored the vessel off Piraeus with a full crew ready to sail until the charter expired, and then sold the vessel for scrap. The charterers succeeded in recovering the hire charges which they had paid from the time the vessel was repaired, on the ground that the owners had 'no legitimate interest' in continuing performance of the contract,[18] or that continued performance was 'wholly unreasonable' and damages would be an adequate remedy.[19] The charterers persuaded the court that it was wholly unreasonable for the owners not to have sought alternative employment for the ship, or lay it up without a crew, or have sold it for scrap without repairs.

These arguments describe what would have comprised the duties to mitigate loss if the owners had accepted the repudiation and merely sought damages, which suggest that economic efficiency considerations colour this qualification. Perhaps the court was also impressed by the futility and waste of resources in repairing the ship and then selling it for scrap.[20] On the other hand, it must be observed that the

16 See: Sale of Goods Act 1979, s 48(2); Torts (Interference with Goods) Act 1977, s 12.
17 [1984] 1 All ER 129, [1983] 2 Lloyd's Rep 645, QB.
18 The test suggested by Lord Reid in *White and Carter (Councils) Ltd v McGregor* [1962] AC 413, [1961] 3 All ER 1178, HL.
19 The test suggested by Kerr J in *The Odenfeld* [1978] 2 Lloyd's Rep 357, QB.
20 See also: *Attica Sea Carriers Corpn v Ferrostaal Poseidon Bulk Reederei GmbH (The Puerto Buitrago)*

owner acted in a way which saved it the trouble of suing for damages for any difference in hire charges, and was able to keep its crew in full employment. Nor could it be said that the charterers had no commercial use for the vessel, for their failure to use it resulted from their choice to break the contract and make alternative arrangements at lower cost.

(d) FAIRNESS

The underlying problem for judicial control over the action for an agreed price concerns the characterisation of the claim. If the creditor's claim is regarded simply as an enforcement of a primary obligation under the contract, the judicial reluctance to rewrite bargains and test them for fairness discourages any scrutiny of the reasonableness of the claim. But once the action for an agreed price is classified, as it should be, as a form of agreed remedy, the courts can employ standards which prevent oppression, waste of resources, and excessive compensation. The courts have used the devices of 'entire obligations', set-off, and 'legitimate interest in performance' to serve this purpose of controlling these claims.

2. Limitation of damages

A simple and common term for specifying the measure of compensation consists of fixing an upper limit to compensation payable in an action for damages in the courts. An alternative is to specify the exact amount payable for breach of contract at a level which falls below the ordinary measure of compensatory damages.[21] Limitation of damages clauses in commercial contracts often serve a useful function in setting the limits of potential liability in advance, so that appropriate insurance arrangements can be taken out.

As a form of exclusion clause, these limitation of damages clauses are subject to a test of fairness and reasonableness under the Unfair Contract Terms Act 1977.[22] In *George Mitchell (Chesterhall) Ltd v Finney Lock Seeds Ltd*,[23] for instance, the contract fixed the maximum liability at £192 which was the price of the seeds being sold, whereas the plaintiff claimed losses of £61,000 as a result of planting the wrong seeds. The House of Lords found the limitation of damages clause unreasonable and invalid. One important consideration operating here was the gross disparity between the fixed measure of compensation and actual measure of

[1976] 1 Lloyd's Rep 250, CA, where the cost of repairs to the ship was twice its market value when repaired.

21 *Cellulose Acetate Silk Co Ltd v Widnes Foundry (1925) Ltd* [1933] AC 20, HL.
22 Unfair Contract Terms Act 1977, s 13(1)(b) provides that the controls over exclusion clauses apply also to any term which restricts any remedy in respect of liability.
23 [1983] 2 AC 803, [1983] 2 All ER 737, HL.

loss. In addition, however, the control also rested on a perception that the plaintiff lacked equality of bargaining power, so that limitation of damages clauses between substantial commercial entities might prove enforceable even if they lead to substantial undercompensation. Those limitation of damages clauses which fall outside the scope of the 1977 Act will normally be enforceable according to their literal meaning, the courts believing that the dangers of oppression and unfairness will not exist in these circumstances.[24]

In consumer contracts, limitation of damages clauses will also be subject to the Unfair Terms in Consumer Contracts Regulations 1999, where the relevant illustration of a presumptively unfair clause speaks of 'inappropriately' limiting the legal rights of the consumer in the event of breach of contract.[25] A limitation of damages clause in a consumer contract may prove valid under the general good faith and fairness standard, however, if the consumer received an inducement to agree to the term or perhaps if the clause fitted into otherwise fair insurance arrangements between the parties.

3. Liquidated damages and penalties

A more ambitious type of clause in a contract which sets a level of agreed compensation fixes in advance the sum of money which will be payable in the event of breach of contract. These liquidated damages clauses serve the valuable purpose of reducing the uncertainties and expense entailed in claims for damages, for they can be enforced as an action for an agreed sum in debt. A fixed level of compensation also has the attraction of determining precisely the potential scale of the financial risk, and of allocating the risk of loss in advance, so that worries about unexpected claims will not deter entry into contracts. They can also ensure that the injured party receives full compensation for losses incurred, even though these might not be fully recoverable in an ordinary action for damages because of difficulties of proof of actual loss. Liquidated damages clauses also benefit from the advantage of employing an action for an agreed sum in securing a simplified legal process for claiming fixed sums of money through the courts. The threat of such an action may help to put pressure on a contractor to reduce delay and may facilitate agreed settlements of compensation payable for breach.[26]

(a) EQUITABLE CONTROL

The courts have, however, devised strict controls over liquidated damages clauses which exceed the normal level of compensatory damages for breach of contract.

---

24 *Ailsa Craig Fishing Co Ltd v Malvern Fishing Co Ltd and Securicor (Scotland) Ltd* [1983] 1 All ER 101, [1983] 1 WLR 964, HL.
25 SI 1999/2083, Sch 2, para 1(b).
26 Beale and Dugdale, 'Contracts between Businessmen' (1975) 2 *British Journal of Law and Society* 45, at p 55.

Unless the clause sets a level of compensation which is a genuine pre-estimate of the loss, then the term will be dubbed a 'penalty clause' and will be unenforceable if the court regards it as unconscionable. The court will replace the agreed compensation with a sum of money representing an accurate assessment of a fair measure of compensation for the injured party's loss, which can then be enforced as a debt.[27] The measure of compensation will be calculated by reference to the ordinary measure of damages payable for that type of breach of contract.

There can be no clear dividing line between agreed price clauses and agreed compensation clauses. Indeed, to avoid judicial control over penalty clauses there is every incentive for a party to attempt to present the fixed sum as a primary obligation under the contract, as the agreed price rather than compensation. In *Interfoto Picture Library Ltd v Stiletto Visual Programmes Ltd*[28] the contractual terms stated that there would be a fixed hire charge per day after the due date for return of the photographs. These terms sought to present a penalty clause as merely an agreed rate of hire, and, although the court left the issue undecided, it seems likely that the jurisdiction over penalty clauses could have been applied. The courts have often revealed little hesitation in cutting through such shams and controlling the disguised penalty clause. In *Willson v Love*[29] a lease provided for the increase of rent in the event of a breach of covenant, but the court treated this term as a penalty clause. This approach makes sense if the purpose of the jurisdiction is to ensure fairness between the parties by controlling the terms of the contract, but is inexplicable if the courts are merely concerned to prevent oppressive remedies from interfering with individual freedom. Yet the courts have proved reluctant to drop the barrier to the jurisdiction to give relief from penalty clauses which requires that the sum of money should be payable on breach of contract.[30] The reason for this reluctance is that dropping this requirement would enable them to test the fairness of the price in all actions for an agreed sum, a jurisdiction which they have systematically declined, no doubt because they believe that it would interfere too greatly with freedom of contract, and weaken the utility of the quick remedy for debt.

This invalidity of penalty clauses does not prevent the level of agreed compensation from being set above an ordinary award of damages. The legal test requires the agreement to contain a genuine pre-estimate of loss, which may in the events which happen deviate from the actual loss. With the benefit of hindsight it may be possible to see that the agreed compensation was excessive, but, provided that the court is convinced that the agreement did try to estimate

---

27 *Beckham v Drake* (1849) 2 HL Cas 579; *Bridge v Campbell Discount Co Ltd* [1962] AC 600, [1962] 1 All ER 385, HL; *Jobson v Johnson* [1989] 1 All ER 621, [1989] 1 WLR 1026, CA.
28 [1989] QB 433, [1988] 1 All ER 348, CA.
29 [1896] 1 QB 626, CA.
30 *Export Credits Guarantee Department v Universal Oil Products Co* [1983] 2 All ER 205, [1983] 1 WLR 399, HL; but compare Lord Denning in *Bridge v Campbell Discount Co Ltd* [1962] AC 600, [1962] 1 All ER 385.

the likely loss accurately, it will enforce the clause as permitted liquidated damages.[31] A strict rule against agreed levels of compensation above ordinary damages would render liquidated damages clauses almost always vulnerable to attack, since at the time of the formation of the contract the parties will not have complete foresight of the consequences of a breach of contract. The courts therefore permit some latitude in the fixing of agreed remedies.

The approach to testing the validity of higher levels of compensation can be described as 'risk averaging'.[32] The degree of tolerance extends to agreed remedies which fix a sum of compensation which represents an average of probable losses resulting from different breaches of the same contract. For example, in *Dunlop Pneumatic Tyre Co Ltd v New Garage and Motor Co Ltd*,[33] the manufacturer of tyres required under its contracts with distributors a payment of £5 for every tyre sold to the public below list price, or sold after tampering with the manufacturer's markings, or supplied to prohibited persons, or exported. The defendant dealer sold to the public below list price, which created the risk to the manufacturer that its other dealers would either demand reduced prices or go to other manufacturers. Although the fixed sum of compensation might have exceeded the manufacturer's loss in any particular breach of contract, since the loss springing from a more competitive market was in any case difficult to assess, the court enforced the fixed sum by way of liquidated damages as a genuine attempt to predict it. The £5 charge was not an extravagant measure of compensation for any of the potential breaches of contract. It was a prediction of the average probable loss resulting from each breach of contract.

This latitude does not extend to cases where the obligation which has been broken merely involves the payment of money or the transfer of ascertained property. In cases involving an obligation to pay money, as in the case of a loan, the courts will simply examine the question of whether the agreed compensation exceeds the creditor's loss. Whenever the agreed compensation exceeds the sums due to the creditor by way of return of principal and payment of interest, the court will scale down the penalty clause. This will be true even if the creditor suggests that his possible losses, as foreseen at the time of the formation of the contract, might have exceeded the repayment of principal and interest. Similarly, where the agreed compensation is described in the form of a transfer of a property right, if the value of the property exceeds the injured party's loss, then the court can order the debtor to sell the property and deliver to the injured party that part of the proceeds which amounts to the sum of the injured party's loss.[34]

31 *Clydebank Engineering and Shipbuilding Co v Castaneda* [1905] AC 6, HL.
32 Collins, 'Fairness in Agreed Remedies' in C Willett (ed), *Aspects of Fairness in Contract* (London, 1996), p 97, at p 116.
33 [1915] AC 79, HL.
34 *Jobson v Johnson* [1989] 1 All ER 621, [1989] 1 WLR 1026, CA.

(b)   CONSUMER CONTRACTS

The origins of the equitable jurisdiction to give relief from penalty clauses lay in loan agreements. Creditors inserted into the loan agreement a term under which the debtor in default agreed to pay a fixed sum greatly in excess of the loan and interest. The creditor would then seek to enforce this 'penal bond' in an action for an agreed sum. But courts of equity prevented these actions on the ground that the loan agreement constituted an unconscionable bargain, and insisted that the only sum recoverable by the creditor was the principal and interest on the loan. In most cases such agreements would now be regulated by the Consumer Credit Act 1974, ss 137–140, which permits a court to reopen and revise an extortionate credit bargain, but the common law jurisdiction could still be applicable outside the field of consumer protection.

Prior to the 1974 Act, the jurisdiction to give relief from penalty clauses was used to regulate transactions such as hire purchase, as in *Bridge v Campbell Discount Co Ltd*.[35] Under this contract for the hire and purchase of a car from a finance company, the terms provided that as compensation for depreciation of the value of the car the finance company should be entitled to retain any instalments paid and also claim the remainder of the payments to the sum of two-thirds of the hire-purchase price. The debtor returned the car after having paid only a few instalments and was then sued for the sum representing the balance of two-thirds of the hire-purchase price. The House of Lords refused to enforce this term for agreed compensation, on the ground that it could not represent a genuine pre-estimate of the creditor's loss, since the sum payable for depreciation in the value of the car actually decreased over time rather than increased. At bottom this contract was objectionable because it sought to guarantee interest on a loan which could far exceed market rates, since the finance company could be sure under the terms of the agreement of gaining both the value of the car at the date of breach of contract and the value of two-thirds of the instalments. This amounted to unjust enrichment of the finance company.

The strict legislative control over fixed measures of compensation in consumer contracts has been expanded under the Unfair Terms in Consumer Contracts Regulations 1999.[36] For example, Sch 2, para 1(e) illustrates a type of term which is presumptively unfair as one which requires a consumer in breach of contract 'to pay a disproportionately high sum in compensation'.

These Regulations also appear to introduce a novel principle derived from European civil law systems. The Regulations imply in the illustrations of terms which may be regarded as unfair contained in Sch 3 a principle that the seller's advantages obtained in agreed remedies should be mirrored by identical or

---

35 [1962] AC 600, [1962] 1 All ER 385, HL. The current law governing this case is contained in Consumer Credit Act 1974, ss 99–103.
36 SI 1999/2083.

equivalent remedial advantages afforded to the consumer. For example, illustration (d) creates a presumption of unfairness and therefore invalidity for a term:

> permitting the seller or supplier to retain sums paid by the consumer where the latter decides not to conclude or perform the contract, without providing for the consumer to receive compensation of an equivalent amount from the seller or supplier where the latter is the party cancelling the contract.

This illustration suggests that while sellers may insist upon advance payments and deposits as security, these terms will only be effective if the consumer receives an equivalent financial assurance of performance from the seller.

(c) FAIRNESS

The equitable and legislative controls over excessive measures of agreed compensation invoke a standard of fairness. Dillon LJ has observed that the courts do not claim a 'general power not to enforce any agreement which the courts regard as unconscionable and extravagant . . . but rules which evolved as to the types of cases in which relief would be given, and one of those rules, now too entrenched to be challenged, is the equitable rule against penalties'.[37] Other justifications for the control over penalty clauses appear less convincing.

One justification is that a penalty clause represents a form of private punishment for breach of contract which is objectionable in the relations of civil society in the market. While this justification is true and explains why terms contrary to moral standards will be invalid on grounds of public policy, an obligation to pay compensation does not constitute punishment except in the sense that it provides for a greater measure of compensation than the ordinary law of damages. Is paying above the normal price for something really a kind of punishment? Another justification for control over penalty clauses is that they constitute an attempt to pressurize a person to perform a contract, which is an invasion of freedom of the individual and which should therefore be strictly controlled and administered by the courts. This criticism certainly makes sense if, for example, in a contract of employment where the weekly wage is £200 the employee agrees to pay £1,000 compensation for any day's absence. But this objection to penalty clauses rarely applies to a carefully constructed commercial agreement. The application of the equitable jurisdiction to such commercial agreements also undermines the possibility of justifying the control on the ground of coercion or oppression during the bargaining process.[38]

---

37 *Jobson v Johnson* [1989] 1 WLR 1026 at 1032, CA.
38 Goetz and Scott, 'Liquidated Damages, Penalties and the Just Compensation Principle' (1977) 77 *Columbia Law Review* 554; Harris, 'Incentives to Perform, or Break Contracts' (1992) 45(2)

The standard of fairness explains better why the courts examine the precise details of the level of compensation provided in commercial agreements. The concept of fairness at stake is one which compares the agreed remedy with the ordinary measure of damages. Attempts to increase the measure of compensation will be invalidated. But this concept of fairness is qualified by respect for the parties' attempts to plan the consequences of breach. This leads to the tolerance of the 'risk averaging' approach under which the agreed compensation may exceed actual loss provided the fixed level represents a genuine estimate of the probable loss arising from a number of possible breaches of contract.

The equitable jurisdiction to give relief from penalty clauses has been criticised on the ground that it interferes with freedom of contract and inhibits the use of contracts for wealth maximization.[39] For example, Rea argues that a party to a contract will charge a higher price if it risks a penalty clause in the event of breach of contract; so the penalty clause is paid for by the higher price for the contract; and the contract is worth more to both parties than a contract without a penalty clause.[40] By invalidating the penalty clause, not only does a court prevent the maximization of wealth through contracts, but the court also causes unfairness by refusing to enforce a promise (the liability to pay a penalty) which has been paid for (by a higher contract price). This argument assumes that the ancillary remedial clauses in contracts will form part of the bargaining over the price, which is unlikely in the case of consumer standard form contracts, so that the controls over consumer contracts will not be vulnerable to this criticism. Indeed the Unfair Terms in Consumer Contracts Regulations 1999 appear to agree with the point in the mirror principle, which insists that the consumer should be awarded an equivalent right. Another criticism of the courts' control over penalty clauses is that the agreed remedy may achieve a remedy for an item of loss which might not be compensated under the ordinary law of damages.[41] This observation is correct, but the courts appear sensitive to this point, as in *Dunlop Pneumatic Tyre Co Ltd v New Garage and Motor Co Ltd*, where one reason for upholding the validity of the £5 charge was that the losses were unpredictable and in many respects speculative, so that the plaintiff's claim for damages might have failed for want of proof of loss.

Current Legal Problems 29; Muir, 'Stipulations for payment of an Agreed Sum' (1983–85) *Sydney Law Review* 503; some support for the relevance of procedural unfairness is given by Mason and Wilson JJ in *AMEV-UDC Finance Ltd v Austin* (1986) 162 CLR 170 at 193, Aust HC.

39 A penalty clause may deter efficient breach of contract, but this seems unlikely if there is post-breach bargaining between the parties: Clarkson, Miller and Muris, 'Liquidated Damages v Penalties: Sense or Nonsense' (1978) *Wisconsin Law Review* 351; Goetz and Scott, 'Liquidated Damages, Penalties and the Just Compensation Principle' (1977) 77 *Columbia Law Review* 554.

40 Rea, 'Efficiency Implications of Penalties and Liquidated Damages' (1984) 13 *Journal of Legal Studies* 147.

41 Goetz and Scott, 'Liquidated Damages, Penalties and the Just Compensation Principle' (1977) 77 *Columbia Law Review* 554.

In some jurisdictions the fairness principle leads to the invalidity of all clauses which fix a level of compensation above the normal level of damages for breach of contract.[42] This approach has the advantage that the parties can apply it themselves in order to test the enforceability of the agreed remedy, but it suffers from the problem that the parties cannot always foresee the likely losses at the time of the formation of the contract. The English Law Commission, however, has rejected any change to the approach of requiring the parties to make a genuine pre-estimate of loss which then permits what we have called 'risk averaging'.[43]

D.   Security

Under the terms of a contract a creditor may seek to acquire an interest in property so that, in the event of breach of contract, the creditor can use the proprietary interest in order to satisfy the debt. This form of agreed remedy has the obvious advantage to the creditor that it provides a security against the debtor's performance of his contractual obligations; the debtor is more likely to perform if he risks some property interest, and if he fails to perform then the creditor can realize the value of the asset in order to ensure compensation for any loss. The creditor's remedy is also likely to be cheaper and quicker, since the creditor can help himself to the proprietary right rather than seek an award of damages through the courts. Some proprietary rights will also accord the creditor priority over other creditors in the event of the debtor's insolvency, so that the risks associated with the debtor's insolvency are greatly reduced. The enormous advantage of these types of secured transactions to a market system should be obvious. Without the facility of taking security, credit arrangements would be far less common, with a substantial diminution in transactions overall. The law permits considerable flexibility to the parties to determine the precise scope and incidents of these types of proprietary security.

The nature of a proprietary right can range from absolute ownership to a much lesser interest such as possession. We have noted, for instance, that in a hire-purchase contract the finance company retains ownership of the goods, merely giving the debtor possessory rights under a contract of hire. The positions can be reversed. Under a lien, for instance, the debtor retains title to the goods, but the creditor enjoys the right to possess the goods until the debt has been paid. English law has developed a remarkably subtle system of proprietary rights, so that it can distribute many different types of interests in property such as ownership and possession to different persons at the same time. This flexibility

---

42 See The International Institute for the Unification of Private Law (Working Group for the Preparation of Principles for International Commercial Contracts) *Principles for International Commercial Contracts* (1992) 40(3) *American Journal of Comparative Law* 703, Art 7.4.14.

43 Law Commission, *Penalty Clauses and Forfeiture of Monies Paid*, Working Paper No 61.

permits the parties to a contract to shape the agreed remedies in a host of ways which distribute the proprietary interests in numerous patterns.

Although the complexity of the different patterns and species of proprietary interests which may be distributed between creditor and debtor prevents any comprehensive and simple classification of these contractual arrangements, it is possible to provide a preliminary guide to the principal types of proprietary distributions adopted as agreed remedies. We can divide proprietary rights into four basic forms: full title (which includes both legal and equitable proprietary interests in property); bare legal title; equitable proprietary interests; and mere possessory rights. These four basic categories of proprietary interests can be distributed between creditor and debtor by a contract, which results in a matrix as illustrated by the following table:

	Creditor's Right	Debtor's Right	Example
(1)	full title	possessory right	hire purchase
(2)	legal title	equitable interest	lease
(3)	equitable interest	legal title	home loan, floating charge
(4)	possessory right	full title	lien

A common example of (1) is the hire-purchase contract, where the creditor retains full ownership of the goods, but grants the debtor a contract of hire which entitles the debtor to use the goods. Breach of contract by the debtor leads to loss of the possessory right. The arrangement in (2) is typified by a lease of property under which the tenant (debtor) acquires an equitable proprietary interest, but the landlord retains legal ownership of the property. Failure to pay rent or breach of some other covenant leads to forfeiture of the tenant's equitable proprietary interest.

Under arrangement (3), the creditor is granted an equitable charge over property owned by the debtor, as in the typical case of a home loan, so that, on the debtor's failure to repay the loan, the creditor may rely upon the charge to secure possession of the property and sell it and use the proceeds to satisfy the debt. A particularly startling and sophisticated device of this kind is the 'floating charge' over the assets of a company. This charge gives a creditor of a company the right to seize and sell all the assets of the company subject to the charge through a receiver in the event of breach of the credit arrangement, but prior to the breach the management of the company is left at liberty to use and dispose of the assets as it sees fit.

The arrangement in (4) corresponds to the lien, where the creditor is entitled to retain possession of the goods until the debt has been paid. A vendor of goods, for instance, can arrange to retain possession of the goods until full payment has been received. In the absence of express provision in the contract, by law the vendor of goods is given an implied lien which permits the vendor to retain possession of the goods until payment is made.[44] The lien does not give the right to sell the goods, although a power of sale (after certain procedures have been followed) is provided for by statute.[45] Similarly, a pawnbroker enjoys the right to possession of the goods which have been pledged until he receives repayment of the loan. Of course, these rights to retain possession and to sell the goods in the event of default can be combined. In the case of a pawnbroker, if the pawn is not redeemed within six months or a longer period provided for by contract, in general the pawnbroker may sell the pawn after giving the statutory prescribed notice.[46]

It should be stressed, however, that these four broad patterns of the distribution of property rights conceal considerable subtleties in the varieties of agreed remedies. The parties to a contract may divide the incidents of ownership between them in a myriad of ways, according to such considerations as the need for strong proprietary security, avoidance of taxation, and simplicity such as avoidance of registration requirements. Nor is it easy to fit every type of contract with its division of proprietary interests into these four basic categories.[47]

It is difficult, for instance, to classify the practice of giving deposits of money as advance payment for goods and services. If, for example, a person pays 10% of the price of a holiday in advance, by way of security or earnest of future performance, then this payment will be classified as a deposit.[48] On receipt of the payment from the debtor, the creditor receives legal title to the money, but it seems that the creditor is under an obligation to devote the money towards satisfaction of the debt. If the debtor fails to pay the balance of the debt, then the money is forfeited to the creditor. This arrangement fits most closely the pattern in (2), but it is not clear from the cases that the debtor enjoys an equitable interest in the money. The position seems to be that the debtor merely enjoys a contingent claim to repayment in the event of the creditor's breach of contract, a claim which is regarded simply as return of money on the ground of unjust enrichment. A deposit differs from an advance payment or a payment of an instalment, because the deposit will be forfeited on breach of contract, whereas other types of pre-payment will be recoverable if there has been no consideration received for them.[49]

---

44 Sale of Goods Act 1979, s 39. A lien also arises in favour of the repairer of goods, and proves an effective security even if the owner of the goods did not make the contract for repairs: *Green v All Motors Ltd* [1917] 1 KB 625, CA.

45 Torts (Interference with Goods) Act 1977, s 12.

46 Consumer Credit Act 1974, ss 114–121.

47 S Worthington, *Proprietary Interests in Commercial Transactions* (Oxford, 1996).

48 *Howe v Smith* (1884) 27 Ch D 89, CA.

49 *Dies v British and International Mining and Finance Corpn* [1939] 1 KB 724; *Hyundai Shipbuilding & Heavy Industries Co Ltd v Papadopoulos* [1980] 2 All ER 29, [1980] 1 WLR 1129, HL.

What interests us here, however, is not a taxonomy of all the types of agreed distributions of proprietary interests, but rather the nature and extent of the controls exercised by the law over the freedom of the parties to create such proprietary remedies. The question is whether any clear principles can be discerned for limiting the freedom of the parties to contracts to agree any type of distribution of proprietary interests between them. There are three principal grounds for control over this type of agreed remedy which should be considered:

(i)   promoting certainty of proprietary rights;
(ii)   protection of possessory interests; and
(iii) prevention of unjust enrichment arising from excessive compensation.

1. Certainty of proprietary rights

As indicated in the introduction to this chapter, a complex division of proprietary interests poses a threat to the institution of the market. Uncertainties about the location of ownership and rights to dispose of property can deter beneficial transactions. Here the position of third parties is the crucial concern. If a third party wishes to deal with goods or assets which are subject to a complex division of proprietary interests, then it will be difficult for the third party to be sure whether he will acquire the desired form of proprietary rights over the goods. The legal principle that no one can sell a proprietary right which they do not own has an attractive logic, but it renders the position of third parties dealing with persons who are the apparent owners, but who in fact enjoy lesser rights, rather precarious.

One solution to this difficulty lies in systems of registration of interests in property. Once a system of registration has been established, a failure to register a particular kind of interest can be used as a ground to protect a third party who acquires an interest in property without notice of another's prior claim. Two important systems of registration in England are the compulsory registration of interests in land,[50] and proprietary interests in the assets of companies.[51] Proprietary interests in goods, such as a mortgage of a ship, created by individuals are also registrable under the Bills of Sale Act (1878) Amendment Act 1882. This complex and patchy scheme of registration is certainly due for reform, to ensure that it becomes simplified in its coverage of security interests.[52] Yet systems of registration are objectionable because they are expensive and time-consuming, so that compulsory registration of interests should be used as sparingly as possible.

Another solution is to permit ostensible ownership arising from possession of property to confer certain powers to make contracts with respect to the property,

---

50 Land Registration Act 1925.
51 Companies Act 1985, Part XII, as amended by Insolvency Act 1985 and Companies Act 1989.
52 Company Law Review Steering Group, Final Report, *Modern Company Law for a Competitive Economy*, URN 01/942 (2001); Law Commission, Consultation Paper, *Registration of Security Interests: Company Charges and Property other than Land* (2002).

so that the third party dealing in good faith acquires good title. In the case of hire purchase, for instance, by statute the consumer can give good title over goods to a third party.[53] Obviously this solution cannot be available frequently, for otherwise it would render the security afforded to creditors of proprietary interests in the debtor's property illusory, which in turn would deter entry into these secured credit arrangements.

A good illustration of these competing policy concerns and how the courts have sought to reconcile them arises in the context of commercial contracts of sale containing retention of title clauses. The pattern of the creditor retaining full legal and equitable proprietary interests and merely conferring possessory rights on the debtor has a long history. This is the form of a hire-purchase contract and other conditional sales. It is also the underlying structure of a mortgage agreement, under which the debtor transfers title to property in return for a loan and a right to repurchase the property on repayment of the loan. By virtue of his ownership, the creditor can sell the property in the event of the debtor's default, realize the value of the asset, and secure repayment of the debt from its proceeds. In principle this scheme of retention of title can apply to any type of property except money (where ownership is normally tied to possession). Under the Sale of Goods Act 1979, s 19, the law leaves it to the parties to the contract to choose at what point in time ownership of the goods passes between them.

In recent years creditors have favoured the strategy of retention of title in the context of the sale of goods between commercial parties in order to secure priority in the event of insolvency. With repeated and deep economic recessions and credit squeezes, this has perhaps been an inevitable response by creditors. Under these contracts, known as Romalpa Clauses after a leading case,[54] a seller of goods includes a term in the contract to the effect that legal title to the goods remains the seller's until the debtor has paid for the goods in full. This allows the debtor to acquire goods on credit without having to seek a loan from a bank to pay for them, whilst at the same time affording the protection of a proprietary right to the creditor. These Romalpa Clauses have the advantage to the creditor that they fall outside any requirement of registration, since the debtor does not receive any proprietary interest until full payment has been made. As a consequence, the proliferation of retention of title clauses in commercial sales results in considerable uncertainty with respect to the rights of ownership in goods. A third party cannot be sure whether or not goods on sale by a person in possession of them in fact belong to the possessor or a third party.

These Romalpa Clauses create especially severe difficulties when the purchaser uses the goods in a production process, so that they become mixed up with other

53 Hire-Purchase Act 1964, s 27 (as amended by Consumer Credit Act 1974, s 192(3)).
54 *Aluminium Industrie Vaassen BV v Romalpa Aluminium Ltd* [1976] 2 All ER 552, [1976] 1 WLR 676, CA; the technique of retaining legal title was accorded validity initially in *McEntire v Crossley Bros Ltd* [1895] AC 457, HL.

goods which the debtor owns. For example, in *Clough Mill Ltd v Martin*,[55] the vendor sold yarn to a buyer which used the yarn to manufacture fabrics which were then sold on to third parties. Under the contract for sale of the yarn the seller retained ownership of the yarn, even if it had been mixed up with other goods to make a fabric, until full payment had been received. The contract also provided, however, that the purchaser of the yarn could sell the made-up material. Some of the difficult questions which may arise in such situations are: will the third party who receives the material receive good title to it? who owns the proceeds of such sales, the seller or the buyer of the yarn?[56] who owns the fabric after it has been manufactured if all the suppliers of goods to the manufacturer have insisted upon a retention of title clause?[57]

The answer to these perplexing questions at present turns on the terms of each contract and how it is construed by a court. The question in *Clough Mill Ltd v Martin* was whether the seller owned the yarn when the buyer became insolvent and went into receivership, and, if so, whether the seller could obtain damages against the receiver for using the yarn after the seller had given notice that it sought return of its property for breach of contract. The Court of Appeal upheld the seller's claim, stating that the seller had retained full ownership of the yarn so there was no need for it to have registered its proprietary interest. On the other hand, in so far as the yarn had become mixed up with other goods and made into fabric, then the seller had lost full legal title to the yarn, so its proprietary interest, as an equitable interest or charge, needed to be registered in order to be valid in the event of insolvency. This puzzling result under which legal ownership changes hands as workers on the shop floor open up bundles of yarn and mix them into a fabric reveals how retention of title clauses can provoke considerable confusion in markets.

This need for limitations upon freedom of contract with respect to retention of title clauses becomes all the more apparent when they are employed in an oppressive manner. One striking illustration of oppression even in commercial transactions is where the creditor insists upon retention of title of goods sold until not only full payment for those goods has been received, but also any other debts owed by the debtor to the creditor or members of the creditor's group of companies have been satisfied. If the parties to the contract of sale have long-term business relations with frequent contracts, such a provision will have the effect that the debtor will never acquire title to any goods unless all outstanding credit has been paid off. The creditor can thus achieve a dominant position over the debtor by means of this 'catching bargain'. Nevertheless, the House of Lords in

55 [1984] 3 All ER 982, [1985] 1 WLR 111, CA.

56 *Aluminium Industrie Vaassen BV v Romalpa Aluminium Ltd* [1976] 2 All ER 552, [1976] 1 WLR 676, CA. Despite elaborate contractual provision, the proceeds of a sub-sale will be owned by the buyer, leaving the seller with a registrable charge: *Compaq Computers Ltd v Abercorn Group Ltd* [1991] BCC 484, QB.

57 *Borden (UK) Ltd v Scottish Timber Products Ltd* [1981] Ch 25, [1979] 3 All ER 961, CA.

Armour v Thyssen Edelstahlwerke AG[58] has accepted the validity of such agreements, relying simply on the idea that the parties should be free to set the terms on which property interests in goods will pass.

This striking adherence to freedom of contract with respect to retention of title clauses overlooks the danger which this commercial practice poses to markets. Although the courts may be bound to observe the logic of these retention of title arrangements with respect to the distribution of proprietary interests, the absence of the normal protection afforded to third parties by systems of compulsory registration of interests requires some measure of reform. Either a system of registration for such contractual arrangements should be introduced, or it might be possible to restrict the kinds of retention of title clauses which may be used effectively against third parties.

2. Protection of possessory interests

Under most of these schemes for the distribution of property rights, the debtor risks losing possession of the goods or property in the event of breach of contract. This right to repossess provides one of the principal securities for the creditor against the debtor's default. In practice a creditor is likely to prefer to negotiate a settlement such as a rescheduling of repayments under a loan in order to avoid the costs of a forced sale. But clearly the creditor's proprietary interest provides him with a powerful bargaining chip in securing a favourable settlement. Although the common law invariably respects this right to repossess under a forfeiture clause in a contract, an equitable jurisdiction and various statutory measures have been developed to protect the debtor's possessory interest.

(a) EQUITABLE RELIEF FROM FORFEITURE

The reason for this protection of the debtor's possessory interest reveals a realistic interpretation of the purpose of forfeiture clauses. The purpose of the clause is to provide a security against payment by the debtor. The creditor is unlikely to wish to acquire the property for himself, and will almost certainly on repossession seek to divest himself of the property. In contrast, the debtor will often have a strong interest in maintaining possession of the property. In a contract for a lease, for instance, the debtor or tenant normally wishes to continue occupation of the land. If the lease is forfeited because of failure to pay rent or breach of some other covenant, then the landlord can repossess the property and evict the tenant, resulting in great inconvenience to the tenant. Similarly, under a contract of hire purchase, a consumer will normally wish to retain possession of the car or television set, although this will be forfeited on failure to pay the hire charges.

---

58 [1991] 2 AC 339, [1990] 3 All ER 481, HL; Bradgate, 'Retention of Title in the House of Lords: Unanswered Questions' (1991) 54 *Modern Law Review* 726.

The courts of equity recognized that the creditor did not usually have any interest in possession of the property. The purpose of the forfeiture clause was rather to provide a deterrence against default and a way of securing the debt.

On the basis of this realistic interpretation of forfeiture clauses, equity devised a mechanism for the protection of the debtor's possessory interest. It provided relief from forfeiture on condition that the debtor paid any sums of money owing to the creditor plus interest on the money for late payment. Provided the debtor can produce this sum of money within the time which the court is prepared to allow,[59] the debtor has a complete defence to an action for repossession of the property.[60] This equitable relief from forfeiture is routinely available, for instance, to tenants in arrears of rent.

But the exact scope of the protection of a debtor's possessory interest provided by the equitable jurisdiction remains controversial. Lord Wilberforce in *Shiloh Spinners Ltd v Harding* observed that:

> we should reaffirm the right of courts of equity in appropriate and limited cases to relieve against forfeiture for breach of covenant or condition where the primary object of the bargain is to secure a stated result which can effectively be attained when the matter comes before the court, and where the forfeiture provision is added by way of security for the production of that result.[61]

The courts have subsequently defined the limits to this jurisdiction by reference to two criteria.

The first criterion concerns the urgency of the debtor's performance. If the contract expressly provides that with respect to the debtor's performance 'time is of the essence', then the courts infer that the parties have agreed that the delays envisaged by the jurisdiction to relieve from forfeiture are inappropriate. Thus in *Scandinavian Trading Tanker Co AB v Flota Petrolera Ecuatoriana (The Scaptrade)*,[62] the House of Lords declined to give relief to a charterer of a ship under a time charter when the owner of the vessel sought repossession of the vessel for failure to pay the charges due on time, on the ground that the contract expressly stated that prompt payment was of the essence of the charterer's obligations. To give relief from forfeiture in these circumstances would be to permit the charterer much greater flexibility in the date of payment without fear of losing possession of the ship, whereas under the contract the charterer had expressly agreed to make prompt payments. In short, the courts will not exercise the jurisdiction to relieve from forfeiture where this would undermine the express agreement between the

---

59 *Starside Properties Ltd v Mustapha* [1974] 2 All ER 567, [1974] 1 WLR 816, CA.
60 *In Re Dagenham (Thames) Dock Co* (1873) 8 Ch App 1022, CA; *Kilmer v British Columbia Orchard Lands Ltd* [1913] AC 319, PC.
61 [1973] AC 691 at 723, [1973] 1 All ER 90 at 101, HL.
62 [1983] 2 AC 694, [1983] 2 All ER 763, HL.

parties on the need for prompt payment, even if payment is only ten minutes late,[63] at least if this express agreement has been reached between commercial parties dealing at arm's length.

The second criterion for limiting the scope of relief from forfeiture concerns the nature of the debtor's proprietary or possessory interest. Lord Diplock in *The Scaptrade* insisted that the jurisdiction to relieve from forfeiture was confined to certain proprietary and possessory rights. He concluded that the jurisdiction could not apply to a time charter, because he characterized the arrangement as merely a contract for services under which the ship owner provided a vessel and crew in return for a hire charge, rendering the contract analogous to the hire of a taxi. The equitable jurisdiction appears to have been confined further by the House of Lords in *Sport International Bussum BV v Inter-Footwear Ltd*.[64] Here the debtor's interest was in the right granted under a contractual licence to use the creditor's trademark in the sale of footwear. The debtor breached the contract, not by failing to pay sums due, but by failing to arrange for a bank guarantee of payment by a set date. For this technical breach of contract which caused the creditor no delay in payment, the creditor purported to terminate the licence to use the trademark, thus ruining the debtor's business. The court upheld this termination, partly on the ground of the first criterion that time was of the essence in securing the bank guarantee, but also on the ground that the contractual licence to use a trademark was not the kind of possessory interest for which relief from forfeiture would be given. This is a striking limitation on the jurisdiction, for the possessory interest in the trademark was of the highest commercial interest to the debtor.

The decision contrasts sharply with the acceptance of jurisdiction to grant relief from forfeiture in *BICC plc v Burndy Corpn*,[65] where the proprietary interest at stake was a joint interest between the parties in certain patent rights. Although it is possible to draw a distinction between joint ownership and a mere contractual licence, there is little difference between them from the point of view of the commercial function, for in both cases the point of the transaction is to permit another to exploit a particular form of intellectual property.

Instead of utilizing these formal distinctions concerning the nature of the debtor's proprietary interest in order to define the scope of the equitable jurisdiction to give relief from forfeiture, it would be better if the courts asked themselves three questions:

(i)   Does the debtor have a real commercial or consumption interest in retaining possession of the property?

(ii)   Was the forfeiture clause merely designed to ensure payment rather than to establish a conditional sale of a proprietary interest?

---

63 *Union Eagle Ltd v Golden Achievement Ltd* [1997] AC 514, [1997] 2 All ER 215, PC.
64 [1984] 2 All ER 321, [1984] 1 WLR 776, HL.
65 [1985] Ch 232, [1985] 1 All ER 417, CA.

(iii) Have the parties through the terms of their contract, either expressly or impliedly, indicated that prompt payment is an essential feature of the contract, thereby negativing the possibility of delays afforded by applications for relief from forfeiture?

If the answer to the first two questions is affirmative, and to the last negative, normally relief from forfeiture should be available.

(b) STATUTORY RELIEF

In many specific instances, the power to give relief from forfeiture has been accorded to the courts and regulated by statute. Forfeiture of leases for non-payment of rent is governed by the Common Law Procedure Act 1852, ss 210–212, and forfeiture of leases for other breaches of covenant is regulated by the Law of Property Act 1925, s 146. In consumer credit transactions, the Consumer Credit Act 1974 protects the consumer's interest in possession of property being acquired under a conditional sale agreement or hire purchase in two ways:

(i)   the creditor must follow a statutory procedure under ss 87–89 for giving notice or warning to the debtor that the default in payments risks the creditor's repossession of the goods; and

(ii) the court has a general power under s 129 to allow the debtor time to make good any missing payments, if the court regards it as just to do so.[66]

This latter power of making time orders goes beyond the equitable jurisdiction, because it gives the court much greater flexibility, so that in effect it can reschedule the payment of debts.

3.   Unjust enrichment by over-compensation

The third ground on which a court may control an agreed distribution of property rights as a remedial device contained in a contract is to prevent unjust enrichment of the creditor. For consumer contracts, any device designed to achieve disproportionate compensation is likely to be regarded as an invalid unfair term.[67] Moreover, the mirror principle may require consumer contracts to grant equal or equivalent proprietary interests to both supplier and consumer, so that a deposit without an equivalent assurance to the benefit of the consumer may invalidate an attempt to retain the deposit.[68] Outside statutory protections, however, the existence of a power to prevent excessive compensation is both

---

66 The court is unlikely to make a time order if there is no reasonable prospect of repayment even after rescheduling: *First National Bank plc v Syed* [1991] 2 All ER 250, CA.

67 Unfair Terms in Consumer Contracts Regulations 1999, SI 1999/2083, Sch 2, para 1(e).

68 Unfair Terms in Consumer Contracts Regulations 1999, SI 1999/2083, Sch 2, para 1(d).

controversial and uncertain in its scope.[69] But it is clearly analogous to, and overlaps with, the jurisdiction to control penalty clauses, and doubts about its existence should be put aside. The purpose of the jurisdiction is to ensure that the creditor does not receive a remedy which far exceeds his loss resulting from the debtor's breach of contract. The forfeiture of valuable property rights can risk this result just as much as a contractual penalty clause which specifies high levels of compensation.

(a) UNJUST ENRICHMENT AS A DEFENCE

Where the creditor seeks to enforce an agreed distribution of property rights by applying for a court order to convey or transfer those rights, then the court may decline to make such an order on the ground that this compensatory arrangement is unconscionable, although it will require the debtor to compensate the creditor fully. In *Jobson v Johnson*,[70] for instance, the contractual remedy for breach provided that the debtor should transfer to the creditor some valuable shares in a company owning a football club. The court ordered that if the value of the shares exceeded the loss to the creditor, an order of specific performance would be refused, and instead the court would replicate the technique of scaling down penalty clauses by ordering sale of the shares and payment of the debt out of the proceeds. Similarly, in, *BICC plc v Burndy Corpn*, the court decided that specific performance of the assignment of the patent rights would not be ordered in any event, since the debt owed by the defendant to the plaintiff was less than the amount of money owed by the plaintiff. Here the right of set-off was used to defeat the proprietary remedy, for otherwise enforcement of the proprietary right would result in unjust enrichment to the plaintiff.

In these cases it was easy for the court to detect the risk of over-compensation for the creditor. In other instances, the issue will often be more difficult to assess. Consider, for example, the pattern of commercial contracts known as commercial leases. In recent years leases have been used widely as a form of commercial finance. The finance company purchases the goods selected by the debtor, and then leases them for a fixed term to the debtor in return for periodic payments of rent. This arrangement differs from a hire-purchase agreement both in the absence of the debtor's right to purchase the goods, and in the way that the cost of credit or rate of interest is concealed in the price of the rent. This arrangement may prove attractive as a means of financing a purchase if the value of the goods will quickly depreciate, as in the case of a computer, for then the security provided by ownership of the goods will prove minimal. Under the terms of the lease, the rental payments will continue to be payable during the period of the lease, regardless of the fact that the lessee returns the goods or the lessor repossesses

---

69 Beatson, 'Discharge for Breach: The Position of Instalments, Deposits and Other Payments Due Before Completion' (1981) 97 *Law Quarterly Review* 389.

70 [1989] 1 All ER 621, [1989] 1 WLR 1026, CA.

them for breach. There is a danger for the lessor that a court may regard the term requiring payment of all future rent for the term of the lease as a penalty clause,[71] but it is far from clear that the rent represents anything more than a genuine pre-estimate of the loss, especially if allowances are made for acceleration of payments and the resale value of the goods. In any event, as illustrated by *Lombard North Central plc v Butterworth*,[72] a case concerning the commercial lease of a computer to an accountant, the lessor will be able to claim damages as a secondary obligation for the loss of the bargain amounting to close on the whole amount of rental payments due for the term of the lease. At first sight this result may appear to leave the lessor over-compensated, for it receives most of the rent and return of the goods prior to the end of the term of the lease, but once one recognizes that the goods may not have any commercial value so that the lessor cannot mitigate its loss, this contractual measure of compensation does not result in unjust enrichment.

(b) RESTITUTIONARY CLAIM

The courts have shown themselves more circumspect in providing relief from unconscionable measures of compensation through contractual distributions of proprietary rights when the debtor has already transferred the property and now seeks to claim a sum of money to remedy the unjust enrichment of the creditor. This reluctance is understandable, since the court is not merely being asked to refuse an order for specific performance of a contract, but is required to make a positive order for the creditor to pay money to the debtor because of the over-compensation. In the case of deposits for the purchase of interests in land, this jurisdiction has statutory backing, which gives a court the discretion to order repayment of a deposit.[73] This jurisdiction appears to reflect a more general equitable jurisdiction to provide relief from deposits if the sum forfeited far exceeds the loss and is unreasonable.[74]

A similar protection is afforded to the debtor under transactions regulated by the Consumer Credit Act 1974. Here the general rule is that the creditor cannot repossess the goods being purchased on credit once the debtor has paid to the creditor one-third or more of the total price of the goods without a court order.[75] In making an order, the court then has broad discretionary powers to attach conditions to the order,[76] and may strike it down as an extortionate credit

---

71 *Lombard North Central plc v Butterworth* [1987] QB 527, [1987] 1 All ER 267, CA.

72 [1987] QB 527, [1987] 1 All ER 267, CA.

73 Law of Property Act 1925, s 49(2); *Universal Corpn v Five Ways Properties Ltd* [1979] 1 All ER 552, CA.

74 *Public Works Comr v Hills* [1906] AC 368, PC; *Workers Trust and Merchant Bank Ltd v Dojap Investments Ltd* [1993] AC 573, [1993] 2 All ER 370, PC.

75 Consumer Credit Act 1974, s 90.

76 Consumer Credit Act 1974, s 136.

bargain.[77] In addition, under a hire-purchase agreement where the owner recovers possession, the court enjoys broad powers to order the return of any money paid in respect of the goods by the debtor, if it appears just to do so.[78] But can a restitutionary claim be used more generally for return of money and property forfeited under the terms of a contract?

The question of whether or not this jurisdiction exists was answered affirmatively by a majority of the Court of Appeal in *Stockloser v Johnson*.[79] Under a contract for the sale of machinery, the price was payable by instalments. The contract provided that in the event of breach by the purchaser, the seller was entitled to retain instalments already paid. This forfeiture of instalments was held to be valid on the facts of the case, since in view of the risks accepted by the seller and his losses the retention of the instalments was not unconscionable. But the majority of the court recognized the possibility of a restitutionary claim for return of all or part of the instalments, if the forfeiture clause led to unjust enrichment. Romer LJ, dissenting, denied the existence of any such equitable jurisdiction, arguing that it would give the courts a power to rewrite contracts by dispensing with forfeiture clauses altogether.

But this criticism overlooks the analogous power to control penalty clauses, and misses the point that the aim of judicial control is merely to prevent unjust enrichment through agreed remedies and not to rewrite the terms of contracts in general. The only difference between penalty clauses and these instances of forfeiture of property is that in the latter the creditor has already secured through the contract a proprietary interest representing the agreed compensation. This puts the creditor in a stronger position than a simple claim for agreed compensation, and there may be a case for respecting this choice of the parties in the contract by restricting equitable intervention to severe cases of unjust enrichment caused by forfeiture of deposits and other proprietary interests, but this should not prevent the equitable jurisdiction from operating to give relief from unconscionable agreed remedies.[80] 'This argument leads towards the conclusion that, since a promised penalty cannot be claimed, a penalty which has already passed into the other's hands should be recoverable.'[81]

E.   Guarantees and indemnities

A contract of guarantee provides an agreed remedy against a third party. Subject to the precise terms of the contract, the guarantor promises to a creditor either to

---

77 Consumer Credit Act 1974, s 137.
78 Consumer Credit Act 1974, s 132.
79 [1954] 1 QB 476, [1954] 1 All ER 630, CA; see also Collins LJ, *Cornwall v Henson* [1900] 2 Ch 298 at 302, CA.
80 This view prevails in Australia: *McDonald v Dennys Lascelles Ltd* (1933) 48 CLR 457, Aust HC; and in the USA: Corbin, 'The Right of a Defaulting Vendee to the Restitution of Instalments Paid' (1931) 40 *Yale Law Journal* 1013.
81 P Birks, *An Introduction to the Law of Restitution* (Oxford, 1985), p 215.

procure performance of a debtor's obligations under a contract or to fulfil those obligations himself.[82] A director of a company may, for example, give a personal guarantee of his company's contractual performance to a creditor such as a bank. If the debtor company breaks the contract with the bank, then the bank may enforce the guarantee against the director as guarantor, as if the guarantor were the primary debtor. This is a valuable technique for facilitating market transactions where the debtor cannot offer any valuable proprietary security to the creditor. A performance bond is a type of guarantee under which a bank guarantees a fixed measure of compensation in the event of the defendant's breach of a contract to perform a service, although the plaintiff will only be able to retain under the performance bond an amount equal to the extent of its loss caused by the defendant's breach of contract.[83]

A contract of indemnity performs a similar function to a guarantee. Here the third party normally promises that he will meet any loss suffered by a creditor as a result of contracting with the debtor. This is an independent contract between the third party and the creditor, so that unlike a guarantee its content and enforceability do not depend upon the validity of the contract between the debtor and the creditor.[84] In particular, a contract of indemnity could extend to cover the debtor's tortious liability to a creditor, whereas a contract of guarantee merely promises to meet the debtor's contractual obligations to the creditor. Thus an indemnity not only serves the purpose of encouraging credit transactions, but can also provide a risk allocation device between three parties. It is not an exclusion clause which limits liability, but merely determines which of the three parties should eventually meet the cost of losses incurred during business.[85]

A guarantee is only valid if evidenced by a note or memorandum in writing signed by the guarantor.[86] No formalities are required, however, for a contract of indemnity. The consideration to support the enforcement of both a guarantee and an indemnity is usually discovered in the creditor's entry into a contract with the debtor.

The guarantor, if called upon to perform, enjoys implied rights of indemnity against the debtor except in so far as these are qualified by contract. Thus the director, if called upon to perform the personal guarantee, could then claim an indemnity against the company. Because the guarantor's right to claim an indemnity is his only security, any agreement between the creditor and debtor which alters or extinguishes the value of this indemnity is likely to be held to discharge the guarantor from liability. Unlike a guarantee, a contract of

---

82 *Moschi v Lep Air Services Ltd* [1973] AC 331, [1972] 2 All ER 393, HL.
83 *Cargill International SA v Bangladesh Sugar and Food Industries Corp* [1998] 2 All ER 406, [1998] 1 WLR 461, CA.
84 R Goode, *Commercial Law* (London, 2nd edn, 1995), pp 821–825.
85 *Thompson v T Lohan (Plant Hire) Ltd* [1987] 2 All ER 631, [1987] 1 WLR 649, CA.
86 Statute of Frauds (1677), s 4. *Elpis Maritime Co Ltd v Marti Chartering Co Inc (The Maria D)* [1991] 2 Lloyd's Rep 311, HL.

indemnity given by a third party does not give rise to a similar implied contract of indemnity against the debtor, although of course such an additional indemnity might be agreed as well.

Outside commercial transactions, the risk posed by contract of guarantee is that the debtor may persuade a friend to give a guarantee when the friend does not fully appreciate the potential extent of liability and the nature of the risk. To reduce this danger, the Consumer Credit Act 1974 requires guarantees for consumer credit transactions to be in writing according to a prescribed form and also requires the details of the transaction to be given in writing to the guarantor.[87] This is a slim protection, for it assumes that information is a sufficient bulwark against foolish transactions. In contrast, under the Unfair Contract Terms Act 1977, s 4, a person dealing as a consumer is protected by the test of reasonableness from giving foolish indemnities against his own or another's breach of contract or negligence.

F. Arbitration

Under the terms of a contract the parties may agree that any disputes arising between them should be resolved by a forum other than a public court. International business transactions often prefer private arbitration. For the construction industry, a source of many legal disputes, not only is private arbitration prevalent, but also Parliament has created a special statutory adjudication procedure,[88] as well as a specialist division of the courts, the Technology and Construction Court. Many industries dealing with consumers also prefer to set up an arbitration system or an Ombudsman. Some use of arbitration also occurs in the collective arrangements between management and unions. An arbitration agreement can normally be enforced by a court order to stay any legal proceedings relating to a dispute governed by a written arbitration agreement.[89]

The attractions of private arbitration are numerous. The parties can select an arbitrator who is familiar with the nature of the business and who has their confidence. Arbitration proceedings may prove quicker and more convenient, although they are often more expensive since the parties have to pay the arbitrator. The arbitrator may also be more willing to act as mediator between the parties and help them to reach a settlement. These advantages may prove particularly significant in long-term relational contracts, where the parties wish to avoid any breakdown in the economic relationship, yet need a method of

---

87 Consumer Credit Act 1974, ss 105–112.
88 Housing Grants, Construction and Regeneration Act 1996, Part II; Gould and Cohen, 'ADR: Appropriate Dispute resolution in the UK Construction Industry' (1998) 17 *Civil Justice Quarterly* 103.
89 Arbitration Act 1996, s 9.

dispute resolution to govern the occasional unforeseen divergence of interest. A simple example is the contract of employment, where many employers have established internal arbitration for the grievances of individual employees to be heard and for disciplinary sanctions to be imposed.

The use of arbitration is controlled by legislation for two purposes. In the first place, the legislation reserves to the courts the power to ensure that the arbitrator acts according to the principles of natural justice or procedural due process and within the substantive jurisdiction conferred on it by the parties.[90] Beyond these issues of fair process and jurisdiction, however, the parties are free to agree to exclude review by the courts. A second reason for legislative control concerns the risk that a party dealing with consumers will seek to impose through a standard form contract a biased system of arbitration as the forum for resolving disputes. The bias may lie either in the choice of arbitrator, the absence of procedural safeguards, or more simply in hurdles of procedure and expense which may deter consumers from ever making claims.[91] The Arbitration Act 1996 gives limited protection to consumers against this form of oppression by declaring arbitration clauses in consumer contracts involving small claims invalid as unfair terms contrary to the Unfair Terms in Consumer Contracts Regulations 1999.[92] In the Regulations, Sch 2, para 1(q) indicates that an example of an unfair term may be one:

> excluding or hindering the consumer's right to take legal action or exercise any other legal remedy, particularly by requiring the consumer to take disputes exclusively to arbitration not covered by legal provisions, unduly restricting the evidence available to him or imposing on him a burden of proof which, according to the applicable law, should lie with another party to the contract.

Short of an agreed forum such as arbitration, a contract may provide an alternative optional avenue of redress to litigation. There is no objection on the ground of fairness to such arrangements for they merely augment avenues of redress for consumers and do not detract from any legal rights. In recent years many industries dealing with consumers have established through their trade associations ombudsmen as a relatively informal and inexpensive means by which consumers may seek redress against large organizations such as banks, insurance companies, and building societies. An ombudsman offers the consumer the possibility of a thorough investigation of a complaint, an opinion about the merits of the case without necessarily being tied to the strict contractual terms of a

---

90 Arbitration Act 1996, ss 32–33, 67–68.

91 Thomas, 'Consumer Arbitration Agreements Act 1988' (1991) *Arbitration* 48; Schwartz, 'Enforcing Small Print to Protect Big Business: Employee and Consumer Rights Claims in an Age of Compelled Arbitration' (1997) *Wisconsin Law Rev* 33.

92 Arbitration Act 1996, s 91; SI 1999/2038. This protection does not appear as detailed or as favourable to consumers as the Consumer Arbitration Agreements Act 1988, which was repealed by the Arbitration Act 1996.

standard form contract, and as a last resort a binding decision against the member of the trade association. As the existence of these ombudsmen have become known to consumers, they have been swamped by complaints. Although the trade associations exclude many issues from the purview of ombudsmen, this alternative dispute resolution mechanism seems likely to become a key ingredient in providing a more effective remedy for consumers' complaints about breach of contract.

Chapter 17

Judicial remedies

A.   Judicial enforcement mechanisms
B.   Settlements
C.   Considerations shaping judicial remedies
  1.   Avoidance of deterrence
  2.   Minimizing social cost
  3.   Efficient breach of contract
  4.   Social market
D.   Damages
  1.   The compensatory principle
    (a)   Cost of substituted performance
    (b)   Wasted expenditure
    (c)   Cost of repair
    (d)   Net loss
  2.   Loss of profits
    (a)   Proof of loss
    (b)   Remoteness of loss
  3.   Non-pecuniary losses
  4.   Avoidable losses
    (a)   Time of assessment
    (b)   Causation
    (c)   Contributory negligence
    (d)   Mitigation of loss
  5.   Waste of resources
  6.   Disgorgement and punitive damages
E.   Compulsory performance
  1.   Inadequacy of compensation
  2.   Instrumental purposes of compulsory performance
  3.   Limitations
    (a)   Waste of resources
    (b)   Liberty
    (c)   Fairness
    (d)   Mutuality

A. Judicial enforcement mechanisms

In the absence of any contractually agreed remedies, the party injured by a breach of contract must rely upon judicial remedies. The courts offer compensatory damages as the principal remedy for breach of contract. In some circumstances, it is also possible to obtain an order for compulsory performance, either in the positive form of an order for specific performance of the contractual obligations, or in a negative form of an injunction against breach of contract.

Other judicial remedies might apply to actions for breach of contract in particular cases, such as an order to deliver goods to the injured party,[1] or an order to carry out those formalities known as completion which are necessary to effect a legal transfer of ownership of land, or the appointment of a receiver and manager of property in order to carry out positive obligations under a contract.[2] A breach of contract may also provoke insolvency proceedings against a defendant company, resulting in the court's appointment of an administrator or receiver.[3]

Failure to comply with judicial orders for remedies for breach of contract results in the application of further coercive measures. If an award of damages is not paid by the defendant, the claimant may invoke a court procedure for the seizure and sale of the defendant's goods to the value of the outstanding sum owed. The effectiveness of this remedy, of course, depends upon the claimant's being able to locate the defendant's assets, the existence of such assets, and the speed at which the court's process operates before the defendant's assets are moved and dispersed. The coercive mechanism backing up orders for specific performance and injunctions differs because these orders have their origins in the equitable jurisdiction of the courts. If the defendant defies an order for compulsory performance, the claimant may invoke the sanctions for civil contempt of court. If the court determines that the defendant has committed contempt by failing to comply with its order, it may impose the sanctions of fines, the sequestering of all the assets of the defendant, or imprisonment, in order to coerce performance from the recalcitrant defendant.

B. Settlements

Before these judicial remedies will be required, however, the parties are most likely to engage in bargaining towards a settlement of the dispute. The vast majority of litigation terminates as a result of a settlement before any court order is required. A settlement comprises a species of contract under which both parties agree that the litigation of dispute should be terminated.

1 Torts (Interference with Goods) Act 1977, s 3.
2 *Hart v Emilkirk Ltd* [1983] 3 All ER 15, [1983] 1 WLR 1289, Ch; *Parker v Camden London Borough Council* [1985] Ch 162, [1985] 2 All ER 141, CA.
3 Insolvency Act 1986.

This contract usually satisfies the normal requirements for the formation of a binding contract such as agreement and consideration. One party relinquishes its claim for breach of contract in return for a payment or some other consideration. Mere payment of money to the claimant does not create a contract of settlement unless the claimant agrees that the sum has been accepted in return for abandoning the legal claim, or, in a phrase commonly used, in 'accord and satisfaction'.[4] A promise not to enforce a claim in return for compensation satisfies the requirement of consideration even when the claim is unfounded or turns out to be unenforceable.[5] This rule creates the danger that it might encourage the pursuit of fraudulent or spurious claims, so the courts created an exception where the person offering to refrain from litigation knows that the claim is invalid.[6] This exception is hard to square with the rule that the courts will not test the adequacy of consideration, for in principle they should leave the promisee to determine whether the surrender of an invalid claim has any value to him. The exception seems necessary, however, in order to prevent the enforcement of settlements from becoming an instrument of fraud. A settlement may also be impugned on the ground of economic duress under the principles described in Chapter 15.

The time and expense of litigation normally provide sufficient incentives for the parties to want to arrange a compromise if at all possible. But the available judicial remedies for breach of contract affect the nature of this bargaining process. The likely outcome in court provides the benchmark against which the parties reach a settlement. In crude terms, a party injured by breach of contract will not agree a settlement unless it accords roughly with the remedy which might be provided by a court, discounted by the risk of not being able to establish the claim, and minus the likely costs of litigation. If the defendant is teetering on the edge of insolvency, the injured party may be persuaded to accept an extremely disadvantageous settlement for fear of being left without any substantial remedy as an unsecured creditor. For these reasons, the most important impact of judicial remedies upon the market is the way they determine in part the relative bargaining strength of the parties in post-breach settlements.

Two crucial variables in judicial remedies play a major role in determining this bargaining strength of the parties in settlement of disputes. One variable consists in the likely measure of damages or compensation to be awarded by a court. The greater this potential liability, the higher the financial settlement to which the defendant must agree. To the extent that the measure of compensation falls below the value which the injured party places upon performance of the contract, which often proves to be the case in practice, any settlement is likely to be disadvantageous to the injured party. The second variable concerns the incidence of orders for compulsory performance. If the injured party can obtain an order for

4   *Ferguson v Davies* [1997] 1 All ER 315, CA.
5   *Haigh v Brooks* (1839) 10 Ad & El 309, Ex; *Cook v Wright* (1861) 1 B & S 559, 121 ER 822, QB.
6   *Wade v Simeon* (1846) 2 CB 548.

specific performance or an injunction, this threat increases his or her bargaining power in seeking an advantageous settlement. The availability of compulsory performance gives the injured party something analogous to a property right in the performance of the promise.[7] Since the injured party may ultimately threaten the defendant with the sanctions for contempt of court, the injured party may insist upon a settlement that is equal to the value which he or she places upon performance of the contract. Notice how the bargaining position of the injured party is enhanced by the potential availability of an order for compulsory performance.

One final crucial factor affects the practice of reaching settlements. Representation by a lawyer with expertise in respect of the disputed issue can improve the post-breach bargaining position of a party to a contract. A sophisticated lawyer can raise numerous technical problems, dubious arcane legal points, and elaborate procedural hurdles, in order to dissuade a claimant from pursuing the case. For this reason, consumers, employees, and small businesses tend be at a considerable disadvantage in negotiations for a settlement. Businesses which routinely engage in litigation, such as insurance companies or liquidators of insolvent companies, are likely to be able to extract unusually favourable settlements.[8]

C. Considerations shaping judicial remedies

A general aim of the law of contract is no doubt to support the practice of entering market transactions. But it does not follow from this general aim that the courts should necessarily order the defendant to keep the contractual obligation according to its precise terms. Several important considerations dictate that the courts should confine awards of compulsory performance and limit the measure of compensatory damages awarded.

1. Avoidance of deterrence

In the first place, the courts must bear in mind that stiff penalties for breach of contract might deter parties from entering contracts in the first place. If due performance of the contract lies in the future, uncertainty about market conditions and possible unexpected impediments to performance may deter the formation of the contract when the risk of substantial potential liability looms. The remedy available to the injured party must therefore not be so immense as to

---

7 Calibresi and Melamed, 'Property Rules, Liability Rules, and Inalienability: One View of the Cathedral' (1972) 85 *Harvard Law Rev* 1089; J Coleman, *Markets, Morals and the Law* (Cambridge, 1988), ch 2.
8 S Wheeler, *Reservation of Title Clauses* (Oxford, 1991); M Galanter, 'Why the "haves" Come Out Ahead: Speculations on the Limits of Legal Change' (1974–75) 9 *Law and Society Review* 95.

deter the creation of binding contracts. A balance must be struck between the provision of a judicial remedy which supports the reliability of contractual undertakings, whilst not being so great as to discourage the formation of binding commitments.[9]

This consideration leads the courts both to confine the measure of damages by doctrines such as remoteness of damage, and to limit the availability of orders for specific performance and injunctions. The rule denying recovery for remote losses shares the same purpose as the doctrine of privity of contract. It avoids the deterrence to entry into contracts which might result from the scope of potential liability. In the case of privity of contract, the risk arises from the potential number of claimants injured by breach of contract. In the case of remoteness of loss confining the measure of damages, the rule prevents the single claimant's measure of damages from becoming a potential deterrent to the formation of contracts.

2. Minimizing social cost

Secondly, the courts are concerned to limit the social costs of breach of contract. These costs include the administration of justice, the costs of bargaining towards settlements of claims for breach of contract, and the waste of resources following breach of contract. The costs of administration of justice can be reduced to the extent that the parties can be induced to settle the claim out of court. This consideration argues against the use of specific performance and injunctions, which necessarily require a court order, and in favour of damages, for a financial settlement will achieve the same result without the use of the courts. Against this it must be observed, however, that once the parties are in court, the equitable remedies are often awarded speedily and cheaply by interim proceedings. The consideration of the costs of the administration of justice also supports the enforcement of settlements as binding contracts regardless of the justice achieved, subject perhaps to safeguards described above against fraud and duress.[10] Various rules of civil procedure also induce settlements. In particular, if the defendant pays into a court a sum of money prior to the court hearing and this sum proves equal to or greater than the eventual award of damages, the claimant cannot recover the costs of litigation from the defendant.

The costs of bargaining towards settlement of claims can be reduced in a number of ways. The best method is for the courts to provide an easily reckonable method for ascertaining the likely measure of a judicial award of damages. The greater the certainty of the outcome of the court process, the more likely that the parties will be able to agree a settlement for they will be bargaining under conditions of

---

9   Goetz and Scott, 'Enforcing Promises: An Examination of the Basis of Contract' (1980) 89 *Yale Law Journal* 1261.

10 J Coleman, *Markets, Morals and the Law* (Cambridge, 1988), pp 202–215.

relative certainty. It is difficult to predict whether or not the potential for an award of compulsory performance will reduce or increase the costs of bargaining towards a settlement. Although an injured party entitled to an award of specific performance may be tempted to hold out for an advantageous settlement of any claim, this manoeuvre and its associated costs may not prove any worse in terms of transaction costs than the dickering between the parties over a final settlement of a claim for damages. The costs of bargaining over settlements may also be reduced by the introduction of a neutral conciliator or mediator who will bring the parties together. This method is regularly used in specialized areas, such as the allegation of an employer's breach of the contract of employment, where in Britain the government has provided for a long time a free conciliation and mediation service.[11] It has now been extended to all contractual disputes by conferring the power on judges to manage the processing of cases, including encouragement to use alternative dispute resolution techniques.[12]

With respect to the third aspect of social cost, the waste of resources, this factor tends to argue against the use of awards of compulsory performance and towards the imposition of duties upon the parties to minimize the losses resulting from breach. The objective of the law should be to reduce the total costs resulting from breach of contract. The most common way in which this result may be achieved is to encourage the injured party to seek contractual performance from an alternative source. Substitute performance will reduce losses arising from delays and other losses consequent on breach. For this reason the injured party is under a duty to take reasonable steps to reduce the losses resulting from breach of contract, which is known as the duty to mitigate loss. In addition, this consideration of minimizing social cost argues against the availability of orders for compulsory performance, for such a right would remove the incentive for the injured party to seek alternative sources of supply, which might be available at a lower cost than the cost to the defendant of performance of the contract. The argument against compulsory performance becomes even greater when the injured party no longer has any use for the goods or services acquired under the transaction.

3. Efficient breach of contract

We should also consider why parties to a contract choose to break it. Many breaches of contract will not be intentional, but result from negligence or an unforeseen latent defect. Here the purpose of remedies should include the deterrence of negligence and the allocation of risk onto the person in the best position to avoid or reduce the cost of losses. In these instances, it will be too late

11 Employment Tribunals Act 1996, s 18.
12 *Practice Note (Commercial Court Alternative Dispute Resolution)* [1994] 1 All ER 34; Lord Woolf, *Access to Justice: Interim Report to the Lord Chancellor on the Civil Justice System of England and Wales* (London, 1995); H Collins, *Regulating Contracts* (Oxford, 1999), ch 14.

for an award of specific performance of the original contract, but the courts can provide incentives for the defendant to reduce the losses resulting from breach by duties of repair and replacement. In the case of consumer purchases of defective goods, for instance, the consumer may reject the goods, leaving the seller with a duty to mitigate loss, which may best be satisfied by the supply of a substitute. Breaches of contract may also result from calculated business decisions.

The main reasons for a deliberate breach are likely to comprise either a recognition that performance will cause greater losses than breach and the payment of compensation, or that greater profits can be obtained by breach of contract and entering into a different contractual relationship for the same object. Two important factors have to be included in such an efficiency calculation carried out by a party contemplating deliberate breach of contract:

(i)   The party in breach has to consider the possible harm arising from deliberate breach of contract to business reputation and to long-term business relationships. For these reasons, many contracts are performed even though one party suffers a loss.

(ii)   The cost/benefit analysis has to include the potential liability in damages to the injured party from breach of contract. If this liability exceeds either the potential losses on an uneconomic contract or the profits on an alternative deal, there will be no economic incentive to break the contract.

But even with these two factors included in the efficiency calculus, in some instances deliberate breach of contract may prove the most advantageous course of action. The question is in such cases whether or not the law should discourage or support the deliberate breach of contract?

A wealth maximizing criterion of justice supports the view that the law should permit efficient breaches of contract. This view holds that the wealth of the society will be increased in total by the breach of contract. With the receipt of damages for breach of contract the injured party should be at least no worse off than before, and the defendant should, if his calculations prove correct, be better off. The breach of contract will move goods to those who value them most, without any party being worse off than before, which complies with the standard of Pareto efficiency. Economic arguments, therefore, indicate that the law should support efficient breach of contract.[13] If this wealth maximizing criterion of justice does guide the law in its determination of judicial remedies, what practices does it require?

It suggests that orders for compulsory performance should not be generally available. If the injured party could insist upon compulsory performance of the contract, this right would prevent the defendant from making an advantageous profitable transaction elsewhere. If the effect of the availability of compulsory

---

13 This analysis leaves out transactions costs which are likely to be increased by breach: Friedman, 'The Efficient Breach Fallacy' (1989) 18 *Journal of Legal Studies* 1, at p 6.

performance is merely to change the bargaining strengths of the parties, the injured party would be able to acquire a greater proportion of the profits which the defendant gains by the alternative contract, and this in turn may discourage the defendant from seeking such alternative wealth-enhancing contracts. If the reason for the defendant's breach is simply that the contract has ceased to be an economic proposition, again compulsory performance may be undesirable, for it seems likely (if the defendant has calculated correctly) that the injured party will be able to acquire the performance elsewhere at less cost than performance would cost the defendant. In contrast, an award of compensatory damages leaves the defendant free to seek an alternative beneficial transaction simply on payment of compensation to the injured party. In the case of disadvantageous contracts, the losses to the defendant are minimized by refusing an award of compulsory performance. Awards of damages therefore better support the wealth maximizing properties of markets.

The theory of efficient breach of contract also indicates how the measure of the damages remedy should be calculated. In order to ensure that the injured party is no worse off as a result of the breach of contract, the defendant must pay damages at a level set to ensure that outcome. But an ambiguity plagues this principle, for it is unclear whether the injured party's position should be judged as it was prior to the formation of the contract with the defendant, or as the injured party expected it to be following proper performance of the contract. Advocates of the theory of efficient breach of contract assume that the latter measure is the correct one, but in fact the former measure seems more likely to promote efficient breach of contract. The need to permit efficient breach of contract does, however, rule out firmly the possibility of compensation based upon, not the losses to the injured party, but the gains to the defendant achieved by breach. If these profits were the measure of damages, the defendant could never be better off as a result of deliberate breach of contract, which would obliterate the incentive to search for better market opportunities.

4. Social market

Whatever the precise consequences of the theory of efficient breach, our discussion leaves open the issue whether or not efficiency or wealth maximization should count as a relevant consideration determining the shape of and access to judicial remedies. The problem with this criterion is surely that it assumes that the motive for entering contracts can be reduced to one concerned with wealth, so that the law can afford to be indifferent as to the means by which this wealth is acquired, either through performance of the contract or payment of damages. This analysis may serve well enough in most commercial transactions, but throughout this book I have argued that the field of contract law extends across a wide variety of voluntary undertakings, which cannot always be reduced to a simple analysis of wealth enhancement or preference satisfaction. In a contract of employment, for instance, the employee no doubt enters the contract in the pursuit of wealth in the form of wages, but in addition the employee may seek to acquire status, friendship, skills and training, and the satisfaction achieved by giving meaning to one's life through work. When the theory of efficient breach is applied in this context, we can see its dangers. It suggests that the employer should be entitled to terminate the contract in order to replace the employee by a worker who is either prepared to accept lower wages or who has greater productivity. Although this might prove the efficient result, it ignores the claims of the incumbent employee with respect to those social interests in job security which cannot be reduced to money damages.

This objection to the theory of efficient breach and its reductionism returns us to the theme of the social market and the perception that markets serve a greater purpose than mere preference satisfaction. The judicial remedies for breach of contract should also be guided by the recognition that contracts distribute wealth, establish power relations, and provide opportunities for the realization of meaning in one's life. These considerations may run against the grain of the efficiency arguments. In the case of the dismissed employee, for instance, whereas the efficient result may be to restrict the employee to a claim for damages, the result required by policies informed by the social market may indicate the appropriateness of compulsory performance in some cases, with the effect that an employee obtains reinstatement. At the same time, concern for freedom of the individual may prompt a refusal of specific performance at the behest of the employer. Similarly, the remedy for a tenant facing an eviction in breach of contract may require more than damages, for the premises may represent the tenant's home and the basis of security for the tenant and his or her dependents. In some instances damages may prove the sole practicable remedy, but consideration of the power relation and the risk to important interests and rights of the injured party may indicate that greater compensation than usual should be available, even though this might not prove the efficient outcome.

The social market will also be concerned with the fairness of the outcomes of judicial remedies for breach of contract.[14] Unjust enrichment of the defendant at the expense of the injured party will be avoided. The courts will be reluctant also to order compulsory performance of a contract which is severely disadvantageous to the defendant. We should also consider the possibility that the interests of third parties become important to the formulation of judicial remedies for breach of contract as part of more general policies to control the operation of markets.

In the following discussion of the remedies of damages and compulsory performance, we will examine how these conflicting considerations direct the shape and availability of judicial remedies for breach of contract. But this discussion should be prefaced with a warning. The variety of the subject matter of

---

14 Vernon, 'Expectancy Damages for breach of Contract: A Primer and Critique' (1976) *Washington University Law Quarterly* 179.

contracts for which judicial remedies are sought makes it difficult to establish any firm general rules. When this variety combines with the competing policy considerations described above, it becomes almost impossible to state any general principles applicable to the field of judicial remedies. At best we can only hope to indicate the outline of how these remedies are constructed in the light of the relevant considerations.

D.   Damages

The award of damages is the normal remedy for breach of contract, in the absence of agreed remedies or the availability of an action for the price. This rule applies to contracts supported by consideration or contained in a deed. The position with respect to obligations arising from detrimental reliance encouraged by the promisor remains more ambiguous for, as we noted in Chapter 5, English courts have so far been reluctant to award damages for breach of such obligations, but have achieved various measures of equitable relief instead. In jurisdictions in the USA which have accepted the availability of damages for promissory estoppel, the rules governing quantification have gradually been assimilated to those governing any breach of contract.[15] As Oliver Wendell Holmes observed in a famous essay:

> The duty to keep a contract at common law means a prediction that you must pay damages if you do not keep it – and nothing else.[16]

Although this dictum exaggerates the extent to which orders for compulsory performance are excluded from actions for breach of contract, it does indicate how damages are usually the sole option for the injured party. The question to be addressed here is how is an award of damages calculated?

I.   The compensatory principle

Damages are designed to compensate the injured party for losses flowing from the breach of contract rather than to punish the defendant. The starting point for an assessment of compensation is to identify the economic losses cause to the injured party by the breach of contract. The injured party must prove the items of loss, and demonstrate that they were caused by the defendant's breach of contract. The claimant must also demonstrate that the losses were unavoidable or at least reasonably incurred. These economic losses generally fall into a few simple categories: the cost of substituted performance, wasted expenditure, and the cost of repairing damage to property. But in principle any kind of economic loss, if proven, should be recoverable. For instance, damage to business reputation can

15 Slawson, 'The Role of Reliance in Contract Damages' (1990) 76 *Cornell Law Review* 197.
16 Holmes, 'The Path of the Law' (1897) 10 *Harvard Law Review* 457, at p 462.

provide the basis of a claim, although it is hard for the claimant to prove the possible economic effects such as unknown third parties deciding not to enter into contractual negotiations. For example, employees who had worked unwittingly for fraudulent managers of a bank were permitted to claim for the loss that they were subsequently unable to obtain another job in the banking sector,[17] but they were unable to prove that their prior connection had prevented them from obtaining employment.[18] Having considered the typical forms of economic loss that provide grounds for assessment of compensatory damages, we will consider more controversial items that are sometimes claimed as the basis for compensation.

(a) COST OF SUBSTITUTED PERFORMANCE

In many instances of breach of contract, the claim for compensation coincides with the cost of substituted performance. The injured party seeks the additional cost of buying the goods or services elsewhere. Where the seller of goods fails to deliver all or some of the goods specified by the contract, or the provider of services fails to perform all or some of the services which he has undertaken, the measure of damages under the compensatory principle amounts to the difference between the contract price and the market cost of the substitute goods or services which the injured party is obliged to seek. The injured party recovers sufficient compensation to pay for substitute goods and services at no extra cost to himself. Similarly, where the goods or services supplied prove defective, the injured party may claim the cost of rectifying the fault. We noted, for instance, in the case of *Bolton v Mahadeva*,[19] that the defective installation of a central heating system rendered the defendant liable to pay the cost of curing the defects. In addition, the injured party may claim the costs involved in finding a substitute contracting party.

Since the underlying criterion for the measure of damages is the net loss to the injured party, no damages may be claimed at all, or merely nominal damages claimed, if the sum of the market price, ie the actual cost of the substitute, plus any transaction costs, is the same or lower than the original contract price. In a stable and competitive market, therefore, it is likely that the cost of substituted performance will match the contract price, so that, in the absence of other exceptional claims for losses, no damages will be awarded.

(b) WASTED EXPENDITURE

If the option of substituted performance is unavailable, the injured party can claim for the losses representing wasted expenditure in connection with the

---

17 *Mahmud v Bank of Credit and Commerce International SA* [1998] AC 20, [1997] 3 All ER 1, HL.
18 *Bank of Credit and Commerce International SA v Ali (No 2)* [2000] ICR 1354, Ch.
19 [1972] 2 All ER 1322, [1972] 1 WLR 1009, CA.

contract. The costs of work performed in fulfilment of contractual obligations can be recovered, including incidental expenditure such as the cost of travel to the place of performance. In *McRae v Commonwealth Disposals Commission*,[20] for instance, where the claimant incurred expense seeking a sunk tanker for salvage when it subsequently emerged that no such tanker existed, the claimant recovered this wasted expenditure. The recoverable expenses extend to the costs of preparing for performance of the contract, even apparently where those expenses were incurred in anticipation of the formation of the contract.[21] Compensation will also be payable for any money paid in advance or the value of goods transferred to the defendant.

It is also possible to recover compensation for money paid to the defendant with reference to the contract through an action in the law of restitution or unjust enrichment. This claim is known misleadingly as recovery of money for 'total failure of consideration'. Here consideration means no more than performance of the contract. The action is only available where the plaintiff has not received any of the promised contractual performance or where the contract is itself void for reasons of illegality, public policy, or ultra vires.[22] The restitutionary claim is conceived as a kind of proprietary entitlement to the money rather than compensation for breach of contract. Under the principles of the law of restitution, the defendant may resist the claim on certain grounds such as 'change of position'.[23]

(c) COST OF REPAIR

The breach of contract may also have caused damage to the claimant's property. For example, the negligent installation of electrical wiring may cause a fire in the plaintiff's premises. The costs of repairing the fire damage can be recovered in addition to the cost of substituted performance in have the wiring properly installed.

Notice that this cost of repair is only recoverable where the defendant's breach of contract caused the damage or defect. It will not apply, for instance, where the breach of contract merely failed to alert the injured party to the need for repairs or further work. In *Watts v Morrow*,[24] a negligent survey report failed to alert the purchaser of a house as to its many defects such as the need for a new roof and specialist woodworm treatment. Although this work when completed cost about

20 (1950) 84 CLR 377, Aust HC.
21 *Anglia Television Ltd v Reed* [1972] 1 QB 60, [1971] 3 All ER 690, CA.
22 *Westdeutsche Landesbank Girozentrale v Islington Borough Council* [1996] AC 669, [1996] 2 All ER 961. The requirement of total failure of consideration is removed in cases of frustration: Law Reform (Frustrated Contracts) Act 1943, s 1.
23 *Lipkin Gorman v Karpnale Ltd* [1991] 2 AC 548, [1992] 4 All ER 512, HL; *Woolwich Building Society v IRC* [1993] AC 70, sub nom *Woolwich Building Society v IRC (No 2)* [1992] 3 All ER 737, HL.
24 [1991] 4 All ER 937, [1991] 1 WLR 1421, CA.

agains

£34,000, the surveyor was held liable only for £15,000 representing the difference between the contract price for the house and its actual market value with the latent defects.

A further qualification that limits recovery for cost of repair concerns whether it can be recovered if the claimant has no intention of effecting the reparation. In *Radford v De Froberville*,[25] the defendant failed to build a wall in breach of contract, and the court awarded damages to cover the cost to the claimant of building a wall on his side of the boundary on condition that in fact the wall was built. Failing this condition, it was thought that claimant could only claim for the diminution in the value of the goods provided or the damaged property, which in *Radford v De Froberville* would have merely amounted to the small reduction in the value of a property without a walled boundary. This condition for recovery of the cost of curing defective performance has been doubted in subsequent cases, however, although instead the courts have sometimes applied the idea of waste of resources, discussed below, to prevent such claims.[26]

(d) NET LOSS

In these standard instances of claims for compensatory damages, the emphasis is upon discovery of the net loss to the injured party attributable to the breach of contract. If the original contract was disadvantageous to the injured party, the claimant is likely to receive no compensation at all, since the cost of substitutes will be less than the contract price. The courts avoid putting the injured party in a better position than if the contract had been correctly performed.

In a claim for wasted expenditure during performance of contract, this approach can prevent the recovery of all the wasted expenditure, if those costs exceed the benefits that would have accrued from the defendant's performance of the contract.[27] For example, if the injured party undertakes to perform work for a fixed price but incurs a greater expenditure than the contract price, the claim for compensation is limited to the price. Similarly, where the result of repair of damage to the property is an increase in the value of the property, such as a new building which is worth more than the old one, the damages awarded for the cost of repair will be reduced to reflect that increase in value.

2. *Loss of profits*

In a contract between two business, the objective of the parties is likely to include the opportunity to make a profit from the transaction. Goods are purchased not

---

25 [1978] 1 All ER 33, [1977] 1 WLR 1262, Ch D.

26 *Ruxley Electronics and Construction Ltd Forsyth* [1996] AC 344, [1995] 3 All ER 268, HL.

27 *C & P Haulage v Middleton* [1983] 3 All ER 94, [1983] 1 WLR 1461, CA; *CCC Films (London) Ltd v Impact Quadrant Films* [1985] QB 16, [1984] 3 All ER 298, QB.

for consumption but for resale at a profit. Raw materials may be used in a factory for making products to be sold at a price higher than the cost of the original materials plus other costs of production. Breach of the contract to supply goods in both instances is likely to lead to the loss of those anticipated profits unless substituted performance can be obtained in time. Loss of profits may also be caused by delays, as where a carrier of goods delivers machinery or a component late, causing loss of production in a factory. Similarly, damage to the claimant's property can lead to a loss of profit if the property was a productive asset such as a factory or machinery. Can claims for loss of these anticipated profits be included in the measure of compensatory damages?

In principle, the courts permit claims for loss of anticipated profits resulting from breach of contract. The inclusion of compensation for anticipated profits is regarded as implementing an objective of putting the injured party in as good a position as if the contract had been properly performed.

> The rule of the common law is, that where a party sustains a loss by reason of a breach of contract, he is, so far as money can do it, to be placed in the same situation, with respect to damages, as if the contract had been performed.[28]

The courts are aware, however, that claims for loss of anticipated profits can amount to sums out of all proportion to the original value of the contract to the defendant. A carrier who transports a component for £100, but whose delay in delivery causes a loss of profits amounting to many thousands of pounds, may be deterred from accepting such work if found liable for all this loss. Similarly, an electrical contractor that accidentally burns down a factory may cause losses amounting to millions of pounds as a result of loss of production. Unlimited liability for loss of profits may deter people from undertaking such jobs altogether.

To a considerable extent these concerns can be met by liability insurance and exclusion clauses. But liability insurance for indeterminate amounts of liability may prove extremely costly and, therefore, may also deter entry into contracts where there is a risk of loss of profits. Exclusion clauses, as we have seen, may not always prove effective to protect a business against claims for loss of profits. For these reasons, courts approach claims for loss of anticipated profits circumspectly. In particular, the courts emphasize the need for proof of loss, and deny recovery where the loss of profits is regarded as too remote a consequence of the breach of contract.

(a) PROOF OF LOSS

The injured party needs to establish that the consequence of the breach of contract was the loss of the profits being claimed. It is not enough merely to show

---

28 Parke B, *Robinson v Harman* (1848) 1 Exch 850.

that these losses might have resulted. For instance, if a defective component is supplied, and the finished goods sold on to customers, a claim for loss of profits on the sales to customers needs to establish that the customers have in fact rejected the goods or cancelled the contract.[29]

Although the courts will award compensation for loss of a chance to make a profit, this award may be discounted heavily according to the perceived likelihood of the profit being obtained, and the claim may be rejected entirely if it is regarded as too speculative. For example, an author's claim for loss of royalties resulting from the failure of the publisher to publish her book is likely to fail unless the court is reasonably sure that the author would have earned royalties. In *McRae v Commonwealth Disposals Commission*, where it will be recalled that a salvor wasted money fruitlessly search for non-existent wreck, although the salvor recovered its wasted expenditure, the court rejected the claim for loss of profits expected from a successful salvage on that ground that the claim was too speculative.

Under the ordinary principles of compensation, if a buyer refuses to proceed with a purchase of goods, a seller may recover the difference between the contract price and the price at which the good are eventually sold. That measure of compensation includes the loss of profit on the sale, although of course if the goods are disposed of at a higher price, no compensation would be payable. But in the latter circumstance, a commercial dealer in goods may argue that it has nevertheless incurred a loss of profits resulting from lost throughput. In other words, the seller claims that it has suffered a reduction in the number of sales in total, even though it made the same or a greater profit on the sale of that particular item. A claim for lost throughput failed in *Lazenby Garages Ltd v Wright*.[30] The seller of a used car claimed damages from a buyer who repudiated the contract. The seller mitigated the loss by selling the car to a second purchaser for £100 more. The seller claimed compensation for the loss of profit resulting from the loss of the opportunity to sell two cars rather than one. This claim was rejected by the English Court of Appeal as too speculative. The seller therefore received no damages for breach of contract, since the second sale at a higher price covered its loss of profits wasted expenditure. It is possible, however, that the case might be distinguished where the goods being sold are homogenous, not unique as in the case of used cars, for then the lost volume of sales may be regarded as sufficiently probable to justify the award of compensation at least as the loss of a chance.

(b) REMOTENESS OF LOSS

The test for remoteness of loss originates from *Hadley v Baxendale*.[31] In this case, the owner of a factory claimed damages for loss of profits resulting from a

29 *Bence Graphics International Ltd v Fasson UK Ltd* [1998] QB 87, [1997] 1 All ER 979, CA.
30 [1976] 2 All ER 770, [1976] 1 WLR 459, CA.
31 (1854) 9 Exch 341. Danzig, 'Hadley v Baxendale: A Study in the Industrialisation of the Law'

temporary shut-down caused by delays by the defendant carrier in the transport of a mill-shaft. The claim for loss of profits was rejected. The court applied two rules:

(i)   Recovery for loss of profits would be permitted if those losses were 'such as may reasonably be supposed to have been in the contemplation of both parties, at the time they made the contract as the probable result of the breach of it.'

(ii) In addition, if the claimant had expressly notified the defendant of the risk of loss of profits prior to the formation of the contract, the loss of profits would be recoverable.

The court rejected the claim on the ground that the owner of the mill had not expressly notified the carrier of the risk of shut-down, and nor would such a risk be in the contemplation of the carrier as a probable result of delays, because the carrier could reasonably assume that other mill-shafts were being used or were available.

The purpose of the second rule is plainly to encourage disclosure of the risk of loss of profits.[32] Following such disclosure, the defendant might raise the price and take out suitable liability insurance. In effect, by receiving notice, the defendant accepts the risk of the loss of profits under the contract and becomes liable for the losses resulting from that risk materializing. In *Hadley v Baxendale*, if the carrier had been warned that the mill had to close until the shaft arrived before entering the contract, it would have been liable for the loss of profits, but no doubt would have increased its price accordingly and would have taken greater steps to avoid delay. In what was perhaps an unusually favourable decision for the claimant, in *Jackson v Chrysler Acceptances Ltd*,[33] the purchaser of a new car on hire purchase, which turned out to be seriously defective, succeeded in a claim not only for compensation for fixing the defects in the car, but also for the loss arising from a spoiled holiday in France owing to the breakdown of the car. This consequential loss was recoverable because the claimant had informed the car dealer of his intention to use the car for that purpose.

In the absence of notification of the risk of loss of profits, however, the first rule in *Hadley v Baxendale* applies. This test about the reasonable contemplation of the parties at the time of entering the contract seems to depend upon the foreseeability and probability of the loss. In a modern statement of the rule, Lord Reid explained that:

(1975) 4 *Journal of Legal Studies* 249; Barton, 'Contractual Damages and the Rise of Industry' (1987) 7 *Oxford Journal of Legal Studies* 40; Bishop, 'The Contract-Tort Boundary and the Economics of Insurance' (1983) 12 *Journal of Legal Studies* 241.

32 W Bishop, 'The Contract-Tort Boundary and the Economics of Insurance' (1983) 12 *Journal of Legal Studies* 241.

33 [1978] RTR 474, CA.

The crucial question is whether, on the information available to the defendant when the contract was made, he should, or the reasonable man in his position would, have realised that such loss was sufficiently likely to result from the breach of contract to make it proper to hold that the loss flowed naturally from the breach or that loss of that kind should have been within his contemplation.[34]

Similar formulations of the rule suggest that what is required is that a reasonable person, with the knowledge of the defendant, should have foreseen the loss of profits resulting from the breach as a serious possibility.

These vague formulations, which depend upon the degree of foresight of the hypothetical reasonable man, do not produce easily predictable results. If the contract concerns the sale and delivery of business machinery, the court can infer that the seller accepts the risk of the buyer's loss of profits due to late delivery. In *Victoria Laundry (Windsor) Ltd v Newman Industries Ltd,*[35] the defendant failed to deliver on time a boiler to a commercial laundry. The defendant was held liable for the claimant's loss of usual business profits. Yet the defendant escaped liability for unusually high profits that the claimant had expected to gain from a particularly lucrative contract with the government for cleaning army uniforms. With respect to carriers of goods, the difficulty for the court is to know how much knowledge of the business objectives of the owner of the goods should be attributed to the carrier. In a controversial decision of this type, *Koufos v C Czarnikow Ltd (The Heron II),*[36] the House of Lords allowed recovery for anticipated profits where a carrier regularly transported a commodity from one location to another under instructions from a business which, as the carrier knew, made its profits by moving goods promptly to locations where the price was highest. On account of the carrier's delay in arriving in port, competition had lowered the price of the commodity, thereby reducing profits from resale. The court held the carrier liable for the loss of profits resulting from delay, despite the absence of clear evidence that the carrier had assumed the burden of these losses from the outset. Instead, the court inferred from the nature of the trading relationship that the carrier should bear this responsibility. This decision can be distinguished from *Hadley v Baxendale* on the ground that the carrier had greater knowledge of the owner's business purposes and, therefore, had had the opportunity to allocate the risk. Hence, by not excluding liability for delay, the carrier had implicitly accepted the risk.

---

34 *Koufos v C Czarnikow Ltd, The Heron II* [1969] 1 AC 350 at 385, [1967] 3 All ER 686, 691, HL. See also Sale of Goods Act 1979, s 53(2) 'The measure of damages for breach of warranty is the estimated loss directly and naturally resulting, in the ordinary course of events, from the breach of warranty'.

35 [1949] 2 KB 528, [1949] 1 All ER 997, CA.

36 [1969] 1 AC 350, [1967] 3 All ER 686, HL.

The legal reasoning about reasonable foreseeability and probability seems to obscure the real function of the remoteness rule, which is to determine how the parties implicitly allocated the risk of loss of profits in their agreement. Views on this implicit allocation will no doubt be influenced by a variety of matters including the terms of the contract, the nature of the two businesses involved, their familiarity with each other's business, the probable or customary allocation of the burden of taking out insurance, and so forth. In effect, the courts may be imposing on the parties their views on how the parties ought to have allocated the risk. In so doing, the courts are likely to be influenced by perceptions of what would have been an efficient allocation of risk in the sense that the party in the best position to avoid the loss should be held to have accepted the risk.

If the purpose of the rule of remoteness is to determine implicit allocations of risk, knowledge of the claimant's business and the likely losses resulting from breach of contract should not suffice to render the loss recoverable. The court should also allocate the risk of this loss in the light of further evidence about the implicit understanding between the parties. In *Parsons (H) (Livestock) Ltd v Uttley Ingham & Co Ltd*,[37] the manufacturers and suppliers of a pig food hopper were held liable to a farmer for the death of his pigs by a disease that was caused as a result of negligent installation of the hopper. The farmer recovered the value of the pigs when they died from disease, since that was an unavoidable loss caused by a breach of contract. But the farmer's claim for the anticipated profits for the sale of the pigs when he took them to market failed the test of remoteness. This consequence was surely as foreseeable and as probable as the death of the pigs from disease. The reason why the court rejected the claim for loss of profits was perhaps that the manufacturers of the hopper had not assumed implicitly the position of an insurer against such loss of profits when agreeing to supply the hopper. The hopper was merely one method of feeding the pigs, not an essential tool of the farmer's business like the boiler for a laundry, so that it could not be supposed that the supplier had undertaken to be responsible for the farmer's business profits resulting from rearing the pigs and taking them to market. The implicit allocation of risk, as determined by the court, was that the manufacturer would not negligently injure the pigs, but that it did not undertake to guarantee the farmer's profits if some damage to the pigs occurred. This was not perhaps the most efficient allocation of risk: the farmer could have insured his livestock probably more cheaply than the manufacturer, although it is true that the manufacturer was in a better position to take steps to prevent the damage from occurring at all. Efficient risk allocation may play a crucial role in the application of the remoteness rule, but it seems likely that the courts will also be concerned about other factors that indicate how the parties had implicitly allocated the risks in connection with performance of the contract.

37 [1978] QB 791, [1978] 1 All ER 525, CA.

3. Non-pecuniary losses

The above principles governing the assessment of loss concentrate on economic losses resulting from breach of contract. Although economic loss is the principal concern of commercial parties to contracts, in many types of contract, especially those entered by consumers, the purpose of making the contract may include the expectation of enjoyment, satisfaction, and peace of mind. Examples where such expectations may arise are the purchase of a theatre ticket, a package holiday, the installation of a new kitchen, or the acquisition of a holiday home in the country. Breach of these contracts may cause economic loss, but in addition the consumer may suffer disappointment, vexation, worry, and inconvenience. The traditional approach of the law was to refuse compensation for claims for distress and disappointment resulting from breach of contract. This principle was affirmed in *Addis v Gramophone Co Ltd*,[38] where the House of Lords rejected one part of the claim of a wrongfully dismissed employee for compensation for distress and disappointment resulting from the dismissal. The reason for this limit on the scope of compensation was that by awarding compensation to cover the cost of substitute performance and all financial losses, the law enabled the aggrieved party to take steps to minimise any psychological harm and inconvenience, and the remaining disappointment and vexation was a risk that we all have to accept when we make contracts. This rejection of claims for non-pecuniary loss such as distress, frustration, anxiety, displeasure, tension and aggravation remains the general principle. This exclusion of recovery for non-pecuniary losses, however, does not rule out two particular kinds of claims.

Breach of contract sometimes causes personal injury or physical inconvenience. In connection with personal injuries, the courts permit an additional claim for pain, suffering and loss of amenity. It is also possible on the basis of a claim for negligence to claim compensation for a recognised psychiatric disorder.[39] There is no reason why such claims for psychiatric disorders should not be based upon breach of an implied term that requires a duty of reasonable care, but the courts will apply the same elaborate principles developed in the law of tort to an action for breach of contract. In *McLoughlin v Jones*,[40] the claimant alleged that he had suffered psychiatric illness as a result of the negligence of his solicitors in defending him against serious criminal charges. He had been convicted and sentenced to four years' imprisonment, but when new evidence came to light, he was acquitted on a retrial. The Court of Appeal permitted the claim to proceed, whether based on an implied term or in tort, provided that the principles of negligent recovery for psychiatric loss were applied to the case. In particular, it had to be shown that the solicitors had assumed a duty of care with respect to psychiatric injury, that such injury was a foreseeable consequence of a breach of that duty, and that it would be just, fair, and reasonable to impose liability. One

---

38 [1909] AC 488, HL.
39 *White v Chief Constable of South Yorkshire Police* [1999] 2 AC 455, [1999] 1 All ER 1, HL.
40 [2001] EWCA Civ 1743, [2002] QB 1312.

anomaly seems to remain in this field. Although employers may be liable for causing psychiatric disorders to their employees during the course of employment, as where they impose an excessive workload that will foreseeably cause that type of injury to the employee,[41] such a claim for a harsh and wrongful dismissal or termination of the contract is precluded at common law.[42]

Nevertheless, even if there is no physical injury, compensation for physical inconvenience resulting from breach of contract may be recoverable. In *Hobbs v London and South Western Rly Co*,[43] the claimant had purchased a railway ticket to convey him to Hampton Court, but the train deposited him five miles away at Esher. Unable to find any other form of transport, he and his wife had to walk home. Their claim for compensation for the physical inconvenience of the long trek home was successful and exceeded the cost of a taxi fare. Similarly, in *Watts v Morrow*,[44] when purchasing a second home for weekends and holidays, the purchaser relied on a survey report that indicated that the house was in good condition and required little building work on it. The report was negligently inaccurate, and the purchaser had to pay for extensive building works. One element of the successful claim for compensation included damages for the physical inconvenience and discomfort in having the builders in the house to repair the defects. In these cases, the compensation is not awarded for the mere fact of disappointment and vexation, but for the physical discomfort resulting from breach of contract.

A second qualification to the general principle concerns contracts where one of its main purposes is to give pleasure, relaxation, peace of mind, or freedom from molestation. Where the breach of contract prevents that purpose from being realised, the courts award modest amounts of compensation in recognition that the consumer has been deprived of one of the main objects of the contract. Where a photographer failed to turn up at a wedding, thereby depriving the couple of photographs of their special day, the bride received compensation for her disappointment.[45] Similarly, in *Jarvis v Swans Tours Ltd*,[46] the claimant purchased a skiing holiday, which according to the brochure included a 'house party', a 'resident host', and a 'Yodeller evening'. The holiday turned out badly: full length skis were only available for two days, the claimant found himself alone for much of the time, there was no host, and the yodeller turned out to be a local man who sang only a couple of songs. The claimant won damages for his grave disappointment and loss of enjoyment. Also in *Heywood v Wellers*,[47] the claimant employed the defendant solicitors to obtain an injunction to prevent a man from

41 *Hatton v Sutherland* [2002] EWCA Civ 76, [2002] 2 All ER 1.
42 *Johnson v Unisys Ltd* [2001] UKHL 13, [2003] 1 AC 518, [2001] 2 All ER 801.
43 (1875) LR 10 QB 111, CA.
44 [1991] 4 All ER 937, [1991] 1 WLR 1421, CA.
45 *Diesen v Samson* 1971 SLT 49, Sh Ct.
46 [1973] QB 233, [1973] 1 All ER 71, CA.
47 [1976] QB 446, [1976] 1 All ER 300, CA.

molesting her. The solicitors were negligent in conducting the litigation, with the result that the man carried on molesting her. She obtained damages for mental distress, since the relief from such distress was the main reason why she had engaged the solicitors.

Although these two qualifications to the general principle that damages for vexation are well established, their precise scope remains contested. In *Farley v Skinner*,[48] the claimant wanted to purchase a house in the country, but was concerned that it might be badly affected by noise from the nearby Gatwick airport. He engaged a surveyor to inspect the house, and in particular asked the surveyor to investigate the risk of aircraft noise. The surveyors reported on the condition of the house in general, and included in their report their view that they thought it unlikely that the property would suffer greatly from aircraft noise. Having moved in after extensive building works had been completed, the claimant discovered that in the mornings, when the airport was busy, planes waiting to land would be stacked up in a spiral course that caused the aircraft to fly directly overhead. Despite the inconvenience of the noise, the claimant decided not to move. In principle he could have recovered from the surveyors economic measure of damages comprising the difference between the contract price for the house and its market price, but the trial court found there was no difference in value. The claimant was successful, however, in obtaining £10,000 compensation for non-pecuniary loss. The House of Lords held that the award of compensation could be justified on either exception. The noise of the aircraft counted as a physical discomfort, not merely mental distress or vexation, and so fell within the first exception. In addition, in view of the specific instruction to the surveyor to investigate the question of aircraft noise, the case fell within the exception where one of the main purposes of the contract is to provide peace of mind.

By confirming the application of the second exception to this case, the House of Lords recognised that it represents a broad principle. It is not confined to cases where the main purpose of the contract is to provide the benefit of enjoyment or peace of mind. It includes cases where merely one aspect of the contract was to secure for the claimant a benefit, which although having no economic value, was one of the claimant's hopes or expectations. For example, the House of Lords confirmed its earlier decision in *Ruxley Electronics and Construction v Forsyth*,[49] where the claimant received £2,500 because a swimming pool constructed in his garden was only 6 feet in depth whereas the contract had specified a depth of 7 feet 6 inches. Although the difference in depth did not affect the market value of the pool, the claimant complained that he had specifically requested a deeper pool because, being a tall man, he would feel more comfortable with the greater depth. This decision is hard to explain as one involving physical distress, so it must fit

---

48 [2001] UKHL 49, [2002] 2 AC 732, [2001] 4 All ER 801.
49 [1996] AC 344, [1995] 3 All ER 268, HL.

into the other exception. To justify the use of the second exception, it requires acceptance of a broad principle that where one party has contracted for a particular benefit, even though that benefit has no market value and was not the main object of the contract, if the breach of contract prevents that benefit from being received, compensation should be awarded, subject to the principles of remoteness described above. The European Court of Justice has applied a similar broad conception of compensatable non-material losses in its interpretation of the notion of damage or loss in Directives applicable to contracts.[50]

The acceptance of this principle signals a shift in the common law of contract. Instead of viewing the transaction in purely economic terms, the courts are recognising that the value of contracts to the parties may also encompass benefits that cannot be assessed merely in terms of financial loss. It is possible to explain this development as a use of the remedy of damages to increase the incentives of parties to perform their contractual agreements. But this explanation seems to go too far, because to protect an interest in correct performance of the contract, the courts could use other remedies such as compulsory performance or drop the limits set by the doctrine of remoteness. For instance, the court denied recovery for the cost of rebuilding the swimming pool to the correct depth in *Ruxley Electronics and Construction Ltd v Forsyth* as a disproportionate and unreasonable measure of damages, although such a remedy would have surely provided a strong incentive for builders to comply with their contractual undertakings. A better explanation seems to be that the courts are prepared to differentiate between types of contract and to recognise that individuals acting in order to consume or enjoy a product such as a swimming pool, a holiday, a tranquil house in the country or wedding photographs, have not been deprived by the breach of contract of something with merely economic value, but have been deprived of the enjoyment of consuming the product.[51]

To calculate a sum of money in compensation for this kind of non-material loss is inevitably artificial and arbitrary. It makes no sense to ask the question how much more money the consumer would have been prepared to pay for receiving the goods over and above the market price because it is unlikely that the consumer would have been prepared to pay more than the market price in any circumstances. Even if it were true that the consumer would have been prepared to pay more, as in the case of a rich man who buys a drawing of his stately home for £10, but who would have been prepared to pay £1,000 for it, the courts would surely not grant an award of £990 in compensation to the rich man on the seller's failure to deliver the picture. That economic measure of loss, which is sometimes called the 'consumer surplus',[52] seems unhelpful in describing the object of an

---

50 Case C-168/00 *Simone Leitner v TUI Deutschland GmbH & Co KG* [2002] All ER (EC) 561, ECJ, interpreting EC Directive 90/314/EEC on Package Travel.
51 J Wightman, *Contract: A Critical Commentary* (London, 1996), p 98.
52 Harris, Ogus and Phillips, 'Contract Remedies and the Consumer Surplus' (1977) 95 *Law Quarterly Review* 179.

award of compensation in such cases. In practice the courts try instead to discover the diminution in value to the consumer, ie the difference in the value that the consumer placed on the benefit – the contract price – and the value that the consumer placed on what was in fact received. The need to award damages for this difference in value only arises where the consumer cannot obtain substitute performance, for instance either because it is too late once the holiday is over, or because the purchaser of the house decides to stay there despite the discomfort in view of the vexation involved in moving house, or because the court denies the remedy of compensation for the cost of substitute performance such as a new swimming pool.

4. Avoidable losses

The compensatory principle for the assessment of damages disallows any claim where a court finds that the injured party could have avoided the loss by preventative action after the breach of contract. The reason for this general rule probably depends heavily on the aim to reduce the social costs arising from breach of contract. There is a social interest in providing incentives for efficient use of resources at all times. But this reason is further supported by the aim of encouraging co-operation between the parties. The losses may be reduced by an agreed revision of the contract, and if this is the least costly way of handling the breach, the injured party will be required to reach such an agreement on pain of losing damages for the increased loss.[53] The courts may also regard it as unfair to require compensation to be paid to an injured party for losses which in part are attributable to his own choices after the breach of contract. Four doctrines consolidate this general principle which denies recovery for avoidable losses, and these are outlined below.

(a) Time of assessment

To begin with, courts normally assess the measure of loss at the date when it was first reasonable for the injured party to find substitute performance or take remedial action. The injured party cannot sit back while the costs of substitute performance escalate as a result of inflation or shortages and then claim the higher measure of recovery. The normal time for the assessment of loss is the date of breach of contract, but this will not be true, for example, where either the injured party discovers the breach subsequently,[54] or where it is reasonable to wait to see if the defendant remedies the breach,[55] or where no remedial action is

---

53 *Payzu Ltd v Saunders* [1919] 2 KB 581, CA; Goetz and Scott, 'The Mitigation Principle: Toward a General Theory of Contractual Obligation' 91983) 69 *Virginia Law Rev* 967.
54 *Cehave NV v Bremer Handelsgesellschaft GmbH (The Hansa Nord)* [1976] QB 44, [1975] 3 All ER 739, CA.
55 *Radford v De Froberville* [1978] 1 All ER 33, [1977] 1 WLR 1262, Ch.

immediately possible, such as when the injured party is prevented from taking steps to minimize the damage through his own impecuniosity and inability to obtain credit.[56] In these exceptional cases, the court will determine another appropriate date at which damages should be assessed.[57]

(b) CAUSATION

A second method by which courts prevent recovery for avoidable losses is to hold that the loss results not from the breach of contract but was caused by the injured party's own negligence. For example, the purchaser of a defective product who is injured by it may find that the court holds that his injury was caused not by the defect, but by his own foolishness in using the machine once it was apparent that it was defective. In *Lexmead (Basingstoke) Ltd v Lewis*,[58] a purchaser of a trailer coupling continued to use it even after it was clearly defective, and this resulted in serious personal injuries to a third party. The seller was held not liable to the purchaser for the consequential losses of liability for personal injuries resulting from the defective coupling, since the accident had been caused by the purchaser's act rather than the defect in the product.

Although this argument is framed in terms of causation, it should be clear that it departs from the normal attitude to causation found in the common law. In the law of tort and crime, a person will be held to have caused an event if his actions provided the occasion for the accident and constituted a continuing source of the danger. A murderer cannot escape responsibility, for example, merely by demonstrating that better medical care would have avoided the fatality following the infliction of stab wounds. Where the injured party carelessly adds to his injury or through his negligence increases his risk of harm, in tort his contributory negligence reduces the measure of damages but does not eliminate it entirely. In the law of contract, however, the courts often hold that any unreasonable or careless act on the part of the injured party between breach of contract and loss breaks the chain of causation and thus they deny the claim for damages.[59]

(c) CONTRIBUTORY NEGLIGENCE

This sharp, all-or-nothing result produced by the doctrine of causation has been relieved in recent years by the application of the doctrine of contributory negligence to negligent breaches of contract. Under the Law Reform (Contributory Negligence) Act 1945, s 1(1), subject to contrary contractual agreement:

---

56 *Wroth v Tyler* [1974] Ch 30, [1973] 1 All ER 897, Ch.
57 *Johnson v Agnew* [1980] AC 367, [1979] 1 All ER 883, HL.
58 [1982] AC 225, sub nom *Lambert v Lewis* [1981] 1 All ER 1185, HL.
59 *Quinn v Burch Bros (Builders) Ltd* [1966] 2 QB 370, [1966] 2 All ER 283, CA.

Where any person suffers damage as the result partly of his own fault and partly of the fault of any other person or persons, a claim in respect of that damage shall not be defeated by reason of the fault of the person suffering the damage, but the damages recoverable in respect thereof shall be reduced to such extent as the court thinks just and equitable having regard to the claimant's share in the responsibility for the damage.

Although this provision for apportionment of blame and reduction of damages was designed to reform the law of tort, its terms can also encompass at least cases where a negligent breach of contract also constitutes grounds for an action in tort.[60] But there is a case for extending the coverage of the legislation, so that it excludes the all-or-nothing reasoning of causation when the case involves purely contractual obligations which impose a duty of care.[61] Such a reform would not alter the result in *Lexmead v Lewis*, however, for the retailer's obligation in supplying the coupling was one of strict liability under the Sale of Goods Act 1979, s 14.

(d) MITIGATION OF LOSS

The injured party cannot recover damages for losses where it is shown that by seeking substitutes in the market he could have avoided or reduced the losses. The purchaser of goods can usually find a suitable alternative in the market, and in the absence of unusual circumstances, any unreasonable failure to take advantage of this opportunity will result in the reduction of his damages to the level of unavoidable loss. Once again, special circumstances may prevent the injured party from minimizing his loss. For example, his impecuniosity and inability to borrow money, may prevent him from taking immediate steps to find a substitute or cure the damage. Someone who purchases a new house on a large mortgage and then discovers defects in the foundations may not be able to take remedial steps until the builder has paid damages for breach of contract, because until that time the homeowner lacks the means to finance the building work.

The duty to mitigate loss requires the injured party to take reasonable steps to reduce loss. But this duty may not prevent steps to increase some items of loss in order to reduce others. In *Harbutt's Plasticine Ltd v Wayne Tank and Pump Co Ltd*,[62] the claimant's factory was destroyed by a fire caused by the defendant's breach of contract. In principle the claimant could recover for the cost of repairing the factory and the consequential loss of profits from the factory being shut down. The claimant built a new factory, which was worth substantially more than the old

---

60 *Forsikrigsaktieselskapet Vesta v Butcher Bain Dawles Ltd* [1988] AC 852, [1988] 2 All ER 43, CA; [1989] AC 852, [1989] 1 All ER 402, HL. The statute also applies to claims for misrepresentation: *Gran Gelato Ltd v Richcliff (Group) Ltd* [1992] Ch 560, [1992] 1 All ER 865, Ch.

61 Law Commission, *Contributory Negligence as a Defence in Contract*, Working Paper No 114 (London, 1990).

62 [1970] 1 QB 447, [1970] 1 All ER 225, CA.

one, and succeeded in a claim to recover the cost of the new factory. At first sight this decision breaches the compensatory principle, for the claimant obtained a more valuable property than it had lost. But the court reasoned that by building a new factory the plaintiff was taking reasonable steps to reduce the measure of consequential loss of profits, for without a new factory the claimant might have been able to claim loss of profits for a substantial time.

5. Waste of resources

An important practical qualification to the compensation principle concerns the avoidance of a waste of resources. For the sake of the welfare of the whole community, courts will not award damages amounting to the cost of curing defects in performance where the cost of repair is grossly disproportionate to the value of the benefits gained. In one typical case, when building a large house, the contractor used pipes manufactured by a different firm from those specified in the contract, although in all other respects the pipes were identical. The owner of the house claimed damages for the cost of rebuilding the house with the correct pipes, but the New York Court of Appeals declined to give more than nominal damages since there was no diminution in the value of the house. Cardozo J expressed the correct principle in these terms:

> The owner is entitled to the money which will permit him to complete, unless the cost of completion is greatly out of proportion to the good to be attained. When this is true, the measure is the difference in value.[63]

We should recognize, however, that not all judges are as forthright as Cardozo J. They disguise the refusal to award damages for the cost of curing a defect on the ground that it would be a waste of resources under a variety of arguments, such as the claim that there is no loss, or that the cure would be an unreasonable way to mitigate loss.

In *Ruxley Electronics and Construction Ltd v Forsyth*, the case concerning the swimming pool, we have noted already that the customer's claim for the cost of rebuilding the pool to the depth specified in the contract was rejected. The House of Lords held that it would be unreasonable to reconstruct the pool since the completed pool had the same market value as a pool of greater depth and since both were safe for off-the-side diving. The basis for this decision remains unclear and the discretion provided by the reasonableness test seems broad. It is possible that the court regarded the rebuilding of the pool as an unreasonable way in which to mitigate loss, although there was no other way in which to secure a pool of the required depth. It is also possible that the court doubted that the money would be spent on rebuilding the pool, despite the customer's claims to the contrary, although it is unclear why the way in which damages may be spent

63 *Jacob and Youngs v Kent* 230 NY 239, at p 244, 129 NE 889, at p 891 (1921).

should be of concern to the court. It is hard to avoid the conclusion that the court regarded the rebuilding of the pool as a waste of money, and for that reason declined to satisfy that claim and instead awarded modest compensation for the disappointment.

Especially difficult problems arise with respect to waste of resources in cases where the work which has not been undertaken in breach of contract is designed to improve the environment, for no doubt some regard all environmental endeavours as a waste of resources. Courts will be tempted to confine the measure of recovery to the diminution in the value of the asset, rather than award compensation to cover the costs of the environmental work. In *Tito v Waddell (No 2)*,[64] for instance, the court dismissed a claim to enforce a promise to restore a Pacific Island to its idyllic state prior to extensive phosphate mining, although doubts about the likely success of the re-landscaping also contributed to defeat the claim.

6. Disgorgement and punitive damages

As a general rule, the compensatory principle of damages excludes the possibility of punitive damages for breach of contract, ie a measure of compensation that exceeds the injured party's loss. Moreover, as we have seen in Chapter 16, the courts generally prevent the parties from enforcing an agreed remedy, such as a penalty clause, which provides a greater measure of compensation than is available under the compensatory principles. Traditional understandings of contract law insist that the remedies must be confined to 'corrective justice', ie they should be exclusively directed to compensating the interests of the claimant who has been injured by the breach of contract, and not be concerned with broader issues such as discouraging certain kinds of market practices.

Whether the courts in fact ignore broader social issues when formulating the rules governing the quantification of damages must be doubted. In the rules that we have considered so far – recovery for non-pecuniary loss, mitigation of loss, remoteness of loss, and waste of resources – there are clear signs that the courts are taking into account broader policy issues. They can use the law of quantification of damages in order to regulate market practices. For instance, in *Jarvis v Swan's Tours*,[65] the case of the disappointing skiing holiday, the damages awarded were considerably in excess of the contract price. This result should be seen against the background of numerous press reports of misleading and unreliable holiday brochures. The broadening exception for recovery for non-pecuniary losses seems to be a response to problems arising for consumers from dealing with incompetent tradesmen and professionals. By ensuring that consumers receive compensation, even though they cannot point to an economic

64 [1977] Ch 106, [1977] 3 All ER 129, Ch.
65 [1973] QB 233, [1973] 1 All ER 71, CA.

loss, the court is indirectly regulating these markets by placing additional financial pressures on traders to conform to their contractual undertakings. It is a mistake to overlook the potential afforded by punitive damages, and aspects of existing legal practice which approximate to the idea.

In some states in the USA, the courts have more openly used punitive measures of damages to attempt to regulate the market.[66] The higher level of damages, often left to the discretion of the jury, changes the incentives for efficient breach of contract, preventing the defendant from profiting from a deliberate breach. Punitive damages can sometimes be justified on the ground that they may either improve the competitiveness of markets by discouraging rogue traders, or they may satisfy some goals of the social market. Typical cases involve deliberate procrastination and evasion by insurers in settling claims under insurance policies, and refusals by retailers and manufacturers to repair consumer goods properly contrary to an agreed warranty. These decisions concern instances of an effective bilateral monopoly, where the consumer becomes heavily dependent upon the supplier because no substitutes are available in the market. The client of an insurance company must rely heavily upon the good faith of the company in processing the claim, and the purchaser of a consumer product depends upon the retailer or manufacturer to carry out the warranty of service. In order to justify these awards of punitive damages, the courts in the USA usually treat them as a species of fraud in tort, rather than a mere breach of contract, in order to avoid the limitations of the compensatory principle in contract law.[67] In English law, although damages for fraud are not limited by rules about remoteness of loss, so that the victim can recover compensation for all consequential losses,[68] there is no equivalent to a general discretionary award to punish the defendant.

By statute, of course, Parliament can manipulate levels of compensation in connection with breach of contract in order to pursue social goals. In the law of unfair dismissal, for instance, a dismissed employee can claim higher levels of compensation than those provided by the common law of wrongful dismissal, in order to protect job security against an employer's unreasonable use of the power to terminate contracts of employment. Within this scheme, however, Parliament further manipulates the level of compensation.[69] It fixes an upper limit on the amount of compensation, so that highly paid employees are prevented from recovering all their economic loss, the effect of which is to weaken their greater job security. At the same time Parliament provides for minimum levels of

---

66 Sullivan, 'Punitive Damages in the Law of Contract: The Reality and the Illusion of Legal Change' (1977) 61 *Minnesota Law Rev* 207; Chutorian, 'Tort Remedies for Breach of Contract: The Expansion of Tortious Breach of the Implied Covenant of Good Faith and Fair Dealing into the Commercial Realm (1986) 86 *Columbia Law Rev* 377. The Canadian position has also moved towards punitive damages: Chapman, 'Punitive Damages as Aggravated Damages: The Case of Contract' (1990) 16 *Canadian Business Law J* 269.
67 *Foley v Interactive Data Corp* 47 Cal 3d 654 (1988).
68 *Doyle v Olby (Ironmongers) Ltd* [1969] 2 QB 158, [1969] 2 All ER 119, CA.
69 Employment Rights Act 1996 Part X, Chapter 2.

compensation, regardless of actual loss to the employee, in order to protect basic social rights, such as the right to belong and not to belong to a trade union. Similarly the law of sex and race discrimination permits, in addition to compensation for economic losses awards of compensation for injury to feelings and insulting treatment,[70] matters which would be denied under the ordinary common law principles of compensation for breach of contract. Such measures clearly use the quantification of compensation in the pursuit of social goals.

Although the common law has retained its ostensible adherence to the compensatory principle, a number of techniques can be employed to enable claimants to obtain higher levels of compensation than their economic losses caused by the breach of contract. The scope of some of these exceptions needs to be examined.

In the context of contractual relations which are regarded as establishing a fiduciary relationship, the claimant can obtain a remedy of accounting for secret profits. This remedy requires the fiduciary to hand over any money or property which it has obtained in contravention of its position of trust. It does not matter that the claimant has suffered no loss and could not have obtained the benefit itself. The point is rather that the fiduciary should not put itself in a position where there might be, or might appear to be, a conflict of interest in which it might have to chose between its own interests and those of the beneficiary of the trust. The crucial issue in such instances is to determine whether the contractual relationship establishes such a fiduciary relationship. In many instances, such as trustees and directors of companies, the office is clearly a fiduciary one. But it is possible for fiduciary obligations to arise through particular contractual arrangements in which one party has the responsibility to manage the affairs of another in the best interests of the other party, as in the case of agency and partnership. The boundaries of fiduciary relations remain contested. In one recent case, for instance, the director of a fertility clinic, which formed part of a university, obtained income from providing a similar service when working abroad in foreign clinics. The university tried to obtain that income, but the court decided that although the employee was in breach of contract with the university, he did not owe a fiduciary duty. The university could only claim compensation for its losses which, unless some foreign patients had decided not to visit the university because the employee performed their operation in their home country, would be nominal. The director of the clinic was liable to the university, however, under a duty to account for the income earned by his junior staff when he sent them to perform outside work, because that conduct involved a potential conflict of interest between the director's personal interest and that of the university.[71]

---

70 *Alexander v Home Office* [1988] ICR 685, CA; *City of Bradford Metropolitan Council v Arora* [1991] ICR 226, CA.
71 *Nottingham University v Fishel* [2000] ICR 1462.

For some breaches of contract where the claimant cannot prove any loss, it may be possible to claim a remedy for the 'disgorgement of profits'. Here the measure of damages is the gain to the defendant rather than loss to the claimant. This measure is often described as a restitutionary claim, because it amounts to taking away the unjust enrichment of the defendant. This remedy might be available, for instance, where in breach of contract the defendant uses property, including intellectual property, belonging to the claimant in order to obtain a financial gain.[72] The remedy also seems to be available where, in breach of contract, the defendant uses information, which although not constituting an intellectual property right such as a patent, is regarded as confidential. In *A-G v Blake*,[73] the defendant had been a member of the UK intelligence service, but had acted as a spy for the Soviet Union, and eventually managed to escape there. He published a book of memoirs, and the British government sought to seize all the royalties. The defendant was in breach of contract for publishing anything at all, but none of the information the book contained, which was 50 years old and all public knowledge, could be regarded as being confidential. The majority of the House of Lords permitted the claim, even though the defendant's conduct did not involve the use of confidential information, on the ground that the defendant, in publishing the book, was doing the very thing that he had promised in his contract of employment not to do. Of course, this reasoning cannot be persuasive, for that charge might be levelled against any contract breaker. It is clear that the House of Lords was using the remedy of disgorgement in order to achieve a social purpose, namely to remove any financial incentive for disclosures about the security services to punish this traitor.

Use of the remedy of disgorgement of profits is controversial. Not only does the remedy apparently conflict with the compensatory principle for contract damages, but also it runs headlong into the efficiency justifications for contract remedies that permit an efficient breach of contract. If the use of damages as the primary judicial remedy for breach of contract and their restriction to compensation supports a wealth-maximising goal, the introduction of the remedy of disgorgement of profits, which might prevent breaches of contract simply in order to obtain a greater profit, would conflict with that policy.[74] A remedy of disgorgement can only be justified if it supports other social goals, so that its use necessarily undermines the view that judicial remedies for breach of contract are solely directed towards economic goals.

A remedy of disgorgement has been sought in cases where the most appropriate remedy of an injunction against breach of contract must be withheld for some pressing reason, but the court nevertheless wishes to ensure that the defendant

---

72 *Penarth Dry Dock Engineering Co Ltd v Pounds* [1963] 1 Lloyd's Rep 359, CA; *Strand Electric and Engineering Co Ltd v Brisford Entertainments Ltd* [1952] 2 QB 246, [1952] 1 All ER 796, CA.

73 [2001] 1 AC 268, [2001] 4 All ER 385, HL.

74 Smith, 'Disgorgement of the Profits of Breach of Contract: Property, Contract and "Efficient Breach"' (1994–95) 24 *Canadian Business Law Journal* 121.

cannot take advantage of its breach of contract. In *Wrotham Park Estate Co v Parkside Homes Ltd*,[75] the defendant ignored a covenant not to build on some land without the claimant's permission. The court refused to order destruction of the 14 houses that had been built and were now occupied. The claimant could not prove any loss, such as diminution of the value of the claimant's neighbouring property. Nevertheless, the court awarded substantial damages that represented the hypothetical price at which the claimant would have consented to the building development. These damages vindicated the proprietary right to control building development, and for this reason were not tied to the claimant's actual loss. But this decision has been interpreted narrowly. A similar claim for the fee of waiving the covenant not to build was rejected by the Court of Appeal in *Surrey County Council v Bredero Homes Ltd*.[76] Steyn LJ reasserted the principle that this restitutionary measure of disgorgement of profits is only available for the misuse of the plaintiff's proprietary interest. But in *A-G v Blake*, the House of Lords expressed its approval of *Wrotham Park Estate Co v Parkside Homes Ltd*, denied that the remedy of disgorgement is confined to proprietary rights or instances where an injunction would normally be available, and insisted that in suitable cases damages for breach of contract may be measured by the benefit gained by the wrongdoer from the breach. The court was unwilling, however, to set limits on the categories where an account of profits or some other requirement to hand over a benefit obtained would be required. The courts have a discretion to apply this remedy where this response is required by justice.

One type of case where this response of depriving the defendant of its gain seems to be well established is in relation to the skimped performance of services. In a contract for the supply of goods, if inferior quality goods are supplied, the claimant can obtain the difference in value between the goods supplied and the contract price. In a contract for the supply of services, however, if the defendant supplies a poor service, it may not be possible to identify any economic loss caused by that breach of contract. For example, if a public authority contracts for the cleaning of streets by a private enterprise and the job is done poorly because the contractor does not employ sufficient cleaners, it is difficult to identify what economic loss the public authority has suffered. In contracts of this type, there is often an agreed remedy for this kind of breach, perhaps in the form of performance bonds or bank guarantees of liquidated damages, precisely because proof of loss may be difficult.[77] In the absence of such an agreed remedy, however, it seems likely that a court would be willing to award damages not for the

---

75 [1974] 2 All ER 321, [1974] 1 WLR 798, Ch.
76 [1993] 3 All ER 705, [1993] 1 WLR 1361, CA.
77 P Vincent-Jones and A Harries, 'Limits of Contract in Internal CCT Transactions: A Comparative Study of Buildings Cleaning and Refuse Collection in Northern Metropolitan', in D Campbell and P Vincent-Jones (eds), *Contract and Economic Organisation* (Aldershot, 1996), p 180.

claimant's loss but to the extent of the defendant's saving on labour costs. In effect, this is a disgorgement of profits in the form of savings in the cost of performance of the contract.

The examples of exceptions to the compensation principle considered in this section reveal that the courts use the assessment of damages for instrumental social purposes other than the general efficiency criteria in some instances. Although the courts refrain from simple punitive measures of damages without express statutory authority, they can use devices such as the liability to account for profits to prevent contract breakers from obtaining an economic advantage when some compelling social policy suggests that they should be prevented from so doing.

E. Compulsory performance

Courts seldom issue an order to perform a contract or to refrain from breach of it. In practice, the injured party rarely asks for this remedy, for it is usually possible to locate an alternative source of supply for the goods or services which are available without the costs and delays associated with litigation. Alternatively, if the right to obtain compulsory performance is clear, then this will induce negotiations towards a favourable settlement for the claimant. But even where the injured party seeks compulsory performance, the common law rarely permits the remedies of specific performance and injunctions.

1. Inadequacy of compensation

A series of historical accidents deformed the legal principles governing the award of orders for compulsory performance, thereby rendering it almost impossible to discern the rationale behind the modern law. The general rule is normally stated to be that courts will only order specific performance or an injunction where damages would be inadequate to compensate the claimant's loss. This looks a puzzling rule, since the law of damages should compensate the claimant's loss in most respects unless the defendant is insolvent. The origins of the rule lie in a political accommodation between the common law courts and the king's court of Chancery, under which the latter confined its intervention to cases where the common law failed to provide an adequate remedy. Hence the Chancery courts advanced the rule that specific performance and injunctions would only be granted for breach of contract where common law damages were inadequate.[78]

This rule then raises the embarrassing question of when can damages be inadequate, given that they compensate the injured party for all his losses? One

---

78 Dawson, 'Specific Performance in France and Germany' (1959) 57 *Michigan Law Review* 495.

suggestion is that damages prove inadequate when a claim involves those interests which are excluded from compensation, such as remote losses, avoidable losses, and non-pecuniary losses.[79] An order for specific performance, if it could be made in time, would give the injured party his expected profits or his subjective valuation of the property. But then the question becomes why should we wish to subvert these limitations on awards of damages, which rest on important policies such as the minimization of social cost, by introducing compulsory performance as an available remedy?

The argument based upon the inadequacy of damages may prove more convincing, however, where the claim is likely to be defeated for being too speculative. Here the court can avoid the risk of overcompensation or under-compensation, not by denying any damages at all, but by ordering specific performance.[80] A common kind of case where compulsory performance is ordered for this reason involves transactions for the transfer of an asset which will provide an opportunity to earn an uncertain income. If the injured party cannot provide his losses with sufficient certainty to satisfy the compensatory principle, a court may order specific performance. For example, an aggrieved party may be able to specifically enforce a sale of shares which would give him control over a company, because damages for his loss of the power to control the company are too speculative to be compensatable. Similarly, the loss of the right to be an exclusive distributor of a product may lead to the loss of goodwill and trade reputation, items which are hard to prove and to quantify under the compensatory principle, but which can be protected by an injunction. In such cases, the award of compulsory performance overcomes difficulties in proving loss with sufficient certainty to establish a claim for damages.

In practice it has become well established that the only type of contract which will be routinely enforced by an order for specific performance is one concerning the transfer of an interest in land. This practice is hard to square with the rule that damages must be inadequate. Given that the purchaser of a house is likely to be able to discover a satisfactory substitute fairly quickly, then it is hard to see how damages could be inadequate. Even more strangely, the vendor of property can also obtain specific performance, although his claim will only be one for payment of money. The general rule therefore encounters difficulty in explaining the major case where it is invariably satisfied.

Another instance where it is often suggested that specific performance will be routinely ordered concerns unique goods.[81] One possible reason why damages may prove inadequate here is because the uniqueness of the goods prevents a clear market price from being established. But this argument appears weak, for it

79 Harris, Ogus and Phillips, 'Contract Remedies and the Consumer Surplus' (1977) 95 *Law Quarterly Review* 581.
80 Kronman, 'Specific Performance' (1978) 45 *University of Chicago Law Review* 351.
81 *Falcke v Gray* (1859) 4 Drew 651, Ch.

should be possible to obtain a reliable estimate of the current market value for even a rare work of art. In fact the courts do not rely upon this category of uniqueness frequently, but assume that satisfactory substitutes can be obtained in the market, so that damages will be an adequate remedy.[82] The argument based upon the uniqueness of the goods seems likely to succeed only when the claimant can persuade the court of a particular personal reason for seeking possession of that particular item, such as that it has a sentimental value or significance which cannot be replaced by a substitute.

Although the courts frequently repeat the rule that damages must be inadequate before they will award an order for compulsory performance, the rule has been subtly modified in recent years. In *Beswick v Beswick*,[83] an elderly and ailing coal merchant sold his business to his nephew in return for various promises including a promise to pay his widow £5 per week after his death. When the nephew refused to pay, the widow in her capacity as administratrix of her husband's estate claimed specific performance of the contract. Since the estate had lost nothing by the nephew's breach of contract, because the payments were owed to the widow personally, it was hard to justify a substantial award of damages. The House of Lords ordered specific performance of the contract because this remedy achieved a just result, for otherwise the nephew would have been unjustly enriched by being entitled to hold onto his uncle's business without paying his aunt a penny. The modern judicial test asks the question: is it just in all the circumstances that the claimant should be confined to his remedy in damages?[84] This test squarely raises the issue of describing the circumstances and policies that induce a court to find the award of the remedy of specific performance more just than damages?

2. Instrumental purposes of compulsory performance

The key to the law of compulsory performance lies in recognizing that such a remedy is not designed to compensate the injured party for his losses, but to force performance of the contract. Normally a court declines to order performance because damages provide a sufficient incentive to complete most contracts except where the defendant hopes to achieve unusual economic benefits from breach, in which case to compel performance would only serve to discourage contracts and to reduce the combined wealth of the contracting parties. A remedy of compulsory performance therefore deliberately overrides these normal considerations governing remedies in order to serve different policies. These policies are rarely articulated fully by the courts. They may include the prevention of what is perceived as unjust enrichment or the protection of third parties, as in *Beswick v Beswick*. The policy may include the protection of interests that would not be recognised in the law of damages, such as vexation and disappointment. One

---

82 *Societe des Industries Metallurgiques SA v Bronx Engineering Co Ltd* [1975] 1 Lloyd's Rep 465, CA.
83 [1968] AC 58, [1967] 2 All ER 1197, HL.
84 Sachs LJ, *Evans Marshall & Co Ltd v Bertola SA* [1973] 1 All ER 992, [1973] 1 WLR 349, CA.

important policy to note here, however, is that the grant of an order of compulsory performance considerably increases the post-breach bargaining position of the claimant. The award of the remedy can therefore serve the purpose of combating unequal relations of power in contracts.

In transactions which are performed over a period of time, such as output and requirements contracts or distributorships, because of transaction costs and the opportunity costs one party may become heavily dependent upon the other for proper performance of the contract. For example, the retailer of petrol under a franchise agreement may be closely tied to one oil company because he is bound to satisfy all his requirements from it. If the oil company refuses to deliver petrol to satisfy his requirements, then the retailer must make the difficult choice between either going out of business or terminating the contract and seeking a new franchise and sources of supply, which may not be readily available and may appear unreliable. In these circumstances, the relation of dependence may be counterbalanced by an order to the oil company to perform its side of the requirements contract.[85] In other words, having forged a relation of domination through freedom of contract, the oil company makes itself vulnerable to orders for compulsory performance to achieve a more even balance in the transaction. Notice that damages could be a sufficient compensatory remedy in this case, for the oil company would be liable for the full range of opportunity costs and expenses. The principal reason for ordering compulsory performance is not to compensate economic loss or indeed to compensate anything at all, but to control the exercise of power established through contractual agreement by requiring that power to be exercised fairly in the light of the interests of the subordinate party. The courts adjust the rules governing termination of contracts by insisting that paternalist considerations should override the ordinary principles based upon the value of co-operation in order to strengthen the hand of the dependent party.

This pattern of transaction which justifies the use of specific performance can be glimpsed in many other instances. In the contract of employment, an employee may invest a considerable amount of time and effort in acquiring skills specific to the employer's enterprise. This investment of human capital in the job makes the employee peculiarly vulnerable to threats of dismissal, for he may not be able to command the same wages and status in life elsewhere, so he must relinquish any control over his behaviour which the employer desires. Although specific performance is not usually granted in contracts of employment on the ground that a breakdown of mutual trust and confidence renders such orders impracticable, this need for protection explains both the availability of reinstatement as a possible remedy for the statutory claim for unfair dismissal,[86] and the occasional use of injunctions by courts to prevent a dismissal until the

---

85 *Sky Petroleum Ltd v VIP Petroleum Ltd* [1974] 1 All ER 954, [1974] 1 WLR 576, Ch.
86 Employment Rights Act 1996, s 113.

employer has completed a contractual disciplinary procedure or has otherwise followed a fair procedure.[87] This pattern of domination, which can be relieved by specific performance, repeats itself in some consumer transactions. Where a consumer purchases a product, which, by virtue of its complexity and mechanical parts, can only be maintained and repaired by skilled contractors trained by the manufacturer, the service contractor enjoys a relation of domination over the consumer, which can be effectively constrained by orders of compulsory performance of express promises to repair the product. A step in this direction is the right conferred on consumers to require the seller to repair or replace defective goods, unless the cost would be disproportionate in comparison with mere compensation.[88] This remedy of specific performance of an obligation to repair or replace goods strengthens the position of consumers against traders who do not respond to complaints.

The origins of the routine enforcement of contracts for the sale of interests in land may also lie in this purpose of preventing oppression. Some of these contracts do fit the pattern of relief from domination, since between the contract and the formal legal conveyance of the property, both parties are heavily committed to the transaction in terms of expenditure and opportunity costs, so that the threat of compulsory performance removes the potential for domination and exploitation by, for example, demands for a higher price or a delay in completion. Where none of these considerations apply to a sale of land, however, as in the case of a sale of one among many identical apartments by a developer, some American decisions have refused specific relief to the vendor.[89]

3. Limitations

Although the courts possess a broad discretion to make compulsory orders for performance, they observe a number of important limitations on the exercise of this jurisdiction.

(a) WASTE OF RESOURCES

One limitation upon compulsory performance which is common to this branch of remedies as well as damages is that the courts will not countenance a waste of resources. Just as they will not award damages to pay for remedying a defect where the work is pointless or wholly disproportionate to the resulting benefit, so too no court would order specific performance of a wasteful enterprise. In the past, the courts have often hidden behind the pretence that they were unable to

---

87 *Irani v Southampton and South West Hampshire Health Authority* [1985] ICR 590, Ch.
88 Sale of Goods Act 1979, s 48B, as amended by the Sale and Supply of Goods to Consumers Regulations 2002, SI 2002/3045.
89 Van Hecke, 'Changing Emphases in Specific Performance' (1961) 40 *North Carolina Law Rev* 1.

supervise such works and so could not properly order performance. But since the court may always appoint agents, such as receivers, to act for it, these days this argument concerning the difficulties of supervision is seldom heard:

> Where it is necessary, and in my opinion right, to move away from some nineteenth century authorities, is to reject as a reason against granting relief, the impossibility for the courts to supervise the doing of work.[90]

The point is rather that the costs of supervision and performance far exceed any worthwhile benefit emerging from proper performance of the contract. Thus in *Tito v Waddell (No 2)*,[91] the court declined to order specific performance of the mining company's promise to restore the land to its former state partly on the ground that it considered the venture unlikely to succeed and partly on the ground that the benefits of restoration were uncertain. The same concern to avoid a waste of resources led the court in *Wrotham Park Estate Co v Parkside Homes Ltd*,[92] to decline to order the destruction of 14 homes in order to enforce a covenant. This restriction on orders for compulsory performance should be approached cautiously, however, for the effect of the order for compulsory performance will be to strengthen the claimant's bargaining position in achieving a satisfactory settlement. No one actually wanted to knock down the homes: the point was rather to obtain a just level of compensation in a settlement.

(b) LIBERTY

A second limitation upon orders for compulsory performance concerns the protection of individual liberty. A court will be reluctant to order performance of a contract involving the personal performance of services on the ground that this restricts the freedom of an individual too severely. By statute the courts are prevented from making such orders against employees.[93] At one time this limitation was thought to preclude orders for compulsory performance of any contracts involving personal service. But the rule has become more refined. An injunction may be ordered against an employee to prevent breach of a negative covenant in the contract of employment, such as a promise not to work for certain competitors of the employer.[94] A court can also enforce a contractual promise to appoint a person to perform a particular job, such as an undertaking to provide a porter for a building.[95] In recent years injunctions have also been issued against breach of disciplinary procedures by employers: the court's order does not require

---

90 Lord Wilberforce, *Shiloh Spinners Ltd v Harding* [1973] AC 691 at 724, [1973] 1 All ER 90 at 102, HL.
91 [1977] Ch 106, [1977] 3 All ER 129, Ch.
92 [1974] 2 All ER 321, [1974] 1 WLR 798, Ch.
93 Trade Union and Labour Relations (Consolidation) Act 1992, s 236.
94 *Warner Bros Pictures Inc v Nelson* [1937] 1 KB 209, Ch; Stevens, 'Involuntary Servitude by Injunction' (1921) 6 *Cornell Law Quarterly* 235.
95 *Posner v Scott-Lewis* [1987] Ch 25, [1986] 3 All ER 513, Ch.

the employer to keep on the employee, but simply to comply with the agreed remedial procedure under the contract.[96] The modern approach to the question of whether an injunction will be issued against breach by termination of contracts involving the performance services appears to be whether the order is workable or practicable.[97]

(c) FAIRNESS

A third special limitation on awards of compulsory performance insists that it must be fair to enforce the contract at the date of judgment. In *Patel v Ali*,[98] for example, after the defendant had agreed to sell her house, she suffered an injury requiring amputation of her leg, she became pregnant, and her husband was judged bankrupt and sent to prison. Despite the normal practice of awarding specific performance for sales of land, the court declined to order compulsory performance on the ground that it would inflict on the vendor hardship amounting to injustice.

(d) MUTUALITY

The final special limitation upon compulsory performance requires the court to check that by ordering specific performance they do not replace one relation of domination with another. Unless the interests of the defendant are adequately secured, by forcing him to perform the contract, he may be left then with no reliable remedy against the claimant. For example, if the defendant refuses to perform a contract for services because he reasonably believes that the claimant cannot afford to pay him for his work, a court will decline to order compulsory performance unless the claimant either pays in advance or provides adequate security for performance.[99]

---

96 *Jones v Lee* [1980] ICR 310, CA.
97 Eg *Powell v London Borough of Brent* [1988] ICR 176, [1987] IRLR 466, CA; *Hughes v London Borough of Southwark* [1988] IRLR 55, QB. Ewing and Grubb, 'The Emergence of a New Labour Injunction?' (1987) 16 *Industrial Law Journal* 145.
98 [1984] Ch 283, [1984] 1 All ER 978, Ch.
99 *Price v Strange* [1978] Ch 337, [1977] 3 All ER 371, CA.

Index